T0141282

Bioinformatics and Computational Biology

Bioinformatics and Computational Biology: Technological Advancements, Applications and Opportunities is an invaluable resource for general and applied researchers who analyze biological data that is generated, at an unprecedented rate, at the global level. After careful evaluation of the requirements for current trends in bioinformatics and computational biology, it is anticipated that the book will provide an insightful resource to the academic and scientific community. Through a myriad of computational resources, algorithms, and methods, it equips readers with the confidence to both analyze biological data and estimate predictions.

The book offers comprehensive coverage of the most essential and emerging topics:

- Cloud-based monitoring of bioinformatics multivariate data with cloud platforms
- Machine learning and deep learning in bioinformatics
- Quantum machine learning for biological applications
- Integrating machine learning strategies with multiomics to augment prognosis in chronic diseases
- Biomedical engineering
- Next-generation sequencing techniques and applications
- Computational systems biology and molecular evolution

While other books may touch on some of the same issues and nuances of biological data analysis, they neglect to feature bioinformatics and computational biology exclusively, and as exhaustively. This book's abundance of several subtopics related to almost all of the regulatory activities of biomolecules from where real data is being generated brings an added dimension.

Bioinformatics and Computational Biology

Technological Advancements,
Applications and Opportunities

Edited by
Tiratha Raj Singh
Hemraj Saini
Moacyr Comar Junior

CRC Press
Taylor & Francis Group
Boca Raton London New York

CRC Press is an imprint of the
Taylor & Francis Group, an **informa** business

A CHAPMAN & HALL BOOK

First edition published 2024
by CRC Press
2385 NW Executive Center Drive, Suite 320, Boca Raton FL 33431

and by CRC Press
4 Park Square, Milton Park, Abingdon, Oxon, OX14 4RN

CRC Press is an imprint of Taylor & Francis Group, LLC

ISBN: 978-1-032-36158-1 (hbk)
ISBN: 978-1-032-36303-5 (pbk)
ISBN: 978-1-003-33124-7 (ebk)

DOI: 10.1201/9781003331247

Typeset in Times
by SPi Technologies India Pvt Ltd (Straive)

Contents

SECTION A   Computer Science Techniques and Their Biological Applications

Section B Algorithms for Sequence and Structure Analysis

Section C Advanced Computational Biology Techniques and Applications

Editors

Dr. Tiratha Raj Singh is Professor of Bioinformatics in the Department of Biotechnology and Bioinformatics, Jaypee University of Information technology (JUIT), Waknaghat, Solan, HP. He also holds the position of Media In-charge, JUIT and coordinator of the Centre of Excellence in Healthcare Technologies and Informatics (CEHTI), JUIT. Dr. Singh received his PhD in Bioinformatics from MANIT, Bhopal, and his joint research work for PhD was completed at Tel-Aviv University, Tel-Aviv, Israel. Dr. Singh worked with Dr. KR Pardasani and Dr. Tal Pupko in their roles as supervisor and co-supervisor, respectively. After completing his PhD in 2008, Dr. Singh served his fellowship from the planning and budgeting committee (VATAT), Tel Aviv University, Tel-Aviv, Israel, where he did his postdoctoral studies in Functional Genomics and Molecular Evolution in Dr. Dorothee Huchon's lab, TAU, Israel.

In 2009–2010, after returning from Israel, Dr. Singh joined DAVV, Indore, India, for a year. Dr. Singh joined JUIT in July 2010 as an Assistant Professor (Grade II) and has since been working on various aspects of genomics and proteomics regarding their involvement in various human diseases. Dr. Singh is involved in the annotation of complex biological networks through computational systems biology and functional genomics approaches. His current area of research is focused on DNA repair systems and Alzheimer's disease (AD) utilizing a myriad of computational approaches. His lab, by mining huge amounts of genomic, transcriptomic, proteomic, and pathways data, works to generate biologically meaningful information for malignancies associated with the human DNA repair systems. For AD, he is working to rediscover cholinergic hypothesis through acetylcholine esterase and its inhibition activities. Additionally, his lab has proposed multiple inhibitors for the myriad of drug targets for AD through computational means. Dr. Singh completed a DST FASTRACK project and two more projects from ICMR. As a Co-PI in a major DBT funded project, he is associated with the annotation of transcriptomic data for Himalayan medicinal herbs. Dr. Singh has published his research work in various highly reputed journals such as: *Molecular Biology and Evolution, Computers in Biology and Medicine, Nature Scientific Reports, Journal of Molecular Liquids, JBSD, DNA Repair, PlosOne, Phytochemistry, Planta, Gene,* and *Journal of Theoretical Biology.* He has guided several BTech, MTech, and MSc project students for their final-year research projects. Eight PhDs were awarded under his guidance, and his lab has developed important databases for human DNA repair systems, as well as for Alzheimer's disease. Many tools and web-based applications have been developed, in his lab, for the analyses of various biological data. Dr. Singh received multiple awards and recognitions in his academic and research career that include: Young Scientist Award from International Federation of Information Processing

(IFIP), NVIDIA Hardware Award, Bioclues Innovation Research and Development (BIRD) Award, and an international patent. More about Dr. Singh is available at JUIT website and at Bioinfoindia.org/raj.

Dr. Hemraj Saini is Professor in the School of Computing and Dean Research & Consultancy at DIT University in Dehradun, India. Prior to this, he worked in academics, administration, and industry for over 24 years. His research interests include: Information Security, Cyber Security, Edge Computing, and Cloud Computing. He has guided seven PhD degrees to completion, and is currently supervising six more at various universities in India. Dr. Saini is an active member of various professional technical and scientific associations such as IEEE, ACM, and IAENG. He provides his services in various capacities, such as editor, member of editorial boards, member of different subject research committees, reviewer for international journals and conferences (including Springer, Science Direct, IEEE, Wiley, IGI Global, Bentham Science, etc.), and as a resource person for various workshops and conferences. He has published over 160+ research papers in international and national journals and conferences of repute. Dr. Saini has organized various versions of reputed conferences, including ICIIP and PDGC. Currently, he is the General Conference Chair for ISED-2023 (https://isedconf.org/index.php).

Dr. Moacyr Comar Junior is professor in Brazil. He mentioned that "since I was a little boy, while helping my mother to clean the house, I was curious as to how to mix things together to make 'a potion that cleans everything up'." As time passed, I began to understand that I really wanted to know even more – how atoms work together to provide everyday life for us all. Hence, in 1994, I attended a chemistry course, seeking answers to my childhood questions. I soon realized that there were other, more important questions, to which I could not find the answers with only undergraduate knowledge. As a result, I was approved for and attended a graduate course in quantum chemistry. In 2005, I received my PhD and began to work at a university in the middle of the Brazilian Amazon rain forest. Because I was interested in understanding how some biochemical systems work, these were interesting years, years when I began to learn and understand the basis of molecular dynamics simulations. Since that day, and currently at the Federal University of Uberlandia (in the southeast region), I continue to work with molecular dynamics simulations, but, yes, some questions remain to be answered, so … I keep going with the books, and with the simulations, particularly studying molecularly impressed polymers, protein–protein interactions, and inhibition of proteins involved in the Chagas disease."

Foreword

I am delighted and honored to compose the foreword for this remarkable book, as its subject matter aligns perfectly with my area of expertise. Moreover, I have had the privilege of knowing the esteemed editor, Dr. Tiratha Raj Singh, for over eight years. Throughout this time, I have witnessed Dr. Singh's remarkable growth in the fields of bioinformatics and computational biology. Therefore, I am confident that the contents presented in this book will serve as an exceptional resource for readers worldwide.

Bioinformatics stands as a truly remarkable and interdisciplinary domain, seamlessly merging the realms of biological and information sciences with the latest technological advancements. As a computer scientist by training and profession, I embarked on the path of bioinformatics during its nascent stage, and it has been an absolute honor to be a part of this incredible journey witnessing the exponential growth of computational biology and its associated crucial domains. In light of my observations, I can confidently assert that the topics covered in this book hold immense relevance for students, academicians, and researchers alike.

The growing reliance of global bioinformatics infrastructure on information technology is a widely recognized fact. However, the remarkable growth witnessed over the past three decades has also revealed the reciprocal relationship, where numerous new technologies have emerged based on biological and bioinformatics systems. In this context, this book serves as an invaluable resource, offering a detailed exploration of various topics that encompass the essential components required for readers to develop a comprehensive understanding of the current state of the field and its potential for future advancements. It provides a valuable window into the intricate workings of the domain, enlightening readers and paving the way for further development in the field.

Within the pages of this book, readers will encounter a rich amalgamation of both traditional and emerging topics and subtopics. It comprehensively covers a range of subjects including classical algorithms and their applications at the sequence and structure level, NGS data analysis, structural bioinformatics, network biology, and molecular evolution. Additionally, it delves into recent and emerging areas such as cloud-based monitoring of bioinformatics multivariate data using cloud platforms, machine learning, and deep learning techniques in bioinformatics. Furthermore, the book explores diverse subjects such as drug discovery through deep learning and virtual screening, gene regulation, and DNA and RNA structure and sequencing. The inclusion of these comprehensive and diverse topics ensures that readers gain a holistic understanding of the field and its various dimensions.

The challenges faced in the fields of bioinformatics and computational biology are undoubtedly formidable yet captivating. Researchers and professionals tackle these challenges with immense enthusiasm, tenacity, and dedication, continuously striving to develop innovative analysis methods and solutions that can meet the ever-evolving demands of the field. In this era of heightened global interconnectivity and interdependence, it becomes imperative to offer up-to-date knowledge and insights in the realm of bioinformatics. With utmost confidence, I assert that this book takes a significant step in that direction. Its contents provide a wealth of state-of-the-art information, ensuring that readers have access to the latest advancements and discoveries in the field. I wholeheartedly wish all readers a fulfilling and comprehensive journey of reading and learning as they engage with the book's contents.

Professor Gajendra P.S. Raghava
Head, Department of Computational Biology,
IIITD, New Delhi, INDIA

Prof. Gajendra P.S. Raghava is a highly accomplished researcher in the field of Bioinformatics, having received numerous prestigious accolades, including the Shanti Swarup Bhatnagar Award. In stark contrast to traditional researchers who often focus on a specific problem or field, Professor Raghava has made remarkable contributions to multiple problems and fields that are crucial for translational medicine. His expertise lies in developing computational tools and resources, with his research group having created over 300 web servers, databases, and software packages – an unmatched accomplishment.

Preface

Bioinformatics and Computational Biology has emerged as a critical field that has revolutionized the way we understand and analyze biological data at various levels that includes DNA, RNA, genes, proteins, drugs, other biomolecules, and biological systems. Advances in technology have led to an explosion of biological data that requires sophisticated algorithms and computational tools to analyze and interpret it in a meaningful way. This book provides a comprehensive overview of the different aspects of bioinformatics and computational biology, including design and analysis of algorithms, sequence-based algorithms, structure-based algorithms, exact and heuristics, and other algorithms in computational biology.

The book also covers emerging topics such as cloud-based monitoring of bioinformatics multivariate data with cloud platforms, machine learning and deep learning in bioinformatics, quantum machine learning for biological applications, and integrating machine learning strategies with multi-omics to augment prognosis in chronic diseases. Furthermore, the book discusses drug discovery by deep learning and virtual screening, gene regulation, DNA and RNA structure and sequencing, computational prediction of RNA binding proteins, protein annotations at systems level, microarray data analysis, tools and techniques in structural bioinformatics, and the higher-order organization in biological systems.

Additionally, the book explores the advancement and applications of biomedical engineering in human health care, clinical trials in the realm of health informatics, application of genomics in novel microbial species identification, next-generation sequencing data analysis, computational molecular evolution, and, finally, the multifaceted applications of bioinformatics.

This book is intended for researchers, graduate students, and practitioners in the field of bioinformatics, computational biology, and related fields. The book's diverse chapters cover a wide range of topics that will help readers gain a comprehensive understanding of the field's current state and its potential for future development. The authors, who are experts in their respective fields, have contributed their knowledge and expertise to create a valuable resource for those working in computational biology. The authors and editors have answered some questions of the readers and raise many others, leading them to search deeper into this exciting field. Enjoy!!

Prof. Tiratha Raj Singh
Prof. Hemraj Saini
Prof. Moacyr Comar Junior

Acknowledgment

We the editors of this book first of acknowledge CRC press for shaping up and accomplishing this in a timely manner. We anticipate that this book will provide a comprehensive overview of the different aspects of bioinformatics and computational biology its readers.

Special thanks to Ms. Isha Singh, Mr. Rajesh Dey, Ms. Sherry Thomas and Ms. Divya Muthu for their continuous efforts and support during the processing and production.

We know that this book explores the advancement and applications of biomedical engineering in human health care, clinical trials in the realm of health informatics, application of genomics in novel microbial species identification, next-generation sequencing data analysis, computational molecular evolution, and, finally, the multifaceted applications of bioinformatics.

Editors Dr. Hemraj Saini and Dr. Moacyr Comar Junior would like to acknowledge their friends, students, and family members for the continuous support and encouragement during the course of this book. Support from each other is also appreciated by all the three editors for the accomplishment of this tedious and important assignment.

Dr. Tiratha Raj Singh, who served as the lead and corresponding editor of this book, would like to acknowledge the contribution of his own PhD student Rohit Shukla for helping in the initial phase of this project. Prof. Singh mentioned that "I dedicate my first book to my caring parents and beloved wife Ragini. She is a source of inspiration and source of enthusiasm for my whole work. My two lovely kids Priyamvada and Amitva are also part of this beautiful journey as they completed our family. Learning from my own life time mentors Prof. KR Pardasani, Prof. RK Pandey, Prof. Tal Pupko, Prof. Dorothee Huchon and Prof. Yosi S. Diamand also needs a special mention."

As this book is intended for researchers, graduate students, and practitioners in the field of bioinformatics, computational biology, and related fields, therefore, we acknowledge our students with whom we were involved in lots of teaching and research and that practice made the foundation for this book. We are sure that some questions of our readerships to other books were also an additional content designer for this book and it may inspire others also to write such books in near future. Enjoy!!

Prof. Tiratha Raj Singh
Prof. Hemraj Saini
Prof. Moacyr Comar Junior

Contributors

Aman Akash
University of Würzburg
Germany

Anna Almasi
University of Würzburg
Germany

Himanshu Avashthi
ICAR-Indian Agricultural Statistics
    Research Institute
India

Piyush Baindara
University of Missouri
USA

Johannes Balkenhol
University of Würzburg
Germany

Himanshu Bansal
USI Università della Svizzera italiana
Switzerland

Deepika Bhardwaj
All India Institute of Medical Sciences
India

Harshita Bhargava
IIS (deemed to be University)
India

Jyotika Bhati
ICAR-Indian Agricultural Statistics
    Research Institute
India

Deepa Bhatt
National Institute for plant
    Biotechnology
India

Aayushi Chandra
CCS University
India

Megha Chaudhary
All India Institute of Medical Sciences
India

Divya Chauhan
ICAR-Indian Agricultural Statistics
    Research Institute
India

Laxmi N. Chavali
Sri Venkateshwara College of
    Pharmacy
India

Thomas Dandekar
University of Würzburg
Germany

Lipika Das
All India Institute of Medical Sciences
India

Sushanta Deb
All India Institute of Medical
    Sciences
India

Shishir K. Gupta
University of Würzburg
Germany

Sahil Jain
Tel-Aviv University
Israel

Smita Jain
Banasthali Vidyapith
India

Ravi Shankar Jha
DIT University
India

Moacyr Comar Junior
Universidade Federal de Uberlândia
Brazil

Anil Kant
Jaypee University of Information
  Technology
India

Nivedha Karthikeyan
Sri Ramachandra Institute of Higher
  Education and Research (DU)
India

Rekha Khandia
Barkatullah University
India

Laxmi Kirola
Banaras Hindu University
India

Gunasekaran Krishnasamy
University of Madras
India

Ajay Kumar
Jaypee University of Information
  Technology
India

Ashwani Kumar
Chandigarh University
India

Utsang Kumar
Barkatullah University
India

Shweta Kumari
Chandigarh University
India

Priya N. Madhana
Sri Ramachandra Institute of Higher
  Education and Research (DU)
India

Eduardo Habib Bechelane Maia
Universidade Federal de São João del
  Rei
Brazil

Prabina Kumar Meher
ICAR-Indian Agricultural Statistics
  Research Institute
India

Rashmi Minocha
All India Institute of Medical Sciences
India

Shikha Mittal
Jaypee University of Information
  Technology
India

Navnit Kumar Mishra
Chandigarh University
India

Tiago Alves de Oliveira
Universidade Federal de São João del
  Rei
Brazil

Özge Osmanoglu
University of Würzburg
Germany

Sai Padma
Bhavan's Vivekananda College of
  Science
India

Sarvesh Paliwal
Banasthali Vidyapith
India

Swati Paliwal
Banasthali Vidyapith
India

Megha Katare Pandey
All India Institute of Medical
  Sciences
India

Astha Pareek
IIS (deemed to be University)
India

Kshitij Pareek
Rajasthan University of Veterinary and
  Animal Sciences
India

Samiya Parkar
University of Würzburg
Germany

Aparna Pottikkadavath
University of Würzburg
Germany

Upendra Kumar Pradhan
ICAR-Indian Agricultural Statistics
    Research Institute
India

Utkarsh Raj
Dr. D. Y. Patil Vidyapeeth
India

Magesh Ramasamy
Sri Ramachandra Institute of Higher
    Education and Research (DU)
India

Pradeep Singh Rawat
DIT University
India

Dinata Roy
Mizoram University
India

Hemraj Saini
DIT University
India

Anukriti Saran
Banasthali Vidyapith
India

Aishwarya Sekar
Stella Maris College (Autonomous)
    and University of Madras
India

Amita Sharma
IIS (deemed to be University)
India

Ashish Sharma
JECRC
India

Swapnil Sharma
Banasthali Vidyapith
India

Vinamrata Sharma
Jaypee University of Information
    Technology
India

Alisson Marques da Silva
Universidade Federal de São João del
    Rei
Brazil

Ankita Singh
Jaypee University of Information
    Technology
India

Shubhendra Singh Chauhan
ICAR-National Bureau of Plant Genetic
    Resources
India

Tiratha Raj Singh
Jaypee University of Information
    Technology
India

Vikram Singh
Central University of Himachal Pradesh
India

Palak Singhal
University of Bern
Switzerland

Shailja Singhal
Barkatullah University
India

Leyla Sirkinti
University of Würzburg
Germany

Mugdha Srivastava
University of Würzburg
Germany

Prashanth Suravajhala
Amrita Vishwa Vidyapeetham
India

Renuka Suravajhala
Amrita Vishwa Vidyapeetham
India

Alex Gutterres Taranto
Universidade Federal de São João del
  Rei
Brazil

Prithivi Jung Thapa
University of Würzburg
Germany

Kumar D. Thirumal
Meenakshi Academy of Higher
  Education and Research
India

Praveenya Tirunagari
IIT Kharagpur
India

Saumya Tyagi
Jaypee University of Information
  Technology
India

Ananthi Vanaraj
Sri Ramachandra Institute of Higher
  Education and Research (DU)
India

Sunita Verma
All India Institute of Medical Sciences
India

Neetu Verma
National Institute for plant
  Biotechnology
India

Anushri Vijay
IIS (deemed to be University)
India

Arvind Kumar Yadav
Jaypee University of Information
  Technology
India

Section A

Computer Science Techniques and Their Biological Applications

1 Design and Analysis of Algorithms in Computational Biology

Saumya Tyagi, Vinamrata Sharma and Tiratha Raj Singh

Jaypee University of Information Technology, India

1.1 WHAT IS AN ALGORITHM?

The term "algorithm" is derived from the Persian scholar Abu Ja'far Muhammad ibn Musa al-Khwarizmi, who produced a mathematics textbook in 825 AD. This term has gained specific relevance in computer science, where the term "algorithm" now refers to a technique that a computer may apply to solve a problem. So informally, a collection of instructions called an algorithm is what a computer must follow in order to conduct computations or other problem-solving tasks. To put it simply and informally, it is an explanation in the model of a flowchart or pseudocode; it isn't the entire program or piece of code. Algorithms existed prior to the invention of the computer; they are at the core of computing. Algorithms are used not only in computer science but also in your day-to-day life; for example, if you want to make a cup of tea you have to follow a set of instructions such as:

1) Take a pan.
2) Add some water to it.
   a) Do we have water?
      i) If yes, fill the pan with water.
      ii) If not, go and get some water, etc.

So here you are following a proper set of procedures. As we said, an algorithm is a collection or set of instructions or steps to accomplish a task, so here in our example the procedure is the set of instructions and the task is to make tea. So like this everywhere you are using an algorithm. So now, in the procedure of making tea, are the steps finite or infinite? So, the steps are finite.

Thus the formal definition of an algorithm: "it is a finite set of instructions carried out in a specific order to perform a particular task."

1.2 ANALYSIS OF AN ALGORITHM

Analysing an algorithm involves determining its effectiveness. Suppose you have to travel from place "X" to "Z" and you have many options to choose the path to reach

DOI: 10.1201/9781003331247-2

your destination. Depending on your convenience, whichever path takes less time, we have to choose that path. Like this, there are many solutions to a single problem. Choosing the most suitable one from all the options is why we just have to analyse which is the most suitable.

Let's take another example to understand the analysis of the algorithms. Suppose you are given a problem and you have to write code for that in a programming language like C++; before writing the code you need to make the blueprint that will be describing your code in an English-like language so that before implementing it, it should be made more clear and understood, which is nothing more than the idea of an algorithm. The best strategy would be to compare each algorithm in regard to time, which refers to which one might run faster, and storage, which refers to which is going to use less memory. To put it formally, the goal of the analysis of the algorithms is to compare the best solutions not only in terms of running time but also by including other factors such as memory, disk usage, etc. Keep in mind the analysis of the algorithms is just an approximation; it is not exact or perfect.

Typically, we conduct the following categories of analysis:

Worst-case: The most actions performed on any instance of size a.
Best-case: A scenario where just one step is required for each instance of size a.
The average case: An average amount of steps taken for every instance of size a.

Based on these two key factors, we can analyse the algorithm:

Space complexity: Space complexity is the quantity of space required for an algorithm to execute entirely.
Time complexity: The time that it takes for an algorithm to execute its computation is proportional to the input size n.

Let's dig deeper into these terms.

1.3 THE COMPLEXITY OF AN ALGORITHM

How many steps an algorithm needs to take in order to solve a particular problem is measured by the phrase "algorithm complexity". It assesses an algorithm's count of operations concerning the volume of input data. Instead of counting the exact steps, the order of the operations is always taken into consideration when determining the complexity. O(f) notation, often known as "Big O" notation or asymptotic notation, is a way of expressing how complex an algorithm is. The size of the function, in this case, denoted by the letter f, matches the size of the input data [1].

1.4 CLASSIFICATION OF THE ALGORITHM

There are two different sorts of algorithms, based on the structure of computers:

1.4.1 Parallel Algorithms

An approach that can carry out many instructions concurrently on various processing devices and then aggregate all of the discrete outputs to produce the ultimate outcome is known as a parallel algorithm. The rapid processing of large amounts of data is made possible by the use of parallel algorithms [2].

1.4.2 SEQUENTIAL ALGORITHMS

An algorithm that is run sequentially – once through – from beginning to end without any other processes running, i.e., collections of instructions are executed in a chronological arrangement to resolve a problem, is known as a serial algorithm [3].

It is difficult to break a big problem down into smaller ones. There may be data dependency between subproblems. As a result, in order to remedy the issue, the processors must talk to one another. It has been discovered that the time required by processors for communication with one another exceeds the processing time itself. In order to create an effective parallel algorithm, proper CPU utilization should be taken into account.

1.5 ANALYSING PARALLEL ALGORITHMS

An algorithm's analysis enables us to decide whether or not it is useful. An algorithm is often evaluated based on how long it takes to execute (time complexity) and how much space it takes up (space complexity). Now there is no shortage of storage space because sophisticated memory devices are now affordable. As a result, not as much emphasis is placed on space complexity. The purpose of parallel algorithms is to increase a computer's processing speed. The following parameters are typically taken into account while examining a parallel algorithm: the overall quantity of processors utilized, execution time and overall cost [4].

Time complexity: Reduced calculation time was the primary driver behind the development of parallel algorithms. Therefore, assessing an algorithm's execution time is crucial to determining its effectiveness. The total execution time is the period from when the first processor began to execute until the final processor stopped if all processors do not begin or end at the same time [4].

An algorithm's time complexity is divided into three types:

Worst-case complexity: when an algorithm takes the longest possible time to complete for a given input.

When an algorithm takes an average amount of time for a given input, this is known as **average-case complexity**.

Best-case complexity is when an algorithm takes the least amount of time to run given an input [4].

Quantity of processors utilized: When evaluating the effectiveness of a parallel method, the number of processors used is a crucial consideration. The cost of purchasing, operating, and maintaining the computers is calculated. The more processors used in an algorithm to solve a problem, the more expensive the outcome is [4].

Total Cost: The sum of a parallel algorithm's time complexity and processor count is known as the total cost of that algorithm [4].

Total Cost = Time Completion Complexity × Used Processors

Design Methods for Parallel Algorithms: The hardest and most critical task in the construction of a parallel algorithm is to go for a suitable design technique. Let's look into these techniques one by one.

1.5.1 DIVIDE AND CONQUER APPROACH

The idea behind divide and conquer is to take the problem that involves substantial input and break down the input into smaller pieces or subproblems. On every smaller piece, find the solution and then combine the separate solutions to form a complete solution of the large input.

The following three steps are used in a dispute utilizing the divide and conquer method.

Divide: Dividing the native problem into a set of subproblems.
Conquer: Repetitively and independently solve each subproblem.
Combine: To reach the optimum solution, integrate the solutions into several subproblems [5].

Let us understand this with the help of an example: -
In this example, we will be sorting a given array using the above-mentioned approach, i.e., using merge sort.

1. Let the given array be as shown in Figure 1.1
2. Now, divide the given array into two parts as shown in Figure 1.2.
   Again, divide each subdivided part recursively into two parts until you get individual elements as in Figure 1.3.
3. Now put the different pieces together in sorted order as shown in Figure 1.4.

The steps of combining and conquering go hand in hand here.

- *Advantages of Divide and Conquer*:
  One of the toughest issues, like the mathematical riddle known as the Tower of Hanoi, is frequently resolved using the divide and conquer strategy. Compared to other algorithms, this one is far faster as well because it resolves

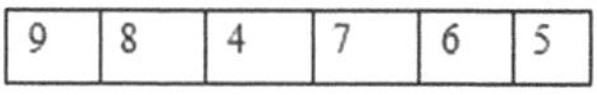

| 9 | 8 | 4 | 7 | 6 | 5 |

FIGURE 1.1   This figure shows an array with six numbers.

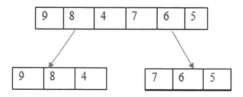

FIGURE 1.2   This figure shows the array is divided into two parts.

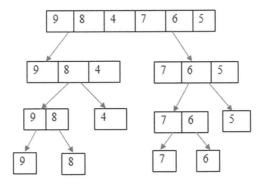

FIGURE 1.3 This figure shows how the subparts are further divided.

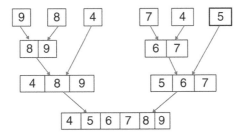

FIGURE 1.4 This figure shows the subparts are merged in a sorted manner.

straightforward smaller problems within the cache memory rather than contacting the main memory which is much slower, and it makes optimal use of cache memory while taking up little space.

- *Disadvantages of Divide and Conquer*:
  It uses recursion in various algorithms; therefore, it needs intensive memory maintenance also the system may crash if the recursion is strictly continued past the CPU stack.
  Applications of Divide and Conquer: Quick Sort, Binary Search, Merge Sort, Karatsuba Algorithm, Strassen's Matrix multiplication.

1.5.2 GREEDY APPROACH

A greedy algorithm is a method of problem-solving that chooses the best choice at the time. It is unconcerned with whether the most excellent result at the moment will produce the final best result. The algorithm never goes back, regardless of how wrong the selection was. It operates in a top-down manner. It's entirely conceivable that employing a greedy strategy won't work for all issues. It does this by consistently attempting to select the best result at the local level.

- *Advantages of the Greedy Approach*:
  It is easier to explain the algorithm and in comparison to other algorithms that are present, this approach yields better outcomes (but, not in all cases) [6].

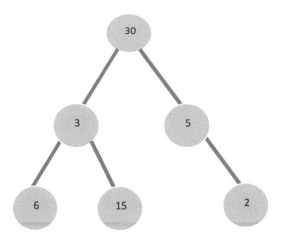

FIGURE 1.5   Greedy approach application to find the longest route through a tree.

- *Disadvantages of the Greedy Approach*:
  The main drawback of the greedy approach is that it may not always give the optimal result. Consider an example where we wish to get the longest path from parent to children in the graph as shown in Figure 1.5. Use the greedy algorithm in this situation as shown in Figure 1.5.

Greedy Approach Procedure:

1. Let us start with node 30, the parent node. The right child weighs 5, whereas the left child weighs 3.
2. The challenge is to identify the longest route. And 5 is currently the best option. Thus, the greedy algorithm will select 5.
3. Finally, the weight of the only child of 5 is 2. Our outcome is 30 + 5 + 2 = 37 as a result of this.
4. It is not, however, the best option. As seen in the graph in Figure 1.6, there is another route that carries additional weight (30 + 3 + 15 = 48).
   - *Different Types of Greedy Algorithms*:
     Knapsack Problem, Selection Sort, Single-Source Shortest Path Problem, Minimum Spanning Tree, Prim's Minimal Spanning Tree Algorithm, Kruskal's Minimum Spanning Tree Algorithm, Dijkstra's Minimum Spanning Tree Algorithm, Huffman Coding, etc.

1.5.3   DYNAMIC PROGRAMMING

Dynamic programming is a way that divides the given problem into smaller problems and updates the solution to use at a later time so we don't have to calculate it again. The optimal substructure property refers to the optimization of the subproblems in order to maximize the overall solution. This type of programming is mostly used to take care of optimization issues. In this view, optimization issues refer to situations where we are trying to find or determine the minimal or maximum solution to

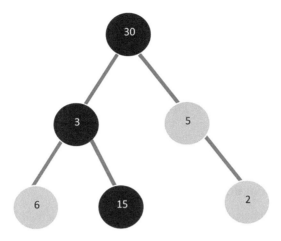

FIGURE 1.6 This figure shows the longest route using the Greedy approach.

a problem. If a solution does exist, dynamic programming makes sure that the best solution will be found. According to the definition of dynamic programming, it is a method for solving difficult problems by first decomposing them into several simpler subproblems, solving each subproblem only once, and then storing the answers to prevent having to perform the same calculations repeatedly. Dynamic programming is one of the most popular algorithms used in bioinformatics [7].

- *What is the methodology behind dynamic programming?*
  The steps that dynamic programming takes are as follows:
  - It separates the difficult problem into smaller, more manageable problems.
  - It effectively addresses these interrelated problems.
  - The results of the lesser problems are preserved (memorization). The method of memorizing involves recalling the solutions to smaller problems.
  - Due to their reuse, the same subproblem is calculated more than once.
  - The difficult problem's solution should be calculated last[8].
  - *Approaches of dynamic programming*: Top-down approach and bottom-up approach.

Top-down approach: The top-down approach uses memorization. Recursion plus caching in this case equals memorizing. While caching entails keeping the interim results, recursion entails calling the method directly. It makes use of the recursion approach, which utilizes an additional call stack memory.

Bottom-up approach: It applies the dynamic programming strategy using the tabulation method. It eliminates the recursion while still solving the same kind of issues. Recursive functions have no overhead or stack overflow problem if recursion is removed. In this method of tabulation, we answer the issues and put the solutions into a matrix. The recursive algorithm begins at the end and works backwards and the bottom-up algorithm begins at the beginning. In the bottom-up method, we begin with the simplest instance and work our way up to the solution.

1.5.4 BACKTRACKING ALGORITHM

Backtracking is an efficient algorithm for handling combinatorial problems. It is used to tackle programmatic and practical problems. Backtracking commences with a probable solution that satisfies all the prerequisites. Then, if the level after that does not produce the desired outcome, we go back to one level and start over with a different option. It is used when there isn't enough information at hand to make the optimal decision.

- *Applications of Backtracking*: N-queen problem, Hamilton cycle, Graph colouring, Sum of subset problem.

1.5.5 BRANCH AND BOUND

A branch and bound algorithm is an optimization technique that identifies the best approach to the problem. In order to get the optimal solution to any given problem, it examines the whole solution space. The boundaries of the function that has to be optimized are merged with the value of the previous best solution. It can be used by the algorithm to precisely locate regions of the solution space. The cheapest way to reach a destination is tracked via a branch and bound search. A solution can be refined after it has been obtained.

1.5.6 LINEAR PROGRAMMING

The optimization task is known as linear programming when the criterion of optimization and the restrictions are linear functions. It is a strategy to get the best outcomes, including the maximum price, the quickest route or the lowest cost. We must give absolute values to several variables in this programming in order to optimize or minimize a given linear objective function and meet a linear programming problem.

1.6 PARALLEL SEARCH ALGORITHM

- **Depth-First Search**: It is an algorithm for evaluating a tree or an undirected graph data structure (or DFS). The goal is to go as far up on that branch as you can by starting from the root. We return to the vertex, which has not yet been visited if a node has no successor nodes.
- **Breadth-First Search**: It is an algorithm for evaluating a tree or an undirected graph data structure (or BFS). We start with one of the nodes and visit all of its neighbouring nodes located on the same level and then move on to the successor node that is immediately adjacent to it on the next level.
- **Best-First Search**: This method moves over a graph in search of the shortest route to a target. Best-First Search provides an evaluation function to determine which node is best to traverse after that, in contrast to BFS and DFS.

1.7 BASIC ALGORITHMS IN COMPUTATIONAL BIOLOGY

Computational biology is the application of computer science, mathematics and statistics to problems in biology. Genetics, evolution, cell biology and biochemistry are a few examples of biological challenges. The field of computational biology encompasses a wide range of traditional disciplines, including biology, chemistry, physics, statistics and computer science. From the perspective of computation, the tasks include algorithmic theory, which concentrates on biologically relevant topics, to the development of tools of computation for particular biological tasks, to experimental work, which replaces a laboratory with test tubes and microscopes with a quick computer and a hard disk full of computational tools written to analyse enormous quantities of biological data in order to support or refute a particular hypothesis.

The term "bioinformatics" is often used to describe the field of computational biology. Although the terms "computational biology" and "bioinformatics" are frequently used interchangeably, there appears to be an emerging consensus that computational biology refers to activities primarily focused on building algorithms to address problems with biological relevance and bioinformatics refers to activities primarily focused on building and using computational tools to analyse available biological data. A few examples of the algorithm used in computational biology are described below; however, their respective detailed versions will be made available in the further specific chapters of this book [9]:

Needleman–Wunsch and Smith–Waterman algorithms are used in implementation of local and global alignment. These algorithms are used to align protein or nucleotide sequences. These are an application of dynamic programming which is used to compare biological sequences [5]. For optimal global alignment, the Needleman-Wunsch algorithm is still frequently utilized, especially where the accuracy of the global alignment is crucial. Local sequence alignment, or finding similar regions between two sequences of nucleic acid or protein sequences, is what the Smith-Waterman method does.

1.7.1   CLASSIFICATION ALGORITHM

Classification is one of the most studied machine learning tasks. The projected attribute acts as the basis for classification by predicting the category of the user-specified target entity.

Classification of genomes and sequence annotation are the two most significant issues in genomics. The many generic categorization models include neural networks, decision trees, naive Bayesian networks and rule learning with evolutionary algorithms [10].

1.7.2   DNA SEQUENCE CLASSIFICATION

A key mining task in machine learning is classification. In order to predict the classification of incoming, unidentified samples, it aims to build a model using the sample set. The identification of biological sequences as a certain data category is a problem that frequently arises in data mining. Sequence classification helps identify genes in DNA molecules by predicting the type of DNA sequence based on how similar its structure or function is to that of other sequences [10].

1.7.3 CLUSTERING ALGORITHMS

Machine learning's clustering technique may group sequences that share certain features and investigate the useful information of unidentified sequences from well-known structures and functionalities. As a result, the grouping of biological sequences has a significant impact on bioinformatics research. Clustering differs from classification in that it does not use a predetermined category. Each cluster has a set of shared traits. With the help of cluster analysis, data with similar features are grouped into one category and then subjected to further analysis [10].

1.7.4 DNA SEQUENCE CLUSTERING

One of the machine learning techniques that are most frequently employed is cluster analysis. In contrast to categorization, we are not aware of the precise categories in advance. Cluster analysis is the unsupervised learning of data patterns. Sequence similarity analysis is the foundation for DNA sequence grouping. DNA sequences with comparable traits are grouped in a cluster using cluster analysis, and the roles of the biological sequences are then examined. The results of DNA sequence clustering are influenced by several parameters, and much recent research on the topic is centred on regional DNA features for grouping. It will be crucial for the future study of DNA sequence clusters if a design can be created that takes into account the general features of DNA sequences. This will significantly increase the accuracy of clustering [10].

1.7.5 ALIGNMENT METHODS

Global alignments and local alignments are the two types of computational methods to align sequences. The alignment was "forced" to cover the whole length of all query sequences so that a global alignment must be calculated. On the other hand, local alignments highlight regions of similarity within long sequences, which are typically highly different collectively. Local alignments generally are the best choice, but due to the additional difficulty of detecting the regions of similarity, they may be more complicated to calculate. Sequence alignment is a subject that has been addressed using a variety of computational approaches. These include formal correct but time-consuming methods such as dynamic programming. These also include efficient probabilistic or heuristic methods designed for extensive database searches, but they need more assurance that they will uncover the best results.

1.7.6 DNA SEQUENCE PATTERN MINING

The fact that the sequence patterns of DNA have remained relatively constant throughout evolution is very important for biological research. The DNA sequence patterns are frequently a section of the DNA sequence with a specific function. The structure and function of these sequences are crucial because, during DNA evolution, more conserved sections in the majority of sequences will establish certain sequence patterns. This explains the evolutionary link between DNA sequences and helps predict how DNA sequences will function. Finding these patterns in DNA sequences and identifying the genes and their activities are the goals of DNA sequence pattern mining.

The key determinants in whether it is possible to discover an exact solution to a challenge as compared to a suboptimal one are the type of problem, the specific instance of the problem to be handled and the computational resources available. This is because certain issues can be addressed optimally in a reasonable amount of time, while others are too hard to solve, leading to only suboptimal results. Heuristics is a term used to describe a variety of potential practical solutions.

1.7.7 LONGEST COMMON SUBSEQUENCE (LCS)

Determining the longest subsequence shared by all of the sequences in a set of sequences is known as the longest common subsequence (LCS) issue (often just two sequences). Contrary to substrings, which must occupy successive positions inside the source sequences, subsequences are not needed to do so, which is how it differs from the longest common substring problem. The LCS issue has an ideal substructure, which makes it possible to separate it into smaller, simpler subproblems, which in turn can be separated into even simpler subproblems, and so on until the solution is finally easy. Dynamic programming techniques, in which subproblem solutions are memorized, or preserved for reuse, apply to problems with these two qualities.

1.7.8 NUSSINOV ALGORITHM

The Nussinov method is a dynamic programming-based nucleic acid structure prediction algorithm used in computational biology to forecast how an RNA molecule will fold. Nussinov's dynamic programming method involves backtracking, which is an extra step. As soon as it is obvious that our "in progress" solution cannot become a complete solution, backtracking enables us to drop incomplete solutions [6, 8].

1.7.9 HEURISTICS

Finding a suboptimal solution to a real-world problem is frequently the only viable alternative because, even with a polynomial algorithm, doing so would take too much time available. Heuristics are typically used in the design of methods that sacrifice accuracy, completeness and optimality for speed.

Local search algorithms, greedy algorithms and probabilistic algorithms are traditional examples of heuristic methods used to address various issues. An illustration of a greedy heuristic for the problem of clustering data points is the frequently utilized agglomerative technique in hierarchical clustering. As opposed to other heuristics, approximation algorithms ensure the quality of the solution by indicating how far away it is from the ideal one. Therefore, more general heuristic approaches, like local search algorithms, do not offer this information, whereas approximation algorithms ensure the quality of the returned suboptimal answer. Finding solutions to challenges in computational biology depends on developing methods that do not suffer from the exponential explosion inherent in the exhaustive search strategy.

Software methods that were previously built for serial computation could now quickly improve in cost performance due to increased transistor count and power dissipation gains [11]. More details about all these algorithms are provided in coming chapters. Exact implementations of all bioinformatics related algorithms are also provided in further chapters with their respective applications for real biological problems.

1.8 CONCLUSION

The recent rapid advancements in hardware technology have given life scientists new opportunities to gather data in a variety of application areas, including omics, biological imaging, medical imaging, etc. The development of life science technologies has also brought up enormous obstacles. The creation of machine learning algorithms, data mining architectures and new data mining analysis functionality studies appropriate for processing biological information is currently a research hotspot. The advancement of machine learning has also been aided by the interdisciplinary approach. Deep learning, reinforcement learning and artificial neural networks have also advanced machine intelligence for several applications. There is a need to understand all these topics in great detail to implement these methods for the analysis of complex biological data and problems. This book provides a basic level understanding of recent developments in all the relevant areas of computer science for the analysis of biological, biotechnological and biomedical data. This chapter is a foundation chapter for algorithms, and other chapters further enhance the reader's understanding of all the mentioned topics. It is anticipated that systematic reading of this book will prove to the user a comprehensive text for teaching and research purposes.

REFERENCES

[1] Java T point. (2011–2021). *The complexity of the Algorithm*. JavaTpoint[online], www.javatpoint.com/daa-complexity-of-algorithm

[2] Blelloch, Guy E., & Maggs, Bruce M. "Parallel Algorithms" (PDF). USA: School of Computer Science, Carnegie Mellon University. Retrieved 2015-07-27.

[3] "A Dictionary of Computing at Encyclopedia.com".

[4] Tutorialspoint. (2022). *Parallel Algorithm – Analysis*. [online], www.tutorialspoint.com/parallel_algorithm/parallel_algorithm_analysis.htm

[5] Gotoh, Osamu. (1982). An improved algorithm for matching biological sequences. *Journal of Molecular Biology* 162 (3): 705–708. https://doi.org/10.1016/0022-2836(82)90398-9

[6] Nussinov, R., & Jacobson, A. B. (Nov 1980). Fast algorithm for predicting the secondary structure of single-stranded RNA. *Proceedings of the National Academy of Sciences of the United States of America* 77 (11): 6309–6313. https://doi.org/10.1073/pnas.77.11.6309

[7] Cormen, Thomas H., Leiserson, Charles E., Rivest, Ronald L., & Stein, Clifford. *Introduction to algorithms*, 3rd edition, pp. 360–395, 2009, The MIT Press, Cambridge, Massachusetts.

[8] Nussinov, R. et al., Predicting RNA secondary structure: The Nussinov Algorithm. *SIAM Journal of Applied Mathematics*, 943, 1978.

[9] Pedersen, Christian N. S. *Algorithms in Computational Biology*. BRICS, pp. 1–15, 2000.

[10] Yang, A., Zhang, W., Wang, J., Yang, K., Han, Y., & Zhang, L. (2020). Review on the Application of Machine Learning Algorithms in the Sequence Data Mining of DNA. *Frontiers in Bioengineering and Biotechnology*, 8. https://doi.org/10.3389/fbioe.2020.01032

[11] Papadimitriou, C. H., & Steiglitz, K. *Combinatorial Optimization: Algorithm and Complexity*, 1982, Prentice-Hall, Inc., Upper Saddle River, NJ.

2 Sequence-Based Algorithms in Computational Biology

Ashwani Kumar and Navnit Kumar Mishra
Chandigarh University, India

Utkarsh Raj
Dr. D. Y. Patil Vidyapeeth, India

Tiratha Raj Singh
Jaypee University of Information Technology, India

2.1 ALGORITHM-INTRODUCTION

Essentially, an algorithm is just a collection of instructions that must be taken in order to solve a particular kind of problem. We'll describe issues with inputs and outputs. Well-stated topics are unambiguous. The steps that another entity must take in order to solve a problem are laid forth in an algorithm. Pen and paper could achieve this, but humans are slow, make mistakes, and despise repetitive tasks. Computers can complete routine tasks fast and accurately despite their lower intelligence. As computers cannot understand English, algorithms must be translated into C or Java. Algorithms demand accurate computer input and are hard to express. A computer would need to know which shoes to place on which feet and how to tie them (Locey & Lennon, 2016). Computational biology sequence algorithms tackle biological problems. Non-formal descriptions of algorithm steps help understand them. Computer scientists explain algorithms using "pseudocode" to avoid programming. Subroutines simplify issues by grouping intractable operations. Our pseudocode uses arguments, variables, and arrays. Algorithm variables vary. An n-element array is an ordered collection of n variables $a1, a2...a_n$. On emphasizing, array elements are ai, with i from 1 to n. After the algorithm's name and required arguments, pseudocode describes its actions, invoking an algorithm with its arguments. Their efforts include creating efficient computer program algorithms. Computational biology algorithms require two steps. The first is developing a biological reality model from a physiologically intriguing computational task. Step two involves designing and implementing a computational problem-solving algorithm. The first phase requires biological reality and the second computational theory. Time and space required to solve the problem determine algorithm quality.

DOI: 10.1201/9781003331247-3

The algorithm's responses should be biologically appropriate since it solves a physiological problem. Specialists from different domains must balance the algorithm's running time, space, and answer relevancy when creating a biological algorithm. One must characterize biological reality and create the algorithm until a balance is reached between its running time and space assumption and its biological relevance.

2.1.1 CLASSIFICATION OF BIOLOGICAL ALGORITHM

Sequence and structure-based analysis techniques for biological problems are developed periodically. Classification is understudied. Sequence-based and structure-based biological algorithms are the most common. This chapter discusses bioinformatics algorithms and methods for understanding biological systems. We can understand complex biological problems by comparing poly-nucleic acid or protein sequences. Dynamic programming investigates local alignment and HHblits. Machine learning algorithms and AI have revealed many biological processes, including protein structural feature identification, active site detection, protein functional classification, and disease prediction.

2.2 ALGORITHMS RELATED TO SEQUENCE ANALYSIS

Inventing alignment is crucial since biological sequencing and string comparisons are similar. Mutations, insertions, deletions, and mismatches evolve genetic sequences. An alignment shows how two biological sequences differ at each evolution stage.

2.2.1 DYNAMIC PROGRAMMING ALGORITHM FOR PAIRWISE ALIGNMENT

Pairwise alignment optimizes sequences. Matches, mismatches, and indels give sites points. Matches score highest, insertions lowest. This is because matches are favored over deletions. Pairwise alignment indels and mismatches decrease sequence similarity. Several scoring algorithms use amino acid conversion's statistical significance. Alignment scoring is simple—2 for insertion, 0 for mismatch, and +1 for match—but many alternative scoring procedures have been modeled.

2.2.1.1 Needleman–Wunsch Algorithm

Needleman and Wunsch's 1970 dynamic programming approach allows pairwise sequence alignment globally or end-to-end. Initialization, computation, and trace back comprise the approach. A matrix with dimensions i and j—the sequence lengths being compared—is initialized. The highest score for each comparison will be determined at each position in the second phase, which is the calculation of $F(i, j)$.

$$F(i,j) = \max\left\{F(i-1,j-1) + s(x_i, y_i), F(i-1,j) - d, F(I, j-1) - d\right\}$$

where "$s(x_i, y_i)$" is the score for match or mismatch score, whereas "d" is the deletion penalty.

Tracing backward begins with the cell at the bottom right of the matrix after determining the highest possible score for each point in the matrix. Each level requires moving from the current cell to the nearest cell that scored the current cell. If the diagonal cell scores highest, that cell is a match or mismatch. Insertion/deletion is assigned to problems with top or left cell scores. After the trace back, we will have two sequences aligned end-to-end with the highest alignment score.

2.2.1.2 Smith–Waterman Algorithm

Smith and Waterman's (1981) Needleman–Wunsch-like algorithm enables local sequence alignment. More compact segments of two sequences can be brought into alignment via local sequence alignment. Finding a domain or pattern in longer sequences may be challenging in biological settings. The Needleman–Wunsch method has the same steps, but there are two major differences. In addition, the value 0 can be used in the computation of the maximum score:

$$F(i,j) = \max\{0, F(i-1, j-1\} + s(x_i, y_j), F(i-1, j) - d, F(I, j-1) - d\}$$

"0" as the maximum score starts a new alignment. It lets alignments end wherever in the matrix, which is convenient. Hence, the trace back begins at the matrix point with the greatest $F(i, j)$ value and continues until it reaches 0.

2.2.2 Heuristic Local Alignment

The sheer quantity and length of sequences present challenges for bioinformatics sequence analysis. Over 100 million protein and DNA sequences from animals across the evolutionary tree have been collected. Pairwise local sequence alignment tools based on dynamic programming algorithm are accurate and promise the best alignment, but they are too slow for large sequence databases. Dynamic programming approaches take O(mn) sequence lengths to complete. In the early days of sequence comparison studies, BLAST (Altschul et al., 1990), BLAT (Kent, 2002), and FASTA (Lipman & Pearson, 1985) were utilized. Several recent works have enhanced the effectiveness of similarity search algorithms, including LSCluster (Pearson & Lipman, 1988), Usearch (Edgar, 2010), Vsearch (Rognes et al., 2016), Diamond (Buchfink et al., 2014), and Ghostx (Suzuki et al., 2014). In order to predict the maximum possible score, these algorithms look for exact matches and, depending on those matches, improve the alignment.

The Simple Tool for Finding Alignments in a Local Database was developed by Altschul and his group (1990). One of the main tenets of this method is that the best-scoring sequence alignment will have the greatest number of perfect matches and/or highly scoring sub-alignments. The algorithm operates as follows: the first step is to divide the query sequence into seeds, look up exact matches in the database, and then repeatedly stretch the string matches for an alignment free of indels. This process is repeated until the highest possible score is obtained. Although seeds expedite the search for exact matches, the un-gapped alignment only loses a small fraction of meaningful matches. This is especially true in the field of biology, where the accuracy and sensitivity of BLAST search algorithms have made them indispensable. The PSI-BLAST method is an extension of the original BLAST algorithm (Altschul et al., 1997). PSI-BLAST performs repeated iterations of BLAST, with the results of the previous round serving as queries for the subsequent rounds. PSI-BLAST may be sluggish, yet it is an effective method for finding distant homology links.

BLAST and PSI-BLAST are widely used, although newer methods are more accurate and sensitive. HMMs, or hidden Markov models, have been used in many biological data analysis applications. Since 2012, HHblits has searched remote homology sequences using iterative HMM-HMM comparison (Remmert et al., 2012). It is compatible with BLAST and PSI-BLAST and has 50–100 times higher sensitivity. The method, which compares HMM representations of sequences, gives the gadget its high sensitivity. HHblits' prefilter reduces the amount of alignments from millions to thousands, making it faster. HHblits creates profile HMMs for each database sequence. This methodology reduces HMM comparisons for similarity search by prefiltering target sequences with ungapped alignment searched through Smith–Waterman considering E-value. Selecting target sequences does this.

2.2.3   SEQUENCE ANALYSIS THROUGH MACHINE LEARNING

The best situation is using AI and ML algorithms to biological data. Computational biology and bioinformatics research data are usually interpreted biologically by statistical analysis. Comparative genomics studies use maximum likelihood (Needleman & Wunsch, 1970) and neighbor joining (Saitou & Nei, 1987). While Sequence analysis uses Naive Bayes and Markov chains; Random forests, SVMs, and logistic regressions are also employed in many applications. Some applications include protein sequence prediction and structural and functional class prediction. Long short-term memory (LSTM) (Hochreiter & Schmidhuber, 1997) and convolutional neural networks (CNN or ConvNet) (Krizhevsky et al., 2017) are being used again to predict biochemical and biomolecular features. Protein contact prediction and post-translational modifications are examples for such processes, and deep neural networks have enabled this surge in algorithm optimal utilization.

Several machine learning algorithms are based on supervised and unsupervised learning. Unsupervised learning can classify unlabeled data if the data cannot be categorized. Proteins are categorized by their amino acid sequence similarity. K-means clustering (Forgy, 1965) and Markov clustering (van Dongen, 2000) are feasible unsupervised classification methods. If the data are classified into various sets, the computer program is trained by examining both positive and negative cases. Showing the computer marked data does this. After training, data similar to the training dataset but not in it can be used to assess training correctness. Assisted machine learning involves using labeled data to train and evaluate a computer to classify. This includes SVM, HMM, random forest, and CNN.

2.2.4   HIDDEN MARKOV MODELS

The Hidden Markov Model (HMM) predicts future events using probability. HMMs underlie numerous complicated models for sequence element detection, profile searches, and multiple sequence alignment. These models can explore biological sequences for numerous key elements. In biological data processing, Viterbi Algorithm HMMs recognize binding sites on DNA sequences. The right order of nucleotides hides a binding site. We know the nucleotide sequence but not the binding location. HMMs are good at discovering binding sites because they categorize hidden states using transition and emission probabilities from observed frequencies. HMMs have emission and transition probabilities. Transition probability is the probability of switching states. Emission or output probability is the likelihood of witnessing a variable in a state.

HMMs have built sequence profiles and probabilistic model representations of protein clusters. Pfam employs HMM to represent proteins based on their functional components. Hidden Markov models (HMMs) cannot depend on occurrences from a long time ago. This limits the use of standard HMMs in composite settings where sequence strings affect each other even if they are sequentially distant but structurally close. Autocomplete and word recommendations are examples outside of biology. The word that preceded the suggestion directly affects the words that follow.

2.2.5 NEURAL NETWORKS

Computational biology uses artificial neural networks, another categorization method. Neurons form artificial neural networks. Each neuron has several input connections with various weights. Activation functions determine neuron output. Each layer of a neural network may have several neuronal connections. Guided learning and categorization employ neural networks. This strategy makes use of labeled data and proceeds through the primary steps outlined below:

   I. Dataset: Separate the information into a training dataset and a testing dataset (usually using a 70 and 30 split or a 60 and 40 split, respectively).
  II. Training: Utilize the training data to go throughout the neuron and estimate the output.
 III. Calculate the error based on the difference between the actual output and the estimated output, and then modify the weights so that they are consistent with the error. Repeat step II.
  IV. Testing: Once the model has been trained via several iterations that fall between steps II and III, the model is ready to be evaluated. When computing the result, use the test set, which consists of data that the model has not seen before. Since the actual label is available, it is possible to derive the accuracy and sensitivity of the test by comparing the number of wrong classifications (false negative or false positives) with the number of correct (true negatives or true positives).
   V. During validation, the splits between the training set and the test set are shuffled about, and new sets are generated from the original dataset. After that, this new test-train split is employed once more, and the process is repeated over stages II–IV. The goal is to develop a model that can be applied to generalized datasets independently. It is possible for there to be several iterations for this stage, which is why it is referred to as k-fold cross validation.

The model's efficacy is assessed using many activation functions or neural network designs. Best-performing models should have high recall rates. AI and machine learning depend on data quality. Homogeneous, low-noise data is good. Biological data noise might result from mislabeled sequencing fragments. Homogeneity spreads data variability evenly across divisions. Data scientists must assess data quality before training models, which takes time. Models may categorize skewedly if the training dataset is not representative of the population. Biased models may perform well on the testing dataset but poorly in reality. The model classified just the training cases. The model's biased sample distorts reality. Dataset size and iterations affect neural network classification accuracy. High-powered processing has improved over the past decade, but neural networks with massive biological data can train accurate classifiers. "Dense Networks" or "Deep Learning" are the latest neural networks. LSTM deep networks feature several hidden layers. Network profundity enhances quality, but model training requires more computational resources.

2.3   NEXT-GENERATION SEQUENCING

Over 30 years, sequencing technology have improved. First with Sanger sequencing, then Craig Venter's whole genome shot gun sequencing, and lastly next-generation sequencing (NGS) (Craig Venter et al., 2001). The Nanopore, the latest sequencing instrument, is compact, efficient, and USB-connected. It fits on a small laptop and is portable. Technology that once cost thousands of dollars per nucleotide is now cheaper. A bioinformatics technique drives a sequence and its biological information, whereas an experimental section isolates, amplifies, and sequences a sample. Each section is a "workflow." The bioinformatics pipeline analyzes NGS sequences using statistical and heuristic algorithms. This section focuses on the bioinformatics pipeline of NGS, which uses a variety of computational methods and algorithms to ensure accurate and efficient sequencing. High-throughput sequencing is NGS. This approach can accurately analyze big RNA and DNA genomes in less time and at a cheaper cost than Sanger sequencing. Different types of platform technologies used in NGS all adhere to the same eight primary processes:

I.   The first step in NGS is preparing the library so that it can yield many high-quality sequences reads. Pieces of genomic DNA or RNA are separated into 150–5000 base pairs (bp) using the sequencing platform. The library can be made through either mechanical shearing or enzyme-based fragmentation (Head et al., 2014; Knierim et al., 2011). Nebulization, acoustic shearing, needle shearing, and sonication are all examples of mechanical shearing techniques. Shearing using restriction enzymes (endonucleases) and transposons is an example of an enzyme-based method (Marine et al., 2011). The short, sticky ends of a read are $5'$-phosphate and $3'$-hydroxl. Adapter ligation and amplification are made possible by adenylation of $3'$ ends, which corrects damaged ends. Several sample types can be sequenced in a single run when individual barcodes are assigned to each fragment during library preparation (Dodt et al., 2012).

II.   This stage generates thousands of copies of every read. After a library has been deposited on a flow cell, fragments can be amplified using emulsion PCR or bridge amplification. The library is amplified in a water-oil emulsion using emulsion PCR Dressman et al., 2003). According to a group of researchers (Nakano et al., 2003), library single-stranded DNA is amplified by hybridizing to forward and reverse oligos attached to the surface of a flow cell. Library adapter sequences are complemented by these oligos. Single-stranded DNA forms a bridge by folding over and binding to adapter-complementary oligos. After the original DNA strand is removed, the complementary extended DNA strands still connected to the flow cell cluster together to form a clonal population. The enzyme DNA polymerase increases DNA copy number by joining together nucleotides (Pemov et al., 2005). Using sequencing technologies like Roche 454, Illumina (Solexa) and Ion Torrent (Proton/PGM), we can determine the correct order of bases in an amplified sequence. Illumina (Solexa) sequencing can distinguish between four different types of DNA bases (A, T, C, or G) and it generates a fluorescent signal for each one that is added to the growing strand of nucleic acid. The typical length of a sequencing read generated by Illumina is 100–150 bases.

III. The main difference between Illumina variations is how much DNA can be read in one run. Roche 454 uses pyrosequencing. Pyrosequencing uses fluorescence to detect pyrophosphate production after polymerase integrates nucleotides into a new DNA strand. Roche 454 sequencing produces 1000-base-pair sequences. It scans optical signals as bases are introduced and sequences multiple reads like Illumina. Ion Torrent (PGM or Proton sequencing) counts the direct release of H+ (protons) by DNA polymerase during nucleotide polymerization, unlike the other two methods, which measure light intensity. This distinguishes Ion Torrent from the other two methods. NGS fragments DNA or RNA into 100–200 base pairs. These sequencing technologies produce FASTQ-formatted 20–1000-bp raw sequencing reads. This format stores nucleotide sequences and quality scores. Reads can be "single-ended" or "paired-ended" depending on organization. Paired end reads result from sequencing fragments longer than 250 base pairs.

IV.   Quality assurance and filtering of reads the readings are converted to an electronic format and used in a bioinformatics NGS procedure to construct the genome or gene sequence after sequencing. Quality control and filtering come first in a bioinformatics NGS pipeline, despite being the fourth step in getting a complete analyzable sequence. Datasets can be cleaned up by using read filters to get rid of any reads with low confidence or that are clearly incorrect. FastQC (Simon Andrews, 2020) runs a quality control check on the amplified reads and reports the coverage, quantity, and quality of the reads. The majority of these algorithms derive read frequency and quality scores by clustering short reads. Following this step, software like as CutAdapt (Martin, 2011), trimmomatic (Bolger et al., 2014), and others are used to remove adapter sequences, filter out low-quality base pairs, and shorten reads.

V.   De novo or reference-based assemblies are used to align and map paired-end or single-end reads. After a good read, this happens (in the absence of a reference sequence). BWA (Li, 2013), Bowtie (Langmead et al., 2009), and TopHat align sequence reads of various lengths (Trapnell et al., 2009). Heuristic-based aligners swiftly align sequences and generate consensus sequences. They find overlapping reads and combine them into longer reads to create a genome or gene string. This stage aims to create a consensus sequence from millions of reads. A consensus sequence describes the individual's genetic makeup at sample collection. This completes the genome sequence. Do the steps below to undertake a comprehensive inquiry that goes beyond a single sequence.

VI. NGS is great for variant discovery since it saves time and provides data for sequencing analysis. Variant analysis uses the reads file to identify fixed and changing nucleotides. Statistical computations spanning millions of images make this approach time-consuming and computationally expensive. Variant calling scores can be assessed using bootstrap re-sampling. SAMtools (Li et al., 2009), GATK (Head et al., 2014) and VarScan (McKenna et al., 2010) are used to analyze genomic sequences and identify variations. Indels, SNVs, and SNPs are these alterations (SNPs) (Li et al., 2009; Koboldt et al., 2009; Koboldt et al., 2012). SAMtools and GATK employ Bayesian statistical methods to find genuine alignment errors. VarScan uses heuristics. Most Next Generation Sequencing methods for SNV identification detect germline genomic alterations. SNPs are population variations.

VII. Annotation: The genetic variants that were found have been given annotations based on published research that was subjected to peer review as well as public genetic variant databases.

VIII. The meaning of the variants is as follows: In the end, to arrive at the most precise diagnosis possible, professionals in the medical field will analyze these variants and gather the patient's clinical history. This includes conducting an analysis of gene networks, looking at the many disease pathways, and locating the specific mutations that are responsible for a disease.

2.3.1 Application

Next-generation sequencing can help researchers solve several biological problems. NGS data analysis includes genome sequencing, gene expression, transcriptome profiling, and epigenetics. Researchers can sequence huge genomes using NGS (also known as whole-genome sequencing). This helps detect and understand genetic variants like SNPs, insertions, and deletions of DNA, as well as rearrangements like translocations and inversions, which are linked to diseases for targeted research (Peng et al., 2015). Scientists utilize RNASeq to characterize and profile genome-wide transcriptomes (Koh et al., 2015). Genome-wide gene expression studies (transcription, translation, and post-transitional alterations) and molecular pathway research help understand gene regulation in immunological, neurological, and other chronic disorders. This method can also study heritable gene regulation alterations without DNA sequence changes. Epigenetics affects growth, development, and disease. Cancer epigenetic research has illuminated several essential disease pathways.

2.4 CONCLUSION

Subdomains split sequence analysis research. Aligning sequences reveals important structural and functional information. Identifying orthologous and homologous sequences can be used to study sequence evolution. Sequence analysis uses machine learning to categorize and predict elements. Sequence profiles and distantly related sequences are identified using statistical approaches. Next-generation sequencing technologies provide tailored medication and haplotype and quasi-species identification. If NGS processes are properly set up, drugs can be analyzed at the sequence level.

REFERENCES

Altschul, S. F., Gish, W., Miller, W., Myers, E. W., & Lipman, D. J. (1990). Basic local alignment search tool. *Journal of Molecular Biology*, *215*(3). https://doi.org/10.1016/S0022-2836(05)80360-2

Altschul, S. F., Madden, T. L., Schäffer, A. A., Zhang, J., Zhang, Z., Miller, W., & Lipman, D. J. (1997). Gapped BLAST and PSI-BLAST: A new generation of protein database search programs. *Nucleic Acids Research*, *25*(17). https://doi.org/10.1093/nar/25.17.3389

Bolger, A. M., Lohse, M., & Usadel, B. (2014). Trimmomatic: A flexible trimmer for Illumina sequence data. *Bioinformatics*, *30*(15). https://doi.org/10.1093/bioinformatics/btu170

Buchfink, B., Xie, C., & Huson, D. H. (2014). Fast and sensitive protein alignment using DIAMOND. *Nature Methods*, *12*(1). https://doi.org/10.1038/nmeth.3176

Craig Venter, J., Adams, M. D., Myers, E. W., Li, P. W., Mural, R. J., Sutton, G. G., Smith, H. O., Yandell, M., Evans, C. A., Holt, R. A., Gocayne, J. D., Amanatides, P., Ballew, R. M., Huson, D. H., Wortman, J. R., Zhang, Q., Kodira, C. D., Zheng, X. H., Chen, L., … Zhu, X. (2001). The sequence of the human genome. *Science*, *291*(5507). https://doi.org/10.1126/science.1058040

Dodt, M., Roehr, J. T., Ahmed, R., & Dieterich, C. (2012). FLEXBAR-flexible barcode and adapter processing for next-generation sequencing platforms. *Biology*, *1*(3). https://doi.org/10.3390/biology1030895

Dressman, D., Yan, H., Traverso, G., Kinzler, K. W., & Vogelstein, B. (2003). Transforming single DNA molecules into fluorescent magnetic particles for detection and enumeration of genetic variations. *Proceedings of the National Academy of Sciences of the United States of America*, *100*(15). https://doi.org/10.1073/pnas.1133470100

Edgar, R. C. (2010). Search and clustering orders of magnitude faster than BLAST. *Bioinformatics*, *26*(19). https://doi.org/10.1093/bioinformatics/btq461

Forgy, E. W. (1965). Cluster analysis of multivariate data: Efficiency versus interpretability of classifications. *Biometrics*, *21*(3).

Head, S. R., Kiyomi Komori, H., LaMere, S. A., Whisenant, T., Van Nieuwerburgh, F., Salomon, D. R., & Ordoukhanian, P. (2014). Library construction for next-generation sequencing: Overviews and challenges. *BioTechniques*, *56*(2). https://doi.org/10.2144/000114133

Hochreiter, S., & Schmidhuber, J. (1997). Long short-term memory. *Neural Computation*, *9*(8). https://doi.org/10.1162/neco.1997.9.8.1735

Kent, W. J. (2002). BLAT—The BLAST-Like Alignment Tool. *Genome Research*, *12*(4). https://doi.org/10.1101/gr.229202

Knierim, E., Lucke, B., Schwarz, J. M., Schuelke, M., & Seelow, D. (2011). Systematic comparison of three methods for fragmentation of long-range PCR products for next generation sequencing. *PLoS ONE*, *6*(11). https://doi.org/10.1371/journal.pone.0028240

Koboldt, D. C., Chen, K., Wylie, T., Larson, D. E., McLellan, M. D., Mardis, E. R., Weinstock, G. M., Wilson, R. K., & Ding, L. (2009). VarScan: Variant detection in massively parallel sequencing of individual and pooled samples. *Bioinformatics, 25*(17). https://doi.org/10.1093/bioinformatics/btp373

Koboldt, D. C., Zhang, Q., Larson, D. E., Shen, D., McLellan, M. D., Lin, L., Miller, C. A., Mardis, E. R., Ding, L., & Wilson, R. K. (2012). VarScan 2: Somatic mutation and copy number alteration discovery in cancer by exome sequencing. *Genome Research, 22*(3). https://doi.org/10.1101/gr.129684.111

Koh, Y., Park, I., Sun, C. H., Lee, S., Yun, H., Park, C. K., Park, S. H., Park, J. K., & Lee, S. H. (2015). Detection of a distinctive genomic signature in rhabdoid glioblastoma, A Rare disease entity identified by whole exome sequencing and whole transcriptome sequencing. *Translational Oncology, 8*(4). https://doi.org/10.1016/j.tranon.2015.05.003

Krizhevsky, A., Sutskever, I., & Hinton, G. E. (2017). ImageNet classification with deep convolutional neural networks. *Communications of the ACM, 60*(6). https://doi.org/10.1145/3065386

Langmead, B., Trapnell, C., Pop, M., & Salzberg, S. L. (2009). Ultrafast and memory-efficient alignment of short DNA sequences to the human genome. *Genome Biology, 10*(3). https://doi.org/10.1186/gb-2009-10-3-r25

Li, H. (2013). [Heng Li—Compares BWA to other long read aligners like CUSHAW2] Aligning sequence reads, clone sequences and assembly contigs with BWA-MEM. *ArXiv Preprint ArXiv*.

Li, H., Handsaker, B., Wysoker, A., Fennell, T., Ruan, J., Homer, N., Marth, G., Abecasis, G., & Durbin, R. (2009). The sequence alignment/map format and SAMtools. *Bioinformatics, 25*(16). https://doi.org/10.1093/bioinformatics/btp352

Lipman, D. J., & Pearson, W. R. (1985). Rapid and sensitive protein similarity searches. *Science, 227*(4693). https://doi.org/10.1126/science.2983426

Locey, K. J., & Lennon, J. T. (2016). Scaling laws predict global microbial diversity. *Proceedings of the National Academy of Sciences of the United States of America, 113*(21). https://doi.org/10.1073/pnas.1521291113

Marine, R., Polson, S. W., Ravel, J., Hatfull, G., Russell, D., Sullivan, M., Syed, F., Dumas, M., & Wommack, K. E. (2011). Evaluation of a transposase protocol for rapid generation of shotgun high-throughput sequencing libraries from nanogram quantities of DNA. *Applied and Environmental Microbiology, 77*(22). https://doi.org/10.1128/AEM.05610-11

Martin, M. (2011). Cutadapt removes adapter sequences from high-throughput sequencing reads. *EMBnet Journal, 17*(1). https://doi.org/10.14806/ej.17.1.200

McKenna, A., Hanna, M., Banks, E., Sivachenko, A., Cibulskis, K., Kernytsky, A., Garimella, K., Altshuler, D., Gabriel, S., Daly, M., & DePristo, M. A. (2010). The genome analysis toolkit: A MapReduce framework for analyzing next-generation DNA sequencing data. *Genome Research, 20*(9). https://doi.org/10.1101/gr.107524.110

Nakano, M., Komatsu, J., Matsuura, S. I., Takashima, K., Katsura, S., & Mizuno, A. (2003). Single-molecule PCR using water-in-oil emulsion. *Journal of Biotechnology, 102*(2). https://doi.org/10.1016/S0168-1656(03)00023-3

Needleman, S. B., & Wunsch, C. D. (1970). A general method applicable to the search for similarities in the amino acid sequence of two proteins. *Journal of Molecular Biology, 48*(3). https://doi.org/10.1016/0022-2836(70)90057-4

Pearson, W. R., & Lipman, D. J. (1988). Improved tools for biological sequence comparison. *Proceedings of the National Academy of Sciences of the United States of America, 85*(8). https://doi.org/10.1073/pnas.85.8.2444

Pemov, A., Modi, H., Chandler, D. P., & Bavykin, S. (2005). DNA analysis with multiplex microarray-enhanced PCR. *Nucleic Acids Research, 33*(2). https://doi.org/10.1093/nar/gnh184

Peng, L., Bian, X. W., Li, D. K., Xu, C., Wang, G. M., Xia, Q. Y., & Xiong, Q. (2015). Large-scale RNA-Seq Transcriptome Analysis of 4043 Cancers and 548 Normal Tissue Controls across 12 TCGA Cancer Types. *Scientific Reports, 5*. https://doi.org/10.1038/srep13413

Remmert, M., Biegert, A., Hauser, A., & Söding, J. (2012). HHblits: Lightning-fast iterative protein sequence searching by HMM-HMM alignment. *Nature Methods*, *9*(2). https://doi.org/10.1038/nmeth.1818

Rognes, T., Flouri, T., Nichols, B., Quince, C., & Mahé, F. (2016). VSEARCH: A versatile open source tool for metagenomics. *PeerJ*, *2016*(10). https://doi.org/10.7717/peerj.2584

Saitou, N., & Nei, M. (1987). The neighbor-joining method: A new method for reconstructing phylogenetic trees. *Molecular Biology and Evolution*, *4*(4). https://doi.org/10.1093/oxfordjournals.molbev.a040454

Simon Andrews. (2020). Babraham Bioinformatics—FastQC a quality control tool for high throughput sequence data. *Soil*, *5*(1).

Smith, T. F., & Waterman, M. S. (1981). Identification of common molecular subsequences. *Journal of Molecular Biology*, *147*(1). https://doi.org/10.1016/0022-2836(81)90087-5

Suzuki, S., Kakuta, M., Ishida, T., & Akiyama, Y. (2014). GHOSTX: An improved sequence homology search algorithm using a query suffix array and a database suffix array. *PLoS ONE*, *9*(8). https://doi.org/10.1371/journal.pone.0103833

Trapnell, C., Pachter, L., & Salzberg, S. L. (2009). TopHat: Discovering splice junctions with RNA-Seq. *Bioinformatics*, *25*(9). https://doi.org/10.1093/bioinformatics/btp120

van Dongen, S. M. (2000). Graph clustering by flow simulation. *Computer Science Review*, *1*(1), https://dspace.library.uu.nl/bitstream/handle/1874/848/full.pdf?sequen

3 Structure-Based Algorithms in Computational Biology

Navnit Kumar Mishra and Ashwani Kumar
Chandigarh University, India

Utkarsh Raj
Dr. D. Y. Patil Vidyapeeth, India

Tiratha Raj Singh
Jaypee University of Information Technology, India

3.1 BASIC CONTEXT: AN INTRODUCTION

We have come a long way in the field of computational biology. For example, we have learned about patterns in human health by combining different types of "big data," and we have located and categorized genes that are linked to certain diseases. On a separate track, research into the central topic of how the genome is regulated is elucidating the dynamic architecture of chromatin. The development of potent conformational sampling tools has also provided a molecularly precise perspective of biological processes. The Computational Structural Biology Group uses cutting-edge methods from a variety of fields to understand the molecular underpinnings of disease and the therapeutic potential of newly discovered drugs. The free energy landscape is the foundation of recent efforts in structural bioinformatics. The ensemble of conformations that make up a protein molecule and their relative population defines its function, as described by the landscape.

As an alternative to the induced-fit model, the section developed the dynamic free energy landscape, conformational selection, and population shift to explain molecular recognition and allosteric regulation. Experiments verified many of the algorithms developed based on these concepts. Scientists have contributed significantly to our understanding of structure, function, and gain-of-function by extending the ensemble model to catalysis, disease activation, and inhibitory processes. With their fresh take, we can better grasp both experimental and clinical observations. Genetics, software, and molecular biology comprise structural bioinformatics. Combinatorial algorithms and machine learning analyze protein structure alignment, DNA, RNA, genome, gene expression, gene prediction, and phylogeny. This chapter explores real-world data applications. Complex molecular biology computational issues demand approximation (Liang et al., 2019), and constraint logic programming (CLP) solves NP-hard biological computer issues.

3.2 ALGORITHMS FOR RNA STRUCTURE PREDICTION AND ANALYSIS

RNA structure prediction helps develop new drugs and identify genetic diseases. Several computational methods—deterministic and soft—predict RNA structure from sequence. Soft computing methods can approximate RNA structures due to dynamics, post-transcriptional folding, and thermodynamic parameter estimation issues. Transcript data analytics relies on soft computing RNA secondary structure prediction. Internal loop, helix, hairpin loop, bulge, and multiloop are anticipated RNA secondary structures. RNA soft computing uses artificial neural networks, genetic algorithms, and fuzzy logic. Metaheuristics methods like particle swarm optimization, simulated annealing, tabu search, and ant colony optimization investigate the 3D structure of RNA. Backbones and secondary structure require base pairing. The bases are aligned based on compatibility to get the optimum arrangement computationally (Yu et al., 2020).

Dynamic programming predicts the optimum RNA or pseudoknot 3D structure. Most dynamic algorithms have O(N4) space and temporal complexity (N6). Quantum field theory's Feynman diagrams represent Pseudoknots' 3D structure, simplifying the method. This approach uses well-established thermodynamic parameters for RNA folding and a few pseudoknots thermodynamic stability factors to generate the best native RNA structure in global minima from RNA sequence. Short pseudoknotted and non-pseudoknotted RNAs predict algorithm characteristics. Both time- and memory-intensive, this thermodynamic technique precisely folds pseudoknotted RNAs into its best global energy minimum.

3.2.1 RNA FOLDING ALGORITHMS

ViennaRNA and MFOLD are most used bioinformatics tools to predict secondary structures of RNA. Both the tools are based on RNA folding algorithms (Eddy, 2004). The RNA folding algorithms simply finds the structure or strings with maximum numbers of nucleotide base paring. There is a fundamental relationship between algorithms for pairwise interactions of palindrome like RNA string to RNA folding algorithms. This algorithm uses a scoring system of +1 per base pair and 0 for anything to identify the RNA structure with a string of nucleotide bases.

3.2.1.1 Nussinov Algorithm to Predict Secondary RNA Structures

Computational biology uses RNA secondary structure prediction from nucleotides. Nussinov-Jacobson predicts and builds RNA secondary fold from RNA sequence (Haleš et al., 2017; Clote, 2005). This dynamic programming technique for RNA structure prediction handles computationally demanding RNA combinatorics. The Nussinov algorithm maximizes nucleotide base pairs to predict RNA secondary structure. This approach predicts pseudoknots, non-crossing RNA structures, which is a strength. One half of a stem is intercalated between stacking two parts of another stem to form a pseudoknot. Algorithm scores input RNA structure in L x L matrix, Nij. Scores are +1 or 0 for nucleotide pairs. The algorithm aims to optimize scores by employing a backtrack strategy on nucleotide strings that yield the highest scores. Nussinov method compares nucleotides using only four rules to maximize base pairs score. Recursively calculating secondary structures for short contigs, the Nussinov algorithm reaches larger ones.

3.2.1.2 Machine Learning Solves RNA Puzzles

In just a few years, machine learning algorithms have transformed structural biology, the study of biomolecule's three-dimensional structure. Experimentalists employ machine learning models to anticipate structures to speed up structure identification (such as computer vision algorithms for cryo-electron microscopy) to solve biological issues (such as AlphaFold) (e.g., large language models for protein design). The field still needs to model protein dynamics, anticipate higher-order complexes, generalize protein folding physics, and connect protein structure to function in vivo and in context. The great diversity and interwoven nature of these problems has spurred researchers to construct breakthrough machine learning algorithms and create and refine industry-wide standards and datasets.

Experimentally or computationally, RNA molecules fold into complex three-dimensional shapes. Understanding these structures may help find cures for incurable diseases. Townshend et al machine's learning method significantly improves RNA structure prediction. Most recent deep learning achievements need massive data training (Townshend et al., 2021b). With such little training data, comparable solutions could tackle issues in many fields.

3.2.1.3 Geometric Deep Learning of RNA Structure

Drug design and RNA function depend on their three-dimensional structures. Computationally predicting the few experimentally known RNA structures is difficult. A novel machine learning method based on 18 known RNA structures predicted 3D RNA structures (Townshend et al., 2021b). In community-wide blind RNA structure prediction contests, Atomic Rotationally Equivariant Scorer (ARES) outperforms previous methods. They overcome a major drawback of deep neural networks by learning from a small dataset. Because it only uses XYZ coordinates and ignores RNA information, this technique is applicable to many problems in chemistry, materials science, structural biology, and more.

3.2.1.4 GPU-Based Acceleration of an RNA Tertiary Structure Prediction Algorithm

Using X-ray crystallography, cryo-electron microscopy, and nuclear magnetic resonance, the RNA tertiary structure is determined in 3D. Due to the huge sample size needed, such an experimental approach is difficult to use for RNA structure prediction. Computational techniques predicted RNA tertiary structure. These experiment methods cannot be used for high-throughput structure determination since they require many pure samples. Hence, computer methods dominate RNA tertiary structure prediction. Several computationally intensive prediction systems need speeding up. The FARNA algorithm predicts RNA 3D structures well. The FARNA algorithm was parallelized recently. A parallelization technique optimizes GPU and multi-core CPU utilization (Jeon et al., 2013). They tested their approach on several RNA sequences and found that it considerably reduces the time needed to estimate RNA molecule structure. The fundamental architecture with a single CPU core was speeded up by 24x. GPUs accelerate 12x faster than quad-core CPUs. Modern PCs with GPUs and multi-core CPUs make their method computationally cost-effective.

Computational methods are better for creating ribozymes that sense oligonucleotides. Allosteric ribozymes help biosensors, designer gene control systems, gene therapy, and molecular computation. IFRG and RG generate allosteric ribozymes. The RG predicts the secondary structure of allosteric ribozyme sequences in the hammerhead ribozyme by recognizing OBS strings in the second stem. Inverse folding program IFRG provides allosteric ribozyme sequences with varying OBS and equivalent folding. Random search generates OBS sequences. The Ribozyme Generator's allosteric ribozyme sequence feeds the IFRG program. Thermodynamic characteristics predict allosteric ribozymes with 90% accuracy using RNAfold and RNAinverse. Both approaches involve dynamic programming and partition function random search.

3.2.2 OTHER IMPORTANT ALGORITHMS FOR RNA STRUCTURE PREDICTION USING VARIOUS METHODS

3.2.2.1 Prediction of Structured Motifs in the Genomic Promoter Strings using an Efficient Algorithm

A genomic sequence cis-regulatory module algorithm has been created. Box-links are used to store information about conserved parts in RISO method dataset sequences (Marsan & Sagot, 2000). Structured motifs—conserved portions used to build promoter models—are vital to gene regulatory research. Complexity study shows exponential time and space gains over the most exact methods. The new computational linguistics algorithm beats previous ones and is accessible online by more than four orders of magnitude. Biological dataset experiments show that the approach can extract useful consensuses.

3.2.2.2 Fast and Accurate Structure Probability Estimation for Simultaneous Alignment and Folding of RNAs with Markov Chains

Non-coding RNA structure and analysis is standardized by simultaneous alignment and folding (SA&F). Sankoff's $O(n6)$ solution solves theoretically. Lower energy models or Sankoff algorithm alignment constraints minimize the program's extraordinary complexity.

De novo protein design employs PMcomp simplifications and hybrid energy function loop models. Sankoff's new algorithm combines both. Bayesian nucleotide pair probabilities—structure element probabilities with expectation of conditional state—calculate energy instead of pseudo-energies. Pankov's Markovian chain method aligns and folds RNAs quickly (Miladi et al., 2020). Pankov accelerates by reducing unstable base-pairing without affecting Sankoff's loop-based free energy. Pankov outfolds LocARNA and SPARSE.

Sankoff's RNA alignment and folding is best. For computational efficiency, the methods use simplified structure energy models or alignment and structure generation limitations instead of the theoretical full loop-based nearest-neighbor energy model, low-energy PMcomp model. These findings show that PMcomp-like approaches can significantly reduce the computational weight of accurate thermodynamic folding details, enabling algorithmic optimization and sparing (Torarinsson et al., 2007). PMcomp assumes base-pairing event independence, violating the closest neighbor energy model. Deconstructed loop-probabilities accurately predicted RNA secondary structure. This energy model simulates loop breakdown using precomputed in-loop probabilities to avoid multi-loop computational complexity. This energy model uses nearest neighbor thermodynamics. The revolutionary model is empirically tested against the full-loop energy model based on non-coding RNAs. This energy model influenced the Pankov RNA folding and alignment algorithm. Benchmark data reveals Pankov predicts secondary structure from homologous RNA pairs better than its predecessors.

3.2.2.3   An Efficient Simulated Annealing Algorithm for the RNA Secondary Structure Prediction with Pseudoknots

Biochemical processes require RNA pseudoknot structures. Pseudoknot structure prediction in RNA secondary structure is currently unreliable. Adding non-consecutive base pairs does not diminish free energy (Kai et al., 2019). This algorithm searches using successive base pairs. The ESA algorithm calculates and archives all successive base pairs in a triplet data structure if the number exceeds a specified minimum stem length. The annealing schedule is adjusted to get the lowest free energy solution. The final approach is tested on PseudoBase. Experimental results are equivalent to the most advanced RNA structure prediction methods.

3.2.2.4   RNA Secondary Structure Prediction through Deep Neural Network Algorithm with Free Energy Perturbation or Thermodynamic Integration

Secondary structure predictions help identify functional non-coding RNA activities. Despite their high prediction accuracy, machine learning-based models still overfit. Turner's nearest-neighbor free energy parameters reduce overfitting. Thermodynamic regularization brings the model's folding scores and computed free energy as close as possible (Sato et al., 2021). Compared to previous methods, MXfold2 predicts secondary structures for newly discovered non-coding RNAs with the highest accuracy and efficiency. Thermodynamic and deep neural network algorithms accurately predict RNA secondary structure.

3.2.2.5   Energy-Directed RNA Structure Prediction

Even though the partition function predicts all secondary structures, dynamic programming algorithm calculates optimal RNA structure folding through energy minimization. Minimum free energy (MFE) structure prediction is imprecise yet essential for RNA folding since it may be used to construct reliability measures that give the projected structure a confidence grade (Hofacker, 2014). MFE uses centroid structures and maximum anticipated accuracy (MEA). Dynamic programming approaches assume RNA thermodynamic equilibrium. Not necessarily, especially for long RNAs. Lastly, energy-directed RNA structure prediction algorithm predicts co-transcriptional and RNA folding kinetics.

3.2.2.6 Chemical Reaction Optimization Algorithm for RNA Secondary Structure Prediction with Pseudoknots

Pseudoknots operate RNA molecules. The least free energy method can predict pseudoknots in RNA secondary structure. This is NP-hard. Chemical Reaction Optimization (CRO) metaheuristic algorithm accurately predicts RNA pseudoknotted structure (Islam et al., 2021). The CRO algorithm's response operators were modified and used to the population to find the structure with the lowest free energy. The Repair Operator, a new operator, also affects CRO algorithm validity. Its benefits include increasing the number of true positive base pairs and decreasing false-positive and -negative base pairs. Four energy models calculate RNA free energy. The CRO algorithm was evaluated on four datasets of pseudoknotted RNA sequences from the RNA STRAND and Pseudobase++ databases. CRO-based model outperformed other algorithms in accuracy and efficiency studies.

3.2.2.7 An Algorithm for Ranking RNA 3D Structures

RNA research is accelerating. New soft-computing methods and approaches have opened new avenues in illness research, vaccine development, therapeutics, and architecture by revealing unique RNA structures. RNAs and proteins share structure and function. RNA's complexity requires a deeper structure research. Cutting-edge experimental and computational structure-probing methods provide a variety of RNA shapes that match experimental data. Yet, determining the best structure is difficult. Tan et al.'s innovative approach—rsRNASP—recently exhibited progress in both areas (Wienecke & Laederach, 2022). rsRNASP, a residue separation-based statistical potential, outperforms other methods for three-dimensional structure evaluation.

3.2.2.8 Effectiveness of the Thermodynamics Algorithms for RNA Secondary Structure Prediction

Many cell activities require RNA molecule gene regulation, enzyme catalysis, and protein synthesis. Given that folded RNA serves a functional role, it becomes possible to predict the RNA secondary structure based on its underlying base sequence. MFE projections use Mathews, Turner, and Andronescu thermodynamic parameters. Structure precision is the goal of partition function calculation methods (called MEA or pseudo-MEA). New prediction algorithms analyze sensitivity, positive predictive value, and their harmonic mean, the F-measure, using reference structures. We need to know how reference datasets affect accuracy metrics and whether algorithmic or thermodynamic parameter improvements boost computational prediction system benchmarks statistically. Novel energy parameters and datasets have increased MFE and (pseudo-)MEA knowledge (Hajiaghayi et al., 2012). MFE and MEA algorithm improvements cannot be deduced from average accuracy on 89 Group I introns in previously benchmarked RNAs. Huge datasets demonstrate the generalized centroid base pair estimator's accuracy. MFE accuracy depends on energy parameters. MFE-, MEA-, and pseudo-MEA-based techniques exhibited the highest accuracy with the Andronescu et al.'s thermodynamic parameter set, BL*, with accuracy values of 0.68, 0.68, and 0.71 (on a scale of 0 to 1, with 1 representing perfect structural predictions) (named after the Boltzmann likelihood method by which the parameters were derived). Due to small datasets, group I introns and tRNAs should be appraised using the proper algorithm for average accuracy. MFE with Andronescu et al.'s is less accurate than MEA-based methods. For our massive datasets, Hamada et al.'s pseudo-MEAs with the BL* parameter set beat MFE and MEA-based techniques.

3.2.3 A Novel Algorithm for RNA Secondary Structure Design

Many RNAs are structurally dependent on their function. Hence, RNA molecules with a certain structural feature can be used to create ribozymes or nanostructures with RNA properties. An algorithm can find secondary structure folding sequences (if any are available). Like the pseudoknot-free secondary structure prediction challenge, this is computationally complex (Andronescu et al., 2004). Stochastic local search is a well-known general approach for tackling complex combinatorial problems. Scientifically, the best-known solution for this problem—RNAinverse from Vienna RNA Package—is dramatically surpassed in an empirical examination of computationally predicted biological sequence structures, artificially manufactured RNA structures, and empirically modeled biological structures. The novel method solves structures that RNAinverse cannot. The RNASoft website calls RNA-SSD "RNA Designer" (www.rnasoft.ca).

3.2.3.1 MoiRNAiFold: A Computational Tool for RNA Design

New computational modeling tools for Riboregulators an RNA string are needed for diagnostic and therapeutic advances. MoiRNAiFold helps develop novel RNA molecules. MoiRNAiFold's Large Neighborhood Search variable types, heuristics, and restart methods use Constraint Programming (Minuesa et al., 2021). This application improves Translation Efficiency Calculation, which manages design limits and quality measures for RNA regulating gene expression. MoiRNAiFold outperforms other EteRNA programs. The program constructs biologically relevant RNA sequences using RNA riboregulators, ensuring its in vitro and in vivo functionality. Finally, the web server for de novo complex RNA construction is https://moiraibiodesign.com/design/.

3.3 ALGORITHMS FOR PROTEIN STRUCTURE ANALYSIS

3.3.1 Fast Quantum Hydrophobic and Hydrophilic Algorithm for Protein Structure Prediction

Unfolded proteins are amino acids. Drugs and vaccines are made through protein structure prediction. NP-complete protein structure prediction is unsolved. Quantum computing improves classical algorithms. Quantum hydrophobic-hydrophilic model on two-dimensional square lattice solves problem for any N-amino acid sequence with quadratic speedup over classical equivalent. Grover's quantum search (Wong & Chang, 2022). Any amino acid sequence works. Building a superposition state, computing potential energy for each conformation and selecting the lowest energy consumer are necessary. Quadratic speed leads to asymptotic spatial complexity. IBM Quantum's Qiskit SDK-based qasm simulator effectively predicts protein structure (Wong & Chang, 2021). Quantum approach computes theoretical conformation probability. Quantum methods quadruple protein tertiary structure prediction.

Models that incorporate polynomially spaced quantum characteristics for hydrophobic and hydrophilic interactions. IBM quantum simulators verified the algorithm. Theoretical probability supports experimental confirmation.

3.3.2 DEEP LEARNING INTER-RESIDUE ORIENTATIONS ALGORITHM FOR PROTEIN STRUCTURE PREDICTION

Protein structure prediction has long plagued computational biology. By using Rosetta's constrained optimization and extending deep learning-based prediction to include residue orientations and distances, more accurate models can be created. Based on 18 proteins developed utilizing the inter-residue orientations method, de novo protein design difficulties can be addressed. Deep learning predicts coevolutionary distance-based inter-residue interactions, improving protein structure predictions. A Rosetta-constrained energy-minimization of conformations and deep residual network for predicting inter-residue orientations and distance maps have been developed to quickly and accurately produce structure models guided by these constraints (Yang et al., 2020). Benchmark testing using Continuous Automated Model Evaluation (CAMEO)-derived sets and 13th Critical Assessment of protein Structure Prediction showed that the approach was one of the best disclosed (CASP13). The network trained solely on natural proteins awards higher likelihood to de novo-designed proteins, providing an independent quantitative assessment of a protein structure's "ideality." The method should be useful for protein structure prediction and design challenges.

3.3.3 HOMOLOGY MODELING ALGORITHMS FOR PROTEIN STRUCTURE PREDICTION

As many as ten times of protein structures of three-dimensional protein sequences are known. Large-scale genome sequencing, protein crystallization issues, or resource shortages may be at blame. Homology modeling programs can create protein computational models. Scientists model proteins using similar architectures. Homology modeling systems must create high-quality models using user-defined target–template sequence alignments under various scenarios when working with proteins or small molecules (Dolan et al., 2012). Prime, SWISS-MODEL, MOE, MODELLER, and ROSETTA were tested. Modeled proteins were chosen to test a variety of sequence identities, lengths, and protein motifs. HIV-1 protease contains VCP and factor Xa. Most programs yield equivalent results. Good models can be created with sequence identities of at least 30%, but comprehensive models cannot (Twilight Zone). Certain apps perform better in certain situations.

3.3.4 AN EFFICIENT ANT COLONY OPTIMIZATION ALGORITHM FOR PROTEIN STRUCTURE PREDICTION

Predicting 3D protein structure from amino acids is bioinformatics' oldest problem. Free energy hydrophobic-polar model and Miyazawa-Jernigan model with efficient ant colony optimization estimate protein structure using face-centered cubic lattice coordinates. Reinforcement learning and heuristic information increase energy in a k-order Markov model. This method outperformed cutting-edge algorithms on benchmark proteins (Duc et al., 2018). A novel hybrid genetic technique predicts protein structure on 2D triangular lattice.

Three-dimensional structure determines protein function. Protein structure prediction from amino acid sequence is difficult but important in many fields. Combinatorial optimization is the hydrophobic-polar model's description. Genetic algorithm, tabu search method, and local search algorithms are combined to predict protein structure. A quality-of-answer experiment assessed the strategy. The proposed methodology matched state-of-the-art methods based on benchmark cases.

3.3.5 Ab Initio Protein Structure Prediction through Genetic Algorithm using Low-Resolution Model

Proteins are amino acid chains. Protein folding allows specialized functions. Ab initio or de novo protein structure prediction (PSP) can help unravel the sequence–structure relationship. A genetic algorithm accurately predicts protein structure from sequencing (Hoque et al., 2009). Twin elimination, intelligence in coding, domain-specific heuristics from model features, and protein core creation are low-resolution models.

3.4 POPULAR ALGORITHMS IN DRUG DISCOVERY

3.4.1 LEADD: Lamarckian Evolutionary Algorithm for De Novo Drug Design

Goal-directed de novo molecular design can identify molecules that maximize or minimize an objective function that predicts essential molecule properties. These technologies often yield synthesizable molecules. LEADD evolves drug design (Kerstjens & De Winter, 2022). This approach considers optimization, chemical synthesis, and computing efficiency. LEADD represents molecules as graphs of molecular fragments and restricts their bonds using knowledge-based pairwise atom type compatibility rules to maximize synthetically accessible compound construction. A drug-like chemical reference library provides fragments, preferences, and compatibility guidelines. New genetic operators effectively enforce these principles. The method efficiently examines a Lamarckian evolutionary mechanism that alters molecule reproduction to better explore chemical space. LEADD outperformed virtual screening and an evolutionary algorithm in discovering chemicals with higher fitness using a defined benchmark set.

3.4.2 Drug Discovery and Development using Graph Machine Learning Algorithm

Graph machine learning (GML) can effectively predict biomolecular structures, their functional connections, and integrate multi-omics datasets, which is attracting pharmaceutical and biotechnology businesses (Gaudelet et al. 2021). Target discovery, small molecule and biologic formulation, and pharmaceutical repurposing eased medicine creation with graph machine learning (GML). GML will dominate biomedical machine learning due to repurposed drugs used in in vivo research and other breakthroughs.

3.5 CONCLUSION

Computational structural algorithms are growing in molecular biology. These programs produce protein or nucleotide sequences that can fold into a desired 3D shape and perform a desired biological activity. The biophysical model and algorithm used to predict biomolecular structure are key. Improved model and algorithm can only improve successful programs. Structural bioinformatics algorithms offer great potential for developing therapeutic oligonucleotide and oligopeptide assemblies, as this chapter indicates.

REFERENCES

Afanasyeva, A., Nagao, C., & Mizuguchi, K. (2019). Prediction of the secondary structure of short DNA aptamers. *Biophysics and Physicobiology*, *16*. https://doi.org/10.2142/biophysico.16.0_287

Andronescu, M., Fejes, A. P., Hutter, F., Hoos, H. H., & Condon, A. (2004). A new algorithm for RNA secondary structure design. *Journal of Molecular Biology*, *336*(3). https://doi.org/10.1016/j.jmb.2003.12.041

Busch, A., & Backofen, R. (2006). INFO-RNA – A fast approach to inverse RNA folding. *Bioinformatics*, *22*(15). https://doi.org/10.1093/bioinformatics/btl194

Clote, P. (2005). An efficient algorithm to compute the landscape of locally optimal RNA secondary structures with respect to the Nussinov-Jacobson energy model. *Journal of Computational Biology*, *12*(1). https://doi.org/10.1089/cmb.2005.12.83

Dolan, M. A., Noah, J. W., & Hurt, D. (2012). Comparison of common homology modeling algorithms: Application of user-defined alignments. *Methods in Molecular Biology*, *857*. https://doi.org/10.1007/978-1-61779-588-6_18

Duc, D. D., Dinh, P. T., Anh, V. T. N., & Linh-Trung, N. (2018). An Efficient Ant Colony Optimization Algorithm for Protein Structure Prediction. *International Symposium on Medical Information and Communication Technology, ISMICT, 2018-March*. https://doi.org/10.1109/ISMICT.2018.8573710

Eddy, S. (2004). How do RNA folding algorithms work? *Nature Biotechnology*, *22*, 1457–1458. https://doi.org/10.1038/nbt1104-1457

Gaudelet, T., Day, B., Jamasb, A. R., Soman, J., Regep, C., Liu, G., Hayter, J. B. R., Vickers, R., Roberts, C., Tang, J., Roblin, D., Blundell, T. L., Bronstein, M. M., & Taylor-King, J. P. (2021). Utilizing graph machine learning within drug discovery and development. *Briefings in Bioinformatics*, *22*(6). https://doi.org/10.1093/bib/bbab159

Hajiaghayi, M., Condon, A., & Hoos, H. H. (2012). Analysis of energy-based algorithms for RNA secondary structure prediction. *BMC Bioinformatics*, *13*(1). https://doi.org/10.1186/1471-2105-13-22

Haleš, J., Héliou, A., Mañuch, J., Ponty, Y., & Stacho, L. (2017). Combinatorial RNA design: Designability and structure-approximating algorithm in Watson–Crick and Nussinov–Jacobson energy models. *Algorithmica*, *79*(3). https://doi.org/10.1007/s00453-016-0196-x

Hofacker, I. L. (2014). Energy-directed RNA structure prediction. In J. Gorodkin, & W. Ruzzo (Eds.), *RNA sequence, structure, and function: Computational and bioinformatic methods*. Methods in Molecular Biology, vol 1097. Humana Press, Totowa, NJ. https://doi.org/10.1007/978-1-62703-709-9_4

Hoque, M. T., Chetty, M., & Sattar, A. (2009). Genetic algorithm in Ab initio protein structure prediction using low resolution model: A review. *Studies in Computational Intelligence*, *224*. https://doi.org/10.1007/978-3-642-02193-0_14

Islam, M. R., Islam, M. S., & Sakeef, N. (2021). RNA secondary structure prediction with Pseudoknots using chemical reaction optimization algorithm. *IEEE/ACM Transactions on Computational Biology and Bioinformatics*, *18*(3). https://doi.org/10.1109/TCBB.2019.2936570

Jeon, Y., Jung, E., Min, H., Chung, E. Y., & Yoon, S. (2013). GPU-based acceleration of an RNA tertiary structure prediction algorithm. *Computers in Biology and Medicine*, *43*(8). https://doi.org/10.1016/j.compbiomed.2013.05.007

Kai, Z., Yuting, W., Yulin, L., Jun, L., & Juanjuan, H. (2019). An efficient simulated annealing algorithm for the RNA secondary structure prediction with Pseudoknots. *BMC Genomics*, *20*. https://doi.org/10.1186/s12864-019-6300-2

Kerstjens, A., & De Winter, H. (2022). LEADD: Lamarckian evolutionary algorithm for de novo drug design. *Journal of Cheminformatics*, *14*(1). https://doi.org/10.1186/s13321-022-00582-y

Liang, X., Zhu, W., Lv, Z., & Zou, Q. (2019). Molecular computing and bioinformatics. *Molecules*, *24*(13). https://doi.org/10.3390/molecules24132358

Marsan, L., & Sagot, M. F. (2000). Algorithms for extracting structured motifs using a suffix tree with an application to promoter and regulatory site consensus identification. *Journal of Computational Biology*, *7*(3–4). https://doi.org/10.1089/106652700750050826

Miladi, M., Raden, M., Will, S., & Backofen, R. (2020). Fast and accurate structure probability estimation for simultaneous alignment and folding of RNAs with Markov chains. *Algorithms for Molecular Biology*, *15*(1). https://doi.org/10.1186/s13015-020-00179-w

Minuesa, G., Alsina, C., Garcia-Martin, J. A., Oliveros, J. C., & Dotu, I. (2021). MoiRNAiFold: A novel tool for complex in silico RNA design. *Nucleic Acids Research*, *49*(9). https://doi.org/10.1093/nar/gkab331

Sato, K., Akiyama, M., & Sakakibara, Y. (2021). RNA secondary structure prediction using deep learning with thermodynamic integration. *Nature Communications*, *12*(1). https://doi.org/10.1038/s41467-021-21194-4

Torarinsson, E., Havgaard, J. H., & Gorodkin, J. (2007). Multiple structural alignment and clustering of RNA sequences. *Bioinformatics*, *23*(8). https://doi.org/10.1093/bioinformatics/btm049

Townshend, R. J. L., Eismann, S., Watkins, A. M., Rangan, R., Karelina, M., Das, R., Dror, R. O. (2021a). Geometric deep learning of RNA structure. *Science*, 373(6558), 1047–1051. https://doi.org/10.1126/science.abe5650

Townshend, R. J. L., Eismann, S., Watkins, A. M., Rangan, R., Karelina, M., Das, R., & Dror, R. O. (2021b). Geometric deep learning of RNA structure. *Science*, *373*(6558). https://doi.org/10.1126/science.abe5650

Wienecke, A., & Laederach, A. (2022). A novel algorithm for ranking RNA structure candidates. *Biophysical Journal*, *121*(1). https://doi.org/10.1016/j.bpj.2021.12.004

Wong, R., & Chang, W. L. (2021). Quantum speedup for protein structure prediction. *IEEE Transactions on Nanobioscience*, *20*(3). https://doi.org/10.1109/TNB.2021.3065051

Wong, R., & Chang, W. L. (2022). Fast quantum algorithm for protein structure prediction in hydrophobic-hydrophilic model. *Journal of Parallel and Distributed Computing*, *164*. https://doi.org/10.1016/j.jpdc.2022.03.011

Yang, J., Anishchenko, I., Park, H., Peng, Z., Ovchinnikov, S., & Baker, D. (2020). Improved protein structure prediction using predicted inter-residue orientations. *Proceedings of the National Academy of Sciences of the United States of America*, *117*(3). https://doi.org/10.1073/pnas.1914677117

Yu, B., Lu, Y., Zhang, Q. C., & Hou, L. (2020). Prediction and differential analysis of RNA secondary structure. *Quantitative Biology*, 8(2). https://doi.org/10.1007/s40484-020-0205-6

4 Exact, Heuristics and Other Algorithms in Computational Biology

Shubhendra Singh Chauhan
ICAR-National Bureau of Plant Genetic Resources, India

Shikha Mittal
Jaypee University of Information Technology, India

4.1 INTRODUCTION

A sequence alignment is a manner of arranging RNA, DNA, or amino acid sequences in order to discover similarity regions which might be the result of functional, structural, or phylogeny links between the sequences (Phillips, Janies, and Wheeler 2000; Fukuda and Tomii 2020; Hu et al. 2022). Nucleotide or amino acid residue sequences that are aligned frequently represent rows of a matrix. To align similar/identical characters in successive columns, gaps are introduced between the residues. It is also possible to use sequence alignments for non-biological sequences, such as calculating the cost of distance between spoken language strings or financial data (Wong, Suchard, and Huelsenbeck 2008).

Mutation and natural selection are used for evolution of biological sequences. We can tell if two sequences have a common evolutionary origin if their resemblance is unlikely to be due to chance by comparing them. Before we get into how this is done, it's important to remember that sequences can have a variety of evolutionary relationships (Xie et al. 2005). The first is similarity, which corresponds to the intuitive concept of the level of similarity between two sequences. However, we can use the term "identity" to refer to more precise instances, such as having the same subsequence. The state of sharing a common evolutionary origin is referred to as homology. If two sequences share a common ancestor, we call them homologous. Homology can be divided into two categories. To begin, orthology refers to homologous sequences that evolved from a shared ancestral gene during speciation. For example, the plant Flu regulatory protein is present both in *Arabidopsis* and *Chlamydomonas*. Second, paralogy refers to the situation of being homologous sequences that resulted from gene duplication from a common ancestral gene. The human hemoglobin gene and chimpanzee's myoglobin gene are paralogs.

DOI: 10.1201/9781003331247-5

TABLE 4.1
Different Methods of Sequence Alignment

Alignment Scheme	Description
Dot matrix	Helpful for simple alignments – uses graphical manner, simple to understand and applicable.
Dynamic Programming	Starts an alignment from one end and keeps track of all likely best alignments to that point to provide an optimal alignment.
Heuristics methods	Methods for computing data quickly. It's possible that it's not as precise as dynamic programming.

4.2   ALIGNMENTS METHODS

When the query sequences are comparable and almost equal in size, global alignments are proven to be quite helpful. The Needleman–Wunsch algorithm is a general global alignment technique based on dynamic programming (Needleman and Wunsch 1970). Whereas local sequence alignments are more valuable for divergent sequences supposed of containing similar sequence motifs or similarity patches within their bigger context. The local alignment (Smith–Waterman algorithm) is a dynamic programming–based approach (Smith and Waterman 1981).

Moreover, to find the matching regions between two sequences, pairwise sequence alignment is used (Mullan 2006). As the sequence number increases, it is impossible to compare each and every sequence to every other. Consequently, multiple sequence alignment (MSA) is needed. The fundamental idea is to align the sequences on top of one another to form a matrix, where each row corresponds to a protein sequence and each column corresponds to a certain place of amino acid residue within each sequence. Sequence alignment can be done in a variety of ways. The strategy, computing complexity, and accuracy of the outcomes differ between these methods (Table 4.1). Alignment methods are divided into three categories.

4.3   DOT MATRIX METHOD

A dot matrix method is used for analyzing two sequences and attempting to discover likely character alignment between them. A diagonal on an identity matrix can be used to detect similarity between two sequences. Graphic similarity comparisons make use of a computer's power to visualize relationships between sequences in a way that allows a human researcher to spot patterns in the data. If we want to see if two sequences are comparable, we must compare every portion of one with every part of the other. This can be done by sliding one sequence over the top of the other and counting the number of identities at each alignment. The optimal alignment would be the one with the highest number of identities (Manohar and Singh 2012).

To demonstrate the concept of similarity, a dot plot is employed using these sequences given above (Figure 4.1). Dot plots are used to visually compare two sequences and identify areas of high similarity. Two sequences are organized on the axes of a simple

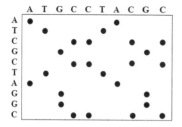 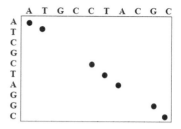

FIGURE 4.1   Representation of dot plots.

graph. A dot is inserted at every spot where the two sequences are identical. A diagonal stretch of dots denotes areas where the two sequences are comparable.

4.4   DYNAMIC PROGRAMMING

Dynamic programming (DP) is a method of problem solving for a set of problems that can be resolved by separating them into simpler sub-problems (Zhou and Zhongwen 2013). It resolves the best alignment by comparing two sequences for all likely character pairings between them. By creating a 2D alignment matrix, it functions similarly to the dot matrix method. In order to do this, a dot matrix is transformed into a score matrix, and matches and mismatches between the sequences are taken into account. The ideal solution is to look for the set of maximum scores in this matrix to obtain best alignment.

Creating a 2D matrix with the two sequences to be aligned as its axes is the first step in dynamic programming. The residues are matched using a specific scoring matrix. One row at a time, the scores is computed. This starts by examining the first row of one sequence, which is then used to look at the entire length of the other sequence, and then the secondrow is examined. The corresponding scores are computed. The scores from the first round are taken into account while scanning the second row. In an intermediate matrix, the optimal score is placed in the lower right corner of the matrix. This method is repeated until all of the cells have been filled with values. As a result, the points are added up all along the diagonal from the topmost left to the lowermost right corner. The next stage is to find out the path that represents the perfect alignment after the scores have been aggregated in a matrix. This is accomplished by tracing back throughout the matrix in turn around order from the bottom right-hand cell to the top left-hand cell, where the matrix's origin is located. The path with the highest overall score is the best match. At a particular point, the path can move either vertically or horizontally, leading to the creation of a gap, an indel (insertion/deletion) for one of the two sequences.

4.5   GAP PENALTIES

Gaps that reflect insertions and deletions are frequently used to attain most favorable alignment between sequences. As there is no evolutionary hypothesis available to set up an accurate cost for adding indels, usage of penalty levels can be rather arbitrary.

If the level of penalties is too low, gaps can accumulate to the point that yet unrelated sequences can be aligned with high match scores. If the levels of penalty are put too high, gaps may turn out to be impossible to detect, making logical alignment impossible.

The cost distinction between gap opening and gap extension is another aspect to consider. It is well recognized that extending a gap that has already been established is easy. As a result, opening of gap should be penalized far more severely than extension of gap. Affine gap penalties are another name for differential gap penalties. For establishing and extending gaps, the standard strategy is to employ predefined gap penalty levels. For example, a −12/−1 method could be used, with the opening of gap penalty being −12 and the extension of gap penalty being −1. The overall gap penalty is determined using the formula:

$$W = \gamma + \delta \times (k-1)$$

Here, W = gap penalty; γ = gap opening penalty; δ = gap extension penalty, and k = gap length.

A constant gap penalty, which gives the equal score to each gap in spite of whether it is opening or expanding, is occasionally employed in addition to the affine gap penalty. However, it has been discovered that this penalty scheme is less reasonable as compared to affine penalty.

4.6 NEEDLEMAN–WUNSCH GLOBAL ALIGNMENT ALGORITHM

A classic global alignment algorithm, i.e., Needleman–Wunsch algorithm, uses DP (Needleman and Wunsch 1970). In this method, an optimal alignment is obtained using the full lengths of the 2 sequences. To obtain best score for $A(i,j)$ of an alignment, three possible ways are available. If $A(i-1,j)$, $A(i-1,j-1)$, and $A(i, j-1)$ are known, $A(i, j)$ can then be calculated. To do this, begin from the top left hand corner and fill each cell according to the following rule:

$$A(i,j) = \max\left[A(i-1,j-1) + s(X_i,Y_j), A(i,j-1) + d, A(i-1,j) + d \right]$$

Here, $A(i,j)$ represents the value in the ith and jth row and column respectively; $s(X_i, Y_j)$ represents the score for the residues being matched; d = gap penalty; $A(i-1,j-1) + s(X_i, Y_j)$ = path graph diagonal move, in which two residues X_i aligned with Y_j; $A(i,j-1) + d$ = path graph horizontal move, in which a residue of the first sequence (x) is matched with a gap of the second sequence; $A(i-1,j) + d$ = path graph vertical move, in which a residue in the second sequence (y) is aligned with a gap in the first sequence.

The top score of (i,j) will be biggest of these three options. This equation is constantly used to fill the matrix values as shown in Figure 4.2. The alignment path has to move from the bottom right cell to the topmost left cell of the matrix. The disadvantage of concentrating on obtaining the highest possible score for the whole length sequence is that you risk lost out on the best local similarity. The technique does not generate optimal alignment for dissimilar sequences. GAP is one of the few web servers that focus on global pair wise alignment.

Here, A is the maximum score from one of the three directions plus matching score at the current position

	A	C	G	T	C
A	1	0	0	0	0
T	0	1			
G					
C					

	A	C	G	T	C
A	1	0	0	0	0
T	0	1	1		
G					
C					

	A	C	G	T	C
A	1	0	0	0	0
T	0	1	1	2	2
G					
C					

	A	C	G	T	C
A	1	0	0	0	0
T	0	1	1	2	
G					
C					

	A	C	G	T	C
A	1	0	0	0	0
T	0	1	1	2	2
G	0	1	2	2	2
C	0	2	2	2	3

	A	C	G	T	C
A	1	0	0	0	0
T	0	1	1	2	2
G	0	1	2	2	2
C	0	2	2	2	3

FIGURE 4.2   Illustration of dynamic programming algorithm.

4.7   DYNAMIC PROGRAMMING FOR LOCAL ALIGNMENT

For local pairwise alignment, the Smith–Waterman approach is used (Smith and Waterman 1981). Between two sequences, the algorithm returns the highest-scoring local match. For matching two sequences that have a matched region that is merely a fraction of their lengths, that have different lengths, that overlap, or where one sequence is a fragment of the other, Smith–Waterman DP algorithm is preferred as compared to Needleman–Wunsch (Gotoh 1982). In this scenario, the rules for determining score matrix values are different:

i.   The scoring system must have negative scores for mismatches.

ii. When the value of a score matrix goes negative, it is set to zero, thus ending the alignment up to that point, i.e.,

$$A(i,j) = \max\left[A(i-1,j-1) + s(X_j, Y_j), A(i,j-1) + d, A(i-1,j) + d, 0 \right]$$

In local alignment algorithm, an analogous tracing-back method is utilized. The alignment path, on the other hand, may start and finish within the major diagonal. It starts at the spot with the highest score and goes diagonally up to the left until it hits a cell with zero in it. If necessary, gaps are created. The affine gap penalty is frequently utilized in this situation. Occasionally, many perfectly matched segments with the highest scores are discovered. The goal of local alignment is to obtain the highest alignment score locally, possibly at the expense of obtaining the highest alignment score globally. This method could be useful for aligning highly diverged sequences or sequences with many domains from several sources. The local alignment approach is employed by most commonly used web servers, such as SIM, SSEARCH, and LALIGN.

4.8 HEURISTIC METHODS

Although accurate and trustworthy, searching a huge database by dynamic programming algorithms is exceptionally time-consuming and unreasonable when computational resources are forced. In a study carried out more than ten years ago, it took 2–3 hours on a normal computer system to query a database of 400,000 sequences with a sequence of 150 residues. Heuristic approaches must be employed to speed up the comparison. Heuristic algorithms are speedier since they only look at a part of the likely alignments that ordinary dynamic programming.

For database searches, there are currently two primary heuristic algorithms: BLAST (Altschul et al. 1990) and FASTA (Lipman and Pearson 1985; Pearson and Lipman 1988). When it comes to discovering the best alignment and true homologs, these database searching techniques outperform dynamic programming by a factor of 50–100. The enhanced computational pace comes at a reasonable cost in terms of search specificity and sensitivity, which working molecular scientists can easily accept.

For quick pairwise alignment, a third approach, i.e., heuristic approach is used by both BLAST and FASTA. It operates by comparing two sequences for brief sections of identical or nearly similar letters. Words are the short sequence of characters, equivalent to the windows applicable in the dot matrix method. By extending similarity regions from the words, a longer alignment can be obtained by first finding word matches. After finding regions with high sequence similarity, contiguous high-scoring sections can be put together to form a full alignment.

4.9 BLAST (BASIC LOCAL ALIGNMENT SEARCH TOOL)

In 1990, BLAST program was developed by Stephen Altschul (Altschul et al. 1990). BLAST, by using heuristic approach, aligns a query sequence with all the database sequences. The goal is to locate un-gapped segments with high scores among closely related sequences. Above a certain threshold value, the presence of such segments suggests pair wise similarity that is not due to chance, which aids in distinguishing related from unrelated sequences in a database. It offers exceptionally quick, precise, and sensitive database searching as a free service through the Internet.

4.10   HEURISTIC APPROACHES

4.10.1   BLAST Algorithm

BLAST is a word-based approach, similar to FASTA. One significant difference is that BLAST requires a search database that has been pre-formatted. The BLAST steps are summarized below:

1. **Query Preprocessing**: Finding ungapped similarity regions between the query sequences and database sequences is the first step. Similar to this, all of the query's words of length w are compared to all of the database sequences. For instance, using amino acid sequences, if $w = 2$ there are $20^2 = 400$ potential words, and $20^3 = 8000$ if $w = 3$, each query word is matched with each word of this comprehensive set, and a threshold T is set for the similarity between words. A list of words that score higher than T when compared to the word of the query commencing at this location is linked to each position of the query sequence. The neighbors are another name for the similar terms. The second step is to look for these phrases in a sequence database.

2. **Generation of the hits**: Assume Q is the query sequence and D is a database sequence. Following the first stage, each location in the query sequence Q is now represented by a list of its neighbors. In order to compare Q and D, one must first seek for similarities between each of Q's neighbors in each position and each of D's words. Therefore, every word in D is compared to every position of Q, and if one of the neighboring words at that position of Q is the same as a word in D, a hit is recorded. A hit is made with one

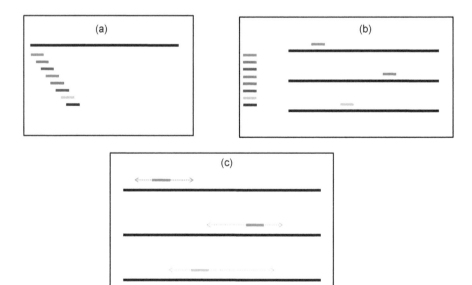

FIGURE 4.3   The BLAST algorithm (a) Query preprocessing (b) Generation of hits (c) Hits extension (Source: Pertsemlidis and Fondon 2001).

or more subsequent (overlapping) pairs of words that are identical, and it is identified by where it appears in the two sequences. In this manner, all potential matches between the query sequence and database sequences are determined.

3. **Extension of the hits**: In order to determine whether a given hit could be a part of a larger portion of similarity, every hit that has been generated has now been enlarged, without any gaps. As a result, each hit is extended in both directions. To make this extension step go as rapidly as possible, an extension is halted as soon as the score of the extended hit drops below the best score that has been reached during the extension process by more than X.

4.10.2 STEPS INVOLVED IN THE BLAST TOOL

To search a query sequence against a database, the following steps must be performed.

4.10.3 BLAST VARIANTS

1. **BLASTN –** queries nucleotide sequences with a nucleotide sequence database.
2. **BLASTP –** compares a amino acid query sequence with a amino acid sequence database.

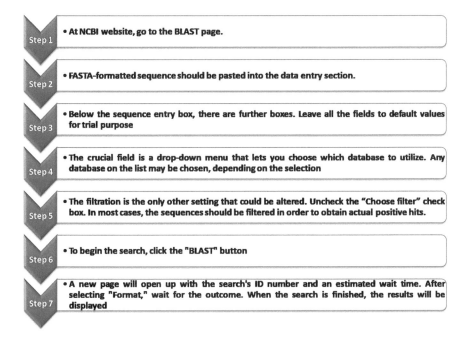

FIGURE 4.4 Steps involved in BLAST tool.

3. **BLASTX** – compares a nucleotide query sequence (6 frames translation) to an amino acid sequence database.
4. **TBLASTN** – compares a nucleotide query sequence (6 frames translation) to an amino acid sequence database.
5. **TBLASTX** – compares a nucleotide query sequence (6 frames translation) to a nucleotide sequence database (6 frames translation).

In a 2D picture illustrating the overall alignment between the two sequences, the output in graphical form consists of horizontal bars and a diagonal. The programs are organized on the basis of query sequences, i.e., amino acid (protein), nucleotide (DNA), or nucleotide sequences that need to be translated. In addition, distinct groups are created for programs used for specific tasks, such as VecScreen, and IgG BLAST which removes contaminated vector sequences. A technique called VecScreen quickly identifies nucleic acid sequence fragments that might have a vector origin. Whereas IgG BLAST, a webtool, has been designed for the analysis of variable (V) domains of Immounoglobulin (IG) (Ye et al. 2013).

4.10.4 STATISTICAL SIGNIFICANCE

A list of pairwise sequence matches, graded by statistical importance, is included in the BLAST result. The significance scores assist in differentiating between sequences that are evolutionary related and those that are not. Generally, only hits above a certain threshold are displayed.

Since there are more unrelated sequence alignments in larger databases, the statistical measure is calculated slightly differently than for a single paired sequence alignment. The statistical parameter, referred to as the E-value (expectation value) in BLAST searches, shows the likelihood that the alignments obtained by database searching are the result of random chance. Since BLAST aligns a sequence of query to every database sequence, the following formula is used to get the E-value:

$$E = m \times n \times P$$

where $E = E$-value; m = total no. of residues in a database; n = no. of residues in the query sequence; and P = probability that an HSP alignment is a result of random chance

The E-value tells us how likely it is that a given sequence match is the result of pure chance. The database match is considered to be more significant and less likely to be an outcome of random chance, the lower the E-value is. The following is an observed elucidation of the E-value. The match can be regarded as the outcome of homology if E falls within the range of 0.01 and 1e-50. The match is not regarded significant if E is between 0.01 and 10. If E is greater than 10, the sequences under consideration are either unrelated or related by relationships that are so far apart that they are below the current method's limit of detection (Table 4.2).

Due to the proportional relationship between the E-value and database size, it is evident that as the database expands, the E-value for a particular sequence match also does. Since the two sequences actual evolutionary relationship does not change over

TABLE 4.2
Empirical Interpretation of *E*-values

E-value	Interpretation	Significance
$E < 1e - 50$	Database match is a result of homologous relationships	Highly significant
E is between 0.01 and $1e - 50$	The match can be considered a result of homology	Significant
E is between 0.01 and 10	Hints at a tentative remote homology relationship but may hint at a tentative remote homology relationship	Not significant
$E > 10$	sequences under consideration are either unrelated or related by extremely distant relationships	Not significant

time, one may "lose" previously discovered homologs as the database expands due to the decline in the reliability of the sequence match. Therefore, a replacement for *E*-value calculations is required.

In addition to the *E*-value in a BLAST result, another notable statistical indicator is called a bit score. The bit score, which is normalized based on the raw pairwise alignment score, assesses sequence similarity irrespective of query sequence length and database size. The following formula is used to calculate the bit score (*S*):

$$S = \left(\lambda \times S - \ln K \right)/\ln 2$$

where *K* is a constant related to the scoring matrix employed, *S* is the raw alignment score, and is the Gumble distribution constant. It is obvious that the bit score (*S*) and the raw alignment score are linearly connected (*S*). Therefore, the match is more highly relevant the higher the bit score. For searching various databases of various sizes or for searching the same database at various times as the database grows, the bit score offers a continuous statistical signal.

4.10.5 BLAST OUTPUT

The BLAST output comprises a text description of the alignment, a matching list, and a graphical summary box.

Colored horizontal bars in the graphical overview box make it easy to quickly see how many database results there are and how similar they are to one another. The ranking of sequence similarity hits is indicated by the color coding of the parallel bars (red: closely related; green and blue: reasonably related; black: dissimilar). The bars length shows the ranges of sequence matching in relation to the query sequence. The pairwise alignment is linked to for each bar in the report's text section. A list of matching hits is presented below the graphical box, arranged in ascending order by the *E*-values.

Following this list is the description of text, composed of three classes: the header, the statistics, and the alignment. The header part includes a single-line summary of the database sequence together with the reference number/gene index of the database hit. The output summary of the search comprises the bit score, *E*-value, identity percentage,

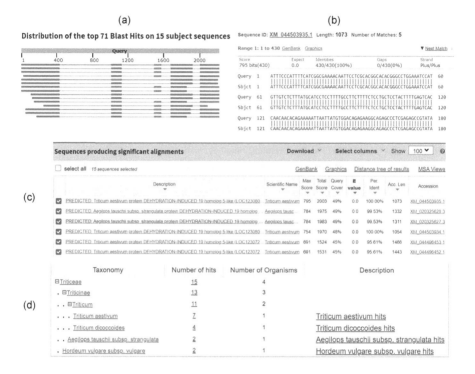

FIGURE 4.5   A BLAST output example with four sections, including the graphical overview box, the text section with header and statistics, and the list of matches that matched the query, and the actual alignment and taxonomy classification.

similarity ("Positives"), and gaps is then presented. The database sequence designated as subject is at the bottom of the pair, whereas the query sequence is at the top of the pair.

4.11   FASTA

The Lipman method is used by FASTA (FAST ALL) to look for matches between a query sequence and database sequences of the same type according to the query sequence. Although FASTA is typically the greatest tool for comparing proteins to proteins, it can also be used for the comparison of nucleotide sequences to nucleotide databanks (Pearson 2016). A protein query sequence can be compared to DNA databanks using the related application TFASTA. For a brief segment of identical residues having k length, FASTA employs a "hashing" method to locate matches. The string of residues is referred to as a ktuple, which is shorter than a word but is equivalent to a word in BLAST. A ktup typically consists of six and two residues for DNA and protein sequences respectively.

The hashing approach is used to find ktups between two sequences as the first phase in the FASTA alignment process. This method operates by creating a lookup table that displays each key's location for the two sequences under consideration.

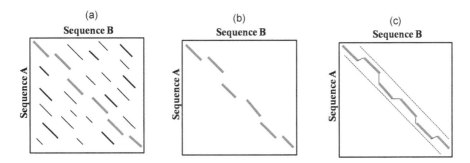

FIGURE 4.6 FASTA Algorithm: The hashing method is used in the first phase to find any potential ungapped alignments between two sequences. The alignments are graded in the second stage using a specific scoring matrix. The top ten alignments are the only ones chosen. The final stage involves selecting and joining the alignments that are on the same diagonal to create a single gapped alignment that is then optimized using a dynamic programming strategy.

The offset is an expression for the positional variation between each word in the two sequences, which is calculated by deducting the first sequence position from the second sequence position. Linking the ktups with the same offset values reveals an identical sequence region that is contiguous and corresponds to a section of the diagonal of a 2D matrix (Lipman and Pearson 1985).

The next stage is to focus on the areas where the two sequences are most similar. High similarity regions are those that have the top 10 highest diagonal densities. A substitution matrix is used to score the diagonals in these areas. A single alignment is created by choosing and joining adjacent high-scoring segments that are on the same diagonal. Applying gap penalties at this stage allows for the introduction of gaps between the diagonals. The gapped alignment score is once more computed. Step 3 involves applying the Smith–Waterman technique to further improve the gapped alignment to create the final alignment.

The final step is to do the final alignment statistical analysis, just like BLAST does, to determine the E-value.

FASTA features a lot of variants, just like BLAST. Two of the program's available forms include FASTX, which translates a nucleotide sequence and uses the translated amino acid sequence to query a protein database, and TFASTX, which matches an amino acid query sequence to a translated nucleotide database.

4.12 STATISTICAL SIGNIFICANCE

Bit scores and E-values are also used by FASTA. The Z-score, however, is a further statistical metric offered by the FASTA result. This indicates how many standard deviations there were from the database search's mean score. The majority of alignments with the query sequence are with dissimilar sequences, therefore the more important the match, the high the value of Z-score for a reported match, the further away from the mean of the score distribution. With a Z-score of greater than 15, the match might be assumed to be exceedingly significant and to be homologous. The sequences can be referred to as very likely homologous if Z is between 5 and 15.

4.13 COMPARISON OF BLAST AND FASTA

It has been demonstrated that BLAST and FASTA work nearly equally well when searching databases manually. The two strategies do differ in several significant ways, though. The key distinction is that while FASTA finds identical matched words using the hashing process, BLAST finds matching words using a substitution matrix. FASTA scans smaller window sizes by default. As a result, it provides more accurate results than BLAST and has a higher homolog coverage rate. The BLAST technique may offer higher specificity than FASTA because potential false positives are decreased by the use of low-complexity masking. While FASTA only produces one final alignment, BLAST occasionally returns numerous best-scoring alignments from the same sequence.

4.14 CONCLUSION

The quality of a particular alignment strategy is determined by the accurate assessment of match, mismatch, and gap (Bawono et al. 2015). The topic of optimal sequence matching is complicated. For sequence comparison, dynamic programming optimization and its numerous refined forms are the best option. The alignment and analysis of computational sequences are crucial. Numerous techniques and technologies, as well as various sequence alignment methodologies, are used for this goal. The difficult task of multiple sequence alignment is made simple by parallel processors and specialized hardware (Sebastião, Roma, and Flores 2012). All different types of alignments and analysis techniques greatly benefit from the use of online bioinformatics resources. The parallel processing of algorithms is the aim of the next-generation sequence alignment. The use of various algorithms simultaneously or a hybrid strategy also guarantees the effectiveness of matching strategies. Almost all computational methods involve mathematical or statistical probabilistic estimations. Multiple sequence alignment's computational overhead is removed by parallel genetic methods. Both word-based and structure-based MSA use genetic algorithms that are capable of self-improving and evolution (Rost and Sander, 1994). The time commitment is lessened, and productivity is increased, using hybrid computing and parallel computing. Researchers are currently competing to create and propose optimal alignment libraries or packages in various programming languages.

REFERENCES

Altschul, Stephen F., Warren Gish, Webb Miller, Eugene W. Myers, and David J. Lipman. 1990. "Basic Local Alignment Search Tool." *Journal of Molecular Biology* 215 (3): 403–10. doi:10.1016/S0022-2836(05)80360-2

Bawono, Punto, Arjan Van Der Velde, Sanne Abeln, and Jaap Heringa. 2015. "Quantifying the Displacement of Mismatches in Multiple Sequence Alignment Benchmarks." *PLoS ONE* 10 (5). doi:10.1371/JOURNAL.PONE.0127431

Fukuda, Hiroyuki, and Kentaro Tomii. 2020. "DeepECA: An End-to-End Learning Framework for Protein Contact Prediction from a Multiple Sequence Alignment." *BMC Bioinformatics* 21 (1): 1–15. doi:10.1186/S12859-019-3190-X/FIGURES/7

Gotoh, Osamu. 1982. "An Improved Algorithm for Matching Biological Sequences." *Journal of Molecular Biology* 162 (3): 705–8. doi:10.1016/0022-2836(82)90398-9

Hu, Guibing, Junting Feng, Xiang Xu, Jiabao Wang, Jarkko Salojärvi, Chengming Liu, Zhenxian Wu, et al. 2022. "Two Divergent Haplotypes from a Highly Heterozygous Lychee Genome Suggest Independent Domestication Events for Early and Late-Maturing Cultivars." *Nature Genetics* 54 (1): 73–83. doi:10.1038/s41588-021-00971-3

Lipman, David J., and William R. Pearson. 1985. "Rapid and Sensitive Protein Similarity Searches." *Science* 227 (4693): 1435–41. doi:10.1126/SCIENCE.2983426

Manohar, Parshant, and Shailendra Singh. 2012. "Protein Sequence Alignment: A Review." *World Applied Programming*, (2): 141–45. www.waprogramming.com

Mullan, Lisa. 2006. "Pairwise Sequence Alignment—It's All about Us!" *Briefings in Bioinformatics* 7 (1): 113–15. doi:10.1093/BIB/BBK008

Needleman, Saul B., and Christian D. Wunsch. 1970. "A General Method Applicable to the Search for Similarities in the Amino Acid Sequence of Two Proteins." *Journal of Molecular Biology* 48 (3): 443–53. doi:10.1016/0022-2836(70)90057-4

Pearson, W. R., and D. J. Lipman. 1988. "Improved Tools for Biological Sequence Comparison." *Proceedings of the National Academy of Sciences* 85 (8): 2444–48. doi:10.1073/PNAS.85.8.2444

Pearson, William R. 2016. Finding Protein and Nucleotide Similarities with FASTA. *Current Protocols in Bioinformatics*. doi:10.1002/0471250953.bi0309s53

Pertsemlidis, A., and J. W. Fondon. 2001. "Having a BLAST with Bioinformatics (and Avoiding BLASTphemy)." *Genome Biology* 2 (10). doi:10.1186/GB-2001-2-10-REVIEWS2002

Phillips, Aloysius, Daniel Janies, and Ward Wheeler. 2000. "Multiple Sequence Alignment in Phylogenetic Analysis." *Molecular Phylogenetics and Evolution* 16 (3): 317–30. doi:10.1006/MPEV.2000.0785

Rost, Burkhard, and Chris Sander. 1994. "Combining Evolutionary Information and Neural Networks to Predict Protein Secondary Structure." *Proteins: Structure, Function, and Bioinformatics* 19 (1): 55–72. doi:10.1002/PROT.340190108

Sebastião, Nuno, Nuno Roma, and Paulo Flores. 2012. "Hardware Accelerator Architecture for Simultaneous Short-Read DNA Sequences Alignment with Enhanced Traceback Phase." *Microprocessors & Microsystems* 36 (2): 96–109. doi:10.1016/J.MICPRO.2011.05.003

Smith, T. F., and M. S. Waterman. 1981. "Identification of Common Molecular Subsequences." *Journal of Molecular Biology* 147 (1): 195–97. doi:10.1016/0022-2836(81)90087-5

Wong, Karen M., Marc A. Suchard, and John P. Huelsenbeck. 2008. "Alignment Uncertainty and Genomic Analysis." *Science* 319 (5862): 473–76. doi:10.1126/SCIENCE.1151532/SUPPL_FILE/WONG.SOM.PDF

Xie, Xiaohui, Jun Lu, E. J. Kulbokas, Todd R. Golub, Vamsi Mootha, Kerstin Lindblad-Toh, Eric S. Lander, and Manolis Kellis. 2005. "Systematic Discovery of Regulatory Motifs in Human Promoters and 3' UTRs by Comparison of Several Mammals." *Nature* 434 (7031): 338–45. doi:10.1038/NATURE03441

Ye, Jian, Ning Ma, Thomas L. Madden, and James M. Ostell. 2013. "IgBLAST: An Immunoglobulin Variable Domain Sequence Analysis Tool." *Nucleic Acids Research* 41: 34–40. doi:10.1093/nar/gkt382

Zhou, Zhi-Min, and Chen Zhongwen. 2013. "Dynamic Programming for Protein Sequence Alignment." *Sematic Scholar*.

5 Cloud-Based Monitoring of Bioinformatics Multivariate Data with Cloud Platforms

Ravi Shankar Jha, Pradeep Singh Rawat and Hemraj Saini
DIT University, India

5.1 INTRODUCTION

In addition to reshaping next-generation technologies and altering the biology environment, biologists are also dumping enormous volumes of unprocessed sequencing data into databases. This exponential increase in datasets is turning into a major bottleneck. Biomedical researchers are exploring more dependable, dynamic, and practical techniques for carrying out sequencing analysis since the unpredictability in data volume leads to fluctuating computation and storage needs. The necessity of storage and data archiving with advancement in analysis on distributed computing and storage systems has expanded due to quick accumulation of sequencing and genotype data generated by high-throughput systems. A business process management system is necessary for effective data management across platforms. It supports an automation of analysis, makes large-scale bioinformatics analysis accessible, and allows accurate results. Each and every researcher is facing problems in analysis of their statistical data due to unavailability of computing resource. High cost need to be paid for a small start-up research. The collected raw datasets must be dispersed over a computer cluster or server farm for the current computing devices to operate in parallel with them in order to extract the desired results from the data. A second thought of various streams of biology cloud helping researchers deal with the computation of this data flood of various sector of bio filed data like genomic data, as it has become increasingly difficult to store and analyse massive amounts of genome data, easily access biomedical analysis tools, effectively share data, and efficiently retrieve data. Here the cloud computing solves the problem with its service model which offers various services. Many bioinformatics companies are moving towards cloud computing to give leverage to their research work. The features of cloud computing enable biologists to perform data analysis task without caring about computing resources with respect to architecture and other related issues like system administration and sharable resource allocation [1]. In the field of bioinformatics many players like Amazon, Microsoft Azure, Salesforce, etc. are providing various categories of tools which extend the researcher.

DOI: 10.1201/9781003331247-6

Cloud service models are embedded with huge and shareable resource pools where on-demand services are available at cheap price as compared to buying the whole system. Cloud provides a variety of services, and these services are divided in the cloud module [2]. As we already know, cloud services are in today's era being used by every field research and also providing a global platform which can be accessed and utilized independent of geographic access location and highest availability. Cloud platforms are capable of fulfilling the requirements of software, hardware, storage space, and other computation units. flexibility, and utility-based service modules are much more rigid and efficient as compare to other computing module [3]. They are also powered by various technologies like artificial intelligence services, network optimized techniques, machine learning, deep learning, natural language processing, quantum computing. Still it is growing with additional features which are helpful to serve the bioinformatics industry as well as taking it to the top priority.

This chapter is divided into five segments; the next segment covers the motivation toward integration of cloud services and bioinformatics research components. The third section includes the basic components and system architecture which is further divided in three segments. These three sub-segments discuss layered use and user interface with workflow and respective process, then cloud integration with multivariate bioinformatics which lead to next segments of SaaS modeller of container orchestration. Afterwards basics of bioinformatics are covered. It includes the compute and data resources with subsection of cloud service provider giant Amazon EC2 cloud services for container management and execution. The fourth segment contains details of bioinformatics applications which are served by cloud platform computing paradigm. The real time application using Kubernetes Platform is also covered in a detailed manner.

This chapter will end with a conclusive analysis of cloud services' role in bioinformatics industries and its impact on research outcomes with respect to cloud service.

5.2 MOTIVATION TO USE CLOUD COMPUTING

Cloud computing is a type of computing that uses the internet to deliver data, software, and other services. It is a model for enabling ubiquitous, on-demand access to shared pools of configurable computing resources. It allows users to access applications and data from any location. Cloud computers are typically accessed by means of a web browser or other client computer program such as those running on a mobile device or desktop computer.

Cloud computing can be divided into three types: public cloud, private cloud, and hybrid cloud. The main difference between them is the level of control that the user has over the service provider or, in other words, vendor of infrastructure and where their data is stored.

Public clouds offer shared processing power and storage space for all users with an internet connection. Private clouds are only accessible by one organization, while hybrid clouds offer some combination of public and private options for accessing data stored in the cloud.

The term "cloud" comes from the idea that these resources are not all stored on one computer or server, but instead they are spread out over many different servers.

It has many benefits, such as being able to access data from anywhere with an internet connection as mentioned earlier; it also helps companies save money because they do not need to buy expensive hardware and software licenses for each of their employees. Bioinformatics is the application of computer science and computational methods to problems in biology, medicine, and other sciences involving sequences of nucleic acids (DNA or RNA). The traditional idea of cloud computing is shifting as a result of recent advancements in new technologies including high throughput computing based on multi-core/multi-process architecture, cost-effective memory and data capacity, and virtualization approaches. As a result, cloud computing is increasingly crucial in data-intensive analysis conducted in academia and industry. Research communities have long depended primarily on regional, compact computer systems for data processing. Such small groupings of computer nodes, however, are unable to keep up with the quick output of such a vast volume of data given the data burst we are presently witnessing. By using parallelism or a type of many computers known as computer clusters or grids for data-intensive computing, many academics are currently attempting to utilize the maximum potential of computing resources.

Elasticity, which enables customers to buy processing power just for the capacity and duration they require, is another crucial aspect of cloud computing. This is a significant new possibility, particularly for tiny research laboratories without high-performance computer capacity.

Only a small number of cloud computing services are currently open to the general public or will be soon. The first cloud computing service that allows customers to "rent" a number of computing units on demand is the Amazon Elastic Compute Cloud (commonly known as EC2). Make adjustments and applications have been made solely to operate in Amazon EC2, as can be seen in our earlier work [4] and Amazon's report [5]. In order to create an Internet-scale cloud service platform, Microsoft is also exploring a cloud computing service named Azure. Microsoft has unveiled a cloud computing test bed named M45 in collaboration with academics, HP, Intel, and Yahoo to offer a globally dispersed Internet-scale testing environment to serve various academic projects.

5.3   COMPONENTS AND SYSTEM ARCHITECTURE

In cloud computing cloud services are divided into three parts as IaaS (Infrastructure as a Service), PaaS (Platform as a Service), and SaaS (Software as a Service). System architecture for bioinformatics in divided into three parts. The first part is considered as bioinformatics with multivariate data which is raw data collected by researcher to be processed for data analytics and further going to use or going to consider as in put value for cloud computing [6]. This raw data directly utilizes the cloud SaaS (software as a service) which can be used at first service of cloud computing; it has bidirectional utilization for optimize the result and also can be valued the data, i.e., pre-processing can be done at this point and that can be used for further processes.

Intelligent cloud system is the combination of cloud services with its AI-powered services where the data is processed with available services like ML, storage, network, computing, which are offered by cloud providers [7]. Each part of this system is divided into different layers, and each layer is advanced with embedded features of cloud computing.

5.3.1 Layer Use for User Interfaces

The delivery of data, software, and other services through the internet is referred to as cloud computing. It is a framework for allowing constant, on-demand access to shared, configurable computer resource pools. Users may access data and apps from anywhere. A web browser or another client computer software, such as one operating on a mobile device or desktop computer, is usually used to access cloud computers. The top layer is completely dedicated to all aspect or branches of bioinformatics where all respective data is collected. Here comes the cloud storage as service, as said flooded data requires a huge amount of storage which are served by cloud storage units. Storage services can be utilized using web apps, mobile apps, and any other platform provided by cloud service providers. Easy interaction allows users to access or store data over cloud using SaaS or, in other words, a predefined cloud-enabled platform, which can be utilized for further processing over the second layer.

Layer two is cloud PaaS enabled with other cloud utility applications like ML, storage optimization, network bandwidth services, core elements of computing like Central Processing Unit (CPU), General Processing Unit (GPU) which are available to do processing work means computational work done in this layer. Data which are collected for predefined computations on the basis of dedicated algorithms are applied here and it compiles in a short period. This module can be an AI-powered on-demand service module which will use the AI capability to enhance the result and optimize the process. This process utilizes the cloud PaaS service module and generates the output with a refined dataset. The user does not need to worry about how this data is being scheduled, how the task is being scheduled, or what kind of technique is used; all these questions will be solved by vendor or service provider. Even if the user feels that these resources are not enough to process the data they can scale their requirement with any latency with the on-demand feature of cloud service. The last layer in this architecture is the result of bioinformatics data analysis which can be utilized by researchers to provide the desired destination to the computed data.

At present Bio-VLAB [8] is the real example of cloud computing and utilization of it in the field of bioinformatics. This Bio VLAB concept is cloud-based service architecture to utilize the cloud service architecture for their lab experiments.

5.3.1.1 Workflow and Process

As discussed earlier, the flow of process is based on Figure 5.1 which is divided into various segments, and each segment plays its crucial role to complete the task. It starts with the actuation of data. At the first stage the data are collected and stored in a cloud storage unit. Here cloud storage saves data with cloud security; only authorized users can see or access the data. At this stage the data could be further processed using cloud PaaS-enabled data refinement capable services.

After the refinements, data is processed for cloud computational unit to apply predefined algorithm-based computation. At this stage the user may apply dedicated algorithms and also call for special predefined services to improvise their work. All the computation, data, network, other services will be available here. The result of the upper layer is generating the output of process data which could be used by users for further processes. Resultant data uses again cloud storage which gives the immense of cloud services at its best.

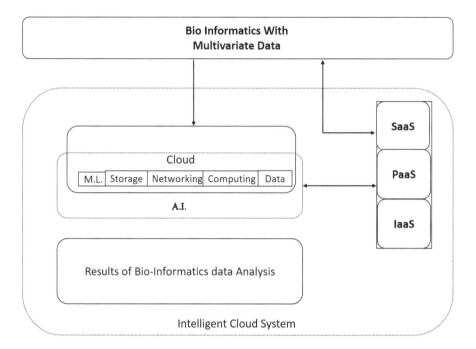

FIGURE 5.1   Components and system architecture.

5.3.1.2   Cloud Integration with Multivariate Bioinformatics

In bioinformatics, there is a large number of extra multivariate data that is usually very redundant and devoid of any discernible pattern. Because it is challenging to analyse this data using standard calculations, professionals in the sector are gradually turning to machine learning and artificial intelligence methods along with cloud computing. Because cloud computing successfully addresses the issue of a shortage of processing power and storage space, it has emerged as the most practical choice for bioinformatics data analysis. This chapter examines how cloud computing and the emergence of the intelligent cloud have improved bioinformatics [9].

Research in bioinformatics is commonly associated with computation, enormous data collections, and expensive computing tools. To address the computing demands of the research staff, these computational requirements call for high-end laboratories.

As a result, the requirement for an expensive setup is becoming a computational bottleneck in biological discovery [10]. Therefore, cloud computing offers researchers in the field of bioinformatics a practical answer. By minimizing processing time and maximizing cost, cloud computing lessens the workload for bioinformatics researchers. Scientists may simply and rapidly obtain results with the use of cloud computing without having to spend time and money on costly laboratory settings.

As we can see in Figure 5.2, bioinformatics research management blocks representation of a model where a researcher can utilize cloud services as shown in Figure 5.1. Here this interaction is divided into two portions: one is Bios (Bio Interface System); it is completely a user interface where an application framework will interact with cloud system.

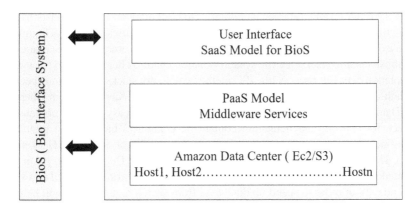

FIGURE 5.2   Bioinformatics Research Management Services

User interface SaaS Model for Bios is software as a service model; at this point the user is powered with thousands of software/tools which are completely dedicated to bioinformatics research and researcher utilizes the related software utility service module to access the privileges of cloud computing [11]. The second layer is PaaS (Platform as a Service) which is middleware which utilizes the core computing elements like CPU, GPU, and cache. These middleware services provide accessibility and management of core computing elements in a sharable fashion. This middleware software manages and provides rich connectivity with CDN (content delivery network), SDN (Software Defined Network), etc. It also manages the VM (Virtual Machine) and other key aspect required by the middleware to have full utilization and distribute the workload over the data centres.

5.3.1.3   SaaS Modeller using Container Orchestration

The use of Docker containers in the business to streamline software deployment has grown recently [6, 12, 13]. Nearly concurrently, container orchestration middleware has evolved which enables automated container deployment, scaling, and supervision. Samples include Kubernetes [14], Docker Swarm, Mesos, and Openshift 3.0 [12]. The question of whether and how this container technology may play a key architectural role in the creation and management of multi-tenant SaaS systems is becoming ever more pertinent for SaaS providers, This problem is difficult since there are so many factors that must be taken into account while taking part. For instance, the common shared-everything multi-tenant design is more affordable than containers. Such shared-everything designs maintain the isolation with high availability and scalability.

When opposed to virtual machine technology like Xen, VMWare, and KVM, container technology such as Docker, LXC, and OpenVZ offers a distinct trade-off between cost-efficiency and security isolation, which is a major factor for its recent rise in popularity [15, 16]. One distinguishing factor between virtual machines and containers is that virtual machines run on a hypervisor, which isolates the computer hardware architecture and linked peripherals, whereas containers run on a common Linux kernel. As a result, virtual machine images are heavier since they include an additional operating system on top of which the application runs. Contrarily, containers simply require the program and its dependent libraries to be contained. The hypervisor handles isolation between virtual machines, but the Linux kernel uses several techniques to handle isolation between containers. Cgroups, chroot, and kernel namespaces are used to establish resource isolation, file system isolation inside a chroot-enabled file system, and isolation between process ids, IPC methods, network stacks, and mount spaces. A thorough description of these technologies is provided by Xavier et al. in Chapter 8 [15]. Thanks to Docker, which provides a daemon and an easy-to-use command line interface for starting and managing containers, containers have gained popularity. Images include the application and libraries that are packaged for use in Docker containers. These images are kept in either a nearby or a distant Docker registry. A picture is created as a collection of incremental layers that may be communicated and stored independently in order to speed up download from such a registry. This will help you out to have a better understanding of these technological terminologies.

Now, as we can see in Figure 5.3, each user interacts with SaaS model interface and post collected data over the Kubernetes framework; framework assigns it to pods (a pod is a group of containers that are always deployed on the same node together since they logically belong together) which are responsible to accumulate the container images. These pods work in an isolated manner. Kubernetes framework lead its processed data to clusters which are responsible to schedule the process to desired clusters. Each cluster is ensembled with its Host OS which leads to the container and processed data is collected and analytics result collected or processed output presented to the user.

5.3.2 MIDDLEWARE SERVICES FOR SERVICE INTERFACE WITH MULTIVARIATE DATA ANALYSIS

Process industries need maximized valuable products while maintaining high quality and lowering necessary energy consumption in today's competitive refining and

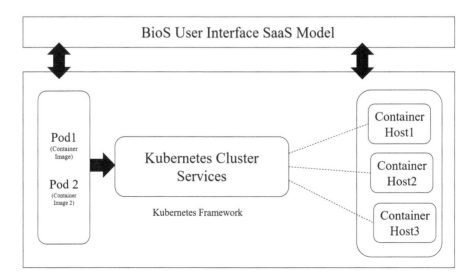

FIGURE 5.3 Bioinformatics system application on Kubernetes.

petrochemical production environment, which is also backed by tight government rules and environmental requirements. This demanding need necessitates the use of cutting-edge agile and strict process control technologies to boost production, enhance quality, and save costs [12].

5.3.2.1 Bioinformatics

Bioinformatics is a young, expanding branch of study that employs computer methods to respond to biological queries. In order to get true, biological answers to these questions, researchers must carefully use vast, diverse datasets (both public and private). Such an approach has the potential to significantly alter the way that basic science is conducted and may be used to more effectively direct laboratory experiments. The study of fundamental biomedical issues is becoming more and more reliant on the area of bioinformatics due to the explosion of sequence and structural data that is now readily available to researchers. The challenge for computational biologists will be to support the discovery of new genes and the development of molecular modelling, site-directed mutagenesis, and other types of experiments that may reveal interconnection here between structure and function of genes and proteins that were not previously known. Given the immense quantity of data generated by the Human Genome Project and other systematic sequencing efforts to date, this task becomes very difficult [17].

5.3.3 Compute and Data Resources

For the purpose of the bioinformatics data analysis a huge amount of processing and storage capacity is required. The capacity and storage requirement is not fulfilled by using traditional computing and storage paradigm. The service-oriented computing paradigm is used to provide the unlimited resources in an on demand fashion. The computing power and storage can be fulfilled using public, private, hybrid, or community cloud deployment model. In the present scenario, Amazon, Google, and Microsoft provide infinite resources in the form of instances. The common example, i.e., biological study of human body with DNA sequencing [18], cloud service providers provides instances with service level agreement. For the gene expression analysis, GEO2R online platform is used which requires cloud storage and computing capability for gene expression analysis. The key bucket feature of Google cloud stores the bioinformatics data for real-time predictive modelling. Figure 5.4 shows the flow diagram of the flow of the information from bioinformatics tool to cloud infrastructure for analysis.

5.3.3.1 Amazon EC2 Cloud Services for Container Management and Execution

The public cloud service provider Amazon provides the services of storage, computing, and network resources. For the execution of the bioinformatics application, cloud services are used which are provided by the service providers using pay-as-you-go model. The Amazon EC2 service provides the compute service to run the application. The lightweight virtual machines handle the user requests. The lightweight virtual machine acts as a container. The container running across 23 datacentres of the cloud provides the Amazon machine images as a service to handle the complex bioinformatics applications. The Amazon EC2 compute cloud provides the Amazon machine

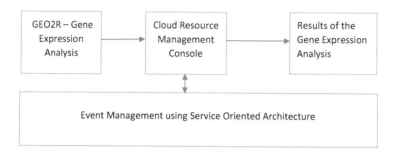

FIGURE 5.4   Flow process of the gene sequence analysis in cloud environment.

image, i.e., JCVI Cloud Bio-Linux [17, 19]. The AMI provides the bioinformatics packages to the researchers and scientist. It includes glimmer (Microbial Gene-Finding System), hmmer package for bio sequence analysis. For the RNA sequence analysis is also performed using Amazon web services. Hence this leading cloud service provider provides unlimited computing and storage resources to the end users through EC2 and S3 services.

5.4 BIOINFORMATICS APPLICATIONS HANDLING USING SERVICE-ORIENTED COMPUTING PARADIGM

The service-oriented computing paradigm provides the optimal platform for the bioinformatics applications. It includes DNA sequence analysis, RNA sequence analysis, and gene sequence Analysis. The following components are used for the integration of the cloud services with bioinformatics. Figure 5.5 shows the clear picture of the BioS integration with Cloud [20].

For storage purpose, we can use Amazon storage service or Google buckets which provide the on-demand data as a service to the BioS application.

5.4.1 BIOINFORMATICS APPLICATIONS (BIOVLAB-PROTEIN, BIOVLAB-MICROARRAY, BIOVLAB-MMIA) HANDLING USING KUBERNETES PLATFORM

The lightweight virtualization plays an important role in cloud computing environment. Kubernetes orchestration open source platform provides the container or pods

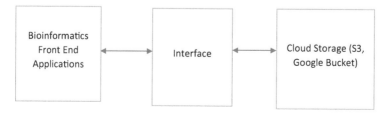

FIGURE 5.5   Cloud storage integration with BioS system.

for bioinformatics management. As shown in Section 5.3.1.3, Kubernetes cluster handle the bioinformatics applications on pods. The number of pods required depends on application requests on SaaS model. The most commonly used bioinformatics applications include BioVLAB-Protein, BioVLAB-Microarray, and BioVLAB-MMIA [8].

The BioVLAB provides genomes rapid sequencing. The protein sequence can be analysed using this technology for rapid sequencing. The applications in bioinformatics including Gibbs [21] can be executed also. The workflow and Gateway system with cloud computing environment provides the optimal solution of the Protein sequence analysis. The workflow events include configuration, input file, and output files of the sequence analysis [22].

Another Bioinformatics application, BioVLAB-Microarray, covers the technology to handle the cell dynamics. It can handle multiple genes in a single step. This is efficient with high throughput. It provides a prominent feature to identify the gene patterns and detect the genes associated with particular type of diseases. The NCBI-Geo databases provide the data for applying the machine learning approaches inside the cloud. K Means Clustering provides the solution to analyse the bioinformatics data.

BioVLAB-MMIA is a cloud computing–based environment which provides the solution for microRNA analysis and gene analysis. It also provides the feature to analyse the mRNA. Hence for such types of bioinformatics application analysis which includes the study of the pattern in protein, RNA, and DNA for disease detection, cloud computing provides the solution.

5.5 CONCLUSION

Cloud computing environment provides the solution to researches and scientist for computational purpose. The integration of workflow composer with cloud provides high throughput. The bioinformatics application service management is handled using lightweight virtual machines provided at the end of cloud service providers. This chapter presents the role of cloud platform in bioinformatics system. The cloud computing environment provides the service-oriented feature to handle the bioinformatics-based scientific applications. Data-driven scientific applications of bioinformation, i.e., BioVLAB-Protein, BioVLAB-Microarray, and BioVLAB-MMIA are focused for the analysis of real time data and analysis. The focus of the chapter shows that the kubernetes platform provides an optimal solution to handle the biological data for detection of diseases and prediction. In future our objective will be to test the presented cloud-oriented framework using real-time monitoring of the bioinformatics system.

REFERENCES

1. Ekanayake, J., Gunarathne, T., & Qiu, J. (2010). Cloud technologies for bioinformatics applications. *IEEE Transactions on Parallel and Distributed Systems*, 22(6):998–1011.
2. Moreno, P., Pireddu, L., Roger, P., Goonasekera, N., Afgan, E., Van Den Beek, M., & Neumann, S. (2019). Galaxy-Kubernetes integration: Scaling bioinformatics workflows in the cloud. BioRxiv, 488643.
3. Zhou, S., Liao, R., & Guan, J. (2013). When cloud computing meets bioinformatics: A review. *Journal of Bioinformatics and Computational Biology*, 11(5):1330002–1330028.

4. Yang, Y., Choi, J. Y., Choi, K., Pierce, M., Gannon, D., & Kim, S. (2008, December). Biovlab-microarray: Microarray data analysis in virtual environment. In *2008 IEEE Fourth International Conference on eScience* (pp. 159–165). IEEE.
5. Case Studies, http://aws.amazon.com/solutions/case-studies/
6. Kratzke, N. A lightweight virtualization cluster reference architecture derived from open source PaaS platforms. *Open Journal of Mobile Computing and Cloud Computing*, 1(2):17–30, 2014.
7. Oh, M., Park, S., Kim, S., & Chae, H. (2021). Machine learning-based analysis of multi-omics data on the cloud for investigating gene regulations. *Briefings in Bioinformatics*, 22(1), 66–76.
8. Yang, Y., Choi, J. Y., Herath, C., Marru, S., & Kim, S. (2010). Biovlab: Bioinformatics data analysis using cloud computing and graphical workflow composers. *Cloud Computing and Software Services*, 309.
9. Dai, L., Gao, X., Guo, Y., Xiao, J., & Zhang, Z. (2012). Bioinformatics clouds for big data manipulation. *Biology Direct*, 7(1):1–7.
10. Yazar, S., Gooden, G. E., Mackey, D. A., & Hewitt, A. W. (2014). Benchmarking undedicated cloud computing providers for analysis of genomic datasets.
11. Taylor, R. C. (2010). An overview of the Hadoop/MapReduce/HBase framework and its current applications in bioinformatics. *BMC Bioinformatics*, 11(12):1–6.
12. Coulouris, G. (2011). *Distributed Systems: Concepts and Design*, Addison-Wesley.
13. Ali, A. A., El-Kalioby, M., & Abouelhoda, M. (2016, April). The case for Docker in multicloud enabled bioinformatics applications. In *International Conference on Bioinformatics and Biomedical Engineering* (pp. 587–601). Springer, Cham.
14. Burns, B., Grant, B., Oppenheimer, D., Brewer, E., & Wilkes, J. Borg, omega, and kubernetes. *Communications of the ACM*, 59(5):50–57, 2016.
15. Xavier, M. G. et al. A Performance Comparison of Container-Based Virtualization Systems for MapReduce Clusters. *2014 22nd Euromicro International Conference on Parallel, Distributed, and Network-Based Processing*, pp. 299–306, 2014.
16. Zhang, M., Marino, D., & Efstathopoulos, P. Harbormaster: Policy Enforcement for Containers. *2015 IEEE 7th International Conference on Cloud Computing Technology and Science (CloudCom)*, pp. 355–362, 2015.
17. Calabrese, B., & Cannataro, M. (2015). Bioinformatics and microarray data analysis on the cloud. *Microarray Data Analysis*, 25–39.
18. Angiuoli, S. V., Matalka, M., Gussman, A., Galens, K., Vangala, M., Riley, D. R., ... Fricke, W. F. (2011). CloVR: A virtual machine for automated and portable sequence analysis from the desktop using cloud computing. *BMC Bioinformatics*, 12(1):1–15.
19. Krampis, K., Booth, T., Chapman, B., Tiwari, B., Bicak, M., Field, D., & Nelson, K. E. (2012). Cloud BioLinux: pre-configured and on-demand bioinformatics computing for the genomics community. *BMC Bioinformatics*, 13(1):1–8.
20. Gamarra, M., Zurek, E., Nieto, W., Jimeno, M., & Sierra, D. (2017, April). A service-oriented architecture for bioinformatics: An application in cell image analysis. In *World Conference on Information Systems and Technologies*, Volume 15 pp. 724–734. Springer, Cham.
21. W. Hompson, E. C. Rouchka, & C. E. Lawrence (2003). Gibbs recursive sampler: Finding transcription factor binding sites. *Nucleic Acids Research*, 31:3580–3585.
22. Novella, J. A., Emami Khoonsari, P., Herman, S., Whitenack, D., Capuccini, M., Burman, J., ... Spjuth, O. (2019). Container-based bioinformatics with Pachyderm. *Bioinformatics*, 35(5):839–846.

6 Machine Learning and Deep Learning in Bioinformatics

Swati Paliwal
Banasthali Vidyapith, India

Ashish Sharma
JECRC, India

Smita Jain and Swapnil Sharma
Banasthali Vidyapith, India

6.1 INTRODUCTION

Bioinformatics is an interdisciplinary field that can be considered an amalgamation of computer science, biology, mathematics, and statistics. Technological advancements have led to an upsurge in the accumulation of massive databases that has motivated the development of robust software tools and algorithms (Larrañaga et al., 2006; Hinton and Salakhutdinov, 2006; LeCun et al., 2015; Nussinov, 2015). Advanced high-throughput sequencing platforms have led to a massive increase in gene and protein sequence data, gene expression data, microarray data, signaling pathway data, and gene ontology data (Baldi et al., 1999; Pan et al., 2008; Alipanahi et al., 2015). Several machine learning and deep learning algorithms can be applied to these datasets to identify various associations between protein-DNA, protein-RNA, DNA-binding motifs, pattern recognition, and protein-ligand binding in drug discovery and precision medicine (Cao et al., 2018; Zhang et al., 2017). Furthermore, detecting methylation patterns in epigenomics, gene variants, genetic polymorphisms, drug-ligand binding motifs pattern recognition, and biomedical image screening libraries has led to significant advancements in biomedicine and novel drug discoveries (Zhang et al., 2018; He et al., 2019; Hu et al., 2019). This massive inflow of data has presented a few challenges for storage, organization, management, and analysis of both structured and unstructured datasets in a streamlined manner. Artificial intelligence mimics cognitive human brain functions for smartly interpreting large datasets using advanced machine learning models and algorithms. Machine learning and deep learning are components of artificial intelligence that have shown promising outcomes in analyzing biological datasets (Angermueller et al., 2016; Schmidhuber,

DOI: 10.1201/9781003331247-7

2015). They have allowed faster and more sophisticated supercomputers that have revolutionized the field of bioinformatics for analyzing a high-throughput dataset. It uses training data to unravel the existing patterns within the data using algorithms and predictive models based on basic models such as Bayesian networks, Markov models, and Gaussian networks. Deep learning is a subset of machine learning based on complex multilayered neural networks-based algorithms for raw data extraction and its interpretation in various fields of biomedical sciences. Scientific advancements have generated a plethora of databases comprising transcriptome, genome, and proteomics variation in several diseases, protein-ligand binding libraries in drug development, and biomarker and biomedical image patterns related to many diseases (Alipanahi et al., 2015; Akhavam et al., 2018; Angermueller et al., 2017). These accruing databases demand the development of advanced computer-based algorithms and models that can provide novel strategies to utilize the existing knowledge to empower the advancement in bioinformatics. The application of machine learning and deep learning occurs in several areas of bioinformatics, including genomics, microarray, RNA-seq analysis, proteomics, system biology, phylogenetics analysis, text mining, bioimage analysis, biomedical signal processing, and drug discovery. Applying machine learning and deep learning in bioinformatics is useful in genome sequence analysis, molecular medicine, personalized medicine, oncology, animal physiology, signaling pathways, gene ontology, and drug discovery (Figure 6.1). Genomics is the branch of bioinformatics that studies and regulates gene sequence, gene expression, RNA-binding motifs, and their classifications (Libbrecht and Noble, 2015). There is a demand for using machine learning and deep learning tools in various fields of bioinformatics. **Genome sequencing** has led to an exponential increase in data explosion using following gen high-throughput sequencing platforms such as Illumina and Affymetrix. **Structural genomics** utilizes experimental results and computational biology data to predict the 3D structure of proteins, including primary, secondary, and tertiary models. **Functional genomics** related to gene interaction and classification of their functions also used these tools to interpret results better. **Gene editing**: The correction of genes by deletion, insertion, and replacement is possible due to CRISPR technology. Machine learning aids in identifying the correct target sequencing, reducing cost, and increasing the workflow's efficacy. Thus, it has dramatically impacted clinical therapeutic application by analyzing personal sequence data of patients, identifying susceptibility to disease, single nucleotide polymorphic variants, and mutations, and making appropriate therapeutic predictions. **Microarray** and **RNA-seq** datasets studies (transcriptomics), gene expression analysis, differentiation of various stages of genes, cell-specific gene expression, and the relationship between gene expression and disease progression are possible due to advanced machine learning tools. **Proteomics** used the analysis of data generated from mass-spectroscopy and scanned for peptide masses as biomarkers that can be helpful in the diagnosis and treatment of different diseases. In addition, these algorithms are applicable in MRI, CT, PET scans, and histopathological image analyses in **biomedicine**. Biosignal processing of ECG and EEG signals, electronic records, paper charts, and other tool kits use machine learning (Schmidt and Andreas, 2021).

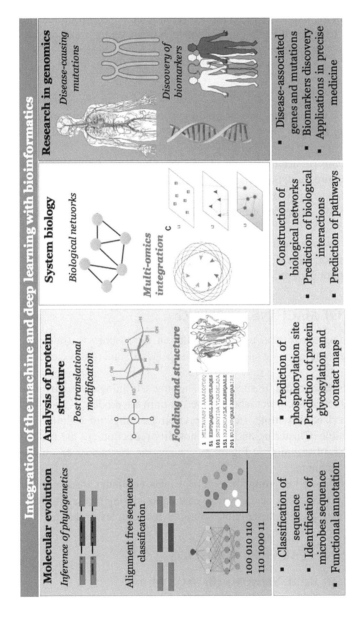

FIGURE 6.1 Machine learning and deep learning tools applied to several aspects of bioinformatics.

6.2 MACHINE LEARNING

Machine learning is the subset of artificial intelligence techniques that learn from the data and employ the learning capability to make a decision. Machine learning comprises several algorithms and statistical inference, which helps the machine to learn itself without being explicitly programmed (Hinton et al., 2006). In machine learning, the aim is to create the relationship between input vector x and output vector y given as:

$$y = f(x)$$

Here the x and y vectors may have large dimensions. The following are a few examples of the input vector.

- x may comprise health parameters of a large number of humans like diabetes, blood pressure, body mass index, etc., and $f(x)$ may be 1 for the person to be diabetic and 0 if not.
- x can be the sequence of amino acids and $f(x)$ can define the function of proteins.
- x can be an image dataset and $f(x)$ can be 1 or 0 for a person to have breast cancer or not. Here $f(x)$ is the complex function used as the model for training the input dataset.

6.3 TYPES OF MACHINE LEARNING

Machine learning algorithms use three different approaches to train themselves. These learning techniques are supervised, unsupervised, and reinforcement learning.

- **Supervised learning**: In supervised learning, a training dataset having various samples with correct labels is used to train the model.
- **Unsupervised learning**: In unsupervised learning, no training datasets are available. Clustering and dimensionality reduction are the two famous unsupervised techniques. Figure 6.2 shows the various types of machine learning techniques.
- **Reinforcement Learning**: It requires robust computer machinery to perform highly complex mathematical calculations using trial-and-error-based prediction to provide sustainable solutions for complex problems.

6.4 MACHINE LEARNING METHODS

6.4.1 BAYESIAN BELIEF NETWORKS (BAYESIAN MODEL)

In bioinformatics or computational biology, the data are noisy and complex. Traditional statistical techniques are unable to generate meaningful results while dealing with massive unstructured input data. Bayesian networks are developed on the basis of the concept of probability.

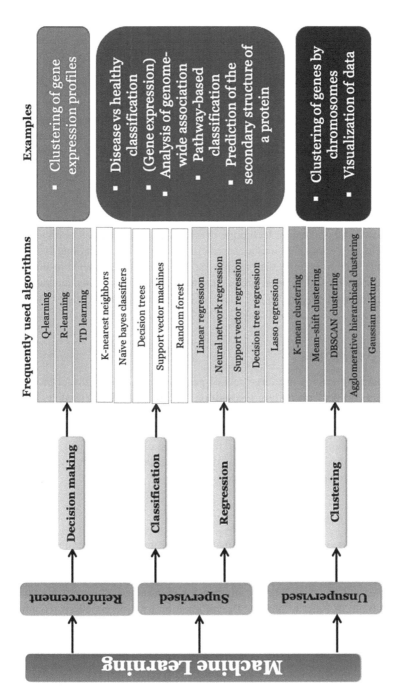

FIGURE 6.2 Application of different tools of machine learning in bioinformatics.

6.4.2 Hidden Markov Model

The hidden Markov model (HMM) describes multinomial distributions using a first-order Markov chain. It is used for modeling biological sequences in computational biology.

6.4.3 Gaussian Mixture Model

It assumed that a mixture of datapoints is obtained from finite Gaussian data distribution and can be applied to genome-wide association studies for genome analysis (Zeng et al., 2018) and quantification of unsupervised and asymmetric peptide peaks data in LC-MS data (Yu and Hesen, 2010).

6.4.4 Clustering Methods

Clustering is the classification technique in which the given dataset is divided into groups where each group has similar characteristics. It is a vital technique in machine learning. It is used to identify the patterns and structure of the labeled or unlabeled dataset. It can be applied to better understand noisy gene expression data and cluster them according to their gene functions, signaling pathways, and cellular processes categories (Steuer et al., 2006; Tseng, 2007; Miller et al., 2008).

6.5 DEEP LEARNING

Deep learning algorithms use large sets of genomic, proteomic, transcriptomic, or imaging data and perform pattern recognition to create a tool that predicts the outcome of an input dataset. The training datasets are then used to analyze a plethora of databases available at multiple sources. It, thus, appears as a readily available tool required to comprehend extremely large and complex datasets which cannot be handled by the human brain. The training datasets are then used to analyze a plethora of databases available at multiple sources.

6.6 NEURAL NETWORKS

Artificial neural networks (ANN) are mathematical models having interconnected nodes inspired by the interconnection of neurons in the human brain. It should be noted that these algorithms are basically based on a predictive model that comprises neurons arranged as nodes relaying information in a pattern similar to neurons in the human brain in order to analyze the information by hidden pattern recognition (Figure 6.3). The input to the neurons is given as x_1, x_2, and x_3 with weights w_1, w_2, w_3, and bias b. Mathematically it is given as

$$O = w_1 x_1 + w_2 x_2 + w_3 x_3 + b$$

$$O = \sum_{i=1}^{n} w_i x_i + b_i$$

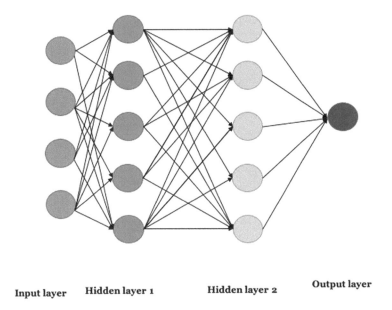

Input layer   Hidden layer 1   Hidden layer 2   Output layer

FIGURE 6.3 An example of a neural network displaying multiple filters and layers through which input information is relayed to optimize the result and arrive at a coherent output.

6.7 MAIN TYPES OF NEURAL NETWORKS AND THEIR APPLICATIONS IN BIOINFORMATICS

6.7.1 DEEP NEURAL NETWORKS

Deep neural networks (DNN) comprise the input layer, an output layer, and multiple hidden layers, as shown in Figure 6.4. When the input data is applied, the output data is sequentially calculated and forwarded to the next layer of neurons as input. The input is multiplied by the associated weight vector of each unit in the current layer and generates the weighted sum of output. These are used to understand genomics, proteomics, and various aspects of bioinformatics for predicting drug-target binding, pharmacokinetics, and tissue microenvironment (Shi et al., 2019; Ludwig et al., 2019; Alfaro-Ponce and Isaac, 2020; Wang et al., 2020; Tegner and David, 2022).

6.7.2 CONVOLUTION NEURAL NETWORKS

Convolutional neural network (CNN) is the type of deep neural network used to analyze multiple arrays of data, especially images. CNN has multiple optimizable filters that transform the hidden layers. The number of filters defines the depth of the convolutional neural network. The major aim of CNN is to identify the patterns in the data which are decisive in particular problems. CNN has been applied to both microarray and RNA-seq data to identify sequence binding motifs (Park et al., 2016; Singh et al., 2019). Different software is now being made that can use CNN-based algorithms to differentiate between live and dead cells, as shown in Figure 6.4 (Webb, 2018; Linsley et al., 2021). CNN is fundamentally designed for image interpretation,

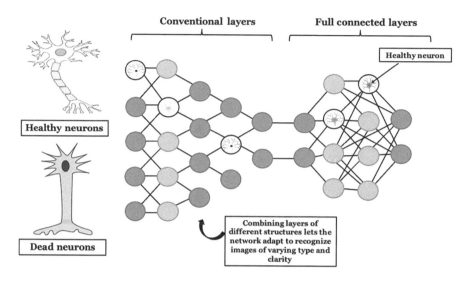

FIGURE 6.4   Software and tools based on CNN are used for cellular image detection to differentiate between healthy and dead neurons. (Adapted from Webb, 2018, Linsley et al., 2021.)

and therefore, most of its applications are in the field of bioimage analysis. It can be applied to MRI scans, CT scans, and various cellular and histological image analysis.

6.7.3   RECURRENT NEURAL NETWORK (RNN)

Recurrent neural networks (RNN) use sequential information on which a recurrent computation is performed on input data using hidden units forming a cyclic connection that can be applied for both gene expression and image analysis (Table 6.1). Machine learning and deep learning tools have a wide variety of applications in bioinformatics-related areas as depicted in Table 6.1.

6.8   DEEP LEARNING TOOLS AND MACHINE LEARNING–BASED COMPANIES

Visualization of gene sequences can be done by several tools such as **Deep motif, DeepDiff, Deep Variant, Deep Target, DeepNet, D-GEX_RNN** (Lanchantin et al., 2016; Sekhon et al., 2018; Lee et al., 2016); micro-RNA-expression analysis is done using **Deepmir**, and molecular signatures can be identified by **ADAGE** (histone modifications and methylation identifications detection by **DeepCHROME** and **DeepCpG** (Chen et al., 2016; Miotto et al. (2016); Singh et al., 2016; Angermueller et al., 2017). **Google Life Sciences, now known as Verily Life Sciences**, has developed a tool for analysis of single nucleotide variation for a gene variant associated with any disease trait. It is named as **Deep Variant software** that represents genomic information as images-like patterns which are then analyzed as images (Webb, 2018). Another **Canada-based company** has developed a tool called **Deep Genomics** that uses genomic information for prediction of diseases. A company named **Atomwise** at

TABLE 6.1

Different Methods of Machine Learning (ML) Tools and Their Applications in Bioinformatics-Related Research Areas

Methods of Machine Learning	Category Related to the Problem	Research Area	References
Convolutional neural networks	Clustering and analysis of biological sequences/proteins	Prediction of a protein family, pathogenicity, and genomes	Seo (2018), Auslander (2020), Fang (2019)
Deep neural networks	Identification of system biology networks, biomarkers and biomedical imaging	Prediction of regulatory genes, proteins, drug target effects or side effects and association with genes	Marbach (2012), Chen (2019), Aghakhani (2018), Xiao (2018), Gao (2018)
Recurrent Neural Network	Signaling of biomedicals and OMICS	Decoding of brain signal, Interpretation of EEG signal and Identifying DNA-binding motifs, RNA-splice variants using RNA-seq data	Li (2019), Liu (2017), Liang and Hu (2015)

San Fransico uses precise atomic structures of carbon atoms and hydrogen bonds in 3D structures of proteins to identify binding to the target ligands. A massive library of ten million compounds is used for molecular screening protein of interest (Smalley, 2017). **Google Accelerated Science** and **Contour** uses millions of biological images as a training dataset any relevant deviation in cellular images. The field of artificial intelligence and machine learning is evolving at a tremendous rate and these advancements will facilitate better understanding of complex gene structures, gene expression, and disease manifestation and eventually promote therapeutic advancements.

REFERENCES

Aghakhani, S., Qabaja, A., and Alhajj, R. (2018). Integration of k-means clustering algorithm with network analysis for drug-target interactions network prediction. *International Journal of Data Mining and Bioinformatics* 20:185.

Akhavam, M., Sharifi, A., and Pedram, M.M. (2018). Combination of RS-fMRI and sMRI data to discriminate autism spectrum disorders in young children using deep belief network. *Journal of Digital Imaging* 31:895–903. DOI: 10.1007/s10278-018-0093-8

Alfaro-Ponce, M., and Isaac, C. (2020). Bioinformatics-inspired non-parametric modelling of pharmacokinetics-pharmacodynamics systems using differential neural networks. *International Joint Conference on Neural Networks (IJCNN)*, Glasgow, UK, 2020, pp. 1–6. DOI: 10.1109/IJCNN48605.2020.9207669

Alipanahi, B., Delong, A., Weirauch, M.T., and Frey, B.J. (2015). Predicting the sequence specificities of DNA- and RNA-binding proteins by deep learning. *Nature Biotechnology* 33:831–838. DOI: 10.1038/nbt.3300

Angermueller, C., Heather, J.L., Wolf, R., and Oliver, S. (2017). DeepCpG: accurate prediction of single-cell DNA methylation states using deep learning. *Genome Biology* 18(1):1–13.

Angermueller, C., Pärnamaa, T., Parts, L., and Stegle, O. (2016). Deep learning for computational biology. *Molecular Systems Biology* 12:878. DOI: 10.15252/msb.20156651

Auslander, N., Gussow, A.B., Benler, S., Wolf, Y.I., and Koonin, E.V. (2020). Seeker: alignment-free identification of bacteriophage genomes by deep learning. *Nucleic Acids Research* 48:e121.

Baldi, P., Brunak, S., Frasconi, P., Soda, G., and Pollastri, G. (1999). Exploiting the past and the future in protein secondary structure prediction. *Bioinformatics* 15:937. DOI: 10.1093/bioinformatics/15.11.937

Cao, Z., Xiaoyong, P., Yang, Y., Yan, H., and Hong-Bin, S. (2018). The lncLocator: a subcellular localization predictor for long non-coding RNAs based on a stacked ensemble classifier. *Bioinformatics* 34(13):2185–2194.

Chen, C., Zhang, Q., Ma, Q., and Yu, B. (2019). LightGBM-PPI: predicting protein-protein interactions through LightGBM with multi-information fusion. *Chemometrics and Intelligent Laboratory Systems* 191:54–64.

Chen, Y., Yi, L., Narayan, R., Subramanian, A., and Xiaohui, X. (2016). Gene expression inference with deep learning. *Bioinformatics* 32(12):1832–1839.

Fang, Z., Tan, J., Wu, S., Li, M., Xu, C., Xie, Z., and Zhu, H. (2019). PPR-Meta: a tool for identifying phages and plasmids from metagenomic fragments using deep learning 8(6), giz066.

Gao, M., Bagci, U., and Lu, L. (2018). Holistic classification of CT attenuation patterns for interstitial lung diseases via deep convolutional neural networks. *Computer Methods in Biomechanics and Biomedical Engineering: Imaging and Visualization* 6:1–6.

He, F., Wang, R., Gao, Y., Wang, D., Yu, Y., Xu, D., and Zhao, X. (2019). Protein ubiquitylation and sumoylation site prediction based on ensemble and transfer learning. *International Conference Bioinformatics and Biomedicine BIBM)*, San Diego, CA, USA, 2019, pp. 117–123. DOI: 10.1109/BIBM47256.2019.8983329

Hinton, G.E., Osindero, S., and Teh, Y.W. (2006). A fast-learning algorithm for deep belief nets. *Neural Computation* 18:1527–1554. DOI: 10.1162/neco.2006.18.7.1527

Hinton, G.E., and Salakhutdinov, R.R. (2006). Reducing the dimensionality of data with neural networks. *Science* 313:504–507. DOI: 10.1126/science.1127647

Hu, S., Chenglin, Z., Peng, C., Pengying, G., Jun, Z., and Bing, W. (2019). Predicting drug-target interactions from drug structure and protein sequence using novel convolutional neural networks. *BMC Bioinformatics* 20(25):1–12.

Lanchantin, J., Singh, R., Zeming, L., and Yanjun, Q. (2016). Deep motif: visualizing genomic sequence classifications. *arXiv preprint arXiv* 1605.01133.

Larrañaga, P., Calvo, B., Santana, R., Bielza, C., and Galdiano, J. (2006). Machine learning in bioinformatics. *Briefings in Bioinformatics* 7(1):86–112. DOI: 10.1093/bib/bbk007

LeCun, Y., Bengio, Y., and Hinton, G. (2015). Deep learning. *Nature* 521(7553):436–444. DOI: 10.1038/nature14539

Lee, B., Junghwan, B., Seunghyun, P., and Sungroh, Y. (2016). DeepTarget: end-to-end learning framework for microRNA target prediction using deep recurrent neural networks. *Proceedings of the 7th ACM International Conference on Bioinformatics, Computational Biology and Health Informatics* 434–442.

Li, G., Lee, C.H., Jung, J.J., and Youn, Y.C. (2019). Deep learning of EEG data analytics: a survey. *Concurrent Computing* 32:1–15.

Liang, M., and Hu, X. (2015). Recurrent convolutional neural network for object recognition. *Conference on Computer Vision and Pattern Recognition* 3367–3375. DOI: 10.1109/CVPR.2015.7298958

Libbrecht, M.W., and Noble, W.S. (2015). Machine learning applications in genetics and genomics. *Nature Reviews Genetics* 16:321–322. DOI: 10.1038/nrg3920

Linsley, J.W., Drew, A., Linsley, J.L., Gennadi, R. Kevan, S., Nicholas, A., and Castello, V. (2021). Superhuman cell death detection with biomarker-optimized neural networks. *Science Advances* 7(50):eabf8142.

Liu, X. (2017). Deep recurrent neural network for protein function prediction from a sequence. *BioRxiv*. 103994.

Ludwig, N., Tobias, F., Fabian, K., Manfred, G., Walter, M., Stephanie, D., and Simone, G. (2019). Machine learning to detect Alzheimer's disease from circulating non-coding RNAs. *Genomics, Proteomics and Bioinformatics* 17(4):430–440.

Marbach, D., Costello, J.C., Küffner, R., Vega, N.M., Prill, R.J., Camacho, D.M., Allison, K.R., Kellis, M., Collins, J.J., and Stolovitzky, G. (2012). Wisdom of crowds for robust gene network inference. *Nature Methods* 9:796–804.

Miller, J., Yue, W., and George, K. (2008). Emergent unsupervised clustering paradigms with potential application to bioinformatics. *Frontiers in Bioscience-Landmark* 13(2): 677–690.

Miotto, R., Li, L., Kidd, B.A., and Dudley, J.T. (2016). Deep patient: an unsupervised representation to predict the future of patients from the electronic health records. *Scientific Reports* 6:26094. DOI: 10.1038/srep26094

Nussinov, R. (2015). Advancements and challenges in computational biology. *PLoS Computational Biology* 11:e1004053. DOI: 10.1371/journal.pcbi.1004053

Pan, Q., Shai, O., Lee, L.J., Frey, B.J., and Blencowe, B.J. (2008). Deep surveying of alternative splicing complexity in the human transcriptome by high-throughput sequencing. *Nature Genetics* 40:1413–1415. DOI: 10.1038/ng.259

Park, S., Seonwoo, M., Hyunsoo, C., and Sungroh, Y. (2016). DeepMiRGene: deep neural network-based precursor microRNA prediction. *arXiv preprint arXiv:1605.00017*.

Schmidhuber, J. (2015). Deep learning in neural networks: an overview. *Neural Network* 61:85. DOI: 10.1016/j.neunet.2014.09.003

Schmidt, B., and Andreas, H. (2021). Deep learning in next-generation sequencing. *Drug Discovery Today* 26(1):173–180.

Sekhon, A., Singh, R., and Qi, Y. (2018). DeepDiff: DEEP-learning for predicting differential gene expression from histone modifications. *Bioinformatics* 34:i891–i900. DOI: 10.1093/bioinformatics/bty612

Seo, S., Oh, M., Park, Y., and Kim, S. (2018). DeepFam: deep learning-based alignment-free method for protein family modelling and prediction. *Bioinformatics* 34:i254–i262.

Shi, Q., Weiya, C., Siqi, H., Fanglin, J., Yinghao, D., Yan, W., and Zhidong, X. (2019). DNN-Dom: predicting protein domain boundary from sequence alone by a deep neural network. *Bioinformatics* 35(24):5128–5136.

Singh, J., Hanson, J., Paliwal, K., and Zhou, Y. (2019). RNA secondary structure prediction using an ensemble of two-dimensional deep neural networks and transfer learning. *Nature Communications* 10:5407.

Singh, R., Jack, L., Gabriel, R., and Yanjun, Q. (2016). DeepChrome: deep-learning for predicting gene expression from histone modifications. *Bioinformatics* 32(17):i639–i648.

Smalley, E. (2017). AI-powered drug discovery captures pharma interest. *Nature Biotechnology* 35(7):604–606.

Steuer, R., Peter, H., and Joachim, S. (2006). Validation and functional annotation of expression-based clusters based on gene ontology. *BMC Bioinformatics* 7(1):1–12.

Tegner, J.N., and David, G.C. (2022). Data-driven bioinformatics to disentangle cells within a tissue microenvironment. *Trends in Cell Biology* 32(6):467–469.

Tseng, C. (2007). Penalized and weighted K-means for clustering with scattered objects and prior information in high-throughput biological data. *Bioinformatics* 23(17):2247–2255.

Wang, J., Hao, W., Xiaodan, W., and Huiyou, C. (2020). Predicting drug-target interactions via FM-DNN learning. *Current Bioinformatics* 15(1):68–76.

Webb, S. (2018). Deep learning for biology. *Nature* 554(7690):555–558.

Xiao, Q., Luo, J., Liang, C., Cai, J., and Ding, P. (2018). A graph regularized non-negative matrix factorization method for identifying microRNA-disease associations. *Bioinformatics* 34: 239–248.

Yu, T., and Hesen, P. (2010). Quantification and deconvolution of asymmetric LC-MS peaks using the bi-Gaussian mixture model and statistical model selection. *BMC Bioinformatics* 11(1):1–10.

Zeng, P., Xingjie, H., and Xiang, Z. (2018). Pleiotropic mapping and annotation selection in genome-wide association studies with penalized Gaussian mixture models. *Bioinformatics* 34(16):2797–2807.

Zhang, S., Hailin, H., Tao, J., Lei, Z., and Jianyang, Z. (2017). TITER: predicting translation initiation sites by deep learning. *Bioinformatics* 33(14): i234–i242.

Zhang, Y., Shaojie, Q., Shengjie, J., and Jiliu, Z. (2018). Ensemble-CNN: predicting DNA binding sites in protein sequences by an ensemble deep learning method. *International Conference on Intelligent Computing* 301–306.

7 Quantum Machine Learning for Biological Applications

Anushri Vijay, Harshita Bhargava and Astha Pareek
IIS (deemed to be University), India

Prashanth Suravajhala
Amrita Vishwa Vidyapeetham, India

Amita Sharma
IIS (deemed to be University), India

7.1 INTRODUCTION

Artificial intelligence (AI) research has been ongoing since the late 1940s. The goal of artificial intelligence is to figure out how to make machines think and feel like humans. With the dawn of the internet era, data in numerous areas has exponentially risen in volume, variety, and viscosity, and hence the phrase "Big Data." These ML-based systems have remarkably handled this "Big Data," delivering an astonishing amount of hidden knowledge and frequently occurring trends. Various businesses, the pharmaceutical industry, bioinformatics, astrology, remote sensing, and other sectors, are all engaged with an unfathomable amount of data. Among these, the bioinformatics realm is one of the most critical data generators. "Omics" is a term that refers to technologies used to study various types of molecules in an organism's cells, such as genes, proteins, and metabolites (Suravajhala et al. 2016). In omics, QC is expected to be more effective than traditional computing at predicting and simulating the structure and behavior of molecules. We aim to compare the classical machine learning approach in omics data to the quantum computing approach.

7.2 CLASSICAL MACHINE LEARNING AND DEEP LEARNING APPROACH

ML is a modernized form of data mining that was intended to discover hidden patterns in data warehouses (a collection of historical datasets generally concerned with business transactions). Learning concepts govern ML techniques, which are also

DOI: 10.1201/9781003331247-8

regarded as a subdomain of AI. Major factors distinguishing different types of ML algorithms are learning paradigms and mathematical techniques for learning from tasks.

As data size and complexity increase, standard hardware struggles to process it in a timely manner. Cloud-based ML solutions are built to handle large amounts of data. Omics data, being multidimensional, requires powerful hardware for effective pattern retrieval. The multilayer perceptron (MLP) approach is often used in omics data analysis because it can handle incomplete data and mimic the human nervous system. Neural network models are inspired by neurobiology and consist of units that aggregate inputs to produce a single output, with MLP being a popular type. MLP's layered architecture and rapid supervised learning approach make it an attractive option. However, ANN faces challenges when processing omics data.

Modern biomedical research is experiencing a molecular data explosion as a result of the emergence of omics approaches. Extraction of relevant knowledge from the massive amounts of data in biomedical and omics datasets is by far the most difficult task for researchers (Wang et al. 2021). Traditional ANN networks were unable to handle these challenging tasks; hence, deeper ANN networks were designed for effective remedies. A massive volume of high-dimensional and complicated structured data has rendered traditional machine learning techniques ineffective. Fortunately, deep learning technology can help to solve these problems.

7.2.1 Deep Learning Approaches

DL is a type of ML that uses ANN. DL algorithms can handle unstructured data and extract features automatically, while ML algorithms require structured and labeled data. DL is becoming popular in both supervised and unsupervised environments for learning from complex data. DL has made progress in traditional AI tasks like language processing, speech recognition, and image recognition (Silaparasetty, 2022). Deep neural networks use complex layer-based architectures for more advanced activities. Figure 7.1 shows the differences between ML and DL.

Types of Deep Networks: Deep networks can be categorized into various classes, each with its own architectural style (Quinn et al. 2020). Table 7.1 discusses the various deep networks (Ou et al. 2019).

DL techniques have already proven to be more sensitive, specific, and effective than earlier approaches in omics analysis including a wide area of diseases such as inherited disorders (Iddamalgoda et al. 2016) and neurodegenerative diseases (Myszczynska et al. 2020) to mention a few. But these algorithms face challenges when combining multiple omics layers in addition to examining each type of information separately (Kang, Ko, and Mersha 2021).

The demand for programmability and the high dimensionality both lead to a rise in computation and data mobility (Sze et al. 2017). As a consequence of this, more data is generated, and the network weights must also be retrieved and preserved. Even training takes a substantial amount of data and many iterations to fix weights. When designing ANN and DNN-based systems, it's always crucial to strike a balance between the demands for accuracy, energy, throughput, and cost. So, more effective hardware will produce better outcomes. ASICs, FPGAs, CPUs, and GPUs

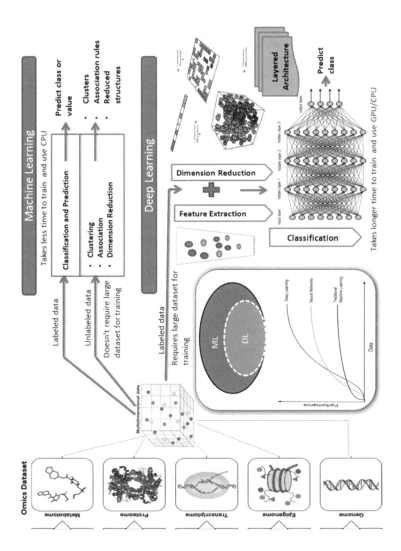

FIGURE 7.1 A pictorial representation of machine learning vs. deep learning.

TABLE 7.1
Popular Classes of Deep Networks (Ou et al. 2019)

Name of Deep Neural Network	Concept	Layers	Mathematical Functions/ Algorithm	Purpose
Multilayer Perceptron (MLP)	Multilayer units	An input layer, a hidden layer and an output layer	Feedforward and back propagation	To approximate any continuous function and can solve problems which are not linearly separable
Convolutional Neural Network (CNN)	Based on Convolution and sampling	Input layer, convolutional layer, pooling layer, fully connected layer, and output layer	Convolution and sampling	Image processing, classification, and segmentation
Recurrent Neural Network (RNN)	The state of the art algorithm for sequential data	• Simple RNN • GRU • LSTM	Back propagation algorithm	Modeling sequence data
Deep Belief Network (DBN)	Hybrid generative graphical model	One input and one output layer, and at most one hidden layer in between	Gradient descent algorithm	Unsupervised technique used in video and motion data

are all being employed in cloud-based training research to deliver the best ANN/DNN solutions (Turanli et al. 2021). To effectively analyze omics data, there is a need for ultrafast ANN/DNN systems that can handle platform-specific measures, normalize various data distributions, and handle small sample sizes. Such systems are necessary to address the challenges associated with omics analytics.

7.3　QUANTUM COMPUTING (QC)

High-performance computing (HPC) systems, with parallel heterogeneous designs, are leading the way for omics applications. HPC computers are used for complex problems such as disease research, cancer treatment, and material discovery. The fastest supercomputers, including Frontier, Fugaku, and Lumi, all use HPC-based node designs with accelerators like FPGA and GPU (Bertels et al. 2020). Quantum-based accelerators are being explored for even greater computing power (Britt et al., 2017). The term "quantum computing" refers to a type of computing that uses the probabilistic computations and principles of quantum mechanics to process data. It seeks to address challenging issues that even the most potent supercomputers in the world cannot be able to address. The tiniest discrete unit of any physical attribute is called a quantum in physics. In most cases, it alludes to the characteristics of atomic or subatomic particles like electrons, neutrinos, and photons. In QC, a qubit is the fundamental unit of information. Although they function similarly to bits in classical

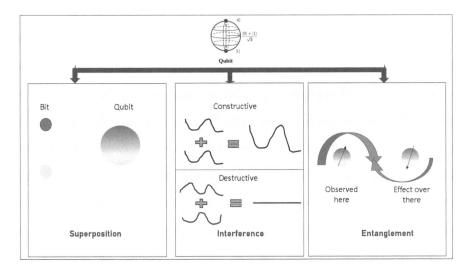

FIGURE 7.2 A pictorial representation of three concepts of QC.

computing, qubits exhibit completely distinct behavior with a store of all possible states (generated by superimposition) instead of binary states. ("What Is Quantum Computing | Microsoft Azure," n.d.). There are three concepts associated with QC: superposition, entanglement, and quantum interference (Gamble 2019). Figure 7.2 shows the diagrammatic concepts of QC (Giani and Eldredge 2021).

1) Superposition: Many waves of various frequencies superposed. It leads to the formation of a new genuine quantum state.
2) Entanglement: When two particles' quantum states are inseparable, it is said to be entangled (s).
3) Interference: Interference is a technique for manipulating the quantum states in a quantum machine by enhancing or weakening the wave functions of quantum particles.

A quantum circuit uses quantum gates to modify the quantum state of one or more qubits. There are single-qubit, two-qubit, and multi-qubit gates. A measurement on one or more qubits marks the end of the circuit. Quantum algorithms are reversible and can solve some problems more efficiently than classical algorithms, such as Shor's and Grover's algorithms.

7.3.1 Quantum Machine Learning (QML)

QML is the intersection of quantum computing and machine learning, aiming to leverage quantum computing power to process data more quickly than traditional computers. QML explores how concepts from QC and ML can interact to create more powerful quantum technologies, with the goal of solving machine learning problems more efficiently. Three prominent ways of ML are: (1) quantum versions

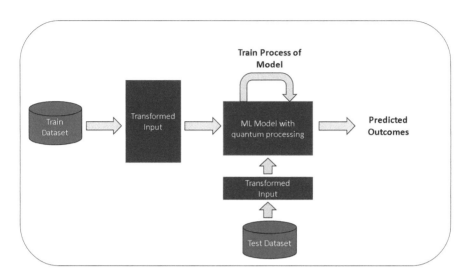

FIGURE 7.3   Processing cycle of QML.

of existing ML algorithms; (2) ML algorithms influenced by quantum mechanics; and (3) hybrid quantum-classical ML, which combines quantum algorithms and ML algorithms to enhance performance (Suryotrisongko and Musashi 2022). Figure 7.3 shows the processing cycle of QML. The input data is transformed before supplying to a quantum-based model and the model is trained using the transformed input. The model is designed using the quantum circuit. This model explains the quantum-inspired ML algorithm.

7.3.2   Deep Quantum Learning (DQL)

Deep learning and quantum computing can be coupled to speed up neural network training. This approach allows us to do underlying optimization and create a new framework for deep learning (Beer et al. 2020; Ganguly 2021; Hung and Tang 2017). The idea behind DQL is to use quantum computing devices, such as quantum processors and quantum simulators, as the computing substrate for deep learning algorithms. A quantum computing system comprises qubits that help to maintain the performance of deep learning algorithms. Qubits behave like neurons and mimic the deep learning network to deliver the required outcomes.

7.4   QUANTUM MACHINE LEARNING MODEL FOR BIOLOGICAL APPLICATIONS

7.4.1   Drug Discovery

The conventional drug discovery pipeline is expensive and takes many years to complete. Due to the complexity of these compounds and databases and the fact that a large portion of the screening data is not directly accessible, discovering significant relationships and novel compounds requires an associative approach (Amiri-Dashatan et al., 2018). Another approach is exploring images via image profiling using deep neural networks. With the help of image-based profiling, the affluence of underlying data in biological images is condensed into a multidimensional profile, or a set of extracted image-based features. Such an approach requires high-performance systems like GPU and the training quality of learning tasks may be improved by using quantum computers, which cannot be efficiently produced by classical machines. In research articles generative adversarial networks (GAN), convolutional neural networks (CNN), and variational auto-encoders (VAE) are combined with a quantum approach to create drug molecules (Li et al. 2021). The quantum GAN is one of the primary applications in quantum computers for molecule generation.

Generator (G) and discriminator (D) are networks of GAN. While the discriminator uses a binary classifier to indicate whether a given sample is realistic, the generator creates artificial data samples using noise as input. In contrast, discriminator $D(l;\theta d)$ outputs a indicates the likelihood that l originates from original data as opposed to data space pg (synthetic chemical). Generator $G(o; \theta g)$ maps randomized input noise o to pg, a fake dataset. G is intended to reduce the gap between original and fake by learning it. "$log(1-D(G(o)))$" while D has been taught to maximize the likelihood of assigning the correct label. Implementation of quantum GAN depends on execution environments. And also classical data cannot be supplied directly to quantum systems and it has to undergo preparation, typically through amplitude encoding as shown in Figure 7.4. This stage requires K log(L) qubits (K:size of train dataset and L: feature dimension). The QM9 (quantum molecule data) dataset is the one of popularly used dataset in QML studies. The Quantum GANs' learning outcomes can be assessed using the Frechet distance metric, which assesses the similarity in generated and real molecules distribution. Either a simulator or a real quantum machine can be used to run the quantum circuits.

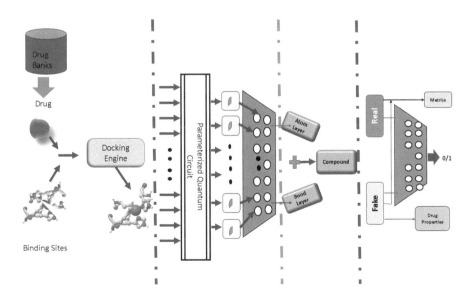

FIGURE 7.4 A pictorial representation of quantum GAN approach in drug discovery.

7.4.2   PROTEIN FUNCTION PREDICTION

Although there are currently many models for classifying protein realms, one disadvantage of these approaches is that they are premised on the conformity of linear sequence alignment and do not take into account interactions among amino acids in various regions of protein sequences. Bileschi (2022) suggested dilated convolutional neural networks (CNNs) to model non-local pairwise amino-acid interactions. This network is easily deployable on GPU-powered systems. To predict the structure of the proteins, Ben Geoffrey AS et al. developed a quantum-classical hybrid Keras deep neural network model. ProteinNet's CASP dataset was utilized in this system (Geoffrey AS 2021). A quantum machine learning library called TensorFlow Quantum (TFQ) is used to quickly prototype hybrid quantum-classical ML models. The TFQ includes the Quantum Keras Library. For working with quantum computers at the level of pulses, circuits, and application modules, there is another tool called Qiskit, which is an open-source SDK. It can also be used to create hybrid quantum classical ML by integrating the pytorch framework's library ("Hybrid Quantum-Classical Neural Networks with PyTorch and Qiskit" n.d.; Figure 7.5).

7.4.3   DRUG TARGET INTERACTION

One of the most difficult aspects of drug repositioning is determining how well-known drugs interact with targets. By supplying the most effective DTIs, in silico drug–target interaction prediction (DTI) can expedite the costly and time-consuming

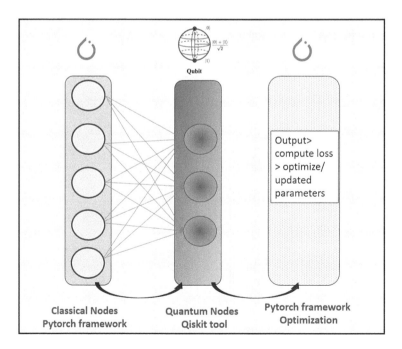

FIGURE 7.5   Hybrid quantum-classical neural network.

experimental work. Proteochemometrics (PCM) and network-based methods are well-known hybrid approaches that collaborate with ML to produce anticipated results in DTI. QML can be applied to this issue to speed up the process. When data is transformed into a quantum circuit format, a hybrid quantum-classical neural network can be created where drug features, protein features, and interaction matrix can be proven as inputs.

7.5 TOOLS FOR QML

While traditional machine learning methods process vast volumes of data, quantum machine learning uses qubits, quantum processes, or particular quantum systems to speed up processing and data storage. There are five popular open-source tools available to explore quantum machine learning (*Review of Open Source Quantum Machine Learning Tools* 2021). Table 7.2 summarizes QML tools.

In addition to proprietary quantum hardware and publicly available cloud quantum computers, other open-source quantum computing frameworks based on Python include PROJECTQ, Q-CTRL PYTHON OPEN CONTROLS, QUIPPER, QUTIP, QUCAT (Quantum Circuit Analyzer Tool), Bayesforge, QUANTUM INSPIRE, PERCEVAL, QCIRCUITS, and Mitiq. The QuTiP library needs the top-notch Numpy, Scipy, and Cython numerical packages. Other freely accessible libraries include Matplotlib, which generates graphical output, FermiLib, a tool for solving

TABLE 7.2
Open-Source Quantum Machine Learning Tools (Dargan, 2022b)

Tool	Purpose	quBit Processor
Braket	Quantum algorithms can be built using Amazon's fully managed quantum computing service.	80-qubit processor
Cirq	The Noisy Intermediate Scale Quantum (NISQ) circuit design, updating, and invocation are made possible by the Cirq Python framework, which is available as a GitHub repository. Cirq is also compatible with the Open Fermion-Cirq platform for developing quantum algorithms for chemical problems.	Not Available
Forest	Rigetti computing gives software libraries for creating, modeling, compiling, and running quantum applications.	30-qubit processor
Ocean	D-Wave System's suite for using quantum computers to solve challenging tasks.	Not Available
OpenQL	With algorithm libraries, optimizers, schedulers, QECs, mapping, and micro-code generators, OpenQL is a compiler framework for high-level quantum programming in C++/Python.	Not Available
QUANTUM INSPIRE	It can create, run, and explore quantum algorithms on various hardware chips using one of QuTech's simulators or hardware backends, giving them hands-on experience with the quantum computing possibilities. IBM's Qiskit and Quantum Inspire have integrated, allowing users to run QI-developed applications on both IBM's quantum simulators and quantum hardware (Wille et al., 2019)	37-qubit processor

fermionic quantum simulation issues, and others. QuTiP is the best tool for teaching pupils about quantum dynamics and mechanics because it doesn't demand any licenses. In addition to supporting the creation of Jupyter Notebooks in Python, R, and Octave, Bayesforge is accessible as a docker image on the Amazon and Tencent clouds. Programs for photonic quantum computers are developed using the open-source Perceval programming environment. The quantum circuit notion is the foundation of QCircuits, a Python quantum simulation and research tool for quantum computers. Error mitigation strategies are applied through the use of an open-source toolbox called Mitiq (James Dargan 2022b).

7.6 CHALLENGES AND FUTURE SCOPE

The fundamental ideas of QC with regard to ML and DL were presented in this chapter together with traditional machine learning approaches. The use of QC in biological applications such as drug discovery, protein function prediction, and predicting drug-target interactions is highly significant. Protein function prediction is yet underdeveloped, whereas drug discovery is done by a few researchers. A significant issue that has yet to be addressed utilizing QML is the research of hypothetical protein. QML is a strong system for omics analysis, but it faces significant obstacles such qubit availability, data processing, and choosing the right QML approach for a given issue. Another crucial area for research in this area is the optimization and selection of architecture. Although there are multiple open-source tools available for QC which help researchers create QML solutions, it is time we have better training modules at the quantum level.

REFERENCES

Amiri-Dashatan, Nasrin, Mehdi Koushki, Hojjat-Allah Abbaszadeh, Mohammad Rostami-Nejad, and Mostafa Rezaei-Tavirani. 2018. "Proteomics Applications in Health: Biomarker and Drug Discovery and Food Industry." *Iranian Journal of Pharmaceutical Research: IJPR* 17 (4): 1523–36. https://www.ncbi.nlm.nih.gov/pmc/articles/PMC6269565/

Beer, Kerstin, Dmytro Bondarenko, Terry Farrelly, Tobias J. Osborne, Robert Salzmann, Daniel Scheiermann, and Ramona Wolf. 2020. "Training Deep Quantum Neural Networks." *Nature Communications* 11 (1): 808. https://doi.org/10.1038/s41467-020-14454-2

Bertels, Koen, A. Sarkar, T. Hubregtsen, M. Serrao, A.A. Mouedenne, A. Yadav, A. Krol, I. Ashraf, and C. Garcia Almudever. 2020. "Quantum Computer Architecture toward Full-Stack Quantum Accelerators." *IEEE Transactions on Quantum Engineering* 1: 1–17. https://doi.org/10.1109/tqe.2020.2981074

Bileschi, Maxwell. 2022. Review of Using Deep Learning to Annotate the Protein Universe. *Google AI Blog* (blog). March 2, 2022. https://ai.googleblog.com/2022/03/using-deep-learning-to-annotate-protein.html

Britt, Keith A., Fahd A. Mohiyaddin, and Travis S. Humble. 2017. "Quantum Accelerators for High-Performance Computing Systems." *2017 IEEE International Conference on Rebooting Computing (ICRC)*, November. https://doi.org/10.1109/icrc.2017.8123664

Dargan, James. 2022a. "35 of the Top Quantum Computing Software Tools [2022]." *The Quantum Insider*. May 27, 2022. https://thequantuminsider.com/2022/05/27/quantum-computing-tools/

Dargan, James. 2022b. Review of Top 35 Open Source Quantum Computing Tools [2022]. *The Quantum Insider*. https://thequantuminsider.com/2022/05/27/quantum-computing-tools/

Gamble, Sara. 2019. Quantum Computing: What It Is, Why We Want It, and How We're Trying to Get It. www.ncbi.nlm.nih.gov. National Academies Press (US). https://www.ncbi.nlm.nih.gov/books/NBK538701/#:~:text=Quantum%20computers%20have%20the%20potential

Ganguly, Santanu. 2021. "Deep Quantum Learning." *Quantum Machine Learning: An Applied Approach*, 403–59. https://doi.org/10.1007/978-1-4842-7098-1_8

Geoffrey AS, Ben. 2021. "Protein Structure Prediction Using AI and Quantum Computers," May. https://doi.org/10.1101/2021.05.22.445242

Giani, Annarita, and Zachary Eldredge. 2021. "Quantum Computing Opportunities in Renewable Energy." *SN Computer Science* 2 (5). https://doi.org/10.1007/s42979-021-00786-3

Hung, Che-Lun, and Chuan Yi Tang. 2017. "Bioinformatics Tools with Deep Learning Based on GPU." 2017 *IEEE International Conference on Bioinformatics and Biomedicine (BIBM)*, November. https://doi.org/10.1109/bibm.2017.8217950

"Hybrid Quantum-Classical Neural Networks with PyTorch and Qiskit." n.d. Community. qiskit.org. Accessed November 22, 2021. https://qiskit.org/textbook/ch-machine-learning/machine-learning-qiskit-pytorch.html

Iddamalgoda, Lahiru, Partha S. Das, Achala Aponso, Vijayaraghava S. Sundararajan, Prashanth Suravajhala, and Jayaraman K. Valadi. 2016. "Data Mining and Pattern Recognition Models for Identifying Inherited Diseases: Challenges and Implications." *Frontiers in Genetics* 7 (August). https://doi.org/10.3389/fgene.2016.00136

Kang, Mingon, Euiseong Ko, and Tesfaye B Mersha. 2021. "A Roadmap for Multi-Omics Data Integration Using Deep Learning." *Briefings in Bioinformatics* 23 (1). https://doi.org/10.1093/bib/bbab454

Li, Junde, Mahabubul Alam, Congzhou M. Sha, Jian Wang, Nikolay V. Dokholyan, and Swaroop Ghosh. 2021. "Invited: Drug Discovery Approaches Using Quantum Machine Learning." *2021 58th ACM/IEEE Design Automation Conference (DAC)*, December. https://doi.org/10.1109/dac18074.2021.9586268

Myszczynska, Monika A., Poojitha N. Ojamies, Alix M. B. Lacoste, Daniel Neil, Amir Saffari, Richard Mead, Guillaume M. Hautbergue, Joanna D. Holbrook, and Laura Ferraiuolo. 2020. "Applications of Machine Learning to Diagnosis and Treatment of Neurodegenerative Diseases." *Nature Reviews Neurology* 16 (8): 440–56. https://doi.org/10.1038/s41582-020-0377-8

"Open Source Quantum Machine Learning Tools." 2021. Emcor. July 21, 2021. https://www.emcorsoft.com/blog-us/open-source-quantum-machine-learning-tools/

Ou, Jishun, Jiawei Lu, Jingxin Xia, Chengchuan An, and Zhenbo Lu. 2019. "Learn, Assign, and Search: Real-Time Estimation of Dynamic Origin-Destination Flows Using Machine Learning Algorithms." *IEEE Access* 7: 26967–83. https://doi.org/10.1109/access.2019.2901289

Quinn, Joanne, Joanne Mceachen, Michael Fullan, Mag Gardner, and Max Drummy. 2020. *Dive into Deep Learning : Tools for Engagement*. Thousand Oaks, California: Corwin, A Sage Company.

Review of Open Source Quantum Machine Learning Tools. 2021. July 21, 2021. https://www.emcorsoft.com/blog-us/open-source-quantum-machine-learning-tools

"Semantic Scholar." n.d. www.semanticscholar.org. https://www.semanticscholar.org/reader/3d679a99b70ebfb50af886df0efda9b36a6b601a

Silaparasetty, Mohan Kumar. 2022. Beginning with Deep Learning Using Tensorflow A Beginners Guide to Tensorflow and Keras For… Practicing Deep Learning Principles and Application. [S.l.]: BPB PUBLICATIONS.

Suravajhala, Prashanth, Lisette J. A. Kogelman, and Haja N. Kadarmideen. 2016. "Multi-Omic Data Integration and Analysis Using Systems Genomics Approaches: Methods and Applications in Animal Production, Health and Welfare." *Genetics Selection Evolution* 48 (1). https://doi.org/10.1186/s12711-016-0217-x

Suryotrisongko, Hatma, and Yasuo Musashi. 2022. "Evaluating Hybrid Quantum-Classical Deep Learning for Cybersecurity Botnet DGA Detection." *Procedia Computer Science* 197: 223–29. https://doi.org/10.1016/j.procs.2021.12.135

Sze, Vivienne, Yu-Hsin Chen, Joel Emer, Amr Suleiman, and Zhengdong Zhang. 2017. "Hardware for Machine Learning: Challenges and Opportunities." IEEE Xplore. April 1, 2017. https://doi.org/10.1109/CICC.2017.7993626

Turanli, Beste, Esra Yildirim, Gizem Gulfidan, Kazim Yalcin Arga, and Raghu Sinha. 2021. "Current State of 'Omics' Biomarkers in Pancreatic Cancer." *Journal of Personalized Medicine* 11 (2): 127. https://doi.org/10.3390/jpm11020127

"Using Deep Learning to Annotate the Protein Universe." n.d. *Google AI Blog*. Accessed July 21, 2022. https://ai.googleblog.com/2022/03/using-deep-learning-to-annotate-protein.html

Wang, Haiying, Estelle Pujos-Guillot, Blandine Comte, Joao Luis de Miranda, Vojtech Spiwok, Ivan Chorbev, Filippo Castiglione, et al. 2021. "Deep Learning in Systems Medicine." *Briefings in Bioinformatics* 22 (2): 1543–59. https://doi.org/10.1093/bib/bbaa237

"What Is Quantum Computing | Microsoft Azure." n.d. Azure.microsoft.com. https://azure. microsoft.com/en-in/overview/what-is-quantum-computing/#introduction

Wille, R., Van Meter, R., and Naveh, Y. (2019, March). IBM's Qiskit Tool Chain: Working with and Developing for Real Quantum Computers. In *2019 Design, Automation & Test in Europe Conference & Exhibition (DATE)* (pp. 1234–1240). IEEE.

8 Integrating Machine Learning Strategies with Multiomics to Augment Prognosis of Chronic Diseases

Aishwarya Sekar
Stella Maris College (Autonomous) and University of Madras, India

Gunasekaran Krishnasamy
University of Madras, India

8.1 INTRODUCTION

Chronic diseases also termed as non-communicable diseases (NCD) in humans are illnesses that last more than a year, are not generally curable and demand progressive medical intervention with compensated everyday activities. As per the information from National Centre for Chronic Disease Prevention and Health Promotion, USA, six out of ten endure a chronic disease and four out of ten have two or more NCDs (Raghupathi and Raghupathi 2018). The life-threatening chronic diseases are cancer, cardiovascular disease (CVD), type 2 diabetes, respiratory diseases, stroke, Alzheimer's disease and kidney diseases. Among them the first four are the foremost reasons with 60% greater mortality and incur up to 80% of the total health care costs (www.cdc.gov). Obvious lifestyle risk behaviours that negatively impact the occurrence of chronic diseases are tobacco usage, malnourishment, passive smoking, lifestyle changes, physical inactivity, increased life expectancy and alcohol abuse (Flarup et al. 2014). Metabolic risk factors include obesity, increased blood pressure, blood sugar and blood fats. Though the chronic illnesses were predominantly seen in the western countries, they have now spread across the globe and enforced a serious impact on the public health and economies of the low- and middle-income countries, attributing to 77% of all deaths every year (Harris 2019). According to the World Health Organisation, 41 million annual deaths are due to NCDs and more than 15 million deaths occur in the people with ages of 30 to 69. Every year, approximately 17.9 million annual deaths are reported due to cardiovascular diseases, 9.3 million in cancer, 4.1 million in respiratory disorders and 1.5 million due

DOI: 10.1201/9781003331247-9

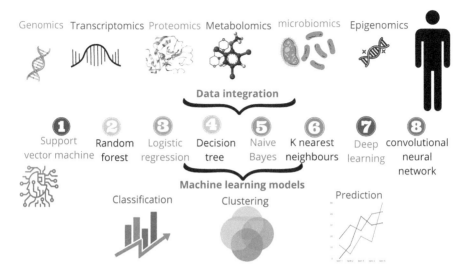

FIGURE 8.1   Graphical abstract.

to diabetes (Budreviciute et al. 2020). The U.S. Food and Drug Administration has approved the use of certain medical device software developed based on AI and ML models to assist in diagnosis of disease. Arterys Cardio DL developed by Arterys Inc. is a software developed from deep learning algorithms for analysing cardiovascular images from MR. They also have a deep learning enabled Arterys Oncology DL to diagnose cancers at the early stage. Automated algorithm–enabled EnsoSleep, developed by EnsoData, Inc., assists in diagnosing the sleep disorders in patients. EchoMD Automated Ejection Fraction Software from Bay labs adopted ML models to the Echocardiogram analysis. To support ECG analysis, an AI-based software AI-ECG Platform, developed by Shenzhen Carewell Electronics, Ltd., was approved in 2018. Another AI-based software called DreaMed, developed by DreaMed Diabetes, Ltd., was approved in July 2018 to manage type I diabetes monitoring and assist in endocrinology (Benjamens, Dhunnoo, and Meskó 2020). There is an urgent need to improve detection, prevention, prognostic measures, medical interventions and health care infrastructures such as palliative care units for the effective management of chronic diseases (Farmer 2013).

8.1.1   MULTIOMICS TECHNOLOGY, ARTIFICIAL INTELLIGENCE AND MACHINE LEARNING APPROACHES

Prognostic measures are the most significant part of NCD management and can be effectively addressed with the revolutionising high-throughput medical technologies. The 'omics' technologies that integrate and evaluate the genomes in large-scale, transcriptomes-based differential diagnosis, proteomics, metabolomics and microbiomics are the most promising advances in clinical research (Tuteja and Soares 2021). Any given disease phenotype involves complex molecular mechanisms, interaction of various biomolecules, faintly altered gene patterns and underlying pathways in progression, all of which yield more promising information about the disease when understood together. Single-omics analysis in such cases would be unfathomable, and integrated multi omics analysis accomplishes inter-relational understanding of the disease phenotype (Misra et al. 2019). Multiomics now offer cost-efficient and high-throughput parallel analysis of disease aetiology with opportunities to unravel the hidden interconnected disease mechanism (Hasin, Seldin, and Lusis 2017).

Artificial intelligence (AI) inspired by the functioning of the human brain is the recent technology that is revolutionising the world with its enormous health care applications. Machine learning (ML) strategies, a part of AI, has found its way into clinical research due to its accurate predictive power by the use of statistical, probabilistic and optimization techniques (Patel and Shah 2021). ML techniques learn, process, identify, predict and decide the outcomes based on the input and have an immense responsibility in predictive, preventive, personalised and participatory medicine. In personalised medicine, it is significant to infer as much information from all these data types and ML methods offer a wide scope to understand, analyse and interpret multiple types of biomedical data. ML strategies have the prospects to transform clinical research into a new horizon and should be made accessible as a pivotal tool in the interpretation of comprehensive puzzles in biomedical research.

Both multiomics and ML approaches are irreplaceable techniques in the diagnosis, prediction and treatment of chronic diseases as seen in Figure 8.2. The biomedical information represented in matrix forms of data grouped by the omics type demands skilful ML models that can handle high-dimensional noisy data. One effective and significant step in handling multiomics data would be a dimensionality reduction step that removes noisy and repeating data. A promising solution to dimensionality reduction is the use of feature selection technique that identifies the smaller, yet more relevant, data variables from each of the omics types, thereby reducing the complexity and dimension of the dataset (Zierer et al. 2016; Wu et al. 2019).

8.2 MULTIOMICS AND INTEGRATED MACHINE LEARNING IN RESPIRATORY DISORDERS

8.2.1 COVID-19

COVID-19 the ongoing pandemic caused by the SARS COV-2 virus has resulted in over 6,416,023 deaths globally. Though it is a communicable disease, the severe impact of the virus on the respiratory system induces acute respiratory distress syndrome (ARDS) and also damages organs like intestine, brain and heart and results in multi-organ failure. Multiomics and machine learning have been integrated in predicting the disease severity and outcomes. RNA sequencing, lipidomic, proteomic and metabolomic data were collected from 128 blood samples of COVID-19 positive and negative patients. The annotations were mapped and compared with clinical outcomes and 219 significant features such as dysregulated lipid transport, complement activation, and neutrophil activation, citrate, protein gelsolin, plasmalogens and apolipoproteins were identified as striking features of COVID-19 severity. In order to enhance prognosis, a ML model was constructed from the multiomic data from 100 patients and grouped them into less severe and severe. ExtraTrees classifier was

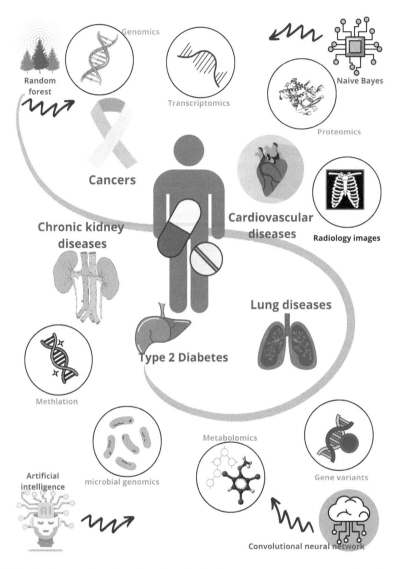

FIGURE 8.2 Integration of multiomic technologies such as genomics, transcriptomics, proteomics, metabolomics, genetic variants, microbiomics, epigenetics and methylation data with the machine learning strategies like Random forest, Naive Bayes and convolutional neural network offers effective management of chronic diseases and sets forth a successful plan to implement personalised medicine.

constructed for each of the omic dataset with a fivefold cross validation and combined multiomics resulted in a better prediction of severity with an AUC of 0.93 and average precision of 0.96 (Overmyer et al. 2021). From the peripheral blood and plasma samples of 66 COVID-19 infected and 17 healthy control individuals, a combination of transcriptomics, proteomics and metabolomics analysis were used to infer DEGs, DEPs, metabolites and extracellular RNAs (exRNAs). Enrichment of neutrophils, inflammatory cytokines and T cell responses were significant in disease severity. The predicted results were validated with a two-layer validation for the two assigned groups of individuals based on the date of admission and outcome. Four classifiers – k-nearest neighbours (KNN), nearest mean classification (NMC), random forest (RF) and support vector machine (SVM) – were used and a 50-fold cross validation was performed. The AUC was 0.79, 0.80, 0.90 and 0.91 for the exRNA dataset, transcriptome, proteome and clinical datasets respectively. The predictive models were robust and accurate in predicting each datasets to patients with prognostic differences. Increased levels of D-dimer and fibrinogen and decreased levels of *F13A1* (coagulation factor XIII A chain) were significant biomarkers of COVID-19 progression. RNA-based results suggested the reduced levels of *CD3E* (CD3 epsilon subunit of T-cell receptor complex), and *increased OLAH* (oleoyl-ACP hydrolase) and let-7 family were significant biomarkers of COVID-19 prognosis (Chen et al. 2020). With the sera of 46 COVID-19 and 53 control individuals, proteomic and metabolomic profiling was done and was validated with a ML model. The omic datasets correlated with the clinical results and exhibited an increase in C-reactive protein, alanine transferase, total bilirubin, direct bilirubin, aspartate aminotransferase, creatine and glucose. In the identification of severe cases an RF model was implemented to analyse the complete multiomic datasets from 18 severe and 13 non-severe patients that resulted in an AUC of 0.957 that also prioritised 22 promising proteins and 7 metabolites involved in the severity of infection (Shen et al. 2020). An integrated multiomic ML model is under clinical trial to quantify plasma metabolome, immunocytokines and single nucleotide polymorphism. ML models were created to integrate cytokines and multiomics data to infer pathogen specific prognosis (NCT05305469). This retrospective study was performed in 900 patients within the age range of 18–85 and the study is still in progress.

8.2.2 Tuberculosis

Tuberculosis (TB) is the deadly respiratory disease caused by the bacterial pathogen whose mortality increases day by day as it can spread to other organs like spine and brain if not treated. In a randomised control trial, 23 cases of TB patients were analysed for their miRNAs, metabolites, cytokines and chemokines. Abundance of *TNFα* and *IP-10/CXCL10* in TB, and *MDC/CCL22* in controls were identified along with 11 altered miRNAs. A decision tree algorithm with a 1000, leave-one out cross-validation was performed along with a principal component analysis that resulted in identification of gamma-glutamyl threonine and hsa-miR-215-5p as significant biomarkers with an AUC of 0.965. Thus these two biomarkers were capable of discriminating TB from the controls (Krishnan et al. 2021).

8.2.3 Chronic Obstructive Pulmonary Disease

Chronic obstructive pulmonary disease (COPD) is a heterogeneous disease that causes significant mortality in the United States. In a large-scale attempt to investigate the clinical heterogeneity of COPD, a study with 3,278 subjects was conducted for their whole blood transcriptomes (2,650), proteomes (1,013), plasma metabolomes

(1,136) and 489 subjects with all three profiles. An autoencoder was used to cluster the subspace both individually and combined. Single omics analysis was performed for each profile and was integrated using covariate filtering, dimensionality reduction, clustering and evaluated based on clinical variables for two subtypes. There were discriminations in oxygen supply, red blood cell counts and wall thickness of airway based on transcriptomics profiles. Metabolomic profiles unravelled the discrimination in blood pressure, carbon monoxide diffusing capacity, coronary artery disease and diabetes, while proteomic results showed differences in the kidney disease, coronary artery disease and quality of life measurements. Integration of all the three profiles was done by clustering them with AE and mineClus that differentiated the subtypes based on wheezing and smoking status. The most significant variations were age at enrolment, blood pressure, distance walked, sex, reported kidney disease, reported coronary artery disease and smoking pack-years. Post clustering integration resulted in two clusters – one large and other small – with eight new subtypes of COPD. The individuals in the large cluster had no significant differences, while those on the smaller cluster were younger and healthier. They walked a longer average distance, had higher diffusing capacity of the lungs for carbon monoxide (DLCO) and less gas trapping. ML methods were successful in classifying the COPD subtypes with respect to lung function and age (Gillenwater et al. 2021).

In a study by Matsumura and Ito (2020) the transcriptomic data of the human bronchial epithelial cells were integrated with the ML technique to classify the COPD and non-COPD patients based on smoking risk. There was a common expression of 15 altered genes related to DNA damage, inflammation, oxidative stress and exposure to cigarette smoke, and ten among them were novel biomarkers of COPD. A logistic regression–based numerical index called Potential Risk Factor (PRF) was predicted that accurately identified 65% of COPD patients from the non-COPD patients but was able to discriminate only 29% of smokers. An RF algorithm with a fivefold cross validation was later applied which resulted in the significant PRF scores of 0.5 for COPD, 0.30 for smokers and 0.02 for non-smokers. The ML method was robust and efficient in inferring the smoking-related COPD (Matsumura and Ito 2020).

Table 8.1 lists the various diseases and the multiomic-based ML integration details.

8.3 MULTIOMICS AND INTEGRATED MACHINE LEARNING APPROACHES IN CARDIOVASCULAR DISORDERS

As per the American Heart Association, cardiovascular problems are the serious diseases of heart and blood vessels that are related to accumulation of plaques in the arteries by blocking the blood flow by a process called as atherosclerosis. This can lead to several complications, including heart attack, a haemorrhagic or ischemic stroke of the brain, heart failure or congestive heart failure due to insufficient blood flow, abnormal heart rhythm called arrhythmia or bradycardia with lower heart rate and heart valve problems. According to the WHO, in 2019, there were 17.9 million deaths due to CVD; among them 85% was due to heart attack and stroke. Hence, there is a great necessity in the early prognosis of CVD, and integrative techniques would enable faster and accurate prediction.

TABLE 8.1

Details of Diseases Where the Multiomic Data Was Integrated with Machine Learning Models

No	Disease	Classification	Multiomics Data	Machine Learning Model	Area Under Curve
1	COVID-19	Severity	Transcriptomics	Extra Trees classifier	0.93
2	COVID-19	Prognosis	Transcriptomics, proteomics and metabolomics	SVM	0.91
3	COVID-19	Severity	Transcriptomics, proteomics and metabolomics	Random forest classifier	0.957
4	Tuberculosis	Severity	MiRNAs, metabolites, cytokines and chemokines	Decision tree algorithm	0.965
5	COPD	Subtype differentiation	Whole blood transcriptomes, proteomes and plasma metabolomes	Autoencoder	Accuracy 75%
6	Heart failure	Diastolic and systolic volume	DNA sequencing, variants of CVD associated genes, and volatilomics in plasma samples and urine	Convolutional neural network	0.95
7	Atrial fibrillation and valvular heart disease	Prognostic biomarkers	Transcriptomics, proteomics and metabolomics	Naive bayes classifier	0.995
8	Type II diabetes	Insulin resistance	Transcriptomics, proteomics, cytokines, clinical data and microbiomics	Deep neural network classifiers	0.994
9	Acute kidney injury	Onset of AKI	Patient's electronic health record	Sequential organ failure assessment (SOFA) scoring system	0.86
10	Acute kidney injury	AKI and non AKI classification	Genomics, transcriptomics, proteomics and metabolomics	General linear model (GLM)	0.89

8.3.1 HEART FAILURE

A total of 46 patients with reduced ejection fraction (HFrEF) and heart failure and 20 healthy controls were analysed in a multiomic study. The metabolomics, DNA sequencing, variant of 174 CVD-associated genes and volatilomics in plasma and urine samples were analysed. The patients were subjected to advanced electrocardiography (AECG) and artificial intelligence echocardiography (Echo AI) and underwent a five-minute virtual reality mental stress test. Left ventricular (LV) global longitudinal strain, EF (ejection fraction) and N terminal prohormone B-type natriuretic peptide (NT-BNP) define the HFrEF. An AI pipeline constructed with a convolutional neural network classified, segmented and analysed LV volumes and LVEF. The classifiers with AECG showed a diagnostic accuracy of 95% and AUC of 0.95 for N-terminal prohormone BNP for HFrEF that correlated with LV (r = 0.77). Echo AI measurements correlated with LV end diastolic volume (LVEDV) (r = 0.77), LV end systolic volume (LVESV) (r = 0.8), and LVEF (r = 0.71). The discriminating biomarkers for HFrEF showed an AUC of 0.88 and VR mental stress test predictive prognostic arrhythmic biomarkers on AECG (Gladding et al. 2021).

8.3.2 ATRIAL FIBRILLATION AND VALVULAR HEART DISEASE

The most common type of arrhythmia that is poorly understood is atrial fibrillation. In a study, four microarray datasets were retrieved from GEO (gene expression omnibus) that had 130 atrial (AF) samples and sinus rhythm (SR) from individuals affected with valvular heart disease to infer the differentially expressed genes (DEG). Qualitative and quantitative proteomic profiles of 18 patients who had valvular surgery (9 each with AF and SR) were inferred to evaluate differentially expressed proteins (DEP). An integrated correlation-based feature selection (CFS) and Naive Bayes classifier evaluated the omics samples. A total of 863 DEGs and 482 DEPs obtained revealed 30 significant prognostic biomarkers. The CFS method validated *CD44, FHL2, CHGB, GGT5, YWHAQ, NRAP, IGFBP2, SEPTIN6* as upregulated and *TNNI1*, and *TRDN* was the downregulated biomarkers of AF. The NB classifier accurately classified the AF from SR with a precision of 87.5% and an AUC of 0.995. Some promising therapeutic and prognostic biomarkers were inferred in the study by Liu et al. (2021).

8.4 CHALLENGES

The demand for faster, accurate and earlier prognosis of chronic diseases is rising exponentially and integration of multiomic data with machine learning techniques are the best offer that are readily available. They aim at improving the understanding of the genotype–phenotype relationships during pathology. Though the technology is fast developing, there are significant limitations that restrict the full-fledged employability of machine learning methods in personalised medicine (MacEachern and Forkert 2021). The data need to be maintained private. It is challenging to infer the genetic and phenotypic relationships, especially the genetic variation involved in the altered anatomy of the imaged organs from the imaging data. A perfect ML model depends on a large number of datasets and in turn requires larger machines for effective and timely prediction (Martorell-Marugán et al. 2019). Any complex and diverse dataset demands extensive interpretation abilities to achieve better prediction. The problem of overfitting can be disastrous as ML models conveniently get adapted to training sets rather than test sets. Similarly underfitting problems can erupt if there is a lack of accuracy when dealing with training dataset. There is no regulatory authority to monitor the wrong decision made by the ML models. Currently, the medical devices that use ML models are allowed to be used only as support tools and not as actual diagnostic tools in decision making. The most serious limitation is the huge financial cost that is required to implement personalised medicine (Zafar et al. 2021).

8.5 ADVANTAGES

Handling the data formats used in multiple omics projects is easy as ML models can effectively combine binary, categorical, discrete, continuous and discontinuous data without too many processing requirements. Though noisy data are to be discarded, ML models can offer quicker and accurate predictions even with smaller datasets. A complex and extensive ML model can predict multinodal, non-linear and irregular patterns of data during training which might be impossible for a physician to discover (Zafar et al. 2021; Ahmed 2020).

8.6 FUTURE DIRECTIONS

The field of biomedicine has become a data science due to its complexity and diversity. The latest technological developments that range from imaging, omics, genetic testing, biomarker research, therapeutic targets to personalised medicine are measurement of thousands of variables (Safari and Motavaf 2021). With growing numbers of clinical data, the demands for implementation of artificial intelligence, deep learning and machine learning strategies are increasing leaps and bounds owing to high accuracy, sensitivity, speed and their applicability on high dimensional datasets (Nicora et al. 2020). The integration of the multiomic data that includes genomics, transcriptomics, metabolomics, proteomics, epigenomics, microbiomics, gene variants and machine learning has enormous impacts on clinical research, pharmaceutical sector, early prognosis and diagnosis, treatment, differential and overlapping annotations, biomarker discovery, stratification of patients, clinical trials, disease mechanisms, drug discovery, lifestyle changes and comorbid conditions (Jajin 2021).

8.7 CONCLUSION

Multiomic technologies have introduced novel analytical challenges, and deep learning promises to analyse the complex and heterogeneous data obtained from the former to achieve personalised medicine. The review sheds light on the various machine learning models that were adapted to handle multiomic datasets in the management of chronic diseases such as respiratory disorders, cancer, kidney diseases and cardiovascular diseases. Though the various methods discussed here showed promising results, they have to be reproduced with significant considerations. The future of clinical research focuses on precision medicine, and deep learning models are promising components to allow disease classification based on severity, prognosis and survival. Thus the integration of machine learning and multiomics has miles to advance in understanding human health in chronic diseases.

REFERENCES

Ahmed, Zeeshan. 2020. "Practicing Precision Medicine with Intelligently Integrative Clinical and Multi-Omics Data Analysis." *Human Genomics* 14 (1): 35.

Benjamens, Stan, Pranavsingh Dhunnoo, and Bertalan Meskó. 2020. "The State of Artificial Intelligence-Based FDA-Approved Medical Devices and Algorithms: An Online Database." *NPJ Digital Medicine* 3 (September): 118.

Budreviciute, Aida, Samar Damiati, Dana Khdr Sabir, Kamil Onder, Peter Schuller-Goetzburg, Gediminas Plakys, Agne Katileviciute, Samir Khoja, and Rimantas Kodzius. 2020. "Management and Prevention Strategies for Non-Communicable Diseases (NCDs) and Their Risk Factors." *Frontiers in Public Health* 8. https://doi.org/10.3389/fpubh.2020. 574111

Chen, Yan-Mei, Yuanting Zheng, Ying Yu, Yunzhi Wang, Qingxia Huang, Feng Qian, Lei Sun, et al. 2020. "Blood Molecular Markers Associated with COVID-19 Immunopathology and Multi-Organ Damage." *The EMBO Journal* 39 (24): e105896.

Farmer, Paul E. 2013. "Shattuck Lecture. Chronic Infectious Disease and the Future of Health Care Delivery." *The New England Journal of Medicine* 369 (25): 2424–36.

Flarup, Lone, Anders Helles Carlsen, Grete Moth, Morten Bondo Christensen, Mogens Vestergaard, Frede Olesen, and Peter Vedsted. 2014. "The 30-Day Prognosis of Chronic-Disease Patients after Contact with the out-of-Hours Service in Primary Healthcare." *Scandinavian Journal of Primary Health Care* 32 (4): 208–16.

Gillenwater, Lucas A., Shahab Helmi, Evan Stene, Katherine A. Pratte, Yonghua Zhuang, Ronald P. Schuyler, Leslie Lange, et al. 2021. "Multi-Omics Subtyping Pipeline for Chronic Obstructive Pulmonary Disease." *PloS One* 16 (8): e0255337.

Gladding, Patrick A., Suzanne Loader, Kevin Smith, Erica Zarate, Saras Green, Silas Villas-Boas, Phillip Shepherd, et al. 2021. "Multiomics, Virtual Reality and Artificial Intelligence in Heart Failure." *Future Cardiology* 17 (8): 1335–47.

Harris, Randall E. 2019. *Epidemiology of Chronic Disease: Global Perspectives*. Jones & Bartlett Learning.

Hasin, Yehudit, Marcus Seldin, and Aldons Lusis. 2017. "Multi-Omics Approaches to Disease." *Genome Biology*. https://doi.org/10.1186/s13059-017-1215-1

Jajin, Elnaz Amanzadeh. 2021. "Data Science for Healthcare: A Brighter Clinical Future." *Precision Medicine and Clinical OMICS*. https://doi.org/10.5812/pmco.114871

Krishnan, Sonya, Artur T. L. Queiroz, Amita Gupta, Nikhil Gupte, Gregory P. Bisson, Johnstone Kumwenda, Kogieleum Naidoo, et al. 2021. "Integrative Multi-Omics Reveals Serum Markers of Tuberculosis in Advanced HIV." *Frontiers in Immunology*. https://doi.org/10.3389/fimmu.2021.676980

Liu, Yaozhong, Fan Bai, Zhenwei Tang, Na Liu, and Qiming Liu. 2021. "Integrative Transcriptomic, Proteomic, and Machine Learning Approach to Identifying Feature Genes of Atrial Fibrillation Using Atrial Samples from Patients with Valvular Heart Disease." *BMC Cardiovascular Disorders* 21 (1): 52.

MacEachern, Sarah J., and Nils D. Forkert. 2021. "Machine Learning for Precision Medicine." *Genome / National Research Council Canada = Genome / Conseil National de Recherches Canada* 64 (4): 416–25.

Martorell-Marugán, Jordi, Siham Tabik, Yassir Benhammou, Coral del Val, Igor Zwir, Francisco Herrera, and Pedro Carmona-Sáez. 2019. "Deep Learning in Omics Data Analysis and Precision Medicine." In *Computational Biology*, edited by Holger Husi. Brisbane (AU): Codon Publications.

Matsumura, Kazushi, and Shigeaki Ito. 2020. "Novel Biomarker Genes Which Distinguish between Smokers and Chronic Obstructive Pulmonary Disease Patients with Machine Learning Approach." *BMC Pulmonary Medicine* 20 (1): 29.

Misra, Biswapriya B., Carl Langefeld, Michael Olivier, and Laura A. Cox. 2019. "Integrated Omics: Tools, Advances and Future Approaches." *Journal of Molecular Endocrinology.* https://doi.org/10.1530/jme-18-0055

Nicora, Giovanna, Francesca Vitali, Arianna Dagliati, Nophar Geifman, and Riccardo Bellazzi. 2020. "Integrated Multi-Omics Analyses in Oncology: A Review of Machine Learning Methods and Tools." *Frontiers in Oncology* 10 (June): 1030.

Overmyer, Katherine A., Evgenia Shishkova, Ian J. Miller, Joseph Balnis, Matthew N. Bernstein, Trenton M. Peters-Clarke, Jesse G. Meyer, et al. 2021. "Large-Scale Multi-Omic Analysis of COVID-19 Severity." *Cell Systems* 12 (1): 23–40.e7.

Patel, Vandana, and Ankit K. Shah. 2021. "Machine Learning for Biomedical Signal Processing." *Machine Learning and the Internet of Medical Things in Healthcare.* https://doi.org/10.1016/b978-0-12-821229-5.00002-1

Raghupathi, Wullianallur, and Viju Raghupathi. 2018. "An Empirical Study of Chronic Diseases in the United States: A Visual Analytics Approach." *International Journal of Environmental Research and Public Health* 15 (3). https://doi.org/10.3390/ijerph15030431

Safari, Saeid, and Mahsa Motavaf. 2021. "The Era of OMICs, Big Data, and Precision Medicine: Keep Pace with Future Medicine and Cutting-Edge Science." *Precision Medicine and Clinical OMICS.* https://doi.org/10.5812/pmco.114370

Shen, Bo, Xiao Yi, Yaoting Sun, Xiaojie Bi, Juping Du, Chao Zhang, Sheng Quan, et al. 2020. "Proteomic and Metabolomic Characterization of COVID-19 Patient Sera." *Cell* 182 (1): 59–72.e15.

Tuteja, Geetu, and Michael J. Soares. 2021. "Editorial: Multi-Omics Approaches to Study Placental Development and Disease." *Frontiers in Cell and Developmental Biology.* https://doi.org/10.3389/fcell.2021.798966

Wu, Cen, Fei Zhou, Jie Ren, Xiaoxi Li, Yu Jiang, and Shuangge Ma. 2019. "A Selective Review of Multi-Level Omics Data Integration Using Variable Selection." *High-Throughput* 8 (1). https://doi.org/10.3390/ht8010004

Zafar, I., M. A. Rather, Q. U. Ain, and R. A. Rayan. 2021. "Precision Medicine and Omics in the Context of Deep Learning." *Deep Learning for Biomedical Applications.* https://doi.org/10.1201/9780367855611-1

Zierer, Jonas, Tess Pallister, Pei-Chien Tsai, Jan Krumsiek, Jordana T. Bell, Gordan Lauc, Tim D. Spector, Cristina Menni, and Gabi Kastenmüller. 2016. "Exploring the Molecular Basis of Age-Related Disease Comorbidities Using a Multi-Omics Graphical Model." *Scientific Reports* 6 (November): 37646.

9 Deep Learning Piloted Drug Design
An Advantageous Alliance

Palak Singhal
University of Bern, Switzerland

Himanshu Bansal
USI Università della Svizzera italiana, Switzerland

Shweta Kumari
Chandigarh University, India

Sahil Jain
Tel-Aviv University, Israel

9.1 INTRODUCTION

Deep learning (DL), a subset of machine learning (ML), enables rapid and efficient collection, analysis, and interpretation of huge data with the help of statistics and predictive modeling (Jakhar and Kaur 2020). DL uses multiprocessing layers called artificial neural networks (ANNs) to extract beneficial features from the datasets. These hierarchical algorithms apply non-linear transformation to input and create statistical models based on what they learn. Various DL algorithms, including deep neural networks (DNNs), convolutional neural networks (CNNs), recurrent neural networks (RNNs), graph neural networks (GNNs), and generative adversarial networks (GANs), may be applied for feature extraction and predictions from complex, large datasets.

DL is becoming increasingly prevalent in computational biology. In the last decade, DL approaches have been extensively applied in various fields, such as biological sequence data analysis, gene mutation analysis, protein engineering, genetic engineering, biomedical imaging, protein structural analysis, and drug design and discovery. Especially in drug discovery, DL methodologies facilitate learning and engineering molecular features directly from raw data, avoiding the human-engineered features, which are required for traditional ML algorithms. Application of DL encompasses all stages of the drug discovery pipeline: target identification and validation, lead optimization, virtual screening, toxicity prediction, and quantitative structure-activity relationship (QSAR). DL models can estimate the effect of molecular derivatives on bioactivity during lead optimization and QSAR modeling studies (de Souza Neto et al. 2020). Also, prediction of ADMET properties of a target molecule

DOI: 10.1201/9781003331247-10

by application of DL architectures has proved to be more efficient than conventional methods (Montanari et al. 2019). Further, de novo drug designing, de novo peptide sequencing, and synthesis planning have been greatly benefited by DL application. This is evident from the growing collaboration between various multinational pharmaceutical companies and IT companies, such as Boehringer Ingelheim-Google, Novartis-Microsoft, IBM and Pfizer, and UCB Belgium-Microsoft partnerships.

Several factors have spurred the application of DL in drug discovery and development, including the massive growth of available data, the advancement of computational hardware (especially generally programmable graphics processing units, or GPUs), advances in techniques enhancing back-propagation stability for larger architectures (such as dropout, rectified linear units (ReLUs), long short-term memories networks (LSTMs), and batch normalization), and availability of open-source software platforms and libraries (Goodfellow, Bengio, and Courville 2016). Also, emerging infectious pathogens, such as SARS-CoV-2, Ebola virus, and Monkeypox virus, require quick and efficient combative measures. But conventional drug research and development approaches are inefficient and require around 15 years and $2.5 billion investment. On the other hand, computer-aided drug design (CADD) facilitates rapid identification of potent drug candidates at minimal costs. This further emphasizes the need of an amalgamation between computational techniques and biological processes.

In this chapter, we discuss the application of various DL approaches in different drug design stages, namely, target identification and validation, lead optimization, virtual screening, predictive toxicology, and quantitative structure-activity relationship (QSAR). Further, we brainstorm on the advantages conferred by the application of DL in the drug designing process as compared to traditional approaches and highlight the extensive scope of DL-based prediction programs in offering rapid, novel, and efficient treatment options.

9.2 APPLICATION OF DL METHODOLOGIES AT VARIOUS STAGES OF DRUG DESIGN

The process of drug discovery is intended to discover novel therapeutic agents against a particular disease. This process starts with identification and validation of a target, which is crucial for the disease progression and pathogenesis. After selecting a plausible target, drug candidates (known as lead compounds) are identified. For this purpose, high-throughput screening (HTS) is carried out for huge chemical libraries against the selected target. The molecules selected from HTS, known as hit compounds, are validated via in vitro experiments for potency against the target molecule. The successful molecules, known as lead compounds, are then processed through lead optimization (Hughes et al. 2011). Next, the compounds are screened for chemical absorption, distribution, metabolism, excretion, and toxicity (ADMET) properties. Finally, the shortlisted compounds are validated for their therapeutic response in animal models and humans, followed by approval as a drug molecule upon exhibiting a desirable safety and immunogenicity profile (Hughes et al. 2011). In early stages of the drug discovery process, application of various DL approaches presents an unprecedented scope in analysis of raw, complex biological data, facilitating deeper exploration in molecular mechanisms (Table 9.1).

TABLE 9.1

Some Examples of Drug Design and Discovery Studies Applying DL Methodologies

Objective	Target Disease	Program	Method	Result	Reference
Drug repurposing	Alzheimer's disease	KG-DTI	Knowledge graph-based method	Fostamatinib	(Wang et al. 2022)
Drug repurposing	Alzheimer's disease	deepDR	Network-based method	Risperidone and aripiprazole	(Zeng et al. 2019)
Drug repurposing	Parkinson's disease	deepDR	Network-based method	Methylphenidate and pergolide	(Zeng et al. 2019)
Drug-target interaction	Covid-19	MT-DTI	Self-attention mechanism	Atazanavir, remdesivir, efavirenz, ritonavir and dolutegravir	(Beck et al. 2020)
Virtual screening	Covid-19	–	DFCNN	Meglumine, vidarabine, adenosine, D-sorbitol, D-mannitol, sodium gluconate, ganciclovir and chlorobutanol	(Zhang et al. 2020)
Drug-target interaction	Covid-19	MT-DTI	Self-attention mechanism	Enalaprilat, ombitasvir, daclatasvir and paritaprevir	(Choi et al. 2020)
Drug discovery	Covid-19	–	Multitask deep model	Abacavir, almitrine mesylate and roflumilast	(Hu, Jiang, and Yin 2020a)
de novo drug design	Covid-19	–	LSTM	Four novel compounds	(Arshia et al. 2021)
de novo drug design	Covid-19	–	Advanced deep Q-learning network with a fragment-based drug design (ADQN–FBDD)	Forty-seven lead compounds	(Tang et al. 2022)
Drug repurposing	Covid-19	–	GCN	Mefuparib	(Ge et al. 2021)
Drug repurposing	Bactericidal	–	D-MPNN	Halicin	(Stokes et al. 2020)
Target identification	Multiple sclerosis	deepDTnet	Network-based method	Topotecan	(Zeng et al. 2020)
Drug repurposing	Lung adenocarcinoma	GPSnet	Network-based method	Ouabain	(Cheng et al. 2019)
Drug repurposing	Breast cancer	GraphRepur	GNN	Selinexor, pitavastatin, etravirine, ibrutinib, sunitinib and vismodegib	(Cui et al. 2021)
Drug repurposing	Non-small cell lung cancer	–	DNN	Pimozide	(Li et al. 2020)
Drug repurposing	Covid-19	–	DNN	Baricitinib	(Richardson et al. 2020)

9.2.1 Target Identification and Validation

A drug target is an enzyme, receptor, substrate, transport protein, ion channel, metabolite, DNA, RNA, or ribosome, known to play a crucial role in a particular disease progression. The desirable properties in a prospective target include safety, commerciality, clinical approval, and accessibility to drugs (Hughes et al. 2011). The drug molecule should be able to interact with the predicted target and generate a statistically measurable immune response upon interaction with it (Hughes et al. 2011). Researchers can predict drug targets and drug-target interactions (DTIs) more quickly and efficiently by application of DL methods, thereby reducing the amount of time spent on extensive experimental work (Table 9.2). Also, unintended targets of a particular drug molecule may be predicted by DTI studies.

TABLE 9.2
Some DL-based Servers for Prediction of Drug-Target Interactions

Year	Server	URL	Method	References
2017	DeepWalk	https://github.com/ zongnansu1982/ drug-target-prediction	Linked Tripartite Network (LTN)	(Zong et al. 2017)
2018	DeepAffinity	https://github.com/ Shen-Lab/DeepAffinity	Multilayer perceptron (MLP)	(Karimi et al. 2019)
2018	DeepNP	–	Deep Neural Representation	(Gao et al. 2018)
2018	DLSCORE	https://github.com/ sirimullalab/dlscore.git	DNN	(Hassan, Mogollon, and Fuentes 2018)
2018	PADME	https://github.com/ simonfqy/PADME	MLP	(Feng et al. 2018)
2018	DeepDTA	https://github.com/ hkmztrk/DeepDTA	CNN	(Öztürk, Özgür, and Ozkirimli 2018)
2018	AutoDNP	http://web.kuicr.kyoto-u. ac.jp/supp/yoshi/ drugtarget	Stacked autoencoder	(Wang et al. 2018)
2019	MT-DTI	https://mt-dti.deargendev. me/	MLP	(Shin et al. 2019)
2019	DeepConv-DTI	https://github.com/ GIST-CSBL/ DeepConv-DTI	CNN	(Lee, Keum, and Nam 2019)
2019	LASSO-DNN	–	LASSO-DNN (Least absolute shrinkage and selection operator-DNN)	(You, McLeod, and Hu 2019)
2020	DeepDrug	https://github.com/ wanwenzeng/deepdrug	GCN	(Yin et al. 2022)
2020	DeepACTION	–	CNN	(Hasan Mahmud et al. 2020)
2020	DeepH-DTA	https://github.com/ Hawash-AI/deepH-DTA	Heterogeneous graph attention (HGAT)	(Abdel-Basset et al. 2020)
2022	DeepFusion	–	CNN	(Song et al. 2022)

Zeng et al. introduced deepDTnet, a network-based DL method, which was trained on 732 small molecule drugs for target identification. It was employed by the authors to predict a new inhibitor (topotecan) of human retinoic-acid-receptor-related orphan receptor-gamma t (ROR-γt), complementing other studies against multiple sclerosis (Zeng et al. 2020). Peng et al. introduced a DTI-CNN method for DTI prediction. This CNN-based model uses feature vectors of the drug-protein pairs to predict the relation between a pair of drugs and proteins. The efficacy of this model is based on using a complex heterogeneous-network-based feature extractor, denoising-auto encoder-based feature selector, and a CNN based drug-protein interaction predictor (Peng, Li, and Shang 2020). In a recent study, Wang et al. proposed KG-DTI, a knowledge graph based on nearly 30,000 positive DTIs, for drug repurposing. The authors applied the model to identify drugs against Apolipoprotein E (APOE) protein for Alzheimer's disease (AD) treatment. Fostamatinib, an FDA-approved drug for chronic immune thrombocytopenia, was predicted from the model against the APOE protein, and this finding was supported by molecular docking analysis (Wang et al. 2022).

9.2.2 LEAD IDENTIFICATION AND OPTIMIZATION

After target identification and validation, the next step is to identify a promising, lead compound. In order to qualify as a lead compound, a prospective molecule must exhibit appropriate physicochemical properties, selectivity, pharmacodynamics, non-toxicity, and novelty. Prior to its development as a drug, the lead compound is optimized to improve its efficacy and pharmacokinetics. DL methodologies have been applied to predict lead molecules and systematically access their bioactivity, ADMET, selectivity and side effects.

Green et al. introduced DeepFrag (http://durrantlab.com/deepfragmodel), a CNN model to carry out fragment-based lead optimization. They trained a 3-D CNN on experimentally derived dataset of drug-target crystal structures. Their model gives an acceptable accuracy on a dataset containing 6,500 or more fragments, for predicting the missing fragments used in lead optimization (Green, Koes, and Durrant 2021). In another interesting study, a DL-based single user interface called Deep2Lead was proposed. This web-based application combines Variational Autoencoder (VAE) and DeepPurpose (Huang et al. 2021) to perform a lead optimization task (Chawdhury, Grant, and Jin 2021). Recently, Erikawa et al. developed a simplified molecular input line entry system (SMILES) based on generative model using Monte carlo tree search (MCTS) and RNN approach. Their automated hit-to-lead model, named MERMAID (https://github.com/sekijima-lab/mermaid), can generate molecules optimized for quantitative estimate of drug-likeness (QED) and penalized octanol-water partition coefficient (PLogP) (Erikawa, Yasuo, and Sekijima 2021).

9.2.3 VIRTUAL SCREENING

Virtual screening (VS) is a computational technique to identify compounds that are more likely to bind with a specific drug target. Compounds are screened based on biological, topological, and physicochemical properties of both the target and the drug candidate. Essentially, VS can be categorized into two types: (a) Structure-based virtual screening (SBVS), which models and visualizes the interactions between a target and chemical compound in 3D, and (b) Ligand-based virtual screening (LBVS), which uses structure-activity data to identify plausible candidates for QSAR and pharmacophore analysis (Lavecchia and Di Giovanni 2013). VS is an important step of the drug designing process and DL approaches fasten the process with effective prediction and screening.

Pereira et al. proposed DeepVS, a DNN model to improve VS based on docking. In this approach, the authors used the docking output of Autodock Vina 1.1.2 and Dock 6.6 to extract useful and relevant features from the protein-ligand complexes. DeepVS also doesn't require any feature engineering, making it simpler to apply (Pereira, Caffarena, and dos Santos 2016). Gonczarek et al. proposed a DL architecture for SBVS, used to estimate the binding affinity of a drug-target pair. Their model can be applied to identify novel drugs for target proteins (Gonczarek et al. 2018). Recently, Kumari and Subbarao proposed a CNN model to identify novel drug molecules against the M_{pro} protein of SARS-CoV-2. Interestingly, they elucidated nine flavonoids with potential anti-M_{pro} activity (Kumari and Subbarao 2021).

9.2.4 PREDICTIVE TOXICOLOGY

Toxicology studies are a significant part of drug designing process. The toxicity profile, including carcinogenicity, mutagenicity, oral toxicity, cardiotoxicity, hepatotoxicity, respiratory toxicity, and ecotoxicity, of a lead compound is important from the safety and clinical perspective. During drug development, ~33% of lead compounds are screened out owing to the preclinical toxicity (Guengerich 2011). Predicting toxicity profile before conducting experimental validation will save time, reduce economic burden, as well as increase the chances of gaining approval for marketing of a drug candidate. Multitask learning in DL architectures allows them to generate complex features automatically, which make DL approaches a suitable method for toxicity prediction.

Asilar et al. targeted prediction of liver toxicity by application of a DL architecture. They proposed a stringent CNN-based model and used image recognition to bridge the gap between chemical composition and geometrical structure of a compound. Using this model, they predicted liver toxicity of prospective compounds, providing their images as input (Asilar, Hemmerich, and Ecker 2020). In 2018, a 2D CNN model was proposed, which utilized 2D images of chemical compounds for training. The model was used by the authors for identification of toxic compounds amongst Prestwick chemical library entries, wherein they found multiple antiandrogen compounds (Fernandez et al. 2018). Recently, a combination of feedforward neural networks (FNNs) and GNNs was applied to design a toxicity prediction model. This model was validated against the data obtained from Tox21 challenge, and the results indicated efficient toxicity predictions of the minority class (Zhang, Norinder, and Svensson 2021).

9.2.5 Quantitative Structure-Activity Relationship (QSAR)

Quantitative structure-activity relationship (QSAR) is a ligand-based drug design methodology to associate the structural properties of bioactive compounds with their biological activities. Various mathematical models are employed to statistically link structural properties of a molecule to its toxicity, negative log of IC_{50} (pIC_{50}), negative log of EC_{50} (pEC_{50}), and dissociation constant (K_i). QSAR studies help to enlist various prospective candidates according to their bioactivity potential, saving a lot of time and money spent on in vivo experimentation.

Many DL architectures have addressed the QSAR analysis in the drug design process. Hu et al. proposed a novel DL-based approach where they combined CNN and end-to-end encoder-decoder architectures for QSAR prediction. This model works in two steps: In the first step, the end-to-end encoder-decoder architecture generates features to represent chemical compounds, while in the second step, the generated features are fed as an input into CNN architecture for training an intact and stable model. Thereafter, the model may be applied to predict the active compounds, which can be further used for drug designing (Hu et al. 2020b). Chakravarti and Alla presented descriptor-free QSAR modeling by using various LSTMs trained on new linear molecular notations. The authors modeled three endpoints: Ames mutagenicity, *P. falciparum* inhibition, and hepatitis C virus (HCV) inhibition. The model displayed results similar to fragment-based models and efficiently predicts test chemicals which are dissimilar to the training set compounds (Chakravarti and Alla 2019). Recently, Ghasemi et al. employed a deep belief network to initialize DNN models in a bid to address primary parameter computation challenge in drug designing. Their model also helps in overcoming the over-fitting challenge in bioactivity predictions (Ghasemi et al. 2018).

9.3 BENEFITS OF DL IN DRUG DESIGNING

In the current paradigm of drug-design approaches, the focus is on extracting maximum information from the available data. This has been complemented by a steep rise in the application of artificial intelligence during drug development. Specifically, a plethora of DL-based drug design and discovery studies have been reported in the last decade (Yang et al. 2021; Pham et al. 2021). This is partly due to better accountability of the highly diverse and complex biochemical data by DL approaches, as compared to traditional ML methodologies. Also, DL approaches require smaller datasets and facilitate solving problems end to end without feature extraction from a sample dataset. Neural networks facilitate development of robust prediction models, catering to specific problems related to drug design. Additionally, DL algorithms learn a target rapidly from the group of hidden layers in ANN, as compared to traditional ML methods, which rely on domain experts to identify features in the dataset (Sarker 2021). Moreover, DL algorithms can learn high-level features incrementally and automatically from a dataset. The use of DL models also revealed pharmacokinetic and toxicity parameters as target properties. The ability of multitask learning enables DL models to perform toxicity predictions with high efficacy (Unterthiner et al. 2015). In virtual screening and QSAR analysis, DL approaches effectively

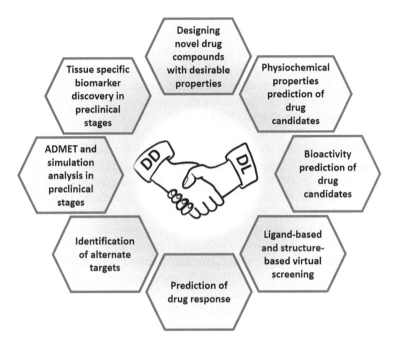

FIGURE 9.1 A handshake between drug design and deep learning, surrounded by benefits of the alliance.

handle large chemical libraries, provide predictive computational models, and facilitate efficient modeling of properties of potential drug candidates.

DL approaches have been successfully applied to screen favorable drug candidates, to estimate the synergistic effects of various drug combinations, and for estimation of the binding affinity of a drug candidate for its target (Figure 9.1). Altae-Tran et al. proposed an advantageous architecture, an iterative refinement LSTM in combination with GCNs, for low-data drug discovery. This architecture allowed reducing the amount of training dataset required for predicting bioactivity of small drug molecules (Altae-Tran et al. 2017). In 2019, a faster region-based convolutional neural network (Faster R-CNN)-based protein binding site prediction method, called FRSite, was proposed. This method allows prediction of the center and size of a drug-binding site, thus assisting in molecular docking analysis to predict the binding affinity of a drug for its target (Jiang et al. 2019). Also, GNINA 1.0, a CNN-based open source (https://github.com/gnina/gnina) molecular docking platform, reportedly outperformed the popular Autodock Vina (Jain and Baranwal 2019a, 2019b; Kaushal, Jain, and Baranwal 2022) during flexible docking and whole protein docking analysis (McNutt et al. 2021). Jin et al. suggested a combination therapy of remdesivir-reserpine, and remdesivir-IQ-1S as an effective treatment against SARS-CoV-2 infection. The grounds for their report were DL-based drug-drug synergy predictions, which they further validated under experimental conditions (Jin et al. 2021). Recently, D3AI-CoV, a freely available web platform (http://www.d3pharma.com/D3Targets-2019-nCoV/D3AI-CoV/index.php) for identification of effective drug molecules against SARS-CoV-2, was proposed. This platform is based on a combination of DL models, namely, MultiDTI, MPNN-CNN, and MPNN-CNN-R models, and exhibited high predictive performance during target identification and virtual screening studies (Yang et al. 2022). In another recent study, Mi and Shukla suggested the application of the one-shot learning method to predict the excipient-target interactions. This allowed them to screen various interactive excipients, which might interfere with the target protein functionality (Mi and Shukla 2022).

Drug repurposing studies have largely benefited from application of various DL models. Novel drug candidates against coronary artery disease were suggested upon implementation of a customized framework based on LSTM and inverse probability of treatment weighting (IPTW). This framework performs a retrospective analysis of the real-world data, and emulates randomized clinical trials, to identify multiple candidates suitable for drug repurposing (Liu, Wei, and Zhang 2021). In another study, pimozide, a known anti-dyskinesia agent, was proposed for treatment of non-small cell lung cancer, based on a DNN model-based drug repurposing approach utilizing the available transcriptomic data and chemical structures. The effect of pimozide was validated on A549 cell line (adenocarcinomic human alveolar basal epithelial cell line), achieving an IC_{50} value (~20 uM) comparable to that of a known inhibitor, gemcitabine (~14 uM) (Li et al. 2020). A combination of pirfenidone (used to treat pulmonary fibrosis) and melatonin (used to treat insomnia) was proposed as an effective therapy alternative for SARS-CoV-2 infection, based on the drug repurposing analysis via therapeutic performance mapping system-artificial neural network (TPMS-ANN) model (Artigas et al. 2020). Also, a dedicated DL-based resource, named PolypharmDB, was developed by Redka et al. in 2020 to identify potential drug repurposing candidates to fight the SARS-CoV-2 infection. Thirty candidates, including sirolimus (used to treat lymphangioleiomyomatosis), cefoxitin (used to treat urinary tract infection), colchiceine (used to treat Behcet's disease), and meropenem (an antibiotic), were identified and proposed for experimental validation (Dar'ya et al. 2020). In the same year, DeepPurpose was proposed by Huang et al. for drug repurposing studies. This package offers a flexible framework, including DNN, CNN, message-passing neural network, and CNN-RNN, takes input in the most accessible SMILES format, and returns binding activity of the drug-target complex (Huang et al. 2020). Another study proposed risperidone (used to treat mood disorders) and aripiprazole (used to treat schizophrenia) for the treatment of Alzheimer's disease, based on a network-based DL approach, termed deepDR (Zeng et al. 2019).

Overall, it can be said that application of DL models in drug design and discovery opens an abundance of hitherto unknown avenues, expediting and complementing novel drug development efforts. Further, the simultaneous consideration of pharmacokinetic simulations, metabolomic mechanisms, ADMET properties, structural information, target properties, and molecule-target interaction dynamics might enable development of comprehensive, state-of-the-art DL approaches for drug designing. Also, a combination of DL and ML models may provide solutions to development of biologically optimized drug discovery systems. Such models shall facilitate a quicker transition of novel drugs from bench to bedside.

REFERENCES

Abdel-Basset, Mohamed, Hossam Hawash, Mohamed Elhoseny, Ripon K Chakrabortty, and Michael Ryan. 2020. "DeepH-DTA: deep learning for predicting drug-target interactions: a case study of COVID-19 drug repurposing." *IEEE Access* 8:170433–170451.

Altae-Tran, Han, Bharath Ramsundar, Aneesh S. Pappu, and Vijay Pande. 2017. "Low data drug discovery with one-shot learning." *ACS Central Science* 3 (4):283–293. doi: 10.1021/acscentsci.6b00367

Arshia, Amir Hossein, Shayan Shadravan, Aida Solhjoo, Amirhossein Sakhteman, and Ashkan Sami. 2021. "De novo design of novel protease inhibitor candidates in the treatment of SARS-CoV-2 using deep learning, docking, and molecular dynamic simulations." *Computers in Biology and Medicine* 139:104967. doi: https://doi.org/10.1016/j.compbiomed.2021.104967

Artigas, L., M. Coma, P. Matos-Filipe, J. Aguirre-Plans, J. Farrés, R. Valls, N. Fernandez-Fuentes, J. de la Haba-Rodriguez, A. Olvera, J. Barbera, R. Morales, B. Oliva, and J. M. Mas. 2020. "In-silico drug repurposing study predicts the combination of pirfenidone and melatonin as a promising candidate therapy to reduce SARS-CoV-2 infection progression and respiratory distress caused by cytokine storm." *PLoS One* 15 (10):e0240149. doi: 10.1371/journal.pone.0240149

Asilar, Ece, Jennifer Hemmerich, and Gerhard F. Ecker. 2020. "Image based liver toxicity prediction." *Journal of Chemical Information and Modeling* 60 (3):1111–1121. doi: 10.1021/acs.jcim.9b00713

Beck, Bo Ram, Bonggun Shin, Yoonjung Choi, Sungsoo Park, and Keunsoo Kang. 2020. "Predicting commercially available antiviral drugs that may act on the novel coronavirus (SARS-CoV-2) through a drug-target interaction deep learning model." *Computational and Structural Biotechnology Journal* 18:784–790. doi: https://doi.org/10.1016/j.csbj.2020.03.025

Chakravarti, S. K., and S. R. M. Alla. 2019. "Descriptor free QSAR modeling using deep learning with long short-term memory neural networks." *Frontiers in Artificial Intelligence* 2:17. doi: 10.3389/frai.2019.00017

Chawdhury, Tarun Kumar, David J. Grant, and Hyun Yong Jin. 2021. "Deep2Lead: A distributed deep learning application for small molecule lead optimization." *ArXiv* abs/2108.05183.

Cheng, Feixiong, Weiqiang Lu, Chuang Liu, Jiansong Fang, Yuan Hou, Diane E. Handy, Ruisheng Wang, Yuzheng Zhao, Yi Yang, Jin Huang, David E. Hill, Marc Vidal, Charis Eng, and Joseph Loscalzo. 2019. "A genome-wide positioning systems network algorithm for in silico drug repurposing." *Nature Communications* 10 (1):3476. doi: 10.1038/s41467-019-10744-6

Choi, Yoonjung, Bonggun Shin, Keunsoo Kang, Sungsoo Park, and Bo Ram Beck. 2020. "Target-centered drug repurposing predictions of human angiotensin-converting Enzyme 2 (ACE2) and Transmembrane Protease Serine Subtype 2 (TMPRSS2) interacting approved drugs for Coronavirus Disease 2019 (COVID-19) treatment through a drug-target interaction deep learning model." *Viruses* 12 (11):1325.

Cui, Chen, Xiaoyu Ding, Dingyan Wang, Lifan Chen, Fu Xiao, Tingyang Xu, Mingyue Zheng, Xiaomin Luo, Hualiang Jiang, and Kaixian Chen. 2021. "Drug repurposing against breast cancer by integrating drug-exposure expression profiles and drug–drug links based on graph neural network." *Bioinformatics* 37 (18):2930–2937. doi: 10.1093/bioinformatics/btab191

Dar'ya, S. Redka, Stephen S. MacKinnon, Melissa Landon, Andreas Windemuth, Naheed Kurji, and Vijay Shahani. 2020. "PolypharmDB, a deep learning-based resource, quickly identifies repurposed drug candidates for COVID-19."

de Souza Neto, Lauro Ribeiro, José Teófilo Moreira-Filho, Bruno Junior Neves, Rocío Lucía Beatriz Riveros Maidana, Ana Carolina Ramos Guimarães, Nicholas Furnham, Carolina Horta Andrade, and Floriano Paes Silva Jr. 2020. "In silico strategies to support fragment-to-lead optimization in drug discovery." *Frontiers in chemistry* 8:93.

Erikawa, Daiki, Nobuaki Yasuo, and Masakazu Sekijima. 2021. "MERMAID: an open source automated hit-to-lead method based on deep reinforcement learning." *Journal of Cheminformatics* 13 (1):94. doi: 10.1186/s13321-021-00572-6

Feng, Qingyuan, Evgenia Dueva, Artem Cherkasov, and Martin Ester. 2018. "Padme: A deep learning-based framework for drug-target interaction prediction." *arXiv preprint arXiv:1807.09741.*

Fernandez, Michael, Fuqiang Ban, Godwin Woo, Michael Hsing, Takeshi Yamazaki, Eric LeBlanc, Paul S. Rennie, William J. Welch, and Artem Cherkasov. 2018. "Toxic colors: The use of deep learning for predicting toxicity of compounds merely from their graphic images." *Journal of Chemical Information and Modeling* 58 (8):1533–1543. doi: 10.1021/acs.jcim.8b00338

Gao, Kyle Yingkai, Achille Fokoue, Heng Luo, Arun Iyengar, Sanjoy Dey, and Ping Zhang. 2018. "Interpretable Drug Target Prediction Using Deep Neural Representation." IJCAI.

Ge, Yiyue, Tingzhong Tian, Suling Huang, Fangping Wan, Jingxin Li, Shuya Li, Xiaoting Wang, Hui Yang, Lixiang Hong, and Nian Wu. 2021. "An integrative drug repositioning framework discovered a potential therapeutic agent targeting COVID-19." *Signal Transduction and Targeted Therapy* 6 (1):1–16.

Ghasemi, Fahimeh, Alireza Mehridehnavi, Afshin Fassihi, and Horacio Pérez-Sánchez. 2018. "Deep neural network in QSAR studies using deep belief network." *Applied Soft Computing* 62:251–258. doi: https://doi.org/10.1016/j.asoc.2017.09.040

Gonczarek, Adam, Jakub M. Tomczak, Szymon Zaręba, Joanna Kaczmar, Piotr Dąbrowski, and Michał J. Walczak. 2018. "Interaction prediction in structure-based virtual screening using deep learning." *Computers in Biology and Medicine* 100:253–258. doi: https://doi.org/10.1016/j.compbiomed.2017.09.007

Goodfellow, Ian, Yoshua Bengio, and Aaron Courville. 2016. *Deep Learning*: MIT Press.

Green, H., D. R. Koes, and J. D. Durrant. 2021. "DeepFrag: a deep convolutional neural network for fragment-based lead optimization." *Chemical Science* 12 (23):8036–8047. doi: 10.1039/d1sc00163a

Guengerich, F. P. 2011. "Mechanisms of drug toxicity and relevance to pharmaceutical development." *Drug Metab Pharmacokinet* 26 (1):3–14. doi: 10.2133/dmpk.dmpk-10-rv-062

Hasan Mahmud, S. M., Wenyu Chen, Hosney Jahan, Bo Dai, Salah Ud Din, and Anthony Mackitz Dzisoo. 2020. "DeepACTION: A deep learning-based method for predicting novel drug-target interactions." *Analytical Biochemistry* 610:113978. doi: https://doi.org/10.1016/j.ab.2020.113978

Hassan, Mahmudulla, Daniel Castaneda Mogollon, and Olac Fuentes. 2018. "DLSCORE: A deep learning model for predicting protein-ligand binding affinities."

Hu, F., Jiaxin Jiang, and Peng Yin. 2020a. "Prediction of potential commercially inhibitors against SARS-CoV-2 by multi-task deep model." *arXiv: Molecular Networks.*

Hu, S., P. Chen, P. Gu, and B. Wang. 2020b. "A deep learning-based chemical system for QSAR prediction." *IEEE Journal of Biomedical and Health Informatics* 24 (10):3020–3028. doi: 10.1109/JBHI.2020.2977009

Huang, K., T. Fu, L. M. Glass, M. Zitnik, C. Xiao, and J. Sun. 2021. "DeepPurpose: a deep learning library for drug-target interaction prediction." *Bioinformatics* 36 (22–23):5545–5547. doi: 10.1093/bioinformatics/btaa1005

Huang, Kexin, Tianfan Fu, Cao Xiao, Lucas Glass, and Jimeng Sun. 2020. "Deeppurpose: a deep learning based drug repurposing toolkit." *arXiv preprint arXiv:2004.08919.*

Hughes, J. P., S. Rees, S. B. Kalindjian, and K. L. Philpott. 2011. "Principles of early drug discovery." *British Journal of Pharmacology* 162 (6):1239–1249. doi: 10.1111/j.1476-5381.2010.01127.x

Jain, Sahil, and Manoj Baranwal. 2019a. "Computational analysis in designing T cell epitopes enriched peptides of Ebola glycoprotein exhibiting strong binding interaction with HLA molecules." *Journal of Theoretical Biology* 465:34–44. doi: https://doi.org/10.1016/j.jtbi.2019.01.016

Jain, Sahil, and Manoj Baranwal. 2019b. "Conserved peptide vaccine candidates containing multiple Ebola nucleoprotein epitopes display interactions with diverse HLA molecules." *Medical Microbiology and Immunology* 208 (2):227–238. doi: 10.1007/s00430-019-00584-y

Jakhar, Deepack, and Ishmeet Kaur. 2020. "Artificial intelligence, machine learning and deep learning: definitions and differences." *Clinical and Experimental Dermatology* 45 (1):131–132.

Jiang, Mingjian, Zhiqiang Wei, Shugang Zhang, Shuang Wang, Xiaofeng Wang, and Zhen Li. 2019. "FRSite: protein drug binding site prediction based on faster R–CNN." *Journal of Molecular Graphics and Modelling* 93:107454. doi: https://doi.org/10.1016/j.jmgm.2019.107454

Jin, W., J. M. Stokes, R. T. Eastman, Z. Itkin, A. V. Zakharov, J. J. Collins, T. S. Jaakkola, and R. Barzilay. 2021. "Deep learning identifies synergistic drug combinations for treating COVID-19." *Proceedings of the National Academy of Sciences of the United States of America* 118 (39). doi: 10.1073/pnas.2105070118

Karimi, Mostafa, Di Wu, Zhangyang Wang, and Yang Shen. 2019. "DeepAffinity: interpretable deep learning of compound–protein affinity through unified recurrent and convolutional neural networks." *Bioinformatics* 35 (18):3329–3338.

Kaushal, Neha, Sahil Jain, and Manoj Baranwal. 2022. "Computational design of immunogenic peptide constructs comprising multiple human leukocyte antigen restricted dengue virus envelope epitopes." *Journal of Molecular Recognition* n/a (n/a):e2961. doi: https://doi.org/10.1002/jmr.2961

Kumari, Madhulata, and Naidu Subbarao. 2021. "Deep learning model for virtual screening of novel 3C-like protease enzyme inhibitors against SARS coronavirus diseases." *Computers in Biology and Medicine* 132:104317. doi: https://doi.org/10.1016/j.compbiomed.2021.104317

Lavecchia, A., and C. Di Giovanni. 2013. "Virtual screening strategies in drug discovery: a critical review." *Current Medicinal Chemistry* 20 (23):2839–2860. doi: 10.2174/09298673113209990001

Lee, Ingoo, Jongsoo Keum, and Hojung Nam. 2019. "DeepConv-DTI: Prediction of drug-target interactions via deep learning with convolution on protein sequences." *PLoS Computational Biology* 15 (6):e1007129.

Li, Bingrui, Chan Dai, Lijun Wang, Hailong Deng, Yingying Li, Zheng Guan, and Haihong Ni. 2020. "A novel drug repurposing approach for non-small cell lung cancer using deep learning." *PLOS ONE* 15 (6):e0233112. doi: 10.1371/journal.pone.0233112

Liu, Ruoqi, Lai Wei, and Ping Zhang. 2021. "A deep learning framework for drug repurposing via emulating clinical trials on real-world patient data." *Nature Machine Intelligence* 3 (1):68–75. doi: 10.1038/s42256-020-00276-w

McNutt, Andrew T., Paul Francoeur, Rishal Aggarwal, Tomohide Masuda, Rocco Meli, Matthew Ragoza, Jocelyn Sunseri, and David Ryan Koes. 2021. "GNINA 1.0: molecular docking with deep learning." *Journal of Cheminformatics* 13 (1):43. doi: 10.1186/s13321-021-00522-2

Mi, Xuenan, and Diwakar Shukla. 2022. "Predicting the activities of drug excipients on biological targets using one-shot learning." *The Journal of Physical Chemistry B* 126 (7):1492–1503. doi: 10.1021/acs.jpcb.1c10574

Montanari, Floriane, Lara Kuhnke, Antonius Ter Laak, and Djork-Arné Clevert. 2019. "Modeling physico-chemical ADMET endpoints with multitask graph convolutional networks." *Molecules* 25 (1):44.

Öztürk, Hakime, Arzucan Özgür, and Elif Ozkirimli. 2018. "DeepDTA: deep drug–target binding affinity prediction." *Bioinformatics* 34 (17):i821–i829. doi: 10.1093/bioinformatics/bty593

Peng, Jiajie, Jingyi Li, and Xuequn Shang. 2020. "A learning-based method for drug-target interaction prediction based on feature representation learning and deep neural network." *BMC Bioinformatics* 21 (13):394. doi: 10.1186/s12859-020-03677-1

Pereira, Janaina Cruz, Ernesto Raúl Caffarena, and Cicero Nogueira dos Santos. 2016. "Boosting docking-based virtual screening with deep learning." *Journal of Chemical Information and Modeling* 56 (12):2495–2506. doi: 10.1021/acs.jcim.6b00355

Pham, Thai-Hoang, Yue Qiu, Jucheng Zeng, Lei Xie, and Ping Zhang. 2021. "A deep learning framework for high-throughput mechanism-driven phenotype compound screening and its application to COVID-19 drug repurposing." *Nature Machine Intelligence* 3 (3): 247–257.

Richardson, Peter, Ivan Griffin, Catherine Tucker, Dan Smith, Olly Oechsle, Anne Phelan, Michael Rawling, Edward Savory, and Justin Stebbing. 2020. "Baricitinib as potential treatment for 2019-nCoV acute respiratory disease." *The Lancet* 395 (10223):e30–e31. doi: https://doi.org/10.1016/S0140-6736(20)30304-4

Sarker, Iqbal H. 2021. "Deep learning: a comprehensive overview on techniques, taxonomy, applications and research directions." *SN Computer Science* 2 (6):420. doi: 10.1007/s42979-021-00815-1

Shin, Bonggun, Sungsoo Park, Keunsoo Kang, and Joyce C. Ho. 2019. "Self-attention based molecule representation for predicting drug-target interaction." *Machine Learning for Healthcare Conference*.

Song, Tao, Xudong Zhang, Mao Ding, Alfonso Rodriguez-Paton, Shudong Wang, and Gan Wang. 2022. "DeepFusion: A deep learning based multi-scale feature fusion method for predicting drug-target interactions." *Methods* 204:269–277. doi: https://doi.org/10.1016/j.ymeth.2022.02.007

Stokes, Jonathan M., Kevin Yang, Kyle Swanson, Wengong Jin, Andres Cubillos-Ruiz, Nina M. Donghia, Craig R. MacNair, Shawn French, Lindsey A. Carfrae, Zohar Bloom-Ackermann, Victoria M. Tran, Anush Chiappino-Pepe, Ahmed H. Badran, Ian W. Andrews, Emma J. Chory, George M. Church, Eric D. Brown, Tommi S. Jaakkola, Regina Barzilay, and James J. Collins. 2020. "A deep learning approach to antibiotic discovery." *Cell* 180 (4):688–702.e13. doi: https://doi.org/10.1016/j.cell.2020.01.021

Tang, Bowen, Fengming He, Dongpeng Liu, Fei He, Tong Wu, Meijuan Fang, Zhangming Niu, Zhen Wu, and Dong Xu. 2022. "AI-aided design of novel targeted covalent inhibitors against SARS-CoV-2." *Biomolecules* 12 (6):746.

Unterthiner, Thomas, Andreas Mayr, Günter Klambauer, and Sepp Hochreiter. 2015. "Toxicity prediction using deep learning." *arXiv preprint arXiv:1503.01445*.

Wang, L., Z. H. You, X. Chen, S. X. Xia, F. Liu, X. Yan, Y. Zhou, and K. J. Song. 2018. "A computational-based method for predicting drug-target interactions by using stacked autoencoder deep neural network." *Journal of Computational Biology* 25 (3):361–373. doi: 10.1089/cmb.2017.0135

Wang, Shudong, Zhenzhen Du, Mao Ding, Alfonso Rodriguez-Paton, and Tao Song. 2022. "KG-DTI: a knowledge graph based deep learning method for drug-target interaction predictions and Alzheimer's disease drug repositions." *Applied Intelligence* 52 (1):846–857. doi: 10.1007/s10489-021-02454-8

Yang, Liuqing, Xifeng Wang, Qi Guo, Scott Gladstein, Dustin Wooten, Tengfei Li, Weining Z Robieson, Yan Sun, Xin Huang, and Alzheimer's Disease Neuroimaging Initiative. 2021. "Deep learning based multimodal progression modeling for Alzheimer's disease." *Statistics in Biopharmaceutical Research* 13 (3):337–343.

Yang, Yanqing, Deshan Zhou, Xinben Zhang, Yulong Shi, Jiaxin Han, Liping Zhou, Leyun
    Wu, Minfei Ma, Jintian Li, Shaoliang Peng, Zhijian Xu, and Weiliang Zhu. 2022.
    "D3AI-CoV: a deep learning platform for predicting drug targets and for virtual screen-
    ing against COVID-19." *Briefings in Bioinformatics* 23 (3):bbac147. doi: 10.1093/bib/
    bbac147

Yin, Qijin, Xusheng Cao, Rui Fan, Qiao Liu, Rui Jiang, and Wanwen Zeng. 2022. "DeepDrug:
    A general graph-based deep learning framework for drug-drug interactions and drug-
    target interactions prediction." *biorxiv*:2020.11. 09.375626.

You, Jiaying, Robert D. McLeod, and Pingzhao Hu. 2019. "Predicting drug-target interaction
    network using deep learning model." *Computational Biology and Chemistry* 80:90–101.

Zeng, Xiangxiang, Siyi Zhu, Xiangrong Liu, Yadi Zhou, Ruth Nussinov, and Feixiong Cheng.
    2019. "deepDR: a network-based deep learning approach to in silico drug reposition-
    ing." *Bioinformatics* 35 (24):5191–5198. doi: 10.1093/bioinformatics/btz418

Zeng, Xiangxiang, Siyi Zhu, Weiqiang Lu, Zehui Liu, Jin Huang, Yadi Zhou, Jiansong Fang,
    Yin Huang, Huimin Guo, and Lang Li. 2020. "Target identification among known drugs
    by deep learning from heterogeneous networks." *Chemical Science* 11 (7):1775–1797.

Zhang, Haiping, Konda Mani Saravanan, Yang Yang, Md Tofazzal Hossain, Junxin Li, Xiaohu
    Ren, Yi Pan, and Yanjie Wei. 2020. "Deep learning based drug screening for novel
    Coronavirus 2019-nCov." *Interdisciplinary Sciences: Computational Life Sciences* 12
    (3):368–376. doi: 10.1007/s12539-020-00376-6

Zhang, Jin, Ulf Norinder, and Fredrik Svensson. 2021. "Deep learning-based conformal pre-
    diction of toxicity." *Journal of Chemical Information and Modeling* 61 (6):2648–2657.
    doi: 10.1021/acs.jcim.1c00208

Zong, Nansu, Hyeoneui Kim, Victoria Ngo, and Olivier Harismendy. 2017. "Deep mining
    heterogeneous networks of biomedical linked data to predict novel drug–target associa-
    tions." *Bioinformatics* 33 (15):2337–2344. doi: 10.1093/bioinformatics/btx160

10 Drug Discovery by Deep Learning and Virtual Screening
Review and Case Study

Tiago Alves de Oliveira, Alisson Marques da Silva and Eduardo Habib Bechelane Maia
Universidade Federal de São João del Rei, Brazil

Moacyr Comar Junior
Universidade Federal de Uberlândia, Brazil

Alex Gutterres Taranto
Universidade Federal de São João del Rei, Brazil

10.1 INTRODUCTION

Computer-assisted drug design (CADD), known as molecular modeling (MM) and sometimes called in silico methods, provides a quick and valid way for scientific research on new compounds with pharmacological potential [1]. CADD makes it possible to analyze many molecules quickly, demonstrating how they connect to targets of pharmacological interest even before their synthesis. In short, the rational process of developing new drugs begins with identifying molecular targets for a particular compound (natural or synthetic), followed by careful molecular analysis of the main molecular recognition forces between the ligand and the target and then, finding more promising molecules addressed to pre-clinical and clinical experimental tests [2]. In other words, CADD tools can select the most promising compounds in a chemical library with millions of compounds. On the other hand, MM tools have yet to find a needle in a haystack but shrunk the haystack.

Among the techniques and methods of CADD, virtual screening (VS) has been highlighted, which has played a prominent role among current strategies for identifying promising bioactive compounds [3]. VS is a fast and cost-effective approach used for screening a virtual database. It is one of the main techniques in developing new drugs [4]. In addition, VS uses scalable docking methods. In short, VS tools assist in the discovery of bioactive molecules by searching a database to find compounds more likely to present biological activity against a specific molecular target. VS has

DOI: 10.1201/9781003331247-11

two distinct approaches: Ligand-Based Virtual Screening (LBVS) and Structure-Based Virtual Screening (SBVS). This chapter focuses essentially on the LBVS approach.

The LBVS can be divided according to the algorithms based on similarity or machine learning–based algorithms (ML). The similarity-based algorithms select compounds structurally similar to another whose biological activity is known. Thus, they can share similar pharmacological activity as well [5]. This approach considers that ligands with previously known biological activity are compared with other ligands of a chemical library, verifying their structural similarity. As a result, a probability score is generated against the target of interest. However, two highly similar molecules can have different biological activities. Therefore, small changes in the molecule can generate an active or inactive compound [6].

Several studies have been proposed employing ML techniques in developing new drugs. Among the various ML techniques used, we can mention Artificial Neural Networks (ANNs), Support Vector Machines (SVM), Bayesian Networks (BN), Decision Trees (DT), k-Nearest Neighbors (KNN), Kohonen's Self-Organizing Maps (SOMs), Counterpropagating ANNs, Ensemble Methods (EM), Genetic Algorithms (GA), Differential Evolution (DE), Ant Colony Optimization (ACO), Particle Swarm Optimization (PSO), and Deep Learning (DL). In addition, various review articles explore the use of ML techniques in drug development, for example [7].

After this brief introduction, the rest of the chapter is organized as follows: Section 10.2 presents some algorithms based on machine learning. Section 10.3 presents and discusses the use of a case study in which a convolutional neural network (CNN) is used to determine whether a compound can be a drug of the non-steroidal anti-inflammatory class or not. Finally, Section 10.4 presents the final considerations about deep learning in VS.

10.2   MACHINE LEARNING–BASED ALGORITHMS

Large databases of molecules are currently available that store information, such as the structure and biological activity of molecules, allowing the use of predictive models based on Machine Learning (ML). Thus, ML techniques have been increasingly used in VS due to the expansion of chemical libraries, new molecular descriptors, and similarity search techniques [8].

The reliability of VS results has increased with ML because it allows, instead of performing computationally costly simulations or exhaustive similarity searches, to track predicted hits much faster [9]. Although there are several methods and techniques, we must select some due to the chapter's limitations. Thus, in the following sections, we present a brief review of the use of ANNs, SVM, SOMs, EM, and DL in drug discovery.

10.2.1   ARTIFICIAL NEURAL NETWORKS (ANNs)

ANNs represent a technology rooted in many disciplines, such as neuroscience, mathematics, statistics, physics, computer science, and engineering [10]. With inspiration from the human brain, ANNs are massively distributed parallel networks that can learn and generalize from examples. ANNs construct a network of interconnected artificial neurons that communicate and work together to solve a problem [11].

In the medicinal chemistry context, ANNs were used in compound classification, quantitative structure–activity relationship studies, potential target identification, and the localization of structural and functional characteristics of biopolymers. Lobanov [12] authored a review paper discussing how ANNs can be used in the virtual screening of combinatorial libraries. In addition, Tayarani et al. [13] proposed an ANN model based on molecular descriptors that obtain the binding energy using physical and chemical descriptions of the selected drugs. The results of the experiments demonstrated that ANN is a powerful tool for predicting the binding energy in the drug design Process. Recently, Mandlik, Bejugam, and Singh [14] wrote a book chapter to show the applications that can be made of artificial neural networks to aid in developing new drugs.

10.2.2   Support Vector Machine (SVM)-Based Techniques

SVM is a supervised machine learning algorithm that can be applied to classification or regression problems [15]. Plotting each data point in n-dimensional space (where n is the number of features), with each feature being the value of a given coordinate, is how the SVM algorithm works. After that, the classification was performed by locating the hyperplane that clearly distinguishes the two classes. SVMs have recently been cited as a promising technique for VS [16].

Silva et al. [17] used Autodock Vina in the docking process but proposed an alternative SVM-based scoring function. They showed that while Autodock Vina offers a prediction of acceptable accuracy for most targets, classification using SVM was better, illustrating the potential of using SVM-based protocols in virtual screening. Finally, Li et al. [18] show ID-Score, a new scoring function based on a set of descriptors related to protein-ligand complexes.

10.2.3   Kohonen's Self-Organizing Maps (SOMs)

SOMs [9] are competitive networks formed by a two-layered structure of neurons organized in a dependent arrangement of the object to be mapped. SOMs are formed by connected nodes with an associated vector corresponding to the map's input data (e.g., molecular descriptors). SOMs are unsupervised self-organized neural networks since they can decrease the size of a data group while maintaining the actual representation concerning the relevant properties of the input vectors, resulting in a set of characteristics of the input space [19].

Noeske et al. [20] used SOMs to discover new targets for metabotropic glutamate receptor antagonists (mGluR). Experiments have revealed distinct subclusters of mGluR antagonists and localization overlap with ligands known to bind to histamine (H1R), dopamine (D2R), and various other targets. In another research, Noeske et al. [21] use SOMs to map drug-like chemical space using pharmacophore descriptors. The experiments demonstrated that other G protein-coupled receptors (GPCRs) could interact with mGluR ligands (mGluR1: dopamine D2 and D3 receptors, histamine H1 receptor, mACh receptor; mGluR5: histamine H1 receptor). Hristozov et al. [22] use SOMs in LVBS to rule out compounds with a low probability of having biological activity. The proposed idea can be used, according to the authors, to improve the recovery of potentially active compounds; to discard compounds that are unlikely to have a specific biological activity; and to select potentially active compounds from a large dataset. Palos et al. [23] applied SOMs in ligand clustering to do a drug repositioning in FDA-approved drugs. This research suggests four FDA drugs could be used in *Trypanosoma cruzi* infection.

10.2.4 ENSEMBLE METHODS

Ensemble methods (EM) use various ML algorithms with intuit to obtain better predictive performance than the isolated application of any learning algorithms [24]. As a result, EM usually produces more accurate solutions than a single model would.

In a previous report, Helguera [25] described that using EM, such as Bagging and Boosting, provides better predictions than the other methods as ANN, KNN, and SVM. Thus, an ensemble method based on genetic algorithms was proposed by this group. Furthermore, to investigate potential Parkinson's disease therapeutics, an LBVS of dual-target A2A adenosine receptor antagonists and MAO-B inhibitors model was proposed showing that the ensemble method outperformed individual models.

10.2.5 DEEP LEARNING

DL is a technique that teaches computers to do what comes naturally to humans: learn by example [11, 26, 27]. DL is a subset of ML that employs multiple layers to extract greater features from input data. The main difference between ANN and DL was the number of hidden layers. DL can transform data between the various layers of a deep learning neural network, which generally follows the same architecture as neural networks.

In the context of drug discovery, numerous models based on DL, such as Deep Learning Neural Networks (DNN) [28], Recurrent Neural Networks (RNN) [29], Deep Convolutional Neural Networks (CNN) [30], and Autoencoder Neural Networks (AEN) [31], can be used. Each model can be used for a specific task.

Ashtawy and Mahapatra [32] proposed a novel multitask deep neural network (MT-Net) trained to simultaneously predict binding poses, affinities, and activity levels. They showed that the performance of MT-Net is superior to conventional Scoring Functions and on par with or better than models based on single-task neural networks.

10.3 A CASE STUDY: UTILIZATION OF CNN TO CLASSIFY COMPOUNDS

In this case study, a Convolutional Neural Network (CNN) was used to classify compounds that belong to non-steroidal anti-inflammatory drugs (NSAIDs). The objective is to calculate whether a given 2D structure of a compound is an NSAID or not. In addition, this approach can use other tools to assess Druggability Prediction and improve system utilization. Furthermore, with this approach, it is possible to perform reverse docking to assess which pharmacological class or classes are recommended to perform VS experiments on a given set of compounds (evaluate which target or targets would be interesting to perform VS).

The first step in using a neural network is to create a dataset corresponding to true and false samples, which is necessary to perform its training and validation. In this process, parameters are configured and adjusted to make the network more generalist and less specialist. In this case study, the dataset of the 2D structures of the compounds was built according to experiments using the training-validation sets. In training-validation, the dataset is divided into three subsets: (i) training dataset – used for model learning, that is, to adjust the ML parameters; (ii) validation dataset – used to provide an unbiased assessment while fitting the model's hyperparameters. It also plays a role in other forms of model preparation, such as feature selection and clipping boundary selection; (iii) test dataset – used to evaluate the model performance. For example, a dataset can be divided into 60% for training, 20% for validation, and 20% for testing.

In this case study, the dataset was formed by 310 drug 2D structure images retrieved from the Drug Bank [33] and ChEMBL [34] divided as follows: 155 structures belong to non-steroidal anti-inflammatory drugs (NSAIDs), the pharmacological class targeted by this study, and 155 structures are outside the class (structures of another class, such as diuretics and false positives generated by DUD-e [35]. In addition to classes, it is separated into Training-Test-Validation, with 186, 64, and 60 images for training, testing, and validation. Figure 10.1 shows selected drugs present in the dataset, which are a) a compound of class (NSAIDs) and b) a compound out of class.

After creating the dataset, it is essential to filter the data to avoid noise and improve the quality of the model. In this stage, it was necessary to pre-process the images, removing those that did not correspond to small molecules and those with many atoms. In other words, a curated process is essential to keep only the organic structures of drugs and eliminate the inorganic contra-ion, for instance.

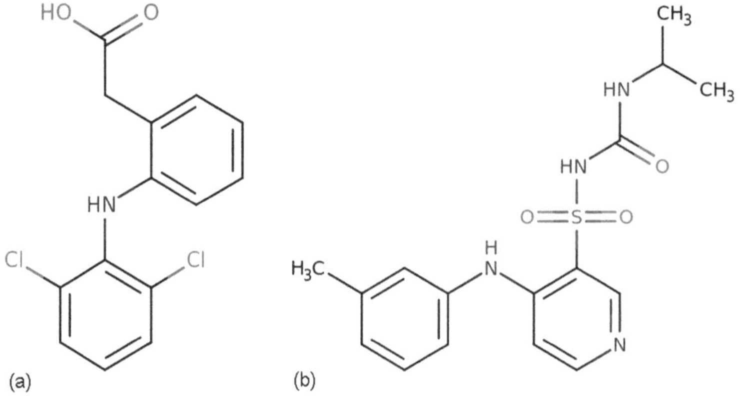

FIGURE 10.1   Examples of NSAIDs images used in the dataset. The structures of the respective compounds are (a) Diclofenac and (b) Torasemide.

TABLE 10.1
Results of the Classifiers with the Respective Algorithm

Method	Accuracy
K-Means	52.57%
Random Forest	55.93%
Decision Tree	49.15%
Gaussian Process	42.37%
Adaboost	50.84%
Naïve Bayes	45.76%

The next step is to train and validate the network. Thus, this study used the Tensorflow framework to implement a CNN. A CNN has kernel layers, convolution, pooling, and fully connected components to extract features and make classification [36]. So, to use a CNN, it is necessary to plan the neural network's architecture, train it, validate the results, and improve the parameters.

After defining the architecture, the next step is evaluating the performance of a model and thus informing the classifier's quality. To evaluate the performance, one or more of the following metrics can be chosen: Accuracy; Confusion Matrix; Precision; Recall; F1-Score; AUC-ROC.

The classifier can be done by binary classifier or multiclass. In this case study, one binary classifier was used, i.e., whether it belongs to a specific class. In the initial step, a CNN using an architecture VGG16 [37] was used to extract the features and evaluated across the following classifier algorithms: K-Means, Random Forest, Decision Tree, Gaussian Process, Adaboost, and Naïve Bayes. The results are summarized in Table 10.1 and demonstrate that all utilized algorithms provide low accuracy, with values below 60%. Values near 50% indicate that the classifier cannot generally classify the results. Through several tests, the algorithms were optimized and did not improve the results.

These preliminary results motivated the search for another algorithm to execute the process to classify if a determined 2D structure belongs to the NSAIDs class or not. A CNN was the chosen algorithm in this case to continue the process. To improve the results by CNN, execute tests with several network architecture configurations and metrics to optimize the process. So, multiple tests were conducted to test various architectures varying the kernel, convolutions, pools, and size of the layers in fully connected (components) to evaluate the CNN.

In the CNN architecture used in this study, the input is an image of 180x180 pixels in three channels. First, the input data is resized to keep values between 0 and 1. Then, data normalization is performed. After that, seven convolutions with a total of filters in each layer: 32, 32, 64, 64, 128, 128, and 256, respectively, are applied. After the convolutions, a dropout is performed (to discard any features to improve the classifier), followed by a Flatten (to do the classification); finally, the model is tested with three dense layers, with sizes of 16348, 4096, and 1 neuron in each layer, respectively. All layers use a ReLU function except the last layer, which uses a sigmoid function to produce the result. In the tests, the CNN was trained with 300 epochs.

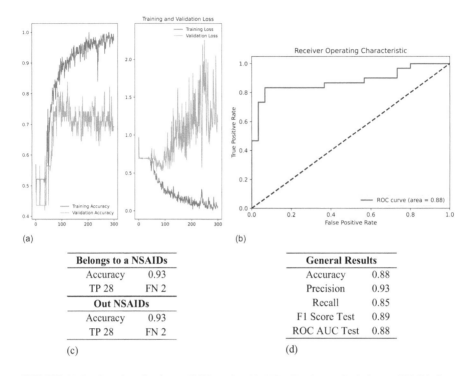

FIGURE 10.2 Results of using a CNN to classify NSAIDs for (a) Training and Validation, (b) AUC-ROC of Testing, (c) Accuracy and values of TP, TN, FP, and FN, and (d) the general results of the test.

The results are summarized in Figure 10.2. Figure 10.2a presents the values of accuracy and loss to train and validation. Figure 10.2b shows the AUC-ROC to test, with values near 90%, which indicates a great result. Figure 10.2c details the accuracy of the results in each class (belong to NSAIDs or not). Finally, Figure 10.2d presents the general Accuracy, Precision, Recall, F1-Score, and ROC-AUC results. These results demonstrated with a CNN could be used to evaluate whether a compound belongs to a determined class. However, this system reduces the time for finding possible search candidates for drugs and helps repurpose existing drugs. Also, this creates an opportunity to evaluate other pharmacophoric classes and use this methodology to perform reverse docking.

10.4 FINAL CONSIDERATIONS

This chapter presented various methods and applications that utilize deep learning techniques in VS. A brief introduction was presented to show how CADD can help in drug discovery and how VS can be applied in this process. Then a detailed description of how LBVS methods can be utilized and how methodologies can be applied utilizing ML techniques. Also, Section 10.2 presented a review of ML-based algorithms and explained the contribution of each technique in drug discovery allied with the use of VS techniques.

The study case presented here demonstrates that a CNN can classify whether a determined compound belongs to an NSAIDs class. The results showed that the network had an accuracy above 90% with F1-Score and AUC-ROC values close to this value. The following steps are creating a CNN for another class, trying new architectures of CNN, evaluating usage together with Virtual Screening values (MolAr Consensus [38]), evaluating the use of descriptors together with CNN information, and evaluating other types of neural networks, compare the QSAR results with the CNN values, integration of classifiers to the MolAr workflow [38], integrate Fast Druggabillity Assessment (FADRA) [39] into the process, test LUDe [39] to generate decoys. However, this system reduces the time for finding possible drug candidates and helps repurpose existing drugs. Also, this creates an opportunity to evaluate other pharmacophoric classes and use this methodology to perform reverse docking.

REFERENCES

1. Hinkle, K.; Wang, X.; Gu, X.; Jameson, C.; Murad, S. Computational Molecular Modeling of Transport Processes in Nanoporous Membranes. *Processes* 2018, *6*, 124, doi:10.3390/pr6080124
2. Duffy, B.C.; Zhu, L.; Decornez, H.; Kitchen, D.B. Early Phase Drug Discovery: Cheminformatics and Computational Techniques in Identifying Lead Series. *Bioorg Med Chem* 2012, *20*, 5324–5342, doi:10.1016/j.bmc.2012.04.062
3. Carregal, A.P.; Maciel, F. V.; Carregal, J.B.; dos Reis Santos, B.; da Silva, A.M.; Taranto, A.G. Docking-Based Virtual Screening of Brazilian Natural Compounds Using the OOMT as the Pharmacological Target Database. *J Mol Model* 2017, *23*, 111, doi:10.1007/s00894-017-3253-8
4. Lourenço, B.L.A.; Silva, M.V.A.S.; de Oliveira, E.B.; de Soares, W.R.A.; Góes-Neto, A.; Santos, G.; Andrade, B.S. Virtual Screening and Molecular Docking for Arylalkylamine-N-Acetyltransferase (AaNAT) Inhibitors, a Key Enzyme of Aedes (Stegomyia) Aegypti (L.) Metabolism. *Comput Mol Biosci* 2015, *05*, 35–44, doi:10.4236/cmb.2015.53005
5. Willett, P. Similarity-Based Virtual Screening Using 2D Fingerprints. *Drug Discov Today* 2006, *11*, 1046–1053, doi:10.1016/j.drudis.2006.10.005
6. Kristensen, T.G.; Nielsen, J.; Pedersen, C.N.S. Methods for Similarity-Based Virtual Screening. *Comput Struct Biotechnol J* 2013, *5*, e201302009.
7. Elton, D.C.; Boukouvalas, Z.; Fuge, M.D.; Chung, P.W. Deep Learning for Molecular Design - a Review of the State of the Art. *Mol Syst Des Eng* 2019, *4*, 828–849, doi:10.1039/C9ME00039A
8. Dara, S.; Dhamercherla, S.; Jadav, S.S.; Babu, C.M.; Ahsan, M.J. Machine Learning in Drug Discovery: A Review. *Artif Intell Rev* 2021, *55*, 1947–1999, doi:10.1007/S10462-021-10058-4
9. Carpenter, K.A.; Huang, X. Machine Learning-Based Virtual Screening and Its Applications to Alzheimer's Drug Discovery: A Review. *Curr Pharm Des* 2018, *24*, 3347–3358, doi:10.2174/1381612824666180607124038
10. Keller, J.M.; Liu, D.; Fogel, D.B. *Fundamentals of Computational Intelligence: Neural Networks, Fuzzy Systems, and Evolutionary Computation*; 1st ed.; Wiley-IEEE Press, 2016; ISBN 978-1119214342.
11. Aggarwal, C.C. *Neural Networks and Deep Learning*; Springer International Publishing, 2018.
12. Lobanov, V. Using Artificial Neural Networks to Drive Virtual Screening of Combinatorial Libraries. *Drug Discov Today Biosilico* 2004, *2*, 149–156, doi:10.1016/S1741-8364(04)02402-3

13. Tayarani, A.; Baratian, A.; Naghibi Sistani, M.-B.; Saberi, M.R.; Tehranizadeh, Z. Artificial Neural Networks Analysis Used to Evaluate the Molecular Interactions between Selected Drugs and Human Cyclooxygenase2 Receptor. *Iran J Basic Med Sci* 2016, *16*, 1196–1202, doi:10.1016/j.jpba.2008.11.005

14. Mandlik, V.; Bejugam, P.R.; Singh, S. *Application of Artificial Neural Networks in Modern Drug Discovery*; Elsevier Inc., 2016; ISBN 9780128015599.

15. Cortes, C.; Vapnik, V.; Saitta, L. Support-Vector Networks. *Mach Learn* 1995, *20*, 273–297, doi:10.1007/BF00994018

16. Deshmukh, A.L.; Chandra, S.; Singh, D.K.; Siddiqi, M.I.; Banerjee, D. Identification of Human Flap Endonuclease 1 (FEN1) Inhibitors Using a Machine Learning Based Consensus Virtual Screening. *Mol Biosyst* 2017, *13*, 1630–1639, doi:10.1039/c7mb00118e

17. Silva, C.; Simoes, C.; Carreiras, P.; Brito, R. Enhancing Scoring Performance of Docking-Based Virtual Screening Through Machine Learning. *Curr Bioinform* 2016, *11*, 408–420, doi:10.2174/1574893611666160212234816

18. Li, G.B.; Yang, L.L.; Wang, W.J.; Li, L.L.; Yang, S.Y. ID-Score: A New Empirical Scoring Function Based on a Comprehensive Set of Descriptors Related to Protein-Ligand Interactions. *J Chem Inf Model* 2013, *53*, 592–600, doi:10.1021/ci300493w

19. Zupan, J.; Novič, M.; Ruisánchez, I. Kohonen and Counterpropagation Artificial Neural Networks in Analytical Chemistry. *Chemom Intell Lab Syst* 1997, *38*, 1–23, doi:10.1016/S0169-7439(97)00030-0

20. Noeske, T.; Sasse, B.C.; Stark, H.; Parsons, C.G.; Weil, T.; Schneider, G. Predicting Compound Selectivity by Self-Organizing Maps: Cross-Activities of Metabotropic Glutamate Receptor Antagonists. *ChemMedChem* 2006, *1*, 1066–1068, doi:10.1002/cmdc.200600147

21. Noeske, T.; Jirgensons, A.; Starchenkovs, I.; Renner, S.; Jaunzeme, I.; Trifanova, D.; Hechenberger, M.; Bauer, T.; Kauss, V.; Parsons, C.G.; et al. Virtual Screening for Selective Allosteric MGluR1 Antagonists and Structure-Activity Relationship Investigations for Coumarine Derivatives. *ChemMedChem* 2007, *2*, 1763–1773, doi:10.1002/cmdc.200700151

22. Hristozov, D.; Oprea, T.I.; Gasteiger, J. Ligand-Based Virtual Screening by Novelty Detection with Self-Organizing Maps. *J Chem Inf Model* 2007, *47*, 2044–2062, doi:10.1021/ci700040r

23. Palos, I.; Lara-Ramirez, E.E.; Lopez-Cedillo, J.C.; Garcia-Perez, C.; Kashif, M.; Bocanegra-Garcia, V.; Nogueda-Torres, B.; Rivera, G. Repositioning FDA Drugs as Potential Cruzain Inhibitors from Trypanosoma Cruzi: Virtual Screening, in Vitro and in Vivo Studies. *Molecules* 2017, *22*, doi:10.3390/molecules22061015

24. Dietterich, T.G. Ensemble Methods in Machine Learning. *Lecture Notes in Computer Science (including subseries Lecture Notes in Artificial Intelligence and Lecture Notes in Bioinformatics)* 2000, *1857 LNCS*, 1–15, doi:10.1007/3-540-45014-9_1/COVER

25. Helguera, A.M.; Perez-Castillo, Y.; Cordeiro, M.N.D.S.; Tejera, E.; Paz-Y-Miño, C.; Sánchez-Rodríguez, A.; Teijeira, M.; Ancede-Gallardo, E.; Cagide, F.; Borges, F.; et al. Ligand-Based Virtual Screening Using Tailored Ensembles: A Prioritization Tool for Dual A2A Adenosine Receptor Antagonists/Monoamine Oxidase B Inhibitors. *Curr Pharm Des* 2016, *22*, 3082–3096, doi:10.2174/1381612822666160302103542

26. Deng, L.; Yu, D. Deep Learning: Methods and Applications. *Found Trends Signal Process* 2014, *7*, 197–387, doi:10.1561/2000000039

27. Haykin, S. *Neural Networks and Learning Machines*; 3rd ed.; Prentice Hall, 2007; Vol. 3; ISBN 9780131471399.

28. Li, F.; Wan, X.; Xing, J.; Tan, X.; Li, X.; Wang, Y.; Zhao, J.; Wu, X.; Liu, X.; Li, Z.; et al. Deep Neural Network Classifier for Virtual Screening Inhibitors of (S)-Adenosyl-L-Methionine (SAM)-Dependent Methyltransferase Family. *Front Chem* 2019, *7*, 324, doi:10.3389/FCHEM.2019.00324

29. Yasonik, J. Multiobjective de Novo Drug Design with Recurrent Neural Networks and Nondominated Sorting. *J Cheminform* 2020, *12*, 1–9, doi:10.1186/S13321-020-00419-6/FIGURES/9

30. Mendolia, I.; Contino, S.; Perricone, U.; Pirrone, R.; Ardizzone, E. A Convolutional Neural Network for Virtual Screening of Molecular Fingerprints. *Lecture Notes in Computer Science (including subseries Lecture Notes in Artificial Intelligence and Lecture Notes in Bioinformatics)* 2019, *11751 LNCS*, 399–409, doi:10.1007/978-3-030-30642-7_36/COVER

31. Nasser, M.; Salim, N.; Saeed, F.; Basurra, S.; Rabiu, I.; Hamza, H.; Alsoufi, M.A. Feature Reduction for Molecular Similarity Searching Based on Autoencoder Deep Learning. *Biomolecules* 2022, *12*, 508, doi:10.3390/BIOM12040508

32. Ashtawy, H.M.; Mahapatra, N.R. Task-Specific Scoring Functions for Predicting Ligand Binding Poses and Affinity and for Screening Enrichment. *J Chem Inf Model* 2018, *58*, 119–133, doi:10.1021/acs.jcim.7b00309

33. Wishart, D.S.; Feunang, Y.D.; Guo, A.C.; Lo, E.J.; Marcu, A.; Grant, J.R.; Sajed, T.; Johnson, D.; Li, C.; Sayeeda, Z.; et al. DrugBank 5.0: A Major Update to the DrugBank Database for 2018. *Nucleic Acids Res* 2018, *46*, D1074–D1082, doi:10.1093/NAR/GKX1037

34. Mendez, D.; Gaulton, A.; Bento, A.P.; Chambers, J.; de Veij, M.; Félix, E.; Magariños, M.P.; Mosquera, J.F.; Mutowo, P.; Nowotka, M.; et al. ChEMBL: Towards Direct Deposition of Bioassay Data. *Nucleic Acids Res* 2019, *47*, D930–D940, doi:10.1093/NAR/GKY1075

35. Mysinger, M.M.; Carchia, M.; Irwin, J.J.; Shoichet, B.K. Directory of Useful Decoys, Enhanced (DUD-E): Better Ligands and Decoys for Better Benchmarking. *J Med Chem* 2012, *55*, 6582–6594, doi:10.1021/JM300687E/SUPPL_FILE/JM300687E_SI_004.TXT

36. Albawi, S.; Mohammed, T.A.; Al-Zawi, S. Understanding of a Convolutional Neural Network. *Proceedings of 2017 International Conference on Engineering and Technology, ICET 2017* 2018, January, 1–6, doi:10.1109/ICENGTECHNOL.2017.8308186

37. Szegedy, C.; Liu, W.; Jia, Y.; Sermanet, P.; Reed, S.; Anguelov, D.; Erhan, D.; Vanhoucke, V.; Rabinovich, A. Going Deeper with Convolutions. *Proceedings of the IEEE Computer Society Conference on Computer Vision and Pattern Recognition* 2014, 7–12 June 2015, 1–9, doi:10.48550/arxiv.1409.4842

38. Maia, E.H.B.; Medaglia, L.R.; da Silva, A.M.; Taranto, A.G. Molecular Architect: A User-Friendly Workflow for Virtual Screening. *ACS Omega* 2020, *5*, 6628–6640, doi:10.1021/acsomega.9b04403

39. Gori, D.N.P.; Alberca, L.N.; Rodriguez, S.; Alice, J.I.; Llanos, M.A.; Bellera, C.L.; Talevi, A. LIDeB Tools: A Latin American Resource of Freely Available, Open-Source Cheminformatics Apps. *Artif Intell Life Sci* 2022, *2*, 100049, doi:10.1016/J.AILSCI.2022.100049

Section B

Algorithms for Sequence and Structure Analysis

11 Gene Regulation, DNA and RNA Structure and Sequencing

Neetu Verma and Deepa Bhatt
National Institute for plant Biotechnology, India

Laxmi Kirola
Banaras Hindu University, India

11.1 THE INTRODUCTION AND PRINCIPLES OF GENE REGULATION

Gene regulation is an integral and fundamental process for the development of all organisms. This is a turning on and off mechanism of gene expression in a spatiotemporal manner, resulting in the organism's development, adaptation, and homeostasis (Spector 2003). Here, we briefly describe the basics of gene regulation at the level of transcription, post-transcription, and epigenetic modification. The genes are the regions of genomic DNA that can be transcribed into different RNAs such as rRNA, mRNA, tRNA, and noncoding RNA (Figure 11.1a). The mRNAs are used as the main template for protein translation while other RNAs carry out secondary functions. Gene regulation occurs mainly in two major steps: transcription and translation. There are multiple checkpoints from where gene expression can be regulated. These checkpoints are the transcription start site (TSS), the RNA polymerase binding sites, upstream regions from the start codon (activators, enhancers, and silencers), and the RNA processing (splicing, capping, and tailing) sites. In prokaryotes, most of the gene regulation is negative (i.e., turn off of the gene expression) in which a small protein called the regulatory molecule (for example, activators or repressors) binds near the regulatory targets and decides whether the gene expression is required or not (Figure 11.1b). Intriguingly, in eukaryotes by default, the gene expression system is "off" whereas in prokaryotes the expression system is always "on". This is due to the complexity of eukaryotic development which requires the genes to express in a specified cell group within a defined interval. Such regulation requires the involvement of both the DNA and histone proteins that bind together and makes a complex structure called chromatin. These histone proteins are abandonly bound to the DNA that forms silent chromatin; thus, the expression of any gene gets "turned off" by default (Carlberg and Molnár 2020). The gene expression starts only when some modification in histone proteins takes place, for example, the positively charged

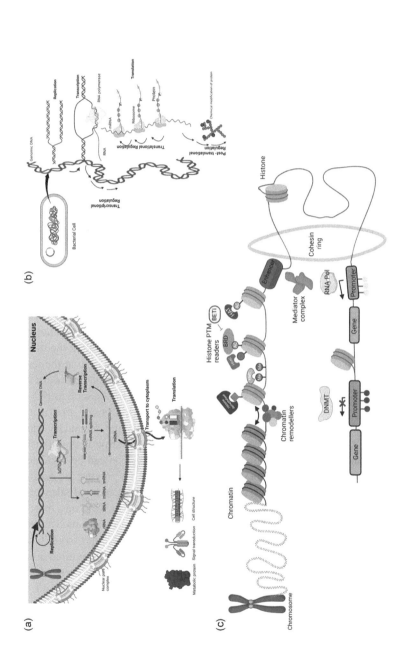

FIGURE 11.1 (a) Shows the eukaryotic gene expression and regulation, (b) Prokaryotic gene expression and regulation, and (c) Shows the compact chromatin packing of gene regulation in eukaryotic system and the epigenetic modifications.

amino acids present on the surface of histone protein induce conformational changes in the chromatin structure to release the bound DNA, and thus, the transcription is started (Figure 11.1c).

11.1.1 ESSENTIALS OF GENE REGULATION AT THE TRANSCRIPTIONAL LEVEL IN EUKARYOTES

Transcriptional regulation has many essential components such as chromatin (DNA and histone proteins) and nuclear proteins (RNA polymerase and transcription factors). Transcriptional regulation has two main interrelated steps: the first step involves chromatin modifications, and the second step involves the transcriptional machinery (RNA Polymerase II) and associated factors (transcription factors, mediators, cofactors).

11.1.2 THE BASAL TRANSCRIPTIONAL MACHINERY IN EUKARYOTES

Basal transcription machinery in eukaryotes comprises TSS, TATA box, RNA polymerase, and the TATA-binding proteins (TBP). Information on the TSS region and TBPs are prerequisite to understanding gene regulation. The transcriptional regulatory factors are mainly divided into two types: the cis-regulatory elements (the short-conserved DNA sequences, the noncoding DNA part such as promoters, enhancers, and silencers) and the trans-regulatory elements (mostly complexes of TFs, DNA bound TFs/coregulators which bind to short and degenerate sequences in the genome). In most organisms, both cis and trans regulatory differences play an important role in gene regulation and phenotypic variations among species. For example, species like mice, *Drosophila*, *Coffea*, etc. have been used for allele-specific expression analysis. Similarly, genome imprinting has been seen in mammals, and some plants, but it is almost absent in birds. Likewise, dosage compensation exists mostly in a diploid organism, and there are many other examples that have supported the complex and unique gene regulations in various organisms.

11.1.3 POST-TRANSCRIPTIONAL GENE REGULATION

Post-transcriptional gene regulation occurs at the RNA level. Post-transcriptional modification of RNA plays a pervasive role in various biological processes including the regulation of genes and modification of mRNA (e.g., nuclear processing of RNA, splicing out of introns, 5′capping, splicing of RNA) to increase the efficiency of translation.

11.1.4 REGULATORY NONCODING RNA

The noncoding elements such as small noncoding RNAs (sncRNAs) and long noncoding RNAs (lncRNAs) are key components of post-transcriptional regulation. The siRNAs, miRNAs, piRNAs, and snoRNAs are sncRNAs, while lncRNAs include linc RNA, circ RNA, Nat, and eRNA. Some of these ncRNAs take part in various transcriptional and post-transcriptional processes such as RNA processing by snoRNAs, protein synthesis by rRNAs and tRNAs, and gene regulation by miRNAs (Riley et al. 2008).

11.1.5 INTRODUCTION OF BIOINFORMATIC ANALYSIS AND ALGORITHMS OF GENE REGULATION

Biological science is deeply addressed in a data-intensive manner from a computational point of view. A simple pipeline that can be used to deal with biological data is as follows:

A statistical survey of biological data

↓

Development of a suitable computational model

↓

Resolve the modeling hitch

↓

Analysis by a computational algorithm

To elucidate the expression, regulation patterns, function, and signaling of a gene, precise in silico prediction of promoters and regulatory elements is mandatory. For in silico identification of promoter regions, different databases are available for example a popular and primitive bacterial database is Regulon DB, which is not only used as a promoter database but also provides information about the genomic regulatory investigations, tools to analyze upstream regulatory regions, tools for microarray, and many more. EDP database, ENSEMBL, and PlantProm database are other collections of non-redundant proximal RNA pol II promoter sequences of eukaryotes. The wide tools used for motif prediction are Scan for Motifs, MEME Suits, and STAMP (Mahony and Benos 2007). On the other hand, clustering is a data learning technique that is a combination of different algorithms applied in different fields such as data mining, image analysis, bioinformatic data analysis, and many more. The most popular algorithms for different clustering techniques are K-means, Self-Organizing Maps, Gaussian Mixture Model (Rasmussen 2000), PAM, etc. Gene regulation is the central area of functional genomics; there are several databases that store gene regulation information. The common databases for nucleotide sequence search are GenBank, NCBI, and EMBL. An important source of information on regulation related to the functional explanation of transcription factors is present in the protein databases PIR and Swiss-Prot. We can divide gene regulation-related databases into three broad specialized groups.

1. Databases that store information about gene regulatory regions, regulatory sequences, promoters, transcription factors, and their binding sites, for example – EDP, JASPAR, and TRANSFAC (Wingender 2004; Périer et al., 2000).
2. Databases that contain information about the signal transduction pathways and regulatory networks, for example – TRANSPATH and CSNDB (Wingender 2004).
3. Databases that are related to expression patterns across the tissues based on microarray data, for example – GO, CYTOMER, and Genevestigator (Wingender 2004).

Several regulatory databases along with clustering algorithms and popular tools/software have been used to understand the gene regulation process in multiple organisms including plants, animals, and some prokaryotes have been given in Table 11.2.

11.2 DEOXYRIBONUCLEIC ACID (DNA) STRUCTURE, INTRODUCTION, AND FUNDAMENTALS

In the 1940s, DNA was described as a long polymer consisting of just four types of sub-units that resembled chemically to each other (Avery, MacLeod, and McCarty 1944). Early in the 1950s, two English researchers Rosalind Franklin and Maurice Wilkins utilized X-ray crystallography to delineate the three-dimensional structure of this molecule (Klug 1968). The results of X-ray crystallography were of crucial significance and further used to predict that DNA had two strands of polymer which are interwound as a helix. The observation that DNA was double-stranded led Watson and Crick to propose the double-helical model of DNA (Watson and Crick 1953). After that, it is well known that the primary structure of DNA consists of four nucleotides known as adenine (A), cytosine (C), guanine (G), and thymine (T). These nucleotides are named by their respective nitrogen bases, i.e., adenine or guanine are purines, and cytosine or thymine are pyrimidines. Each nitrogen base is joined to deoxyribose sugar via a glycosidic bond. Deoxyribose sugar with nitrogen base is known as nucleoside which is attached to the phosphate group to form a nucleotide. Further, these four nucleotides in a single-stranded DNA are connected to each other by covalent 5′-3′ phosphodiester bonds formed between 5′ phosphate group and 3′ hydroxyl group of adjacent deoxyribose sugars (Figure 11.2a). Different forms of DNA are represented below.

Properties	Forms of DNA				
Parameters	A Form	B Form	C Form	D Form	Z Form
Base pair per turn	11	10	9.33	8	12
Rotation per bp	+32.7°	+36.0°	+38.6°	−	−30.0°
Vertical rise per bp	2.56 Å	3.38 Å	3.32 Å	3.03 Å	3.71 Å
Helical diameter	23 Å	20 Å	19 Å	−	18 Å
Pitch of the helix	28.15 Å	34 Å	31 Å	−	45 Å
Tilt of bp sugar puckering	20.2 Å	6.3°	−7.8°	−16.7°	7°

DNA is the genetic material and also carries the biological information in the chemical form from parent cells to daughter cells each time a cell divides. Many unanswered questions related to the evolutionary biology of the origin of humans had been answered after the discovery of the structure of the DNA double helix by Watson and Crick. The information stored in the DNA molecule is transmitted to the daughter cells during cell division. Before cell division starts, the DNA of the original cell divides using the DNA replication process into two identical replicas of DNA for each of the two daughter cells. During replication, an enzyme called helicase unwinds the double helix of DNA. Then, each strand of DNA acts as a template for the replication of its complementary strand. Thus, the replication of DNA is referred to as semiconservative which means the new helix generated after replication contains an original DNA strand winding to the newly synthesized strand. DNA replication starts at specific sites in the genome, known as the origins of replication. At the origin of the replication site, both the strands of DNA unwind to form a replication fork which is bidirectional in nature. At the replication fork, both strands start replication in both directions from the origin as shown in Figure 11.2c. Many proteins, like RNA primase, DNA polymerase,

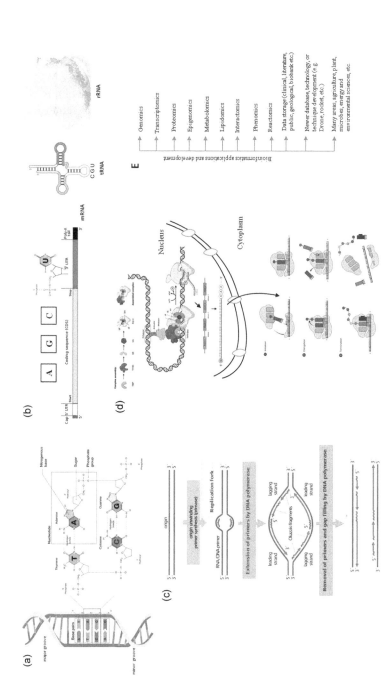

FIGURE 11.2   (a) Shows the double helical model of DNA and four different bases, A, T, C and G, that make the DNA structure; (b) Shows three different types of RNAs, mRNA, tRNA and rRNA, and four different bases, A, C, G and U that build the RNA structure; (c) Schematic representation of DNA replication in eukaryotes; (d) Shows typical modular mechanism of RNA transcription, processing, and translation, and (e) Shows numerous applications of bioinformatics and the advancements of omics technologies.

and RNase, are recruited at the replication fork for the initiation of DNA replication by adding more nucleotides complementary to the template strand (Figure 11.2c and d). The RNA primase recruits RNA primers to the template strands. Only one RNA primer is recruited at the 5'-3' leading strand which is extended continuously from that RNA primer by the enzyme called DNA polymerase. While many RNA primers are recruited in the replication of the 3'-5' lagging strand which is further extended discontinuously in the form of Okazaki fragments using DNA polymerase. Then, the RNase enzyme removes the RNA primers, and the gaps are filled by the DNA polymerase, completing the newly replicated 5'-3' and 3'-5' DNA strands. All the steps involved in DNA replication are shown in Figures 11.2c and d.

11.2.1 Phylogenetic, Computational, and Evolutionary Aspects of DNA Structure

The objective of DNA-based phylogenetics is to construct a tree-like pattern that infers the evolutionary relationships between any two or multiple organisms. DNA-based phylogenetics started early in 1980 when DNA sequencing began to provide gene sequences. DNA-based phylogenetics is predominant over protein sequences-based phylogenetics because many mutations are the result of non-synonymous changes which alter the DNA sequences and it might not necessary if these have an impact on the protein sequences. Moreover, the ease of DNA extraction along with sequence analysis using a range of molecular tools like PCR, RFLP, and SSR have made the predominance of DNA in modern molecular phylogenetics. Many computational tools which are used for phylogenetic tree constructions include Custal W, MegAlign Pro (DNASTAR), BEAST, and fastDNAml (Suchard et al. 2018). Multiple computational tools have evolved in recent years, and with the help of these tools, biologists have designed their own synthetic genes, oligos, constructs, etc. The BLAST (basic local alignment search tool) is a very famous computational tool for comparing the nucleotide sequence (query sequence) of particular gene/genes of an organism with a library of sequences, and it recognizes sequences that show some degree of conservation (similarity) with the query sequence. Some tools for oligo designing have focused on selecting the oligonucleotide sequences with or without the prediction of secondary structures and optimization of GC content. Primer 3 and Oli2go are popular web-based tools that are used for oligo designing and testing. Another popular tool, Primer blast is used to analyze the specificity of the primer sequences which should amplify only target gene sequences without any nonspecific binding to other genes. Certain tools for designing synthetic genes such as Synthetic Gene Designer, GeneDesign, OPTIMIZER, and Visual Gene Developer are some popular web-based computational tools (Jung and McDonald 2011; Wu et al., 2005). These tools have optimization functionalities such as codon usage optimization, removal of repetitive segments, and restriction site optimization.

11.2.2 Algorithms for DNA Structure Prediction and Analysis

The genome sequence data of different organisms are assembled and available in several databanks such as GenBank at the National Centre for Biotechnology Information (NCBI), UCSC browser, the Ensemble, etc. Many algorithms have been developed to comprehend the information stored in databanks and use this information for DNA structure prediction and analysis. A mathematical operation based on digital signal processing (DSP) transforms the gene information of a sequenced genome into a digital signal and predicts biologically noteworthy information on new genomic sequences being sequenced. The principle behind digital signal processing is that the DNA sequences are alphabetical (A, T, C, and G) in nature. The nucleotide sequence of DNA can be converted into numerical sequences using digital signal processing for structural analysis. Identification of coding (exonic) and the noncoding (intronic) portions of a gene is the most important and initial step to unraveling the genetic processes. The exonic region of a gene can be predicted using this algebraic operation. This information also helps in the designing of personalized drugs for several diseases. Algorithms, TESTCODE and Gene Scan to predict the coding regions of DNA, are based on the probability of coding region by analyzing the local signal-to-noise ratio of the peak within a sliding window (Tiwari et al. 1997). Wavelet-based filtering approach is very popular to recognize protein-coding regions (Bao and Yuan 2015; Fickett 1982). In DNA structure analysis, it was found that coding regions of DNA exhibit the period-3 (three-base periodicity property) property (Chen and Ji 2014), while the noncoding regions do not have this characteristic. Therefore, this characteristic is utilized as a marker to distinguish the coding regions of DNA sequences. To predict the coding region of a DNA sequence, the sequences are collected from the NCBI site and transformed into a numeric sequence which is now known as EIIP (electron-ion interaction pseudopotentials) sequence. EIIP represents the distribution of free electrons in the DNA sequence. In a DNA sequence, the EIIP value is calculated for every nucleotide (A, T, C, and G) to generate a numeric sequence. Due to the period-3property, the coding regions of DNA produce larger amplitude coefficients in the transformed sequence (Chen and Ji 2014). Therefore, the transformed sequence yields discrete energy-concerted regions at the time-frequency level.

11.2.3 Pathophysiology of DNA Structure and Clinical Significance

Many genetic disorders are also caused by mutations in the DNA sequences inherited from the parents to their offspring. Genetic disorders can be monogenic (result from a mutation in one gene) or multifactorial inheritance disorders (result from mutations in multiple genes). One very popular example of a genetic disorder is sickle-cell anemia which is caused by a single point mutation (A-T) in the gene encoding a protein called beta-globin. An individual homozygous for this mutation has defective hemoglobin resulting in the aggregation of erythrocytes into a sickle-like shape which blocks the capillaries and leads to hemolytic anemia. Another popular example of an inherited genetic disorder is cystic fibrosis. Inheritance of this disorder is also autosomal recessive. Some genetic disorders are caused by changes in chromosome numbers. Some examples of chromosome-related disorders include Down syndrome, Turner syndrome, etc. Otherwise, environmental factors that can lead to mutation in DNA sequences include chemical exposure, smoking, UV exposure, radiation exposure, etc. These DNA-related pathologies can be identified by genetic testing in which the genome of an affected individual is sequenced to detect the gene(s) mutation(s), which causes the disorder(s).

11.2.4 DNA SEQUENCING

The order of nucleotides in DNA is delineated by DNA sequencing. DNA sequencing has become an essential part of basic biological research and applied research such as biotechnology, forensic biology, and medical diagnosis. Numerous new methods of DNA sequencing including next-generation" or "second-generation" sequencing (NGS) techniques have evolved to help researchers in the medical field along with other areas and are responsible for personalized medicine advances in the future.

11.3 RIBONUCLEIC ACID (RNA) STRUCTURE, INTRODUCTION, ARCHITECTURE, AND FUNDAMENTALS

In 1868, Friedrich Miescher discovered nucleic acids, and he called this material "nuclein" as this material was seen inside the nucleus (Dahm 2005). In 1939, it was suspected that RNA played a role in protein synthesis (Caspersson and Schultz 1939). Severo Ochoa discovered that RNA was synthesized by an enzyme that can be used in the synthesis of RNA in the laboratory and for this discovery he was awarded the Nobel Prize (Severo Ochoa and Arthur Kornberg) in medicine in 1959 (KARLSON 1960). Subsequently, many discoveries happened in the RNA world, which is documented in Table 11.1. RNA is another molecule like DNA and proteins which play a major role in making different life forms. RNA has three major groups that contain ribosomal, messenger, and transfer RNAs. Here, we describe the three standard RNAs in detail and other small and long noncoding RNAs briefly.

mRNA: mRNA is the main molecule that carries the chemical blueprint of genetic information from DNA to ribosomes for the synthesis of a protein product.

rRNA: rRNAs are the core parts of the ribosome which are the main sites of protein synthesis in all living creatures. In eukaryotes, the ribosome has two submits, the smaller is the 40S and the larger is 60S consisting of mainly 18s and 28s rRNAs, respectively.

tRNA: tRNA is made of around 73–95 nucleotides which are constantly involved in polypeptide chain formation at the larger subunit of the ribosome. tRNA contains an anticodon site that matches with the corresponding codon present in the mRNA.

11.3.1 REGULATION AND POST-TRANSCRIPTIONAL MODIFICATIONS IN RNAS

Other groups of RNA molecules include small nuclear ribonucleic acid (snRNA). This group is present mostly in the nucleus and coded by RNA pol II and III. The main functions of these RNAs are gene regulation (e.g., 7SK RNA, B2 RNA, NA splicing, etc.) and telomere maintenance.

11.3.2 PHYLOGENETIC, COMPUTATIONAL, AND EVOLUTIONARY ASPECTS OF RNA STRUCTURE

The different forms of RNAs are not just intermediatory molecules to transfer genetic information. The help of advanced tools along with newer algorithms has allowed for performing homology searches, RNA–RNA interaction prediction, in silico genome-scale screens of ncRNAs, RNA folding, and design of interfering RNAs (Rivas 2021). However, with the advent of the latest in genomic, transcriptomic, and other omics data, more application-based computational tools for RNA biology and experimental data processing have been developed to enrich RNA bioinformatics. Multiple methods have been used for finding the stable folds in RNA that include Mfold, RNA structure, Sfold, ViennaRNA, NUPACK, or GTfold, CONTRAfold, or RNAsoft. A phylogenetic tree can be constructed on the basis of similarity (rooted) and dissimilarity (unrooted) that is based on the DNA or RNA sequences and the evolutionary time.

11.3.3 Algorithms for Analysis of RNA Structure Prediction and Analysis

The RNA tertiary structure is a complex phenomenon that requires both basic primary structures along with representative models. Presently, the RNA secondary structure can be attained by using mainly NMR experiments as well as X-ray diffraction. Two major algorithms for structure prediction are deterministic dynamic programming and the comparative sequence analysis method. The first one uses an algorithm called dynamic programming or the Nussinov algorithm. This includes a total count of base pairs as well as the free energy of the system (Nussinov et al. 1978). Examples include mfold web server and RNAfold. However, it works better with shorter RNAs while for longer RNAs, the accuracy gets compromised (Zuker and Stiegler 1981). Lately, the artificial intelligence (AI) methods (genetic algorithm, neural network algorithm, and neural network algorithm) along with additional methods can also be utilized for RNA secondary structure predictions (Zhang, Deng, and Song 2006). However, further validations are required with larger samples and to check the prediction accuracy. With the advancements of AI-based deep learning methods, the prediction and accuracies can effectively be improved and at present, breakthroughs are coming in the area of protein secondary structure predictions.

11.3.4 Pathophysiology of RNA Structure and Clinical Significance

Many diseases in humans are reported due to dysfunctions of RNA biology that include cardiomyopathies, neuropathies, and other complex diseases like diabetes, cancer, etc. For example, in the maturation of miRNA inhibition by using conditional experiments in the murine heart, miRNA expression-related studies in human hearts have shown the involvement of miRNAs in developmental processes. Similarly, other miRNAs (miR-124, miR-132, and miR-134) are involved in nervous system development, including synapse formation and maturation, dendritogenesis, etc. For example, altered miRNA expression has been seen in schizophrenia. Moreover, the importance of miRNA in cancer has increased several fold in terms of both as a regulatory factor and in diagnostics and early prognostic markers. For example, dysregulation in miRNAs in cMyc regulatory network has been shown in a variety of cancers, e.g., prostate cancer, breast cancer, etc. Recently, a novel miRNA expression assay has been generated against early stage of colorectal cancer detection and other studies related to clinical trials are under process (Wang, Chen, and Sen 2016). RNA interference (RNAi) technology was shown to be used in the treatment of respiratory syncytial virus and macular degeneration in the mouse model. RNAi is used in treating microbial infections such as herpes simplex virus type 2, and hepatitis A and B gene silencing. Additional examples are the knockdown of host receptors and coreceptors for HIV, silencing of influenza inhibition of measles viral replication, and the inhibition of viral gene expression in cancerous cells. Potential treatments are also being proposed for neurodegenerative diseases such as polyglutamine diseases (for example, Huntington's disease).

11.3.5 RNA SEQUENCING

Unlike DNA, RNA creates short helices and other forms of RNA structures that are quite packed and fashioned together to create a chemical catalyst like ribozyme. With advanced high-throughput approaches such as CLIP-Seq and RBPome (i.e., the network of protein–RNA interactions), it is now possible to find out the binding sites of RNA on the RNA binding proteins (Backofen et al. 2017). In addition, other high-throughput methods include RIP-seq, CLIP-seq, RiboSeq, Shape-Seq, or ChIRP-Seq. RNA bioinformatics is expanding as new analysis tools and analysis protocols are advancing.

11.4 LATEST IN SEQUENCING AND BIOINFORMATICS TOOLS/ TECHNOLOGIES TO STUDY OMICS DATA

Bioinformatics is the combination of many scientific disciplines that work together and leads to bigger changes in many areas of human biology and understanding of complex diseases. To solve such complex biological problems, we need advanced bioinformatics tools along with newer sequencing technologies. Over the last decades, high-throughput sequencing (DNA, RNA, protein, etc.) technologies have evolved the bioinformatics advancements in many areas including clinical, medical, animal, and plant sciences, as well as energy, and environmental fields, etc. Bioinformatics has many interdisciplinary fields of science that include research, diagnostics, development, clinics, biomedical, agricultural applications, and many more. Mostly, it has evolved due to the excessive advancement of genomics, transcriptomics, proteomics, metabolomics data, etc. along with the need for data storage, analysis, and integration for future research and therapeutics. Other omics tools include Hi-C, ATac-seq, mass spectrometry, MS-MS, microarrays, DNA and RNA deep sequencing, single-cell sequencing, single molecule Helioscope, the Nanopore, SMRT, RNAP sequencing, etc. Whole genome sequencing, de novo sequencing, genome-wide structural variations, carrier screening, mutation detection, and sequencing of the mitochondrial genome, as well as human genomes for inherited and complex disorders, are other examples of new advancements in the bioinformatics (Pareek, Smoczynski, and Tretyn 2011). Alongside, many tools and algorithms along with pipelines have also been developed with extremely sophisticated computational and mathematical approaches, and techniques. Many of these tools and programs are provided in Tables 11.1 and 11.2.

TABLE 11.1

Timeline of Major Milestones in Discoveries and Technologies in Gene Regulation, DNA, and RNA, along with the Latest Bioinformatics Implication

Year	Technologies/ Discoveries	Scientist Name	Key Information/Importance	References
			Gene Regulation	
1957	Central dogma	Francis Crick	DNA was discovered as a genetic material and it codes for a molecule that is necessary for life.	Crick (1958)
1970	Reverse transcriptase	David Baltimore, Howard Temin and S Mizutani	Autonomous and concurrent discovery of reverse transcriptase in retroviruses.	Baltimore (1970); Temin and Mizutani (1970)
1961	Gene regulation system	Francois Jacob and Jacques Monod	The discovery of Lac operon system has shown that some enzymes express only either the absence of glucose or the presence of lactose.	Jacob and Monod (1961)
1942	Epigenetics	Conrad Waddington	Epigenetic mechanisms contain DNA methylation, histone modification, and ncRNAs; these have impact on gene expression.	Waddington (1942)
			DNA	
1944	Transforming principle	Avery, MacLeod, and McCarty	Remarkable discovery on DNA, and DNA as the material of inheritance.	Avery et al. (1944)
1968	DNA structure discovery	Rosalind Franklin	Contribution of Rosalind Franklin in making the discovery of DNA structure.	Klug (1968)
1958	Discvoery of DNA	Watson & Crick	Double-helical structure of DNA.	Watson and Crick (1953)
2006	Coevolution of genetic codes	Guy Sella & David H. Ardell	Coevolution of Genes and Genetic Codes.	Sella and Ardell (2006)
			RNA	
1868	Discovery of the nucleic acids	Friedrich Miescher	Discovered the nucleic acids called "nuclein."	Friedrich Miescher (1879)

1939	RNA as an interplaying molecule between nucleus and cytoplasm	T. Caspersson and Jack Schultz	RNA played a role in protein synthesis.	Caspersson and Schultz (1939)
1958	Discovery of ribosome	George E Palade	Protein synthesis can be performed within the small compartments in the cytoplasm.	Palade (1958)
1959	Synthesis of DNA and RNA	S. Ochoa and A. Kornberg	Two enzymes are responsible for synthesis of DNA and RNA.	S. Ochoa and A. Kornberg (1959)
1965	Structure of a Ribonucleic Acid	Robert Holley and group	Isolated first and complete nucleotide sequence of an alanine transfer RNA from yeast.	Holley et al. (1965)
1960	RNA Polymerase	Jerard Hurwitz, Sam Weiss, Audrey Stevens, and James Bonner	Synthesizes RNA molecules from DNA.	J. Hurwitz (2005)
1964	Genetic code	Nirenberg and Philip Leder	Discovered the first triplet that codes for one of the 20 amino acids.	Nirenberg and Leder (1962)
1993	Discovery of first miRNA	Ambros and Ruvkun groups	Noncoding and post-transcriptional gene regulation.	Lee et al. (1993); Wightman et al. (1993)
Genome Sequencing and Bioinformatics				
1978	Bioinformatics	Paulien Hogeweg and Ben Hesper	The term "Bioinformatics" was invented.	Hogeweg (1978)
2000	Fruit fly genome	M. Adams and their group	Drosophila melanogaster full genome sequences.	Adams et al. (2000)
2001	Human genome sequencing	Craig Venter and their group	First draft published on Human genome.	Venter et al. (2001)
2002	Mouse genome	R. H. Waterson and their group	Draft sequence released on *Mus musculus*.	Waterson et al. (2002)
2004	Metagneomics	Jo Handelsman	Metagenomics first appeared.	Handelsman (2004)
2005	HapMap	David Altshuler & Peter Donnelly	Phase I draft of international HapMap was released.	David and Peter (2005)
2005	NGS	Thomas Jarvie	First next-generation sequencing technology was developed.	Thomas Jarvie (2005)

(Continued)

TABLE 11.1   (CONTINUED)

Gene Regulation

Year	Technologies/ Discoveries	Scientist Name	Key Information/Importance	References
2007	ChIP-Seq	Elaine R Mardis	ChIP-seq data map was released on DNA-protein binding.	Elaine R Mardis (2007)
2008	Transcriptomics	Zhong Wang and group	Transcriptomics came into picture.	Wang et al. (2009)
2010	DNA-Seq	Drmanac Radoje and group	DNA sequencing started.	Radoje et al. (2010)
2012	ENCODE	Ian Dunham & Anshul Kundaje & group	ENCODE provided functional genome information.	Dunham et al. (2012)
2013	ATAC-Seq	Jason D Buenrostro and group	ATAC-seq used for epigenome multimodal profiling.	Buenrostro et al. (2013)
2015	Epigenome	Anshul Kundaje and group	Human epigenome roadmap published.	Kundaje et al. (2015)
2020	Full human genome sequence	Karen H. Miga and group	First human gapless chromosome assembled using telomere-to-telomere assembly.	Miga et al. (2020)

TABLE 11.2

Different Programs (Algorithm/Databases/Tools) have been Utilized for Gathering Various Information on Gene Regulation, the DNA and RNA Structure and Function, and the Latest on Sequencing Tools in the Bioinformatic Application

Program	Application	Weblink	References
Gene Regulation			
Gaussian Mixture Model	Mostly used in gene expression that include learning recognition patterns, machine learning, data minimizing, and statistical analysis	https://www. geeksforgeeks.org/ gaussian-mixture-model/	C. Rasmussen (1999)
MICRAT	used in analysis of dependency of expression in different time series in relation to the gene regulatory network.	https://bmcsystbiol. biomedcentral.com/ articles/10.1186/ s12918-018-0635-1	Yang et al. (2018)
Partition around medoids	Used in finding medoids, cluster sequence localization of objects.	https://www.xlstat.com/ en/solutions/features/ partitioning-around-medoids	Van et al. (2003)
K-means	This algorithm is used to facilitate and generate structured data, and to make clusters in the data with different subgroup comparison.	http://weka.sourceforge. net/doc.dev/weka/ clusterers/Simple-KMeans.html	I. Dabbura (2018)
Self-Organizing Maps	Help in simplification in high dimensional datasets to low-dimensional datasets without changing the topological structures.	https://www.cs.hmc. edu/~kpang/nn/som. html	Willighagen et al. (2007)
DBSCAN	This uses density-based clustering in machine learning and data mining and also uses distance-based measurements for groupings	https://www.jstatsoft.org/ article/view/v091i01	Hahsler et al. (2019)
Hierarchical Clustering	Data tree clustering can be done in addition to assemble similar data parts into one group.	https://doi.org/10.1007/ 978-3-642-13672-6_22	Murtagh and Contreras (2012)
GenBank and EMBL Nucleotide sequence database	Provides information on the TSS, the promoter elements as well as transcription factor binding sites.	http://www.ncbi.nlm.nih. gov/We%20b http://www.ncbi.nlm. nih.gov/Web/Genbank/ index.html/Genbank/ index.html http://www.ebi.ac.uk/ embl.html	Kanz et al. (2005); Benson et al. (2013)
SWISS PROT	Help in finding the function and structure of proteins as well as protein domain structure	http://www.expasy.ch	Bairoch et al. (2000)
TRANSFAC	Helps in finding structure and sequences of many gene regulatory regions, the weight matrices, and to retrieve information on transcription factors and binding sites.	http://www.biobase.de	Wingender (2004)

(Continued)

TABLE 11.2 (CONTINUED)

Program	Application	Weblink	References
RegulonDB	This contains information on transcriptional regulation network of *E. coli*, operon, regulon, and other regulatory units.	http://www.cifn.unam.mx/Computational_Biology/regulondb	Tierrafria et al. (2022)
TRANSPATH	Contains information regarding reactions and molecules related to signal transduction.	http://www.biobase.de	Wingender (2004)
GeneNet	Provides information on the number of regulatory networks of a gene and gives an object oriented details	http://wwwmgs.bionet.nsc.ru/systems/MGL/GeneNet/	Kolpakov et al. (1998)
GRTD: Gene Transcription Regulation Database	This includes complete collection and information on ChIP-seq data, transcription factors and their binding site of human and mouse.	http://gtrd.biouml.org/	Kulyashov et al. (2020)
BART: Binding analysis for regulation of transcription	Helps in functional transcriptional factor prediction tool.	http://faculty.virginia.edu/zanglab/bart/	Amaral et al. (2018)
TargetFinder	Gene expression pattern prediction tool.	http://targetfinder.org/	Lavorgna et al. (1999)
MATCH	Weight matrix-based program to predict binding sites for transcription factors.	http://gene-regulation.com/pub/programs.html#match	Kel et al. (2003)
ScanForMotifs	Predict regulatory elements in UTRs by combining multiple data sources.	bioanalysis.otago.ac.nz/sfm	Biswas et al. (2014)
GlobalScore	Predicts interaction of protein and large noncoding RNAs.	service.tartaglialab.com/grant_submission/omixcore	Cirillo et al. (2017)
NucleicNet	Predict binding preference protein and RNA constituents.	github.com/NucleicNet/NucleicNet	Lam et al. (2019)
DNA			
CLUSTAL W	Multiple sequence alignment using Clustal W.	https://www.genome.jp/tools-bin/clustalw	Thompson et al. (1994)
fastDNAml	Phylogenetic trees construction using DNA sequences	https://www.life.illinois.edu/gary/programs/fastDNAml.html	Olsen et al. (1994)
BEAST software package	Phylogenetic and phylodynamic analysis using Bayesian Evolutionary Analysis by Sampling Trees (BEAST)	https://www.beast2.org/	Suchard et al. (2018)
GeneDesign	synthetic gene design using huge sequences	http://slam.bs.jhmi.edu/gd	Richardson et al. (2006)
OPTIMIZER	web server used for codon usage optimization	http://genomes.urv.es/OPTIMIZER/	Puigbò et al. (2007)
Visual gene developer	bioinformatics and programmable software used for optimization of synthetic gene.	http://www.visualgenedeveloper.net	Jung and McDonald (2011)

(Continued)

TABLE 11.2 (CONTINUED)

Program	Application	Weblink	References
GeneScan	Use of Fourier analysis in prediction of probable genomic sequences in genes.	http://hollywood.mit.edu/ GENSCAN.html	Tiwari et al. (1997)
wavelet-based feature vector model	The alignment-free method uses DNA sequence for similarity check.	http://dx.doi. org/10.4238/2015	Bao and Yuan (2015)
self-adaptive spectral rotation method	Eliminate the noise and detection of a potential coding sequence pattern.	10.1155/2014/176943	Chen and Ji (2014)
RNA			
Mfold	Optimal and suboptimal secondary structures for an RNA molecule	http://rothlab.ucdavis. edu/genhelp/mfold.html	Zuker and Sankoff (1984)
RNA structure	prediction of secondary RNA structure and its analysis	http://rna.urmc.rochester. edu/RNAstructure.html	Reuter and Mathews (2010)
Sfold	statistical prediction of RNA secondary structure.	http://www.bioinfo.rpi. edu/applications/sfold	Ding et al. (2004)
Rfam	It provides multiple sequence alignments collections and performs covariance modeling for many noncoding RNA families	https://rfam.xfam.org/	Jones et al. (2003)
Noncode	knowledge and experimental-based dedicated database to ncRNAs.	http://www.noncode.org/	Liu et al. (2005)
SILVA	Major comprehensive and up-to-date web-based information for rRNA sequences across species from bacteria to eukaryotes.	https://www.arb-silva.de/	Pruesse et al. (2007)
Sequencing and Bioinformatics Advances			
FASTP algorithm	A Fast Algorithm for the Two-Variable Integer Programming Problem.	https://github.com/ OpenGene/fastp	Sidnie Dresher Feit (1984); Chen et al. (2018)
BLAST program	It is rapid sequence alignment and comparison of a query sequence to the available database sequences.	https://blast.ncbi.nlm.nih. gov/Blast.cgi	Altschul et al. (1990)

REFERENCES

Adams, M. D., and S. E. Celniker, et al. 2000 Mar 24. "The Genome Sequence of Drosophila Melanogaster". *Science* 287 (5461), 2185–95. doi: 10.1126/science.287.5461.2185. PMID: 10731132.

Avery, Oswald T., Colin M. MacLeod, and Maclyn McCarty. 1944. "Studies on the Chemical Nature of the Substance Inducing Transformation of Pneumococcal Types." *Journal of Experimental Medicine* 79 (2). doi:10.1084/jem.79.2.137

Backofen, Rolf, Jan Engelhardt, Anika Erxleben, Jörg Fallmann, Björn Grüning, Uwe Ohler, Nikolaus Rajewsky, and Peter F. Stadler. 2017. "RNA-Bioinformatics: Tools, Services and Databases for the Analysis of RNA-Based Regulation." *Journal of Biotechnology* doi:10.1016/j.jbiotec.2017.05.019

Baltimore, D. 1970. "Viral RNA-dependent DNA Polymerase: RNA-dependent DNA Polymerase in Virions of RNA Tumour Viruses". *Nature* 226, 1209–1211. https://doi.org/10.1038/2261209a0

Bao, J. P., and R. Y. Yuan. 2015. "A Wavelet-Based Feature Vector Model for DNA Clustering." *Genetics and Molecular Research* 14 (4). doi:10.4238/2015.December.29.26

Buenrostro, J., P. Giresi, L. Zaba, et al. 2013. "Transposition of Native Chromatin for Fast and Sensitive Epigenomic Profiling of Open Chromatin, DNA-Binding Proteins and Nucleosome Position. *Nature Methods* 10, 1213–18. https://doi.org/10.1038/nmeth.2688

Carlberg, Carsten, and Ferdinand Molnár. 2020. *Mechanisms of Gene Regulation: How Science Works. Mechanisms of Gene Regulation: How Science Works*. doi:10.1007/978-3-030-52321-3

Caspersson, T., and J. Schultz 1939. "Pentose Nucleotides in the Cytoplasm of Growing Tissues. *Nature* 143, 602–3. https://doi.org/10.1038/143602c0

Chen, Bo, and Ping Ji. 2014. "An Exploration of the Triplet Periodicity in Nucleotide Sequences with a Mature Self-Adaptive Spectral Rotation Approach." *Journal of Applied Mathematics* 2014. doi:10.1155/2014/176943

Crick, F. 1970. "Central Dogma of Molecular Biology". *Nature* 227, 561–3. https://doi.org/10.1038/227561a0

Dahm, Ralf. 2005. "Friedrich Miescher and the Discovery of DNA." *Developmental Biology* doi:10.1016/j.ydbio.2004.11.028

Drmanac, R., A. B. Sparks, et al.. 2010 Jan 1. "Human Genome Sequencing Using Unchained Base Reads on Self-Assembling DNA Nanoarrays". *Science* 327 (5961), 78–81. doi:10.1126/science.1181498. Epub 2009 Nov 5. PMID: 19892942.

Fickett, James W. 1982. "Recognition of Protein Coding Regions in DNA Sequences." *Nucleic Acids Research* 10 (17). doi:10.1093/nar/10.17.5303

Handelsman, J. 2004 Dec. "Metagenomics: Application of Genomics to Uncultured Microorganisms". *Microbiology and Molecular Biology Reviews*, 68 (4), 669–85. doi:10.1128/MMBR.68.4.669-685.2004. PMID: 15590779; PMCID: PMC539003

Hogeweg, P. 1978. "Simulating the Growth of Cellular Forms". *Simulation* 31 (3), 90–6. doi:10.1177/003754977803100305

Holley RW, Apgar J, Everett GA, Madison JT, Marquisee M, Merrill SH, Penswick JR, Zamir A. 1965 Mar 19. "Structure of A Ribonucleic Acid". *Science* 147 (3664), 1462–5. doi:10.1126/science.147.3664.1462. PMID: 14263761.

Hurwitz, E. L., H. Morgenstern, and C. Chiao. 2005 Oct. Effects of Recreational Physical Activity and Back Exercises on Low Back Pain and Psychological Distress: Findings from the UCLA Low Back Pain Study. *American Journal of Public Health* 95 (10), 1817–24. doi: 10.2105/AJPH.2004.052993. PMID: 16186460; PMCID: PMC1449442

Jacob, François, Jacques Monod. 1961. "Genetic Regulatory Mechanisms in the Synthesis of Proteins". *Journal of Molecular Biology* 3 (3), 318–56, ISSN 0022-2836, https://doi.org/10.1016/S0022-2836(61)80072-7

Jarvie, T. 2005 Autumn. "Next Generation Sequencing Technologies". *Drug Discovery Today: Technologies* 2 (3), 255–60. doi: 10.1016/j.ddtec.2005.08.003. PMID: 24981944.

Jung, Sang Kyu, and Karen McDonald. 2011. "Visual Gene Developer: A Fully Programmable Bioinformatics Software for Synthetic Gene Optimization." *BMC Bioinformatics* 12. doi:10.1186/1471-2105-12-340

Karlson, P. 1960. "Nobel Prize Winners for Medicine in 1959 (S. Ochoa and A. Kornberg)." *Münchener Medizinische Wochenschrift (1950)* 102.

Klug, A. 1968. "Rosalind Franklin and the Discovery of the Structure of DNA." *Nature* 219 (5156). doi:10.1038/219808a0

Kornberg, A, S. B. Zimmerman, S. R. Kornberg, and J. Josse. 1959 Jun. "Enzymatic Synthesis of Deoxyribonucleic Acid. Influence Of Bacteriophage T2 On The Synthetic Pathway In Host Cells. *Proceedings of the National Academy of Sciences of the United States of America*. 45 (6), 772–85. doi: 10.1073/pnas.45.6.772. PMID: 16590443; PMCID: PMC 222636.

Lee, R. C., R. L. Feinbaum, V. Ambros. 1993 Dec 3. "The C. Elegans Heterochronic Gene Lin-4 Encodes Small RNAs with Antisense Complementarity to Lin-14". *Cell* 75 (5), 843–54. doi: 10.1016/0092-8674(93)90529-y. PMID: 8252621.

Mahony, Shaun, and Panayiotis V. Benos. 2007. "STAMP: A Web Tool for Exploring DNA-Binding Motif Similarities." *Nucleic Acids Research* 35 (SUPPL.2). doi:10.1093/nar/gkm272

Mardis, E. R. 2007 Aug. "ChIP-Seq: Welcome to the New Frontier". *Nature Methods* 4 (8), 613–4. doi: 10.1038/nmeth0807-613. PMID: 17664943.

Miga, K. H., S. Koren, A. Rhie, et al. 2020. "Telomere-to-Telomere Assembly of a Complete Human X Chromosome". *Nature* 585, 79–84. https://doi.org/10.1038/s41586-020-2547-7

Mouse Genome Sequencing Consortium, R. H. Waterston, K. Lindblad-Toh, et al.. 2002 Dec 5. "Initial Sequencing and Comparative Analysis of the Mouse Genome". *Nature* 420 (6915), 520–62. doi: 10.1038/nature01262. PMID: 12466850.

Nirenberg, M. W., J. H. Matthaei, O. W. Jones. 1962 Jan 15. "An Intermediate in the Biosynthesis of Polyphenylalanine Directed by Synthetic Template RNA". *Proceedings of the National Academy of Sciences of the United States of America* 48 (1), 104–9. doi: 10.1073/pnas.48.1.104. PMID: 14479931; PMCID: PMC285511

Nussinov, Ruth, George Pieczenik, Jerrold R. Griggs, and Daniel J. Kleitman. 1978. "Algorithms for Loop Matchings." *SIAM Journal on Applied Mathematics* 35 (1). doi:10.1137/0135006

Olsen, Gary J., Hideo Matsuda, Ray Hagstrom, and Ross Overbeek. 1994. "FastDNAml: A Tool for Construction of Phylogenetic Trees of DNA Sequences Using Maximum Likelihood." *Bioinformatics* 10 (1). doi:10.1093/bioinformatics/10.1.41

Pareek, Chandra Shekhar, Rafal Smoczynski, and Andrzej Tretyn. 2011. "Sequencing Technologies and Genome Sequencing." *Journal of Applied Genetics* doi:10.1007/s13353-011-0057-x

Périer, Rouaïda Cavin, Viviane Praz, Thomas Junier, Claude Bonnard, and Philipp Bucher. 2000. "The Eukaryotic Promoter Database (EPD)." *Nucleic Acids Research* doi:10.1093/nar/28.1.302

Puigbò, Pere, Eduard Guzmán, Antoni Romeu, and Santiago Garcia-Vallvé. 2007. "OPTIMIZER: A Web Server for Optimizing the Codon Usage of DNA Sequences." *Nucleic Acids Research* 35 (SUPPL.2). doi:10.1093/nar/gkm219

Rasmussen, Carl Edward. 2000. "The Infinite Gaussian Mixture Model." In S. A. Solla, T. K. Leen, K. Müller *Advances in Neural Information Processing Systems*. MIT Press, Cambridge, MA, United States. doi:10.5555/3009657.3009736

Richardson, Sarah M., Sarah J. Wheelan, Robert M. Yarrington, and Jef D. Boeke. 2006. "GeneDesign: Rapid, Automated Design of Multikilobase Synthetic Genes." *Genome Research* 16 (4). doi:10.1101/gr.4431306

Riley, Todd, Eduardo Sontag, Patricia Chen, and Arnold Levine. 2008. "Transcriptional Control of Human P53-Regulated Genes." *Nature Reviews Molecular Cell Biology* 9 (5). doi:10.1038/nrm2395

Rivas, Elena. 2021. "Evolutionary Conservation of RNA Sequence and Structure." In *Wiley Interdisciplinary Reviews: RNA*. doi:10.1002/wrna.1649

Roadmap Epigenomics Consortium, A. Kundaje, and W. Meuleman et al. 2015. "Integrative Analysis of 111 Reference Human Epigenomes". *Nature* 518, 317–30. https://doi.org/10.1038/nature14248

Sella, G., and D. H. Ardell. 2006 Sep. The Coevolution of Genes and Genetic Codes: Crick's Frozen Accident Revisited. *Journal of Molecular Evolution* 63(3), 297–313. doi: 10.1007/s00239-004-0176-7. Epub 2006 Jul 12. PMID: 16838217.

Siekevitz, P., and G. E. Palade. 1958 Sep 25. "A Cyto-Chemical Study on the Pancreas of the Guinea Pig. III. In Vivo Incorporation of Leucine-1-C14 into the Proteins of Cell Fractions". *The Journal of Biophysical and Biochemical Cytology* 4 (5), 557–66. doi: 10.1083/jcb.4.5.557. PMID: 13587549; PMCID: PMC2224556.

Spector, David L. 2003. "The Dynamics of Chromosome Organization and Gene Regulation." *Annual Review of Biochemistry* doi:10.1146/annurev.biochem.72.121801.161724

Suchard, Marc A., Philippe Lemey, Guy Baele, Daniel L. Ayres, Alexei J. Drummond, and Andrew Rambaut. 2018. "Bayesian Phylogenetic and Phylodynamic Data Integration Using BEAST 1.10." *Virus Evolution* 4 (1). doi:10.1093/ve/vey016

Temin, H. M., and S. Mizutani. 1970 Jun. "RNA-Dependent DNA Polymerase In Virions of Rous Sarcoma Virus". *Nature*. 27;226(5252):1211–3. doi: 10.1038/2261211a0. Erratum in: Nature 1970 Jul 4;227(5253):102. PMID: 4316301.

The ENCODE Project Consortium. 2012. "An Integrated Encyclopedia of DNA Elements in the Human Genome. *Nature* 489, 57–74. https://doi.org/10.1038/nature11247

Thompson, Julie D., Desmond G. Higgins, and Toby J. Gibson. 1994. "CLUSTAL W: Improving the Sensitivity of Progressive Multiple Sequence Alignment through Sequence Weighting, Position-Specific Gap Penalties and Weight Matrix Choice." *Nucleic Acids Research* 22 (22). doi:10.1093/nar/22.22.4673

Tiwari, Shrish, S. Ramachandran, Alok Bhattacharya, Sudha Bhattacharya, and Ramakrishna Ramaswamy. 1997. "Prediction of Probable Genes by Fourier Analysis of Genomic Sequences." *Bioinformatics* 13 (3). doi:10.1093/bioinformatics/13.3.263

Venter, J. C., M. D. Adams, et al.. 2001 Feb 16. "The Sequence of the Human Genome". *Science* 291 (5507), 1304–51. doi: 10.1126/science.1058040. Erratum in: *Science* 2001 Jun 5;292 (5523), 1838. PMID: 11181995.

Waddington, C. 1942. Canalization of Development and The Inheritance Of Acquired Characters. *Nature* 150, 563–5. https://doi.org/10.1038/150563a0

Wang, Jin, Jinyun Chen, and Subrata Sen. 2016. "MicroRNA as Biomarkers and Diagnostics." *Journal of Cellular Physiology* doi:10.1002/jcp.25056

Wang, Z., M. Gerstein, and M. Snyder. 2009 Jan. "RNA-Seq: A Revolutionary Tool for Transcriptomics". *Nature Reviews. Genetics* 10 (1), 57–63. doi: 10.1038/nrg2484. PMID: 19015660; PMCID: PMC2949280

Watson, J. D., and F. H.C. Crick. 1953. "Molecular Structure of Nucleic Acids: A Structure for Deoxyribose Nucleic Acid." *Nature* 171 (4356). doi:10.1038/171737a0

Wightman, B., I. Ha, and G. Ruvkun. 1993 Dec 3. "Posttranscriptional Regulation of the Heterochronic Gene Lin-14 by Lin-4 Mediates Temporal Pattern Formation in C. elegans". *Cell* 75 (5), 855–62. doi: 10.1016/0092-8674(93)90530-4. PMID: 8252622

Wingender, Edgar. 2004. "TRANSFAC®, TRANSPATH® and CYTOMER® as Starting Points for an Ontology of Regulatory Networks." *In Silico Biology* 4 (1), 55–61.

Wu, Gang, Nabila Bashir-Bello, and Stephen Freeland. 2005. "The Synthetic Gene Designer: A Flexible Web Platform to Explore Sequence Space of Synthetic Genes for Heterologous Expression." In *2005 IEEE Computational Systems Bioinformatics Conference, Workshops and Poster Abstracts*. doi:10.1109/CSBW.2005.133

Zhang, Xiuwei, Zhidong Deng, and Dandan Song. 2006. "Neural Network Approach to Predict RNA Secondary Structures." *Qinghua Daxue Xuebao/Journal of Tsinghua University* 46 (10).

Zuker, Michael, and Patrick Stiegler. 1981. "Optimal Computer Folding of Large RNA Sequences Using Thermodynamics and Auxiliary Information." *Nucleic Acids Research* 9 (1). doi:10.1093/nar/9.1.133

12 Computational Prediction of RNA Binding Proteins
Features and Models

Upendra Kumar Pradhan and Prabina Kumar Meher

ICAR-Indian Agricultural Statistics Research Institute, India

12.1 INTRODUCTION

Although most species today rely on DNA as their primary genetic building block, RNAs were responsible for the beginning of life and are still used by them to carry out active forms of genetic expression. Besides the two major layers of gene regulation, i.e., (i) transcription regulation by transcription and epigenetic factors and (ii) post-transcription regulation by various classes of small RNA, there is a third layer which is primarily controlled by RNA binding proteins (RBPs).

The discovery of heterogeneous nuclear ribonucleoproteins (hnRNP) and other pre-mRNA/mRNA-binding proteins enabled the identification of amino acid motifs and functional domains that confer RNA binding (Burd & Dreyfuss, 1994). RBPs have one or, more frequently, many RNA-binding domains (RBD). Using the well-characterised RBDs as a foundation, computational analyses have showed that eukaryotic genomes encode a large number of RBPs (Keene, 2001). The majority of RBPs have a range of diverse functions that result from these domains' combinatorial effects (Gerstberger et al., 2014). RBPs are involved in every step of RNA biology, from transcription to translation (Pradhan et al., 2021). RBP dysfunction has been linked to a variety of human diseases, including cancer, neurological disorders, and muscle atrophy (Lukong et al., 2008). But, since RBPs are still mostly unknown, further research is needed to fully understand the underlying mechanisms of the RNA regulatory system and RBP-related human diseases.

With the introduction of high-throughput molecular techniques for *in vivo* RBP discovery, such as the interactome capture method, the current repertoire of human RBPs has been rapidly expanding in recent years (Castello et al., 2016). Cutting-edge experimental approaches are being developed to recognise RBPs, which include UV crosslinking methods (Castello et al., 2012), photo-reactive nucleotide-enhanced UV crosslinking and oligo (dT) purification method (Baltz et al., 2012), and mass spectrometry (Mitchell et al., 2013). Though these experiments for RBP identification have greatly expanded our knowledge, they are costly and labour-intensive. Furthermore, the massive effort put into genome sequencing has resulted in a plethora of protein sequences and generation of an unprecedented amount of genomic information, which

DOI: 10.1201/9781003331247-14

145

has outpaced the tasks required to annotate their functions. As a result, faster and more accurate computational techniques for RBP annotation are required.

12.2 COMPUTATIONAL METHODS FOR PREDICTING RBPS

Wet-lab experimental techniques like RNA Interactome Capture (RIC) can be used to accurately detect RBPs (Castello et al., 2016). However, these methods require a lot of time and money, making them unsuitable for the high-throughput detection of RBPs. The fact that RIC can only work on RBPs with fully implemented crosslink-enhancing artificial nucleotides, but functioning poly (A) tails on transcripts further restricts its application to prokaryotic RBPs. In this situation, computational methods for in silico high-throughput RBP prediction can aid in directing hypothesis-driven experimental RBP studies.

Prediction methods for RBPs based on sequence similarity have been the main focus of the majority of earlier investigations. In order to determine whether a query protein is an RBP, databases were searched for homologous sequences to the query protein. The other commonly used computational approaches for identifying RBPs are those based on predicted structural and sequence information. If the 3D structure of a target protein is known, structure-based prediction was employed to distinguish RBPs (Zhao et al., 2011a).

Computational approaches are typically used in addition to biological procedures to improve the effectiveness and efficiency of the RBP discovery process (i.e. experiment-based approaches). The RBP classifier's predictions can be applied easily to many other biological conditions using machine learning techniques, which experiment-based approaches cannot. This is due to the fact that a robust RBP classifier can provide high-quality RBP candidates, hence narrowing the search space for experimental validation (Han et al., 2004). For development of a computation model for prediction of RBPs, construction of benchmark dataset and generation of highly discriminative features are two most important aspects besides choosing learning algorithm for classification for RBPs and non-RBPs.

12.2.1 Dataset for RBP Recognition

The sequence and structure of protein-RNA complexes can be accessed in the PDB database and other specific protein-RNA interaction databases (Lewis et al., 2011). The largest dataset currently available is RB344. Another dataset, PRIPU, was collected by Cheng et al. (2015) which was different from earlier datasets. We summarised the datasets from several prior studies (Table 12.1).

12.2.2 Feature Representation

Machine learning models cannot accommodate the sequence data directly, and hence numerical representation of the RBP sequence is an essential step for developing sequence-based computational model. The numerical representation also determines the effectiveness of the prediction model to a large extent as far as prediction accuracy is concerned. Majorly, three types of features have been used for prediction of RBPs which are sequence-derived features, structural features, and features

TABLE 12.1

Data Sets Commonly Used for RNA-Binding Protein Prediction

Dataset	Reference	Brief Description
PRIPU	Cheng et al. (2015)	The dataset contains both positive and negative sequences, which is an innovation because previous ones only contained negative samples. Such negative samples are not true negative samples; in fact, some of them might be unknown positive samples.
RB344	Ren and Shen (2015)	At 30% sequence identity, 344 RBPs have been almost entirely non-redundant.
RB172	Nagarajan and Gromiha (2014)	172 RBPs with sequence identity of less than 25%
RB75	Puton et al. (2012)	75 non-redundant RNP complexes from the PDB database with 40% sequence identity.
RB199	Lewis et al. (2011)	Protein dataset from the Protein Data Bank. Proteins with more than 30% sequence identity as well as high resolution (>3.5 Å).
RB86	Ahmad and Sarai (2011)	86 RBP chains
RB109	Petrey and Honig (2003)	109 RNA-protein complexes extracted from X-ray crystallography structures of known RNA-protein complexes in the PDB.

based on physicochemical properties. Each category of feature is briefly described as follows.

12.2.2.1 Sequence-Based Features

12.2.2.1.1 Amino Acid Composition (AAC)

The AAC descriptor has been successfully applied for RBP prediction in earlier studies (Kumar et al., 2011; Zhang and Liu, 2017; Sun et al., 2020). The AAC is simply the frequency of 20 amino acids in a protein sequence. The frequency of each amino acid is computed as:

$$f(t) = \frac{N(t)}{N}, \quad t \in \{A, C, D, ..., Y\},$$

where $N(t)$ is the number of amino acid type t, while N is the length of the protein sequence.

12.2.2.1.2 Tri-peptide Composition (TPC)

The Tripeptide Composition (TPC) gives 8000 descriptors, defined as:

$$f(r, s, t) = \frac{N_{rst}}{N-2}, \quad r, s, t \in \{A, C, D, ...Y\},$$

where N_{rst} is the number of tripeptides represented by amino acid types r, s and t. The tripeptide composition was successfully implemented to develop the TriPepSVM method for prediction of RBP (Bressin et al., 2019).

12.2.2.1.3 Evolutionary Features

For the prediction of RBPs, evolutionary features derived from the position-specific scoring matrix (PSSM) profiles have been successfully employed as input in many studies (Zhang et al., 2021, 2022; Mishra et al., 2021). PSSMs have been widely used in prediction studies due to their ability to predict the likeliness of a specific residue substitution based on evolutionary information. PSSM recognises the conservation pattern in multiple alignments and stores it as a score matrix for each position in the alignment. The PSSM profile is an $L{\times}20$ dimensional matrix, which can be written as

$$\text{PSSM}_{L\times 20} = \begin{bmatrix} p_{1,1} & p_{1,2} \cdots & p_{1,20} \\ p_{2,1} & p_{2,2} \cdots & p_{2,20} \\ \vdots & \vdots \ldots & \vdots \\ p_{L,1} & p_{L,2} \cdots & p_{L,20} \end{bmatrix}$$

where L is the protein length, $P_{i,j}$ denotes the occurrence probability of amino acid j at position i of the protein sequence. Some of the important PSSM-based features are represented in Table 12.2.

12.2.2.2 Structure-Based Features

12.2.2.2.1 The Secondary Structure (SS)

Local and geometric patterns are provided by the secondary structure (SS). When the protein structure is known, the DSSPcont (Carter et al., 2003) can be used for calculating the secondary structure. When the protein structure is unknown, a method like PSIPRED (Liam et al., 2000) can be used to predict the secondary structure. In several studies to predict RBP (Peng et al., 2022; Zhao et al., 2011b; Yang et al., 2014), secondary structure has been used as an encoding feature.

TABLE 12.2
Ten Important PSSM-Based Features Descriptors

Sl.	Feature Class	Dimension	References
1	PSSMBLOCK	20	An et al. (2017)
2	AADP-PSSM	420	Liu et al. (2010)
3	PSSM-DWT	80	Wang et al. (2017)
4	EDP-EEDP-MEDP	420	Zhang et al. (2014)
5	MBMGAC-PSSM	560	Liang et al. (2015)
6	PSSM400	400	Nanni et al. (2014)
7	PSSM-AC	200	Zou et al. (2013)
8	RPSSM	110	Ding et al. (2014)
9	SOMA-PSSM	160	Liang and Zhang (2017)
10	DFMCA-PSSM	290	Liang et al. (2018)

12.2.2.2.2 Accessible Solvent Area (ASA)

Calculating solvent accessibility is important in RBP prediction since RNA-binding residues often become accessible and interact with proteins (Lam et al., 2019). While the protein structure is given, the relative ASA could be calculated using NACCESS (Yu et al., 2006). It is crucial to note that without the presence of the DNA molecule, the relative ASA could not be determined.

12.2.2.3 Physicochemical Features

12.2.2.3.1 Hydrophobicity

RBP predictors commonly employ hydrophobicity, which stands for the percentage of residues attracted to water (Zhang & Liu, 2017; Zheng et al., 2018; Mishra et al., 2021). The definition of the hydrophobicity scale included a numerical number for each amino acid (Kyte and Doolittle, 1982).

12.2.2.3.2 Electrostatic Patches

Electrostatic patches can also be used to describe the state of a protein's surface. Usually, positively charged electrostatic patches are more common near nucleic acid-binding surfaces (Stawiski et al., 2003). GRASP (Petrey & Honig, 2003), GRASS (Nayal et al., 1999), and the web server PFplus (Shazman et al., 2007) can be used to compute electrostatic patches. In a couple of studies, electrostatic patches are successfully employed for RBP prediction (Shazman & Mandel-Gutfreund, 2008; Paz et al., 2016).

12.2.3 Computational Models Available for Prediction of RBPs

The discovery of RNA-binding proteins has been explored on multiple occasions, and effective computational prediction techniques have been developed. Template-based and methods based on machine learning or deep learning are the two primary categories into which these methods can be classified. Template-based method identifies RBPs by calculating the similarity score between a query protein and the template RBPs or RNA-binding domains (RBDs). However, the predefined RBDs cannot be found in almost half of the experimentally identified RBPs. Also, proteins with the presence of the RBDs may not necessarily correspond to RBPs (Hentze et al., 2018). Thus, the template-based methods would be ineffective in these two cases.

In contrast to template-based methods, machine learning techniques develop their predictive models by searching for patterns in the input feature space. This category of methods uses annotated training datasets with both RBPs and non-RBPs to train models using machine learning techniques. Due to their attractive nature in successfully handling high-dimensional features, machine learning techniques have gained in popularity in recent years. The extraction of pertinent features and the choice of an appropriate classification algorithm are two crucial steps in the machine learning-based approach for the prediction of RBPs. The current prediction approach can also be divided into two groups, depending on the feature extraction, i.e. (i) features derived from the protein structure and (ii) features obtained from the sequence.

Deep learning models have been successfully applied to many big dataset classification tasks. Deep learning method has incomparable advantages in the computation of large-scale biological sequence data. For instance, Zheng et al. (2018) developed Deep-RBPPred, a deep learning model using the protein feature of RBPPred and Convolutional Neural Network (CNN). This model achieved the MCC values of 0.82 (0.82), 0.65 (0.69), and 0.85 (0.80) for testing the balance model (imbalance model) in the proteomes of *A. thaliana*, *S. cerevisiae*, and *H. sapiens*, respectively. In order to tackle the cross-prediction problem and improve the predictive performance of DBPs and RBPs, several deep learning–based models are developed in recent time. Furthermore the transformer model and its variations, which were more recently shown to have a considerable potential for utilising the power of big data, were pre-trained on a large number of protein sequences using self-supervision methodologies. For the purpose of identifying RBPs, several methods are reported based on transfer learning. Table 12.2 lists all currently available computational methods (both template- and sequence-based) for RBP prediction. Despite substantial advancements, the majority of RBP prediction methods developed in the past have limitations when it comes to explaining how protein-RNA interactions take place. Therefore, it is crucial to find novel features, efficient encoding methods, and cutting-edge machine learning approaches that can aid in

TABLE 12.3

List of Computational Methods Available for Prediction of RNA Binding Proteins (RBPs)

Feature Type	Name of the Tool	Prediction Model	Reference
Structural-based	SPalign	Template-based	Yang et al. (2012)
	SPOT-stru		Zhao et al. (2011a)
Sequence-based	SPOT-seq		Zhao et al. (2011b)
	SPOT-Seq-RNA		Yang et al. (2014)
	APRICOT		Sharan et al. (2017)
Structural-based	NAbind	SVM–Gist	Shazman and Mandel-Gutfreund (2008)
	BindUP	SVM–Gist	Paz et al. (2016)
	NucleicNet	ResNet	Lam et al. (2019)
Sequence-based	RNApred	SVM	Kumar et al. (2011)
	RBPPred	SVM	Zhang and Liu (2017)
	TriPepSVM	SVM	Bressin et al. (2019)
	RBPro-RF	RF	Sun et al. (2020)
	IDRBP-PPCT	RF	Wang et al. (2022)
	iDRBP_MMC	CNN	Zhang et al. (2020)
	Deep-RBPPred	CNN	Zheng et al. (2018)
	DeepDRBP-2L	LSTM and CNN	Zhang et al. (2021)
	AIRBP	Ensemble model	Mishra et al. (2021)
	PreRBP-TL	Motif CNN	Zhang et al. (2022)
	RBP-TSTL	Two-stage deep transfer learning	Peng et al. (2022)

enhancing the precision of RBP predictors and, in turn, expand our understanding of RNA-protein interactions and their functions.

12.3   CONCLUSIONS AND FUTURE PERSPECTIVES

The previous decade has seen a tremendous improvement in prediction accuracy, and experimental scientists now have access to several web servers for predicting RBPs. Nevertheless, there are at least issues that need to be addressed in the field RBP prediction. The first important issue is how to distinguish DNA-binding proteins (DBPs) from RBPs. Generally, the prediction approaches that use templates are more effective than those using machine learning methods for distinguishing RBPs from DBPs. Conversely, for those RBPs that could not be detected successfully using template-based methods, machine learning methods can detect RNA-binding residues. Therefore, combining the strengths of two approaches has the potential to obtain better performance of RBP prediction. The second important issue is that which feature vectors contribute more and which ones offer less to the predictor in machine learning methods remains unclear. It is certain that selection of novel and effective features could be one of the most important aspects in RBPs prediction. The third issue is that all existing protein–RNA docking approaches do not take into account conformational changes that may occur in the combination process of protein and RNA molecules. The ability to model the 3D RNA structure using several RNA folding simulations and accommodating those methods to refold RNA fragments to simulate protein–RNA interaction and optimise minimum energy would be useful. Finally, further comparison studies are required to adequately evaluate the advantages and disadvantages of various methods.

REFERENCES

Ahmad, S., & Sarai, A. (2011). Analysis of electric moments of RNA-binding proteins: Implications for mechanism and prediction. *BMC Structural Biology*, *11*(1), 8.

An, J.-Y., Zhang, L., Zhou, Y., Zhao, Y.-J., & Wang, D.-F. (2017). Computational methods using weighed-extreme learning machine to predict protein self-interactions with protein evolutionary information. *Journal of Cheminformatics*, *9*(1), 47.

Baltz, A. G., Munschauer, M., Schwanhäusser, B., Vasile, A., Murakawa, Y., Schueler, M., Youngs, N., Penfold-Brown, D., Drew, K., Milek, M., Wyler, E., Bonneau, R., Selbach, M., Dieterich, C., & Landthaler, M. (2012). The mRNA-bound proteome and its global occupancy profile on protein-coding transcripts. *Molecular Cell*, *46*(5), 674–690.

Bressin, A., Schulte-Sasse, R., Figini, D., Urdaneta, E. C., Beckmann, B. M., & Marsico, A. (2019). TriPepSVM: De novo prediction of RNA-binding proteins based on short amino acid motifs. *Nucleic Acids Research*, *47*(9), 4406–4417.

Burd, C. G., & Dreyfuss, G. (1994). Conserved structures and diversity of functions of RNA-binding proteins. *Science (New York, N.Y.)*, *265*(5172), 615–621.

Carter, P., Andersen, C. A. F., & Rost, B. (2003). DSSPcont: Continuous secondary structure assignments for proteins. *Nucleic Acids Research*, *31*(13), 3293–3295.

Castello, A., Fischer, B., Eichelbaum, K., Horos, R., Beckmann, B. M., Strein, C., Davey, N. E., Humphreys, D. T., Preiss, T., Steinmetz, L. M., Krijgsveld, J., & Hentze, M. W. (2012). Insights into RNA Biology from an Atlas of Mammalian mRNA-Binding Proteins. *Cell*, *149*(6), 1393–1406.

Castello, A., Fischer, B., Frese, C. K., Horos, R., Alleaume, A.-M., Foehr, S., Curk, T., Krijgsveld, J., & Hentze, M. W. (2016). Comprehensive Identification of RNA-Binding Domains in Human Cells. *Molecular Cell*, *63*(4), 696–710.

Cheng, Z., Zhou, S., & Guan, J. (2015). Computationally predicting protein-RNA interactions using only positive and unlabeled examples. *Journal of Bioinformatics and Computational Biology*, *13*(3), 1541005.

Ding, S., Li, Y., Shi, Z., & Yan, S. (2014). A protein structural classes prediction method based on predicted secondary structure and PSI-BLAST profile. *Biochimie*, *97*, 60–65.

Gerstberger, S., Hafner, M., & Tuschl, T. (2014). A census of human RNA-binding proteins. *Nature Reviews Genetics*, *15*(12), Article 12.

Han, L. Y., Cai, C. Z., Ji, Z. L., Cao, Z. W., Cui, J., & Chen, Y. Z. (2004). Predicting functional family of novel enzymes irrespective of sequence similarity: A statistical learning approach. *Nucleic Acids Research*, *32*(21), 6437–6444.

Hentze, M. W., Castello, A., Schwarzl, T., & Preiss, T. (2018). A brave new world of RNA-binding proteins. *Nature Reviews. Molecular Cell Biology*, *19*(5), 327–341.

Keene, J. D. (2001). Ribonucleoprotein infrastructure regulating the flow of genetic information between the genome and the proteome. *Proceedings of the National Academy of Sciences*, *98*(13), 7018–7024.

Kumar, M., Gromiha, M. M., & Raghava, G. P. S. (2011). SVM based prediction of RNA-binding proteins using binding residues and evolutionary information. *Journal of Molecular Recognition: JMR*, *24*(2), 303–313.

Kyte, J., & Doolittle, R. F. (1982). A simple method for displaying the hydropathic character of a protein. *Journal of Molecular Biology*, *157*(1), 105–132.

Lam, J. H., Li, Y., Zhu, L., Umarov, R., Jiang, H., Héliou, A., Sheong, F. K., Liu, T., Long, Y., Li, Y., Fang, L., Altman, R. B., Chen, W., Huang, X., & Gao, X. (2019). A deep learning framework to predict binding preference of RNA constituents on protein surface. *Nature Communications*, *10*(1), Article 1.

Lewis, B. A., Walia, R. R., Terribilini, M., Ferguson, J., Zheng, C., Honavar, V., & Dobbs, D. (2011). PRIDB: A Protein-RNA interface database. *Nucleic Acids Research*, *39*(Database issue), D277–282.

Liam, J., McGuffin, K.B., & David T.J. (2000). The PSIPRED protein structure prediction server. *Bioinformatics*, *16*(4), 404–405.

Liang, Y., Liu, S., & Zhang, S. (2015). Prediction of protein structural classes for low-similarity sequences based on consensus sequence and segmented PSSM. *Computational and Mathematical Methods in Medicine*, *2015*, e370756.

Liang, Y., & Zhang, S. (2017). Predict protein structural class by incorporating two different modes of evolutionary information into Chou's general pseudo amino acid composition. *Journal of Molecular Graphics & Modelling*, *78*, 110–117.

Liang, Y., Zhang, S., & Ding, S. (2018). Accurate prediction of Gram-negative bacterial secreted protein types by fusing multiple statistical features from PSI-BLAST profile. *SAR and QSAR in Environmental Research*, *29*(6), 469–481.

Liu, T., Zheng, X., & Wang, J. (2010). Prediction of protein structural class for low-similarity sequences using support vector machine and PSI-BLAST profile. *Biochimie*, *92*(10), 1330–1334.

Lukong, K. E., Chang, K., Khandjian, E. W., & Richard, S. (2008). RNA-binding proteins in human genetic disease. *Trends in Genetics: TIG*, *24*(8), 416–425.

Mishra, A., Khanal, R., Kabir, W. U., & Hoque, T. (2021). AIRBP: Accurate identification of RNA-binding proteins using machine learning techniques. *Artificial Intelligence in Medicine*, *113*, 102034.

Mitchell, S. F., Jain, S., She, M., & Parker, R. (2013). Global analysis of yeast mRNPs. *Nature Structural & Molecular Biology*, *20*(1), Article 1.

Nagarajan, R., & Gromiha, M. M. (2014). Prediction of RNA binding residues: An extensive analysis based on structure and function to select the best predictor. *PLOS ONE*, *9*(3), e91140.

Nanni, L., Lumini, A., & Brahnam, S. (2014). An empirical study of different approaches for protein classification. *The Scientific World Journal*, *2014*, e236717.

Nayal, M., Hitz, B. C., & Honig, B. (1999). GRASS: A server for the graphical representation and analysis of structures. *Protein Science: A Publication of the Protein Society*, *8*(3), 676–679.

Paz, I., Kligun, E., Bengad, B., & Mandel-Gutfreund, Y. (2016). BindUP: A web server for non-homology-based prediction of DNA and RNA binding proteins. *Nucleic Acids Research*, *44*(W1), W568–W574.

Peng, X., Wang, X., Guo, Y., Ge, Z., Li, F., Gao, X., & Song, J. (2022). RBP-TSTL is a two-stage transfer learning framework for genome-scale prediction of RNA-binding proteins. *Briefings in Bioinformatics*, *23*(4), bbac215.

Petrey, D., & Honig, B. (2003). GRASP2: Visualization, surface properties, and electrostatics of macromolecular structures and sequences. *Methods in Enzymology*, *374*, 492–509.

Pradhan, U. K., Sharma, N. K., Kumar, P., Kumar, A., Gupta, S., & Shankar, R. (2021). miRbiom: Machine-learning on Bayesian causal nets of RBP-miRNA interactions successfully predicts miRNA profiles. *PLoS ONE*, *16*(10), e0258550.

Puton, T., Kozlowski, L., Tuszynska, I., Rother, K., & Bujnicki, J. M. (2012). Computational methods for prediction of protein–RNA interactions. *Journal of Structural Biology*, *179*(3), 261–268.

Ren, H., & Shen, Y. (2015). RNA-binding residues prediction using structural features. *BMC Bioinformatics*, *16*(1), 249.

Sharan, M., Förstner, K. U., Eulalio, A., & Vogel, J. (2017). APRICOT: An integrated computational pipeline for the sequence-based identification and characterization of RNA-binding proteins. *Nucleic Acids Research*, *45*(11), e96.

Shazman, S., Celniker, G., Haber, O., Glaser, F., & Mandel-Gutfreund, Y. (2007). Patch Finder Plus (PFplus): A web server for extracting and displaying positive electrostatic patches on protein surfaces. *Nucleic Acids Research*, *35*(Web Server issue), W526–W530.

Shazman, S., & Mandel-Gutfreund, Y. (2008). Classifying RNA-Binding Proteins Based on Electrostatic Properties. *PLOS Computational Biology*, *4*(8), e1000146.

Stawiski, E. W., Gregoret, L. M., & Mandel-Gutfreund, Y. (2003). Annotating nucleic acid-binding function based on protein structure. *Journal of Molecular Biology*, *326*(4), 1065–1079.

Sun, X., Jin, T., Chen, C., Cui, X., Ma, Q., & Yu, B. (2020). RBPro-RF: Use Chou's 5-steps rule to predict RNA-binding proteins via random forest with elastic net. *Chemometrics and Intelligent Laboratory Systems*, *197*, 103919.

Wang, N., Zhang, J., & Liu, B. (2022). IDRBP-PPCT: Identifying nucleic acid-binding proteins based on position-specific score matrix and position-specific frequency matrix cross transformation. *IEEE/ACM Trans Comput Biol Bioinform*, *19*(4), 2284–2293.

Wang, Y., Ding, Y., Guo, F., Wei, L., & Tang, J. (2017). Improved detection of DNA-binding proteins via compression technology on PSSM information. *PLOS ONE*, *12*(9), e0185587.

Yang, Y., Zhan, J., Zhao, H., & Zhou, Y. (2012). A new size-independent score for pairwise protein structure alignment and its application to structure classification and nucleic-acid binding prediction. *Proteins: Structure, Function, and Bioinformatics*, *80*(8), 2080–2088.

Yang, Y., Zhao, H., Wang, J., & Zhou, Y. (2014). SPOT-Seq-RNA: Predicting protein-RNA complex structure and RNA-binding function by fold recognition and binding affinity prediction. *Methods in Molecular Biology (Clifton, N.J.)*, *1137*, 119–130.

Yu, X., Cao, J., Cai, Y., Shi, T., & Li, Y. (2006). Predicting rRNA-, RNA-, and DNA-binding proteins from primary structure with support vector machines. *Journal of Theoretical Biology*, *240*(2), 175–184.

Zhang, J., Chen, Q., & Liu, B. (2020). iDRBP_MMC: Identifying DNA-binding proteins and RNA-binding proteins based on multi-label learning model and motif-based convolutional neural network. *Journal of Molecular Biology*, *432*(22), 5860–5875.

Zhang, J., Chen, Q., & Liu, B. (2021). DeepDRBP-2L: A new genome annotation predictor for identifying DNA-binding proteins and RNA-binding proteins using convolutional neural network and long short-term memory. *IEEE/ACM Transactions on Computational Biology and Bioinformatics*, *18*(4), 1451–1463.

Zhang, J., Yan, K., Chen, Q., & Liu, B. (2022). PreRBP-TL: Prediction of species-specific RNA-binding proteins based on transfer learning. *Bioinformatics*, *38*(8), 2135–2143.

Zhang, L., Zhao, X., & Kong, L. (2014). Predict protein structural class for low-similarity sequences by evolutionary difference information into the general form of Chou's pseudo amino acid composition. *Journal of Theoretical Biology*, 355, 105–110.

Zhang, X., & Liu, S. (2017). RBPPred: Predicting RNA-binding proteins from sequence using SVM. *Bioinformatics (Oxford, England)*, *33*(6), 854–862.

Zhao, H., Yang, Y., & Zhou, Y. (2011a). Structure-based prediction of RNA-binding domains and RNA-binding sites and application to structural genomics targets. *Nucleic Acids Research*, *39*(8), 3017–3025.

Zhao, H., Yang, Y., & Zhou, Y. (2011b). Highly accurate and high-resolution function prediction of RNA binding proteins by fold recognition and binding affinity prediction. *RNA Biology*, *8*(6), 988–996.

Zheng, J., Zhang, X., Zhao, X., Tong, X., Hong, X., Xie, J., & Liu, S. (2018). Deep-RBPPred: Predicting RNA binding proteins in the proteome scale based on deep learning. *Scientific Reports*, *8*(1), Article 1.

Zou, C., Gong, J., & Li, H. (2013). An improved sequence based prediction protocol for DNA-binding proteins using SVM and comprehensive feature analysis. *BMC Bioinformatics*, *14*(1), 90.

13 Fundamental and Best Practices for Protein Annotations

Tiratha Raj Singh

Jaypee University of Information Technology, India

Prashanth Suravajhala

Amrita Vishwa Vidyapeetham, India

13.1 INTRODUCTION

In the recent past, various bioinformatics tools have been developed that allow researchers to compare genomic and proteomic repertoire. Comparative studies using algorithms like Blast[1–3] and databases are carried out to distinguish unique proteins from paralogs which later might have resulted from gene duplication events. The genomes sequenced so far were helpful in predicting not only evolutionary relationships but also identified functions for the genes through functional genomics.[4] Although many methods are being employed by researchers, screening of proteins for novel translatable candidates is not often used and the researcher repeatedly performs the screening with laborious wet-lab experiments. To increase the sensitivity, further clues on tissues and development stages from the queried gene's sequences could be surveyed using tools like gene expression omnibus (GEO) or Unigene-EST or cDNA profile database. Furthermore, proteins linked to genomic location specified by transcript mapping, radiation hybrid mapping, genetic mapping, or cytogenetic mapping as available from GenBank resources would improve the understanding of protein annotation. Besides this, whether or not a protein contains a poly-Adenylation signal could be an added knowledge to meet the criteria of well-annotated proteins. This is because tools like MEME[5] reveal many 3′ UTRs forming conserved motifs, which indicates these regions appear more conserved than expected. This means, higher the conservation, greater is the duplications and greater is the chance of being not annotated or 'hypothetical.' There seems to be many unique genes which are over-represented in the form of duplications; a simple search in GenBank gene list would reveal that there are several accessions duplicated. For example, in case of the gene FusA2a, bona fide accession is mapped to CAD92986 and yet a few of the isoforms/unique genes remain unknown (for example CAD93127). In summary, there could be many proteins less annotated and yet many tools are known to describe the function. This leaves to beg a question, what would be the fate of proteins that cannot be annotated through some tools or in contrast how many best tools amongst them are used to describe or annotate a protein?

13.2   STANDARD TOOLS FOR THE ANALYSIS OF PROTEINS

Apart from BLAST[2] and FASTA,[6] the sequence-based feature annotation is applied by RefSeq using several tools, namely, BEAUTY-X–Blast Enhanced Alignment Utility[7] and PROSITE.[8] While many other variants of BLAST including PSI-Blast and PHI-Blast, sequence alignments using ClustalW, ClustalX and Cobalt are used, not all the tools are used in tandem to eliminate false positives. Whether the protein is soluble or insoluble is known through TopPred;[9] the topology of protein with the orientation and location of transmembrane helices is attributed to the function. Additionally, orthology mapping using tools like HomoMINT[10] are used which increases the chance of protein annotation. With the central dogma beyond the age today in bioinformatics, namely, sequence specifies structure which specifies function, annotations have become mightier to further manually curate allowing researchers to perform experimental analyses for some proteins. The structures of proteins not only provide functions but the shapes exhibited by the proteins allow them to interact selectively with other proteins or molecules. This specificity is the key for the proteins to interact with another protein, thereby inferring the function. However, most of the bioinformatics analyses are misleading unless biochemical characterization is carried out. Further, the protein annotation has gained much importance with the introduction of many metazoan genome sequencing projects in addition to the 1,000 genomes project that is in progress. With 40–50% of identified genes corresponding to proteins of unknown function, the functional-structural annotation screening technology using NMR (FAST-NMR) has been developed to assign a biological function which is based on the principle that a biological function can be described based on the basic dogma of biochemistry that the proteins with similar functions will have similar active sites and exhibit similar ligand binding interactions, even though there is a global difference in sequence and structure. Tools like combinatorial extension which confer structure similarity as DALI for NMR.[11] Finally, to determine the function, PvSOAR,[12] and Profunc can be used conditioned to give a 3D structure, aimed at identifying a protein's function.[13] However, there are many other methods like the Rosetta stone method,[14] phylogenetic profiling method,[15] and conserved gene neighbors[16] that have been widely employed and being accepted by the scientific community.

13.3   BIOLOGICAL AND FUNCTIONAL ANNOTATIONS

Biological functions of proteins would help in the identification of novel drug targets and help reduce the extensive cost of practical examinations on several candidates.

With the enormous amount of sequence and structure information available, innumerable automated annotation tools for proteins have also been generated.[17, 18] One such example is APAT (Automated Protein Annotation Tool), which uses the markup language concept to provide wrappers for several kinds of protein annotations. While Ffpred is available to predict molecular function for orphan and unannotated protein sequences, the method has been optimized for performance using a protein feature–based method through SVMs (support vector machines) that do not require prior identification of protein sequence homologues. It works on the premise of post-translational modifications, gene ontology, and localization features of proteins. Yet another tool, namely, VICMpred aids in broad functional classification of proteins of bacteria into virulence factors, information molecule, cellular process, and metabolism molecule.[19] The VICMpred server uses SVM-based method having patterns, amino acid, and dipeptide composition of bacterial protein sequences. ConSeq and ConSurf have been widely applied in predicting functional/structural sites in a protein using conservation and hyper-variation.[20] Functional annotations could also be related with the differential gene expression analysis and various kind of polymorphisms along with miRNA-based analysis.[21–28] It will help to summarize the genomic-level annotations toward proteomic directions, which will be part of the next section.

The final part of annotation can be studied through interactions and associations. All interactions are associations, while not all associations are interactions. The association tools, namely, *STRING* (Search Tool for the Retrieval of Interacting Genes/Proteins),[29] GeneCards,[30] IntAct,[31] MINT,[32] BIND (Biomolecular Interaction Network Database)[33] which has been enhanced as BOND (Biomolecular Object Network Database), are very popular for the interaction-level annotations. With BIND inside, BOND is a comprehensive database that helps in the annotation of proteins through unique object-based interaction studies. Although there are other variants of some of these databases like GeneAnnot, GeneDecks, or GeneCards, most of them are used for finding genes based on different queries.

Methods for predicting protein antigenic determinants from amino acid sequences were a crucial point for segment-level annotation of proteins.[34,35] Since then, so many computational methods have been developed based on such basic and fundamental methods and pinpoint the importance of basic methods in the area of computational biology. Developed methods are being assorted in applications from sequence-based antigenic determinants[36] to surface-based consensus scoring matrix approach for antigenic epitopes.[37] Such developments significantly contributed to the refinement of existing and development of new and versatile techniques but have roots in indispensable and conventional approaches.

We have incorporated a systematic representation of fundamental and best practiced tools/servers to facilitate users for information (Figure 13.1). Additional features with their respective inputs, outputs, mode of action, and level of annotation have also been compiled (Table 13.1), and will help those experienced as well as beginners in the area of protein annotations and computational biology.

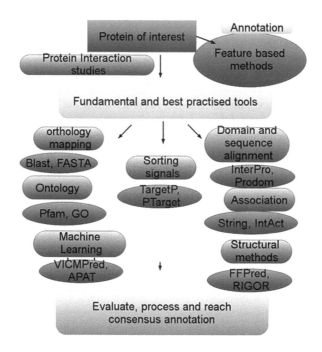

FIGURE 13.1 Systematic representation of various kinds of protein functional annotation tools.

TABLE 13.1
Best Practiced Tools for Myriad of Protein Functional Annotations

Tools/Servers	Interaction/ Association	Output	Comments on Methods	Annotation
Blast/FASTA	Protein sequence Database	Close and distant candidates	Heuristics	Homology
Pfam/GO	Protein sequences	Ontology based	Pattern based	Ontology
VICMPred	Annotated Protein sequences	Functional information	Machine Learning based	Functional annotation
Interpro/ Prodom	Protein sequence motifs and domains	Protein family and domains	Domain based	Structural and functional annotation
MEME	Protein sequence motifs	Protein motifs	Statistical	Motifs identification and analysis
TopPred	Proteins	Protein solubility conditions	Machine Learning based	Solubility/ insolubility of proteins

(Continued)

TABLE 13.1 (CONTINUED)

Tools/Servers	Interaction/ Association	Output	Comments on Methods	Annotation
Profunc	3D structure	Various functions	Machine Learning based	Functional annotation
STRING/ IntAct	PPI and database	Interactors	Pattern and Mining based	Protein-Protein Interactions
TargetP/ PTarget	Annotated Proteins	Inter and intra cellular signals	Quantitative Analytical	Signal sorting
APAT	Proteins	Myriad features	Markup language based	Miscellaneous
FFPred/ RIGOR	Information based	Structural and functional element information	Structural elements based annotation	Structural and Functional annotation
ConSeq/ ConSurf	Protein sequence and 3D structure	MSA, Phylogenetic tree, various statistical scores, conserved residues on sequence and structure of proteins	Sequence and structural Evolutionary conservation and hyper variation	Structural, Functional, and Evolutionary annotation
MINT/BIND/ BOND/ GeneCards	Protein-protein interactions	Interactors and annotated pathways	Miscellaneous	Protein-Protein Interactions and pathways

ACKNOWLEDGMENTS

Inputs from Dr. G.P.S. Raghava, IIIT Delhi, India, are gratefully appreciated.

REFERENCES

1. Altschul, S.F., Gish, W., Miller, W., Myers, E.W., Lipman, D.J., Basic local alignment search tool. *J. Mol. Biol.*, 1990, **215**(3), 403–10.
2. Altschul, S.F., Amino acid substitution matrices from an information theoretic perspective. *J. Mol. Biol.*, 1991, **219**, 555–65.
3. Altschul, S.F., Wootton, J.C., Gertz, E.M., Agarwala, R., Morgulis, A., Schifer, A.A., Yu Y.K., Protein database searches using compositionally adjusted substitution matrices. *FEBS J.* 2005, **272**(20), 5101–9.
4. Link, A.J., Robison, K., Church, G.M., Comparing the predicted and observed properties of proteins encoded in the genome of Escherichia coli K-12. *Electrophoresis*, 1997, **18**(8), 1259–313.
5. Bailey, T.L., Elkan, C., Fitting a mixture model by expectation maximization to discover motifs in biopolymers, *Proceedings of the Second International Conference on Intelligent Systems for Molecular Biology*, AAAI Press, Menlo Park, California, 1994, 28–36.
6. Pearson, W.R., Rapid and sensitive sequence comparison with FASTP and FASTA. *Methods Enzymol.*, 1990, **183**, 63–98.
7. Worley, K.C., Culpepper, C.A., Wiese, B.A., et al. BEAUTY-X – enhanced BLAST searches for DNA queries. *Bioinformatics*, 1998, **14**(10), 890–91.

8. Hofmann, K., Bucher, P., Falquet, L., Bairoch, A., The PROSITE database, its status in 1999. *Nucleic Acids Res.*, 1999, **27**(1), 215–19.

9. Claros, M.G., Vincens, P., Computational method to predict mitochondrially imported proteins and their targeting sequences. *Eur. J. Biochem.*, 1994, **241**, 779–86.

10. Persico, M., Ceol, A., Gavrila, C., et al. HomoMINT: an inferred human network based on orthology mapping of protein interactions discovered in model organisms. *BMC Bioinf.*, 2005, **6**(Suppl. 4), S21.

11. Shindyalov, I.N., Bourne, P.E., Protein structure alignment by incremental combinatorial extension (CE) of the optimal path. *Protein Eng.*, 1998, **11**(9), 739–47.

12. Holm, L., Kaariainen, S., Rosenstrom, P., et al. Searching protein structure databases with DaliLite v.3. *Bioinformatics*, 2008, **24**, 2780–781.

13. Binkowski, T.A., Freeman, P., Liang, J., pvSOAR: detecting similar surface patterns of pocket and void surfaces of amino acid residues on proteins. *Nucleic Acids Res.*, 2004, **32** (Web Server issue), W555–58.

14. Marcotte, E.M., Pellegrini, M., Ng, H.L., et al. Detecting protein function and protein-protein interactions from genome sequences, *Science*, 1999, **285**(5428), 751–3.

15. Pellegrini, M., Marcotte, E.M., Thompson, M.J., et al. Assigning protein functions by comparative genome analysis: protein phylogenetic profiles. *Proc. Natl. Acad. Sci.*, 1999, **96**(8), 4285–8.

16. Overbeek, R., Fonstein, M., D'Souza, M., et al. The use of gene clusters to infer functional coupling. *Proc. Natl. Acad. Sci.*, 1999, **96**(5), 2896–2901.

17. Jensen, J.L., Gupta, R., Blom, N., et al. Prediction of human protein function from post-translational modifications and localization features. *J. Mol. Biol.*, 2002, **319**, 1257–265.

18. Jensen, L.J., Stærfeldt, H.-H., Brunak, S., Prediction of human protein function according to Gene Ontology categories. *Bioinformatics*, 2003, **19**, 635–42.

19. Saha, S., Raghava, G.P.S., VICMpred: SVM-based method for the prediction of functional proteins of gram-negative bacteria using amino acid patterns and composition. *Genomics Proteomics and Bioinformatics*, 2006, **4**(1), 42–7.

20. Ashkenazy, H., Erez, E., Martz, E., et al. ConSurf: calculating evolutionary conservation in sequence and structure of proteins and nucleic acids. *Nucleic Acids Res.*, 2010, **38** (web server issue), W529–33.

21. Pratap, A., Taliyan, S., Singh, T.R., NMDB: network motif database envisaged and explicated from human disease specific pathways. *Journal of Biological Systems*, 2013, **22**(1), 89–100.

22. Vashisht, I., Mishra, P., Pal, T., Chanumolu, S. Singh, T.R., Chauhan, R.S., Mining NGS transcriptomes for miRNAs and dissecting their role in regulating growth, development, and secondary metabolites production in different organs of a medicinal herb, Picrorhiza kurroa. *Planta*, 2015, **241**(5), 1255–68.

23. Sehgal, M., Gupta, R., Moussa, A., Singh, T.R. An integrative approach for mapping differentially expressed genes and network components using novel parameters to elucidate key regulatory genes in colorectal cancer. *PLoS One*, 2015, **10**(7), e0133901.

24. Shukla, A., Moussa, A., Singh, T.R., DREMECELS: a curated database for base excision and mismatch repair mechanisms associated human malignancies. *PlosOne*, 2015, DOI:10.1371/journal.pone.015703

25. Sehgal, M., Singh, T.R., DR-GAS: A database of functional genetic variants and their phosphorylation states in human DNA repair systems. *DNA Repair*, 2013, **16**(2014), 97–103.

26. Bansal, A., Singh T.R., Chauhan, R.S., A novel miRNA analysis framework to analyze differential biological networks. *Scientific Reports*, 2017, **7**(1), 14604.

27. Gupta, A., Suravajhala, P., Singh, T.R., Challenges in the miRNA research, *IJBRA*, 2013, **9**(6), 576–83.

28. Seal, A., Gupta, A., Mahalaxmi, M., Riju, A., Singh T.R., Arunachalam V., Tools, resources and databases for SNPs and indels in sequences: A review. *IJBRA*, 2013, **10**(3), 264–96.

29. Jensen, L.J., Kuhn, M., Stark, M., et al. STRING 8--a global view on proteins and their functional interactions in 630 organisms. *Nucleic Acids Res.*, 2009, **37**(Database issue), D412–16.

30. Rehban, M., Chalifa-Caspi, V., Prilusky, J., et al. GeneCards: a novel functional genomics compendium with automated data mining and query reformulation support. *Bioinformatics*, 1998, **14**(8), 656–64.

31. Aranda, B., Achuthan, P., Alam-Faruque, Y., et al. The IntAct molecular interaction database in 2010. *Nucleic Acids Res.*, 2010, **38**(Database issue), D525–31.

32. Zanzoni, A., Montecchi-Palazzi, L., Quondam, M., et al. MINT: a molecular INTeraction database, *FEBS Let.*, 2002, **513**(1), 135–40.

33. Bader, G.D., Betel, D., Hoque, C.W., BIND: the biomolecular interaction network database. *Nucleic Acids Res.* 2003, **31**(1), 248–50.

34. Thomas, P. H., Kenneth, R. W., Prediction of protein antigenic determinants from amino acid sequences. *Proc. Nati. Acad. Sci.*, 1981, **78**(6), 3824–28.

35. Welling, G.W., Weijer, W.J., Van Der Zee, R. et al. Prediction of sequential antigenic regions in proteins. *FEBS Let.*, 1985, **188**(2), 215–18.

36. Maksyutov, A.Z., Zagrebelnaya, E.S., ADEPT: a computer program for prediction of protein antigenic determinants. *Comput. Appl. Biosci.* 1993, 9(3), 291–97.

37. Liang, S., Zheng, D., Zhang, C. et al. Prediction of antigenic epitopes on protein surfaces by consensus scoring. *BMC Bioinformatics*, 2009, **10**, 302.

14 Microarray Data Analysis
Methods and Applications

Arvind Kumar Yadav, Ajay Kumar, Ankita Singh,
Anil Kant and Tiratha Raj Singh
Jaypee University of Information Technology, India

14.1 INTRODUCTION

Microarray is a high-throughput technology used in molecular biology and genetics to simultaneously analyze the expression levels of thousands of genes or the presence of single nucleotide polymorphisms (SNPs) in a single experiment [1]. It consists of a small glass slide or chip that is spotted with thousands of small, known DNA or RNA sequences, called probes, which are complementary to the target DNA or RNA molecules. In typical microarray experiment, fluorescently labeled DNA or RNA molecules are hybridized to the probes on the microarray, allowing researches to measure the expression level of thousands of genes or the presence of SNPs in a single experiment [2]. The intensity of the fluorescence signal is used to determine the relative abundance of the target molecules. Microarray has many applications, including gene expression profiling, SNP genotyping, and comparative genomics hybridization. They have been used in research to identify disease biomarkers, discover new drug targets, and understand the molecular basis of disease.

The successful application of microarray for the analysis of gene expression came into consideration almost two decades back [3]. Since then, almost all areas of biological research have utilized the microarray technique for expression profiling [4]. Alternative microarray-based approaches have also been developed for application other than transcription analysis, including genotyping, DNA mapping, protein binding, and epigenetic investigations [5]. Due to the high throughput capabilities of microarray technology, biological research has been greatly expanded from the level of single genes to the transcriptome. Microarray is a reliable tool for assessing the transcriptome, according to earlier research [6]. Microarrays are still widely used to measure gene expression, even though RNA-Seq has become more common in recent years [7–9]. Microarray has advantages for clinical investigations, which may require a large number of samples and are more affordable than RNA-Seq.

This chapter describes about the microarray experiment design, important methods, tools, and software available for microarray data analysis. Various types of data are generated during the time of analysis in every step. Various tools and software for microarray data analysis have been summarized. The microarray analysis has various applications in diverse biological fields to find out a significant insight for biological problems. Therefore, we also summarized most frequent and important applications of microarray data analysis.

DOI: 10.1201/9781003331247-16

14.2 MICROARRAY TECHNOLOGY

Microarray technology is an effective tool to analyze the expression of thousands of genes in tissues, organs, or cells, simultaneously. With the help of this technology, thousands of genes' transcript expression levels can be monitored globally in a single experiment. Microarray experiments can be used for categorization studies or to look at changes in gene expression between several groups of people [10]. On a solid glass slide surface known as a microarray chip, DNA molecules have been fixed in an organized pattern at certain locations. A microarray can be used to measure gene expression, and the main steps include sample preparation and labeling, hybridization, cleaning and washing, scanning and image processing. Fluorophores, which fluoresce as green (Cy3) and red (Cy5), are used to co-synthesize co-hybridized samples of mRNA in order to pinpoint the genes that are more or less, or equally, expressed in the two samples. While a laser scanner scans the microarray, fluorophores are ignited. The genes with varying degrees of expression in each sample can then be found using spot colors (Figure 14.1) [11].

At least five different components are necessary when we used microarrays. These components are the tool for creating microarrays through the in-situ production of nucleic acids; a scanner to read the chips; a fluidic system for hybridization to target DNA; chip itself with its distinctive surface; and sophisticated software or applications to analyze and evaluate the findings [12]. The various systems exhibit wildly different levels of dependability and reproducibility are incompatible with one another. Therefore, the expert scientist is needed who can set up the systems, command them, and even run them on a regular basis. The accuracy of the arraying, which has lately been realized by mask less in situ synthesis of or bubble jet technology oligonucleotides, still greatly influences the value of microarray research [13].

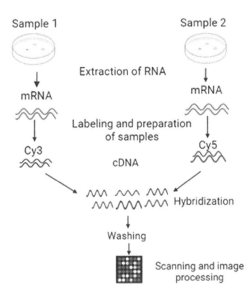

FIGURE 14.1 Generalized depiction of use of microarray for gene expression analysis.

The choice of the nucleic acids that are attached to the microarray surface, as well as the preparation of the probe and target, all affect the results of microarray research. These variables affect the uniformity of the interface and linking chemistries on the chip, the microarray testing, overexposure and background concerns in image analysis, and more [14]. With the exception of low abundant mRNAs, quantitative variations in transcription activity can now be reproducibly in the range of twofold or less. This is due to advances in software and scanner technology [15]. A technique called massively parallel signature sequencing (MPSS) is fluidic microarrays that analyzes millions of cDNA fragments. Because around 250,000 micro-beads are processed all at once, even rare mRNAs can be assessed without knowing their sequence. To add decoder probes for decoding the DNA signatures, many restriction type II cleavage cycles, hybridization reactions and ligation procedures are used [16]. By encoding microbeads with a particular dye signature, several microbeads in a high-density fiber array can be analyzed simultaneously using an imaging fluorescence system [17]. The technology (scanometric) depends on a silver reduction promoted by gold nanoparticles, which they claim is a hundred times more sensitive than fluorescence detection [18]. Large-scale analyses of peptides and proteins have also been performed using microarrays [19]. New protein microarrays can take the role of the yeast 2-hybrid method for analyzing protein-protein interactions in vitro, finding protein kinase substrates, and investigating relationships among proteins and low-molecular-weight molecules [20]. In a single, self-assembling hybridization step, protein microarrays have been created from DNA microarrays using single-stranded nucleic acids connected to proteins [21]. It is anticipated that the technique will speed up research and advance understanding in areas including route engineering, toxicological investigation of food components, and risk assessment of transgenic plants.

14.3   METHODS FOR MICROARRAY DATA ANALYSIS

Large volumes of data are made available to the scientific community through microarray research. Significant information and knowledge that are hidden in these data may be brought forward using systematic approach experimentation and data analysis while minimizing the errors. As a result, techniques that can handle and explore big data volumes are required. For the analysis of massive data sets, the fields of data mining and machine learning offer a multitude of approaches and tools [22, 23]. The process for microarray data acquisition and analysis is shown in Figure 14.2.

A sample containing an intricate mixture of labeled biomolecules that can bind to the probes, an array on which these probes are immobilized at predetermined locations, a detector that can measure the spatially resolved distribution of label after it has bound to the array, and a microarray experiment are the four main components [24]. With arrays, this is made possible by the high sequence-specificity of the hybridization process between complementary DNA strands. The probes are selected such that they attach to certain sample molecules. Usually, a glass slide or nylon membrane serves as the array. The sample molecules may be marked by the addition of fluorescent dyes like phycoerythrin, Cy3, or Cy5. The signal strength at the appropriate probe locations may be used to quantify the quantity of various sample

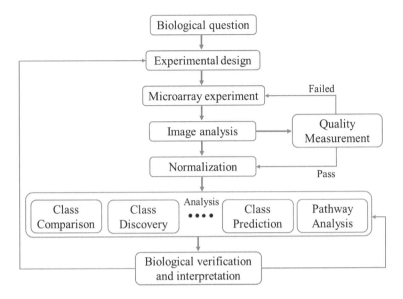

FIGURE 14.2   Microarray data analysis process.

molecule species after the array has been exposed to the sample. A spotted array approach has been developed by combining the simultaneous hybridization of two samples tagged with distinct fluorescent dyes, Detection is performed at the respective wavelengths of these dyes, allowing for a direct comparison [25].

In image quantification, each probe location is represented by a large number of pixels since the detector scans the intensity pictures at a high spatial resolution. The appropriate pixels must be located (segmented) and the intensities must be summed together in order to get a single overall intensity value for each probe (quantification). Additional auxiliary values, such as a spot quality measure or an estimate of the seeming unspecific "local background" intensity, may be computed in addition to the total probe intensity. In the software packages that are now available, several segmentation and quantification techniques are used. They vary from one another in terms of how resilient they are to anomalies and how much they are in demand. Different sorts of abnormalities may arise in various applications of microarray technology, and a segmentation or quantification technique that works well on one platform might not be appropriate on another. For instance, the characteristics of the support (such as glass or nylon), the probe delivery mechanism (such as quill-pen type, pin and ring systems, ink jetting), and the detecting technique all have an impact on the variance of spot shapes and locations. Additionally, compared to mass-produced arrays, home-made arrays might be expected to have greater differences in the spot placing from array to array. Yang et al. presented on an evaluation of image analysis techniques for spotted cDNA arrays [26].

The identification of differentially expressed genes in the comparison of various cell or tissue sample types is one of the fundamental aims of microarray gene expression data analysis. A sufficient number of experimental replications must be used to establish statistical inference in order to control the biological and experimental variability of the measurements. A relevant statistical test may be run on each gene to determine whether genes are differentially expressed in relation to a particular biological process [29]. The biological question and the kind of the available experimental data both influence the test statistic selection. In the most straightforward scenario, one looks for genes whose transcript quantity differs between two situations. One can search for genes whose abundance is linked to multiple factor levels of one or more sample attributes in more complicated circumstances. On the basis of patient survival data, one may also take into account continuous-valued sample characteristics and search for genes that exhibit non-zero coefficients in a regression model, such as a linear model or a Cox proportional hazards model [27]. Different statistical tests may place stronger or weaker restrictions on the replicate measurement distributions. Important considerations include whether or not the distributions are symmetric, how closely or far they resemble normal distributions, and how they compare to other genes or situations [28].

14.4 MICROARRAY DATA ANALYSIS TOOLS AND SOFTWARE

A microarray experiment produces a significant amount of data, first in the form of image files that are later evaluated to provide useful results. To acquire accurate expression levels for each gene, the entire procedure entails a number of processes as well as a variety of software and instruments. Once you have the data, the next logical step is to extract the biological information from it. Many pieces of software have been created to provide an answer. In-depth descriptions of key software and tools for the analysis of microarray data are provided in this section Table 14.1 [29].

14.5 APPLICATIONS OF MICROARRAY ANALYSIS

Microarray analysis is a technique used to study the expression levels of thousands of genes simultaneously. This technique has numerous applications in various fields, including:

- *Gene expression analysis:* Microarray analysis can be used to identify genes that are up- or down-regulated in response to different stimuli or in different disease states. This can provide insight into the molecular mechanisms underlying these processes [41].
- *Disease diagnosis:* Microarray analysis can be used to identify gene expression signatures that are associated with specific diseases, allowing for more accurate diagnosis and personalized treatment [42].
- *Drug discovery:* Microarray analysis can be used to identify potential drug targets by identifying genes that are differentially expressed in disease states compared to healthy controls [43].
- *Toxicology:* Microarray analysis can be used to identify genes that are differentially expressed in response to environmental toxins or drugs, providing insight into their mechanisms of action and potential toxicity [7].

TABLE 14.1
List of Tools and Software for Microarray Data Analysis

Tools/Software	Description	URL	Reference
RMA Express	RMA express software, which works with both Windows and Linux operating systems, implements the RMA normalization method. The program offers a visual user interface with options to choose the Affymetrix raw data files, conduct normalization, and quantify the expression values.	http://rmaexpress.bmbolstad.com/	[30]
dCHIP	DNA-Chip Analyzer (dCHIP) uses a model-based expression analysis for Affymetrix gene expression arrays. Both raw and processed Affymetrix data may be processed by the program.	www.dchip.org	[31]
SNOMAD	For two-channel and single-channel studies, SNOMAD, a web-based program, offers a variety of normalization choices. The right normalization procedures must be chosen and the data must be uploaded in the correct format. The options include removing the background signal, global and local mean normalization across a microarray surface, log transformation, calculating the mean log intensity and log ratio local mean normalization across element signal intensity, and local variance correction across element signal intensity.	http://pevsnerlab.kennedykrieger.org/snomad.php	[32]
TM4	The TM4 toolkit consists of 4 applications: Multiexperiment Viewer, Microarray Data Manager (MADAM), TIGR Spotfinder, and Microarray Data Analysis System (MIDAS) (MeV). Although it may be modified for Affymetrix arrays, this program was primarily created for cDNA chips. They come together to provide an entire process for analyzing microarray data.	https://www.danatm4.com/products/tau-software/	[33]
GenMAPP	Gene expression and other genomic information may be shown on maps that depict biological pathways and gene clusters using the computer program GenMAPP. Incorporating a color-code system based on user-defined criteria, it overlays gene expression data on the paths.	http://www.genmapp.org/	[34]
Genespring	The first commercially accessible tool for analyzing microarray data was Genespring from Agilent. It includes a lot of tools for analyzing microarray data.	https://www.agilent.com/en/product/software-informatics/genomics-software-informatics/gene-expression/genespring	[35]

(Continued)

TABLE 14.1 (CONTINUED)

Tools/Software	Description	URL	Reference
Partek	The Partek Genomics Suite is a collection of software modules for the analysis of gene expression data as well as a number of other types of data, including alternative splicing, copy number, SNP association, and next-generation sequencing.	https://www.partek.com/partek-genomics-suite/	[36]
Genowiz	A comprehensive tool for gene expression analysis, Genowiz from Ocimumbio Solutions is compatible with a wide range of data formats and has a ton of features for diverse analyses.	https://ocimumbio.com/genowiz/	[37, 38]
GenomatixSuite	Software called GenomatixSuite from Genomatix is used to examine the biological significance of the genes of interest discovered by microarray analysis. ElDorado, Gene2Promoter, GEMS Launcher, MatInspector, MatBase, and BiblioSphere are included in the package. The program builds interaction maps between the relevant genes by mining the body of literature.	https://www.genomatix.de/solutions/genomatix-software-suite.html	[39]
Pathway Studio	Ariadne Genomics' Pathway Studio is a program that uses the list of genes from a microarray experiment to visualize and analyze biological pathways, gene regulation networks, and protein interaction maps. It includes a comprehensive database with an overview of all the data in PubMed, with an emphasis on pathways and cell-signaling networks. As a component of Pathway Studio, MedScan aids in the mining of recent literature and the creation of pathways pertaining to the research topic, such as a disease, phenotype, or physiological process.	http://www.ariadnegenomics.com/products	[40]

- *Agricultural research:* Microarray analysis can be used to identify genes involved in crop growth and development, as well as those responsible for resistance to pests and diseases [44].
- *Forensic science:* Microarray analysis can be used to identify genetic markers for human identification, paternity testing, and the detection of genetic disorders [45].
- *Evolutionary biology:* Microarray analysis can be used to compare gene expression profiles between different species or populations, providing insight into the evolution of gene regulation [46].

14.6 CONCLUSION

A popular tool in molecular biology research today is the microarray. To assess gene expression is one of their primary applications. Analyzing gene expression data from microarrays is fundamentally more difficult compared to earlier expression measurement methods like Northern blotting because of the enormous volumes of data they generate. Recent findings indicate that cutting-edge next-generation (NGS) technology may shortly supplant microarrays in a variety of applications. Microarrays are still the method of choice for many researches where the flexibility of NGS may not be necessary, even though NGS seems more reasonable and inexpensive. Applications for the analysis of microarray data are accessible in numerous numbers of specialized databases and software/tools. The microarray technology has various biological and clinical applications. This chapter provides an overview about the microarray experiment, data type tools and software for data analysis, and potential application of microarray in various fields.

REFERENCES

[1] K. Kaliyappan, M. Palanisamy, R. Govindarajan, J. Duraiyan, Microarray and its applications, *Journal of Pharmacy and Bioallied Sciences*. 4 (2012). https://doi.org/10.4103/0975-7406.100283

[2] R. Jaksik, M. Iwanaszko, J. Rzeszowska-Wolny, M. Kimmel, Microarray experiments and factors which affect their reliability, *Biology Direct*. 10 (2015) 46. https://doi.org/10.1186/s13062-015-0077-2

[3] C. Robert, Microarray analysis of gene expression during early development: a cautionary overview, *Reproduction*. 140 (2010) 787–801. https://doi.org/10.1530/REP-10-0191

[4] A.L. Tarca, R. Romero, S. Draghici, Analysis of microarray experiments of gene expression profiling, *American Journal of Obstetrics and Gynecology*. 195 (2006) 373–388. https://doi.org/10.1016/j.ajog.2006.07.001

[5] J.D. Hoheisel, Microarray technology: beyond transcript profiling and genotype analysis, *Nature Reviews Genetics*. 7 (2006) 200–210. https://doi.org/10.1038/nrg1809

[6] S. Zhao, W.-P. Fung-Leung, A. Bittner, K. Ngo, X. Liu, Comparison of RNA-Seq and microarray in transcriptome profiling of activated T cells, *PLoS One*. 9 (2014) e78644. https://doi.org/10.1371/journal.pone.0078644

[7] M.S. Rao, T.R. Van Vleet, R. Ciurlionis, W.R. Buck, S.W. Mittelstadt, E.A.G. Blomme, M.J. Liguori, Comparison of RNA-Seq and Microarray Gene Expression Platforms for the Toxicogenomic Evaluation of Liver From Short-Term Rat Toxicity Studies, *Frontiers in Genetics*. 9 (2019). https://doi.org/10.3389/fgene.2018.00636 (accessed August 22, 2022).

[8] J.H. Malone, B. Oliver, Microarrays, deep sequencing and the true measure of the transcriptome, *BMC Biology*. 9 (2011) 34. https://doi.org/10.1186/1741-7007-9-34

[9] T.R. Singh, B. Vannier, A. Moussa, *Extraction of Differentially Expressed Genes in Microarray Data*, (2015) 335–346. https://doi.org/10.1002/9781119078845.ch18

[10] L.D. Miller, P.M. Long, L. Wong, S. Mukherjee, L.M. McShane, E.T. Liu, Optimal gene expression analysis by microarrays, *Cancer Cell*. 2 (2002). https://doi.org/10.1016/S1535-6108(02)00181-2

[11] A.M. Kbir, F. Rafii, B.D. Rossi Hassani, M. Ait Kbir, Microarray Data Integration To Explore The Wealth Of Sources Generated By Modern Molecular Biology, 2015.

[12] D.H. Blohm, A. Guiseppi-Elie, New developments in microarray technology, *Current Opinion in Biotechnology*. 12 (2001). https://doi.org/10.1016/S0958-1669(00)00175-0

[13] T. Okamoto, T. Suzuki, N. Yamamoto, Microarray fabrication with covalent attachment of DNA using Bubble Jet technology, *Nature Biotechnology*. 18 (2000). https://doi.org/10.1038/74507

[14] J. Schuchhardt, D. Beule, A. Malik, E. Wolski, H. Eickhoff, H. Lehrach, H. Herzel, Normalization strategies for cDNA microarrays, *Nucleic Acids Research*. 28 (2000). https://doi.org/10.1093/nar/28.10.e47

[15] E.S. Lander, Array of hope, *Nature Genetics*. 21 (1999). https://doi.org/10.1038/4427

[16] S. Brenner, M. Johnson, J. Bridgham, G. Golda, D.H. Lloyd, D. Johnson, S. Luo, S. McCurdy, M. Foy, M. Ewan, R. Roth, D. George, S. Eletr, G. Albrecht, E. Vermaas, S.R. Williams, K. Moon, T. Burcham, M. Pallas, R.B. DuBridge, J. Kirchner, K. Fearon, J.I. Mao, K. Corcoran, Gene expression analysis by massively parallel signature sequencing (MPSS) on microbead arrays, *Nature Biotechnology*. 18 (2000). https://doi.org/10.1038/76469

[17] F.J. Steemers, J.A. Ferguson, D.R. Walt, Screening unlabeled DNA targets with randomly ordered fiber-optic gene arrays, *Nature Biotechnology*. 18 (2000). https://doi.org/10.1038/72006

[18] T.A. Taton, C.A. Mirkin, R.L. Letsinger, Scanometric DNA array detection with nanoparticle probes, *Science*. 289 (2000). https://doi.org/10.1126/science.289.5485.1757

[19] B. Hassan, S. Hamzaoui, S. Bouzergane, A. Moussa, Analysis of mass spectrometry data: significance analysis of microarrays for SELDI-MS data in proteomics, *International Journal for Computational Biology*. 4 (2015). https://doi.org/10.34040/IJCB.4.1.2015.46

[20] G. MacBeath, S.L. Schreiber, Printing proteins as microarrays for high-throughput function determination, *Science*. 289 (2000). https://doi.org/10.1126/science.289.5485.1760

[21] C.M. Niemeyer, L. Boldt, B. Ceyhan, D. Blohm, DNA-directed immobilization: efficient, reversible, and site-selective surface binding of proteins by means of covalent DNA-streptavidin conjugates, *Analytical Biochemistry*. 268 (1999). https://doi.org/10.1006/abio.1998.3017

[22] R. Shukla, A.K. Yadav, T.R. Singh, Application of deep learning in biological big data analysis, *Large-Scale Data Streaming, Processing, and Blockchain Security*. (2021) 117–148. https://doi.org/10.4018/978-1-7998-3444-1.ch006

[23] R. Shukla, A.K. Yadav, W.O. Sote, M.C. Junior, T.R. Singh, Chapter 25 – Systems biology and big data analytics, in: D.B. Singh, R.K. Pathak (Eds.), *Bioinformatics*, Academic Press, 2022: pp. 425–442. https://doi.org/10.1016/B978-0-323-89775-4.00005-5

[24] S. Kotoulas, R. Siebes, The chipping forecast. Special supplement to Nature Genetics Vol 21, in: *3rd Intl. IEEE Workshop on Collaborative Service-Oriented P2P Information Systems (COPS Workshop at WETICE07)*, 1999.

[25] D.J. Duggan, M. Bittner, Y. Chen, P. Meltzer, J.M. Trent, Expression profiling using cDNA microarrays, *Nature Genetics*. 21 (1999) 10–14. https://doi.org/10.1038/4434

[26] Y.H. Yang, M.J. Buckley, S. Dudoit, T.P. Speed, Comparison of methods for image analysis on cDNA microarray data, *Journal of Computational and Graphical Statistics*. 11 (2002) 108–136. https://doi.org/10.1198/106186002317375640

[27] J.M. Claverie, Computational methods for the identification of differential and coordinated gene expression, *Human Molecular Genetics*. 8 (1999) 1821–1832. https://doi.org/10.1093/hmg/8.10.1821

[28] W.S. Cleveland, E. Grosse, W.M. Shyu, Local Regression Models, in: Statistical Models in S, Routledge, 1992.

[29] J.P. Mehta, S. Rani, Software and Tools for Microarray Data Analysis, in: L. O'Driscoll (Ed.), *Gene Expression Profiling: Methods and Protocols*, Humana Press, Totowa, NJ, 2011: pp. 41–53. https://doi.org/10.1007/978-1-61779-289-2_4

[30] B.M. Bolstad, R.A. Irizarry, M. Åstrand, T.P. Speed, A comparison of normalization methods for high density oligonucleotide array data based on variance and bias, *Bioinformatics (Oxford, England)*. 19 (2003) 185–193. https://doi.org/10.1093/bioinformatics/19.2.185

[31] C. Li, W.H. Wong, DNA-Chip Analyzer (dChip), in: G. Parmigiani, E.S. Garrett, R.A. Irizarry, S.L. Zeger (Eds.), *The Analysis of Gene Expression Data: Methods and Software*, Springer, New York, NY, 2003: pp. 120–141. https://doi.org/10.1007/0-387-21679-0_5

[32] C. Colantuoni, G. Henry, S. Zeger, J. Pevsner, SNOMAD (Standardization and Normalization of MicroArray Data): Web-accessible gene expression data analysis, *Bioinformatics (Oxford, England)*. 18 (2002) 1540–1541. https://doi.org/10.1093/bioinformatics/18.11.1540

[33] A.I. Saeed, Vasily Sharov, Joseph Andrew White, J. Li, W. Liang, Nirmal Bhagabati, J. Braisted, Maria I. Klapa, T. Currier, M. Thiagarajan, et al. TM4: a free, open-source system for microarray data management and analysis, *BioTechniques*. 34 (2003). https://doi.org/10.2144/03342mt01

[34] S.W. Doniger, N. Salomonis, K.D. Dahlquist, K. Vranizan, S.C. Lawlor, B.R. Conklin, MAPPFinder: using Gene Ontology and GenMAPP to create a global gene-expression profile from microarray data, *Genome Biology*. 4 (2003) 1–12. https://doi.org/10.1186/gb-2003-4-1-r7

[35] O. Gevaert, L.A. Mitchell, A.S. Achrol, J. Xu, S. Echegaray, G.K. Steinberg, S.H. Cheshier, S. Napel, G. Zaharchuk, S.K. Plevritis, Glioblastoma multiforme: exploratory radiogenomic analysis by using quantitative image features, *Radiology*. 273 (2014) 168. https://doi.org/10.1148/radiol.14131731

[36] Tom Downey, Analysis of a multifactor microarray study using Partek genomics solution, *Methods in Enzymology*. 411 (2006). https://doi.org/10.1016/S0076-6879(06)11013-7

[37] Ocimum Biosolution, (n.d.). https://ocimumbio.com/genowiz/ (accessed August 10, 2022).

[38] G6G Directory of Omics and Intelligent Software - Genowiz, (n.d.). https://www.g6g-softwaredirectory.com/bio/genomics/gene-expression/20074R-Ocimum-Biosolutions-Genowiz.php (accessed August 10, 2022).

[39] A. Nazarian, S.A. Gezan, GenoMatrix: a software package for pedigree-based and genomic prediction analyses on complex traits, *Journal of Heredity*. 107 (2016) 372–379. https://doi.org/10.1093/jhered/esw020

[40] Alexander Nikitin, Sergei Egorov, Nikolai Daraselia, Ilya Mazo, Pathway studio--the analysis and navigation of molecular networks, *Bioinformatics (Oxford, England)*. 19 (2003). https://doi.org/10.1093/bioinformatics/btg290

[41] Y. Shen, R. Zhang, L. Xu, Q. Wan, J. Zhu, J. Gu, Z. Huang, W. Ma, M. Shen, F. Ding, H. Sun, Microarray analysis of gene expression provides new insights into denervation-induced skeletal muscle atrophy, *Frontiers in Physiology*. 10 (2019) 1298. https://doi.org/10.3389/fphys.2019.01298

[42] X. Yu, N. Schneiderhan-Marra, T.O. Joos, Protein Microarrays for Personalized Medicine, *Clinical Chemistry*. 56 (2010) 376–387. https://doi.org/10.1373/clinchem.2009.137158

[43] M.V. Chengalvala, V.M. Chennathukuzhi, D.S. Johnston, P.E. Stevis, G.S. Kopf, Gene expression profiling and its practice in drug development, *Current Genomics*. 8 (2007) 262–270.

[44] N.J. Atkinson, C.J. Lilley, P.E. Urwin, Identification of genes involved in the response of arabidopsis to simultaneous biotic and abiotic stresses1[C][W][OPEN], *Plant Physiology*. 162 (2013) 2028–2041. https://doi.org/10.1104/pp.113.222372

[45] G.O. Urtiaga, W.B. Domingues, E.R. Komninou, A.W.S. Martins, E.B. Blödorn, E.N. Dellagostin, R. S. dos Woloski, L.S. Pinto, C.B. Brum, L. Tovo-Rodrigues, V.F. Campos, DNA microarray for forensic intelligence purposes: high-density SNP profiles obtained directly from casework-like samples with and without a DNA purification step, *Forensic Science International*. 332 (2022) 111181. https://doi.org/10.1016/j.forsciint.2022.111181

[46] G. Gibson, Microarrays in ecology and evolution: a preview, *Molecular Ecology*. 11 (2002) 17–24. https://doi.org/10.1046/j.0962-1083.2001.01425.x

15 Tools and Techniques in Structural Bioinformatics

Alex Gutterres Taranto

Universidade Federal de São João del Rei, Brazil

Moacyr Comar Junior

Universidade Federal de Uberlândia, Brazil

15.1 RELATIONSHIP WEBSITES

The first step in this area is known as "Relationship Websites". These sites are very useful to search for new software, discussion lists, congress, tutorials, and principally to search for jobs. Naturally, isolated initiatives have emerged all the time, and all of them are welcome. However, we have to select some of them due to limitations of the chapter.

Among them, Computational Chemistry List (CCL – http://www.ccl.net/) since 1991 has contributed to the growth of the area with an independent electronic forum (1). Likely, the International Society for Computational Biology (ISCB) is an international nonprofit organization. The ISCB provides meetings, publications, and reports on methods and tools and promotes support of scientific endeavors to benefit society at large (https://www.iscb.org/index.php).

Following, it is important to introduce the SIB Swiss Institute of Bioinformatics (2). SIB is an internationally recognized nonprofit organization, dedicated to biological and biomedical data science. It contains a large number of online software (https://www.expasy.org/), with focus in Bioinformatics. The SwissDrugDesign tools (https://www.expasy.org/resources/swissdrugdesign), such as Swiss-Model, SwissDock, Swiss ADME, SwissSimilarity, SwissBioisostere, and SwissTargetPrediction, cover the main methods in drug design. In addition, Click2Drug (https://www.click2drug.org/) contains a comprehensive list of computer-aided drug design (CADD) software, databases, and web services, covering the whole drug design pipeline.

An important organization is the European Bioinformatics Institute (EBI), which is part of European Molecular Biology Laboratory (EMBL – https://www.ebi.ac.uk/), focused on research and services in bioinformatics. Beyond being an important platform to learn bioinformatics and molecular biology, this supports the platform known as ChEMBL (3), which is a manually curated database of bioactive molecules with drug-like properties. Details about ChEMBL will be described in the databases section.

Another initiative to improve the area has come from Dr. B. Villoutreix. The vls3d website (https://www.vls3d.com/index.php) (4) is a huge directory of tools and databases collected over 20 years, counting with, approximately, 500 links. It is noteworthy that these drug discovery tools are free. Many thanks to Dr. Villoutreix for his contribution to CADD and bioinformatics area. Finally, the group coordinated by Prof. A. G. Taranto has released a set of software, such as Molecular Architect (MolAr) (5), Run_mopac, Mini-docking, and Octopus (6), which are free software with simple and intuitive interfaces, decreasing the human intervention, and very useful for beginners (https://www.drugdiscovery.com.br/).

15.2   DATABASES

The second step to perform structural biological studies is the knowledge of the main chemical and biological databases. Even though a formal classification has not been described, the Swiss Institute of Bioinformatics has classified them as Chemical databases, Databases handling, Protein-ligand complexes databases, Target databases, and Pathway databases. To avoid an extensive description of databases, the Chemical databases and Protein-ligand complexes databases will be highlighted due importance in the next steps of Structural Bioinformatics.

Chemical databases, in general, refer to small molecules, which the compounds can be obtained by downloading them in a text format file. This text format file can be in Protein Data Bank (pdb), mol2, Simplified Molecular Input Line Entry System (smiles), and structure-data file format (sdf), for instance, and can be open in any editor software. However, to visualize the structures, a specific software, such as Pymol (available at http://www.pymol.org/pymol), is necessary. It is noteworthy that these format files can be converted to each other by Open Babel software (7), when necessary. Table 15.1 summarizes the most used chemical database.

It is noteworthy that some structures have to be curated before use in simulations. Roughly speaking, except Zinc15, which the molecules are ready to be used, in general, the molecules from the other databases need to be checked if they contain counter ions in their structures, for instance. In addition, it is necessary to include the hydrogens according to the pH of the environment, which can generate tautomer forms. Moreover, molecular mechanics or semi-empirical methods can be used to refine the molecules. Thus, this refinement can be carried out by Run_mopac. Run_mopac (5) which is a Python software developed to refine a set of ligands using the semi-empirical Parametric Method 7 (PM7) (11).

On the other hand, Protein-ligand complexes databases are composed, principally, by Protein Data Bank (PDB: https://www.rcsb.org/) (12) and BindigDB (https://www.bindingdb.org/rwd/bind/index.jsp). PDB is a database of experimentally determined structures of proteins, nucleic acids, and complex assemblies obtained by X-ray diffraction, nuclear magnetic resonance (NMR), and electronic microscopy. During the elaboration of this chapter, PDB has 196,979 retrieved experimental structures. In addition, it has 1,000,361 computed structure models (CSM). All entries in the PDB are composed of four and three alphanumeric codes, for macromolecules and ligands, respectively. In addition, several tools have been developed which require a dedication chapter for it.

BindigDB aims to provide experimental data on the noncovalent association of molecules in solution, focusing on biomolecular systems. This database is very

TABLE 15.1
Select Chemical Database Used in CADD

Name	Description	Link
Zinc15 (8)	A free database of commercially available compounds for virtual screening. ZINC contains over 230 million purchasable compounds in ready-to-doc.	https://zinc15.docking.org/
ChEMBL (3)	A manually curated database of bioactive molecules with drug-like properties. It brings together chemical, bioactivity, and genomic data to aid the translation of genomic information into effective new drugs.	https://www.ebi.ac.uk/chembl/
DrugBank (9)	A comprehensive, free-to-access, online database containing information on drugs and drug targets.	https://go.drugbank.com/about
PubChem (10)	The world's largest collection of freely accessible chemical information.	https://pubchem.ncbi.nlm.nih.gov/
DUD-E (10)	DUD-E is designed to help benchmark molecular docking programs by providing challenging decoys.	http://dude.docking.org/
NuBBE$_{DB}$ (10)	Brazilian natural products were created as the first natural product library from Brazilian biodiversity.	https://nubbe.iq.unesp.br/portal/nubbe-search.html
LUDe (LIDEB's Useful Decoys)	A web app that generates, from a set of active compounds, decoys (putative inactive compounds).	https://github.com/Capigol/LUDe_v1

useful to find active compounds for a specific molecular target, evaluate docking methods, and in the development of predictive Quantitative Structure Activity Relationship (QSAR) models (13).

15.3 TERTIARY STRUCTURE PREDICTION

The release of amino acid sequence motivates the tertiary structure prediction of proteins which are not retrieved into PDB. Of course, this prediction can be performed by experimental methods. However, these processes are expensive and are time-consuming. Moreover, in general, experimental methods have had little success in determining the structure of membrane proteins, due to experimental limitations. Thus, computational methods have been highlighted in this scenario. As the protein folding is an open question, two different approaches have been used by bioinformatics: (a) structure-based template methods (threading and modeling comparative and (b) structure-independent methods free of template (*ab initio* or *de novo*) (14). It is noteworthy that the term *ab initio* used in this section has nothing to do with *ab initio* used by quantum chemistry.

The structure-based template methods assume that the tertiary structure and function of a protein have not changed during the evolution process. Two different approaches have been highlighted in this field. The first one, called comparative or homology modeling, predicts the tertiary structure of the protein of interest (denoted by target or model) using the 3D structure of another similar protein (denoted by template). Three aspects have to be considered: (i) the limit of identity alignment between target and template cannot be less than 25% (15); (ii) it is not essential, however better results can be reached if both target and template belong to the same family; (iii) the experimentally resolved structures has to have high quality (resolution ≤ 2 Å, R factor < 20%) as much as possible, and with the number of amino acids close to each other; (iv) the template structure has already been resolved with its substrate (ligand) for further docking studies, for instance. Of course, not all these considerations can be obtained in the everyday work. Thus, it is possible to build a target protein using more than one template, achieving more robust results (16). Two software packages have been highlighted: Swiss-model (17) (https://swissmodel. expasy.org/) and MODELLER (18), both with different approaches.

The second structure-based template method, known as protein threading or fold recognition, is a method with the same principle as comparative modeling; evolutionarily related proteins tend to present a conserved three-dimensional structure (19). Consequently, target and template share the same fold, but do not have homologous proteins with known structure. This method has used the structures retrieved in the PDB as well. Currently, as the PDB has approximately 200,000 structures, it is difficult not to find a similar structure template with the target protein. Protein Homology/analogY Recognition Engine 2.0 (Pyre2) (20) and the Iterative Threading ASSEmbly Refinement (I-TASSER) (21) software are examples of these methods. These are running on the web to predict and analyze protein structures.

In contrast, in *ab initio* methods (22), which are template-free, two different approaches have been highlighted: molecular dynamics simulations (MD) (23) and deep learning (DL) (24). The first approach, MD, has performed long timescales simulations, which are required for folding processes, around 500 ns, resulting in high computational cost. This computational cost can be overcome by coarse models and implicit solvent. Details about MD simulations methods will be discussed in the further section of this chapter. In contrast, DL methods have been used in the last few years. Details about DL methods are beyond the scope of this chapter. In this field, RaptorX (http://raptorx.uchicago.edu/) have been highlighted to win the Critical Assessment of Protein Structure Prediction (CASP) 12 and 13 competition (25). CASP is a worldwide competition for tertiary prediction of protein each two years since 1994. CASP provides research groups with an opportunity to objectively test their structure prediction methods and delivers an independent assessment of the state of the art in protein structure modeling to the research community and software users. RaptorX (26) is available as a web server developed and standalone program (27).

Finally, independent of the approach used to predict the protein folding, the target models have to be evaluated by two different methods at least. The most popular method is the Ramachandran plot (28), which is possible to visualize the stereochemical quality of the constructed model. Ramachandran plot is implemented into the Procheck software (29), available freely. In addition, the web server software called Verify3D (30) has performed protein evaluation, in which each residue is assigned a structural class based on its location and environment (alpha, beta, loop, polar, nonpolar, etc.). A collection of good structures is used as a reference to obtain a score for each of the 20 amino acids in this structural class. The scores of a sliding 21-residue window (from −10 to +10) are added and plotted for individual residues.

Other methods are Qualitative Model Energy ANalysis (QMEAN) (31) and Atomic Non-Local Environment Assessment (ANOLEA) (32). In addition, several evaluation methods can be found in the Protein Structure Evaluation Suite and Server (PROSESS) (33).

In conclusion, the structures template methods have been applied rather than free-of-template methods. However, it does not mean that good results can be achieved by free-of-templates methods. Actually, more than one model has to be built and evaluated. Noteworthy that for further docking and virtual screening studies, the model has to include the crystallographic ligand. It can be obtained by a simple transfer of the atomic coordinate to the template to the model. Next, the built model can be refined by molecular mechanics methods using steepest descent following conjugate gradient. Chimera (34) is a free software able to perform this calculation, for instance.

15.4 DOCKING, VIRTUAL SCREENING AND VIRTUAL HIGH-THROUGHPUT SCREENING

Molecular docking is the most widely used tool in structure-based drug design. It was described for the first time by Ferrin and collaborators in 1982 (35). In other words, considering biochemistry experimental methods, molecular docking has still continued its improvement. In the beginning of its release, docking simulations were performed for one or few molecules. However, due to the advance of computational resources, it can be performed for a chemical library with hundreds of molecules. Thus, molecular docking has become virtual screening (VS) (36). Similarly, an experimental approach using robotics has performed screening of millions of compounds quickly to recognize active compounds. This experimental method is known as High-throughput Screening (HTS) (37). In this context, drug designers have gotten this term to refer to their in silico studies involving a huge chemical library. Hence, the term HTS was modified for virtual High-throughput Screening (vHTS). In addition, the term vHTS has expanded to perform the simulations for more than one molecular target, similar to experimental phenotype biological assay (36).

Once a clean chemical library and the molecular target, with a crystallographic ligand into the binding site preferentially, are defined (refined or not), the next step is to perform the docking evaluations (38). The most simple evaluation is called redocking, which consists in removing the crystallographic ligand of the binding site cavity and docking it again. As a result, this process shows (i) if the docking methodology can reproduce a pose close to the crystallographic ligand, with the root-mean-square deviation (RMSD) value of atomic positions between them has to be close to 2.0 Å; (ii) if the configurations parameters were set correctly. Docking simulations, in general, are performed to fit ligands into a specific cavity of protein. It can be performed for the whole protein as well. In this situation, we call blinding docking; (iii) a determination of reference affinity value. Summarizing, docking methods have two problems to solve, find the correct ligand pose into the binding site, and sign the corresponding affinity between the pose and molecular target.

Another method used to evaluate the scoring functions of docking methodology is called the receiver operating characteristic curve (ROC curve). The ROC (39) curve is a graphical representation which shows how much the docking method can distinguish between true positives and false positives. In general, the ROC curve for docking methods can be built using five active compounds for the selected molecular target, of which the active values should be less than 1 micromolar. These active compounds can be found at ChEMBL platform or in specific reports. It is noteworthy that the structures from ChEMBL should be refined by molecular mechanics method or a semi-empirical method, at least, following a visual inspection. Run Mopac is a Python software able to refine a set of ligands using Parametric Method 7 (PM7). However, it is necessary to adjust its script for ChEMBL structures.

In contrast, decoys (40) can be generated using two platforms at least, by Directory of Useful Decoys, Enhanced (DUD-E) and LIDEB's Useful Decoys (LUDe) (41). Both of them can generate nonbinding molecules (false-positive), which share similar physicochemical properties, but are topologically different. In general, 50 decoys are generated and used for each active compound. Following, docking simulation can be performed with all compounds, active and decoys. As a result, the area under ROC curve (AUC) values below 0.5 denote a random process and values, whereas values under 0.7 are considered significant.

In conclusion, scoring functions of docking methodologies achieve false positives results, which have been very common in docking studies. There is not a clear explanation for it, but we have concluded that docking methods are structure dependent. Doerksen highlighted the following suggestions: (i) generate the ligand conformers as efficiently as possible and not depend on self-generation approach; (ii) do not minimize the complex protein–ligand. However, several groups have carried out it; (iii) analysis of active site crystal water molecules. Inclusion of water molecules should be considered after studying the hydrogen bonding with non-water residues in multiple crystal structures of the target; (iv) multiple crystal structures should be considered to cover all possible active site conformations, carrying out an ensemble docking or cross-docking (42) protocol. In addition, Taranto and collaborators (43) obtained good docking results by re-score strategy together with consensus using Autodock Vina following Dock 6. In summary, docking has three different levels of challenges to solve. The first one is to find the correct pose of ligands; second, be able to distinguish active compounds from inactive; third, show a proper ranking of compounds.

15.5   MOLECULAR DYNAMICS SIMULATIONS

The biochemical structures constantly work through their interactions, signaling, conformational alterations, inhibition, and other process that, in a way or other, are related to its structure. Hence, the knowledge the tridimensional structure of these biochemical actors is fundamental in the comprehension of its role in the intricated biological mechanism. However, although important, this knowledge is only a part in the study of the biochemical players. Another fundamental point is study how these structures interact between itself, with the solvent or how, for example, their structures will be altered as the time pass. However, obtaining this information in atomistic scale is not so simple if we want to see the time evolution of the interacting parts. Fortunately, for most of these cases, there are an alternative that is the Molecular Dynamics (MD) simulations.

MD is a technique that simulates the time evolution in systems counting hundreds to thousands of atoms, including solvents, ions, and counter ions. The history of MD began evaluating the time evolution of the one-dimensional chain by Fermi-Pasta-Ulan (44). The simulations were gain more complexity as the works of Alder and Wainwright (45, 46), Rahman (47) and Verlet (48), and many other. All these works are milestones that were followed by the works of Stillinger and Rahman (49, 50), who performed the first molecular dynamics simulation of the water in the liquid state. Finally, Karplus and colleague (51) carried out the first simulation of a protein what opened an all new word of possibilities of simulation, since there still are continuous enhancement of the hardware and software as well, allowing that bigger and more complex systems can be simulated.

The properties and observations that can be extracted from the computational simulations, or computational experiments, are the result of a calculation process that can take on count, necessarily, the presence of many different components and the way that they interact between them and the functions that describe these interactions must consider all particularities of these various components. From a formal point of view, the MD are based on the Statistical Thermodynamics to problems that interest to Chemistry, Physics, Material Engineering, Biology and many other disciplines, since concepts like ensemble time and ensemble averages are necessary to understand MD.

From an experimental point of view, any system, no matter how small it can be, contain an enormous number of atoms. In this sense, any analysis is statistical *a priori*, which place the MD, from a theoretical perspective, in the realm of statistical thermodynamics, which must be used every time we ask questions such as "why this primary sequence of residues presents this particular tertiary structure?"

To evaluate the temporal evolution of the system it is necessary that, at each instant of time, the velocity and position of every atom of the system can be calculated. Hence, grossly, any system (no matter its size) can be viewed as a point that describes a path in a multidimensional space defined by the constraints of the system, such as the number of particles, temperature, and pressure (N, P, T) as control variables. These set of conditions, or any others applied to the system, determine the *ensemble* to which the system is related, and the properties has its values given by the *ensemble average*. The most used ensembles are the *canonical ensemble*, which has as control variables the number of particles, N, the pressure, P and the temperature, T; the *micro canonical ensemble*, which has as control variables the number of particles, N, the volume, V and the energy, E and, finally, the *gran canonical ensemble*, where N, V, and the chemical potential, μ, are considered the control variables. Using these *ensembles*, a great number of situations can be simulated.

From a technical point of view, the quality and accuracy of an MD simulation, and as a consequence, the obtained results, depend on three main factors: the model used to describe the interactions between the particles, the calculation of the energies and forces from the considered model, and, equally important, the integrator of the motion equations.

An example of the model used to estimate the potential energy arising from the interactions can be the following equation:

$$V\left(R\right)_{\text{total}} = V\left(R\right)_{\text{internal}} + V\left(R\right)_{\text{external}}$$

$$V(R)_{\text{internal}} = \sum_{\text{bonds}} K_b (b-b_0)^2 \sum_{\text{angles}} K_\theta (\theta-\theta_0)^2 + \sum_{\text{dihedrals}} K_\chi \left[1+\cos(n\chi-\sigma)\right]$$

and

$$V(R)_{\text{external}} = \sum_{\substack{\text{non bonded} \\ \text{atom pairs}}} \varepsilon_{ij} \left[\left(\frac{R_{\min,ij}}{r_{ij}}\right)^{12} - \left(\frac{R_{\min,ij}}{r_{ij}}\right)^{6} \right] + \frac{q_i q_j}{\varepsilon_D r_{ij}}$$

where two principal parts are considered: one used to evaluate the intramolecular interactions that are constituted by the calculation of energy from bonds, angles, and dihedrals, and the other part to potential energy from the intermolecular interactions, through the Lennard-Jones potential and the Coulomb interactions. The necessary parameters to feed the equation come from two sources: one is a file where there are equilibrium values to the bonds, angles, and dihedrals, the values of the atomic partial charges, and other necessary information; these values are placed together the initial structural information from the system that has to be simulated. The union of an equation to model all interactions and the file containing the needed values are known as *force field*. It is important to say that this equation is one between other possibilities and different force fields use different equations (52).

The other factor that can affect the quality of the simulation is the integrator of the motion equations. Using Newton's second law, it is possible follow the trajectory of a system along the time. However, the use of this motion equation is, sometimes, complicated, mainly when using it to simulate atoms and molecules. Hence, in order to make the things feasible we just alter the formulation of the description of the mechanics. In this case the Hamiltonian formulation of Newton's laws of motion can be used with great success, as it can be used in classical and quantum mechanics as well.

The Hamiltonian formulation of the Newton's Laws of movement is an alternative to the Lagrangian formulation, not for been superior, but for allowing its use in several fields of physics. In this case, from a formal point of view, the Hamiltonian equations of motion that must be integrated in order to perform a temporal evolution of the system are derived from the Lagrangian equation

$$\frac{d}{dt}\left(\frac{\partial L}{\partial \dot{q}}\right) - \frac{\partial L}{\partial q_i} = 0$$

where $\dot{q}$ is the velocity and L is the Lagrangian. A system that contains n degrees of freedom must have n the above equations and, from a procedure known as Legendre Transformation, the n Lagrangian equations of motion can be transformed into n following Hamiltonian equations of motion:

$$\frac{\partial H}{\partial p_i} = \dot{q}_i$$

$$\frac{\partial H}{\partial q_i} = -\dot{p}_i$$

These equations are of first order, decreasing the amount computation needed to be done. Particularly a Hamiltonian must be calculated from

$$H = T + U$$

where T and U are the kinetic energy potential energies, respectively.

Using these equations, the initial conditions of the system and one equation to model the interactions between the system particles, the following scheme can be applied to perform a molecular dynamics simulation:

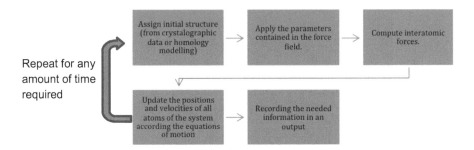

A fundamental step in this process is to use an integrator, or solver, of the Hamiltonian motion equations, which allows to perform the temporal evolution of the system. The easier way to do this is to use a Taylor series:

$$r_i(t + \Delta t) \approx r_i(t) + \Delta t \dot{r}_i + \frac{1}{2}\Delta t^2 \ddot{r}_i(t)$$

where the terms beyond the quadratic term were dropped out (this is because there is no equality in the equation) and each point above r is its time derivative. Using Newton's second law and the time reversibility of the process, the above equation can be rewritten as:

$$r_i(t + \Delta t) = 2r_i(t) - r_i(t - \Delta t) + \frac{\Delta t^2}{m_i} F_i(t)$$

This equation is known as Verlet algorithm, and both the initial coordinates and velocities for each particle i of the system are necessary for the calculation. From this point a trajectory can be generated, and at the end of the process, the desired properties can be calculated. However, despite its simplicity, the Verlet algorithm does not make the velocity calculation explicitly, which must be obtained through a modification of the initial algorithm, done by Swope (53) and known as Verlet velocity algorithm:

$$r_i(t + \Delta t) \approx r_i(t) + \Delta t v_i(t) + \frac{\Delta t^2}{m_i} F_i(t)$$

$$v_i\left(t+\Delta t\right) = v_i\left(t\right) + \frac{\Delta t}{2m_i}\left[F_i\left(t\right) + F_i\left(t+\Delta t\right)\right]$$

These algorithms maintain two fundamental properties to any integrator of the motion equations: the time reversibility, which means that if the algorithm is run backward using a time step of $-\Delta t$, the initial condition of the system must be reestablished; the other property is the symplectic property.

The main purpose in obtaining a trajectory of the system along the phase space is to provide a way to evaluate some properties of interest about the behavior of the system and its interactions or alterations in that amount of time. To calculate the value of any property from the Hamiltonian of the system, it must possess the commutation property, which means that Poisson bracket can be used for this property

$$\frac{dz}{dt} = \left\{z, H\right\}$$

where H is the temporal generator of the temporal evolution of the property $z(x_t)$. There are many mathematical schemes that must be used in order to accomplish this process and to the interested reader the Tuckerman (54) text can provide a lot of details about this subject.

At the conclusion of this section it is worth noting that the use of bioinformatics tools with molecular dynamics simulations can offer a better possibility to achieve important results (55–58), and there are many subjects that can be studied through these approaches.

REFERENCES

1. Gu J, Bourne PE. *Structural Bioinformatics*. 2nd Edition. Wiley-Blackwell; 2011. 1096 p.
2. Gabella C, Duvaud S, Durinx C. Managing the life cycle of a portfolio of open data resources at the SIB Swiss Institute of Bioinformatics. *Brief Bioinform*. 2022;23(1): bbab478.
3. Mendez D, Gaulton A, Bento AP, Chambers J, De Veij M, Félix E, et al. ChEMBL: Towards direct deposition of bioassay data. *Nucleic Acids Res*. 2019;47(D1):D930–40.
4. Villoutreix BO, Lagorce D, Labbé CM, Sperandio O, Miteva MA. One hundred thousand mouse clicks down the road: Selected online resources supporting drug discovery collected over a decade. *Drug Discov Today*. 2013;18(21–22):1081–9.
5. Maia EHB, Medaglia LR, Da Silva AM, Taranto AG. Molecular architect: A user-friendly workflow for virtual screening. *ACS Omega*. 2020;5(12):6628–40.
6. Maia EHB, Campos VA, dos Reis Santos B, Costa MS, Lima IG, Greco SJ, et al. Octopus: A platform for the virtual high-throughput screening of a pool of compounds against a set of molecular targets. *J Mol Model*. 2017;23(1):1–11.
7. O'Boyle NM, Banck M, James CA, Morley C, Vandermeersch T, Hutchison GR. Open Babel: An open chemical toolbox. *J Cheminform*. 2011;3(10):1–14.
8. Sterling T, Irwin JJ. ZINC 15 – Ligand discovery for everyone. *J Chem Inf Model*. 2015; 55(11):2324–37.
9. Wishart DS, Feunang YD, Guo AC, Lo EJ, Marcu A, Grant JR, et al. DrugBank 5.0: A major update to the DrugBank database for 2018. *Nucleic Acids Res*. 2018;46(D1):D1074–82.

10. Kim S, Cheng T, He S, Thiessen PA, Li Q, Gindulyte A, et al. PubChem protein, gene, pathway, and taxonomy data collections: Bridging biology and chemistry through target-centric views of PubChem data. *J Mol Biol*. 2022;434(11):167514.

11. Stewart JJP. Optimization of parameters for semiempirical methods VI: More modifications to the NDDO approximations and re-optimization of parameters. *J Mol Model*. 2013; 19(1):1–32.

12. Burley SK, Bhikadiya C, Bi C, Bittrich S, Chen L, Crichlow G V, et al. RCSB Protein Data Bank: Powerful new tools for exploring 3D structures of biological macromolecules for basic and applied research and education in fundamental biology, biomedicine, biotechnology, bioengineering and energy sciences. *Nucleic Acids Res*. 2021;49(1):D437–51.

13. Muratov EN, Bajorath J, Sheridan RP, Tetko IV, Filimonov D, Poroikov V, et al. QSAR without borders. *Chem Soc Rev*. 2020;49(11):3525–64.

14. Dhingra S, Sowdhamini R, Cadet F, Offmann B. A glance into the evolution of template-free protein structure prediction methodologies. *Biochimie*. 2020;175:85–92.

15. Chothia C, Lesk AM. The relation between the divergence of sequence and structure in proteins. *EMBO J*. 1986;5(4):823–6.

16. Setiawan D, Brender J, Zhang Y. Recent advances in automated protein design and its future challenges. *Expert Opin Drug Discov*. 2018;13(7):587–604.

17. Waterhouse A, Bertoni M, Bienert S, Studer G, Tauriello G, Gumienny R, et al. SWISS-MODEL: Homology modelling of protein structures and complexes. *Nucleic Acids Res*. 2018;46(W1):W296–303.

18. Webb B, Sali A. Comparative protein structure modeling using MODELLER. *Curr Protoc Bioinforma*. 2016;2016:5.6.1–5.6.37.

19. Kaczanowski S, Zielenkiewicz P. Why similar protein sequences encode similar three-dimensional structures? *Theor Chem Acc*. 2010;125(3–6):643–50.

20. Kelley LA, Mezulis S, Yates CM, Wass MN, Sternberg MJE. The Phyre2 web portal for protein modeling, prediction and analysis. *Nat Protoc*. 2015;10(6):845–58.

21. Zheng W, Zhang C, Li Y, Pearce R, Bell EW, Zhang Y. Folding non-homologous proteins by coupling deep-learning contact maps with I-TASSER assembly simulations. *Cell Rep. Methods*. 2021;1(3):100014.

22. Robson B. De novo protein folding on computers. Benefits and challenges. *Comput Biol Med*. 2022;143.

23. Sorokina I, Mushegian AR, Koonin E V. Is protein folding a thermodynamically unfavorable, active, energy-dependent process? *Int J Mol Sci*. 2022;23(1):5553.

24. Pakhrin SC, Shrestha B, Adhikari B, Kc DB. Deep learning-based advances in protein structure prediction. *Int J Mol Sci*. 2021;22(11):5553.

25. Kryshtafovych A, Schwede T, Topf M, Fidelis K, Moult J. Critical assessment of methods of protein structure prediction (CASP)—Round XIV. *Proteins Struct Funct Bioinforma*. 2021;89(12):1607–17.

26. Wang S, Sun S, Li Z, Zhang R, Xu J. Accurate De Novo prediction of protein contact map by ultra-deep learning model. *PLoS Comput Biol*. 2017;13(1):e1005324.

27. Källberg M, Wang H, Wang S, Peng J, Wang Z, Lu H, et al. Template-based protein structure modeling using the RaptorX web server. *Nat Protoc*. 2012;7(8):1511–22.

28. Ramachandran GN, Ramakrishnan C, Sasisekharan V. Stereochemistry of polypeptide chain configurations. *J Mol Biol*. 1963;7(1):95–9.

29. Laskowski RA, MacArthur MW, Moss DS, Thornton JM. PROCHECK: a program to check the stereochemical quality of protein structures. *J Appl Crystallogr*. 1993;26(2): 283–91.

30. Lüthy R, Bowie JU, Eisenberg D. Assessment of protein models with three-dimensional profiles. *Nature*. 1992;356(6364):83–5.

31. Benkert P, Biasini M, Schwede T. Toward the estimation of the absolute quality of individual protein structure models. *Bioinformatics*. 2011;27(3):343–50.

32. Melo F, Feytmans E. Assessing protein structures with a non-local atomic interaction energy. *J Mol Biol*. 1998;277(5):1141–52.

33. Benson G. Nucleic acids research annual web server issue in 2010. *Nucleic Acids Res*. 2010;38(SUPPL. 2):W1–2.

34. Pettersen EF, Goddard TD, Huang CC, Couch GS, Greenblatt DM, Meng EC, et al. UCSF Chimera - A visualization system for exploratory research and analysis. *J Comput Chem*. 2004;25(13):1605–12.

35. Kuntz ID, Blaney JM, Oatley SJ, Langridge R, Ferrin TE. A geometric approach to macromolecule-ligand interactions. *J Mol Biol*. 1982;161(2):269–88.

36. Maia EHB, Assis LC, de Oliveira TA, da Silva AM, Taranto AG. Structure-based virtual screening: From classical to artificial intelligence. *Front Chem*. 2020;8.

37. Zeng W, Guo L, Xu S, Chen J, Zhou J. High-throughput screening technology in industrial biotechnology. *Trends Biotechnol*. 2020;38(8):888–906.

38. Kitchen DB, Decornez H, Furr JR, Bajorath J. Docking and scoring in virtual screening for drug discovery: Methods and applications. *Nat Rev Drug Discov*. 2004;3(11):935–49.

39. Brozell SR, Mukherjee S, Balius TE, Roe DR, Case DA, Rizzo RC. Evaluation of DOCK 6 as a pose generation and database enrichment tool. *J Comput Aided Mol Des*. 2012;26(6):749–73.

40. Réau M, Langenfeld F, Zagury J-F, Lagarde N, Montes M. Decoys selection in benchmarking datasets: Overview and perspectives. *Front Pharmacol*. 2018;9(JAN):11.

41. Llanos MA, Gantner ME, Rodriguez S, Alberca LN, Bellera CL, Talevi A, et al. Strengths and weaknesses of docking simulations in the SARS-CoV-2 Era: The Main Protease (Mpro) case study. *J Chem Inf Model*. 2021;61(8):3758–70.

42. Shamsara J. CrossDocker: A tool for performing cross-docking using Autodock Vina. *Springerplus*. 2016;5(1):1–5.

43. de Oliveira TA, Medaglia LR, Maia EHB, Assis LC, de Carvalho PB, da Silva AM, et al. Evaluation of docking machine learning and molecular dynamics methodologies for DNA-ligand systems. *Pharmaceuticals*. 2022;15(2):132.

44. Fermi E, Pasta P, Ulam S, Tsingou M. *Studies of the Nonlinear Problems*. United States; 1955.

45. Alder BJ, Wainwright TE. Studies in molecular dynamics. I. General method. *J Chem Phys*. 1959;31(2):459–66.

46. Alder BJ, Wainwright TE. Phase transition for a hard sphere system. *J Chem Phys*. 1957; 27(5):1208–9.

47. Rahman A. Correlations in the motion of atoms in liquid argon. *Phys Rev*. 1964;136(2A): A405–11.

48. Verlet L. Computer "experiments" on classical fluids. I. Thermodynamical properties of Lennard-Jones molecules. *Phys Rev*. 1967;159(1):98–103.

49. Stillinger FH, Rahman A. Improved simulation of liquid water by molecular dynamics. *J Chem Phys*. 1974;60(4):1528–32.

50. Stillinger FH, Rahman A. Molecular dynamics study of temperature effects on water structure and kinetics. *J Chem Phys*. 1972;57(3):1281–92.

51. McCammon JA, Gelin BR, Karplus M. Dynamics of folded proteins. *Nature*. 1977;267(5612):585–90.

52. Leach AR. *Molecular Modelling: Principles and applications*. 2nd ed. Longman Pub Group; 1996. 616 p.

53. Swope WC, Andersen HC, Berens PH, Wilson KR. A computer simulation method for the calculation of equilibrium constants for the formation of physical clusters of molecules: Application to small water clusters. *J Chem Phys*. 1982;76(1):637–49.

54. Tuckerman ME. *Statistical Mechanics: Theory and Molecular Simulation*. Oxford University Press; 2010. 696 p.

55. Soté WO, Franca EF, Hora AS, Comar M. A computational study of the interface interaction between SARS-CoV-2 RBD and ACE2 from human, cat, dog, and ferret. *Transbound Emerg Dis*. 2022;69(4):2287–95.

56. Dans PD, Gallego D, Balaceanu A, Darré L, Gómez H, Orozco M. Modeling, simulations, and bioinformatics at the service of RNA structure. *Chem*. 2019;5(1):51–73.

57. Shuli Z, Linlin L, Li G, Yinghu Z, Nan S, Haibin W, et al. Bioinformatics and computer simulation approaches to the discovery and analysis of bioactive peptides. *Curr Pharm Biotechnol*. 2022;23(13):1541–55.

58. de Oliveira Lopes D, de Oliveira FM, do Vale Coelho IE, de Oliveira Santana KT, Mendonça FC, Taranto AG, et al. Identification of a vaccine against schistosomiasis using bioinformatics and molecular modeling tools. *Infect Genet Evol*. 2013;20.

16 A Streamline to New Face of Drug Discovery by Protein–Protein and Protein–Nucleic Acid Interactions

Priya N. Madhana

Sri Ramachandra Institute of Higher Education and Research (DU), India

Kumar D. Thirumal

Meenakshi Academy of Higher Education and Research, India

Nivedha Karthikeyan, Ananthi Vanaraj and Magesh Ramasamy

Sri Ramachandra Institute of Higher Education and Research (DU), India

16.1 INTRODUCTION TO DRUG DISCOVERY

Computer-aided drug discovery (CADD) is a burgeoning research field that considers various elements. In a fascinating and diverse control, several fields of practical and basic research are integrated and enlivened by one another in CADD (Das, 2017). The economic advantage of adopting computational technology is significant in the early stages of drug research (Arodz and Dudek, 2007).

In the past years, CADD has emerged to be very successful. This technology has many applications, including creating compounds with good physiochemical properties and managing compound digital libraries. CADD can be accomplished by structure-based drug discovery (SBDD) or LBDD. SBDD protocols have a huge rise in usage among the research community and a detailed view is given below (Small Molecule Drug Design, 2019).

DOI: 10.1201/9781003331247-18

16.2   STRUCTURE-BASED DRUG DISCOVERY

Structure-based drug design employs 3D structural data to build new, physiologically active molecules of the receptor structures (Seneci, 2018). As a result, the major initial phase of SBDD is identifying target molecules and determining their structure. The target found might be an enzyme associated with the condition under investigation. Based on binding affinity tests, potential medicines that block the target and diminish its activity are identified (Lionta et al., 2014).

In drug discovery, identifying potential drugs occupies a vast space in the research space. All through the world, protein-small molecule interaction is attended to with great interest, but PPi and PNi are not given importance. PPi and PNi lead to great strategies in disease management; one important lead in research is vaccine development which is a part of PPi, implying protein-peptide interactions. Many more therapies and treatments depend on PNi. There are many tools in PPi and PNi (Chai et al., 2021).

16.2.1   Protein Structures (PDB and Modeling)

Many protein structures are determined using techniques such as NMR, EM, X-ray crystallography, and in silico approaches such as homology structure prediction and molecular dynamic simulation (MDS) (Anderson, 2012). As part of the homology modeling method, a known sequence including an unknown structure is matched to a known structure of one or more homologous sequences. Two proteins with the same function and origin should share some structural similarities. As a result, using the known structure as a template, it is feasible to recreate the structure of the unknown structure (Claude Cohen, 1996; Roy, 2019).

16.2.2   Binding Site and Allosteric Site

The initial stage in structure-based design is to locate a potential ligand binding pocket on a target molecule. The ideal target area would be a pocket or disturbance with a diverse set of hydrogen bond (HB) donors and acceptors and hydrophobic characteristics (Usha et al., 2017; Sharma et al., 2021). Understanding binding site residues is critical for understanding biological processes and how drugs interact with the body (Roche, Brackenridge, and McGuffin, 2015).

16.2.3   Interaction Analysis

Additional scoring methods can improve the docking process's expected efficiency by evaluating the solvent and free energy contribution of a target molecule contact. Several docking software packages already have scoring capabilities (Baig et al., 2018). Docking and scoring applications generate a list of ligands with ranks. Docking algorithm evaluation typically depends on "enrichment," or the detection of verified hits in a large collection of bogus data (Anderson, 2012; Sreerama and Kaushik, 2019).

16.3   PROTEIN-PROTEIN DOCKING A NEW ATTEMPT IN DRUG DEVELOPMENT

Using PPi characteristics like physicochemical and steric complementarity, protein-protein docking predicts how two protein structures would interact to produce a protein complex (Hirose, n.d.). Anticipating conformations between complex and apo form structures is a part in the PPi (Meller and Porollo, 2012).

16.3.1   Protein Recognition

The increasing accessibility of protein complex crystal structures has made it feasible to describe the interfaces between proteins in a protein complex. This was done to understand better the interactions that stabilize such complexes and to discover the specificity of the interaction. Protein-protein complex formation can be seen physically as the system's reduced free energy or empirically as a match between multiple phenomenological structural and/or physicochemical motifs (Marshall and Vakser, n.d.).

16.3.2   List of Tools Used

The prediction of PPIs, which may be considered as binary classification issues, may be understood as the objective of identifying protein pairs as either interacting or not (Kangueane and Nilofer, 2018). A list of available tools is provided below based on their working platform:

16.3.2.1   Online Tools

i. **Haddock @ BonvinLab**: HADDOCK is free and capable of handling a wide variety of problems that includes: structure modeling, and docking of receptors with proteins, peptides, DNA, RNA, or small molecules to form complexes.

ii. **PRODIGY @ BonvinLab**: Python and Perl were used to create PRODIGY open source platform. The free SASA open-source program is used to compute the solvent accessible surface area (Mitternacht, 2016; Xue et al., 2016 [Ibid.]).

iii. **FireDock and FiberDock**: The tool offers FireDock, the first online server for dynamic protein-protein docking solution refinement and scoring. It integrates rigid structures and optimized side-chain conformations and high-throughput refining (Mashiach et al., 2008; Andrusier, Nussinov, and Wolfson, 2007).

    The very first docking refinement web service that takes into consideration side-chain and backbone flexibility is FiberDock. FiberDock refines the structure and assigns them a score based on an energy function after modeling the backbones and side-chain motions (Mashiach et al., 2008).

iv. **SymmDock and PatchDock**: Proteins complexed with ligand and co-protein can have their structures predicted using the PatchDock technique. Based on the structure of the given monomeric unit, the homomers' cyclic rotation is predicted via the SymmDock method (Schneidman-Duhovny et al., 2005).

v. **FoXSDock**: Using the complex's SAXS profile, this tool docks double the rigid protein structures. This is an increasingly popular and practical method for analyzing molecule structure (Schneidman-Duhovny et al., 2016).

vi. **HDock Server**: The processing of sequences for inputs, as well as a composite docking approach that allows investigational data on the interacting site as well SAXS integrated docking and post-docking practices, distinguishes the HDOCK server to other online docking domains of a similar nature (Yan et al., 2020; Yan et al., 2017). The HDOCK server is used for efficient and dependable PPi's.

vii. **ZDock**: ZDOCK has excellent predictive accuracy for protein-protein docking benchmarks, with 470% success inside the top 1,000 predictions for restricted situations. ZDock offers users options to control the scoring and choosing of output models, in addition to dynamic docking model and input structure displays (Pierce et al., 2014; Chen et al., 2003; Chen, Li, and Weng, 2003).

viii. **FroDock**: FroDock automatically docks two submitted receptor structures together (in PDB format). As an alternative, to extend the success rates, the user can select the type of docking. The benchmark 4.0 cases average dock running time is two minutes (Ramírez-Aportela, López-Blanco, and Chacón, 2016). FRODOCK 2.0 is a faster alternative for modern servers.

ix. **Hex Server**: First ever Fourier transform (FFT)-based protein docking service driven by graphics processors is the HexServer. A typical docking run takes upto 15s and generates a ranking list of up to 1,000 docking predictions after receiving two protein structures using PDB format (Macindoe et al., 2010).

16.3.2.2   Commercial Software and Offline User Tools

x. **BioLuminate and Piper**: A state-of-the-art protein-protein docking software is available from BioLuminate, providing modes enabling antibody and multimer docking (Beard et al., 2013). PIPER is a cutting-edge protein-protein docking tool that reliably produces precise structures for protein-protein complexes. It is based on a multi-staged methodology and cutting-edge numerical algorithms. The Vajda group at Boston University developed the well-validated docking code used in PIPER (Chuang et al., 2008).

xi. **CombDock**: CombDock receives a collection of ordered protein substructures and forecasts the interactions between them that determine how they are organized overall. It scores the final complexes to prevent repetitive hypotheses and iteratively clusters the answers. The scoring functions combines physicochemical and geometrical characteristics (Inbar et al., 2003).

xii. **F² Dock**: The program is built on expressing affinity functions together in multi-resolution radial basis format. In comparison to conventional FFT-based docking techniques, the smoother particle protein representation and nonequispaced Fast Fourier transformations provide various benefits in efficiency and accuracy trade-offs (Bajaj, Chowdhury, and Siddavanahalli, 2011).

xiii. **MegaDock**: MEGADOCK4.0 is a structural biology FFT-grid-based protein-protein docking performed using many computational clusters and the linear computing CUDA framework of NVIDIA GPUs. It may be used as a technique to expedite the study of the whole interactome (Ohue et al., 2014).

xiv. **BindML/BindML+**: BindML uses data from a protein family's multiple sequence alignment to estimate the stable and transitory forms protein-protein interaction residues of a given protein structure (Wei, La, and Kihara, 2017). BindML attempts to assess and identify surface residues of the structure. Protein residue sites along the MSA are anticipated to be protein interface residues based on the places with the greatest score mutation pattern.

xv. **SPRINT**: A unique sequence-based method and tool called SPRINT (Scoring PRotein INTeractions) are used to predict protein-protein interactions. According to credible human PPI data, it is far more precise, uses far less memory, and operates orders of magnitude more quickly. It takes between 15 and 100 minutes to predict the whole human interactome, making it the only sequence-based software that can do so (Li and Ilie, 2017).

16.4 PROTEIN-PEPTIDE DOCKING AND ITS TOOLS

Protein-peptide interactions are crucial for the functioning of living organisms, and the structural characterization of these interactions is a contentious issue in both experimental and theoretical study today. The two main stages of protein-peptide docking are: identifying the binding pocket and subsequently docking the peptides into the receptor. They have much less interaction affinity. These traits make it challenging to describe the structure of protein-peptide complexes, due to the significant torsional stability of the peptides (Audie and Swanson, 2012).

16.4.1 TYPES OF PROTEIN-PEPTIDE DOCKING

Template-based docking, local docking, and global docking are the three different protein-peptide docking methods (Ciemny et al., 2018; Audie and Swanson, 2012; Ohue, n.d.).

16.4.1.1 Template-based Docking

Receptor structures from PDB are used to model the complex using template-based (comparative) docking techniques. Utilizing a collection of tools for comparing and evaluating sequence structures, template-based docking is frequently done by hand or partially automatically (Kundrotas et al., 2012).

16.4.1.2 Local Docking

The data set on the binding site determines how accurate local docking approaches will be; the more precise the input, the better. A peptide docking posture at a user-specified binding site is sought after by local docking techniques (Schueler-Furman and London, 2017, 2019).

16.4.1.3 Global Docking

Global docking approaches are used to search concurrently for the peptide's binding location and posture. Their workflow typically include three phases: rigid-body docking, input peptide conformation creation, model scoring, and/or refining (Yan, Xu, and Zou, 2016).

16.4.2 Tools for Protein-Peptide Docking

There are a few online and stand-alone software both freely and commercially to perform Protein-Peptide Docking. Given their well-known flexibility as ligands, peptides can be particularly difficult.

16.5 PROTEIN NUCLEIC ACID COMPLEXES: A NEW TREND TO DRUG DISCOVERY

The activities of living things rely on the interconnections of proteins and nucleic acids The majority of biological activities depend critically on the interaction of macromolecules and has led to an evolution in the computational methods to investigate protein–nucleic acid interactions in recent years (Musiani and Ciurli, 2015).

16.5.1 Types of Protein–Nucleic Acid Interactions

Proteins interact with DNA and RNA by a variety of physical forces, including electrostatic contacts, H-bonds, hydrophobic interactions, and dispersion forces.

16.5.1.1 Protein-DNA Interaction

The study of protein-DNA docking is becoming more popular, and attempts are being made to create docking techniques that overcome the drawbacks outlined above. Understanding the biochemistry between recognition and gene expression is crucial given the significance of biomolecular interactions in system biology. A significant problem in protein-DNA docking is maintaining the helical nature of DNA when conformational changes occur in protein and DNA during docking (van Dijk and Bonvin, 2008).

16.5.1.2 Protein-RNA Interaction

Protein-RNA interactions typically serve a vital purpose in the cell. They regulate the activity of important cellular machinery like the RNA-mediated silencing complex and are involved in various biological processes, such as mRNA transcription, replication, or RNA level control (RISC). They make excellent subjects for therapeutic research (Guilhot-Gaudeffroy et al., 2014).

16.5.2 Tools Used

16.5.2.1 NP Dock

The modeling of the protein–nucleic acid complex structure is made automated via the NPDock server. NPDock uses the GRAMM software, a third-party technique, as part of its computational workflow. By default, clustering is performed using the top 100 models (Tuszynska et al., 2015).

16.5.2.2 HDock

The HDOCK pipelines of protein-RNA interactions when compared to other types of interactions with ligand or DNA when top ten interactions were taken into consideration, HDOCK performed better (Yan et al., 2017).

16.5.2.3 HNADock

When modeling the three-dimensional complex structures of two RNAs or DNAs, the user-friendly online platform HNADOCK accepts inputs as sequence or structure for RNAs but only allows structures for DNAs as input. The server has a phenomenal accomplishment record of 71.7% and regularly achieves a task in 10 minutes (He et al., 2019; Parisien, Freed, and Sosnick, 2012).

16.6 CONCLUSION

We have examined the crucial drug discovery pathway based on receptor linkages with certain other proteins and nucleic acids. Though many therapies such as vaccine development, peptide- and nucleic acid–based therapies are based on PPi and PNi, they still remain an unexplored part in SBDD. The world greatly focuses on protein-small molecule interaction, but fails to understand the significance of PPi and PNi. With the growing computer capacity, a better knowledge of the underlying principles governing protein interactions, and the continuous expansion of data and research resources all aid in the creation of more effective and appropriate docking techniques. To focus on the various complex structures with co-proteins or peptides or nucleic acids, these tools mentioned above will pave a new way to understand the interactions might become the new face to drug development.

ACKNOWLEDGMENTS

The authors like to acknowledge Department of Biotechnology, Sri Ramachandra Institute of Higher Education and Research (DU), for their constant support.

AUTHOR CONTRIBUTION STATEMENT

The authors Madhana Priya and Thirumal Kumar were involved in work and in drafting the manuscript. Madhana Priya, Thirumal Kumar, Nivedha, and Ananthi were involved in data collection. Magesh and Thirumal Kumar were involved in supervising the work and critically examined the manuscript for submission.

The authors approve the manuscript at its correct form.

DATA AVAILABILITY

All data generated or analyzed during this study are included in this published article (and its supplementary information files).

COMPLIANCE WITH ETHICAL STANDARDS

This article does not contain any studies with human or animal subjects performed by the any of the authors.

CONFLICT OF INTEREST

The authors declare that there are no conflicts of interest.

SOURCE OF FUNDING

No funding was received for this work.

REFERENCES

Anderson, Amy C. "Structure-Based Functional Design of Drugs: From Target to Lead Compound." *Methods in Molecular Biology* 823 (2012): 359–66.

Andrusier, Nelly, Ruth Nussinov, and Haim J. Wolfson. "FireDock: Fast Interaction Refinement in Molecular Docking." *Proteins: Structure, Function, and Bioinformatics*, 2007. doi:10.1002/prot.21495

Arodz, Tomasz, and Arkadiusz Dudek. "Multivariate Modeling and Analysis in Drug Discovery." *Current Computer Aided-Drug Design*, 2007. doi:10.2174/157340907782799381

Audie, Joseph, and Jon Swanson. "Recent Work in the Development and Application of Protein–peptide Docking." *Future Medicinal Chemistry*, 2012. doi:10.4155/fmc.12.99

Baig, Mohammad Hassan, Khurshid Ahmad, Gulam Rabbani, Mohd Danishuddin, and Inho Choi. "Computer Aided Drug Design and Its Application to the Development of Potential Drugs for Neurodegenerative Disorders." *Current Neuropharmacology* 16, no. 6 (2018): 740–48.

Bajaj, Chandrajit, Rezaul Chowdhury, and Vinay Siddavanahalli. "F2Dock: Fast Fourier Protein-Protein Docking." *IEEE/ACM Transactions on Computational Biology and Bioinformatics / IEEE, ACM* 8, no. 1 (2011): 45–58.

Beard, Hege, Anuradha Cholleti, David Pearlman, Woody Sherman, and Kathryn A. Loving. "Applying Physics-Based Scoring to Calculate Free Energies of Binding for Single Amino Acid Mutations in Protein-Protein Complexes." *PloS One* 8, no. 12 (2013): e82849.

Blaszczyk, Maciej, Mateusz Kurcinski, Maksim Kouza, Lukasz Wieteska, Aleksander Debinski, Andrzej Kolinski, and Sebastian Kmiecik. "Modeling of Protein-Peptide Interactions Using the CABS-Dock Web Server for Binding Site Search and Flexible Docking." *Methods* 93 (2016): 72–83.

Chai, Tsun-Thai, Kah-Yaw Ee, D. Thirumal Kumar, Fazilah Abd Manan, and Fai-Chu Wong. "Plant Bioactive Peptides: Current Status and Prospects Towards Use on Human Health." *Protein and Peptide Letters* 28, no. 6 (2021): 623–42.

Chen, Rong, Li Li, and Zhiping Weng. "ZDOCK: An Initial-Stage Protein-Docking Algorithm." *Proteins: Structure, Function, and Genetics*, 2003. doi:10.1002/prot.10389

Chen, Rong, Weiwei Tong, Julian Mintseris, Li Li, and Zhiping Weng. "ZDOCK Predictions for the CAPRI Challenge." *Proteins: Structure, Function, and Genetics*, 2003. doi:10.1002/prot.10388

Chuang, Gwo-Yu, Dima Kozakov, Ryan Brenke, Stephen R. Comeau, and Sandor Vajda. "DARS (Decoys As the Reference State) Potentials for Protein-Protein Docking." *Biophysical Journal* 95, no. 9 (2008): 4217–27.

Ciemny, Maciej, Mateusz Kurcinski, Karol Kamel, Andrzej Kolinski, Nawsad Alam, Ora Schueler-Furman, and Sebastian Kmiecik. "Protein–peptide Docking: Opportunities and Challenges." *Drug Discovery Today*, 2018. doi:10.1016/j.drudis.2018.05.006

Claude Cohen, N. *Guidebook on Molecular Modeling in Drug Design*. Gulf Professional Publishing, 1996.

Das, Pratik Swarup. "A Review On Computer Aided Drug Design In Drug Discovery." *World Journal of Pharmacy and Pharmaceutical Sciences*, 2017, 279–91.

van Dijk, Marc, and Alexandre M. J. J. Bonvin. "A Protein-DNA Docking Benchmark." *Nucleic Acids Research* 36, no. 14 (2008): e88.

Donsky, Elad, and Haim J. Wolfson. "PepCrawler: A Fast RRT-Based Algorithm for High-Resolution Refinement and Binding Affinity Estimation of Peptide Inhibitors." *Bioinformatics* 27, no. 20 (2011): 2836–42.

Guilhot-Gaudeffroy, Adrien, Christine Froidevaux, Jérôme Azé, and Julie Bernauer. "Protein-RNA Complexes and Efficient Automatic Docking: Expanding RosettaDock Possibilities." *PloS One* 9, no. 9 (2014): e108928.

He, Jiahua, Jun Wang, Huanyu Tao, Yi Xiao, and Sheng-You Huang. "HNADOCK: A Nucleic Acid Docking Server for Modeling RNA/DNA–RNA/DNA 3D Complex Structures." *Nucleic Acids Research*, 2019. doi:10.1093/nar/gkz412

Hirose, Shuichi. "Inferring Protein-Protein Interactions (PPIs) Based on Computational Methods," n.d.

Inbar, Yuval, Hadar Benyamini, Ruth Nussinov, and Haim J. Wolfson. "Protein Structure Prediction via Combinatorial Assembly of Sub-Structural Units." *Bioinformatics* 19 Suppl 1 (2003): i158–68.

Johansson-Åkhe, Isak, and Björn Wallner. "InterPepScore: A Deep Learning Score for Improving the FlexPepDock Refinement Protocol." *Bioinformatics*, 2022. doi:10.1093/bioinformatics/btac325

Kangueane, Pandjassarame, and Christina Nilofer. "Protein-Protein Docking: Methods and Tools." In *Protein-Protein and Domain-Domain Interactions*, edited by Pandjassarame Kangueane and Christina Nilofer, 161–68. Singapore: Springer Singapore, 2018.

Kundrotas, Petras J., Zhengwei Zhu, Joël Janin, and Ilya A. Vakser. "Templates Are Available to Model Nearly All Complexes of Structurally Characterized Proteins." *Proceedings of the National Academy of Sciences of the United States of America* 109, no. 24 (2012): 9438–41.

Lee, Hasup, Lim Heo, Myeong Sup Lee, and Chaok Seok. "GalaxyPepDock: A Protein–peptide Docking Tool Based on Interaction Similarity and Energy Optimization." *Nucleic Acids Research*, 2015. doi:10.1093/nar/gkv495

Lionta, Evanthia, George Spyrou, Demetrios K. Vassilatis, and Zoe Cournia. "Structure-Based Virtual Screening for Drug Discovery: Principles, Applications and Recent Advances." *Current Topics in Medicinal Chemistry* 14, no. 16 (2014): 1923–38.

Li, Yiwei, and Lucian Ilie. "SPRINT: Ultrafast Protein-Protein Interaction Prediction of the Entire Human Interactome." *BMC Bioinformatics* 18, no. 1 (2017): 485.

Macindoe, Gary, Lazaros Mavridis, Vishwesh Venkatraman, Marie-Dominique Devignes, and David W. Ritchie. "HexServer: An FFT-Based Protein Docking Server Powered by Graphics Processors." *Nucleic Acids Research* 38, no. Web Server issue (2010): W445–49.

Marcu, Orly, Emma-Joy Dodson, Nawsad Alam, Michal Sperber, Dima Kozakov, Marc F. Lensink, and Ora Schueler-Furman. "FlexPepDock Lessons from CAPRI Peptide–protein Rounds and Suggested New Criteria for Assessment of Model Quality and Utility." *Proteins: Structure, Function, and Bioinformatics*, 2017. doi:10.1002/prot.25230

Marshall, Garland R., and Ilya A. Vakser. "Protein-Protein Docking Methods." *Proteomics and Protein-Protein Interactions*, n.d. doi:10.1007/0-387-24532-4_6

Mashiach, Efrat, Dina Schneidman-Duhovny, Nelly Andrusier, Ruth Nussinov, and Haim J. Wolfson. "FireDock: A Web Server for Fast Interaction Refinement in Molecular Docking." *Nucleic Acids Research* 36, no. Web Server issue (2008): W229–32.

Meller, Jarek, and Alexey Porollo. "Computational Methods for Prediction of Protein-Protein Interaction Sites." *Protein-Protein Interactions - Computational and Experimental Tools*, 2012. doi:10.5772/36716

Mitternacht, Simon. "FreeSASA: An Open Source C Library for Solvent Accessible Surface Area Calculations." *F1000Research* 5 (2016): 189.

Schueler-Furman, Ora, and Nir London. "Modeling Peptide-Protein Interactions." *Methods in Molecular Biology*, 2017. doi:10.1007/978-1-4939-6798-8

Musiani, Francesco, and Stefano Ciurli. "Evolution of Macromolecular Docking Techniques: The Case Study of Nickel and Iron Metabolism in Pathogenic Bacteria." *Molecules* 20, no. 8 (2015): 14265–92.

Ohue, Masahito. "Re-Ranking of Computational Protein–Peptide Docking Solutions With Amino Acid Profiles of Rigid-Body Docking Results," n.d. doi:10.1101/2020.05.12.092007

Ohue, Masahito, Takehiro Shimoda, Shuji Suzuki, Yuri Matsuzaki, Takashi Ishida, and Yutaka Akiyama. "MEGADOCK 4.0: An Ultra–high-Performance Protein–protein Docking Software for Heterogeneous Supercomputers." *Bioinformatics*, 2014. doi:10.1093/bioinformatics/btu532

Parisien, Marc, Karl F. Freed, and Tobin R. Sosnick. "On Docking, Scoring and Assessing Protein-DNA Complexes in a Rigid-Body Framework." *PloS One* 7, no. 2 (2012): e32647.

Pierce, Brian G., Kevin Wiehe, Howook Hwang, Bong-Hyun Kim, Thom Vreven, and Zhiping Weng. "ZDOCK Server: Interactive Docking Prediction of Protein-Protein Complexes and Symmetric Multimers." *Bioinformatics* 30, no. 12 (2014): 1771–73.

Ramírez-Aportela, Erney, José Ramón López-Blanco, and Pablo Chacón. "FRODOCK 2.0: Fast Protein-Protein Docking Server." *Bioinformatics* 32, no. 15 (2016): 2386–88.

Roche, Daniel, Danielle Brackenridge, and Liam McGuffin. "Proteins and Their Interacting Partners: An Introduction to Protein–Ligand Binding Site Prediction Methods." *International Journal of Molecular Sciences*, 2015. doi:10.3390/ijms161226202

Roy, Kunal. *In Silico Drug Design: Repurposing Techniques and Methodologies*. Academic Press, 2019.

Schneidman-Duhovny, Dina, Michal Hammel, John A. Tainer, and Andrej Sali. "FoXS, FoXS Dock and MultiFoXS: Single-State and Multi-State Structural Modeling of Proteins and Their Complexes Based on SAXS Profiles." *Nucleic Acids Research* 44, no. W1 (2016): W424–29.

Schneidman-Duhovny, Dina, Yuval Inbar, Ruth Nussinov, and Haim J. Wolfson. "PatchDock and SymmDock: Servers for Rigid and Symmetric Docking." *Nucleic Acids Research* 33, no. Web Server issue (2005): W363–67.

Schueler-Furman, Ora, and Nir London. *Modeling Peptide-Protein Interactions: Methods and Protocols*. Methods in Molecular Biology. Springer, 2019.

Seneci, Pierfausto. *Chemical Sciences in Early Drug Discovery: Medicinal Chemistry 2.0*. Elsevier, 2018.

"Small Molecule Drug Design," January 1, 2019, 741–60.

Sreerama, R., and C. Kaushik. "In Silico Drug Design, Molecular Modelling, Synthesis and Characterization of Novel Benzimidazoles." In *Conference on Drug Design and Discovery Technologies*, 271–87, 2019.

Sharma, V., S. Wakode, and Kumar, H. "Structure- and Ligand-Based Drug Design: Concepts, Approaches, and Challenges." In *Chemoinformatics and Bioinformatics in the Pharmaceutical Sciences*, 27–53. Academic Press, 2021. 10.1016/B978-0-12-821748-1.00004-X

Tuszynska, Irina, Marcin Magnus, Katarzyna Jonak, Wayne Dawson, and Janusz M. Bujnicki. "NPDock: A Web Server for Protein–Nucleic Acid Docking." *Nucleic Acids Research* 43, no. W1 (2015): W425–30.

Usha, Talambedu, Dhivya Shanmugarajan, Arvind Kumar Goyal, Chinaga Suresh Kumar, and Sushil Kumar Middha. "Recent Updates on Computer-Aided Drug Discovery: Time for a Paradigm Shift." *Current Topics in Medicinal Chemistry* 17, no. 30 (2017): 3296–3307.

Wei, Qing, David La, and Daisuke Kihara. "BindML/BindML+: Detecting Protein-Protein Interaction Interface Propensity from Amino Acid Substitution Patterns." *Methods in Molecular Biology* 1529 (2017): 279–89.

Xue, Li C., João Pglm Rodrigues, Panagiotis L. Kastritis, Alexandre Mjj Bonvin, and Anna Vangone. "PRODIGY: A Web Server for Predicting the Binding Affinity of Protein–protein Complexes." *Bioinformatics*, 2016. doi:10.1093/bioinformatics/btw514

Yan, Chengfei, Xianjin Xu, and Xiaoqin Zou. "Fully Blind Docking at the Atomic Level for Protein-Peptide Complex Structure Prediction." *Structure* 24, no. 10 (2016): 1842–53.

Yan, Yumeng, Huanyu Tao, Jiahua He, and Sheng-You Huang. "The HDOCK Server for Integrated Protein-Protein Docking." *Nature Protocols*, 2020. doi:10.1038/s41596-020-0312-x

Yan, Yumeng, Di Zhang, Pei Zhou, Botong Li, and Sheng-You Huang. "HDOCK: A Web Server for Protein-Protein and Protein-DNA/RNA Docking Based on a Hybrid Strategy." *Nucleic Acids Research* 45, no. W1 (2017): W365–73.

van Zundert, G. C. P., J. P. G. L. M. Rodrigues, M. Trellet, C. Schmitz, P. L. Kastritis, E. Karaca, A. S. J. Melquiond, M. van Dijk, S. J. de Vries, and A. M. J. J. Bonvin. "The HADDOCK2.2 Web Server: User-Friendly Integrative Modeling of Biomolecular Complexes." *Journal of Molecular Biology* 428, no. 4 (2016): 720–25.

Section C

*Advanced Computational
Biology Techniques and
Applications*

17 From Proteins to Networks
Assembly, Interpretation, and Advances

Shishir K. Gupta, Rashmi Minocha,
Aman Akash, Samiya Parkar, Leyla Sirkinti,
Prithivi Jung Thapa, Anna Almasi,
Johannes Balkenhol, Özge Osmanoglu,
Aparna Pottikkadavath, Mugdha Srivastava
and Thomas Dandekar
University of Würzburg, Germany

17.1 INTRODUCTION

Living organisms consist of millions of wide varieties of proteins and the possibilities of interactions between them are endless. Graph theory provides a mathematical abstraction for describing such relationships [1]. A graph is defined as a set of entities or objects called vertices connected by links. In the omics era of biological research, its exponential data growth necessitates more systematic approaches to data analysis including graph-theoretical and network approaches [2]. As another systemic approach, systems biology views biological entities not only as individual components, but also as emergent properties of interacting systems. In network biology, tools derived from graph theory are used to represent and analyze biological systems. There are many types of data that can be represented by networks. The nodes represent entities like the proteins or genes in biological networks, whereas edges indicate the relationship between nodes as shown in Figure 17.1.

Biological networks are often represented as graphs which are complex sets of binary interactions between different entities. Biological networks are powerful tools to study complex biological systems and can be defined as a global snapshot of the system. A larger system can be easily abstracted by the biological network [3]. It can be used to understand the functions and dysfunctions of biological systems on a molecular level, considering the complexity arising from the interplay of biomolecules. These networks are enormously helpful to study cell-cell interactions [4], ligand-receptor interactions [5], disease gene identification [6], pathway analysis [7], evolution and dynamics of interactions [8], crosstalk-analysis [9], etc. Modeling of

DOI: 10.1201/9781003331247-20

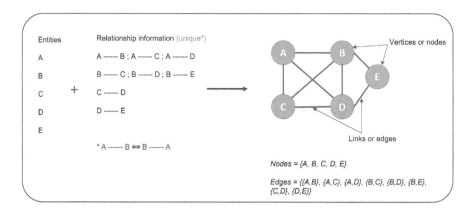

FIGURE 17.1   Schematic diagram of a small network (graph) showing the relationships between entities.

the cellular functionalities can be accomplished by representing information in the form of networks. Some of the most common types of biological networks are signaling network, co-expression network, regulatory network, protein-protein interaction network, and metabolic network. Besides, there are networks which also study interactions between two organisms such as the host-pathogen interaction network [10]. At the genome level, epistasis can be studied by use of epistatic interaction networks of single nucleotide polymorphisms (SNPs) [11]. In this chapter, we particularly focus on protein-protein interactions networks (PPINs). In PPINs, various types of topological and functional analysis can be performed based on the underlying edge information [12]. Therefore, it is important to highlight the main types of edges in a network. Generally, edges are of three types as shown in Figure 17.2. (a) Undirected edges – where the relationship between the nodes is usually a simple connection without a given flow implied, (b) directed edges – where there is a clear flow of signal implied, and the network can be organized hierarchically, and (c) weighted edges – where there can also be a weight, or a quantitative value associated with directed or undirected edges. Undirected edges are very common in PPINs which

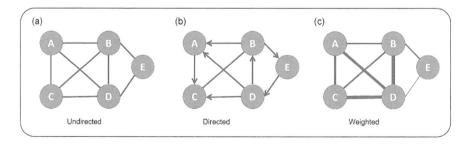

FIGURE 17.2   Schematic diagram of a small network showing (a) undirected, (b) directed, and (c) weighted edges.

also limits the dynamic analysis of network. Directed edges are a specific feature of signaling networks, directed PPINs, and metabolic networks where flux direction is shown with edges. Weighted networks are very useful as interaction confidence scores can be associated with edges and high confidence edges can be prioritized during the network analysis.

Here, we present a detailed review about networks and their importance as a systems biological approach. Our goal is to provide the basics of network biology and show various ways to integrate biological data at different levels. Networks are essential for having a more integrated view on complicated molecular processes and their interactions in a cellular system. We aim to underline the significance of networks for analysis and interpretation of complex biological mechanisms. We give an extensive view on the network reconstruction and analysis followed by integration of omics data to the networks with examples of specific cases, in which networks help discover information that otherwise can be overlooked.

17.2   THE INFORMATION FLOW IN THE CELL

One of the fundamental principles of molecular biology is the central dogma which ensures flow of genetic information from DNA to RNA (known as transcription) and from RNA to proteins (known as translation) [13]. The nucleus of a cell is the site of transcription in eukaryotic cells where DNA serves as a template for encoding the genetic information present in its nucleotide sequence into a messenger RNA (mRNA). The mRNA molecule is a single stranded RNA which stores the genetic information specific to a protein. Once the mRNA molecule is synthesized, it is then transported out of the nucleus to the cytoplasm where it travels and attaches to the ribosomes which leads to protein synthesis. During the translation, the mRNA sequence is used as a guide to make protein polypeptide chains which are assembled on the ribosomes. An activation or an inhibition in any of the two processes of central dogma (transcription or translation) is referred as a perturbation. What will happen, for instance, if a gene coding for a particular protein is knocked out of the cells? As the whole cellular system is completely connected by central dogma, even a small perturbation in a single gene can affect the entire system, which might result in abnormal functioning of the cell [14]. If we can reconstruct the directed network, we can study the effect of these perturbations in more detail.

17.3   PROTEIN-PROTEIN INTERACTION NETWORKS (PPINS)

PPINs are a mathematical representation of stable or transient contact between proteins, where a node represents a protein, and their interaction is represented by a line called edge. The computational analysis of these networks has significant applications in identification of essential proteins or disease genes, inference of pathways and prediction of protein complexes. PPINs, generally, are created from the data obtained from Tandem affinity purification (TAP purification) coupled with mass spectrometry (TAP-MS), yeast two Hybrid (Y2H) or literature mining [15]. However, these only give a static representation of the protein interactions and,

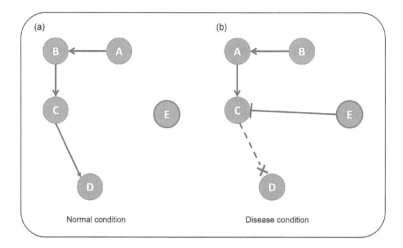

FIGURE 17.3   Schematic diagram of the effect of a perturbation in a PPIN resulting in a disease.

herein lies a critical disadvantage as the biological processes are dynamic in nature. It is safe to assume, at specific times, even if a protein is encoded in the genome, it can only interact with its counterparts if they are also expressed. Furthermore, proteins may undergo modifications during interaction, or some proteins may only interact under certain physiological states like disease conditions, different stages of the cell cycle, or different environmental conditions. For instance, in Figure 17.3, we have a network where in normal condition, the protein E associated with a disease is inactive and thus, we get a resultant network on the left. If the disease-related protein E were to be active, the topology of the network would change as shown on the right. Thus, using only the PPINs in computational studies may yield in biologically meaningful results.

To address these drawbacks, there have been numerous studies that have integrated various omics data (proteomics, genomics, transcriptomics) to represent temporal and spatial states of the proteins more accurately in the network which is somewhat close to the dynamic nature of the real-world protein interaction network [16]. The PPINs mainly give a mathematical representation of the physical contacts between the proteins in a cell. Although genetic interactions can be represented by PPINs, it is important to note that physical contacts are specific: they occur between defined binding regions in the proteins and serve a specific biological purpose. Information about PPIs can represent both the transient and stable interactions [17]. The stable interactions are formed in protein complexes such as ribosomes. These stable interactions are often mediated by domains of proteins and architecture of the complex interactions in an organism. These stable interactions in protein complexes prevent them to dissociate under perturbations. On the contrary, transient interactions are interactions that are part of essential biological processes including different signaling cascades and regulatory biochemical networks such as protein kinase pathways, protein degradation pathways, ligand-receptor binding, etc. These transient interactions constitute the dynamicity of the PPIN (also called interactome). The required information for reconstructing PPIN is interaction data, which can be obtained from various freely available databases (Table 17.1).

For extracting the interaction or genomic information of model organisms, many organism-specific databases are freely available for the scientific community. Some of such widely used databases are listed in Table 17.2.

TABLE 17.1
Widely Used Protein-Protein Interaction Databases

Name	Description	Link	Reference
APID	APID (Agile Protein Interaction DataAnalyzer) is a public resource-wide board protein interactome database of more than 1100 organisms with more than 500 protein physical interactions	http://cicblade.dep. usal.es:8080/APID/ init. action	[18]
BioGRID	Biological General Repository for Interaction Datasets (BioGRID) is an open source that provides protein and genetic interactions and enables to build up complex biological networks associated with human health and diseases. Database created from biomedical literature.	https://thebiogrid.org	[19]
DIP	The Database of Interacting Proteins (DIP) is a protein-protein interaction database that provides information regarding protein functionality, protein-protein relationships, and evolution of the protein-protein interactions	https://dip.doe-mbi. ucla.edu/dip/Main. cgi	[20]
IntAct	IntAct is an open-source database tool for analysis of protein interactions. It has a collaboration with Swiss-Prot team. It enables the investigation of interaction networks within the context of the GO annotations.	https://www.ebi. ac.uk/intact	[21]
MINT	Molecular INTeraction (MINT) database uses the Spokes model to show PPIs based on the binary interactions.	https://mint.bio. uniroma2.it	[22]
String	Search Tool for the Retrieval of Interacting Genes/Proteins (STRING) is another database to provide and predict protein-protein interactions based on enormous experimental and computational data. This tool also provides protein lists submitted by users, utilizing a variety of functional classification such as GO, Pfam, and KEGG.	https://string-db.org	[23]
BIND	The Biomolecular Interaction Network Database (BIND) is a database for biomolecular interactions. It takes information from PDB and, Mass spectrometry, genetic interactions, yeast two hybrid assays, phage display, and several large-scale interactions and complex mapping experiments.	http://bond.unleashed informatics.com	[24]

TABLE 17.2

Organism-Specific Interaction Databases

Name	Description	Link	Reference
AtPID	*Arabidopsis thaliana* Protein Interactome Database (AtPID) contains several bioinformatic prediction methods. It provides protein-protein interactions, protein subcellular localization, ortholog maps, and gene regulation information.	http://atpid. biosino.org	[25]
EcoCyc	Encyclopedia of *E. coli* Genes and Metabolism (EcoCyc) is a model organism database for *Escherichia coli* K-12. It includes gene, protein, and metabolic networks.	https://ecocyc. org	[26]
MGI	Mouse Genome Informatics (MGI) is an online database comprising information from laboratory mice. It provides integrated data based on genetics, genomics, and transcriptomics and facilitates study of human diseases and health.	http://www. informatics. jax.org	[27]
SGD	Saccharomyces Genome Database (SGD) is a model organism database comprising whole genome sequences of the budding yeast *Saccharomyces cerevisiae*. It also provides comprehensive information on functional relationships between the gene and gene products.	https://www. yeastgenome. org	[28]
ZFIN	Zebrafish Information Network (ZFIN) is an online database that provides information for the model organism Zebrafish (*Danio rerio*). It enables to assess genetic, genomic, and developmental information.	https://zfin.org	[29]
FlyBase	It is a model organism database containing information about the fruit fly, *Drosophila melanogaster*. It provides genetic, molecular, genomic, and developmental information about *Drosophila*.	https://flybase. org	[30]
WormBAse	It is a model organism database that provides genetic and genomic information for *Caenorhabditis elegans* and related nematodes.	https:// wormbase. org//#012-34-5	[31]
HumanCyc	It is a curated database that provides information on human metabolic pathways, metabolites, enzymes, and reactions.	https:// humancyc. org	[32]
HPRD	Human Protein Reference Database (HRPD) only focuses on human protein interactions, and provides additional post-translational modifications, disease associations, and enzyme-substrate relationship information.	http://www. hprd.org	[33]

17.4   WHY DO WE NEED COMPUTATIONAL PPINS?

The biological processes in a cell are governed by the interplay between various multi-protein complexes rather than single proteins. To gain deeper insights into these processes, many high-throughput experimental techniques such as the Y2H, TAP-MS, and co-immunoprecipitation (Co-IP) assays are successfully carried out.

Despite their efficiency, due to multiple reasons these techniques limit themselves and may provide false positives or false negatives, and thus may fail to detect many true interactions [34]. It is important to emphasize that significant challenges arise not only due to the size of a biological dataset, but also due to inherent noise and incompleteness in the dataset. Thus, there is a limitation on how many true physiological interactions can be revealed by these PPI detection methods. Other widely used techniques, such as fluorescence resonance energy transfer (FRET) microscopy, X-ray crystallography, atomic force microscopy (AFM), and nuclear magnetic resonance (NMR) spectroscopy, though they provide accurate results, require extensive costly instrumentation as well as huge time consumption [35–38]. Also, experimental methods often have a difficulty in identifying weaker interactions, thus excluding many transient interactions. These limitations have driven the adoption of fast and inexpensive in silico methods. The ability of computational methods to predict PPIs and validate them via experiments has enticed tremendous interest among biologists. There are computational solutions for reconstructing high quality PPINs from scratch or for improving existing PPINs. For instance, gene co-localization information can be used to reduce false positive PPINs which are based on the key idea that related genes are located near one another in the genome. Scoring the interactions is another way by which PPINs quality can be improved.

17.5   RECONSTRUCTION OF A PPI NETWORK

A protein complex is a combination of proteins which closely interact together and play important roles in regulating important cellular processes, functions, and signaling cascades. The complexity and intricacy of these interactions increase as we move from a single protein structure to the genome-level interactome. The representation of numerous functional interactions that can occur in a cell, an organism, or within a specific biological setting is known as an interactome. Due to the development of large-scale PPI screening techniques, such as TAP-MS and Y2H, assays, the amount of PPI data has vastly increased and interactomes have become more intricated. A PPI prediction algorithm thus complements experimental evidence to map interactomes. At a large scale, a global interactome describes all the stable PPIs in a biological system. When reconstructing a PPI network, it is important to be aware of the type and quality of the data used. The reconstruction of high-quality computational PPINs can be achieved through previous studies [10]. After PPI network reconstruction, quality can be assessed by comparing the network with random and real networks [39]. To understand the biological context of PPI data, several tools can be used to integrate gene expression data to the network and analyze it. One of the most popular network analysis tools is Cytoscape [40]. This application is widely used to represent and analyze networks. A non-programmatic option for large networks is Gephi [41]. Even though Gephi can process and draw very large networks, massive amounts of high-performance computational power are required to process and draw networks of this size. Useful tools for the analysis of large networks include packages such as igraph (R, Python and C), NetworkX (Python), and graph-tool (Python).

17.5.1 TRANSCRIPTOME DATA INTEGRATION IN PROTEIN INTERACTION NETWORK

Transcriptomic data can reveal gene expression profiles at different time points and physiological states and can indirectly provide protein activity patterns. The transcriptomics data can be obtained either experimentally through microarray and high throughput RNA sequencing technologies or through various databases such as GEO [42], 4DXpress [43], and ArrayExpress [44] which publish a huge amount of gene expression data, making it convenient for computational biologists to assimilate with the available protein interaction data. Transcriptome data analysis can reveal a multitude of information. Incorporating these knowledges can lead to generation of a PPIN with different topologies and reveal important subnetworks that fits within the context. For example, it can help identify differentially expressed genes (DEGs) or significantly expressed genes (SEGs) and their integration with PPIN can especially be useful in disease studies to identify differences between disease states and cellular processes which, in turn, can help to reveal the underlying disease mechanism and find candidates for drug targeting. In a recent study, to decipher the unclear molecular pathogenesis of very similar diseases like Crohn's disease (CD), inflammatory bowel disease (IBD), and ulcerative colitis (UC), they used the integrative approach and created disease specific subnetworks to identify and differentiate the key players in the disease networks [45]. Transcriptome data can also be integrated with both the metabolic and PPIN to identify the potential drug targets [46, 47].

Another popular approach to identification of drug targets is searching for essential genes. In a static PPI model, essential genes are commonly identified by centrality measures like degree, betweenness, closeness, edge-clustering coefficient, etc. conforming to the centrality-lethality rule. But these analysis methods generate many false positives and false negatives. On the other hand, while gene expression data is also used to identify essential genes, these are also prone to fluctuations due to dynamics of interactions. Methods integrating PPIN and gene expression like PeC [48] and Weighted Degree Centrality (WDC) (both of which use Pearson Correlation coefficient (PCC) to relate PPI and gene expression data) have been shown to outperform the traditional solo PPIN and gene-expression-based prediction of essential genes [48, 49].

Likewise, directed PPINs or/like signaling pathways can also have both transient and stable interactions. Some ligands facilitate in a permanent change while some invoke transient states like cascade reactions. Here, time series gene expression data can be used to find stable modules and active modules in the pathway. From these, either time course PPIN (TC-PPIN) or dynamic PPINs (DPPINs) can be constructed which would be very useful for understanding the molecular mechanisms and functional modules in a given condition [50]. There are many more examples that show the shift from a static to a dynamic point of view in the study of PPIs which greatly improves the understanding and prediction methods of these networks [51–53].

17.6   QUALITY ASSESSMENT OF COMPUTER GENERATED PPINS

Once the PPIN is reconstructed it is crucial to check the quality of the reconstructed PPIN. This ensures the presence of biologically meaningful interactions. The quality can be assessed by comparing the reconstructed PPIN with random networks. For random networks, edges are created based on different algorithms such as the Barabási-Albert Model, Watts–Strogatz, or Erdős-Rényi Model [54–56]. However, the PPIN can also be compared to a real biological network or by accessing the functional similarity between interacting partners.

17.6.1 COMPARISONS WITH RANDOM NETWORKS

The Barabási-Albert Model [54] can be used to create random scale-free networks using a preferential attachment mechanism to mimic a real biological network. On the other hand, completely random networks can be modeled by Watts–Strogatz or Erdős-Rényi Model [55, 56]. Comparison of reconstructed PPI with random networks can give the indication of the goodness of the reconstructed PPIN. Such comparisons can be done by simply analyzing the topological properties of the reconstructed PPIN and random networks followed by calculating the mean of these random properties and then compare it with the reconstructed network using Z statistics [39]. Such calculations are based on the concept that the properties of a biologically meaningful PPIN should be much closer to Barabási-Albert Model.

17.6.2 COMPARISON WITH REAL BIOLOGICAL NETWORKS

Another comparative method is to compare the reconstructed PPIN with an existing PPIN of another species with experimentally verified interactions. Often, there are well-preserved interactions between orthologous proteins in functional modules that are present in different species [57]. Hence, for the quality check it would be appropriate to measure the topological similarity between the reconstructed PPINs with the interactome of other phylogenetically closer species [39].

17.6.3 FUNCTIONAL SIMILARITY-BASED ASSESSMENT

Many functional similarity methods based on Gene Ontology (GO) have been proposed in recent years [58, 59]. A variety of applications have been developed using these measures, including PPIs, network predictions and cellular localization predictions. Two types of measures of gene functional similarity rely on the GO graph: pairwise approaches and groupwise approaches. In pairwise methods, functional similarity between genes is measured in two steps. First, semantic similarity scores are calculated by comparing term pairs. Ten of these semantic similarity scores are integrated into a single functional similarity measure. In groupwise methods, functional similarity is measured by comparing terms that are used to annotate genes in groups. In comparison to random networks, it is then expected that the biologically meaningful network shows higher GO semantic similarity between the interacting proteins [39].

17.7 NETWORK ANALYSIS

Different types of topological analysis of PPIN are possible. Here we define few widely used topological analysis measures.

17.7.1   Hubs

In a scale-free PPI network, only a few proteins or nodes are connected to numerous others while remaining nodes do not show high connectivity. When a node is connected to numerous other nodes, it is known as a hub. The importance of the hub is generally measured by the impact on the network when it is removed [60]. The number of interactions of a protein is commonly known as the degree. Typically, a fixed cutoff of 5–10 interactions is required for a node to be defined as a hub in a network. However, this threshold may differ from study to study, and hence, it is now mostly used in a vague sense. More characteristics can be assigned to hubs apart from the number of interactions, such as centrality, for a more distinguished definition [61]. Protein hubs are quite important to a PPI network due to the huge impact they have on the network. Deletion of a hub can be more fatal to an organism as compared to non-hub proteins referred as the centrality-lethal rule. This could be due to higher number of interactions a hub protein is involved. Therefore, they potentially have more essential interactions than other interactions in the overall network structure [62]. The hub proteins are categorized mostly as 'party' hubs and 'date' hubs. 'Party' hubs are the hubs that interact with other nodes or hubs at the same time whereas 'date' hubs interact with others one at a time [63, 64]. The hub proteins in static protein interaction networks generally interact with proteins; however, with the evolution of networks, dynamic protein interaction networks can also see hubs interacting with other supramolecule components of cells like ribosomes, nucleosomes, etc. A hub protein varies from other proteins structurally as it consists of disordered regions and global flexibility. These disordered regions can explain why some proteins interact with numerous proteins whereas other proteins do not interact [65]. Thus, hub proteins not only play an important role in the network aspects of PPINs but also have essential biological roles important for the survival of an organism. Hubs in host PPINs are one of the preferential targets of different pathogens [10, 66], and the hubs in pathogen PPINs represent potential drug targets [67, 68]. Regulatory hubs can also be identified in PPIN which requires the integration of transcriptome data to the hubs and their primary interactors in PPIN [69, 70].

17.7.2   Bottlenecks

Besides degree, betweenness is one of the widely used topologically measures for the importance of a network node. Proteins with high betweenness are often essential for the network as they were the key links between two subnetworks [71]. Betweenness measures the number of shortest paths that pass-through nodes and edges. Deletion of proteins with high betweenness can impair the network easily and these proteins are called bottlenecks in a network. Connecting two subnetworks, the bottleneck proteins may be more crucial than hub proteins, as their disruption can be lethal to the cell. Bottlenecks can also be hub proteins, thereby increasing their essentiality [72, 73]. Bottlenecks, like hubs, are coded from essential genes. Hence, it is no surprise that a positive correlation (Spearman's $\rho = 0.76$) can be observed between the degree and betweenness of a protein, although differences in evolutionary patterns still exist between hubs and bottlenecks [74].

17.7.3 Shortest Path

The analysis of biological networks is essential for understanding the underlying pathways. Shortest path as the name suggests, states the shortest distance between two nodes in a network. This measure also defines the functional distance [75] and provides insights into network clusters and modules. Core pathways can also be predicted using the shortest path measures of a PPIN. With the rising complexity of networks, these measures can help in easing their analysis [76]. Shortest path analysis of a PPI network revealed that other than helping in understanding the network, it can also reveal meaningful biological pathways, although not all the observations may match fully to the existing system due to high complexity and crosstalk in real biological networks [77]. The two algorithms mostly used for calculating the shortest path are Dijkstra's greedy algorithm and Floyd's dynamic algorithm [2, 78] (their strategies are different, but give the same result).

17.7.4 Centrality

Centrality is another important aspect to measure while studying the topological features of a network. Centrality determines the important parameters of a network and is quite helpful in the analysis of key players like hubs and bottlenecks [79]. There are different types of centrality analyses which deal with different areas of a biological network. For instance, degree centrality analysis is used to find the most connected hubs in a network and their potential impact. Closeness centrality measures the shortest path from one node to other nodes and thus the overall flow of information from a given node in a network. It can also be used to distinguish between the networks and helps define hubs in a network. Furthermore, shortest path betweenness centrality uses the shortest paths through nodes to find the betweenness of a node. This can be used to infer the importance of a hub and calculate modularity in the network [80]. There are several other centralities apart from the core ones that we discussed, and it was found that some of them have more importance when analyzing a PPI network. With the increase in biological data (expression profiles, protein clusters, ontology, localization, etc.), centralities can be analyzed more effectively rather than just using graph theory-based algorithms. Biological data combined with different centrality measures can be more useful in the prediction of important nodes and other parameters in a biological network [81].

17.7.5 Controllability

Controllability in any directed PPI or a signaling network deals with the regulation of the network with preferable inputs. Controllability is based on the mathematical concept of control theory which suggests that a dynamic system can be steered from an initial state to a final state with specific inputs [82]. Thus, interpretation of the network control is important for the regulation of complex networks. In the case of biological networks, regulation of a network may result in desirable phenotypes. An interesting example of a PPI network shows that controlling a node near a hub can be a better alternative than directly controlling a hub which could be lethal (central-lethality rule) [83]. Nodes in such systems can be deemed as indispensable, neutral, or dispensable based on controllability measures [84]. Control methods can be used to reduce the complexity of a network for better understanding. However, controllability analysis in complex networks can be a huge task when calculating the effect of each element of a network with limited knowledge of underlying network dynamics. In PPNs, controllability measures can help pinpoint drug targets and disease-controlling elements [84]. Therefore, controllability is essential to identify nodes and other elements which are crucial to the network apart from hubs, bottlenecks, or ones identified by other parameters. Nodes with high controllability in a dynamic network can be used to drive the system from one state to other state [85, 86].

17.7.6 NETWORK DYNAMICS

Transient networks are dynamic and are mostly associated with external stimuli. Transient networks can be seen in crucial biological processes like signal transduction, receptor binding, enzyme functions, etc. To comprehend this type of network, analysis of the changing dynamics is necessary. There are plenty of applications of dynamic networks in modern biology and medicine. Apart from highlighting the changing parameters of a network during a stimulus, it can also show the onset and progression of any disease and its related parameters in a network. It can also help emphasize/discover the drug targets which do not show up in static networks. A dynamic network has spatial and temporal information and thus contains a more complex framework for biological information discovery. A dynamic PPIN is usually reconstructed by integrating gene expression data to a static PPIN [52]. Understanding the changes in parameters of a network under certain stimuli is essential in understanding the resulting phenotype. Certain proteins tend to participate in dynamic complexes that can result in novel interactions. Analysis of network dynamics also led to the discovery of 'party' and 'date' hubs which are essential for understanding the interactions in a network [83]. Therefore, dynamic interaction analysis can show distinct roles of a single hub. Dynamic protein complexes are also formed in a dynamic network which can shed some light on previously undiscovered interactions as well as on protein localization [87]. These complex network dynamics can only be analyzed using specific computational tools due to very complex nature of the network. Tools like DyNetViewer [88], CellNetAnalyzer (CNA) [89] and Jimena [90] can be used to visualize dynamic networks as well as to analyze network dynamics.

17.8 FUNCTIONAL ANALYSIS

To understand the function of protein group or an unknown protein function in a PPIN, functional analysis is used.

17.8.1 MODULARITY IN BIOLOGICAL NETWORKS

A cell functions in a modular manner, in which the network can be subdivided into groups of physically or functionally connected nodes that are linked through a specific cellular function [75]. In the cell, most molecules are either a function in an intracellular complex or they are part of a functional module regulating a distinct process [75].

If a gene or a molecule is involved in a biological process, its direct interaction partners are also likely to be involved in the same process. Likewise, proteins involved in the same disease apt to interact together [91, 92]. This suggests that a disease can be associated with a specific region of the interactome, known as a disease module [93].

In general, network modules can be classified as topological, functional and disease modules. A topological module is a locally dense region of the network, where the nodes have a higher likelihood to interact with the nodes within the module than with the nodes outside. Network clustering algorithms that identify topological modules do not consider specific functions of the individual nodes. Functional modules, on the other hand, represent groups of nodes with similar function in the same network region. Therefore, a functional module requires defined node characteristics since it assumes that the nodes that are involved in a specific cellular process are more likely to interact and to cluster in the same network region. A disease module represents a group of nodes that together contribute to a particular cellular function and any disruption in this module may result in a disease phenotype. These three types of networks tend to overlap, and therefore, functional modules are mostly comparable to topological modules and a disease can be viewed as the breakdown of a functional module [93].

Different measures exist for the evaluation of topological modularity. These measures can be categorized as local and global measures. Local measures score specific modules of the network. Networks with a higher number of connections within the module and lower number of connections outside of the module have a high modularity score [94].

An example for local measures is the Q measure for modality, which defines the difference between the real connections of the module and the expected connections within a module.

$$Q = \sum_{s=1}^{M} \left[\frac{l_0}{L} - \left(\frac{d_s}{2L} \right)^2 \right]$$

where M is the modules of the partition, l_0 is the number of edges in the module s, L is the number of edges in the network, and d_s is the total degree of nodes in module s.

17.8.2 CLUSTERING OF BIOLOGICAL NETWORKS

While topological module detection divides the graph into densely connected subgraphs, graph clustering algorithms group the network based on the quality of network nodes. Nodes that are like each other are organized into the same cluster and objects that have a low similarity are grouped into a different cluster [95]. Network clustering can be flat or hierarchical: while flat clustering determines all clusters at the same time, hierarchical algorithms find further clusters using previously deter-mined clusters. Flat clustering is based on specifying the number of clusters and iteratively reallocating objects among groups to convergence. Hierarchical cluster-ing requires the specification of how much dissimilarity should be tolerated between the groups. Based on the clustering strategy, it can be agglomerative (bottom-up) or divisive (top-down). Agglomerative clustering starts from the individual objects and groups of objects and clusters of objects, while divisive clustering starts from all objects (as one single cluster) and breaks it down into smaller clusters. For separating the graph into clusters, various heuristic rules are used, such as betweenness central-ity [96], clustering coefficient [97], minimum cut [98], etc. Both types of hierarchical clustering can be represented by a tree structure known as a dendrogram.

17.8.3 NETWORK-BASED PATHWAY ANALYSIS

The discovery of high throughput techniques permits comparison of the gene expres-sion levels between different conditions, such as a healthy state or a diseased state of a cell. While interpreting significantly altered genes between two states, identifica-tion of the activated pathways can provide deeper biological insights. The most pop-ular method determines the overlap between a gene set and a pathway [99]. However, because of the limited and incomplete knowledge of pathways, there is a high false-positive rate [100] and a low detection rate [101] in this technique. Statistical assumptions also require all genes to be equal, which is contradictory to the buildup of complex biological systems [102]. Overlap-based analysis can be improved by functional class scoring [102, 103], or pathway topology methods [104], if gene expression data is available.

Pathway analysis can be improved by using network-based methods, which can detect significant associations between gene sets and pathways even though no shared genes exist. This is based on the enrichment of the interactions and crosstalk between a pathway and a gene set in the network. Network-based pathway analysis relies on the likelihood of functionally associated proteins to be in the same pathway. However, the accuracy of these methods requires high quality of the network. In addition, there is another criterion known as suitability of a statistical model, which determines how efficiently a method can evaluate a correct statistical model and thereby differentiate between pseudo and existing biologically significant observa-tions [101].

17.9   RECENT ADVANCES IN PPI NETWORK

PPINs can be used in different contexts depending on the data being integrated to the network. PPINs specific to a cell type or a complex disease can be reconstructed by integrating proteomics or transcriptomics data and they can be used to look at processes at single cell resolution or intercellular communication between individual cells. Furthermore, on bigger scale, organism-specific PPINs can elucidate commu-nication between a host and a pathogen and thus a better look into a disease mecha-nism. In this section, we provide latest methods on reconstruction and analysis of such networks focusing on single-cell level PPINs and host-pathogen PPINs.

17.9.1 Recent Advances from Single Cell Data

Organism-specific interactomes offer many possibilities for systems biological investigation of complex processes via integration of multiple levels of biological data. These interactomes, however, do not offer cell type specific information. Although methods exist to reconstruct tissue specific PPINs using bulk RNA-sequencing data, they still lack the single-cell resolution needed to extract significant data from the cellular processes occurring at inter- and intracellular levels [105]. Single-cell proteomics presents the most accurate method to decipher PPIs in each context. However, it is a relatively novel technology and one can expect challenges in the generation and subsequent analysis of the data [4]. On the other hand, single-cell RNA sequencing (scRNA-seq) is a widely used method with standardized techniques of data generation and easy protocols of data analysis [4]. Integration of scRNA-seq data to PPINs provides a closer look into context-specific spatiotemporal dynamics of the interactome, which is normally a rather static snapshot of the process [106]. It is now becoming a widely used approach thanks to a high number of PPI databases hosting interactomes of many species.

Multiple network-based methods are available for scRNA-seq data [107]. Most common methods rely on co-expression of two genes to predict an interaction, or of multiple genes to reconstruct a gene regulatory network (GRN). These networks capture transcriptional states of individual cell types and identify cell clusters [107]. Based on co-expression of the genes, they reveal functional relationships by reconstructing GRNs from single-cell gene expression [108–118]. Although very useful to reveal functional clusters, methods based on co-expression do not make use of protein interactions. Since protein interactions vary between cell-types and normal/diseased states, investigating the changes in these interactions is helpful to identify proteins that may be involved in a process but do not show variations at the gene level.

Integrating scRNA-seq to PPINs helps in detecting active modules in different cellular states. It can be used to reconstruct cell-specific, process-specific networks to represent changes in protein interactions. scRNA-seq can also be used to reconstruct cell-cell communication networks (CCCN) that are based on similar expression patterns of a ligand on one cell and the receptor on the other [4]. Zhou et al. constructed a CCCN between different cell types in cancer based on scRNA-seq data from melanoma [119]. More tools have been developed to elucidate context-specific cell-cell communication using scRNA-seq data [120–130]. Nevertheless, these networks focus specifically on ligand-receptor interactions and do not provide information about the rest of the PPIs regulating intracellular processes.

As a more global approach, one can integrate scRNA-seq data into reference PPINs. One of these tools is SCINET, a method used to reconstruct cell-specific PPINs with single-cell transcriptional profile [105]. After analysis of the scRNA-seq data, SCINET shows PPIs according to the expression patterns of the interaction partners. They also exemplify their method by integrating scRNA-seq data [131] into a reference [132] to build cell-specific interactomes of six different blood cell types. Therefore, they reveal changes in the active parts of the reference PPIN based on changes in the expression patterns of interaction partners according to cell type or context [105].

Another large-scale approach from Klimm et al. focuses on finding active modules in a reference PPIN based on cell-specific gene expression [133]. SCPPIN applies methods for clustering the scRNA-seq data and identifying modules in the PPIN based on the DEGs. Thus, they identify in these modules genes which are not differentially expressed but are part of an active module, and thus may be important in the process. Therefore, they present an integrative approach into biological functions behind the specific cell-specific transcriptional states [133].

A similar goal is also pursued by scNetViz, a Cytoscape app for visualization of scRNA-seq data [134]. This approach also finds active modules by mapping the data onto STRING database and visualizes the resulting sub-PPINs. scNetViz then performs further functional analyses.

Integration of scRNA-seq data holds promise to identify cell-specific transcriptional states, from identification of functional modules by GRNs, to cell-cell communication by finding pairwise active ligand-receptor interactions. It also helps to reconstruct cell-specific interactomes at single-cell resolution. However, one must be careful when integrating multi-level omics data. Generally, these do not correspond and correlating transcript level to protein level may be problematic because of the different regulation levels including turnover rates, cellular localization, post-transcriptional and post-translational modifications, etc. [106, 135]. Therefore, when applying these methods to conclude hypotheses, it is ideal to decrease the chances of false-positive interactions with additional data integration or experiments.

17.9.2 Recent Advances in Host–Pathogen PPIN

Host-pathogen interaction networks open space for interspecies, or trans kingdom networks [136] as an extension to the widely studied intraspecies networks [4, 137, 138]. The communication of cells does not stop at the cell border. In particular, studies related to immune system signaling [4, 139] and neuronal cell population [139–142] confirm that external cell-cell signaling is a widely established concept. Intercellular interactions receive a special role, as the intersection at a cell border represents an interaction bottleneck, that is characterized by a high network control, or high betweenness centrality, as many pathways between two cells are interconnected via a limited number of intersection sites [73, 136].

It is only the next logical step that the intercellular intraspecies intersections are not only functional within a species but are valid intersections for cross-species interactions in a highly enriched environment [143–145]. The interaction of species via the intersections is categorized as mutualism, parasitism, or commensalism [146, 147]. Interestingly, similar intersection sites are often linked to harmful (parasitism), as well as beneficial (symbiosis) host effects [145, 148]. Thus, minor changes in interaction can modulate a species relationship [146].

Yet, knowledge on host-pathogen interactions is sparse. Therefore, inference methods display a central complement to experimental methods as described in Section 17.5. There are two different ways to infer host-pathogen PPI: similarity to common PPI and ab-initio prediction based on 3D binding models. Homology targeting paved the way for determining interologs, as a protein interaction analog to protein homology analysis [149, 150]. The interolog method could be easily extended to predict host-pathogen interactions based on sequence similarity of experimentally evaluated interactions [151, 152]. However, sequence similarity is not the only trait to conclude on a conserved interaction site. Several traits such as pathway, complex similarity, high expression, and short sequence can be utilized or combined to find conserved interaction sites [153].

Presently, common interaction prediction algorithms are based on sequence similarity [154], structural similarity [155, 156], and domain interactions [157]. Interactions are refined by further protein annotation such as GO similarity [158], expression profile, pathway correlations, and further features [159–162].

Recently, prediction approaches are using neuronal networks and deep learning to extract conserved intersection site information from experimentally analyzed interactions [163]. The study reveals that vector machines are trained to extract certain features from sequences that allow the prediction of interactions. Another approach uses machine learning on position-specific scoring matrices (PSSM) to extract conserved amino acid patterns of interaction sites [164]. Self-attention with deep neural networks [165] and network-based predictions [166] are good candidates for improved prediction accuracy.

Other than the methods that are based on feature extraction from experimentally analyzed interactions, computational docking simulation can predict protein interactions based on the structure of proteins only (*ab initio interaction prediction*) [167]. However, docking simulations are computationally heavy and are limited to proteins with structure, but can complement similarity-based methods [168].

Recent advances in protein structure prediction by AlphaFold2 thereby support structure-based interaction predictions by delivering homology-based structures of yet not experimentally investigated pathogenic proteins [138].

All the advances in computational prediction of host-pathogen protein helped to decrease the enormous search space of possible protein interactions and shifted the focus from a narrow view on separated intraspecies interactions to a rather holistic view on interactions such as trans-kingdom networks. However, even if the accuracy levels of these predictions are far better than earlier used methods, direct evidence coming out of the experimental data is indispensable.

17.10   OUTLOOK AND FUTURE DIRECTIONS

One of the goals of systems biology is to create theoretical models to represent and investigate cellular behavior at the whole system level. This saves experiments but becomes reliable and strong by including experimental data wherever possible. Here, we have presented reconstruction, analysis, and recent progress in the field of computational prediction of PPIN. Explicitly, we have detailed the recent advances in single cell based PPIN and host-pathogen interactions.

An accurate prediction of functions of proteins involved in a particular disease is a key to understanding its pathogenesis at the molecular level. It is noteworthy to mention that PPINs have been successfully employed to extract new information regarding proteins involved in pathogenesis of various diseases and in predicting potential drug targets. However, owing to their black-box nature, it is recommended to integrate the static PPINs with the multimodality data from the high-throughput technologies like genomics, transcriptomics, and proteomics (multiomics analysis). The dynamic PPINs (DPPINs) thus constructed would not only allow for a more comprehensive and systematic understanding of complex pathogenesis of a disease, but also the prediction model would be more significant from biological point of view for performing experimental research in future [52]. In recent years, DPPINs have shown promising results in understanding molecular pathways, predicting the mechanism of drug action and identifying new drug targets.

As most diseases are not just an effect of a single protein perturbation in isolation but rather the combined result of all these perturbations in a cellular context, recent advancements in the field of network medicine offer new approaches to gain deeper insights into the molecular pathways of complex diseases. Network medicine can provide tools to integrate disease networks with information such as disease symptoms, epidemiology, clinical-based evidence or data from the Electronic Health Records (EHR), thus providing details of disease mechanisms and strategies for prediction and evaluation of novel therapeutic targets [169]. In addition, interactome analysis helps to identify other diseases that target the same interactome vicinity and thus, it may be possible to repurpose a drug corresponding to one disease for another disease. For instance, by measuring the network proximity, Cheng et al. [170] predicted new associations between a non-cardiovascular drug hydroxychloroquine and coronary artery disease, suggesting the possibility of 'multiple-drugs, multiple-targets' approach in future. This would further help to understand the role of a gene or associated protein within one disease and between various diseases and thus also elucidate the connection between different diseases.

Despite tremendous progress made in the field of protein interaction network biology, considerable challenges are required to be addressed in the future in order to develop robust and reliable networks. First, since we have a wealth of new and heterogeneous biological data emerging continuously, it is imperative to develop new methods which could minimize errors such as false positives and false negatives. Second, as the biological systems are highly complex, integration of diversified biological interactions in a composite network is another challenge. For instance, a protein can interact with different set of proteins under different cellular conditions and thus, it is difficult to obtain high-confidence data which incorporates multiple interactions under different conditions into a composite network. Third, a lot of experimental data comes from experiments performed on model organisms such as mice, fruit flies, or zebrafish. It is difficult to integrate the information from animal models into the PPINs which aim to predict a disease in humans. Nevertheless, recent advancements and fast improvements in PPIN approaches will definitely revolutionize our understanding of complex biological systems over the coming decade.

REFERENCES

1. Koutrouli M, Karatzas E, Paez-Espino D, et al. A guide to conquer the biological network era using graph theory. *Front Bioeng Biotechnol*. 2020;8:34.
2. Pavlopoulos GA, Secrier M, Moschopoulos CN, et al. Using graph theory to analyze biological networks. *BioData Min*. 2011;4:10.

3. Alon U. Biological networks: the tinkerer as an engineer. *Science*. 2003;301(5641):1866–7.
4. Armingol E, Officer A, Harismendy O, et al. Deciphering cell-cell interactions and communication from gene expression. *Nat Rev Genet*. 2021;22(2):71–88.
5. Shao X, Liao J, Li C, et al. CellTalkDB: a manually curated database of ligand-receptor interactions in humans and mice. *Brief Bioinform*. 2021;22(4):bbaa269.
6. Gillis J, Pavlidis P. The impact of multifunctional genes on "guilt by association" analysis. *PLoS One*. 2011;6(2):e17258.
7. Lin PL, Yu YW, Chung RH. Pathway analysis incorporating protein-protein interaction networks identified candidate pathways for the seven common diseases. *PLoS One*. 2016;11(9):e0162910.
8. Levy ED, Pereira-Leal JB. Evolution and dynamics of protein interactions and networks. *Curr Opin Struct Biol*. 2008;18(3):349–57.
9. Akhoon BA, Gupta SK, Tiwari S, et al. C. elegans protein interaction network analysis probes RNAi validated pro-longevity effect of nhr-6, a human homolog of tumor suppressor Nr4a1. *Sci Rep*. 2019;9(1):15711.
10. Gupta SK, Osmanoglu Ö, Srivastava M, et al. Pathogen and host-pathogen protein interactions provide a key to identify novel drug targets. In: Wolkenhauer O, editor. *Systems Medicine*. Oxford: Academic Press; 2021. pp. 543–53.
11. Liu Y, Li X, Liu Z, et al. Construction and analysis of single nucleotide polymorphism-single nucleotide polymorphism interaction networks. *IET Syst Biol*. 2013;7(5):170–81.
12. Hakes L, Pinney JW, Robertson DL, et al. Protein-protein interaction networks and biology--what's the connection? *Nat Biotechnol*. 2008;26(1):69–72.
13. Crick F. Central dogma of molecular biology. *Nature*. 1970;227(5258):561–3.
14. Markowetz F. How to understand the cell by breaking it: network analysis of gene perturbation screens. *PLoS Comput Biol*. 2010;6(2):e1000655.
15. Rao VS, Srinivas K, Sujini GN, et al. Protein-protein interaction detection: methods and analysis. *International Journal of Proteomics*. 2014;2014:147648.
16. Snider J, Kotlyar M, Saraon P, et al. Fundamentals of protein interaction network mapping. *Mol Syst Biol*. 2015;11(12):848.
17. Byrum S, Smart SK, Larson S, et al. Analysis of stable and transient protein-protein interactions. *Methods Mol Biol*. 2012;833:143–52.
18. Alonso-Lopez D, Campos-Laborie FJ, Gutierrez MA, et al. APID database: redefining protein-protein interaction experimental evidences and binary interactomes. *Database (Oxford)*. 2019;2019.
19. Oughtred R, Stark C, Breitkreutz BJ, et al. The BioGRID interaction database: 2019 update. *Nucleic Acids Res*. 2019;47(D1):D529–41.
20. Xenarios I, Rice DW, Salwinski L, et al. DIP: the database of interacting proteins. *Nucleic Acids Res*. 2000;28(1):289–91.
21. Del Toro N, Shrivastava A, Ragueneau E, et al. The IntAct database: efficient access to fine-grained molecular interaction data. *Nucleic Acids Res*. 2022;50(D1):D648–53.
22. Calderone A, Iannuccelli M, Peluso D, et al. Using the MINT database to search protein interactions. *Curr Protoc Bioinform*. 2020;69(1):e93.
23. Szklarczyk D, Gable AL, Lyon D, et al. STRING v11: protein-protein association networks with increased coverage, supporting functional discovery in genome-wide experimental datasets. *Nucleic Acids Res*. 2019;47(D1):D607–D613.
24. Bader GD, Betel D, Hogue CW. BIND: the biomolecular interaction network database. *Nucleic Acids Res*. 2003;31(1):248–50.
25. Li P, Zang W, Li Y, et al. AtPID: the overall hierarchical functional protein interaction network interface and analytic platform for Arabidopsis. *Nucleic Acids Res*. 2011;39 (Database issue):D1130–3.

26. Keseler IM, Gama-Castro S, Mackie A, et al. The EcoCyc Database in 2021. *Front Microbiol.* 2021;12:711077.

27. Eppig JT. Mouse Genome Informatics (MGI) resource: genetic, genomic, and biological knowledgebase for the laboratory mouse. *ILAR J.* 2017;58(1):17–41.

28. Cherry JM, Adler C, Ball C, et al. SGD: saccharomyces genome database. *Nucleic Acids Res.* 1998;26(1):73–9.

29. Sprague J, Clements D, Conlin T, et al. The Zebrafish Information Network (ZFIN): the zebrafish model organism database. *Nucleic Acids Res.* 2003;31(1):241–3.

30. Thurmond J, Goodman JL, Strelets VB, et al. FlyBase 2.0: the next generation. *Nucleic Acids Res.* 2019;47(D1):D759–65.

31. Dubaj Price M, Hurd DD. WormBase: A Model Organism Database. *Med Ref Serv Q.* 2019;38(1):70–80.

32. Romero P, Wagg J, Green ML, et al. Computational prediction of human metabolic pathways from the complete human genome. *Genome Biol.* 2005;6(1):R2.

33. Peri S, Navarro JD, Amanchy R, et al. Development of human protein reference database as an initial platform for approaching systems biology in humans. *Genome Res.* 2003; 13(10):2363–71.

34. Farooq QUA, Shaukat Z, Aiman S, et al. Protein-protein interactions: methods, databases, and applications in virus-host study. *World J Virol.* 2021;10(6):288–300.

35. Martino E, Chiarugi S, Margheriti F, et al. Mapping, structure and modulation of PPI. *Front Chem.* 2021;9:718405.

36. Vinogradova O, Qin J. NMR as a unique tool in assessment and complex determination of weak protein-protein interactions. *Top Curr Chem.* 2012;326:35–45.

37. Whited AM, Park PS. Atomic force microscopy: a multifaceted tool to study membrane proteins and their interactions with ligands. *Biochim Biophys Acta.* 2014;1838(1 Pt A): 56–68.

38. Lin T, Scott BL, Hoppe AD, et al. FRETting about the affinity of bimolecular protein-protein interactions. *Protein Sci.* 2018;27(10):1850–56.

39. Gupta SK, Srivastava M, Osmanoglu O, et al. Genome-wide inference of the Camponotus floridanus protein-protein interaction network using homologous mapping and interacting domain profile pairs. *Sci Rep.* 2020;10(1):2334.

40. Shannon P, Markiel A, Ozier O, et al. Cytoscape: a software environment for integrated models of biomolecular interaction networks. *Genome Res.* 2003;13(11):2498–504.

41. Bastian M, Heymann S, Jacomy M. Gephi: An Open Source Software for Exploring and Manipulating Networks. *Proceedings of the International AAAI Conference on Web and Social Media.* 2009;3(1):361–62.

42. Barrett T, Troup DB, Wilhite SE, et al. NCBI GEO: archive for high-throughput functional genomic data. *Nucleic Acids Res.* 2009;37(Database issue):D885–90.

43. Haudry Y, Berube H, Letunic I, et al. 4DXpress: a database for cross-species expression pattern comparisons. *Nucleic Acids Res.* 2008;36(Database issue):D847–53.

44. Rocca-Serra P, Brazma A, Parkinson H, et al. ArrayExpress: a public database of gene expression data at EBI. *C R Biol.* 2003;326(10–11):1075–8.

45. Maden SF, Acuner SE. Mapping transcriptome data to protein-protein interaction networks of inflammatory bowel diseases reveals disease-specific subnetworks. *Front Genet.* 2021;12:688447.

46. Bencurova E, Gupta SK, Sarukhanyan E, et al. Identification of antifungal targets based on computer modeling. *J Fungi (Basel).* 2018;4(3):81.

47. Kaltdorf M, Srivastava M, Gupta SK, et al. Systematic identification of anti-fungal drug targets by a metabolic network approach. *Front Mol Biosci.* 2016;3:22.

48. Li M, Zhang H, Wang JX, et al. A new essential protein discovery method based on the integration of protein-protein interaction and gene expression data. *BMC Syst Biol*. 2012;6:15.

49. Tang X, Wang J, Pan Y, editors. Identifying essential proteins via integration of protein interaction and gene expression data. *2012 IEEE International Conference on Bioinformatics and Biomedicine*; 2012 4–7 October 2012.

50. Tang X, Wang J, Liu B, et al. A comparison of the functional modules identified from time course and static PPI network data. *BMC Bioinform*. 2011;12:339.

51. Wang J, Peng X, Li M, et al. Construction and application of dynamic protein interaction network based on time course gene expression data. *Proteomics*. 2013;13(2):301–12.

52. Wang J, Peng X, Peng W, et al. Dynamic protein interaction network construction and applications. *Proteomics*. 2014;14(4–5):338–52.

53. Zhang J, Zhong C, Lin HX, et al. Identifying protein complexes from dynamic temporal interval protein-protein interaction networks. *Biomed Res Int*. 2019;2019:3726721.

54. Barabási AL. *Network science*. Cambridge University Press, Cambridge. 2016. English.

55. Watts DJ, Strogatz SH. Collective dynamics of 'small-world' networks. *Nature*. 1998;393 (6684):440–2.

56. Erdös P, Rényi A. On random graphs I. *Publ. Math. Debrecen*. 1959;6:290–97.

57. Lee SA, Chan CH, Tsai CH, et al. Ortholog-based protein-protein interaction prediction and its application to inter-species interactions. *BMC Bioinform*. 2008;9(Suppl 12):S11.

58. Tian Z, Fang H, Ye Y, et al. A novel gene functional similarity calculation model by utilizing the specificity of terms and relationships in gene ontology. *BMC Bioinform*. 2022;23 (Suppl 1):47.

59. Zhao C, Wang Z. GOGO: An improved algorithm to measure the semantic similarity between gene ontology terms. *Sci Rep*. 2018;8(1):15107.

60. Albert R, Jeong H, Barabasi AL. Error and attack tolerance of complex networks. *Nature*. 2000;406(6794):378–82.

61. Vandereyken K, Van Leene J, De Coninck B, et al. Hub protein controversy: Taking a closer look at plant stress response hubs. *Front Plant Sci*. 2018;9:694.

62. He X, Zhang J. Why do hubs tend to be essential in protein networks? *PLoS Genet*. 2006; 2(6):e88.

63. Han JD, Bertin N, Hao T, et al. Evidence for dynamically organized modularity in the yeast protein-protein interaction network. *Nature*. 2004;430(6995):88–93.

64. Chang X, Xu T, Li Y, et al. Dynamic modular architecture of protein-protein interaction networks beyond the dichotomy of 'date' and 'party' hubs. *Sci Rep*. 2013;3:1691.

65. Higurashi M, Ishida T, Kinoshita K. Identification of transient hub proteins and the possible structural basis for their multiple interactions. *Protein Sci*. 2008;17(1):72–8.

66. Gupta SK, Ponte-Sucre A, Bencurova E, et al. An Ebola, Neisseria and Trypanosoma human protein interaction census reveals a conserved human protein cluster targeted by various human pathogens. *Comput Struct Biotechnol J*. 2021;19:5292–5308.

67. Gupta SK, Dandekar T. Bioinformatics in Leishmania Drug Design. In: Ponte-Sucre A, Padrón-Nieves M, editors. *Drug Resistance in Leishmania Parasites: Consequences, Molecular Mechanisms and Possible Treatments*. Cham: Springer International Publishing; 2018. pp. 297–317.

68. Gupta SK, Gross R, Dandekar T. An antibiotic target ranking and prioritization pipeline combining sequence, structure and network-based approaches exemplified for Serratia marcescens. *Gene*. 2016;591(1):268–78.

69. da Rocha EL, Ung CY, McGehee CD, et al. NetDecoder: a network biology platform that decodes context-specific biological networks and gene activities. *Nucleic Acids Res*. 2016;44(10):e100.

70. Srivastava M, Bencurova E, Gupta SK, et al. Aspergillus fumigatus challenged by human dendritic cells: Metabolic and regulatory pathway responses testify a tight battle. *Front Cell Infect Microbiol.* 2019;9:168.

71. Joy MP, Brock A, Ingber DE, et al. High-betweenness proteins in the yeast protein interaction network. *J Biomed Biotechnol.* 2005;2005(2):96–103.

72. Nithya C, Kiran M, Nagarajaram HA. Comparative analysis of Pure Hubs and Pure Bottlenecks in Human Protein-protein Interaction Networks. bioRxiv. 2021:2021.04.06.438602.

73. Yu H, Kim PM, Sprecher E, et al. The importance of bottlenecks in protein networks: correlation with gene essentiality and expression dynamics. *PLoS Comput Biol.* 2007;3(4):e59.

74. Pang E, Hao Y, Sun Y, et al. Differential variation patterns between hubs and bottlenecks in human protein-protein interaction networks. *BMC Evol Biol.* 2016;16(1):260.

75. Barabasi AL, Oltvai ZN. Network biology: understanding the cell's functional organization. *Nat Rev Genet.* 2004;5(2):101–13.

76. Ren Y, Ay A, Kahveci T. Shortest path counting in probabilistic biological networks. *BMC Bioinformatics.* 2018;19(1):465.

77. Rubanova N, Morozova N. Centrality and the shortest path approach in the human interactome. *J Bioinform Comput Biol.* 2019;17(4):1950027.

78. https://www.baeldung.com/cs/dijkstra-vs-floyd-warshall

79. Koschützki D, Lehmann KA, Peeters L, et al. Centrality Indices. In: Brandes U, Erlebach T, editors. *Network Analysis: Methodological Foundations.* Berlin, Heidelberg: Springer; 2005. p. 16–61.

80. Koschutzki D, Schreiber F. Centrality analysis methods for biological networks and their application to gene regulatory networks. *Gene Regul Syst Bio.* 2008;2:193–201.

81. Jalili M, Salehzadeh-Yazdi A, Gupta S, et al. Evolution of centrality measurements for the detection of essential proteins in biological networks. *Front Physiol.* 2016;7:375.

82. Liu YY, Slotine JJ, Barabasi AL. Controllability of complex networks. *Nature.* 2011;473(7346):167–73.

83. Yun-Yuan D, Jun Y, Qi-Jun L, et al., editors. Understanding centrality-lethality rule from the distinction of essential party/date hub proteins in yeast protein-protein interaction networks. *2012 IEEE Symposium on Robotics and Applications (ISRA);* 3–5 June 2012.

84. Vinayagam A, Gibson TE, Lee HJ, et al. Controllability analysis of the directed human protein interaction network identifies disease genes and drug targets. *Proc Natl Acad Sci U S A.* 2016;113(18):4976–81.

85. Gupta SK, Srivastava M, Minocha R, et al. Alveolar regeneration in COVID-19 patients: a network perspective. *Int J Mol Sci.* 2021;22(20):11279.

86. Kálmán RE. Mathematical description of linear dynamical systems. *SIAM J Control Optim.* 1963;1:152–92.

87. Celaj A, Schlecht U, Smith JD, et al. Quantitative analysis of protein interaction network dynamics in yeast. *Mol Syst Biol.* 2017;13(7):934.

88. Li M, Yang J, Wu FX, et al. DyNetViewer: a Cytoscape app for dynamic network construction, analysis and visualization. *Bioinformatics.* 2018;34(9):1597–99.

89. Klamt S, von Kamp A. An application programming interface for CellNetAnalyzer. *Biosystems.* 2011;105(2):162–8.

90. Karl S, Dandekar T. Jimena: efficient computing and system state identification for genetic regulatory networks. *BMC Bioinformatics.* 2013;14:306.

91. Goh KI, Cusick ME, Valle D, et al. The human disease network. *Proc Natl Acad Sci U S A.* 2007;104(21):8685–90.

92. Oti M, Snel B, Huynen MA, et al. Predicting disease genes using protein-protein interactions. *J Med Genet.* 2006;43(8):691–8.

93. Barabasi AL, Gulbahce N, Loscalzo J. Network medicine: a network-based approach to human disease. *Nat Rev Genet.* 2011;12(1):56–68.

94. Alcala-Corona SA, Sandoval-Motta S, Espinal-Enriquez J, et al. *Modularity in Biological Networks. Front Genet.* 2021;12:701331.

95. Wang J, Li M, Deng Y, et al. Recent advances in clustering methods for protein interaction networks. *BMC Genomics.* 2010;11(Suppl 3):S10.

96. Girvan M, Newman ME. Community structure in social and biological networks. *Proc Natl Acad Sci U S A.* 2002;99(12):7821–6.

97. Radicchi F, Castellano C, Cecconi F, et al. Defining and identifying communities in networks. *Proc Natl Acad Sci U S A.* 2004;101(9):2658–63.

98. Hartuv E, Shamir R. A clustering algorithm based on graph connectivity. *Inf Process Lett.* 2000;76(4):175–81.

99. Huang DW, Sherman BT, Lempicki RA. Systematic and integrative analysis of large gene lists using DAVID bioinformatics resources. *Nat Protoc.* 2009;4(1):44–57.

100. Gatti DM, Barry WT, Nobel AB, et al. Heading down the wrong pathway: on the influence of correlation within gene sets. *BMC Genomics.* 2010;11:574.

101. Ogris C, Guala D, Helleday T, et al. A novel method for crosstalk analysis of biological networks: improving accuracy of pathway annotation. *Nucleic Acids Res.* 2017;45(2):e8.

102. Subramanian A, Tamayo P, Mootha VK, et al. Gene set enrichment analysis: a knowledge-based approach for interpreting genome-wide expression profiles. *Proc Natl Acad Sci U S A.* 2005;102(43):15545–50.

103. Tarca AL, Draghici S, Bhatti G, et al. Down-weighting overlapping genes improves gene set analysis. *BMC Bioinformatics.* 2012;13:136.

104. Draghici S, Khatri P, Tarca AL, et al. A systems biology approach for pathway level analysis. *Genome Res.* 2007;17(10):1537–45.

105. Mohammadi S, Davila-Velderrain J, Kellis M. Reconstruction of cell-type-specific interactomes at single-cell resolution. *Cell Syst.* 2019;9(6):559–68 e4.

106. Basu A, Ash PE, Wolozin B, et al. Protein interaction network biology in neuroscience. *Proteomics.* 2021;21(3–4):e1900311.

107. Wang M, Song WM, Ming C, et al. Guidelines for bioinformatics of single-cell sequencing data analysis in Alzheimer's disease: review, recommendation, implementation and application. *Mol Neurodegener.* 2022;17(1):17.

108. Chan TE, Stumpf MPH, Babtie AC. Gene regulatory network inference from single-cell data using multivariate information measures. *Cell Syst.* 2017;5(3):251–67 e3.

109. Woodhouse S, Piterman N, Wintersteiger CM, et al. SCNS: a graphical tool for reconstructing executable regulatory networks from single-cell genomic data. *BMC Syst Biol.* 2018;12(1):59.

110. Moignard V, Woodhouse S, Haghverdi L, et al. Decoding the regulatory network of early blood development from single-cell gene expression measurements. *Nat Biotechnol.* 2015;33(3):269–76.

111. Aubin-Frankowski PC, Vert JP. Gene regulation inference from single-cell RNA-seq data with linear differential equations and velocity inference. *Bioinformatics.* 2020;36(18):4774–80.

112. Matsumoto H, Kiryu H, Furusawa C, et al. SCODE: an efficient regulatory network inference algorithm from single-cell RNA-Seq during differentiation. *Bioinformatics.* 2017;33(15):2314–21.

113. Sekula M, Gaskins J, Datta S. A sparse Bayesian factor model for the construction of gene co-expression networks from single-cell RNA sequencing count data. *BMC Bioinformatics.* 2020;21(1):361.

114. Papili Gao N, Ud-Dean SMM, Gandrillon O, et al. SINCERITIES: inferring gene regulatory networks from time-stamped single cell transcriptional expression profiles. *Bioinformatics*. 2018;34(2):258–66.

115. Huynh-Thu VA, Irrthum A, Wehenkel L, et al. Inferring regulatory networks from expression data using tree-based methods. *PLoS One*. 2010;5(9):e12776.

116. Specht AT, Li J. LEAP: constructing gene co-expression networks for single-cell RNA-sequencing data using pseudotime ordering. *Bioinformatics*. 2017;33(5):764–66.

117. Aibar S, Gonzalez-Blas CB, Moerman T, et al. SCENIC: single-cell regulatory network inference and clustering. *Nat Methods*. 2017;14(11):1083–86.

118. Cha J, Lee I. Single-cell network biology for resolving cellular heterogeneity in human diseases. *Exp Mol Med*. 2020;52(11):1798–1808.

119. Zhou JX, Taramelli R, Pedrini E, et al. Extracting intercellular signaling network of cancer tissues using ligand-receptor expression patterns from whole-tumor and single-cell transcriptomes. *Sci Rep*. 2017;7(1):8815.

120. Wang S, Karikomi M, MacLean AL, et al. Cell lineage and communication network inference via optimization for single-cell transcriptomics. *Nucleic Acids Res*. 2019; 47(11):e66.

121. Schiebinger G, Shu J, Tabaka M, et al. Optimal-transport analysis of single-cell gene expression identifies developmental trajectories in reprogramming. *Cell*. 2019;176(4): 928–43 e22.

122. Ramilowski JA, Goldberg T, Harshbarger J, et al. A draft network of ligand-receptor-mediated multicellular signalling in human. *Nat Commun*. 201522;6:7866.

123. Camp JG, Sekine K, Gerber T, et al. Multilineage communication regulates human liver bud development from pluripotency. *Nature*. 2017;546(7659):533–38.

124. Pavlicev M, Wagner GP, Chavan AR, et al. Single-cell transcriptomics of the human placenta: inferring the cell communication network of the maternal-fetal interface. *Genome Res*. 2017;27(3):349–61.

125. Vento-Tormo R, Efremova M, Botting RA, et al. Single-cell reconstruction of the early maternal-fetal interface in humans. *Nature*. 2018;563(7731):347–53.

126. Skelly DA, Squiers GT, McLellan MA, et al. Single-cell transcriptional profiling reveals cellular diversity and intercommunication in the mouse heart. *Cell Rep*. 2018;22(3): 600–10.

127. Wang L, Yu P, Zhou B, et al. Single-cell reconstruction of the adult human heart during heart failure and recovery reveals the cellular landscape underlying cardiac function. *Nat Cell Biol*. 2020;22(1):108–119.

128. Browaeys R, Saelens W, Saeys Y. NicheNet: Modeling intercellular communication by linking ligands to target genes. *Nat Methods*. 2020;17(2):159–62.

129. Kumar MP, Du J, Lagoudas G, et al. Analysis of single-cell RNA-Seq identifies cell-cell communication associated with tumor characteristics. *Cell Rep*. 2018;25(6):1458–68 e4.

130. Choi H, Sheng J, Gao D, et al. Transcriptome analysis of individual stromal cell populations identifies stroma-tumor crosstalk in mouse lung cancer model. *Cell Rep*. 2015; 10(7):1187–201.

131. van der Wijst MGP, Brugge H, de Vries DH, et al. Single-cell RNA sequencing identifies celltype-specific cis-eQTLs and co-expression QTLs. *Nat Genet*. 2018;50(4):493–7.

132. Huang JK, Carlin DE, Yu MK, et al. Systematic evaluation of molecular networks for discovery of disease genes. *Cell Syst*. 2018;6(4):484–95 e5.

133. Klimm F, Toledo EM, Monfeuga T, et al. Functional module detection through integration of single-cell RNA sequencing data with protein-protein interaction networks. *BMC Genomics*. 2020;21(1):756.

134. Choudhary K, Meng EC, Diaz-Mejia JJ, et al. scNetViz: from single cells to networks using Cytoscape. *F1000Res*. 2021;10:ISCB Comm J-448.

135. Ghazalpour A, Bennett B, Petyuk VA, et al. Comparative analysis of proteome and transcriptome variation in mouse. *PLoS Genet*. 2011;7(6):e1001393.

136. Greer R, Dong X, Morgun A, et al. Investigating a holobiont: Microbiota perturbations and transkingdom networks. *Gut Microbes*. 2016;7(2):126–35.

137. Barman RK, Jana T, Das S, et al. Prediction of intra-species protein-protein interactions in enteropathogens facilitating systems biology study. *PLoS One*. 2015;10(12):e0145648.

138. Bryant P, Pozzati G, Elofsson A. Improved prediction of protein-protein interactions using AlphaFold2. Nature *Communications*. 2022;13(1):1265.

139. Martin S, Sollner C, Charoensawan V, et al. Construction of a large extracellular protein interaction network and its resolution by spatiotemporal expression profiling. *Mol Cell Proteomics*. 2010;9(12):2654–65.

140. Rajendran L, Bali J, Barr MM, et al. Emerging roles of extracellular vesicles in the nervous system. *J Neurosci*. 2014;34(46):15482–9.

141. de Curtis I. Neuronal interactions with the extracellular matrix. *Curr Opin Cell Biol*. 1991;3(5):824–31.

142. Yang X, Hou D, Jiang W, et al. Intercellular protein–protein interactions at synapses. *Protein & Cell*. 2014;5(6):420–44.

143. Strand MA, Jin Y, Sandve SR, et al. Transkingdom network analysis provides insight into host-microbiome interactions in Atlantic salmon. *Comput Struct Biotechnol J*. 2021; 19:1028–34.

144. Rodrigues RR, Shulzhenko N, Morgun A. Transkingdom Networks: A Systems Biology Approach to Identify Causal Members of Host–Microbiota Interactions. In: Beiko RG, Hsiao W, Parkinson J, editors. *Microbiome Analysis: Methods and Protocols*. New York, NY: Springer New York; 2018. pp. 227–42.

145. Rodrigues RR, Gurung M, Li Z, et al. Transkingdom interactions between Lactobacilli and hepatic mitochondria attenuate western diet-induced diabetes. *Nature Communications*. 2021;12(1):101.

146. Drew GC, Stevens EJ, King KC. Microbial evolution and transitions along the parasite-mutualist continuum. *Nat Rev Microbiol*. 2021;19(10):623–38.

147. Overstreet RM, Lotz JM. Host–Symbiont Relationships: Understanding the Change from Guest to Pest. In: Hurst CJ, editor. *The Rasputin Effect: When Commensals and Symbionts Become Parasitic*. Cham: Springer International Publishing; 2016. p. 27–64.

148. Herrera P, Schuster L, Wentrup C, et al. Molecular causes of an evolutionary shift along the parasitism-mutualism continuum in a bacterial symbiont. *Proc Natl Acad Sci U S A*. 2020;117(35):21658–66.

149. Nguyen PV, Srihari S, Leong HW. Identifying conserved protein complexes between species by constructing interolog networks. *BMC Bioinform*. 2013;14(Suppl 16):S8.

150. Yu H, Luscombe NM, Lu HX, et al. Annotation transfer between genomes: protein-protein interologs and protein-DNA regulogs. *Genome Res*. 2004;14(6):1107–18.

151. Remmele CW, Luther CH, Balkenhol J, et al. Integrated inference and evaluation of host-fungi interaction networks. *Front Microbiol*. 2015;6:764.

152. Gupta SK, Srivastava M, Osmanoglu O, et al. Aspergillus fumigatus versus Genus Aspergillus: Conservation, adaptive evolution and specific virulence genes. *Microorganisms*. 2021;9(10).

153. Kachroo AH, Laurent JM, Yellman CM, et al. Evolution. Systematic humanization of yeast genes reveals conserved functions and genetic modularity. *Science*. 2015;348(6237): 921–5.

154. Matthews LR, Vaglio P, Reboul J, et al. Identification of potential interaction networks using sequence-based searches for conserved protein-protein interactions or "interologs". *Genome Res.* 2001;11(12):2120–6.

155. Davis FP, Barkan DT, Eswar N, et al. Host pathogen protein interactions predicted by comparative modeling. *Protein Sci.* 2007;16(12):2585–96.

156. Ogmen U, Keskin O, Aytuna AS, et al. PRISM: protein interactions by structural matching. *Nucleic Acids Res.* 2005;33(Web Server issue):W331–6.

157. Ng SK, Zhang Z, Tan SH. Integrative approach for computationally inferring protein domain interactions. *Bioinformatics.* 2003;19(8):923–9.

158. Wu X, Zhu L, Guo J, et al. Prediction of yeast protein-protein interaction network: insights from the Gene Ontology and annotations. *Nucleic Acids Res.* 2006;34(7):2137–50.

159. Chang JW, Zhou YQ, Ul Qamar MT, et al. Prediction of protein-protein interactions by evidence combining methods. *Int J Mol Sci.* 2016;17(11).

160. Rapanoel HA, Mazandu GK, Mulder NJ. Predicting and analyzing interactions between Mycobacterium tuberculosis and its human host. *PLoS One.* 2013;8(7):e67472.

161. Thahir M, Sharma T, Ganapathiraju MK. An efficient heuristic method for active feature acquisition and its application to protein-protein interaction prediction. *BMC Proc.* 2012;6(Suppl 7):S2.

162. Chen K-C, Wang T-Y, Chan C-h. Associations between HIV and Human Pathways Revealed by Protein-Protein Interactions and Correlated Gene Expression Profiles. *PLOS ONE.* 2012;7(3):e34240.

163. Shen J, Zhang J, Luo X, et al. Predicting protein-protein interactions based only on sequences information. *Proc Natl Acad Sci U S A.* 2007;104(11):4337–41.

164. Li Y, Wang Z, Li LP, et al. Robust and accurate prediction of protein-protein interactions by exploiting evolutionary information. *Sci Rep.* 2021;11(1):16910.

165. Li X, Han P, Wang G, et al. SDNN-PPI: self-attention with deep neural network effect on protein-protein interaction prediction. *BMC Genomics.* 2022;23(1):474.

166. Kovacs IA, Luck K, Spirohn K, et al. Network-based prediction of protein interactions. *Nat Commun.* 2019;10(1):1240.

167. Alazmi M, Alshammari N, Alanazi NA, et al. In silico characterization, docking, and simulations to understand host-pathogen interactions in an effort to enhance crop production in date palms. *J Mol Model.* 2021;27(11):339.

168. Llanos MA, Gantner ME, Rodriguez S, et al. Strengths and weaknesses of docking simulations in the SARS-CoV-2 Era: the main protease (Mpro) case study. *Journal of Chemical Information and Modeling.* 2021;61(8):3758–70.

169. Faria do Valle Í. Recent advances in network medicine: From disease mechanisms to new treatment strategies. *Mult Scler.* 2020;26(5):609–15.

170. Cheng F, Desai RJ, Handy DE, et al. Network-based approach to prediction and population-based validation of in silico drug repurposing. *Nat Commun.* 2018;9(1):2691.

18 Higher-Order Organization in Biological Systems
An Introduction

Vikram Singh

Central University of Himachal Pradesh, India

18.1 INTRODUCTION

Selection for function/purpose is the property of biological systems that sets them apart from other non-living phenomena of natural sciences (Hartwell et al. 1999). Although both systems are composed of matter, one (non-living) is a collection of individual elements and the other (living) possesses an emergent behaviour resulting from non-linear interaction among its constituent elements (Editorial 2005). So to gain insights into the complex system, these functional interdependencies among molecular components must be deciphered (Ma and Gao 2012). Network theory is a systems science approach that has been utilized to study emergent, complex system behaviour by examining the relationship among its constituents (Liu et al. 2020). Networks are abstract mathematical representations of complex systems where the elements of the system are represented as nodes and interactions among them as edges. In general, networks and graphs are used interchangeably. However, mathematically graphs can only represent pairwise or direct relationships between two nodes, while networks can represent complex non-linear interactions as well (Klamt, Haus, and Theis 2009). This chapter focuses on higher-order graph theoretic descriptions and their implications for biological networks.

Biological networks exist in many forms ranging from microscopic macromolecular networks, like gene interaction networks (Karlebach and Shamir 2008), protein interaction networks (Uetz et al. 2000), to macroscopic food webs comprising various animal species (nodes) connected by their feeding habits (Martinez 1991). Early research on biological networks has concentrated on describing them using global network descriptors such as density, assortative or disassortative patterns, and node-specific local network properties like node degree, closeness, eccentricity, and centralities that operate at the macroscale. These descriptors are node-specific measurements and do not consider any edge-specific information. Another significant problem with graph-based descriptors is that they can only depict pairwise or dyadic relationships between the nodes. Many examples of group interactions in biological systems, such as protein complexes (Gaudelet, Malod-Dognin, and Pržulj 2018),

DOI: 10.1201/9781003331247-21

neuronal dynamics (Ganmor, Segev, and Schneidman 2011), and competitive interactions between individuals of different species (Levine et al. 2017), cannot be explained by pairwise interactions. Thus efforts have been undertaken more recently to formalize and create mathematical frameworks that can natively characterize and enrich higher-order interactions (Battiston et al. 2020). Frameworks like motifs, graphlets, simplicial complexes, and hypergraphs have been shown to describe node local wiring patterns in biological networks and are the subject of this text.

This chapter attempts to summarize and define a number of fundamental metrics and frameworks to depict higher-order interactions in biological systems, without attempting to be an exhaustive review. The chapter is structured in the following manner: The main focus of this text is on an overview of available mathematical frameworks that may formally depict higher-order organizations, as well as graph-based measurements that can capture higher-order interactions. Specifically, in Section 18.2, we began by giving a general description of an interacting network, then moving to Section 18.2.1 to discuss some graph theoretic terms, Section 18.2.2 to discuss graph theoretic measures that can capture higher-order interactions, and Section 18.2.3 define frameworks that can explicitly represent higher-order interactions. Examples of these frameworks in biological networks are given in Section 18.3, namely protein interaction networks in Section 18.3.1, brain networks in Section 18.3.2, ecological networks in Section 18.3.3, and other biological networks in Section 18.3.4.

18.2   NETWORK THEORETIC CONCEPTS

Consider an interacting system (S) composed of an edge set $E = \{I_0, I_1, ..., I_m\}$ with m sets of interactions or relationships among n elements denoted by the set V. Here, I_i stands for the Ith interaction set consisting of k system components, $i.e.$, $I = \{p_0, p_1, ..., p_{k-1}\}$ and $(k - 1)$ indicates the order or dimensions of interaction. So a self-loop is an interaction of order zero $i.e. \forall v \in V: (v, v) \in E$, a dyadic interaction is an interaction of order one, and an interaction among k elements is an interaction of order $k - 1$. Lower-order interactions are all k-interactions with order one or less, while higher-order interactions are the ones having order two or more. Lower-order systems are generally any systems that merely have interactions between one or two nodes. Higher-order systems, on the other hand, are those that involve interactions among more than two nodes. Consider the example $S(V, E)$, which has five vertices $V = \{a, b, c, d, e\}$ that interact to generate one polyadic interaction of order two and three dyadic interactions $E = \{(a, b, c), (a, d), (d, c), (c, e)\}$ (Figure 18.1a). Different network representations of ($S(V, E)$) are possible, but working with higher-order objects is difficult because there are few well-defined mathematical analysis frameworks for them, in contrast to graphs, which have a large number of analysis tools available. As a result, graphs have been widely used to represent biological systems as sets of binary interactions.

Although many intriguing characteristics of complex systems have been successfully described using graphs, they are unable to represent non-linear interactions. Since interactions of order one are the basic building blocks of graphs, unfolding each interaction into a set of binary interactions between its nodes is the most logical way to represent each higher-order interaction I in the edge set E. As a result, the interacting

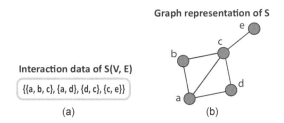

Graph representation of S

Interaction data of S(V, E)

{{a, b, c}, {a, d}, {d, c}, {c, e}}

(a)   (b)

FIGURE 18.1 An example interacting system (a) consisting of a set of higher-order interactions of heterogeneous order represented as a lower-order object called a graph where only pairwise interactions exist (b).

system in the above example can be transformed into a dyadic interaction network, where $IG = \{(a, b), (b, c), (c, a), (a, d), (d, c), (c, e)\}$ (Figure 18.1). While it is simple to describe higher-order interactions as a collection of binary interactions, doing so results in irreversible loss of higher-order structures, making the conclusions reached by such representations either ungeneralizable or, in some situations, requiring additional granularity. The second-order interaction between the nodes $\{a, b, c\}$ in the aforementioned example (Figure 18.1) is permanently destroyed and cannot ever be recovered due to this representation, which also results in the creation of a false interaction $\{a, d, c\}$. Some local network features, such as triangle counts, cliques, communities, sub-graph counts, and motifs, that can express higher-order interactions, have been frequently used to capture these relationships in the past few decades (Battiston et al. 2020). They capture the local wiring patterns of nodes by enumerating the occurrence frequencies of small sub-graphs of order up to k that uniquely describe a network. Global network properties, on the other hand, such as average degree, average path length, and diameter, are statistics that describe the entire network. Regardless of the information they hold, global network properties are very noise-sensitive. They may change in response to modifications to the network's local structure, such as edge or node removal. These small network structural changes would not significantly alter the frequency of sub-graphs, hence local network properties remain unaffected. Similarly, objects, such as simplicial complexes and hypergraphs, that can explicitly express higher-order interactions, have been frequently used to capture these relationships in the past few decades (Battiston et al. 2020).

18.2.1 GRAPH DEFINITIONS

This section begins with a definition of a graph before giving mathematical definitions of key terms used in relation to graphs. Finally, we define graph theoretic local network measures that can capture higher-order interactions. These measures include motifs, graphlets, cliques, and additional frameworks like simplicial complexes and hypergraphs that can formally express higher-order interactions.

18.2.1.1 Graph

A graph $G = (V, E)$ comprises nodes and the edges that connect them, where each edge can only connect two nodes or a node to itself. Here, V denotes a finite set of nodes known as the vertex set of the graph $V(G)$, and E denotes a finite collection of edges known as the edge set of the graph $E(G)$ which is made up of two element subsets of V such that $E \subseteq V \times V$. The first and most popular mathematical framework (construction) used to represent and analyse large biological systems is the graph (Newman 2003). The basic components or aspects of the system that the graph models are represented by nodes. Proteins, genes, transcription factors, metabolites, cortical areas, or even plants can serve as nodes in biological networks. Conversely, interactions describe the functional interdependencies among nodes, such as a transcription factor that may up- or down-regulate a gene's expression or an enzyme that can catalyse a biochemical reaction, etc. (Liu et al. 2020). Directed graphs are those in which the edge orientation is significant $i.e.\forall(u, v) \in E : (u, v) = (v, u)$, while undirected graphs are those in which the edge orientation is irrelevant $i.e.\forall(u, v) \in E : (u, v) * (v, u)$. If the edges of a graph are associated with some characteristic property, the graph is said to be weighted. A k-graph describes a graph of size k, which is defined as the total number of nodes in a graph ($|V(G)|$), also known as network order or size. A self-loop is a connection between one node to itself. An unweighted, undirected graph that forbids self-loops and multiple edges, i.e., more than one edge incident to the same pair of nodes is called simple graph. The neighbourhood ($N(u)$) of a node u is the set of all its neighbouring edges, and the degree of u is denoted by ($|N(u)|$). All the nodes in the neighbourhood of u are called its adjacent nodes.

18.2.1.2   Graph Isomorphism and Orbits

Suppose there is a node bijection $f: V(G) \rightarrow V(H)$ that preserves both adjacency and non-adjacency between the node sets of two graphs G and H. In that case, the graphs are said to be isomorphic, and the bijection is referred to as an isomorphism. Informally, two graphs that are structurally or topologically equivalent regardless of edge labels or outward appearance are said to be isomorphic. An automorphism is an isomorphism of a graph to itself. A graph's collection of automorphisms defines a permutation group known as an automorphism group. The node set of G is considered to be organized into symmetrically equivalent groups (Figure 18.2) termed orbits by the equivalence relationship between two nodes that result from an automorphism mapping them to one another, i.e., the nodes in an equivalence group produce automorphism of the same sub-graph when they are swapped. Identifying if two graphs are isomorphic is known as the graph isomorphism problem.

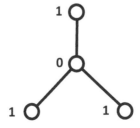

FIGURE 18.2   A four-node tree with two potential equivalence groups, one having the centre node (labelled 0) and an additional node holding all the last three leaf nodes with the designation 1.

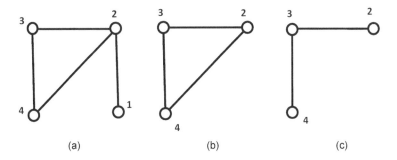

FIGURE 18.3 A three node sub-graph on nodes {2, 3, 4} of a graph G with four nodes and four edges (a) is called an induced sub-graph (b) because it contains all of the edges connecting them in G, but the other sub-graph lacks an edge connecting nodes{2, 4} and is referred to as a partial sub-graph (c).

18.2.1.3 Sub-graphs

A sub-graph $G'(V', E')$ of a graph $G(V, E)$ consists of a subset of nodes (V') from the vertex set $V(G)$ and a subset of edges (E') from the edge set $E(G)$ such that every endpoint of (E') is in the subset of nodes (V') from the vertex set $V(G)$. A sub-graph G' is referred to as an induced sub-graph if and only if the endpoints of all the edges existent between (V') in $E(G)$ are present in (E') (Figure 18.3b). On the other hand, if the sub-graph has any combination of the edges between (V') in $E(G)$ but not all of them, then it is called a partial sub-graph (Figure 18.3c). Sub-graph isomorphism, which belongs to the NP-Complete category, is the process of finding whether a graph that is isomorphic to a particular graph H exists in a graph G. The local topology of a graph, represented by the frequency of sub-graph occurrences, provides valuable information about the underlying process that the graph is modelling and a robust feature vector that describes the network. However, because the number of sub-graphs exponentially grows as k increases, enumerating the frequencies of all the k-sized sub-graphs is only feasible for small k (Ribeiro et al. 2021). The task is made considerably more difficult by counting the frequencies of H, a process known as sub-graph counting.

18.2.2 Graph-Based Measures to Capture Higher-Order Interactions

The fact that graph-based representations can only depict direct interactions is one of their main drawbacks. This has long been mysterious because a significant proportion of biological interactomes is made up of indirect or non-linear interactions. As a result, several graph theoretic metrics that can capture higher-order interactions are the subject of this section.

18.2.2.1 Network Motifs

Motifs have been described as the basic units of complex networks representing the regional node interaction patterns. Specific sub-graphs that appear in real networks much more frequently than in their random counterparts have been referred to as

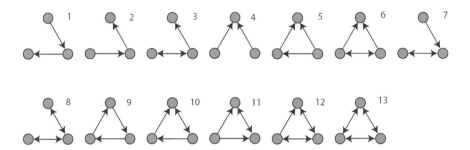

FIGURE 18.4 Directed 3 nodes partial sub-graphs, sub-graph 5 has been found to be over represented in gene regulatory networks and is termed as feed forward loop motif.

network motifs (Figure 18.4). Formally, in any graph $G = (V, E)$, the significantly recurring sub-graphs $G = (V', E')$ are called motifs if $V' \in V$, $E' \in E$ and $V' \ll V$, are called motifs. The resulting vector is known as a motif count vector, and its value of ith element represents the frequency of ith pattern (Shen-Orr et al. 2002; Milo et al. 2002). Random ensembles are typically produced using random graph models that retain the degree sequence of real networks. Z-statistics, frequently more than 2.58, is used to determine the relevance of each overrepresented sub-graph by contrasting its frequency in real networks with that of a null model. It has been demonstrated that the significance profiles produced in this manner yield distinctive network fingerprints that can distinguish between various superfamilies of networks (Milo et al. 2004).

18.2.2.2 Graphlets

Undirected networks, including protein interaction networks, residue interaction networks, disease gene networks, etc., have all benefitted from the widespread use of the graphlet concept. Graphlets were introduced by Pržulj, Corneil, and Jurisica (2004), and a k-graphlet can be defined as a kth order, connected, induced sub-graph of a large network (Figure 18.5).

Like motifs, graphlets capture the local wiring patterns of nodes to describe a network's topology and uniquely characterize a network through these patterns of node interconnections. There exist 30 undirected graphlets for sub-graphs of 2–5 nodes. The nodes of these graphlets can be further grouped into 73 automorphism

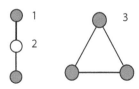

FIGURE 18.5 Undirected 3 nodes induced sub-graphs namely G_1, a path on three nodes, and G_2, represented as a triangle. The numbers here mark symmetrically equivalent nodes in a graphlet and are termed as automorphism orbits.

orbits. These automorphism orbits have been used to extend the notion of node degree where the frequency of occurrence of a node n in ith graphlet orbit represents the ith graphlet degree of n (Pržulj 2007). This 73-dimensional frequency vector, whose elements are graphlet degrees of n for respective orbits, is called graphlet-orbit-signature of n. In this way, any network of order N can be represented through an $N \times O$ matrix called graphlet-orbit-signature-matrix, where O is the number of orbits. Graphlets have two characteristics that set them apart from motifs: first, they are induced subgraphs, and second, they do not have to be overrepresented. But as the study of graphlets materialized, several generalizations of graphlets relevant to directed, dynamic, and heterogeneous networks were discovered (Sarajlić et al. 2016). Induced subgraphs of a directed graph without any antiparallel edges are known as directed graphlets (Sarajlić et al. 2016). Every edge has two possible orientations when we generalize undirected graphlets to directed ones, leading to a total of [$2k$ – the number of isomorphic sub-graphs] directed graphlets. For instance, we obtain three potential directed graphlets from the four directed confirmations of the three-node path, of which two are isomorphic. By utilizing normalized orbit counts, protein interaction networks of the three domains of life have been distinguish into different phyla of biological hierarchy (Singh and Singh 2022).

18.2.2.3 Cliques

A clique is a complete graph of size k. They create the densest motif and a uniform k-node sub-graph. Cliques are the obvious choice to record higher-order interactions because the quantity of graphlets and motifs increases exponentially with the number of nodes in the sub-graph (Derényi, Palla, and Vicsek 2005). The fact that every member of a clique interacts directly with every other member is another interesting characteristic of cliques that best supports group analysis. In our dummy example (Figure 18.1a), there are two 3-cliques, namely $\{a, b, c\}$ and $\{a, d, c\}$ and a 2-clique $\{c, e\}$. As we can see, cliques can capture the interaction $\{a, d, c\}$; however, interaction $\{a, d, c\}$ is an artefact of graph representation and does not actually exist in the system.

18.2.3 Network Representations That Explicitly Represent Higher-Order Interactions

Researchers began seeking mathematical objects that explicitly describe higher-order interactions after realizing the limitations of pairwise network representations. The two objects that have been utilized to express higher-order interactions so far explicitly are hypergraphs and simplicial complexes.

18.2.3.1 Hypergraphs

The most practical way to represent the earlier-described interacting system is a hypergraph. A hypergraph (Figure 18.6b, like a graph, is made up of a finite collection of nodes called V and an edge set called E that is made up of a subset of non-empty hyperlinks called $P(V)$, where $P(V)$ is the power set of V (Figure 18.6a) (Bick et al. 2021).

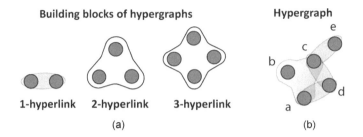

FIGURE 18.6 Different depictions of the components of hypergraphs, known as hyperedges (a), as well as our fictitious example being shown as a hypergraph (b).

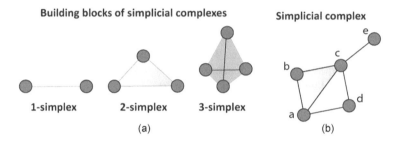

FIGURE 18.7 Different depictions of the components of simplicial complexes, known as simplices (a), as well as our fictitious example being shown as a simplicial complex (b).

18.2.3.2 Simplicial Complexes

Similar to hypergraphs, a simplicial complex (abstract, strictly in a combinatorics sense) is a particular hypergraph whose edge set is closed under inclusion (Figure 18.7b). This means that aside from the null set, every subset of a hyperedge is also a part of the edge set. For instance, if the triangle $\{a, b, c\}$ in our dummy example belongs to edge set E, then all its non-empty subsets $(\{a\}, \{b\}, \{c\}, \{a, b\}, \{a, c\}\{b, c\})$ must also be a part of E. Edges of a simplicial complex are called simplices (Figure 18.7a), where each k-simplex is a finite set of $k + 1$ nodes, similar to the interactions of interacting system § as detailed in (Section 18.2) (Bick et al. 2021).

18.3   EXAMPLES OF HIGHER-ORDER ORGANIZATION IN BIOLOGICAL NETWORKS

The aggregations of biological elements at various dimensions, or levels, from the tiniest atomic to enormous organismal and even higher ecosystem levels, give rise to biological systems, which reflect a complex vertical hierarchy. Components at each level interact with one another to accomplish a variety of functions. These linkages hold great interest and can be represented as networks, where the elements operate as nodes and the connections between them as edges. Given that practically all biological systems can be represented as networks, this hierarchy demonstrates the existence of various biological networks. In the following, we will investigate the effects of higher-order objects on protein interaction, brain, and ecological networks.

18.3.1 PROTEIN INTERACTION NETWORKS (PINs)

Recent developments in high-throughput techniques, such as yeast two-hybrid (Y2H) (Chen et al. 2010) and affinity purification followed by mass spectrometry (AP-MS) (Morris et al. 2014), have produced a significant amount of interaction data, not only increasing network coverage but also enhancing our comprehension of the intricate biological mechanisms. Wuchty, Oltvai, and Barabási (2003) demonstrated that proteins' local wiring patterns network patterns called motifs and functions they carry out are evolutionarily conserved across protein interaction networks of several species in their key work. This structure-function conservation has also been demonstrated using graphlets from Kuchaiev et al.'s. (2010) and Milenković and Pržulj's (2008) work. For the computational discovery of protein–protein interactions, graphlets have been widely used (Lü and Zhou 2011; Lichtenwalter, Lussier, and Chawla 2010; Narayanan, Shi, and Rubinstein 2011). Network comparison is one of the most prevalent applications of graphlet-based measurements in recent years (Ali et al. 2014). One of the early investigations applying higher-order objects to model protein complexes was the introduction of the idea of hypergraphs to biological systems. The protein complexes in this study were represented as hypergraphs, and it was discovered that the hyperedges adhere to the preferential attachment (Wong et al. 2008). Gaudelet, Malod-Dognin, and Pržulj (2018) recently used hypergraphs to represent protein complexes and generalized the concept of graphlets on them called hypergraphlets. Another study has successfully applied a novel framework that makes use of hypergraph kernels to address three distinct prediction issues: vertex classification, (hyper-)edge classification, and edge prediction in biological graphs and hypergraphs, including PINs (Lugo-Martinez et al. 2021).

18.3.2 BRAIN NETWORKS

It is widely known that neurons fire action potentials in groups, and more recently, the significance of high-order correlation to capture brain activities has been demonstrated in neuronal populations (Yu et al. 2011). Huang et al. (2017) showed the presence of weak higher-order connections in a study on the macroscopic functional networks of cortical cells, but due to their weakness, underlying pairwise interactions play a key role in regulating brain processes. In contrast, a test-retest analysis revealed that these non-linear, higher-order structures were crucial for detecting altered connection patterns in neural diseases' networks (Plis et al. 2014). Recently proposed topological data analysis approaches have shown the potential to model more complex brain network aspects. For example, the recent implementation of homology methods to model and differentiate a healthy network from a perturbed one (Lee et al. 2017). Large cliques have been found to be more frequent in white matter fibres than in corresponding random networks, because these units (cliques) are dense and positioned around cavities so aid in information flow. Similarly, using persistent homology, Bendich et al. (2016) described arterial morphology and found age-stratified patterns. Higher-dimensional organizational structures have the potential to discriminate between different functional configurations of neurological disorders (Chung et al. 2017).

18.3.3 ECOLOGICAL NETWORKS

When modelling the horizontal influences of other species on the relationship between two species, approaches to represent higher-order interactions become essential (Levine et al. 2017). According to Kelsic et al. (2015), third species have a stabilizing impact that reduces the severity of harmful interactions between two species and encourages species cohabitation. Additionally, it has been shown that when more species are included in this higher-order interaction, the rate of excluded species declines consequently coexistence increases (De Oliveira and Fontanari 2000). The outcome of higher-order interactions is trait-mediated indirect interactions (TMII), where the cumulative effect of interactions, including non-linear interactions across species, governs the overall dynamics of the system regardless of the pairwise interactions that may exist between species in a system. Recently, hypergraphs have been used to illustrate the process of pest resistance in a coffee agroecosystem that depends on numerous higher-order ecological interactions known as TMIIs (Golubski et al. 2016). Grilli et al. (2017), who modelled the function of higher-order connections in networks of organisms interacting competitively, reported similar findings. They created a general model to represent the competitive dynamics of a dense forest where various tree species battle for space. Fitness estimates of ecological models produced from pairwise interactions alone may be challenging to explain because higher-order interactions can change the fitness of species with other species. In order to estimate the fitness values, Mayfield and Stouffer (2017) reported the role of higher-order interactions. To examine the relationships between pathogen and host ecotypes, a hypergraph containing hyperlinks made up of plants, viruses, and habitats was recently created. The study showed that actual ecosystems exist between modular and nested networks (Valverde et al. 2020).

18.3.4 MISCELLANEOUS

Residue interaction networks (RIN) are built from 3D protein structures in which residues act as nodes, and edges are drawn between nodes if they are close enough to one another in space. Graphlets have been used to compare pairs of RINs (Vacic et al. 2010) and categorize them into distinct functional groups of proteins. GRAFENE (Faisal et al. 2017) has been proposed as an alignment-free network comparison approach that compares the topologies of RINs using relative graphlet frequency vectors generated for graphlets of sizes 3 and 4. Additionally, graphlets have been used to distinguish between the wiring patterns of proteins that cause cancer and those that do not. It was discovered that GDV-central proteins were substantially more enriched in cancer proteins than non-GDV-central proteins (Milenković et al. 2010). Protein connections that organize cellular activities according to cellular requirements transmit information within cells to various constituent parts, producing distinct networks of interactions known as signalling pathways. The utility of hypergraph representations in defining various biological signalling pathway aspects has also been demonstrated. The authors have highlighted the roles of hypergraphs in pathway enrichment, pathway reconstruction, and pathway cross-talk (Ritz et al. 2014).

18.4   CONCLUSION AND FUTURE PROSPECTS

In this chapter, we have outlined different representations to model higher-order interactions and reviewed their applications to biological networks. Since higher-order interactions impart non-linearity to the system, the topology and dynamics of systems possessing higher-order interactions are substantially different. We have seen that there is a substantial loss of interactions when the system is modelled using pairwise interaction, which is certainly not the case with higher-order structures. This new landscape of higher-order systems is still in its infancy, and a large part of it is yet to be explored. Likewise there is a lot to do on the measures used to describe the information contained in the networks because, currently, most of the available measures are the generalization of those used for pairwise networks. Furthermore, most biological systems possess emergent properties, and their underlying driving mechanisms are still unexplored from the perspective of higher-order interactions.

REFERENCES

Ahn, Andrew C, Muneesh Tewari, Chi-Sang Poon, and Russell S Phillips. 2006. "The limits of reductionism in medicine: could systems biology offer an alternative?" *PLoS Medicine* 3 (6): e208.

Albert, Réka, and Albert-László Barabási. 2002. "Statistical mechanics of complex networks." *Reviews of Modern Physics* 74 (1): 47.

Ali, Waqar, Tiago Rito, Gesine Reinert, Fengzhu Sun, and Charlotte M Deane. 2014. "Alignment-free protein interaction network comparison." *Bioinformatics* 30 (17): i430–i437.

Azevedo, Frederico AC, Ludmila RB Carvalho, Lea T Grinberg, José Marcelo Farfel, Renata EL Ferretti, Renata EP Leite, Wilson Jacob Filho, Roberto Lent, and Suzana Herculano-Houzel. 2009. "Equal numbers of neuronal and nonneuronal cells make the human brain an isometrically scaled-up primate brain." *Journal of Comparative Neurology* 513 (5): 532–541.

Babichev, Andrey, Dmitriy Morozov, and Yuri Dabaghian. 2018. "Robust spatial memory maps encoded by networks with transient connections." *PLoS Computational Biology* 14 (9): e1006433.

Bairey, Eyal, Eric D Kelsic, and Roy Kishony. 2016. "High-order species interactions shape ecosystem diversity." *Nature Communications* 7 (1): 1–7.

Battiston, Federico, Giulia Cencetti, Iacopo Iacopini, Vito Latora, Maxime Lucas, Alice Patania, Jean- Gabriel Young, and Giovanni Petri. 2020. "Networks beyond pairwise interactions: structure and dynamics." *Physics Reports* 874: 1–92.

Bendich, Paul, James S Marron, Ezra Miller, Alex Pieloch, and Sean Skwerer. 2016. "Persistent homology analysis of brain artery trees." *The Annals of Applied Statistics* 10 (1): 198.

Bick, Christian, Elizabeth Gross, Heather A Harrington, and Michael T Schaub. 2021. "What are higher-order networks?" *arXiv preprint arXiv:2104.11329.*

Billick, Ian, and Ted J Case. 1994. "Higher order interactions in ecological communities: what are they and how can they be detected?" *Ecology* 75 (6): 1529–1543.

Chen, Jin, Wynne Hsu, Mong Li Lee, and See-Kiong Ng. 2006. "Labeling network motifs in protein interactomes for protein function prediction." In *2007 IEEE 23rd International Conference on Data Engineering*, 546–555. IEEE.

Chen, Yu-Chi, Seesandra Venkatappa Rajagopala, Thorsten Stellberger, and Peter Uetz. 2010. "Exhaustive benchmarking of the yeast two-hybrid system." *Nature Methods* 7 (9): 667–668.

Chung, Moo K, Victoria Villalta-Gil, Hyekyoung Lee, Paul J Rathouz, Benjamin B Lahey, and David H Zald. 2017. "Exact topological inference for paired brain networks via persistent homology." In *International Conference on Information Processing in Medical Imaging*, 299–310. Springer.

Corel, Eduardo, Philippe Lopez, Raphaël Méheust, and Eric Bapteste. 2016. "Network-thinking: graphs to analyze microbial complexity and evolution." *Trends in Microbiology* 24 (3): 224–237.

De Oliveira, Viviane M, and JF Fontanari. 2000. "Random replicators with high-order interactions." *Physical Review Letters* 85 (23): 4984.

de Vico Fallani, Fabrizio, Jonas Richiardi, Mario Chavez, and Sophie Achard. 2014. "Graph analysis of functional brain networks: practical issues in translational neuroscience." *Philosophical Transactions of the Royal Society B: Biological Sciences* 369 (1653): 20130521.

Derényi, Imre, Gergely Palla, and Tamás Vicsek. 2005. "Clique percolation in random networks." *Physical Review Letters* 94 (16): 160202.

Dorogovtsev, Sergey N, and Jose FF Mendes. 2002. "Evolution of networks." *Advances in Physics* 51 (4): 1079–1187.

Editorial. 2005. "In pursuit of systems." *Nature* 435 (7038): 1.

Eldar, Avigdor, and Michael B Elowitz. 2010. "Functional roles for noise in genetic circuits." *Nature* 467 (7312): 167–173.

Faisal, Fazle E, Khalique Newaz, Julie L Chaney, Jun Li, Scott J Emrich, Patricia L Clark, and Tijana Milenković. 2017. "GRAFENE: Graphlet-based alignment-free network approach integrates 3D structural and sequence (residue order) data to improve protein structural comparison." *Scientific Reports* 7 (1): 1–15.

Farahani, Farzad V, Waldemar Karwowski, and Nichole R Lighthall. 2019. "Application of graph theory for identifying connectivity patterns in human brain networks: a systematic review." *Frontiers in Neuroscience* 13: 585.

Ganmor, Elad, Ronen Segev, and Elad Schneidman. 2011. "Sparse low-order interaction network underlies a highly correlated and learnable neural population code." *Proceedings of the National Academy of sciences* 108 (23): 9679–9684.

Gaudelet, Thomas, Noel Malod-Dognin, and Nataša Pržulj. 2018. "Higher-order molecular organization as a source of biological function." *Bioinformatics* 34 (17): i944–i953.

Giusti, Chad, Robert Ghrist, and Danielle S Bassett. 2016. "Twoâăźs company, three (or more) is a simplex." *Journal of computational neuroscience* 41 (1): 1–14.

Giusti, Chad, Eva Pastalkova, Carina Curto, and Vladimir Itskov. 2015. "Clique topology reveals intrinsic geometric structure in neural correlations." *Proceedings of the National Academy of Sciences* 112 (44): 13455–13460.

Goh, Kwang-Il, and In-Geol Choi. 2012. "Exploring the human diseasome: the human disease network." *Briefings in Functional Genomics* 11 (6): 533–542.

Golubski, Antonio J, Erik E Westlund, John Vandermeer, and Mercedes Pascual. 2016. "Ecological networks over the edge: hypergraph trait-mediated indirect interaction (TMII) structure." *Trends in Ecology & Evolution* 31 (5): 344–354.

Grilli, Jacopo, György Barabás, Matthew J Michalska-Smith, and Stefano Allesina. 2017. "Higher-order interactions stabilize dynamics in competitive network models." *Nature* 548 (7666): 210–213.

Hartwell, Leland H, John J Hopfield, Stanislas Leibler, and Andrew W Murray. 1999. "From molecular to modular cell biology." *Nature* 402 (6761): C47–C52.

He, Yong, and Alan Evans. 2010. "Graph theoretical modeling of brain connectivity." *Current Opinion in Neurology* 23 (4): 341–350.

Huang, Hailiang, and Joel S Bader. 2009. "Precision and recall estimates for two-hybrid screens." *Bioinformatics* 25 (3): 372–378.

Huang, Xuhui, Kaibin Xu, Congying Chu, Tianzi Jiang, and Shan Yu. 2017. "Weak higher-order interactions in macroscopic functional networks of the resting brain." *Journal of Neuroscience* 37 (43): 10481–10497.

Kareiva, Peter. 1994. "Special feature: higher order interactions as a foil to reductionist ecology." *Ecology*.

Karlebach, Guy, and Ron Shamir. 2008. "Modelling and analysis of gene regulatory networks." *Nature Reviews Molecular Cell Biology* 9 (10): 770–780.

Kelsic, Eric D, Jeffrey Zhao, Kalin Vetsigian, and Roy Kishony. 2015. "Counteraction of antibiotic production and degradation stabilizes microbial communities." *Nature* 521 (7553): 516–519.

Kiviet, Daniel J, Philippe Nghe, Noreen Walker, Sarah Boulineau, Vanda Sunderlikova, and Sander J Tans. 2014. "Stochasticity of metabolism and growth at the single-cell level." *Nature* 514 (7522): 376–379.

Klamt, Steffen, Utz-Uwe Haus, and Fabian Theis. 2009. "Hypergraphs and cellular networks." *PLoS Computational Biology* 5 (5): e1000385.

Köster, Urs, Jascha Sohl-Dickstein, Charles M Gray, and Bruno A Olshausen. 2014. "Modeling higher- order correlations within cortical microcolumns." *PLoS Computational Biology* 10 (7): e1003684.

Kuchaiev, Oleksii, Tijana Milenković, Vesna Memišević, Wayne Hayes, and Nataša Pržulj. 2010. "Topological network alignment uncovers biological function and phylogeny." *Journal of the Royal Society Interface* 7 (50): 1341–1354.

Kumar, Anuj, and Michael Snyder. 2002. "Protein complexes take the bait." *Nature* 415 (6868): 123–124.

Lee, Hyekyoung, Moo K Chung, Hyejin Kang, Bung-Nyun Kim, and Dong Soo Lee. 2011. "Discrimi- native persistent homology of brain networks." In *2011 IEEE international symposium on biomedical imaging: from nano to macro*, 841–844. IEEE.

Lee, Hyekyoung, Moo K Chung, Hyejin Kang, and Dong Soo Lee. 2014. "Hole detection in metabolic connectivity of Alzheimerââžs disease using k- Laplacian." In *International Conference on Medical Image Computing and Computer-Assisted Intervention*, 297–304. Springer.

Lee, Hyekyoung, Hyejin Kang, Moo K Chung, Seonhee Lim, Bung-Nyun Kim, and Dong Soo Lee. 2017. "Integrated multimodal network approach to PET and MRI based on multidimensional persistent homology." *Human Brain Mapping* 38 (3): 1387–1402.

Levine, Jonathan M, Jordi Bascompte, Peter B Adler, and Stefano Allesina. 2017. "Beyond pairwise mechanisms of species coexistence in complex communities." *Nature* 546 (7656): 56–64.

Lichtenwalter, Ryan N, Jake T Lussier, and Nitesh V Chawla. 2010. "New perspectives and methods in link prediction." In *Proceedings of the 16th ACM SIGKDD international conference on Knowledge discovery and data mining*, 243–252.

Liu, Chuang, Yifang Ma, Jing Zhao, Ruth Nussinov, Yi-Cheng Zhang, Feixiong Cheng, and Zi-Ke Zhang. 2020. "Computational network biology: data, models, and applications." *Physics Reports* 846: 1–66.

Lü, Linyuan, and Tao Zhou. 2011. "Link prediction in complex networks: A survey." *Physica A: Statistical Mechanics and Its Applications* 390 (6): 1150–1170.

Lugo-Martinez, Jose, Daniel Zeiberg, Thomas Gaudelet, Noël Malod-Dognin, Natasa Przulj, and Predrag Radivojac. 2021. "Classification in biological networks with hypergraphlet kernels." *Bioinformatics* 37 (7): 1000–1007.

Ma, Xiaoke, and Lin Gao. 2012. "Biological network analysis: insights into structure and functions." *Briefings in functional genomics* 11 (6): 434–442.

Malod-Dognin, Noël, and Nataša Pržulj. 2014. "GR-Align: fast and flexible alignment of protein 3D structures using graphlet degree similarity." *Bioinformatics* 30 (9): 1259–1265.

Mariani, Manuel Sebastian, Zhuo-Ming Ren, Jordi Bascompte, and Claudio Juan Tessone. 2019. "Nest- edness in complex networks: observation, emergence, and implications." *Physics Reports* 813: 1–90.

Martinez, Neo D 1991. "Artifacts or attributes? Effects of resolution on the Little Rock Lake food web." *Ecological Monographs* 61 (4): 367–392.

Mayfield, Margaret M, and Daniel B Stouffer. 2017. "Higher-order interactions capture unexplained complexity in diverse communities." *Nature Ecology & Evolution* 1 (3): 1–7.

Mazzocchi, Fulvio. 2012. "Complexity and the reductionism–holism debate in systems biology." *Wiley Interdisciplinary Reviews: Systems Biology and Medicine* 4 (5): 413–427.

Milenković, Tijana, Vesna Memišević, Anand K Ganesan, and Nataša Pržulj. 2010. "Systems-level cancer gene identification from protein interaction network topology applied to melanogenesis- related functional genomics data." *Journal of the Royal Society Interface* 7 (44): 423–437.

Milenković, Tijana, Vesna Memišević, Anthony Bonato, and Nataša Pržulj. 2011. "Dominating biological networks." *PLoS one* 6 (8): e23016.

Milenković, Tijana, and Nataša Pržulj. 2008. "Uncovering biological network function via graphlet degree signatures." *Cancer Informatics* 6: CIN–S680.

Milo, Ron, Shalev Itzkovitz, Nadav Kashtan, Reuven Levitt, Shai Shen-Orr, Inbal Ayzenshtat, Michal Sheffer, and Uri Alon. 2004. "Superfamilies of evolved and designed networks." *Science* 303 (5663): 1538–1542.

Milo, Ron, Shai Shen-Orr, Shalev Itzkovitz, Nadav Kashtan, Dmitri Chklovskii, and Uri Alon. 2002. "Network motifs: simple building blocks of complex networks." *Science* 298 (5594): 824–827.

Morris, John H, Giselle M Knudsen, Erik Verschueren, Jeffrey R Johnson, Peter Cimermancic, Alexander L Greninger, and Alexander R Pico. 2014. "Affinity purification–mass spectrometry and network analysis to understand protein-protein interactions." *Nature Protocols* 9 (11): 2539–2554.

Narayanan, Arvind, Elaine Shi, and Benjamin IP Rubinstein. 2011. "Link prediction by de- anonymization: How we won the kaggle social network challenge." In *The 2011 International Joint Conference on Neural Networks, 1825–1834.* IEEE.

Newman, Mark EJ. 2003. "The structure and function of complex networks." *SIAM Review* 45 (2): 167–256.

Pavlopoulos, Georgios A, Panagiota I Kontou, Athanasia Pavlopoulou, Costas Bouyioukos, Evripides Markou, and Pantelis G Bagos. 2018. "Bipartite graphs in systems biology and medicine: a survey of methods and applications." *GigaScience* 7 (4): giy014.

Petri, Giovanni, Paul Expert, Federico Turkheimer, Robin Carhart-Harris, David Nutt, Peter J Hellyer, and Francesco Vaccarino. 2014. "Homological scaffolds of brain functional networks." *Journal of the Royal Society Interface* 11 (101): 20140873.

Plis, Sergey M, Jing Sui, Terran Lane, Sushmita Roy, Vincent P Clark, Vamsi K Potluru, Rene J Huster, et al. 2014. "High-order interactions observed in multi-task intrinsic networks are dominant indicators of aberrant brain function in schizophrenia." *NeuroImage* 102: 35–48.

Pržulj, Nataša. 2007. "Biological network comparison using graphlet degree distribution." *Bioinformatics* 23 (2): e177–e183.

Pržulj, Natasa, Derek G Corneil, and Igor Jurisica. 2004. "Modeling interactome: scale-free or geometric?" *Bioinformatics* 20 (18): 3508–3515.

Ribeiro, Pedro, Pedro Paredes, Miguel EP Silva, David Aparicio, and Fernando Silva. 2021. "A survey on subgraph counting: concepts, algorithms, and applications to network motifs and graphlets." *ACM Computing Surveys (CSUR)* 54 (2): 1–36.

Ritz, Anna, Allison N Tegge, Hyunju Kim, Christopher L Poirel, and TM Murali. 2014. "Signaling hypergraphs." *Trends in Biotechnology* 32 (7): 356–362.

Sarajlić, Anida, Noël Malod-Dognin, Ömer Nebil Yaveroğlu, and Nataša Pržulj. 2016. "Graphlet-based characterization of directed networks." *Scientific Reports* 6 (1): 1–14.

Shen-Orr, Shai S, Ron Milo, Shmoolik Mangan, and Uri Alon. 2002. "Network motifs in the transcriptional regulation network of Escherichia coli." *Nature Genetics* 31 (1): 64–68.

Shimazaki, Hideaki, Shun-ichi Amari, Emery N Brown, and Sonja Grün. 2012. "State-space analysis of time-varying higher-order spike correlation for multiple neural spike train data." *PLoS Computational Biology* 8 (3): e1002385.

Singh, Vikram, and Vikram Singh. 2022. "Characterizing the organizational diversity of protein inter- action networks across three domains of life." *arXiv preprint arXiv:2203. 00999.*

Sizemore, Ann E, Jennifer E Phillips-Cremins, Robert Ghrist, and Danielle S Bassett. 2019. "The importance of the whole: topological data analysis for the network neuroscientist." *Network Neuroscience* 3 (3): 656–673.

Snider, Jamie, Max Kotlyar, Punit Saraon, Zhong Yao, Igor Jurisica, and Igor Stagljar. 2015. "Fundamentals of protein interaction network mapping." *Molecular Systems Biology* 11 (12): 848.

Sporns, Olaf. 2014. "Contributions and challenges for network models in cognitive neuroscience." *Nature Neuroscience* 17 (5): 652–660.

Uetz, Peter, Loic Giot, Gerard Cagney, Traci A Mansfield, Richard S Judson, James R Knight, Daniel Lockshon, et al. 2000. "A comprehensive analysis of protein–protein interactions in Saccharomyces cerevisiae." *Nature* 403 (6770): 623–627.

Vacic, Vladimir, Lilia M Iakoucheva, Stefano Lonardi, and Predrag Radivojac. 2010. "Graphlet kernels for prediction of functional residues in protein structures." *Journal of Computational Biology* 17 (1): 55–72.

Valverde, Sergi, Blai Vidiella, Raul Montanez, Aurora Fraile, Soledad Sacristán, and Fernando García-Arenal. 2020. "Coexistence of nestedness and modularity in host–pathogen infection networks." *Nature Ecology & Evolution* 4 (4): 568–577.

Von Mering, Christian, Roland Krause, Berend Snel, Michael Cornell, Stephen G Oliver, Stanley Fields, and Peer Bork. 2002. "Comparative assessment of large-scale data sets of protein–protein interactions." *Nature* 417 (6887): 399–403.

Weisstein, Eric W. 2002. "Bipartite graph." https://mathworld.wolfram.com/

Wong, Philip, Sonja Althammer, Andrea Hildebrand, Andreas Kirschner, Philipp Pagel, Bernd Geissler, Pawel Smialowski, et al. 2008. "An evolutionary and structural characterization of mammalian protein complex organization." *BMC Genomics* 9 (1): 1–16.

Wootton, J Timothy. 1993. "Indirect effects and habitat use in an intertidal community: interaction chains and interaction modifications." *The American Naturalist* 141 (1): 71–89.

Wuchty, Stephan, Zoltán N Oltvai, and Albert-László Barabási. 2003. "Evolutionary conservation of motif constituents in the yeast protein interaction network." *Nature Genetics* 35 (2): 176–179.

Yildirim, Muhammed A, Kwang-Il Goh, Michael E Cusick, Albert-Laszlo Barabasi, Marc Vidal, et al. 2007. "Drug–target network." *Nature Biotechnology* 25 (10): 1119–1127.

Yu, Shan, Hongdian Yang, Hiroyuki Nakahara, Gustavo S Santos, Danko Nikolić, and Dietmar Plenz. 2011. "Higher-order interactions characterized in cortical activity." *Journal of Neuroscience* 31 (48): 17514–17526.

Zeng, Min, Fuhao Zhang, Fang-Xiang Wu, Yaohang Li, Jianxin Wang, and Min Li. 2020. "Protein–protein interaction site prediction through combining local and global features with deep neural networks." *Bioinformatics* 36 (4): 1114–1120.

Zhang, Han, Xiaobo Chen, Feng Shi, Gang Li, Minjeong Kim, Panteleimon Giannakopoulos, Sven Haller, and Dinggang Shen. 2016. "Topographical information-based high-order functional connectivity and its application in abnormality detection for mild cognitive impairment." *Journal of Alzheimer's Disease* 54 (3): 1095–1112.

19 Advancement and Applications of Biomedical Engineering in Human Health Care

Dinata Roy
Mizoram University, India

Piyush Baindara
University of Missouri, USA

19.1 INTRODUCTION

Biomedical engineering is the interdisciplinary branch of biological sciences that implies the application of engineering principles to design the concepts and techniques to facilitate medicine and therapeutics in health care [1]. Biomedical engineering provides problem-solving approaches to health care that includes diagnosis, monitoring, and therapy [2]. Biomedical engineering is the application of engineering principles and design concepts to medicine and biology for health care purposes. The principle of engineering is applied for the development of new devices, algorithms, processes, and systems that further aid the advancement of the biological and medical sciences so that medical practices and health care delivery are more efficient. Biomedical engineering has risen as its discipline, compared to many other engineering fields. In the recent past, biomedical engineering has become an important vital interdisciplinary area in its sub-disciplines, such as biomechanics, biomaterials, bioinstrumentation, and medical imaging. Biomedical engineers are involved in virtually all aspects of developing new medical technology or process for the advancement of clinical therapeutics. They are involved in the design, development, and utilization of materials, medical devices (pacemakers, lithotripsy, etc.) and techniques (signal processing, artificial intelligence, etc.) for clinical research [3]. Biomedical engineers are serving as members of the health care delivery teams (clinical engineering, medical informatics, rehabilitation engineering, etc.) that are seeking solutions for the difficult and unsolved health care problems for the betterment and advancement of clinical therapeutics confronting our society. The most significant innovation for clinical medicine was the development of X-rays. X-ray technology gave physicians a powerful tool that permitted the accurate diagnosis of a wide variety of diseases and injuries [4]. To bring forward and test new technologies that will help in solving the

DOI: 10.1201/9781003331247-22

worldwide shortage of organs for clinical implantation repairing damaged organs or allowing regeneration of deteriorated organs and tissue biomedical engineering plays an important role [5]. Typical pursuits of biomedical engineers, therefore, include research in new materials for implanted artificial organs.

Computer modeling in biomedical engineering bridges the gap between engineering, biology, and medicine including computational methods for modeling bones, tissues, muscles, cardiovascular components, cartilage, cells, and cancer nanotechnology as well as many other applications [6].

The patient safety improvement in hospitals is to introduce organizational solutions to the existing system which will lead to faster identification of health dangers and efficient therapeutic intervention carried out by personnel trained in intensive care. The proposed system is based on constant telemetric monitoring using objective physiological parameters. Using a low-distance sensor network that covers the body of a patient, the so-called BAN (Body Area Network) is the main innovation of the project. Some preliminary results of ECG analysis and interpretation modules and units of the proposed system will be presented [7].

Further, the typical pursuits of biomedical engineers include writing software for analysis of medical research data, development of new diagnostic instruments, computer-assisted modeling, analysis of medical device-related hazards for safety and efficacy, development of new diagnostic imaging systems, design of telemetry systems for patient monitoring, design of biomedical sensors for measurement of human physiologic systems variables, development of expert systems for disease diagnosis, design of closed-loop control systems for drug administration, modeling of the physiological systems of the human body, design of communication aids for the handicapped, development of material to be used as a replacement, and so on. Overall, biomedical engineering is the need for modern medical sciences and the betterment of human health. Biomedical engineered devices, technologies, and processes are becoming integrated with every field which is further providing ease in the quantitative and qualitative output of the service process with higher accuracy and in lesser time. This chapter is dedicated to the applications and advancement of biomedical engineering and associated fields, dedicated to the betterment of human health.

19.2   BIOINFORMATICS AND BIOMEDICAL ENGINEERING

Bioinformatics is an interdisciplinary field of biomedical engineering and biotechnology that includes computational, mathematical, statistical analysis, and information technology to provide a better solution to biological and biomedical engineering problems. The key research areas of bioinformatics include sequence analysis, genome annotations, computational drug configuration, analysis of gene expression, and computational evolutionary biology RNA structures, TSS prediction, comparative genomics, demonstration of biological frameworks, high throughput image examination, protein-protein docking, and data mining are hot topics of research in developed countries. Medical engineering and bioinformatics are experiencing new development and recognition in the present day. Applied bioinformatics is thus right now a burning, interesting, and attractive field that integrates life sciences, biomedical sciences, computational biology, and software engineering for the better future of mankind.

Bioinformatics is interconnected with biomedical engineering in many views. As a significant part of science, bioinformatics includes software engineering, computer science, mathematics, statistics, and designing to examine and decode natural information. Bioinformatics and computational biology integrate the investigation of biological data, especially in the field of DNA, RNA, and protein engineering study that generates and apply computational biology procedures to break down substantial procurement of biological data, for example, hereditary groupings, cell populaces, or protein tests, to create new forecasts or search new science. Bioinformatics is thus advancing the knowledge of biomedical engineering to the next extent. Further, bioinformatics is also given that prospect to biomedical engineers for enlightening their inventive engineering modeling, technological skills, and engineering experiences. CRISPR (clustered regularly interspaced short palindromic repeats) is paving the way to the bright future of bioinformatics in solving biological problems. At present days bioinformatics provides several key findings to the field of medical biology and biotechnology that advanced the field of biomedical engineering including drug discovery that can be done by using the bioinformatics web servers. Recently in cancer studies, researchers have recognized the role of genes in human cancer using the bioinformatics tool. Bioinformatics is widely used to develop the quality of medicine and to improve more effective antibiotics in biomedical engineering. Additionally, bioinformatics has established aids such as next-generation sequencing, where one can determine the number of mutations very quickly and find out the possible cause of disease and solution. Computational biology and bioinformatics are valuable in the fields of bio-entrepreneurship, biotechnology, and biological engineering for the welfare of human beings. It improves biomedical research and advances preventive pharmaceuticals, and recognizes sustainable information substance in DNA, RNA, protein arrangements, structure, architecture, and substance of genomes. It also incorporates metabolic engineering data processing, data capacity and recovery, database structures, explanation, and also data mining concerning machine learning instruments, neural nets, and computerized reasoning. Bioinformatics is being applied in many interdisciplinary fields connected to biomedical engineering at some points, such as microbial genomics, molecular and personalized medicine, gene therapy, drug development and preventative medicine, and in forensic analysis.

19.3 BIOMEDICAL ENGINEERING IN HUMAN HEALTH CARE

19.3.1 PATIENT MONITORING SYSTEM

A patient monitoring system (PMS) is a dedicated set of devices for monitoring a patient's health by quantitative evaluation of the crucial physiological parameters during critical periods. PMS measures continuously and automatically the values of the patients' important physiological parameters including heart rate and rhythm, blood pressure, temperature, blood oxygen saturation, respiratory rate, body temperature, etc. PMS uses bio-sensors that can detect the various parameters of the patient body's physiological functions. PMS biosensors are biologically derived recognition entities that are coupled to a transducer, which allow the quantitative development of some complex biochemical parameter and further converted to the numeric data, we can see on the screen [8]. The PMS considerably reduced the risk during surgery, as it continuously monitors the physiological parameters of patients and informs the surgeon about the present status of the patient's condition and suitable measures can be taken in time [9]. In the critical care units (CCUs) of hospitals, PMSs are the most important diagnostic devices capable of complex bio-signal processing and interpretation, and are also equipped with some specialized communication interfaces that provide continuous display and interpretation of the patient's vital physiological functions. In the recent past, the rapid evolution of electronics and information technology is resulting in more powerful bedside PMS systems which are efficiently easing the health care monitoring systems [10]. Further, Clinical Decision Support Systems (CDSSs) can evaluate health abnormalities by accessing data of a single vital sign from a patient such as heart rate, blood pressure, respiratory rate, oxygen saturation, electrocardiogram, body temperature, etc. [11, 12]. CDSSs are efficiently capable of sensing clinically abnormal health consequences ahead of time, which is based on the intelligence analysis of recently observed medical data on patient health [13]. Normally, much of serious clinical anomalies are associated with and reflected as abnormalities in multiple physiological vital signs at the same time [14]; therefore, a context-aware remote monitoring application or system could be an accurate and early predictor of abnormalities that occur due to the changes in multiple physiological vital signs [15]. Interestingly, PMSs are an excellent example of biomedical engineering that perfectly serves the health care system (Figure 19.1).

Further, a 24-hour monitoring is difficult for medical personnel therefore, and so, centralized patient monitoring has been introduced in the recent past. In a centralized patient monitoring system, all PMSs are connected with a single server-based patient monitor which can be monitored by a single person at a time. The use of networks in the medical field has become a core component for any hospital system, especially regarding critical issues like data overflow and security issues [16].

19.3.2 TELEMEDICINE

The delivery of health care services and the exchange of health care information across distances are known as telemedicine. "Telecare" is another associated term that is meant for nursing and community support to a patient situated at distance. Similarly, telehealth refers to public health services delivered at a distance, to the required and needy people. Overall, telemedicine, telecare, and telehealth involve the transfer of information about health-related issues between one or more distant places for the betterment of individual or community health. Nowadays, in pandemic situations such as COVID-19, information transfer is generally facilitated by the use of telecommunications networks such as the internet or mobile phones. Further, telemedicine has obvious advantages for distant places such as remote or rural areas where it facilitates health services while avoiding the meeting and travel of patients and health care workers. Also in urban areas, when person-to-person contact should be avoided or in the situation of immediate consultation, telemedicine improves the access to health services and information within time. Additionally, telemedicine confirmed to improve consistency and quality and is also cheaper than conventional health care services. Besides having advantages over conventional practices, telemedicine services should be categorized based on the interaction between patient and health care provider, i.e. live or pre-recorded, and the type of information that need to be transferred i.e. audio, video, or text. Next, telemedicine services are mainly practiced in only developed countries at present, such as the United States; however, there is an increasing interest in developing countries for telemedicine services. As the name suggested "telemedicine" is provided to a distant person, these services are mainly considered effectively in some situations such as in emergencies (environmental, pandemics like COVID-19) when there is no alternative available [17].

In case of emergencies such as COVID-19, especially in remote areas, telemedicine can provide rapid access to health care services; however, there are several associated factors for successful telemedicine services [18]. Some of the factors associated with successful telemedicine are patient data confidentiality, quality of the internet, images, videos, and devices being used. So, first of all, good infrastructure is needed for both patients and health care providers for an effective telemedicine service. Further, some of the patient's diagnoses may be difficult to perform virtually, so a virtually efficient and user-friendly is needed with online assistance [19]. Above all, successful telemedicine required good internet access, Wi-Fi signal, and bandwidth connectivity along with continuous data collection [20, 21] (Figure 19.1).

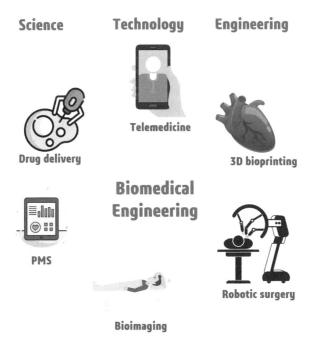

FIGURE 19.1 Examples of biomedical engineering-derived applications, instruments, and strategies in human health care.

19.3.3   3D Bioprinting

Regeneration capabilities of human cells/tissue/organ are less sufficient to deal with any damage while tissue damage and degeneration are common phenomena among humans while on the other side. Traditionally tissue or organ transplantation is the only option that is also dependent upon the availability of a donor and the acceptance or rejection of the graft due to immune response. Biomedical engineering is an emerging field where tissue engineering, regenerative medicine along with 3D bioprinting can work together for the betterment of human health [22]. Tissue engineering uses additive manufacturing that includes the principles of both materials science and life sciences to develop the base of different organs and tissues [23]. 3D bioprinting uses the bio-ink that is solely made of biomaterials such as cells, growth factors, and other essential components required for the manufacturing of the tissues and organs [24]. At present synthetic and natural polymers such as alginate, gelatin, collagen, polyethylene glycol, hydroxyapatite, etc. are being used for 3D bioprinting due to their biocompatibility and physiochemical properties that can be controlled for the formation and structure of the suitable extracellular matrix [25, 26]. The main objective of 3D bioprinting is the reconstruction and restoration of damaged organs and tissues with native complexity to assist cellular differentiation and tissue regeneration. 3D bioprinting is the process of interplay between the cellular interphase and scaffolds where cellular differentiation takes place under the influence of growth factors [27].

Additive manufacturing in 3D printing of biological organs and tissues is further employed in tissue engineering that helps in the production of geometrically accurate organs or tissue with the aid of controlled matter deposition according to the precise 3D model, generated by computer graphics [28]. Biocompatibility of the used material, cell sensitivity toward the printing methods and accurate delivery and infusion of growth factors are the essential parts of 3D bioprinting as it directly deals with and is associated with live cellular entities [29]. 3D bioprinted tissues and organs may be preferred for clinical studies and preclinical trials as pathophysiologically they are more accurate with improved intracellular and intercellular communication, which is precisely accurate to the *in vivo* physiology. On the other side, animal models are not sufficiently decorated to predict the human pathophysiology and also associated with ethical issues [30]. 3D bioprinting along with tissue engineering can be used for the fabrication of fully functional organs and tissues, such as bones, liver, heart, kidney, and skin, which is a revolutionary achievement in the biomedical field for the betterment of human health [31] (Figure 19.1).

The most recent example of 3D printed organ is the human ear pinna which was printed using a computer-aided design and extrusion method. Stereolithography software was used to assist the automated printing and to avoid continuous monitoring. Thermal degradation is a major issue during the 3D printing of ear pinna that was monitored using thermal gravimetric analysis. Next, histology and SEM were used to analyze the cellular proliferation and synthesis of ECM components. Most importantly, the absence of CD14+ expression confirmed the acceptance of xenogenic transplant of 3D bioprinted ear pinna [32]. 3D bioprinting is the bright future of biomedical sciences; however, state-of-the-art technology has several challenges. Vascularization in the bioprinted tissues or organs is the biggest problem that includes blood supply along with gas and nutrient exchange. Further, biocompatibility and biodegradability of the material used in the bio-ink as substrate, shape-fidelity along with preservation and functionality of the printed organs are the major hurdles [33].

19.4 NANOBIOTECHNOLOGY

Nanobiotechnology is the combined application of biotechnology and nanotechnology that uses biological materials and genetic engineering to create tiny synthetic structures along with the rules and tools of basic sciences including physics and chemistry [20, 34]. Fabricated nanosized materials are skillfully integrated into the biomedical device and biological system of nanometer dimensions such as viruses, biomolecules, etc. to attain the desired and designed functionality [35]. Highly efficient and desired functionality biosensors, nanosized microchips, molecular switches, and tissue analogs for skin, bones, muscles, and other organs of the body can be developed with nanobiotechnology. Nanostructured devices and nanomaterials composite of metals, ceramic, and polymers have been developed and explored in various biomedical applications such as tissue engineering scaffolds, targeted drug delivery, and biosensors [36].

TEM, AFM, SIMS, and SPM are advanced instruments that are examples of biomedical engineering used to evaluate the structural and chemical composition of biomaterials and their interfaces with tissue at the nanometer level [37]. Additionally, tools applied in biomedical nanometric and nanomaterials along with computational algorithms and networking are further dissecting the in-depth details of biological systems, such as regulations of metabolic processes [38]. Modified and highly functionalized nanomaterials such as biosensors, imaging agents, and targeted delivery vehicle agents are the core of nanotechnological research and have been used widely in different biomedical applications [39, 40]. Next, a diverse array of nanoparticles such as gold nanoparticles, quantum dots (Qdots), carbon nanotubes/nanofibers, chitosan, dendrimers, liposomes, polymer nanocapsules, and nano-HA have been used in medicine, diagnostics, and therapeutics [41].

19.4.1 Bioimaging

Nanoparticles such as liposomes, dye-doped silica, quantum (Q) dots, and gold nanoparticles are widely used for bioimaging as optical contrast agents. Nanosized metals like gold and silver using surface plasmon resonance as they don't have fluoresced capacity. Nanoparticle-based optical imaging agents have multiple advantages over conventional agents such as enhanced in vitro and in vivo stability, resistance to photobleaching, high quantum yield, high absorbency, resistance to metabolic disintegration, less toxicity, and near-infrared emission; however, metal nanoparticles (gold and silver) don't have fluorescence capacity, they used surface plasmon resonance, instead [42]. Near infrared Q dots have been recently introduced in the bioimaging field showing promising results in cancer detection [43]. The main advantage of Q dots is the large stokes shift value that reduces background signal, permitting sensitive detection of cancers. Additionally, multiplexing capacity allows the detection of more than one cancer-specific receptor at the same time in the range of single excitation significantly improving the cancer diagnosis abilities at an early stage [44].

Further, Q dots have applications in cellular labeling, cell migration tracking, pathogen detection, genomic and proteomic detection, and are also used in fluorescence resonance energy transfer biosensors. Also, the incorporation of different imaging entities into a single nanoparticle probe makes them fit for in-depth imaging of different types of cancers using various imaging platforms such as fluorescence, X-ray, CT, and MRI. Overall, nanoparticles are an excellent example of biomedical engineering that can play an important role for detection and analysis of biomolecules in real-time at a single molecule level (Figure 19.1).

19.4.2 DRUG DELIVERY

Efficient drug delivery to improve the bioavailability and stability of drugs is another area where nanobiotechnology is extensively used. Conventional drug delivery methods or systems have many draw backs such as rapid leakage blood capillaries, opsonization by plasma proteins and nonspecific cell toxicity. Besides, these nanotechnology-based drug delivery systems offer improved drug permeation, controlled release, and targeting. [45] Nanotechnology-based targeted drug delivery increases the chances of nanoparticles reaching the target sites very effectively which reduces drug dosage and toxicity along with enhanced drug stability. These efficient delivery systems are very relevant in cancer chemotherapy, where selective delivery to neoplastic cells is very important to efficiently stop cancer metastasis. Various efficient nanotechnology-based nanoparticle materials such as biodegradable chitosan, liposomes, PEG, dextran, silica, and gelatin have been used in various clinical applications. Additionally, nonbiodegradable polymers such as PMMA, polyacrylamide, polystyrene, polycyanoacrylate, and polyphosphazene derivatives have already been explored for drug and gene delivery in different clinical settings [46].

In the case of brain disorders, efficient drug delivery is challenging due to the presence of the blood-brain barrier (BBB). However, nanoparticles (magnetic nanoparticles)-based delivery is a potentially effective alternative for drug transportation across the blood-brain barrier along with enhanced bioavailability. Nanotechnology provided excellent outcomes in diverse fields such as AIDS, cancer, nutraceutical delivery, and noninvasive imaging. However, the field is still evolving, and advanced in-depth studies and clinical trials are needed for other nanotechnology-based systems such as functionalized carbon nanotubes and nanofibers [47, 48]. Overall, nanotechnology is a good example of an efficient addition in biomedical engineering where scientists of various fields work together in designing and developing various diagnosis methods and novel treatment strategies (Figure 19.1).

19.5 BIOMEDICAL ROBOTICS AND COMPUTER-ASSISTED SURGERY

Biomedical robotics is the rapidly growing field of biomedical engineering in which efficient surgical robots have been developed with multiple skills suitable for clinical settings. Robotic surgery offers significant advantages over handheld open surgery by clinical surgeons and integrated computers help in real-time data collection and analysis that assist future surgical practices. Biomedical robotics systems are precisely accurate as they can position a laser within 10 μm of the target which is at least ten times more efficient than human hands [49]. Human limitations can be overcome during microsurgeries by using surgical robots that result in better assistance and overall improved outputs in medical surgeries. The promising outputs of biomedical robotics can't be achieved without essential communication and mutual understanding of surgeons, engineers, entrepreneurs, and health care administrators. Further, the development of biomedical robotics depends on the quench to evaluate and solve unsolved clinical problems with the aid of promising technologies [50] (Figure 19.1).

Computer-assisted surgery (CAS) is another broad surgical methodology in which computer programs are used to both plan and execute surgical interventions. CAS has been used much in medical therapeutics and dentistry due to its minimally invasive and precise surgical procedures. Volumetric imaging, virtual surgical planning software, instrument tracking, and real-time robotics are the major parts of CAS that assist in the planning and then facilitate the transfer of surgical plans to the precise execution of overall surgery. Due to its excellent assistance and outputs, CAS has been widely used in neurosurgery, cardiology, orthopedic surgery, otolaryngology, ophthalmology, dentistry, and oral and maxillofacial applications [51].

19.6 SYNTHETIC BIOLOGY

Synthetic biology is an emerging discipline of biological sciences that essentially combined the science, technology, and engineering approaches to design manufacture and modification of genetic materials of living organisms to alter or facilitate biological systems [52]. Synthetic biology provides the ease for challenges in biomedical settings such as drug–target specificity, precise drug-dosing regimens, minimizing side effects, shortening the diagnosis-to-treatment timelines, and avoiding drug resistance of pathogens. Synthetic biology avails the complex engineering of biomaterials, high precision devices coupled to sensing and delivery mechanisms, and has the potential to solve the current biomedical problems by providing unique tools [53]. Due to its wide applicability and advancement in ongoing biomedical research, synthetic biology has provided novel strategies for biomedical applications including disease analysis, diagnostics, pathogen characterization, vaccination, screening assays, and drug development [54–59] (Figure 19.2). By using synthetic biology strategies, it is now possible to shorten the drug discovery or development timeline, improve drug delivery, and produce affordable and efficient medicine [60, 61]. Available synthetic biology tools may have incredible output in biomedical applications such as light-activated triggers for accurate therapeutic response and engineered and programmed bacteria to selectively eradicate cancer cells [62, 63]. Next, synthetic biology-derived circuits can regulate the homeostasis of essential metabolites and control the proliferation and destruction of specific cell populations [64, 65]. Using synthetic biology approaches, it is also possible to generate engineered microencapsulated cells with a prosthetic network of predefined functions; however, cells containing engineered prosthetic networks can't be controlled therapeutically and thus limit biomedical applications. However, no synthetic device or prosthetic network has been used in clinical settings yet, and synthetic biology strategies are the future of biomedical engineering for the betterment of human health.

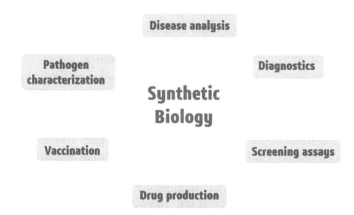

FIGURE 19.2 Biomedical engineering oriented different applications of synthetic biology in human health care.

19.7 SUMMARY

In this chapter, we have summarized and discussed the recent development and prospects of biomedical engineering and associated areas such as telemedicine, 3D bioprinting, nanobiotechnology, robotics, computer-assisted surgery, and synthetic biology. Various applications which have been currently used in the human health care settings have been discussed, including PMSs, nanomedicine, drug engineering, drug delivery, imaging, 3D bioprinted organs, medical devices, genetic manipulation, and cell engineering. Although many promising applications of biomedical engineering and associated areas are under trial and have not yet reached the clinical setting for use, high proficiency and accuracy over conventional methods or materials suggested bioengineered applications as the future of biomedical engineering. Science, technology, and engineering continue to advance, leading to the most cutting-edge and effective applications, technologies, medications, and treatment modalities in human healthcare. Overall, biomedical engineering is the demand of human health care to fight against unsolved medical issues and diseases and for better treatment strategies.

CONFLICT OF INTEREST

The authors declare no conflict of interest.

ACKNOWLEDGMENT

DR acknowledges Department of Zoology, Mizoram University, Aizawl; and PB is thankful to the Department of Molecular Microbiology and Immunology, University of Missouri, Columbia, for providing the space and other facilities for this work.

AUTHOR CONTRIBUTION

DR and PB wrote the manuscript. PB prepared the illustrations. PB conceived the sole idea and led the manuscript.

FUNDING

This study is not supported by any funding source.

REFERENCES

[1] Narayan, R. *Encyclopedia of Biomedical Engineering*; 2019; Vol. 1–3.

[2] Khandpur, R. *Handbook of Biomedical Instrumentation*, 3rd Edition. McGraw-Hill; 2014; Vol. 1, pp. 1–29.

[3] Nisha, S. S.; Meeral, M. N. Applications of Deep Learning in Biomedical Engineering. In *Handbook of Deep Learning in Biomedical Engineering: Techniques and Applications*; 2020; pp. 245–270. https://doi.org/10.1016/B978-0-12-823014-5.00008-9

[4] De Maria, C.; Di Pietro, L.; Ravizza, A.; Lantada, A. D.; Ahluwalia, A. D. Open-Source Medical Devices: Healthcare Solutions for Low-, Middle-, and High-Resource Settings. In *Clinical Engineering Handbook, Second Edition*; 2019; pp. 7–14. https://doi.org/10.1016/B978-0-12-813467-2.00002-X

[5] Jain A, Bansal R. Applications of regenerative medicine in organ transplantation. *Journal of Pharmacy and Bioallied Sciences* 2015;7:188–194. doi:10.4103/0975-7406.160013

[6] Kojić, M.; Filipović, N.; Stojanović, B.; Kojić, N. *Computer Modeling in Bioengineering: Theoretical Background, Examples and Software*; 2009. https://doi.org/10.1002/9780470751763

[7] Kurzyński, M.; Ryba, P.; Markowski, M.; Woźniak, M. Medical Telemetry System for Monitoring and Localization of Patients-Functional Model and Algorithms for Biosignals Processing. *International Journal of Electronics and Telecommunications*, 2010, *56* (4), 445–450. https://doi.org/10.2478/v10177-010-0060-x

[8] Malekloo, A.; Ozer, E.; AlHamaydeh, M.; Girolami, M. Machine Learning and Structural Health Monitoring Overview with Emerging Technology and High-Dimensional Data Source Highlights. *Structural Health Monitoring*. 2022, 1906–1955. https://doi.org/10.1177/14759217211036880

[9] Ferrua, M.; Minvielle, E.; Fourcade, A.; Lalloué, B.; Sicotte, C.; Di Palma, M.; Mir, O. How to Design a Remote Patient Monitoring System? A French Case Study. *BMC Health Services Research*, 2020, *20* (1). https://doi.org/10.1186/s12913-020-05293-4

[10] Várady, P.; Benyó, Z.; Benyó, B. An Open Architecture Patient Monitoring System Using Standard Technologies. *IEEE Transactions on Information Technology in Biomedicine*, 2002, *6* (1), 95–98. https://doi.org/10.1109/4233.992168

[11] Sidek, K. A.; Khalil, I. Enhancement of Low Sampling Frequency Recordings for ECG Biometric Matching Using Interpolation. *The Computer Methods and Programs in Biomedicine*, 2013, *109* (1), 13–25. https://doi.org/10.1016/j.cmpb.2012.08.015

[12] Klingeberg, T.; Schilling, M. Mobile Wearable Device for Long Term Monitoring of Vital Signs. *The Computer Methods and Programs in Biomedicine*, 2012, *106* (2), 89–96. https://doi.org/10.1016/j.cmpb.2011.12.009

[13] Teufel, A.; Binder, H. Clinical Decision Support Systems. *Visceral Medicine*, 2021, 491–498. https://doi.org/10.1159/000519420

[14] Sandra, V. B. Jardim. The Electronic Health Record and Its Contribution to Healthcare Information Systems Interoperability. *Procedia Technology*, 2013, *9*, 940–948.

[15] Forkan, A. R. M.; Khalil, I.; Tari, Z.; Foufou, S.; Bouras, A. A Context-Aware Approach for Long-Term Behavioural Change Detection and Abnormality Prediction in Ambient Assisted Living. *Pattern Recognition*, 2015, *48* (3), 628–641. https://doi.org/10.1016/j.patcog.2014.07.007

[16] Khandpur, R. S. Patient Monitoring System, Central. In *Compendium of Biomedical Instrumentation*; 2020; pp. 1479–1482. https://doi.org/10.1002/9781119288190.ch279

[17] Loeb, A. E.; Rao, S. S.; Ficke, J. R.; Morris, C. D.; Riley, L. H.; Levin, A. S. Departmental Experience and Lessons Learned with Accelerated Introduction of Telemedicine during the COVID-19 Crisis. *Journal of the American Academy of Orthopaedic Surgeons*, 2020, E469–E476. https://doi.org/10.5435/JAAOS-D-20-00380

[18] Chou, E.; Hsieh, Y. L.; Wolfshohl, J.; Green, F.; Bhakta, T. Onsite Telemedicine Strategy for Coronavirus (COVID-19) Screening to Limit Exposure in ED. *Emergency Medicine Journal*, 2020, *37* (6), 335–337. https://doi.org/10.1136/emermed-2020-209645

[19] Li, P.; Liu, X.; Mason, E.; Hu, G.; Zhou, Y.; Li, W.; Jalali, M. S. How Telemedicine Integrated into China's Anti-COVID-19 Strategies: Case from a National Referral Center. *BMJ Health & Care Informatics*, 2020, *27* (3). https://doi.org/10.1136/bmjhci-2020-100164

[20] Shelton, C. J.; Kim, A.; Hassan, A. M.; Bhat, A.; Barnello, J.; Castro, C. A. System-Wide Implementation of Telehealth to Support Military Veterans and Their Families in Response to Covid-19: A Paradigm Shift. *The Journal of Military, Veteran and Family Health*, 2020, *6* (2), 50–57. https://doi.org/10.3138/JMVFH-6.S2-CO19-0003

[21] Contreras, C. M.; Metzger, G. A.; Beane, J. D.; Dedhia, P. H.; Ejaz, A.; Pawlik, T. M. Telemedicine: Patient-Provider Clinical Engagement During the COVID-19 Pandemic and Beyond. *Journal of Gastrointestinal Surgery*, 2020, 1692–1697. https://doi.org/10.1007/s11605-020-04623-5

[22] Wang, C.; Huang, W.; Zhou, Y.; He, L.; He, Z.; Chen, Z.; He, X.; Tian, S.; Liao, J.; Lu, B.; et al. 3D Printing of Bone Tissue Engineering Scaffolds. *Bioactive Materials*, 2020, 82–91. https://doi.org/10.1016/j.bioactmat.2020.01.004

[23] Bandyopadhyay, A.; Mitra, I.; Bose, S. 3D Printing for Bone Regeneration. *Current Osteoporosis Reports*, 2020, 505–514. https://doi.org/10.1007/s11914-020-00606-2

[24] Ozbolat, I. T. Scaffold-Based or Scaffold-Free Bioprinting: Competing or Complementing Approaches? *The Journal of Nanotechnology in Engineering and Medicine*, 2015, *6* (2). https://doi.org/10.1115/1.4030414

[25] Halil Murat, A. Poly(Glycerol-Sebacate) Elastomer: A Mini Review. *Orthoplastic Surgery & Orthopedic Care International Journal*, 2017, *1* (2). https://doi.org/10.31031/ooij.2017.01.000507

[26] Bodhak, S.; Bose, S.; Bandyopadhyay, A. Electrically Polarized HAp-Coated Ti: In Vitro Bone Cell-Material Interactions. *Acta Biomaterialia*, 2010, *6* (2), 641–651. https://doi.org/10.1016/j.actbio.2009.08.008

[27] Satpathy, A.; Pal, A.; Sengupta, S.; Das, A.; Hasan, M. M.; Ratha, I.; Barui, A.; Bodhak, S. Bioactive Nano-Hydroxyapatite Doped Electrospun PVA-Chitosan Composite Nanofibers for Bone Tissue Engineering Applications. *Journal of the Indian Institute of Science*, 2019, pp. 289–302. https://doi.org/10.1007/s41745-019-00118-8

[28] Melchels, F. P. W.; Domingos, M. A. N.; Klein, T. J.; Malda, J.; Bartolo, P. J.; Hutmacher, D. W. Additive Manufacturing of Tissues and Organs. *Progress in Polymer Science*, 2012, 1079–1104. https://doi.org/10.1016/j.progpolymsci.2011.11.007

[29] Murphy, S. V.; Atala, A. 3D Bioprinting of Tissues and Organs. *Nature Biotechnology*, 2014, 773–785. https://doi.org/10.1038/nbt.2958

[30] Shanks, N.; Greek, R.; Greek, J. Are Animal Models Predictive for Humans? *Philosophy, Ethics, and Humanities in Medicine*. 2009. https://doi.org/10.1186/1747-5341-4-2

[31] Guillemot, F.; Guillotin, B.; Fontaine, A.; Ali, M.; Catros, S.; Kériquel, V.; Fricain, J. C.; Rémy, M.; Bareille, R.; Amédée-Vilamitjana, J. Laser-Assisted Bioprinting to Deal with Tissue Complexity in Regenerative Medicine. *MRS Bulletin*, 2011, *36* (12), 1015–1019. https://doi.org/10.1557/mrs.2011.272

[32] Bhamare, N.; Tardalkar, K.; Parulekar, P.; Khadilkar, A.; Joshi, M. 3D Printing of Human Ear Pinna Using Cartilage Specific Ink. *Biomedical Materials*, 2021, *16* (5). https://doi.org/10.1088/1748-605X/ac15b0

[33] Xu, C.; Chai, W.; Huang, Y.; Markwald, R. R. Scaffold-Free Inkjet Printing of Three-Dimensional Zigzag Cellular Tubes. *Biotechnology and Bioengineering*, 2012, *109* (12), 3152–3160. https://doi.org/10.1002/bit.24591

[34] Medvedeva, N. V.; Ipatova, O. M.; Ivanov, Y. D.; Drozhzhin, A. I.; Archakov, A. I. Nano-biotechnology and Nanomedicine. *Biomeditsinskaya Khimiya*, 2006, *52* (6), 529–546. https://doi.org/10.1134/s1990750807020023

[35] Laval, J. M.; Mazeran, P. E.; Thomas, D. Nanobiotechnology and Its Role in the Development of New Analytical Devices. *Analyst*, 2000, *125*, 29–33. https://doi.org/10.1039/a907827d

[36] Wilkinson, C. D. W.; Dalby, M.; Curtis, A. S. G. Making Structures for Cell Engineering. *European Cells and Materials*, 2004, 21–26. https://doi.org/10.22203/eCM.v008a03

[37] Grainger, D. W.; Castner, D. G. Nanobiomaterials and Nanoanalysis: Opportunities for Improving the Science to Benefit Biomedical Technologies. *Advanced Materials*, 2008, *20* (5), 867–877. https://doi.org/10.1002/adma.200701760

[38] Huang, H.; Shen, L.; Ford, J.; Wang, Y.; Xu, Y. Computational Issues in Biomedical Nanometrics and Nano-Materials. *Journal of Nano Research*, 2008, 1, 50–58. https://doi.org/10.4028/www.scientific.net/JNanoR.1.50

[39] Caruthers, S. D.; Wickline, S. A.; Lanza, G. M. Nanotechnological Applications in Medicine. *Current Opinion in Biotechnology*, 2007, 26–30. https://doi.org/10.1016/j.copbio.2007.01.006

[40] Wagner, V.; Dullaart, A.; Bock, A. K.; Zweck, A. The Emerging Nanomedicine Landscape. *Nature Biotechnology*, 2006, 1211–1217. https://doi.org/10.1038/nbt1006-1211

[41] Liu, H.; Webster, T. J. Nanomedicine for Implants: A Review of Studies and Necessary Experimental Tools. *Biomaterials*, 2007, 354–369. https://doi.org/10.1016/j.biomaterials.2006.08.049

[42] Sharma, P.; Brown, S.; Walter, G.; Santra, S.; Moudgil, B. Nanoparticles for Bioimaging. *Advances in Colloid and Interface Science*, 2006, 471–485. https://doi.org/10.1016/j.cis.2006.05.026

[43] Klostranec, J. M.; Chan, W. C. W. Quantum Dots in Biological and Biomedical Research: Recent Progress and Present Challenges. *Advanced Materials*, 2006, *18* (15), 1953–1964. https://doi.org/10.1002/adma.200500786

[44] Yezhelyev, M. V.; Al-Hajj, A.; Morris, C.; Marcus, A. I.; Liu, T.; Lewis, M.; Cohen, C.; Zrazhevskiy, P.; Simons, J. W.; Rogatko, A.; et al. In Situ Molecular Profiling of Breast Cancer Biomarkers with Multicolor Quantum Dots. *Advanced Materials*, 2007, *19* (20), 3146–3151. https://doi.org/10.1002/adma.200701983

[45] Langer, R. Drug Delivery: Drugs on Target. *Science (80-.)*, 2001, *293* (5527), 58–59.

[46] Ray, L. Polymeric Nanoparticle-Based Drug/Gene Delivery for Lung Cancer. *Nanotechnology-Based Targeted Drug Delivery Systems for Lung Cancer*; 2019, 77–93. https://doi.org/10.1016/b978-0-12-815720-6.00004-6

[47] Ray, S. S.; Bandyopadhyay, J. Nanotechnology-Enabled Biomedical Engineering: Current Trends, Future Scopes, and Perspectives. *Nanotechnology Reviews*, 2021, 728–743. https://doi.org/10.1515/ntrev-2021-0052

[48] Saji, V. S.; Choe, H. C.; Yeung, K. W. K. Nanotechnology in Biomedical Applications: A Review. *International Journal of Nano and Biomaterials*, 2010, *3* (2), 119–139. https://doi.org/10.1504/IJNBM.2010.037801

[49] Camarillo, D. B.; Krummel, T. M.; Salisbury, J. K. Robotic Technology in Surgery: Past, Present, and Future. *The American Journal of Surgery*, 2004, *188* (4 SUPPL. 1), 2–15. https://doi.org/10.1016/j.amjsurg.2004.08.025

[50] Satava, R. M. Surgical Robotics: The Early Chronicles: A Personal Historical Perspective. *Surgical Laparoscopy, Endoscopy and Percutaneous Techniques*. 2002, 6–16. https://doi.org/10.1097/00019509-200202000-00002

[51] Chen, Y. W.; Hanak, B. W.; Yang, T. C.; Wilson, T. A.; Hsia, J. M.; Walsh, H. E.; Shih, H. C.; Nagatomo, K. J. Computer-Assisted Surgery in Medical and Dental Applications. *Expert Review of Medical Devices*, 2021, 669–696. https://doi.org/10.1080/17434440.2021.1886075

[52] Shapira, P.; Kwon, S.; Youtie, J. Tracking the Emergence of Synthetic Biology. *Scientometrics*, 2017, *112* (3), 1439–1469. https://doi.org/10.1007/s11192-017-2452-5

[53] Ruder, W. C.; Lu, T.; Collins, J. J. Synthetic Biology Moving into the Clinic. *Science*, 2011, 1248–1252. https://doi.org/10.1126/science.1206843

[54] Gibson, D. G.; Benders, G. A.; Andrews-Pfannkoch, C.; Denisova, E. A.; Baden-Tillson, H.; Zaveri, J.; Stockwell, T. B.; Brownley, A.; Thomas, D. W.; Algire, M. A.; et al. Complete Chemical Synthesis, Assembly, and Cloning of a Mycoplasma Genitalium Genome. *Science (80-.)*, 2008, *319* (5867), 1215–1220. https://doi.org/10.1126/science.1151721

[55] Larman, H. B.; Zhao, Z.; Laserson, U.; Li, M. Z.; Ciccia, A.; Gakidis, M. A. M.; Church, G. M.; Kesari, S.; Leproust, E. M.; Solimini, N. L.; et al. Autoantigen Discovery with a Synthetic Human Peptidome. *Nature Biotechnology*, 2011, *29* (6), 535–541. https://doi.org/10.1038/nbt.1856

[56] Burbelo, P. D.; Ching, K. H.; Bush, E. R.; Han, B. L.; Iadarola, M. J. Antibody-Profiling Technologies for Studying Humoral Responses to Infectious Agents. *Expert Review of Vaccines*, 2010, 567–578. https://doi.org/10.1586/erv.10.50

[57] Gonzalez-Nicolini, V.; Fux, C.; Fussenegger, M. A Novel Mammalian Cell-Based Approach for the Discovery of Anticancer Drugs with Reduced Cytotoxicity on Non-Dividing Cells. *Investigational New Drugs*, 2004, *22* (3), 253–262. https://doi.org/10.1023/B:DRUG.0000026251.00854.77

[58] Ajikumar, P. K.; Xiao, W. H.; Tyo, K. E. J.; Wang, Y.; Simeon, F.; Leonard, E.; Mucha, O.; Phon, T. H.; Pfeifer, B.; Stephanopoulos, G. Isoprenoid Pathway Optimization for Taxol Precursor Overproduction in Escherichia Coli. *Science (80-.).*, 2010, *330* (6000), 70–74. https://doi.org/10.1126/science.1191652

[59] Coleman, J. R.; Papamichail, D.; Skiena, S.; Futcher, B.; Wimmer, E.; Mueller, S. Virus Attenuation by Genome-Scale Changes in Codon Pair Bias. *Science (80-.)*, 2008, *320* (5884), 1784–1787. https://doi.org/10.1126/science.1155761

[60] Noel, J. P. Chemical Biology: Synthetic Metabolism Goes Green. *Nature*, 2010, 380–381. https://doi.org/10.1038/468380a

[61] Runguphan, W.; Qu, X.; O'Connor, S. E. Integrating Carbon-Halogen Bond Formation into Medicinal Plant Metabolism. *Nature*, 2010, *468* (7322), 461–467. https://doi.org/10.1038/nature09524

[62] Nguyen, V. H.; Kim, H. S.; Ha, J. M.; Hong, Y.; Choy, H. E.; Min, J. J. Genetically Engineered Salmonella Typhimurium as an Imageable Therapeutic Probe for Cancer. *Cancer Research*, 2010, *70* (1), 18–23. https://doi.org/10.1158/0008-5472.CAN-09-3453

[63] Ye, H.; Baba, M. D. E.; Peng, R. W.; Fussenegger, M. A Synthetic Optogenetic Transcription Device Enhances Blood-Glucose Homeostasis in Mice. *Science (80-.)*, 2011, *332* (6037), 1565–1568. https://doi.org/10.1126/science.1203535

[64] Chen, Y. Y.; Jensen, M. C.; Smolke, C. D. Genetic Control of Mammalian T-Cell Proliferation with Synthetic RNA Regulatory Systems. *Proceedings of the National Academy of Sciences of the United States of America*, 2010, *107* (19), 8531–8536. https://doi.org/10.1073/pnas.1001721107

[65] Culler, S. J.; Hoff, K. G.; Smolke, C. D. Reprogramming Cellular Behavior with RNA Controllers Responsive to Endogenous Proteins. *Science (80-.)*, 2010, *330* (6008), 1251–1255. https://doi.org/10.1126/science.1192128

20 Clinical Trials in the Realm of Health Informatics

Laxmi N. Chavali
Sri Venkateshwara College of Pharmacy, India

Harshita Bhargava and Amita Sharma
IIS (deemed to be University), India

Prashanth Suravajhala and Renuka Suravajhala
Amrita Vishwa Vidyapeetham, India

20.1 INTRODUCTION

Clinical trials (CT) are used to investigate human subjects and are intended to discover or verify the clinical, pharmacological, and the dynamic effects of a drug, and to identify any adverse reactions on the subjects to ascertain its safety and efficacy. The World Health Organization aims at analyzing the results of specific health-related interventions on health outcomes (https://www.who.int/health-topics, last accessed January 30, 2022). There are various ways the clinical study portfolios could be ascertained. The CT Management System (CTMS) is a cloud-based software that is used to conduct and manage CTs by pharmaceutical/sponsor companies (https://web.archive.org/web/20160624191217/http://www.bio-itworld.com/issues/2007/feb/cover-story/, last accessed on August 29, 2022). One of the impending goals of CTMS is to help reduce cycle times of the trial processes by collaborating with lead clinics and leading-edge information technologies, and by automating the trial processes with workflow technologies. The data acquisition is performed by enabling Interactive Voice Response (IVR) systems, IoT edge devices, and electronic forms (Figure 20.1).

20.2 CT PROCESS

The CT has a sequence of four iterative processes, namely, design process, infrastructure process, execution process, and review process (Rajadhyaksha 2010). The design process is responsible for the development of the CT protocol and resolution of all the ethical issues raised by institutional ethics committee (IEC) and/or

DOI: 10.1201/9781003331247-23

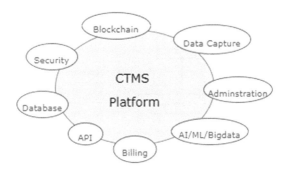

FIGURE 20.1   An overview of modules highlighting various components involved in a CT process.

FDA and producing the final protocol specification for submission to FDA, sites, and IRB (Institutional Review Board). The registration and setup process deals with contractual agreements among sponsors, CROs, SMOs, sites, and patients for conducting efficient CTs, besides ensuring there is an active participation and stakeholders engaged in the trials. Upon completion of these two processes, the platform is ready for users with respective roles to enter the data to make it operational, i.e., ready for execution. Over the years, there is an inherent need for deploying the artificial intelligence (AI) design for CT which is reviewed elsewhere (Harrer et al. 2019).

The protocol for the given trial, which is defined by the sponsor, describes the objectives, methodology, and organization of the trial. The protocol is hosted on the cloud/central server and would then be reviewed by the stakeholders and submitted to FDA before approval of IEC. However, all versions, including the approved version of the protocol, are maintained on the cloud/central platform. Once the protocol is approved by FDA, it is submitted to sites and IRB. On the other hand, report forms (CRF) are used to store, organize, and maintain the forms for conducting the CT. The trial manager is responsible for creating and maintaining CRFs as per protocol. While the CRF templates are designed based on the protocol, after approval from FDA, they are later used for collecting data from patients, and for validation and analysis purposes. Whereas rule-based flows are defined for CRF forms, data capturing mechanisms are used for all other users' transactions. The workflow rules that are associated with a form are defined during the form's design process. In principle, as groups of patients always belong to a site in a trial, it is assumed that more than one site can participate in a trial. A CRF and its template are specific to a given trial. The template describes how a form is organized, stored, and displayed. A template can have more than one section with an associated form for each section. The forms template has a schema for the CT data which is used to create a CT database. The form data of the patients is stored in folders created for each patient (Bellary et al. 2014). Form data is stored with respect to specific form templates for easy display and other form-level processing (Figure 20.2).

The boxes in Figure 20.2 represent the objects and the edges of the static relationships. Edges with a diamond represent the aggregation (set) relationship. Hollow diamond connector represents a three-way relationship between the entities.

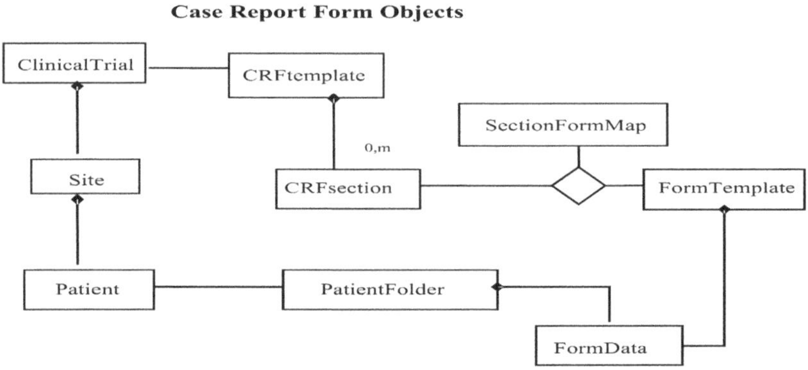

Case Report Form Objects

FIGURE 20.2   A flow diagram of entity relationship for establishing the CRFs.

It is mandatory to register patients and sites before conducting the trial. The site investigation, initiation, maintenance, and termination must be examined during the site qualification process which may lead to defining a checklist by site manager or site coordinator. The checklists have objectives and their respective status set by the rule's engine. The site will be ready for patient recruitment only after the site's initiation checklist is found to be satisfactory during site qualification or registration process. Patient registration or recruitment process involves collecting patient information from various sources including from a CPR/MPR from the hospital. This information is stored in the CTMS on cloud. A patient is assigned the patient/or subject index code issued by FDA when the protocol was approved. The main parts of CT execution are data capture, workflow management, and information portal. Data capture part captures the data from IVR, user browser, smartphones, and through other medical devices. The data received from these sources is put on storage of the cloud and subsequently pushed to the CT database after the necessary transformation of the data. Generally, the data collection agents are responsible for transforming the data collected from the devices/targets. The data is generated in a standard format complying with a framework before finally storing in patient-specific CRF. Workflow is an event monitor and is based on the events registered during the formulation phase. Events can be classified as changes to the database state or objects and messages. Information portal services are meant for each user with a role and profile. These services are accessed over the internet and customized based on profile for user experience. The services include other services like dashboards and group chats. Portal services provide patient-specific and role-specific browsing of the CRF details and other CT information. Figure 20.3 describes an end-to-end high-level overview of the CT process.

A CT is sponsored by an organization and various roles are involved in conducting the trial process. The main actors in CTs are FDA, Sponsor, CRO, SMO, IRB/IEC, sites, patients, and others. Table 20.1 describes the organization roles and responsibilities that participate in CTMS.

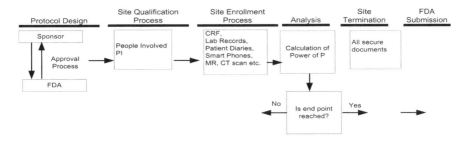

FIGURE 20.3 An overview of the CT processes.

TABLE 20.1

Roles and Responsibilities of Various Stakeholders in CTMS

	Role		
Organization	User	Responsibilities	Remarks, If Any
Sponsor	Trial Manager – TM	Maintenance and registration of user, site, and protocol. Maintenance and creation of CRF forms.	Sponsor is responsible for generating various reports and submitting them to FDA. New Drug approval from FDA.
	Protocol Designer – PD	Creation of protocol document.	
Contract Research Organization (CRO)	TM	Same as above.	
	Clinical Research Associate – CRA	Checklist creation and maintenance. Issues and query resolution of the site.	
	Clinical Data Manager – CDM	Creation and maintenance of queries.	
	Data Analyst – DA	Data analysis	
Site	Study Coordinator -SC	Data entry of the patients and responsible for resolution of the incorrect data entries.	
	Principle / Sub Investigator – PI /SI	Patient recruitment. Review of CRF/ICF/SAE	
	Pharmacist	Patient's data review	
	Administrator	Responsible for the total administration of the CT platform.	
Site Management Organization – SMO		Management of the site that includes	

(Continued)

TABLE 20.1 (CONTINUED)

		Role	
Organization	User	Responsibilities	Remarks, If Any
Institutional Review Board – IRB		Review and analysis of the submitted data and reports	
Independent Ethics Committee – IEC		Same as above	
Data Review Board – DRB		Same as above	
Food and Drug Administration – FDA			

20.3 AUTOMATION METHODS IN CT

20.3.1 SOFTWARE-AS-A-SERVICE

Legacy CTMS (CT Management System) on the Web is a software system that exists even today, which satisfies the needs of biotech and pharmacy companies. CTMS aids the trials from end-to-end in terms of setup, execution, monitoring, and analysis. It is well known that the Software as a Service (SaaS) model emerged from the Application Service Provider (ASP) of the 1990s, which is basically a centralized managed service on the internet. SaaS is more mature in terms of hosting, subscription, and accessing the application services. The key benefits of the SaaS model are round-the-clock access to the application services from anywhere, dynamic scalability and configuration of app services, which provide an opportunity to meet the dynamic demands of client requirements. The regulatory audit has grown more complex due to adoption of digital technologies such as EDC and EHR. Due to the compulsion of new technological trends, business needs and practices, it is inevitable to align the legacy system with the new features that the current leading-edge technologies offer such as mobile-optimized or mobile-version of CTMS and connection to wearable devices. A cloud-based CTMS application provides features like efficient data management, strong security, preventing enrollment in multiple trials. Protocol compliance is the key to conducting a successful trial. CTMS facilitates the internal and external collaboration by process automation and notifies the stakeholders in real time on every change thereby ensuring the legal compliance of the trial (https://langate.com/regulatory-compliance-standards-for-healthcare/, last accessed on August 29, 2022).

Patient data in CTMS is safeguarded by enforcing features such as multi-factor authentication, strong password mechanism, data encryption, virus protection, secure messaging, and secure storage. Multiple enrollments of a patient can be detected and avoided by means of using biometric technologies like facial recognition, fingerprints, and iris. Integrating Electronic Health Records (EHR) with Electronic Data Capture (EDC) by one source model would help the researcher to have a complete view of a patient under trial (https://www.fda.gov/science-research/advancing-regulatory-science, last accessed on August 28, 2022).

In CTs, the sponsor must make sure that the SaaS services of CTMS and its data management must meet all applicable standards. Hence, the sponsor must define SOP in accessing data or managing the data. The users in stakeholder organizations are expected to be aware of the security measures and their processes by the necessary training (https://www.ibm.com/products/clinical-development, last accessed on August 28, 2022).

The major worries for any sponsor or CRO are data security and its compliance, and the integration of clinical systems. These concerns can be addressed by engaging in digital technologies and by adopting the latest trends. eICF (Electronic Informed Consent Form) allows patients to consent on a smartphone or a tablet or a desktop, thereby taking paper out of the equation. It helps the sponsors and CRO reduce the human error of having patients signing the wrong version of paper ICF (Informed Consent Form). There are many eICF solutions available in the market as of today such as Secure Consent, Parallel 6, CRF Health, and Mytrus. EDC enables sponsors and CTO to collect CT data using digital technologies. It replaces paper-based Case Report Form (CRF) with eCRF for collecting patient data. The major hurdles like missing CRF and manually handling volumes of paper-based CRFs can be eliminated by having EDC. Electronic Binder (eBinder) is a useful tool to sponsors and CRO to share their documents, i.e., both study and site-level docs. An eBinder as a cloud-based platform has an advantage which makes the regulatory document management process electronic.

20.3.2 Blockchain

Blockchain technology as a distributed repository is making a big chain of systems enabling direct interactions between various users (Abu-Elezz et al. 2020). Compliance with the regulatory requirements in CTs is all important and immutability of patient records makes it hard for any manipulation and enables faster approvals from Food and Drug Administration (FDA) in the drug discovery process. Blockchains are designed to be appended only, immutable, and ensure the data to be tamper proof (Wong et al. 2019).

CT data in real time on immutable basis minimizes the fraud due to consensus protocol among stakeholders in the network. In traditional trials, all adverse reactions are reported to the regulator or DSMB by CRO after filtering them from CRFs (Baumfeld et al. 2020). As blockchain is decentralized and patient driven, any patient can audit his/her records. This auditability feature helps resolve certain issues like lack of awareness (Meijer and Ubacht 2018).

The blockchain features and smart contract functionality can solve most of the barriers for CT recruitment (Zhuang et al. 2020). It is expected that every stakeholder in the blockchain contributes one node in the network and patients grant permission to access their EHR which can be accessed from the blockchain. Universal Patient ID is the key to getting patient information from different sites in the healthcare ecosystem. Patient recruitment is a good fit for implementing blockchain as it provides public auditability and surveillance by the competent authority (Porsdam et al. 2020). Table 20.2 illustrates the differences between traditional and blockchain-based trials.

A blockchain implementation may provide some benefits such as establishing trust among stakeholders by eliminating mediation, reducing transaction cost, distributed

TABLE 20.2

A Comparison of Models

Feature	Traditional	Blockchain
Data privacy	Data accessed is restricted by login credentials.	Data access is restricted by smart contracts, and by methods of permissioned blockchain.
Data storage	Data is stored at central database and a copy is available at site.	Data is distributed and stored on every node of the stakeholder for transparency.
Data recovery	Regular data backups and data redundancy provide a recovery mechanism.	Data recovery is simple from a decentralized and distributed ledger.
Cost	Low setup and high maintenance.	High setup and low maintenance.

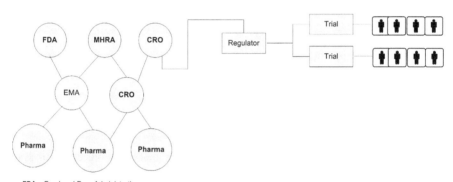

FIGURE 20.4   A pictorial flow diagram of nodes in blockchain trial structure.

network, smart no contracts, and shared and secure data (Dutta et al. 2020). Figure 20.4 displays different nodes that can participate in blockchain.

20.3.3 INTERNET OF THINGS

CT processes are redefined due to the emergence of IoT, and processes have become more efficient and cost-effective. Leveraging IoT in CTs with connected and managed devices will help transform the entire CT process and help in patient recruitment and advertisement process in a big way. Most of the consumers these days have smartphone-connected mobiles, and hence, the patient needs to drive the pharmacy companies to adopt IoT and other innovative technologies which benefit them a great deal. The adoption of IoT in CTs will move up once FDA gives more approvals on wearable devices and gadgets in CTs. "Patient recruitment and online market research are great opportunities that come from IoT," says Malcolm Bohm, CEO of Liquid Grids (https://www.pharmavoice.com, last accessed on August 21, 2022).

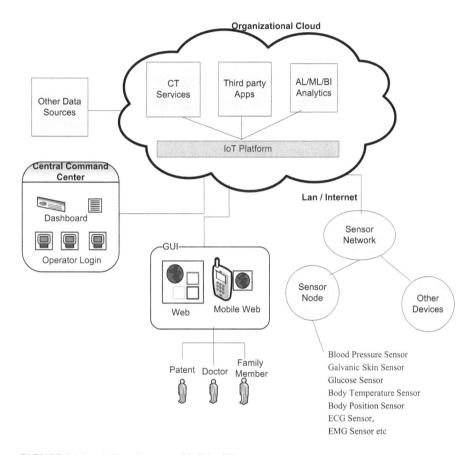

FIGURE 20.5   A flow diagram of IoT in CTs.

Edge computing is evolving, and data acquisition from edge is playing a big role in IoT. The data from edge devices like sensors is relayed to edge infrastructure which in turn pushes it to a central server (i.e., typically cloud). The security of data acquisition from different sources like point of equipment use, point of assay use, and point of room use is taken care of by having redundancies and by employing cyber security practices in place (https://embeddedcomputing.com/, last accessed on August 31, 2022) (Figure 20.5).

Many trials never see the light due to a high failure rate which is caused by factors like lack of participation due to poor results in the early stages of the research. Recruitment of patients in CTs from diverse ethnic backgrounds remains a challenge due to location constraints. However, IoT takes location out of the equation, mitigates the everlasting problem of patient recruitment, and enables patient data collection based on trial choices, which leads to building big data in real time. Analysis of the big data can target the patients more accurately during the recruitment process. The trials with IoT can reap benefits like remote patient monitoring, real time access to data, enhanced study quality, transparency etc. Connected devices such as wearable and ingestible sensors help collect study data, thereby reducing the dropout of study before they are complete.

20.3.4 ARTIFICIAL INTELLIGENCE-BASED DATA ANALYTICS

Before new medications, technologies, and procedures are licensed for widespread applications, CTs are used to evaluate whether they are safe and effective. However, the road from study conception to approval is long, complex, and costly. Traditionally, randomized controlled trials (RCTs) have been used to examine mass-market medications. It lacks the adaptability and analytical skills needed to create sophisticated new medications for smaller, sometimes varied patient populations. Furthermore, poor patient selection, enrollment, and retention, as well as challenges maintaining and monitoring patients efficiently, contribute to high trial failure rates with higher research and development expenditures (https://www2.deloitte.com/us/en/insights/industry/life-sciences/artificial-intelligence-in-clinical-trials.html, last accessed on August 31, 2022). Even though the trial process deals with a lot of operational data, it doesn't give you any insight into the CT portfolio around the world. Consolidating data from diverse sources and putting it on a shared analytics platform based on open data standards can aid in cooperation and integration while also giving insights across key KPIs. Machine learning systems may also deliver proactive analytics views to users when integrated with data visualization tools, enhancing forecasts and recommendations over time (https://www.cbinsights.com/research/clinical-trials-ai-tech-disruption/, last accessed on August 31, 2022) (Figure 20.6).

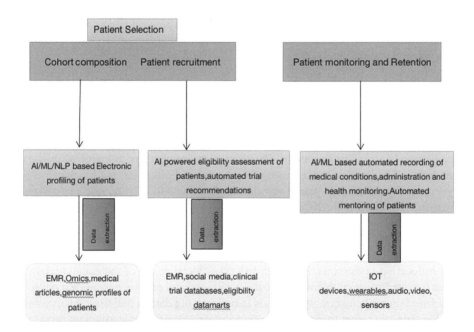

FIGURE 20.6   A pictorial flowchart of AI enabled CT analytical system.

CT generally faces problems related to patient selection for trials. The ML technology has also helped in overcoming such issues by supporting in development of digital twin. The term "digital twin" refers to a living representation of the physical system that continuously adjusts to operational changes using data collected in real time from various IoT sensors and devices. Using AI, it predicts the future of the corresponding physical counterparts.

20.3.5 ROBOTIC PROCESS AUTOMATION (RPA) IN CTs

Companies utilize RPA software to assist employees by automating time-consuming and error-prone repetitive, rule-based processes. Dedicated software bots that have been trained to conduct certain tasks according to rules and directives previously established in a computer program are used to automate tasks. RPA software accelerates and simplifies operations that must be completed during CTs, allowing activities to be completed faster and outcomes to be more accurate. Even regulatory bodies, such as the FDA, have acknowledged the benefits of automation and the use of new technologies, pushing businesses to incorporate them into their strategies and providing help in the form of industry recommendations. RPA software can be utilized at all stages of CTs, not just to optimize trial management and data collecting, analysis, and sharing, but also to match patients and process PV cases, due to its capacity to tackle the problem of systems interoperability. CTMS based on RPA will automate all stages and create a bot to assist with each task in the system. RPA can improve rule-based workflows and processes in CTs. These bots can help with data storage, data manipulation, system calibration, and transaction procedures, among other things. As a result of these advantages, there's a better chance of getting clinical products to market on time and on budget (Figure 20.7).

In a nutshell, RPA-based CTMS speeds up participant recruitment and patient monitoring by integrating data, automating manual operations, and extracting document data. Patient data entry, EHR verification, patient matching to suitable trials based on their provided data, appointment scheduling and notification, and CT report production seem to be just some of the tasks that can be automated with RPA to make CT management easier.

20.4 ARCHITECTURE

CT management software collects data through a variety of data capture systems like Web Forms, telephone (IVR), smartphones, medical devices, and hospital information and management systems/labs. A cloud-based CTMS framework centralizes the data capture mechanism and integrates all data capture systems by API with scalable virtual storage for the collected data. The CT data is critical and sensitive, and hence the security and privacy of the captured data plays a critical role during data audit as the capture is regulated by regulatory bodies like FDA.

Service-based architectures are a significant improvement over monolithic application. service-oriented architecture played a dominant role in IT in the mid-2000s whereas microservices is the emerging technology at present for developing scalable and modular applications. Both SOA and microservices are considered to be

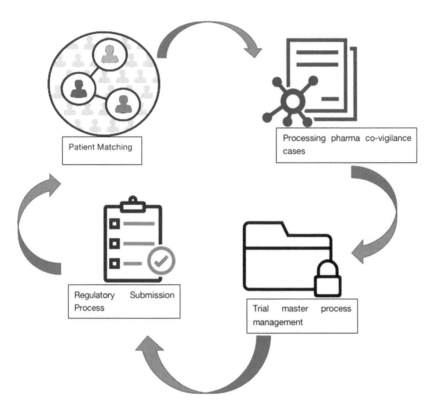

FIGURE 20.7   An overview of RPA based CTMS.

service-based architectures but with different architectural styles and vary greatly in terms of service characteristics (Nageba et al. 2022).

The architectural framework depicted in Figure 20.8 supports microservices architecture with the coexistence of many applications. The detailed design aspects of the architectural layers and its elaboration are beyond the scope of this chapter.

20.5   PROGRESS SO FAR

The CT process is fraught with difficulties and necessitates constant monitoring. Failure is expensive in terms of money and life. Since the process is so crucial, automation can help reduce the risk of failure. The technologies that deal with automation of CT are briefly discussed in this section. Any CT begins with preclinical research. These tests are carried out on the investigational drug to ensure that it is safe and effective in humans. The main challenges in preclinical studies are poor study design, cost compatibility, timeliness, and a lack of pharmacovigilance knowledge. Cost and time issues in pre-CTs can be addressed with advanced computational techniques and existing repositories. Machine learning and cloud-based drug and gene bank repositories can aid in the discovery of suitable drugs for research (https://www.ncbi. nlm.nih.gov/books/NBK195047/).

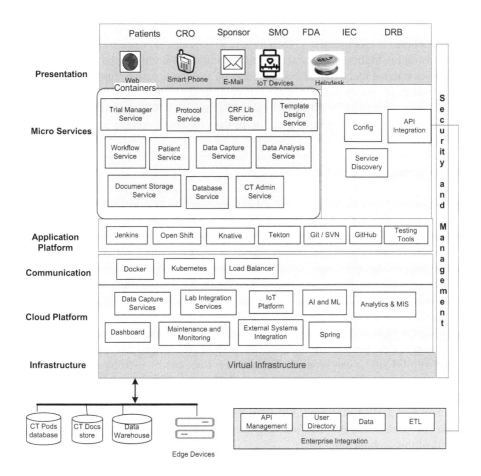

FIGURE 20.8 Microservices architectural framework of CT.

CTs progress through four phases after preclinical approval to test a treatment, determine the proper dosage, and look for side effects. An auditor, usually a doctor, and a team of researchers lead these trials. The FDA approves a drug or other intervention for clinical use and continues to monitor its effects if researchers find it to be safe and effective after the first three phases. CTs are fraught with difficulties and can end up costing pharmaceutical companies far more than they anticipated. CTs are inefficient in many ways around the world; finding the right patients for the right trial is one of the most difficult challenges. Patient recruitment for CTs can go wrong in a variety of ways, causing delays in the trial's completion.

Intelligent CT management systems are alternatives to the most frequent patient recruitment issues, such as underperforming sites and unresponsive patients, that can help you speed up your trial and deliver on time. CTMS applications are built using cloud systems, blockchain, IoT devices and networks, edge computation, data analytics, and other techniques. From patient matching to CTs to data management to drug discovery, these technologies are becoming recognized for their potential to lower costs and speed up every stage of clinical research and drug development. For example, a cloud-based CTMS program provides advantages like fast data administration, high security, and the ability to prohibit multiple trial enrollment. It improves internal and external collaboration by automating procedures and informs stakeholders of any changes in real time, ensuring that the trial is legal. Similarly, blockchain technology in CTMS can assist in keeping CT data in real time on an immutable basis, eliminating fraud, due to the consensus process among network stakeholders.

Recruitment of patients from various backgrounds for CTs remains a challenge due to geographic limits. IoT trials can provide remote patient monitoring, real-time data access, increased research quality, transparency, and other benefits. Wearable and ingestible sensors, for example, aid in the collecting of study data, reducing the number of people who abandon studies before they are finished. The trials process handles a lot of operational data, but it doesn't give any information on the overall CT portfolio. ML algorithms are accessible in several forms for managing massive and heterogeneous data sources, recognizing sophisticated and specialized patterns, and anticipating challenging outcomes. As a result, machine learning could be useful in a variety of settings, including preclinical drug research, trial design and data management, and CT analysis.

Also, the process of constructing a patient population with dynamic inclusion and exclusion is time-consuming, but with the help of robotic process automation software with CTMS, it can be made much faster. Bots can be used to match patients before requiring interaction with employees, effectively speeding up the recruitment process. The CTMS application's microservices architecture, which unites all the technologies, is also explained. The design highlights how each technique serves to make the overall trial process fast, adaptive, secure, and cost effective at numerous layers of this architecture.

20.6   CONCLUSIONS

CTs are increasingly being expected to demonstrate not only efficacy and safety, but also a meaningful influence on patients' lives. This is especially true for increasingly targeted, expensive medicines that target fewer patient populations. Biopharma companies are being pressured by regulators and payers to improve the quality and amount of evidence generated during CTs, which is increasing the complexity of CT design and development. Manual processes have traditionally driven CT processes in prior generations. CT entails several repetitive activities, such as patient data entry, trial data validation, and regulatory submissions to compliance teams and auditors, all of which are difficult to execute manually and provide a risk of failure even with minor errors. The CTMS application, along with other sophisticated technologies, has the potential to influence a wide range of processes, including study design, execution, and decommissioning, as well as regulatory submissions. To reduce money and streamline the CT procedure, the pharmaceutical sector is turning to technology alternatives. The CTMS should essentially log all data changes in the system, including who made them, when they occurred, and what the old and new values were. It generally includes a data warehouse that may be utilized to apply consistent data across data perspectives and studies inside research. The CTMS should also support electronic signatures for records that are critical to a study's regulatory responsibilities. Although most of the CTMS planning and tracking is for the study's efficient and effective execution, regulatory authorities may not find it useful. While CTMS can manage these activities with the help of automation and modern technology, preventing the entire trial from getting corrupted by bad data is a big challenge. As a result, patients receive the medications they require with fewer side effects and lower expenses. Clinical research cannot solve every problem with these computational techniques. However, these technologies can improve the amount of data collected, aggregate data from multiple sources, and ensure the data is clean enough for academics to adequately study. Future trials with CTMS will undoubtedly be more efficient, taking less time to complete while still completing each study stage appropriately.

REFERENCES

Abu-Elezz I, Hassan A, Nazeemudeen A, Househ M, Abd-Alrazaq A. The Benefits and Threats of Blockchain Technology in Healthcare: A Scoping Review. *Int J Med Inform.* 2020;142:104246. doi: 10.1016/j.ijmedinf.2020.104246

Baumfeld AE, Reynolds R, Caubel P, Azoulay L, Dreyer NA. Trial Designs Using Real-World Data: The Changing Landscape of the Regulatory Approval Process. *Pharmacoepidemiol Drug Saf.* 2020;29(10):1201–12. doi: 10.1002/pds.4932

Bellary S, Krishnankutty B, Latha MS. Basics of Case Report form Designing in Clinical Research. *Perspect Clin Res.* 2014;5(4):159–66. doi: 10.4103/2229-3485.140555

Dutta P, Choi TM, Somani S, Butala R. Blockchain technology in supply chain operations: Applications, challenges and research opportunities. *Transp Res E Logist Transp Rev.* 2020;142:102067. doi: 10.1016/j.tre.2020.102067

Harrer S, Shah P, Antony B, Hu J. Artificial Intelligence for Clinical Trials Design. *Trends Pharmacol Sci.* 2019;40(8):577–91. doi: 10.1016/j.tips.2019.05.005

Meijer D, Ubacht J. 2018. The governance of blockchain systems from an institutional perspective, a matter of trust or control? In Proceedings of the 19th Annual International Conference on Digital Government Research: Governance in the Data Age (dg.o '18). Association for Computing Machinery, New York, NY, Article 90, 1–9. doi: 10.1145/320 9281.3209321

Nageba E, Hilka M, Gozlan R, Dubiel J, Baudoin C, Daniel C. Microservices-Based Architecture to Support the Adaptive RECORDS-Trial. *Stud Health Technol Inform.* 2022;294:283–84. doi: 10.3233/SHTI220458

Porsdam MS, Savulescu J, Ravaud P, Benchoufi M. Blockchain, Consent and Prosent for Medical Research. *J Med Ethics.* 2020;47(4):244–50. doi: 10.1136/medethics-2019-105963

Rajadhyaksha V. Conducting feasibility in Clinical Trials: an investment to ensure a good study. *Perspect Clin Res.* 2010;1(3):106–9.

Wong DR, Bhattacharya S, Butte AJ. Prototype of running clinical trials in an untrustworthy environment using blockchain. *Nat Commun.* 2019;10(1):917. doi: 10.1038/s41467-019-08874-y

Zhuang Y, Sheets LR, Shae Z, Chen YW, Tsai JJP, Shyu CR. Applying Blockchain Technology to Enhance Clinical Trial Recruitment. *AMIA Annu Symp Proc.* 2020;2019:1276–85.

21 Application of Genomics in Novel Microbial Species Identification

Lipika Das, Megha Chaudhary,
Deepika Bhardwaj and Sunita Verma
All India Institute of Medical Sciences, India

Praveenya Tirunagari
IIT Kharagpur, India

Sushanta Deb
All India Institute of Medical Sciences, India

21.1 INTRODUCTION

Microbial taxonomy or microbial systematics is the branch of science that deals with the characterization and arrangement of isolates in an existing classification system. Although the term taxonomy and systematic is seen being used interchangeably, the two differ in their meaning. Taxonomy (G: taxis = arrangement or order, nomos = law or nemein = to distribute or govern) is the science of classification, while systematics is the study of diverse organisms and all sorts of relationships and interactions among them (Mayr and Ashlock 1992; Simpson 1961). Identification, classification, and nomenclature are the basic and interrelated concepts of microbial systematics/taxonomy. Classification means arrangements of organisms into different groups or taxa based on similarity and evolutionary relatedness. Assignment of names to the taxonomic group according to the current rule is termed nomenclature. Identification is the discipline of taxonomy that deals with the determination of taxon for a particular isolate.

In prokaryotic nomenclature, proper identification or correct assignment of a taxonomic name can affect both the clinical result and our comprehension of the pathogenicity of a clinical isolate. Identification of species is of interest in a wide range of fields such as forensics, archaeology, food, novel species of great importance, and climate change. Most of the currently used DNA typing techniques for identifying species rely on DNA sources from a single species and are built on pre-PCR amplification using specific primers. However, still there are numerous situations where there is no prior knowledge of the species. In these situations, a universal typing

DOI: 10.1201/9781003331247-24

approach like NGS would be valuable, particularly if it has the ability to identify many species in depth from a mixed source.

21.2 STANDARD PROTOCOLS FOLLOWED FOR PROKARYOTIC NOMENCLATURE

Species are the basic unit of taxonomy and can be scientifically defined as a collection of individuals capable of interbreeding with each other to produce fertile offspring (Mayr 1942). Species can be appropriately characterized as a group of phenotypically similar strains exhibiting less than 70% of DNA–DNA homology value, ∆Tm less than 5°C, G+C difference more than 5% mol, and 16S rRNA gene sequence similarity above 97% (Stackebrandt et al. 2002). In the polyphasic approach, microbes based on chemotaxonomic, genotypic, and phenotypic characteristics are classified into novel taxa and added up to the existing classification system. Classification of particular bacteria to one group depends on the basic similarity and differences between the closely related members of that classification group. The existence of a huge plethora of bacterial species with their own unique characteristics has rendered bacterial taxonomy an ever-evolving field that has continued to perpetuate from 1955 till the current genomics era. Since its inception, Genomic DNA–DNA homology (DDH) calculation has continued to be utilized as the "gold standard" technique for the identification of bacterial species (McCarthy and Bolton 1963).

21.3 16S RRNA GENE SEQUENCE ANALYSIS

The gene sequence of the small ribosomal subunits of any organism acts as a good marker for phylogenetic analysis. The very fact that its function has remained constant over the evolutionary period makes it an accurate marker for predicting temporal changes. In addition to this, its optimum sequence length (>1400 nt) is sufficient for providing substantial information (Stackebrandt and Goebel 1994; Woese et al. 1990). The 16S sequence similarity of the isolate can be matched with databases like BLAST (https://www.ncbi.nlm.nih.gov/BLAST/), EzTaxon (www.eztaxon.org/), and RDP (https://rdp.cme.msu.edu/) for both bacteria and archaea. From the sequence similarity percentage, isolate could be assigned to particular taxa; i.e., a 98.5% sequence similarity was set for species level (earlier the value was 97%) and 95% for genus level (Stackebrandt 2006).

21.4 MULTILOCUS SEQUENCE TYPING (MLST)

Other than the 16S gene sequence, gene sequences of other conserved housekeeping genes, i.e. rpoA, rpoB, rpoC, rpoD, recA, recB, gyrA, etc., have also been employed for microbial identification (Glazunova et al. 2009). Each one of these housekeeping genes fulfills an indispensable role in organisms and has therefore remained conserved over the evolutionary period. In this technique, analysis of five to seven orthologue conserved housekeeping genes was compared among strains of the same genera. The multilocus sequence typing method is widely used for pathogenic strain identification. After the incorporation of WGS, computer-assisted software is now available for proper identification and classification of microbes (Larsen et al. 2012). Multilocus sequence analysis (MLSA) was first introduced in the 1990s and is a sequencing technology based on MLST used for typing pathogenic bacteria (Maiden 2006). In this technique, isolates are characterized based on the distinct features of housekeeping genes (Maiden 2006). Currently, there are about 50 individual MLST patterns available for specific pathogenic bacteria as well as fungi (e.g., http://www.mlst.net/ and http://www.pubmlst.org). In an epidemiology study, MLST aims not only to calculate the phylogenetic relationship but rather it cluster pathogenic strains based on their allelic profiles (Gevers et al. 2005).

21.5   NEXT-GENERATION SEQUENCING (NGS) APPROACH FOR MICROBIAL TAXONOMY

The ultimate goal of microbial taxonomy is to set a more stable and readily usable system for the classification and identification of novel species. Huge developments in the establishment of cost-effective next-generation sequencing platforms (Illumina, Pacbio, and Oxford) have contributed to the growing availability of whole genome sequence data in public databases. The introduction of genomics has profoundly enhanced the knowledge in the field of bacterial taxonomy and has enabled us to gain deeper insights into understanding complex phylogenetic relationships among prokaryotes (Chun and Rainey 2014). It provides an accurate method for species delineation as well as helps in phylogenetic analysis of taxa belonging to subspecies level to higher taxonomic rank. Establishing a database that is easily searchable and comparable is a fundamental requirement of next-generation taxonomy (Whitman 2014; Rosselló-Móra and Amann 2015). In addition to taxonomic analysis, genome sequence information can be used to explore in multiple ways for subsequent comparative analysis (Auch et al. 2010). Our limited knowledge in the field of genomics and its innumerable applications has considerably been enriched after the dawn of next-generation sequencing. It has enabled us to dig deeper into the identification of bacterial pathogens including their evolutionary advances, behavioral patterns, and pathogenesis as well as designing therapeutic interventions.

A robust taxonomic framework has been developed known as "taxogenomics" in which digital genome comparisons are taken place. The earlier DNA-DNA hybridization procedure was substituted by ANI (Average Nucleotide Identity) and GGDC (Genome-to-Genome Distance Calculator), now considered the two gold standards in bacterial taxonomy (Konstantinidis and Tiedje 2005; Meier-Kolthoff et al. 2013; Richter and Rosselló-Móra 2009). The advantages of in silico DNA-DNA hybridization are that it provides a depository for accessible data in a publicly available database.

Most importantly analysis of nucleotide sequence has allowed a natural system of bacterial classification, where evolutionary traits gained an advantage over phenotypic traits (Lalucat et al. 2020). The fact that evolutionary pressure works on the organism as a whole rather than a subset of genes makes the usage of whole genome sequences preferable over the subsets of genes for phylogenetic studies. Phylogenomics is used to study evolutionary relationships among a group of studied bacteria by aligning multiple homologous core gene sequences and extrapolating corresponding phylogenetic trees. Recently, Parks and collaborators performed the phylogenetic analysis of 120 amino acid sequences of 120 proteins encoding genes and proposed a standardized bacterial taxonomy (GTDB taxonomy) (2018).

After the incorporation of genomics in microbial taxonomy lot of reclassification has been occurring. Genome-based indices like DNA–DNA homology, ANI, and AAI complemented with core genome phylogeny resulted in the amendmentation of several taxa into new species and genera. Several taxa merge with or separate from the existing taxa. The amendmentation of earlier taxa has occurred based on the genomic reclassification of families like *Micrococcaceae* and *Staphylococcaceae*, which have been reported. The genome-based study of phylum *Actinobacteria* alone leads to the recognition of two orders, 10 families and 17 genera, as well as the transfer of over 100 species to other genera (Nouioui et al. 2018).

The explosion of genome sequence in the database has made conventional methods and set of rules used in bacterial polyphasic taxonomy seem as obsolete. Time-consuming, labor-intensive, expensive traditional methods that were used earlier did not perform well in the fields like clinical microbiology, epidemiology, and environmental and evolutionary microbiology. The gold standards used in the polyphasic approach (DDH value less than 70%, 16S sequence similarity less than 98.6%, and 5°C Tm) are not reliable for all prokaryotes species delineated (Ludwig 2010). Several reports suggest that the 16S sequence-based classification showed resolution problems at the genus or species level classification in members of the family Enterobacteriaceae, Mycobacteria, the *Acinetobacter baumannii–A. calcoaceticus* complex, Achromobacter, Stenotrophomonas, and Actinomyces. The DDH cutoff value could not be applied to members of the genus Rickettsia where strains show a DDH value of more than 70% (Fournier and Raoult 2009). Similarly, in the case of *Wolbachia* (Ellegaard et al. 2013), *Burkholderia* (Vandamme and Peeters 2014), *Pseudomonas* (Alvarez-Perez et al. 2013), and marine bacterioplankton (Woyke et al. 2009), polyphasic approach alone is insufficient for their classification. In addition, the lack of reproducibility and the inability to be used as a reference for future database is the limiting factor in the wet lab-based polyphasic approach. So the polyphasic approach of prokaryotic taxonomy needs to be revisited and the incorporation of sequence data-based analysis possibly could fill the gap in prokaryotic taxonomy.

21.6   OVERALL GENOME RELATEDNESS INDICES (OGRI)

The OGRI concept for species identification was first introduced by Chun and Rainey (2014), it uses a set of algorithms to estimate the similarity among genome sequences (Chun and Rainey 2014). OGRI provides a general guideline on the use of whole genome sequence data for prokaryote taxonomic delineation (Chun et al. 2018). OGRI comprises three major genomic indices, such as Average nucleotide identity (ANI), Average amino acid identity (AAI), and in silico DDH (isDDH). Nowadays several web services and standalone tools are available to calculate those genomic indices. ANI and isDDH are among the most widely used indices applied for taxonomic classification. Genome relatedness between two genomes is calculated by nucleic acid hybridization known as DNA-DNA Homology, which was first introduced by Johnson and Ordal (1968) and is been considered the 'gold standard' for species delineation. Comparative studies suggest that 97% 16S rRNA sequence similarity resembles 70% DDH value (Stackebrandt and Goebel 1994). To date about 50% of type strains have genome sequences available in the database in contrast to almost a complete dataset for 16S rRNA gene sequences is available for the type strains of prokaryotic species (Yoon et al. 2017). So both 16S and OGRI are being used in a systematic process to identify and recognize a new species. In this approach, the selection of species that will be compared is selected based on 16S sequence similarity, i.e., strains that show 16S sequence similarity equal to or more than 98.7% are taken for calculating OGRI. Earlier the cutoff value was 97% but this optimization in the 16S value is to assure the quality of the 16S sequence. It is also recommended to obtain a genome sequence for that organism that shows sequence similarity of more than 98.7% and whose sequences are not present not only to calculate OGRI but to extend and improve the public genome database for taxonomic purposes.

21.7   AVERAGE NUCLEOTIDE IDENTITY (ANI)

The most commonly used OGRI algorithm is the ANI used to mimic the experimental DDH, therefore termed the digital version of DDH (Goris et al. 2007; Konstantinidis and Tiedje 2005). The concept of ANI was proposed by Goris et al. (2007) which calculates the pairwise overall sequence similarity between two genomes. In the original method, the query sequence is fragmented in silico into 1020-bp-long sequences and then blast against the intact subject sequence present in the NCBI database to find the homologous region. Then the final mean homology value between the two sequences is considered. Usually, BLASTn and MUMMER software are used to calculate ANI; however, BLASTn is the most accepted one. Then the percentage identity value between the query and the subject is calculated. ANI value $\geq 95\%$ is equivalent to $\geq 70\%$ DDH value used for species delineation (Goris et al. 2007).

21.8   DIFFERENT ALGORITHMS USED FOR AVERAGE NUCLEOTIDE IDENTITY (ANI) ESTIMATION

With the steep increase in submissions of whole genome sequences in databases, ANI has become popularized among researchers for novel species identification. With time ANI algorithm has been upgraded and different ANI software tools have been reported. The proposed ANI threshold values are 95–96% to set the species boundary to define novel species (Richter and Rosselló-Móra 2009).

21.8.1   ORIGINAL ANI

Average Nucleotide Identity (ANI) is an estimate to deduce similarity between the coding regions of genomes. To estimate the ANI between genome pairs, pairwise bidirectional best hits (BBHs) with > 70% identity and 70% coverage were determined.

Formula for Alignment Fraction (AF):

$$\underset{G1\rightarrow G2}{AF} = \frac{\text{Lengths of BBH genes}}{\sum \text{Length of genes in genome 1}}$$

Formula for Average Nucleotide Identity (ANI):

$$\underset{G1\rightarrow G2}{gANI} = \frac{\sum_{bbh}\left(\text{Percent identity} * \text{Alignment length}\right)}{\text{Length of BBH genes}}$$

21.8.2 OrthoANI

OrthoANI algorithm is the upgraded version of Original ANI with faster delivery of results. Lee et al. (2015) first reported the OrthoANI algorithm. Standalone software tools are freely available for OrthoANI calculation (https://www.ezbiocloud. net/tools/orthoani) (Lee et al. 2015).

21.8.3 OrthoANIu

OrthoANIu tool is the faster version of OrthoANI, which uses USEARCH instead of the BLAST algorithm for OrthoANI calculations (Yoon et al. 2017).

21.8.4 ANIm

ANIm tool is different from all other ANI types in the context of the used algorithm for ANI analysis. ANIm calculation is based on the MUMmer algorithm and does not require prior genome slicing for ANI calculation (Richter and Roselló-Móra 2009).

21.8.5 Average Amino Acid Identity (AAI)

The average amino acid identity (AAI) genomic index can be applied to delineate species boundaries and is widely used for microbial taxonomic classification (Kim et al. 2021). EzAAI web tool can calculate the AAI values in prokaryotic genome sequences (Kim et al. 2021). The AAI tool provides a proper resolution of the two genomes of closely or distantly related species at the amino acid level. Previously it was used for only phase taxonomy but now it's been widely used in bacterial taxonomy. In this technique genome relatedness of the query, the genome is calculated based on a comparison of conserved protein-coding signature genes using pairwise alignment in BLAST. AAI value $\geq 96\%$ correlates with values $\geq 95\%–96\%$ ANI and $\geq 70\%$ DDH value.

21.8.6 In Silico DNA-DNA Hybridization (insDDH)

DDH is the ultimate concept in prokaryotic taxonomy and majorly used technique in microbiology to assign a new strain to existing taxa. In almost all bacteria and archaea threshold values for species, delineation is fixed at ≥ 70% to declare the novelty of a particular strain. The wet lab DDH calculation was cumbersome and restricted to a few specialized laboratories only, and also the results obtained in DDH vary with changes in the method. Recent progress in genome sequencing makes it possible to calculate DDH using bioinformatics methods. In silico or digital genome-to-genome distance (GGD) calculation has now replaced the wet-lab DDH (Meier-Kolthoff et al. 2013). The in silico GGDC can be calculated between two bacterial and archaeal genomes and the value of 70% has been set as the threshold value for species delineation. The DDH threshold value is equivalent to the 95% ANI and AAI threshold value. An online web program Genome-to-Genome Distance Calculator (https://ggdc.dsmz.de/ggdc.php#) is used to estimate digital DDH value, which gives differences in G+C content value along with the GGD value. This value provides an opportunity to delineate a strain at the species and subspecies level in addition it also gives insight into the relatedness of novel strain with already existing known type strain.

21.8.7 Maximal Unique Matches Index (MUMi)

Another new genome distance calculation technique is the Maximal Unique Matches Index (MUMi) which gives ideas about bacterial genome variability. This method calculates distance based on the number of Maximum Unique Matches (MUMs). The values are represented as MUMi–MUM index which varies between 0 and 1 (0 for very similar and 1 for distant genome). These MUMi values are correlated with ANI values (Konstantinidis and Tiedje 2005). In the case of *E. coli* and *S. aureus* the tree generated in the MUMi distance matrix was mostly similar to the tree generated in MLST and perfectly congruent with the tree generated in ANI. Fast algorithms are present to calculate MUMs; e.g., to calculate the MUMs between two *E. coli* genomes requires only a few seconds. MUMi can help us understand the

21.9 WEB-BASED TOOLS FOR TAXONOMIC ANALYSIS OF WHOLE GENOME SEQUENCES

In recent times in silico DDH (*is*DDH) have gained priority over average nucleotide identity (ANI) for microbial species demarcation due to its ability for in-depth taxonomic delineation even at the subspecies level (Meier-Kolthoff et al. 2014). At present time, several online platforms are available with automated genome analysis features for taxonomic demarcation and classification of the prokaryotic genomes (Table 21.1). For example, the JspeciesWS server can analyze multiple genome sequences (maximum fifteen) at a time, but it only gives ANI values and doesn't have any internal type strain genome database, which limits its capability to identify the closest type strain genomes to the query genomes (Richter et al. 2016).

In addition, the EzBioCloud database allows users to upload 16S rRNA as well as whole genome sequences of type strains for species identification (Yoon et al. 2017). However, only 16S rRNA genes were compared against a curated database dedicated to type species 16S rRNA sequences; for genome sequences, there is no internal database, and it only reports the ANI values between the uploaded genomes. The Type

TABLE 21.1

Web Tool Available for Taxonomic Classification of Microbial Genomes

Si. No.	Web Tool	URL	Purpose/Feature	References
1	16S-based ID (EZbiocloud)	https://www. ezbiocloud.net/	Identify bacterial isolates using 16S rRNA sequences	Yoon et al. (2017); Kim et al. (2012); Chun et al. (2007)
2	ContEst16S	https://www. ezbiocloud.net/ tools/contest16S	Detect 16S rRNA from whole genome sequence	Lee et al. (2017)
3	ANI Calculator	https://www. ezbiocloud.net/ tools/ani	Average Nucleotide Identity calculator between two prokaryotic genome sequences	Yoon et al. (2017)
4	Pairwise Nucleotide Sequence Alignment For Taxonomy	https://www. ezbiocloud.net/ tools/pairAlign	Pairwise alignment of genetic sequences to obtain sequence similarity value for taxonomic delineation.	Yoon et al. (2017)
5	UBCG	https://www. ezbiocloud.net/ tools/ubcg	Phylogenomic trees can be obtained from the genome assemblies.	Na et al. (2018)
6	EzAAI	http://leb.snu. ac.kr/ezaai	Average amino acid sequence identity tool	Kim et al. (2021)
7	OrthoANI-usearch tool	https://www. ezbiocloud.net/ tools/orthoaniu	This tool gives priority to USEARCH instead of BLAST to obtain OrthoANI value and considerably decrease computational time.	Yoon et al. (2017)
8	ANItools 2.0	http://ani. mypathogen.cn/	Compare bacterial genomes and calculate their average nucleotide identity (ANI)	Wen et al. (2014)
9	GTDB-Tk	https:// github.com/ ecogenomics/ gtdbtk	Assignment of taxonomic rank to prokaryotic genome using the Genome Database Taxonomy	Parks et al. (2018)
10	TYGS	https://tygs.dsmz. de/	Genome-based identification of prokaryotic strains	Meier-Kolthoff & Göker (2019)
11	JSpeciesWS	https://jspecies. ribohost.com/ jspeciesws/	This web tool can report Average Nucleotide Identity (ANI) and Tetra-nucleotide signatures in genome sequences	Richter et al. (2016)

Strain Genome Server (TYGS) has come forward with a number of collective features, such as the comprehensive database of validly published type strain genomes and an integrated automatic pipeline for taxonomic classification and phylogeny analysis (Meier-Kolthoff & Göker 2019). A new toolkit named GTDB-Tk has been specifically designed to assign a taxonomic rank to archaeal and bacterial genomes

(Chaumeil et al. 2019). This advanced tool is capable of analyzing hundreds of single-cell genomes as well as metagenome-assembled genomes (MAGs) in a single attempt. It employs an alignment-free computation-based FastANI algorithm to calculate the whole genome ANI among the genomes.

21.10   CONCLUSION

Taxonomy is an integral part of bacteriology that arranges the bacteria into suitable groups and provides precise names to bacteria so that bacteriologists can efficiently work and communicate. Bacterial taxonomy contributes significantly to the area of clinical microbiology. Treatment of bacterial disease could often become exceptionally difficult if the pathogen is not properly identified. The conventional methods and set of rules used in bacterial polyphasic taxonomy are facing serious competition after the explosion of genome sequences in the database. Time-consuming, labor-intensive, expensive traditional methods that were used earlier did not perform well in fields like clinical microbiology, epidemiology, and environmental and evolutionary microbiology. Recently the use of bacterial whole genomes, as well as analysis of their specific gene sequences, has gained superior value over phenotypic traits for bacterial classification and identification. The easy access to microbial genome sequence has upgraded the taxonomic classification concept to taxogenomics. NGS analysis coupled with genomics comparison has facilitated the analysis of overall as well as fraction of genetic content greatly providing super-resolution in the identification of microbial species. Along with the taxonomic status, the genome sequence gives a detailed idea about the metabolic pathway or genes responsible for interesting properties such as microbial resistance and metal resistance. Obtaining the genome sequence, therefore, reduces extensive preliminary work to confirm the presence of any given gene for specific metabolic pathways.

REFERENCES

Alvarez-Perez, Sergio, Clara de Vega, and Carlos M. Herrera. "Multilocus sequence analysis of nectar pseudomonads reveals high genetic diversity and contrasting recombination patterns." *PloS One* 8, no. 10 (2013): e75797.

Auch, Alexander F., Mathias von Jan, Hans-Peter Klenk, and Markus Göker. "Digital DNA-DNA hybridization for microbial species delineation by means of genome-to-genome sequence comparison." *Standards in Genomic Sciences* 2, no. 1 (2010): 117–134.

Beaulaurier, John, Xue-Song Zhang, Shijia Zhu, Robert Sebra, Chaggai Rosenbluh, Gintaras Deikus, Nan Shen et al., "Single molecule-level detection and long read-based phasing of epigenetic variations in bacterial methylomes." *Nature Communications* 6, no. 1 (2015): 1–12.

Chun, J., J. H. Lee, Y. Jung, M. Kim, S. Kim, B. K. Kim, and Y. W. Lim, EzTaxon: a web-based tool for the identification of prokaryotes based on 16S ribosomal RNA gene sequences. *International Journal of Systematic and Evolutionary Microbiology* (2007): 57, 2259–2261.

Chun, Jongsik, Aharon Oren, Antonio Ventosa, Henrik Christensen, David Ruiz Arahal, Milton S. da Costa, Alejandro P. Rooney et al., "Proposed minimal standards for the use of genome data for the taxonomy of prokaryotes." *International Journal of Systematic and Evolutionary Microbiology* 68, no. 1 (2018): 461–466.

Chun, Jongsik, and Fred A. Rainey. "Integrating genomics into the taxonomy and systematics of the Bacteria and Archaea." *International Journal of Systematic and Evolutionary Microbiology* 64, no. Pt_2 (2014): 316–324.

Ellegaard, Kirsten Maren, Lisa Klasson, Kristina Näslund, Kostas Bourtzis, and Siv GE Andersson. "Comparative genomics of Wolbachia and the bacterial species concept." *PLoS Genetics* 9, no. 4 (2013): e1003381.

Fang, Gang, Diana Munera, David I. Friedman, Anjali Mandlik, Michael C. Chao, Onureena Banerjee, Zhixing Feng et al., "Erratum: Genome-wide mapping of methylated adenine residues in pathogenic Escherichia coli using single-molecule real-time sequencing (Nature Biotechnology (2012) 30 (1232-1239))." *Nature Biotechnology* 31, no. 6 (2013): 566.

Fournier, Pierre-Edouard, and Didier Raoult. "Current knowledge on phylogeny and taxonomy of Rickettsia spp." *Annals of the New York Academy of Sciences* 1166, no. 1 (2009): 1–11.

Gevers, Dirk, Frederick M. Cohan, Jeffrey G. Lawrence, Brian G. Spratt, Tom Coenye, Edward J. Feil, Erko Stackebrandt et al., "Re-evaluating prokaryotic species." *Nature Reviews Microbiology* 3, no. 9 (2005): 733–739.

Glazunova, Olga O., Didier Raoult, and Veronique Roux. "Partial sequence comparison of the rpoB, sodA, groEL and gyrB genes within the genus Streptococcus." *International Journal of Systematic and Evolutionary Microbiology* 59, no. 9 (2009): 2317–2322.

Goris, Johan, Konstantinos T. Konstantinidis, Joel A. Klappenbach, Tom Coenye, Peter Vandamme, and James M. Tiedje. "DNA–DNA hybridization values and their relationship to whole-genome sequence similarities." *International Journal of Systematic and Evolutionary Microbiology* 57, no. 1 (2007): 81–91.

Ide, Keigo, Yohei Nishikawa, Masato Kogawa, Eisuke Iwamoto, Ashok Zachariah Samuel, Yoshikatsu Nakano, and Haruko Takeyama. "High-quality draft genome sequence of a Rickettsiales bacterium found in Acropora tenuis Coral from Okinawa, Japan." *Microbiology Resource Announcements* 9, no. 48 (2020): e00848–20.

Kim, Dongwook, Sein Park, and Jongsik Chun. "Introducing EzAAI: a pipeline for high throughput calculations of prokaryotic average amino acid identity." *Journal of Microbiology* 59, no. 5 (2021): 476–480.

Kim, O. S., Y. J. Cho, K. Lee, S. H. Yoon, M. Kim, H. Na, S. C. Park, Y. S. Jeon, J. H. Lee, et al.. Introducing EzTaxon-e: a prokaryotic 16S rRNA gene sequence database with phylotypes that represent uncultured species. *International Journal of Systematic and Evolutionary Microbiology* 62 (2012): 716–721.

Konstantinidis, K. T., and J. M. Tiedje. Towards a genome-based taxonomy for prokaryotes. *Journal of Bacteriology* 187, no. 18 (2005): 6258–6264.

Kumar, Sudhir, Glen Stecher, and Koichiro Tamura. "MEGA7: molecular evolutionary genetics analysis version 7.0 for bigger datasets." *Molecular Biology and Evolution* 33, no. 7 (2016): 1870–1874.

Lalucat, Jorge, Magdalena Mulet, Margarita Gomila, and Elena García-Valdés. "Genomics in bacterial taxonomy: impact on the genus Pseudomonas." *Genes* 11, no. 2 (2020): 139.

Larsen, Mette V., Salvatore Cosentino, Simon Rasmussen, Carsten Friis, Henrik Hasman, Rasmus Lykke Marvig, Lars Jelsbak et al., "Multilocus sequence typing of total-genome-sequenced bacteria." *Journal of Clinical Microbiology* 50, no. 4 (2012): 1355–1361.

Lee, I., M. Chalita, S.M. Ha, S.I. Na, S.H. Yoon, and J. Chun. ContEst16S: an algorithm that identifies contaminated prokaryotic genomes using 16S RNA gene sequences. *International Journal of Systematic and Evolutionary Microbiology* 67, no. 6 (2017): 2053–2057.

Lee, Imchang, Yeong Ouk Kim, Sang-Cheol Park, and Jongsik Chun. "OrthoANI: an improved algorithm and software for calculating average nucleotide identity." *International Journal of Systematic and Evolutionary Microbiology* 66, no. 2 (2016): 1100–1103.

Maiden, Martin C.J. "Multilocus sequence typing of bacteria." *Annual Review of Microbiology* 60 (2006): 561–588.

Mayr, E., and P.K. Ashlock. *Principles of Systematic Zoology*. McGraw-Hill, Inc., New York, 1992.

Mayr, Ernst. *Systematics and the Origin of Species, from the Viewpoint of a Zoologist*. Harvard University Press, 1999.

McCarthy, Brian J., and Ellis T. Bolton. "An approach to the measurement of genetic relatedness among organisms." *Proceedings of the National Academy of Sciences* 50, no. 1 (1963): 156–164.

Meier-Kolthoff, J.P., A.F. Auch, H.P. Klenk, and M. Göker. Genome sequence-based species delimitation with confidence intervals and improved distance functions. *BMC Bioinformatics* 14 (2013): 60.

Meier-Kolthoff, J. P., R. L. Hahnke, J. Petersen, C. Scheuner, V. Michael, A. Fiebig, … H. P. Klenk. Complete genome sequence of DSM 30083 T, the type strain (U5/41 T) of Escherichia coli, and a proposal for delineating subspecies in microbial taxonomy. *Standards in Genomic Sciences*, 9, no. 1 (2014): 1–19.

Meier-Kolthoff, Jan P., and Markus Göker. "TYGS is an automated high-throughput platform for state-of-the-art genome-based taxonomy." *Nature Communications* 10, no. 1 (2019): 1–10.

Na, S. I., Y. O. Kim, S. H. Yoon, S. M. Ha, I. Baek, and J. Chun. UBCG: Up-to-date bacterial core gene set and pipeline for phylogenomic tree reconstruction. *Journal of Microbiology* (2018): 56.

Nouioui, Imen, Lorena Carro, Marina García-López, Jan P. Meier-Kolthoff, Tanja Woyke, Nikos C. Kyrpides, Rüdiger Pukall, Hans-Peter Klenk, Michael Goodfellow, and Markus Göker. "Genome-based taxonomic classification of the phylum Actinobacteria." *Frontiers in Microbiology* (2018): 2007.

Parks, Donovan H., Maria Chuvochina, David W. Waite, Christian Rinke, Adam Skarshewski, Pierre-Alain Chaumeil, and Philip Hugenholtz. "A standardized bacterial taxonomy based on genome phylogeny substantially revises the tree of life." *Nature Biotechnology* 36, no. 10 (2018): 996–1004.

Richter, M., R. Rosselló-Móra, F. Oliver Glöckner, and J. Peplies. JSpeciesWS: a web server for prokaryotic species circumscription based on pairwise genome comparison. *Bioinformatics* 32, no. 6 2016: 929–931.

Richter, Michael, and Ramon Rosselló-Móra. "Shifting the genomic gold standard for the prokaryotic species definition." *Proceedings of the National Academy of Sciences* 106, no. 45 (2009): 19126–19131.

Rosselló-Móra, Ramon, and Rudolf Amann. "Past and future species definitions for Bacteria and Archaea." *Systematic and Applied Microbiology* 38, no. 4 (2015): 209–216.

Simpson, George Gaylord. 1961. *Principles of Animal Taxonomy*. Columbia University Press.

Slatko, Barton E., Andrew F. Gardner, and Frederick M. Ausubel. "Overview of next-generation sequencing technologies." *Current Protocols in Molecular Biology* 122, no. 1 (2018): e59.

Stackebrandt, EaBMG, and Brett M. Goebel. "Taxonomic note: a place for DNA-DNA reassociation and 16S rRNA sequence analysis in the present species definition in bacteriology." *International Journal of Systematic and Evolutionary Microbiology* 44, no. 4 (1994): 846–849.

Stackebrandt, Erko. "Taxonomic parameters revisited: tarnished gold standards." *Microbiology Today* 33 (2006): 152–155.

Stackebrandt, Erko, Wilhelm Frederiksen, George M. Garrity, Patrick A.D. Grimont, Peter Kämpfer, Martin C.J. Maiden, Xavier Nesme et al., "Report of the ad hoc committee for the re-evaluation of the species definition in bacteriology." *International Journal of Systematic and Evolutionary Microbiology* 52, no. 3 (2002): 1043–1047.

Vandamme, Peter, and Charlotte Peeters. "Time to revisit polyphasic taxonomy." *Antonie Van Leeuwenhoek* 106, no. 1 (2014): 57–65.

Whitman, William B. "The need for change: embracing the genome." In *Methods in Microbiology*, vol. 41, pp. 1–12. Academic Press, 2014.

Woese, Carl R., Otto Kandler, and Mark L. Wheelis. "Towards a natural system of organisms: proposal for the domains Archaea, Bacteria, and Eucarya." *Proceedings of the National Academy of Sciences* 87, no. 12 (1990): 4576–4579.

Woyke, T., G. Xie, A. Copeland, J.M. González, C. Han, H. Kiss, J.H. Saw, P. Senin, C. Yang, S. Chatterji, J.F. Cheng, J.A. Eisen, M.E. Sieracki, and R. Stepanauskas Assembling the marine metagenome, one cell at a time. *PLoS One* 4, no. 4 2009: e5299. doi: 10.1371/journal.pone.0005299

Yoon, S. H., S.M. Ha, J. Lim, S. Kwon, and J. Chun. A large-scale evaluation of algorithms to calculate average nucleotide identity." *International Journal of General and Molecular Microbiology* 110 (2017a): 1281–1286.

Yoon, Seok-Hwan, Sung-Min Ha, Soonjae Kwon, Jeongmin Lim, Yeseul Kim, Hyungseok Seo, and Jongsik Chun. "Introducing EzBioCloud: a taxonomically united database of 16S rRNA gene sequences and whole-genome assemblies." *International Journal of Systematic and Evolutionary Microbiology* 67, no. 5 (2017b): 1613.

Zhao, Huilin, Jiangfan Shan, Taojie Wang, Yue Tian, Yingjian Shen, Zongjun Du, Boqing Li, and Xiaofei Ji. "Vibrio marinisediminis sp. nov., Isolated from Marine Sediment." *Current Microbiology* 78, no. 2 (2021): 810–815.

22 Next-Generation Sequencing Data Analysis

Jyotika Bhati, Himanshu Avashthi and Divya Chauhan

ICAR-Indian Agricultural Statistics Research Institute, India

Shikha Mittal

Jaypee University of Information Technology, India

22.1 INTRODUCTION – GENOMICS

Researchers may now examine the complete genome or exome since NGS can detect mutations that traditional sequencing technologies cannot. Structural variation can be discovered using whole genome NGS data or "targeted" data such as exomes. Hence, targeting of sequencing greatly increases sequencing depth or coverage of individual genes and can introduce biases in the data for further computational analysis. There have been significant breakthroughs in approaches for identifying structural variants and a comprehensive coverage of changes from SNVs in recent years. Also, with the advancement of low-cost and high-throughput sequencing techniques, a number of genome-wide scans for selection signatures can be performed. It enhances the search for genomic variants and selection signals across the entire genome that can reveal new information about genes.

22.2 ANALYSIS OF WHOLE GENOME AND EXOME SEQUENCING DATA

Genetic variation can be determined using a variety of methods for diagnostic purposes. The bioinformatics techniques utilized in the study of whole genome and exome sequencing will be discussed further. The sequencing instrument's creation of the FASTQ files constitutes primary analysis. Secondary analysis involves trimming of raw read sequences and tertiary analysis involves collecting data on each detected genetic variation to produce a subset of relevant variants. The methodology for DNA-Seq is represented in Figure 22.1.

Several algorithms have been created for aligning sequences, and the choice of aligner will be based on parameters, including the type of sequencer and preparation of the DNA library. The Burrows-Wheeler Aligner (BWA) and Bowtie 2 are two of

DOI: 10.1201/9781003331247-25

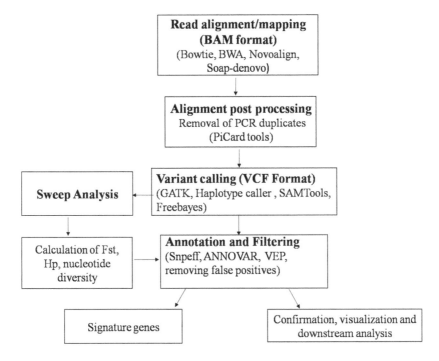

FIGURE 22.1   Flow chart depicting the analyses of DNAseq data (whole genome and exome).

the most popular, freely available alternatives for short read sequences whereas Novo-align and Soap-*denovo* are used for de novo assembly and Hisat2 is a fast and sensitive alignment program for mapping NGS reads. The alignment algorithm will affect speed, performance, and accuracy. A SAM file will be made after the alignment step which can be converted to BAM format.

Variant calling is the major step of secondary analysis. Advanced variant callers take into account certain parameters like various quality scores, depth over coverage at a specific site, and probabilities of different types of mutations. Software like the GATK, Samtools, and Freebayes are the most well-known free variant callers. Since, variant calling is a rapidly evolving field where numerous new variant callers, including GATK and SNVer that combine developments in bioinformatics and computer science (such Apache Hadoop/Spark). For particular circumstances, such as the detection of significant insertions and deletions and the detection of copy number variations, software such as Amplicon Indel Hunter is developed as a specialized variant caller.

Finding meaning and importance in the enormous data sets pose a real challenge since sequencing and variant identification have become common. This mostly entails annotating a VCF against different annotation software such as SnpEff, Variant Effect Predictor, and ANNOVAR which are open-source tools for annotating a VCF file. These tools identify the association between a variant, the gene and "canonical" transcript that it affects, and their impact at the codon level. Several studies have been performed using whole genome sequencing, a study by Lai et al. (2015)

TABLE 22.1
The List of Software Used for DNA-Seq Analysis

Software	Description	References
Novoalign	Aligner for de novo assembly	Yu et al. (2012)
Soap-denovo		Liang et al. (2012)
Genome Analysis Toolkit Haplotype Caller	Call germline SNPs and indels via local re-assembly of haplotypes	Pirooznia et al. (2014)
Samtools mpileup	Summarizes of the coverage of mapped reads on a reference sequence at a single base pair resolution	Li et al. (2009)
Freebayes	Variant Caller	Marth et al. (1999)
GATK	Identifies SNPs and indels in germline DNA and RNAseq data.	McKenna et al. (2010)
SnpEff	Genetic variant annotation and functional effect prediction toolbox	Cingolani et al. (2012)
SNVer	calling common and rare variants in analysis	Wei et al. (2011)
Amplicon Indel Hunter	Detects Indels in amplicon-based paired-end data	Sabah et al. (2015)
Variant effect predictor	determines the effect of variants (SNPs, insertions, deletions, CNVs or structural variants)	McLaren et al. (2016)
ANNOVAR	Functional annotation of genetic variants	Wang et al. (2010)
Integrated Genome Viewer	Variant calling, microarray data, and genome annotations	Gulledge et al. (2012)

revealed more than 4 million SNPs (intervarietal) across the group 7 chromosome of bread from the whole genome shotgun sequencing platform. A list of software used for DNA-Seq analysis is given in Table 22.1.

22.3 SELECTIVE SWEEP

It is a process where a new mutation increases in frequency and becomes fixed in the population leading to elimination of genetic variants among nucleotide sequences which are present near the mutation. In case of positive selection, the mutation reaches fixation and the near gene exhibits hitchhiking effect and becomes fixed in nature. Therefore, a region of the genome with a significant reduction in genetic variation in that chromosome region is the result of a selective sweep caused by a strongly selected allele that emerged on a single genomic background (Barrett R. D. and Schluter D 2008). With whole-genome resequencing data, selective sweeps analysis can also be performed to identify candidate genetic sequences that underlie complex traits. Selective sweeps are classified into three main categories: (a) when mutations are few, a process known as the "classic selected sweep" or "hard selective sweep" will take place, (b) a "soft sweep from standing genetic variation" can place when an environmental change makes a population's previously neutral mutation advantageous, (c) "many origin soft sweep" can occur when mutations are frequent (for instance, in a large population) and the same or comparable advantageous mutations occur on different genomic backgrounds such that no single genomic background can hitchhike to high frequency.

22.4 APPROACHES FOR GENOME WIDE SCAN TO IDENTIFY SIGNATURE GENES

Recent selection in a population can also result in significant levels of genetic divergence between groups. Two approaches can be explored to identify signatures of positive selection between different populations. Fst (F statistic) is a popular method for determining genetic differences across populations. First, identification of selective sweeps is performed by calculating pairwise Fst between breeds. It is performed by calculating the Fst value for each window using VCFtools (Danecek et al. 2011). For example, a sliding window of 40-kb window with 20-kb step size can be used to determine pairwise-Fixation index (FST) between populations. Therefore, a Z transformation of Fst can be used to find genome-wide outliers with high degrees of differentiation in whole-genome resequencing data.

Further, heterozygosity (ZHp) is an alternate way to estimate nucleotide diversity (Rubin et al., 2012). To identify regions with high levels of homozygosity and genomic sequences that can influence phenotypic traits of a particular group. Therefore, whole genome sequencing data can be used to identify cross-group comparison through ZHp. For calculation of heterozygosity (Hp), sliding windows where, $\sum$nMAJ and $\sum$nMIN are the sums of nMAJ and nMIN for all the SNPs are selected for a particular window. Then, the expected heterozygosity within each window using in-house R scripts will be calculated. Further, candidate genes can be identified using Ensemble BioMart (Kinsella et al. 2011). Genes that partially or completely spanned the window regions will be regarded as putative candidate genes under positive selection. A study conducted by Erik Axelsson et al. (2013) identified candidate domestic regions with 122 genes in dogs having low ZHp and Zfst scores. Annotation of the genes showed enrichment of pathways related to fat and starch metabolism.

22.5 DETECTION

Occurrence of a selective sweep can be investigated in various ways. One such method is linkage disequilibrium that identifies the presence of a haplotype if fit is overrepresented in the population. This haplotype will change as a result of genetic recombination under neutral evolution, and no haplotype will predominate in the population. However, selection for a positively selected gene variant will also lead to selection of nearby alleles during a selective sweep, thereby decreasing the chance for recombination. Strong LD may therefore be a sign of a recent selective sweep and can be used to pinpoint the locations of selective sites.

There are various frequently used tests for sweep detection, namely, CLR test that detects a single selective sweep (Qanbari et al. 2014). Moreover, the GOF test is used in combination with the CLR test to control for demography. In case of whole-genome sequencing, the CLR test also accounts for background selection, whereas the SweeD test uses SweepFinder algorithm to detect sweeps (Qi et al. 2021). However, the iHS haplotype-based test detects ongoing selective sweep (Günther and Schmid 2011). For example, the phytoene synthase gene Y1 in maize is responsible for the yellow endosperm color, and a recent comparison of yellow and white corn genotypes nearby provides strong evidence for a selective sweep in yellow germ-plasm that reduced diversity at this locus and linkage disequilibrium in neighboring regions (Andersson and Purugganan 2022). Therefore, increased diversity was seen in white maize lines, and there was no sign of linkage disequilibrium brought on by a selective sweep.

22.6 TRANSCRIPTOMICS

The transcriptome is the complete set of transcripts expressed in a particular cell, tissue, or organism under a certain developmental phase or physiological condition (Ozsolak and Milos 2011). Transcriptome analysis is essential to decipher functional parts of the genome and to understand the mechanisms behind disease and development of organisms by identifying differentially expressed genes (DEGs). Previously, microarray technology was used to identify DEGs between healthy and diseased samples (Marioni et al. 2008). Due to its hybridization-based nature, it reduced the ability to identify and measure RNA molecules expressed under different conditions (Avashthi et al. 2018). RNA-seq has quickly overtaken microarray technology because it identifies alternative splicing events, novel genes, and fusion transcripts. RNA-seq analysis workflow may include the following steps (Figure 22.2).

We should evaluate the quality of raw reads before data analysis. Similar to whole genome sequencing data, thereafter read alignment can be done to map the reads to

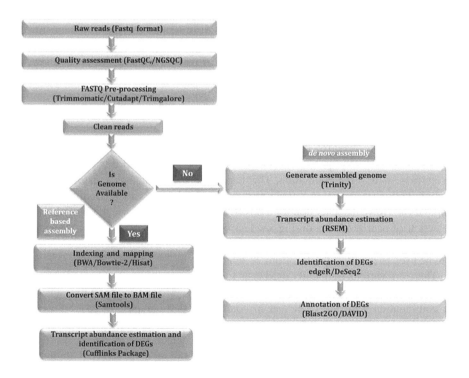

FIGURE 22.2 Workflow of RNA-Seq data analysis.

TABLE 22.2
List of Widely Used Software for Transcriptomic Data Analysis

S.No.	Software	Description	References
1	Fastqc	Quality assessment	Leggett et al. (2013)
2	NGSQC-Toolkit		Patel and Jain (2012)
3	Cutadapt	FASTQ Pre-processing (Remove adapter	Martin (2011)
4	Trimmomatic	sequences, contamination, and low-quality reads)	Bolger (2014)
5	Oases	*de novo* transcriptome assembly	Schulz et al. (2012)
6	SOAPdenovo-Trans		Xie et al. (2014)
7	Trans-ABySS		Robertson et al. (2010)
8	Trinity		Haas et al. (2014)
9	Bowtie	Mapping of RNA-seq reads	Langmead (2010)
10	BWA		Li and Durbin (2010)
11	Hisat		Kim et al. (2015)
12	Tophat		Trapnell et al. (2012)
13	Cufflinks package	Transcript assembly, transcript abundance estimation, and differential expression analysis	Trapnell et al. (2012)
14	RSEM	Transcript abundance estimation	Li and Dewey (2011)
15	DESeq2	differential expression analysis	Love et al. (2014)
16	edgeR		Robinson et al. (2010)
17	Blast2GO	Gene ontology annotation and pathway enrichment analysis	Conesa et al. (2005)
18	DAVID		Sherman et al. (2022)

the reference genome. The next step is transcript reconstruction in which we identify the transcripts that are expressed in the samples. Based on the availability and unavailability of reference genome, transcriptome reconstruction can be categorized into two parts, namely, reference-based and de novo assembly approach (Bhati et al. 2022). De novo assembly approach is used when the reference genome is not available. Once assembled transcripts have been identified, their abundance can then be estimated. Furthermore, differential expression analysis can be performed using different available software. In this chapter, we have attempted to describe the typical RNA-seq workflows well as listed the bioinformatics tools and software associated with each step in Table 22.2.

22.7 QUALITY ASSESSMENT AND PRE-PROCESSING OF RAW READS

RNA-seq data is obtained in FASTQ format. The first step of typical RNA-Seq analysis involves quality assessment of raw reads. There are a lot of software available such as FastQC, PRINSEQ (Schmieder and Edwards 2011), NGSQC-Toolkit, and HTQC-Toolkit (Yang et al. 2013) which are used to check the quality of raw reads. These software help in assessing the overall and per-base quality of each read of each sample. In addition, trimming can be performed to remove adapter sequences, contamination and low-quality reads which ultimately provides clean reads to the users. This step can be performed using Trimmomatic, FASTX-Toolkit (Liu et al. 2019), TrimGalore (Lindgreen 2012), Cutadapt, etc.

22.8   READ ALIGNMENT

Clean reads must first be aligned or mapped to a reference genome or transcriptome to identify the exact genomic positions (origin) with respect to that reference. The alignment can only be used to identify known exons and junctions as it does not identify splicing events associated with novel exons. Whereas, taking the genome as reference, spliced aligners permit a wider range of gaps which helps in aligning the reads at exon–exon junctions. By using this method, the possibility of discovering novel transcripts may be increased. There are several spliced aligners available that can be used to align reads to the genome are TopHat, STAR (Dobin et al. 2013), Bowtie, and BWA.

22.9   TRANSCRIPTOME RECONSTRUCTION

Identification of all transcripts expressed in a particular sample is known as transcriptome reconstruction. It is of two types i.e., reference-guided and the reference-free. The reference-guided method has two consecutive steps: (i) alignment of clean reads to the reference and (ii) assembly of overlap reads for transcript reconstruction. This method is useful when reference genome and their annotation information are well-known, for instance in wheat, rice, human and mouse. On the other hand, the reference-free method simply constructs consensus transcripts from clean reads without reference genome or transcriptome using a *de Brujin* graph algorithm.

22.10   EXPRESSION QUANTIFICATION

Several methods have been developed to quantify expression using RNA-seq data. Based on the target, methods are of two types, namely, isoform-level and gene-level quantification. According to the type of reference and alignment results, isoform-level quantification method is categorized into three groups. RSEM is included in the first group which requires the alignment results between clean reads and reference transcriptome. Cufflinks and StringTie are included in the second group which requires the alignment results between clean reads and reference whole genome. Sailfish (Patro et al. 2014) comes in the last group which is an alignment-free method.

22.11   RSEM

RSEM quantify expression in two steps: (i) generation and pre-processing of reference transcripts and (ii) read alignment to the reference transcripts thereafter estimates transcript abundances. RSEM provides estimates for both genes and isoforms levels as the main output.

22.12   CUFFLINKS

Cufflinks is the most popular software for transcript assembly and quantification, and it includes a variety of programs like Cuffdiff, Cuffmerge, and CummeRbund. Abundance information is obtained in the form of FPKM (fragments per kilobase per million mapped fragments) for paired-end reads and RPKM for single-end reads. Cuffdiff use mapped reads along with the reference genome file to obtain differentially expressed genes and transcripts.

22.13   DIFFERENTIAL EXPRESSION ANALYSIS

Differential expression (DE) analysis is a last step of RNA-Seq data analysis. A number of software are available for DE analysis includes DESeq2, edgeR, EBSeq (Leng et al. 2013), NOIseq (Tarazona et al. 2015), SAMseq (Li et al. 2013), and Cuffdiff. These programs provide two standard parameters, i.e., Log2 fold change and p-value. Many programs have been developed despite having different input types.

22.14   ANNOTATION AND PATHWAY ENRICHMENT ANALYSIS

To understand the biological context of the DEGs, it is necessary to perform pathway enrichment analysis. Functional enrichment analysis relies on various annotation tools and databases such as DAVID, ShinyGO (Ge et al. 2020), KOBAS (Xie et al. 2011), and Blast2GO. These tools interpret a set of genes and provide gene ontology information by categorizing into biological processes, molecular function, and cellular components.

22.15   METAGENOMICS

Metagenomics is the study of microbes isolated from a particular environment using functional gene screening or sequencing analysis. Studies on metagenomics concentrate on the diversity of microbes, the composition of communities, the genetic and evolutionary linkages, the functional activities, and the interactions and relationships with the environment. Metagenomics has emerged as a powerful tool that can be used to study microbial communities regardless of the ability of member organisms to be cultured in the laboratory using conventional isolation. It has also provided the chance to describe the diversity of microbial life in the environment because many are still unable to be cultured (Yasir et al. 2014). Metagenomics, which involves the direct extraction and cloning of DNA from a collection of microorganisms in the majority of the planet's habitats, such as water or soil, is also known as environmental and community genomics. Most often, environmental genomes are separated, fragmented, and then cloned into an organism using its plasmid, which has the ability to multiply. After being cultured, organisms are used to build metagenomic libraries, which are then analyzed using DNA sequencing (Nazir 2016).

The concept of cloning DNA directly from environmental samples was first proposed by Pace and his colleagues in 1985 (Pace et al. 1985), and Schmidt and his colleagues employed this method in 1991 (Schmidt et al. 1991) to clone DNA from picoplankton in a phage vector for ensuing 16S rRNA gene sequence studies. The first productive function-driven metagenomic libraries were screened in 1995 and were known as zoolibraries (Healy et al. 1995). Metagenomic refers to the community genome, with the ultimate goal of obtaining a comprehensive understanding of how the microbial world functions. Metagenomic provides a strategy approach that integrates research at three primary levels, sample processing, DNA sequencing, and functional analysis (Maria-Eugenia et al. 2009). Up to 99% of the total number of microorganisms in environmental samples can be read using this technique to determine their diversity (Prayogo et al. 2020). Community genomics, environmental genomics, and population genomics are further terminology for metagenomics.

22.16 FRAMEWORK OF METAGENOMICS

Figure 22.3 shows the direction in a metagenomics study. Metagenomic has been separated into two strategies: functional based and sequence based (Jimenez et al. 2012). The study of sequence metagenomics is concerned with the composition of microbial communities. Understanding the connections between the various elements that go into creating a community in a given context is the main goal of the

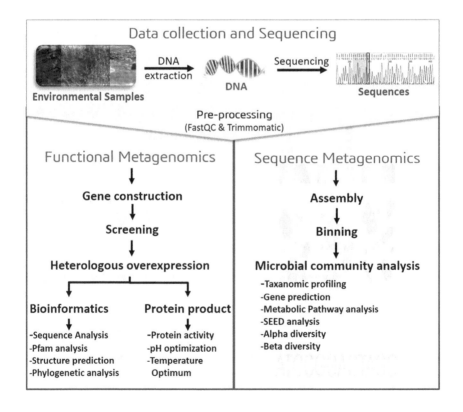

FIGURE 22.3 Framework for a metagenomic study.

study of community structure. Assembly, binning, and microbial community analysis approaches such as taxonomic profiling, gene prediction, and metabolic pathways make up the fundamental structural metagenomics techniques (Alves et al. 2018).

Functional metagenomics is devoted to the usage of genes that produce a specific protein. Exploring natural substances that can be used in the biotechnology sector presents a new challenge with the science of functional metagenomics. Gene construction, screening, and gene expression are some of the fundamental techniques used in functional metagenomics to find novel enzymes. As a method for examining microbial communities in ecology and biotechnology investigations, structural and functional metagenomics work hand in hand in metagenomics studies. The bioinformatics tools and software (Table 22.3) play a crucial part in metagenomics study. SqueezeMeta and MGRAST are a complete package-based tools which perform all the analysis starting from quality check, assembly, identification, and annotation. Following are a few approaches of bioinformatics analysis used in metagenomics approaches:

Assembly – Before going for assembly, the raw reads are quality-checked and trimmed. To recover the genome of uncultured organisms, assembly is necessary to retrieve the longer genomic contents from short trimmed read fragments. The long sequences are termed contigs. The two common methods used in metagenome assembly are OLC and the de Bruijn graph. Few software such as SequeezeMeta are based on sequential, coassembly, and hybrid assembly approaches. The other assembly tools are IDBA_UD, MetAMOS, Megahit, and MetaQuast.

Binning – Binning is the process of grouping DNA sequences that could represent a single genome or genomes from closely related organisms. Contigs are grouped by binning into classes to represent a biological taxon. Software used for binning analysis are MetaWatt and CONCOCT. MetaWatt has a higher accuracy, while CONCOCT can group complicated microbial communities.

Sequence Analysis – Sequence analysis is used to compare the sequences of various types of organisms using simple alignment and multiple alignments. The most commonly used tool is BLAST. The alignments are scored statistically based on expectation value (*e-value*) (Altschul et al. 1990). Further the sequences are analyzed for taxonomic profiles, COGs and KEGG pathways.

Protein family identification – To look for the relationship between protein sequences at family level, Pfam database is used. It uses a hidden Markov model to identify the protein families (Khandelwal et al. 2017).

Protein structure prediction – Understanding the structure of proteins is essential to comprehending how proteins work. The primary structure of proteins comes from the sequences of the genes that encode it. Bioinformatics' prediction study of protein structure can assist in comprehending a protein's physical properties and functions (Raza 2012).

Phylogenetic analysis – In order to reconstruct the evolutionary links between groups of protein molecules and to forecast certain properties of a molecule, phylogenetic analysis is performed (Mehmood et al. 2014). The tools widely used in phylogenetic analysis are MEGA (Molecular Evolutionary Genetics Analysis) (Tamura et al. 2011) and PHYLIP (Felsenstein 1989).

TABLE 22.3
Metagenomics Tools and Software Grouped as per Their Functionality

Tools	Description	References
Metagenomic assembly		
MetaVelvet	Linux/Unix command-line tool; requires large amounts of RAM; may take several days to run	Namiki et al. (2012)
Meta Velvet-SL	Extension to MetaVelvet with similar characteristics; improved detection of chimeras	Afiahayati and Sakakibara (2014)
IDBA-UD	Linux/Unix command-line tool; requires large amounts of RAM; may take several days to run	Peng et al. (2012)
Megahit	Linux/Unix command-line tool; lower memory and processor requirements, though only for certain options	Dinghua et al. (2015)
MetAMOS	Linux/Unix command-line tool; depends on many other software tools; may require large amounts of RAM depending on the assembler used	Treangen et al. (2013)
MetaQuast	Linux/Unix command-line tool; high performance	Alla et al. (2016)
Binning		
MetaBAT	Linux/Unix command-line; designed to run on simple commodity/desktop PCs in a reasonable time	Kang et al. (2015)
MaxBin	Linux/Unix command-line; requires 50Gb RAM and 24 hours to build models	Wu et al. (2014)
MetaWatt	GUI-based; designed to run on desktop hardware	Strous et al. (2012)
CONCOCT	Linux/Unix command-line; depends on other software; initially used Ray Meta for assembly	https://arxiv.org/abs/1312.4038
Gene Prediction		
MetaGene Annotator	Available as Linux/Unix command-line or through web interface (web interface limited to 10Mb)	Hideki et al. (2008)
Orphelia	Available as Linux/Unix command-line or through web interface (web interface limited to 30Mb)	Hoff et al. (2009)
FragGenScan	Available as Linux/Unix command-line; designed to run on commodity/desktop hardware in minutes/hours	Rho et al. (2010)
Prokka	Available as Linux/Unix command-line; depends on other software; uses parallel processing	Torsten (2014)
Domain DBs		
InterPro	A consortium of 14 protein/domain/family databases	https://www.ebi.ac.uk/interpro/
InterProScan	Available as Linux/Unix command-line; or web-interface; or via API	Quevillon et al. (2005)
Pathway Databases		
KEGG	Online resource for reactions/pathways; data available to download for a fee; accessible via web interface or via APIs	Ogata et al. (1999)
MetaCyc	Online resource for reactions/pathways; data available to download; accessible via web interface or via APIs	Caspi et al. (2020)
Analysis Pipeline		
MG-RAST	Online system with graphical user interface	Keegan et al. (2016)
EBI Meta genomics	Online system with graphical user interface; requires data to be in EBI ENA	Hunter et al. (2014)

(Continued)

TABLE 22.3 (CONTINUED)

Tools	Description	References
IMG/M	Online system with graphical user interface	Markowitz et al. (2014)
SqueezeMeta	Linux/Unix command-line tool; requires large amounts of RAM; may take several days to run	Tamames and Puente-Sanchez (2019)
SILVA	GUI-based; designed to run on desktop hardware	Pruesse et al. (2007)
MEGAN	GUI-based; designed to run on desktop hardware	Huson and Weber (2013)

22.17 APPLICATIONS

Metagenomics research is advancing in domains including medicine, agriculture, environmental protection, and other areas (Figure 22.4). Functional metagenomics is important in order to identify novel bioactive compounds and functional genes from microbial metabolites. Metagenomics technology has found many new genes, including the biocatalyst gene, polyketide synthase coding gene, and antibiotic resistance genes (ARGs).

The sequence metagenomics is helpful in studying the uncultured microorganisms. By examining the diversity of the microbial community, it is possible to learn about the species, genetics, and evolutionary history of microorganisms. The existing diagnosis of medical infections can be improved by new pathogenic microbial evidence (Kasper et al. 2020). Functional metagenomes aid in the discovery of novel members of existing enzyme families or enzymes that are only active under particular physicochemical conditions, both of which are more useful for industrial applications (Bekele et al. 2021). Metabolomics and functional metagenomics were coupled to analyze the C, N, and S cycle metabolism of environmental bacteria (Zhang et al. 2021).

The study of microbes in soils, deep oceans, glaciers, craters, and other habitats is one application of environmental metagenomics. The discovery of harmful bacteria in the gastrointestinal tract, bloodstream infections, lung infections, central nervous system infections, and other diseases are only a few of the medical field's many uses for metagenomics. Antibiotic-resistant bacteria (ARB), antibiotic-resistant genes,

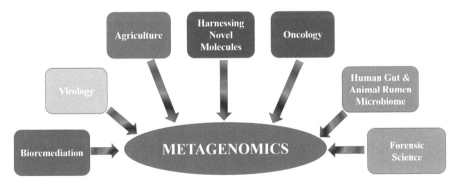

FIGURE 22.4 Applications of metagenomics in various scientific fields.

biocatalysts, and medicines are the current focus of metagenomic research (Duarte et al. 2020). Research on agriculture, biology, pollution prevention, energy, the environment, the atmosphere, and other areas makes use of metagenomics (Suttner et al. 2020).

22.18 CONCLUSION

Numerous bioinformatics tools and databases have been developed using different algorithms for NGS data analysis. In this chapter, we described the routine NGS data analysis workflow, focusing on whole-genome sequencing, sweep selection, transcriptome reconstruction, expression quantification, and identification of differentially expressed genes along with their annotation and also discussed related bioinformatics programs. Therefore, we anticipate that this chapter will be useful to establish a specific pipeline for genomic, transcriptomic, and metagenomic data analysis and allow the design of new biological experiments. Functional metagenomics screening technique is a robust research tool with the ability to mine biocatalyst that is both environmentally and commercially significant.

REFERENCES

Afiahayati, K. Sato, and Y. Sakakibara. 2014. MetaVelvet-SL: an extension of the Velvet assembler to a de novo metagenomic assembler utilizing supervised learning. *DNA Res* 22(1):69–77.

Alla, M., S. Vladislav, and G. Alexey. 2016. MetaQUAST: evaluation of metagenome assemblies. *Bioinformatics* 32(7):1088–1090.

Altschul, S.F., W. Gish, W. Miller, et al. 1990. Basic local alignment search tool. *J Mol Biol* 215(3):403–410.

Alves, L.D.F., C.A. Westmann, G.L. Lovate, et al. 2018. Metagenomic Approaches for understanding new concepts in microbial science. *Int J Genomics* 2018:1–15.

Andersson, L. and M. Purugganan (2022). Molecular genetic variation of animals and plants under domestication. *Proceedings of the National Academy of Sciences*, 119:e2122150119.

Avashthi, H., R. K. Pathak, N. Pandey, et al. 2018. Transcriptome-wide identification of genes involved in Ascorbate–Glutathione cycle (Halliwell–Asada pathway) and related pathway for elucidating its role in antioxidative potential in finger millet (Eleusinecoracana (L.)). *3 Biotech* 8:1–18.

Axelsson, E., A. Ratnakumar, M.L. Arendt, et al. 2013. The genomic signature of dog domestication reveals adaptation to a starch-rich diet. *Nature*, 495:360–364.

Barrett, R. D. and D. Schluter 2008. Adaptation from standing genetic variation. *Trends in ecology & evolution*, 23:38–44.

Bekele, W., A. Zegeye, A. Simachew, et al. 2021. Functional Metagenomics from the Rumen Environment—A Review. *Adv Biosci Biotechnol* 12:125–141.

Bhati, J., H. Avashthi, A. Kumar, et al. 2022. Protocol for Identification and Annotation of Differentially Expressed Genes Using Reference-Based Transcriptomic Approach. In *Genomics of Cereal Crops* ed. S. H. Wani and A. Kumar, 175–193. New York: Humana Press.

Bolger, A. M., M. Lohse and B. Usadel. 2014. Trimmomatic: a flexible trimmer for Illumina sequence data. *Bioinformatics* 30:2114–2120.

Caspi, R., B. Richard, I.M. Keseler, et al. 2020. The MetaCyc database of metabolic pathways and enzymes - a 2019 update. *Nucleic Acids Res* 48(D1):D445–D453.

Cingolani, P., A. Platts, L. Wang, et al. 2012. A program for annotating and predicting the effects of single nucleotide polymorphisms, SnpEff: SNPs in the genome of Drosophila melanogaster strain w1118; iso-2; iso-3. *Fly* 6, 80–92.

Conesa, A., S. Gotz, J. M. Garcia-Gomez, J. Terol, M. Talon, and M. Robles. 2005. Blast2GO: a universal tool for annotation, visualization and analysis in functional genomics research. *Bioinformatics* 21:3674–3676.

Danecek, P., A. Auton, G. Abecasis, et al. 2011. The variant call format and VCF tools. *Bioinformatics*, 27:2156–2158.

Dinghua, Li, L. Chi-Man, L. Ruibang, et al. 2015. MEGAHIT: an ultra-fast single-node solution for large and complex metagenomics assembly via succinct de Bruijn graph. *Bioinformatics* 31(10):1674–1676.

Dobin, A., C. A. Davis, F. Schlesinger, et al. 2013. STAR: ultrafast universal RNA-seq aligner. *Bioinformatics* 29:15–21.

Duarte, A.S.R., K.D. Stark, P. Munk, et al. 2020. Addressing learning needs on the use of metagenomics in antimicrobial resistance surveillance. *Front Public Health* 8:38.

Felsenstein, J. 1989. PHYLIP–Phylogeny Inference Package (Version 3.2). *Cladistics* 5: 164–166.

Ge, S. X., D. Jung, and R. Yao. 2020. ShinyGO: a graphical gene-set enrichment tool for animals and plants. *Bioinformatics* 36:2628–2629.

Günther, T., and K.J. Schmid, 2011. Improved haplotype-based detection of ongoing selective sweeps towards an application in Arabidopsis thaliana. *BMC Research Notes*, 4:1–11.

Haas, B. J., A. Papanicolaou, M. Yassour, et al. 2013. De novo transcript sequence reconstruction from RNA-seq using the Trinity platform for reference generation and analysis. *Nature Protocols* 8:1494–1512.

Healy, F.G., R.M. Ray, H.C. Aldrich, et al. 1995. Direct isolation of functional genes encoding cellulases from the microbial consortia in a thermophilic, anaerobic digester maintained on lignocellulose. *Appl Microbiol Biotechnol* 1995:667–674.

Hideki, N., T. Takeaki, and I. Takehiko. 2008. MetaGeneAnnotator: Detecting Species-Specific Patterns of Ribosomal Binding Site for Precise Gene Prediction in Anonymous Prokaryotic and Phage Genomes. *DNA Res* 15(6):387–396.

Hoff, K.J., T. Lingner, P. Meinicke, et al. 2009.Orphelia: predicting genes in metagenomic sequencing reads. *Nucleic Acids Res* 37:W101–105.

Hunter, S., M. Corbett, H. Denise, et al. 2014. EBI metagenomics – a new resource for the analysis and archiving of metagenomic data. *Nucleic Acids Res* 42:D600–D606.

Huson, D.H., and N. Weber. 2013. Microbial community analysis using MEGAN. *Methods Enzymol* 531:465–485.

Jimenez, D.J., F.D. Andreote, D. Chaves, et al. 2012. Structural and functional insights from the metagenome of an acidic hot spring microbial planktonic community in the Colombian Andes. *PLoS One* 7:1–15.

Kang, D.D., J. Froula, R. Egan, et al. 2015. MetaBAT, an efficient tool for accurately reconstructing single genomes from complex microbial communities. *PeerJ* 3:e1165.

Kasper, C.,D. Ribeiro, A.M.D. Almeida, et al. 2020. Omics Application in Animal Science—A Special Emphasis on Stress Response and Damaging Behaviour in Pigs. *Genes* 11:920.

Keegan, K.P., E.M. Glass, F. Meyer. 2016. MG-RAST: A Metagenomics Service for Analysis of Microbial Community Structure and Function. *Methods MolBiol* 399:207–233.

Khandelwal, I., A. Sharma, P.K. Agrawal, et al. 2017. Bioinformatics Database Resources. In: *Library and information services for bioinformatics education and research*. IGI Global, Hershey, pp. 45–90.

Kinsella, R.J., A. Kähäri, S. Haider, et al. 2011. Ensembl BioMarts: a hub for data retrieval across taxonomic space. *Database*, 2011.

Lai, K., M.T. Lorenc, H.C. Lee, et al. 2015. Identification and characterization of more than 4 million intervarietal SNP s across the group 7 chromosomes of bread wheat. *Plant Biotechnology Journal*, 13:97–104.

Langdon, W. B. 2015. Performance of genetic programming optimised Bowtie2 on genome comparison and analytic testing (GCAT) benchmarks. *BioData Mining*, 8:1–7.

Langmead, B. 2010. Aligning short sequencing reads with Bowtie. *Current Protocols in Bioinformatics* 32:11–17.

Leggett, R. M., R. H. Ramirez-Gonzalez, B. J. Clavijo, D. Waite, and R. P. Davey. 2013. Sequencing quality assessment tools to enable data-driven informatics for high throughput genomics. *Frontiers in Genetics* 4:288.

Li, H., and R. Durbin. 2010. Fast and accurate long-read alignment with Burrows–Wheeler transform. *Bioinformatics* 26:589–595.

Li, J., and R. Tibshirani 2013. Finding consistent patterns: a nonparametric approach for identifying differential expression in RNA-Seq data. *Stat Methods Med Res*. 22:519–536.

Liang, C., X. Liu, S. M. Yiu, and B. L. Lim. 2013. De novo assembly and characterization of Camelina sativatranscriptome by paired-end sequencing. *BMC Genomics* 14:1–11.

Lindgreen, S. 2012. Adapter Removal: easy cleaning of next-generation sequencing reads. *BMC Research Notes* 5:1–7.

Liu, X., Z. Yan, C. Wu, et al. 2019. FastProNGS: fast preprocessing of next-generation sequencing reads. *BMC Bioinformatics* 20:1–6.

Love, M., S. Anders, and W. Huber. 2014. Differential analysis of count data–the DESeq2 package. *Genome Biol* 15:10–1186.

Maria-Eugenia, G., B. Ana, N.G. Peter, et al. 2009. Metagenomics as a new technological tool to gain scientific knowledge. *World J Microbiol Biotechnol* 2009:945–954.

Marioni, J. C., C. E. Mason, S. M. Mane, M. Stephens, and Y. Gilad. 2008. RNA-seq: an assessment of technical reproducibility and comparison with gene expression arrays. *Genome Res*. 18:1509–1517.

Markowitz, V.M., I.M. Chen, K. Chu, et al. 2014. IMG/M 4 version of the integrated metagenome comparative analysis system. *Nucleic Acids Res* 42:D568–D573.

Marth, G. T., I. Korf, M. D. Yandell, et al. 1999. A general approach to single-nucleotide polymorphism discovery. *Nature Genetics*, 23:452–456.

Martin, M. 2011. Cutadapt removes adapter sequences from high-throughput sequencing reads. *EMBnet Journal* 17:10–12.

McKenna, A., M. Hanna, E. Banks, et al. 2010. The Genome Analysis Toolkit: a MapReduce framework for analyzing next-generation DNA sequencing data. *Genome Research*, 20:1297–1303.

McLaren, W., L. Gil, S. E. Hunt, et al. 2016. The ensembl variant effect predictor. *Genome Biology*, 17:122.

Mehmood, M.A., U. Sehar, and N. Ahmad. 2014. Use of bioinformatics tools in different spheres of life sciences. *Data Mining Genom Proteomics* 5:1–13.

Namiki, T., T. Hachiya, H. Tanaka, et al. 2012. MetaVelvet: an extension of Velvet assembler to de novo metagenome assembly from short sequence reads. *Nucleic Acids Res* 40(20):e155.

Nazir, A. 2016. Review on Metagenomics and its Applications. *Imp J Intersd Res* 2(10).

Ogata, H., S. Goto, K. Sato, et al. 1999. KEGG: Kyoto encyclopedia of genes and genomes. *Nucleic Acids Res* 27(1):29–34.

Ozsolak, F. and P. M. Milos 2011. RNA sequencing: advances, challenges and opportunities. *Nat Rev Genet*. 12:87–98.

Pace, N. R., D. A. Stahl, D. J. Lane, et al. 1985. Analyzing natural microbial populations by rRNA sequences. *ASM News* 1985:4–12.

Papudeshi, B., J.M. Haggerty, M. Doane, et al. 2017. Optimizing and evaluating the reconstruction of Metagenome-assembled microbial genomes. *BMC Genomics* 18:915.

Patel, R. K. and M. Jain. 2012. NGS QC Toolkit: a toolkit for quality control of next generation sequencing data. *PloS one* 7:e30619.

Patro, R., S. M. Mount, and C. Kingsford 2014. Sailfish enables alignment-free isoform quantification from RNA-seq reads using lightweight algorithms. *Nat Biotechnol.* 32:462–464.

Peng, Y., H.C. Leung, S.M. Yiu, et al. 2012. IDBA-UD: a de novo assembler for single-cell and metagenomic sequencing data with highly uneven depth. *Bioinformatics* 28(11): 1420–1428.

Pirooznia, M., M. Kramer, J. Parla, et al. 2014. Validation and assessment of variant calling pipelines for next-generation sequencing. *Human Genomics* 8:1–10.

Prayogo, F.A., A. Budiharjo, H.P. Kusumaningrum, et al. 2020. Metagenomic applications in exploration and development of novel enzymes from nature: a review. *J Genet Eng Biotechnol* 18:39.

Pruesse, E., C. Quast, K. Knittel, et al. 2007. SILVA: a comprehensive online resource for quality checked and aligned ribosomal RNA sequence data compatible with ARB. *Nucleic Acids Res* 35(21):7188–7196.

Qanbari, S., H. Pausch, S. Jansen, et al. 2014. Classic selective sweeps revealed by massive sequencing in cattle. *PLoS Genetics*, 10:1004148.

Qi, X., H. An, T.E. Hall, et al. 2021. Genes derived from ancient polyploidy have higher genetic diversity and are associated with domestication in Brassica rapa. *New Phytologist*, 230:372–386.

Quevillon, E., V. Silventoinen, S. Pillai, et al. 2005. InterProScan: protein domains identifier. *Nucleic Acids Res* 33(suppl_2):W116–W120.

Raza, K. 2012. Application of data mining in bioinformatics. *Indian J Comp Sci Eng* 1:114–118.

Rho, M., H. Tang, and Y. Ye. 2010. FragGeneScan: predicting genes in short and error-prone reads. *Nucleic Acids Res* 38(20):e191.

Robertson, G., J. Schein, R. Chiu, et al. 2010. De novo assembly and analysis of RNA-seq data. *Nature Methods* 7:909–912.

Robinson, M. D., D. J. McCarthy and G. K. Smyth. 2010. edgeR: a Bioconductor package for differential expression analysis of digital gene expression data. *Bioinformatics* 26:139–140.

Rubin, C.J., H.J. Megens, A.M. Barrio, et al. 2012. Strong signatures of selection in the domestic pig genome. *Proceedings of the National Academy of Sciences*, 109:19529–19536.

Kadri, S., C. J. Zhen, M. N. Wurst, et al. 2015. Amplicon Indel Hunter Is a Novel Bioinformatics Tool to Detect Large Somatic Insertion/Deletion Mutations in Amplicon-Based Next-Generation Sequencing Data. *The Journal of Molecular Diagnostics*, 17:635–643.

Schmidt, T. M., E. F. DeLong, and N. R. Pace. 1991. Analysis of a marine picoplankton community by 16S rRNA gene cloning and sequencing. *J Bacteriol* 1991:4371–4378.

Schmieder, R., and R. Edwards. 2011. Quality control and preprocessing of metagenomic datasets. *Bioinformatics* 27:863–864.

Schulz, M. H., D. R. Zerbino, M. Vingron and E. Birney. 2012. Oases: robust de novo RNA-seq assembly across the dynamic range of expression levels. *Bioinformatics* 28:1086–1092.

Sherman, B. T., M. Hao, J. Qiu, et al. 2022. DAVID: a web server for functional enrichment analysis and functional annotation of gene lists (2021 update). *Nucleic Acids Res* 10.

Strous, M., B. Kraft, R. Bisdorf, et al. 2012. The binning of metagenomiccontigs for microbial physiology of mixed cultures. *Front Microbiol* 3:1–11.

Suttner, B., E.R. Johnston, L.H. Orellana, et al. 2020. Metagenomics as a public health risk assessment tool in a study of natural creek sediments influenced by agricultural and livestock runoff: potential and limitations. *App Environ Microbiol* 86(6):e02525–e02519.

Tamames, J. and F. Puente-Sanchez. 2019. SqueezeMeta: A Highly Portable, Fully Automatic Metagenomic Analysis Pipeline. *Front Microbiol* 9:3349.

Tamura, K., D. Peterson, N. Peterson, et al. 2011. MEGA5: Molecular Evolutionary Genetics Analysis Using Maximum Likelihood, Evolutionary Distance, and Maximum Parsimony Methods. *Mol Biol Evol* 28(10):2731–2739.

Tarazona, S., P. Furio-Tari, D. Turra, et al. 2015. Data quality aware analysis of differential expression in RNA-seq with NOISeq R/Bioc package. *Nucleic Acids Res.* 43:e140.

Torsten, S. 2014. Prokka: rapid prokaryotic genome annotation. *Bioinformatics* 30(14): 2068–2069.

Trapnell, C., A. Roberts, L. Goff, et al. 2012. Differential gene and transcript expression analysis of RNA-seq experiments with TopHat and Cufflinks. *Nature Protocols* 7:562–578.

Treangen, T.J., S. Koren, D.D. Sommer, et al. 2013. MetAMOS: a modular and open source metagenomic assembly and analysis pipeline. *Genome Biol* 14(1):R2.

Wang, K., M. Li, and H. Hakonarson. 2010. ANNOVAR: functional annotation of genetic variants from high-throughput sequencing data. *Nucleic Acids Research*, 38:e164–e164.

Wei, Z., W. Wang, P. Hu, G.J. Lyon and H. Hakonarson. 2011. SNVer: a statistical tool for variant calling in analysis of pooled or individual next-generation sequencing data. *Nucleic Acids Research*, 39:31–35.

Wu, Y.W., Y.H. Tang, S.G. Tringe, et al. 2014. MaxBin: an automated binning method to recover individual genomes from metagenomes using an expectation-maximization algorithm. *Microbiome* 2:26.

Xie, C., X. Mao, J. Huang, et al. 2011. KOBAS 2.0: a web server for annotation and identification of enriched pathways and diseases. *Nucleic Acids Research* 39:W316–W322.

Xie, Y., G. Wu, J. Tang, et al. 2014. SOAPdenovo-Trans: de novo transcriptome assembly with short RNA-Seq reads. *Bioinformatics* 30:1660–1666.

Yang, X., D. Liu, F. Liu, et al. 2013. HTQC: a fast quality control toolkit for Illumina sequencing data. *BMC Bioinformatics* 14:33.

Yasir, B., S.P. Singh, and B.K. Konwar. 2014. Metagenomics: An Application Based Perspective. *Chinese J Biol* 2014:146030.

Yu, X., K. Guda, J. Willis. 2012. How do alignment programs perform on sequencing data with varying qualities and from repetitive regions? *BioData Mining*, 5:1–12.

Zhang, L., F. Chen, Z. Zeng, et al. 2021. Advances in Metagenomics and Its Application in Environmental Microorganisms. *Front Microbiol* 12:766364.

23 Computational Molecular Evolution
A Detailed View of Phylogenetic Methods

Vinamrata Sharma, Saumya Tyagi and Tiratha Raj Singh

Jaypee University of Information Technology, India

23.1 INTRODUCTION

The mechanisms governing evolution at the molecular level are the subject of molecular evolution. This chapter starts off by detailing how organic stuff came to be on our planet. The next topics explored are the emergence of informational macromolecules and the RNA world theory for the genesis of life. When DNA became the primary genetic material, it was possible to compare DNA sequences to determine the main evolutionary pathways. The degrees of molecular evolution are numerous [1]. The fundamental level is concerned with the processes that produced the bio-elements. At this level, cosmology and astrophysics are important. We can only hope to understand how heavier elements evolved from the cloud of hydrogen, deuterium, and helium that made up the early Universe after the "big-bang" approximately 18 billion years ago through these disciplines (always assuming that the "big-bang" is a true model of the origin of the Cosmos). This stage of molecular evolution also contributes to highlighting the fundamental unity of the physical Universe [2].

The nuclear furnaces in the innards of the first-generation stars melted the original light elements into heavier ones. These stars' decomposition resulted in the return of many of its constituent elements to interstellar space through supernova explosions, the shedding of material after gravitational collapse, etc. Astronomical systems, including our solar system, were created as a result of the incorporation of this cosmic debris into second-generation heavenly bodies, such as planetary nebulae. As a result, the heavier elements found inside the Sun (which is not a first-generation star) and the solar system's building blocks must have originated from stars that have since long since degenerated into white dwarfs, neutron stars, or black holes. Similar to this, the primary bio-elements of terrestrial life, such as carbon, nitrogen, oxygen, phosphorus, iron, and sulfur, which make up every living thing on Earth today, including humans, were cooked inside a massive star billions of years ago [3].

The process by which bio-elements, which were present on the primordial Earth, joined together to form biomolecules is explored in the subsequent stage of molecular evolution (or chemical evolution). Lehninger (1) lists 20 proteinaceous amino acids (Gly, Ala, Val, Leu, Ile, Ser, Met, Thr, Phe, Tyr, Trp, Cys, Pro, Asn, Asp, Glu, Gln, His, Arg, Lys), 3 pyrimidines (uracil, thymine, and cytosine), 2 purines (adenine and guanine), and 2 sugars (alpha-D-glucose and alpha-D-ribose).

Since the 1980s, the techniques for determining the nucleotide sequences of DNA have advanced significantly and largely automated. The entire genomes of multiple species, ranging from humans to viruses, have had their many genes and number of organisms sequenced. The study of gene duplications has benefited greatly from the usage of DNA sequences. A notable example are the genes that are responsible for human and other mammal hemoglobins.

Reconstructing the evolutionary past of the replications that gave rise to the relevant genes has been made possible thanks to understanding of the amino acid sequences of the myoglobin chains and the hemoglobin chains. However, a closer look at the nucleotide sequences of genes that code for these proteins has revealed that the circumstances are more refined and fascinating than the protein sequences suggest.

The two concepts of molecular evolution and phylogenetics are related. The process of selecting molecular (genes, proteins, etc.) changes (mutations) occurring across different branches of the tree of life is known as molecular evolution (evolution). Molecular phylogenetics creates a phylogenetic tree by drawing conclusions about the evolutionary links that derive from molecular evolution.

23.2 MOLECULAR PHYLOGENETICS

Molecular phylogenetics is the technological know-how of the use of molecular information that is DNA, RNA, and protein sequences to deduce the phylogenetic relationships among species. While historically morphological characters had been used to infer species phylogenies, these days molecules are the dominating sort of facts for almost all species corporations. Molecular phylogenetics anticipates DNA sequencing from many years. It is obtained through the conventional techniques of grouping organisms as per their similarities and dissimilarities. It was first used fully by Linnaeus during the 18th century. Linnaeus became a systematist rather than an evolutionist, aiming to place all recognized organisms into a logical type, but he inadvertently laid the foundation for later evolutionary schemes by dividing organisms directly into a hierarchical set of taxonomic categories. Therefore, the classification system proposed by Linnaeus was rethought into physiology, which now shows not only the similarities between different species but the similarities between their evolutionary relationships as well.

23.3 WHY TO USE MOLECULAR DATA?

Nowadays, nearly all evolutionary relationships are inferred from molecular series records. This is because we all know that DNA is an inherited material and we are all now able to collect the genetic material easily, inexpensively, and reliably. Moreover, sequences are highly rich in evolutionary information.

23.4 MODELS OF MOLECULAR EVOLUTION

23.4.1 JUKES AND CANTOR'S ONE-PARAMETER MODEL

A tree is fitted using distance methods to a matrix of $N*(N-1)/2$ pairwise evolutionary distances, with N representing the number of sequences to be considered. The distance is calculated as a single value from the dissimilarity, or the proportion of positions in which both sequences differ, for every two sequences. This dissimilarity is actually an underestimation of the actual evolutionary distance because some of these sequence differences are the result of multiple events. In this way, one generally attempts to gauge the quantity of replacements that have really occurred by applying a particular developmental model that makes suspicions about the idea of transformative changes. However, accurate estimation of the evolutionary distance is not automatic because there is no precise historical record of sequence evolution events [4].

Jukes and Cantor's (1969) substitution model was one of the first to be used to estimate evolutionary distances. All substitutions are assumed to be independent; all sequence positions are equally susceptible to change, substitutions occur at random among the four types of nucleotides, and there have been no insertions or deletions in this model. Equation to estimate evolutionary distances from observed dissimilarity based on these presumptions is shown:

$$d_{AB} = -\frac{3}{4}\ln\left(1-\frac{4}{3}f_{AB}\right)$$

where d_{AB} is the assumed evolutionary distance of sequences A and B and f_{AB} is the dissimilarity (% of differences observed) of sequences A and B.

23.4.2 KIMURA'S TWO-PARAMETER MODEL

A technique for determining evolutionary distance that treats transitions and transversions discretely was given by Kimura in 1980. The equation is shown:

$$d_{AB} = -\frac{1}{2}\ln\left[(1-2P-Q)\sqrt{1-2Q}\right]$$

where P is the percentage of sequence positions that differ by a transition, and Q represents the percentage that differs by a transversion.

23.5 OPPORTUNITIES AND OBSTACLES OF MOLECULAR PHYLOGENETICS

The superiority of nucleotide sequence information for analyzing phylogeny is due to the overall ability available to assess traits, charge independence between molecular and morphological evolution, and to model patterns of nucleotide substitution in molecules. There are also potential problems such as problems in inferring positional homology, discrepancies between organismal and genetic genealogies, and the low likelihood of restoring proper phylogeny with positive patterns in the timing of speciation events.

Sequence data has a lot of potential characteristics that can be used to infer associations, which is a big advantage. A second advantage of nucleotide-based studies is that alterations within structural genes are dissociated from changes in morphology.

Obstacles could be many like before performing evolutionary analysis, orthologous sequences from multiple species must be aligned to determine the homology of their nucleotide positions. It also comprises all subsequent evaluations of tree structure and reliability, as well as more general aspects of sequence comparison. Percent identity and inference of positional homology are essential. Because the degree of sequence similarity during pairwise and multiplex alignments depends on the penalties for insertion-deletion events, conclusions about positional homology are usually more difficult for non-coding nucleotide sequences. It is advisable to do repeated alignment of protein coding nucleotide sequences on the deduced amino acid sequence. Thereafter, gaps corresponding to codon loss or gain can be added using inferred changes in individual amino acids.

The molecular structure is highly modular and expresses complexity with its own degree of molecular organization. While new sequences evolve in sub microseconds, it can take hundreds of thousands of years for entirely new protein folds to emerge at the sequence level.

23.6 MOLECULAR PHYLOGENETIC ANALYSIS

Molecular phylogenetic analysis can be performed via several different techniques. It includes contiguous DNA sequence assembly, amino acid sequence assembly, multiple sequence alignment, model test and reconstruction of phylogenies by making use of Maximum Likelihood Method and Bayesian Inference Method. Unweighted pairwise group method using arithmetic mean (UPGMA) and neighbor joining, which are distance-based approaches, maximum parsimony, which is the feature-form method, and Bayesian inference, which are feature/model-based methods, are examples of common tree-building techniques. Although UPGMA is the simple process, neighbor joining is more precise.

23.7 APPLICATIONS OF PHYLOGENETICS

Phylogenetics is crucial because it enriches our knowledge of how genes, genomes, and species (and especially typically molecular sequences) evolve. With phylogenetics, we are best able to learn not only how sequences evolved as they are today, but also the modern principles that allow us to predict how they will change in the future. This isn't always the simplest of fundamental significance; however, it is additionally extraordinarily useful for several applications.

23.7.1 PHYLOGENETIC TREE

A phylogenetic tree is the visible relational representation among extraordinary being, displaying a course via transformational time from the usual ancestor to distinct successor. [5] Vertical traces, known as branches, form a line and nodes diverge in them, presenting an opportunity for speciation from a not uncommon ancestor. The trunk at the base of the tree is known as the foundation [3]. The root node shows which taxa have the most recent common ancestor. It also tells us how long ago that ancestor lived. The tree also shows which taxa are more closely related to each other than any other taxa. The clade is the group of taxa that share a common ancestor. The clade is also called a monophyletic group. Taxa that are not related to each other are called taxa that are not in the clade.

Figure 23.1 shows different monophyletic (top row) versus polyphyletic (lower left) or paraphyletic (lower right) shrubs.

The diagram (Figure 23.2) beneath indicates a tree of three taxa.

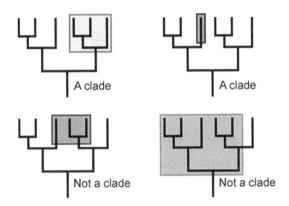

FIGURE 23.1 Image shows different monophyletic (ridge row) versus polyphyletic (lower left) or paraphyletic (lower right).

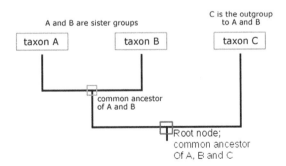

FIGURE 23.2 A representation of tree of three taxa.

23.7.2   RE-CONSTRUCTION OF PHYLOGENETIC TREE

There are two different ways to construct a phylogenetic tree:

- **Character-based method**: This method is based all at once on sequential characters; therefore, it is also known as discrete technique. A person-primary approach uses aligned characters to build a phylogenetic tree. These aligned features include either DNA or protein sequences within the inference tree. The two most popular strategies are: most parsimony and most likelihood.
- **Distance-based method**: This method states the magnitude of the distance or dissimilarity between two aligned sequences. In this method of phylogenetic tree construction, the sequence data are transformed into pairwise distances and then the matrix is used to build the tree.

23.7.3   STEPS TO BUILD A TREE

Building a phylogenetic tree calls for following steps starting with perceiving and gathering a fixed of homologous DNA or protein sequences, orienting the ones sequences, approximating a tree from the aligned sequences [6].

23.7.4   TYPES OF PHYLOGENETIC TREE

Two of the primary forms of phylogenetic trees are cladograms and phylograms. The difference between those sorts of trees is whether or now not they are scaled to symbolize the amount of time among generations.

- Cladograms are not scaled, meaning that the space between every technology at the phylogenetic tree is the equal and does now not represent the actual amount of time between them. Due to this, cladograms are frequently used to depict hypothesized evolutionary relationships especially fast.
- Phylograms are scaled and are used to symbolize the amount of time among generations. Additionally, each cladogram and phylograms can be both rooted and unrooted.
- Rooted trees (shown in Figure 23.3) show the evolutionary relationships of one lineage stemming from an unmarried common ancestor (the foundation of the tree).
- Unrooted (shown in Figure 23.4) bushes display the relationships between taxa without being "rooted" by using a common ancestor.

It is critical to be aware that any kind of phylogenetic tree can be used to painting the evolutionary history of entire species, person organisms, or even genes.

23.7.5   PARTS OF PHYLOGENETIC TREE

Phylogenetic trees are typically made of two additives: branches and nodes. The nodes display points from which the branches, or lineages, diverge to represent entities or

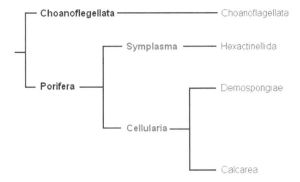

FIGURE 23.3 An example of a rooted phylogenetic tree.

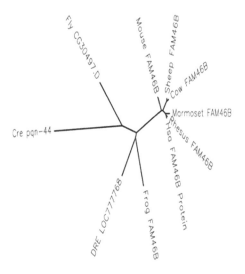

FIGURE 23.4 An example of an unrooted phylogenetic tree.

species involved in the study. Nodes constitute speciation activities, or occasions that bring about the production of two special species from one common ancestor [7].

One trait that rooted trees have that unrooted tree do not is a root. The root is the bottom of the tree, and it constitutes the latest commonplace ancestor of all of the taxa which are portrayed on the tree.

23.8   STRATEGIES OF TREE RECONSTRUCTION

The number of records required for molecular phylogenetic analysis is growing at a logarithmic rate. Since the information units have developed large, it has become more and more important to understand the benefits and drawbacks of using multiple phylogenetic inference methods. There are four inference techniques: Neighbor-joining (NJ), Minimum evolution (ME), Most parsimonious (MP), and Most likely (ML).

The inclusive achievement and overall performance of these techniques in restoring the tree are thought to range with respect to substitution charge, transition-to-transfer ratio, and collection divergence. Computer simulation has proven to be a great way to evaluate the performance of tree-building techniques. It could be used to look at the general overall performance of a method or specific aspects of its overall performance.

23.9 DISTANCE MATRIX METHOD

Remove framework strategies are quick strategies that decide hereditary separations between arrangements. After arrangement comparison utilizing numerous arrangements, the extent of erroneously coordinated positions is calculated. From this, a lattice is developed that portrays the hereditary separate between each serial combine. Within the coming about phylogenetic tree, intentioned related arrangements beneath an indistinguishable inside hub are watched, and department lengths speak to the found hereditary separations between sequences. Neighbor-joining (NJ) and unweighted pair group method with arithmetic mean (UPGMA) procedure are two separate lattice methods. NJ and UPGMA create unrooted and rooted trees. NJ may be a set of rules for bottom-up clustering. The essential points of interest of NJ are its fast pace, notwithstanding of dataset length, and the reality that it not accepts an indistinguishable rate of advancement between all ancestries. Notwithstanding, NJ most productively produces a single phylogenetic tree, although there are a few conceivable outcomes. Let's first discuss the UPGMA method.

23.10 UNWEIGHTED PAIR GROUP METHOD WITH ARITHMETIC MEAN (UPGMA)

UPGMA is a trustworthy approach in constructing a phylogenetic tree from a distance matrix. It miles the best technique of phylogenetic reconstruction for rooted trees. UPGMA is the easiest way to build trees. It was developed to construct taxonomic phenograms, that is, the phylogenetic trees that show phenotypic likenesses between OTUs, but it can moreover also be utilized for developing phylogenetic trees in case rates of advancement between distinctive heredities are around consistent. The number of watched nucleotide or amino corrosive substitutions can be utilized for this reason. UPGMA employs a successive clustering calculation in which nearby topological connections are recognized in the arrangement of likeness and a phylogenetic tree is built consecutively. First, among all OTUs, we identify two OTUs that are most similar to each other, and then treat them as a new single OTU. Such an OTU is referred to as a composite OTU. Subsequently, from the new group of OTUs, we identify the pair with the highest similarity, and so on, until we are left with only two OTUs.

This approach is simple and consists of majorly three steps: (1) Observe any pair of organisms with the smallest dissimilarities. (2) Allot them as a single cluster and hence again calculate the dissimilarities. (3) Redo points (1) and (2) until the tree is complete.

As shown in Table 23.1, notice that there are some empty cells; these values are ignored because they may duplicate other costs in the table. For example, a cell with the row "Monkey" in the "Tiger" column has a similar value as a cell with the row

TABLE 23.1
The Number of Amino Acids in Cytochrome c among Various Organisms

	Tiger	Snake	Rabbit	Monkey	Mouse
Tiger	0	1	12	14	22
Snake		0	11	13	21
Rabbit			0	4	19
Monkey				0	18
Mouse					0

"Tiger" in the "Monkey" column. In Table 23.1, the smallest difference between the two clusters is 1, which takes place between the tiger and the snake. Then group them into clusters and recompute the differences. To do this, replace the tiger cluster and snake cluster with a large cluster containing each tiger and snake respectively. To compute the new value resulting from the intersection of the tiger-snake cluster with the other clusters, compute the average of the values between the intersections of the tiger-snake cluster with this cluster and the intersections of the snake with this cluster. For example, to find the charge at the intersection of (tiger-snake) and monkey, add the values at the intersections of tiger-monkey and snake-monkey and average them. Do the same for all other intersections and fill them out on a new board. All the various hybrids that do not contain multiple clusters, such as chickens and monkeys, remain the same. After completing this, repeat the above steps again. Note that after finishing those steps, we've got to lower the entire figure of clusters through one, as Tiger and snake have been mixed. In the end, after the final clusters are blended, one large cluster will result, with the intention to be our tree.

23.11   NEIGHBOR-JOINING METHOD

Another method known as the neighbor-joining technique is lodged to reconstruct a phylogenetic tree from evolutionary distance data [4]. The method stated is to find sets of Operational Taxonomic Units (OTUs) that constrain an entire period of separation at every degree of OTU clustering starting from the star-like tree. Branch lengths as well as the topology of the parsimonious tree can be rapidly obtained utilizing this strategy. The unused, neighbor-becoming-member strategy and approach of Sattath and Tversky have appeared to be routinely prevalent in elective techniques.

The neighborhood approach may be an uncommon case of the star decay approach. The data is provided as a remote network and the preparatory tree could be a star tree.

23.12   BENEFITS AND DRAWBACKS OF THE NEIGHBOR-JOINING APPROACH

Benefits include being quick, making it appropriate for huge datasets and bootstrap analyses, allowing lineages with widely disparate branch lengths, and allowing alteration for multiple substitutions. Constricted sequence information results in only one viable tree that is very dependent on the evolution model being used. The example is shown in Figure 23.5.

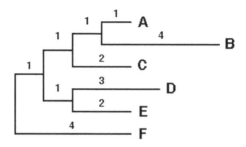

FIGURE 23.5   An example phylogenetic tree generated through NJ approach.

Consider that B and D have amassed mutations more quickly than A. The UPGMA method cannot be applied since it would group together A and C rather than A and B, thus violating the three-point requirement. The neighbor-joining method is one that is suggested in such a situation [2]. The raw tree data is represented by the following distance matrix:

	A	B	C	D	E
B	4				
C	3	7			
D	10	6	5		
E	3	11	4	3	
F	8	7	6	9	8

We have in total 6 OTUs ($N = 6$).

Step 1:   Calculate the $r(i)$ that is the net divergence for each OUT from the rest.

$$r(A) = 4+3+10+3+8 = 28; \ r(B) = 35; \ r(C) = 25; \ r(D) = 33; \ r(E) = 29; \ r(F) = 38$$

Step 2:   Formulate a new distance matrix using the formula:

$$M(ij) = d(ij) - \left[r(i) + r(j) \right] / (N-2)$$

For example: for AB:

$$M(AB) = d(AB) - \left[\left(r(A) + r(B) \right) \right] / (N-2) = -11.75$$

	A	B	C	D	E
B	−11.75				
C	−10.25	−8			
D	−5.25	−11	−9.5		
E	−11.25	−5	−9.5	−12.5	
F	−8.5	−11.25	−9.75	−8.75	−8.75

Step 3:   In the next step consider those OUT's which have the smallest distance in the matrix formed. Here it is A and B as neighbor and thus a new node called U is formed.

Now calculating the branch lengths of A to U and similarly for B to U.

$$S(AU) = d(AB)/2 + \left[r(A) - r(B)\right]/2 \times (N - 2) = 1.125;$$
$$S(BU) = d(AB) - S(AU) = 2.875$$

Step 4:   Now we define new distances from U to other terminal node:

$$d(CU) = d(AC) + d(BC) - d(AB)/2 = 8; \quad d(DU) = d(AD) + d(BD) - d(AB)/2 = 14;$$
$$d(EU) = d(AE) + d(BE) - d(AB)/2 = 12; \quad d(FU) = d(AF) + d(BF) - d(AB)/2 = 13$$

Finally, a new matrix as follows will be created:

	U	C	D	E
C	8			
D	14	5		
E	12	4	3	
F	13	6	9	8

Hence the resulting tree shown in Figure 23.6 will be formed:

$$N = N - 1 = 5$$

The entire procedure is repeated starting at step 1.

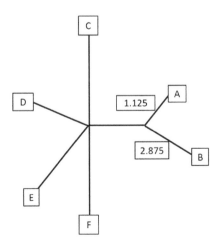

FIGURE 23.6   An example tree generated through UPGMA approach.

23.13   MAXIMUM PARSIMONY METHODS

The evolutionary tree(s) that take the lowest steps to generate the given sequence variation from the common ancestor sequences are calculated using maximum parsimony. Because of this, the technique is also occasionally known as the minimum evolution technique. Multiple sequence alignment is necessary to determine which sequence locations are most likely to match. Assigning multiple sequences will display these positions as vertical bars. Phylogenetic trees which demand fewest evolutionary changes to develop the given sequence changes from the ancestral sequences are found for each aligned site. This method is best suited for sequences that are very similar and is limited to a small number of sequences [9]. Finding the tree in the network with the best parsimony score is one such parsimony criterion, and efficient algorithms have been developed to optimize this criterion on a particular phylogenetic network. These algorithms have been shown to work well in reality, but may only work properly for phylogenetic networks without sister reticulations, as it is easy to find the best tree in this specific class of networks.

23.14   MAXIMUM LIKELIHOOD

There are numerous techniques for rebuilding phylogenetic trees, each with benefits and drawbacks, thus the question of which strategy is the best is not easily answered [11]. Traditional techniques for estimating phylogenies such as maximum parsimony (MP) and maximum likelihood (ML) directly use character information, just like Bayesian approaches do.

The maximum likelihood algorithm will assess different trees, just like maximum parsimony. However, it takes into account the likelihood that each tree, using an evolutionary model, can explain the provided data. In this instance, the tree that has the greatest chance of satisfactorily explaining the data is picked over the others. In comparison to MP, ML studies benefit from the addition of an evolution model since the probability and rate of nucleotide substitutions are taken into account, providing a more accurate explanation of the phylogenetic connections among species. The branch length, which parsimony ignores, is a crucial factor in this approach since changes are more likely to occur along long branches than small ones. This strategy could get rid of long branch attraction and explain why ML is more consistent than MP.

23.15   BAYESIAN INFERENCE OF PHYLOGENY BACKGROUND AND BASES

The term "Bayesian inference" describes a probabilistic approach created by the Reverend Thomas Bayes because of the Bayes theorem. It was the first formulation of inverse probability and a cornerstone of Bayesian reasoning and was published posthumously in 1763. Pierre-Simon Laplace established Bayes' theorem independently and without knowledge of Bayes' work in 1774. The earlier likelihood of the tree P(A) and the likelihood of the information (B) are combined in a Bayesian phylogenetic recreation method to create a back likelihood dispersion on the trees

P(A|B). Given the earlier, the information, and the precision of the likelihood demonstrate, the back likelihood of the tree is the likelihood that the tree is precise.

23.16   RECENT DEVELOPMENTS AND APPLICATIONS IN VARIOUS LIFE DOMAINS

In the last two decades there have been several applications where phylogenetic information contents were generated for several lineages that include animal, plant kingdoms as well as microorganisms [17]. Use of nuclear as well as mitochondrial genomic data was the major focus for these studies. Gene order and gene rearrangement events were also utilized for the analysis of these genomes to either correct the previously existing hypotheses or to propose new ones [18, 19]. There are ample studies to reflect this aspect of the molecular evolutionary analysis. Passerines, tunicates and many other evolutionary orders were studied to generate novel piece of information for their arrangements in classification and systematics [17–20].

23.17   CONCLUSION

Maximum likelihood and Bayesian statistics, as well as other contemporary statistical and computational techniques utilized in molecular evolutionary research, are all thoroughly covered in this chapter. The goal of the chapter is to improve our understanding of the evolution of genes and genomes by describing the models, methods, and algorithms that are most effective for analyzing the vast amount of molecular sequence data. Instead of focusing on mathematical proofs, the chapter focuses on other crucial ideas. Along with numerous illustrations, practical examples, and exercises, it also provides comprehensive data. Students and professionals working in the subjects of molecular phylogenetics, evolutionary biology, population genetics, mathematics, statistics, and computer science will find it useful and relevant.

REFERENCES

[1] Darwin C (1859). *The Origin of Species by Means of Natural Selection, or the Preservation of Favoured Races in the Struggle for Life*. Penguin Books, London.
[2] Darwin C (1871). *The Descent of Man, and Selection in Relation to Sex*. Princeton University Press, Princeton, NJ.
[3] Wain-Hobson S (1998). 1959 and all that. *Nature*, 391:531–532.
[4] vonHoldt BM et al. (2010). Genome-wide SNP and haplotype analyses reveal a rich history underlying dog domestication. *Nature*, 1–5. doi:10.1038/nature08837 [Online], www.pellegrini.mcdb.ucla.edu/wp-ontent/uploads/sites/21/2017/07/week-3c-Phylogenetic_Tree_ConstructionMai-copy.pdf
[5] Saitou N, Nei M (1987). The neighbor-joining method: a new method for reconstructing phylogenetic trees. *Mol Biol Evol*, 4:406–425.
[6] Baum David (2008). Reading a phylogenetic tree: the meaning of monophyletic groups, *Nat Educ*, 1(1):190 [Online], www.nature.com/scitable/topicpage/reading-a-phylogenetic-tree-the-meaning-of-41956
[7] Hall Barry G (2013). Building phylogenetic trees from molecular data with MEGA. *Mol Biol Evol* [Online], https://doi.org/10.1093/molbev/mst012

[8] Susannah Dorrance [Online], study.com/learn/lesson/phylogenetic-tree-parts-types.html#:
~:text=The%20two%20main%20types%20of,can%20be%20rooted%20or%20unrooted

[9] Kannan L, Wheeler WC (2012). Maximum parsimony on phylogenetic networks. *Algorithms Mol Biol* 7:9. doi.org/10.1186/1748-7188-7-9

[10] Dr. Samanthi [Online], www.differencebetween.com/difference-between-maximum-parsimony-and-maximum-likelihood

[11] Yves Van de Peer [Online], bioinformatics.psb.ugent.be/downloads/psb/Userman/treecon_distance.html

[12] Fukami-Kobayashi K, Tateno Y (1991). Robustness of maximum likelihood tree estimation against different patterns of base substitutions. *J Mol Evol* 32:79–91.

[13] Saitou N, Nei M (1987 Jul). The neighbor-joining method: a new method for reconstructing phylogenetic trees. *Mol Biol Evol*, 4(4):406–425. doi:10.1093/oxfordjournals.molbev.a040454

[14] Sourdis J, Nei M (1988). Relative efficiencies of the maximum parsimony and distance-matrix methods in obtaining the correct phylogenetic tree. *Mol Biol Evol* 5:298–311.

[15] Hasegawa M, Yano T (1984). Maximum likelihood method of phylogenetic inference from DNA sequence data. *Bull Biomet Soc Japan.* 5:1–7.

[16] Saitou N, Nei M (1987). The neighbor-joining method: a new method for reconstructing phylogenetic trees. *Mol Biol Evol*, 4:406–425.

[17] Swofford DL (1993). *PAUP: Phylogenetic Analysis Using Parsimony*. Illinois Natural History Survey, Champaign, IL.

[18] Singh TR, Shneor O, Huchon D (2008). Bird mitochondrial gene order: insight from 3 warbler mitochondrial genomes, *Mol Biol Evol*, 25(3):475–477.

[19] Singh TR, Tsagkogeorga G, Delsuc F, Blanquart S, Shenkar N, Loya Y (2009). Tunicate mitogenomics and phylogenetics: peculiarities of the Herdmania momus mitochondrial genome and support for the new chordate phylogeny, *BMC Genomics*, 10(1):534.

[20] Gupta A, Singh TR (2013). SHIFT: Server for hidden stops analysis in frame-shifted translation, *BMC Res Notes*, 6(1):68.

[21] Singh TR, Pardasani KR (2009). Ambush hypothesis revisited: evidences for phylogenetic trends, *Comput Biol Chem*, 33(3):239–244.

24 Exploring Multifaceted Applications of Bioinformatics
An Overview

Anukriti Saran
Banasthali Vidyapith, India

Aayushi Chandra
CCS University, India

Sahil Jain
Tel-Aviv University, Israel

Kshitij Pareek
Rajasthan University of Veterinary and Animal Sciences, India

Sarvesh Paliwal and Swapnil Sharma
Banasthali Vidyapith, India

24.1 INTRODUCTION

Bioinformatics has been playing an emerging role since the last few decades. Analysis part of research of almost all branches of Life Sciences requires bioinformatics. It also helps to predict protein's structure, determine sequence alignment, perform homology modeling, simulation, drug designing, and data mining and manipulation computationally (in silico). Bioinformatics is a combination of many branches, i.e., Biology, Statistics, Mathematics, Computer science (Figure 24.1). Let's take a popular tool, BLAST, of bioinformatics to understand how bioinformatics is a combination of multiple subjects. BLAST performs pairwise sequence alignment and gives local alignment results among sequences from the selected biological databases. BLAST tool was designed using an algorithm that means computer programming was used to

DOI: 10.1201/9781003331247-27

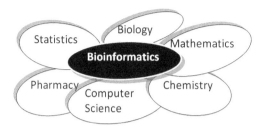

FIGURE 24.1   Bioinformatics is a combination of different branches as shown in the diagram.

develop this. This tool has different versions of BLOSSUM (blocks substitution) and PAM (point accepted mutation) matrices which contain the concepts of mathematics and statistics. BLAST tool was developed at NCBI which is a biological database and contains a huge amount of biological data and facilitates data analysis. Hence, we can say that bioinformatics is a combination of many disciplines. Therefore, if one can say bioinformatics is a subject, that will not be completely true. If we say that bioinformatics is an application, then it seems truer comparatively. To understand the role of bioinformatics we can take two examples. First, suppose a biotechnologist finds a novel protein from an agricultural land. First of all, how can he be sure about the protein's novelty? He must go with sequencing of those proteins that is laboratory as well as in silico work. After getting the sequence of that protein he must go with sequence similarity search that will be done by bioinformatics tools such as BLAST. Another example, suppose a researcher wants to know the evolutionary relationship among different species; he can go with MSA that is again a bioinformatics tool. We have seen above two examples of bioinformatics role in getting the complete results. Nowadays bioinformatics has emerged in a very fine way in life sciences.

Here we will discuss the role of bioinformatics in the field of biotechnological, agricultural, industrial, and biopharmaceutical research. However, bioinformatics is not limited to these disciplines only.

24.2   ROLE OF BIOINFORMATICS IN BIOTECHNOLOGICAL RESEARCH

Biotechnology is the branch of science that deals with a number of techniques that contribute to researchers and scientists to accomplish their research in a polished way. For example let's consider a bacteria; it has its cell wall and cell membrane which are made of specified proteins, which help in their identification on the microbiological aspect (act as an antigen) when they go inside a body they form an antibody (by T cell). Now those antibodies can be used to make vaccine which is a worldwide requirement of animals as well as humans. Additionally those antibodies are used in laboratory tests (for antigen antibody reaction) to confirm the pathogen of a disease (called confirmatory diagnosis). Bioinformatics makes an ease of availability of these kinds of Ag-Ab interactions libraries online. Biotechnology techniques provide a wet laboratory environment to the researcher while bioinformatics provides the way to analyze, store, screen, and annotate to get a complete output.

24.2.1 Comparative Genomics

Bioinformatics can be used to get comparative results of genomic sequence, structural, and functional similarities among different species. It includes comparison of the number of genes, contents, and chromosomal locations of genes.

Alignment is one of the important parts of comparative genomics that provide the root for further research. Alignment actually provides match, mismatch, gaps in two or more protein or nucleotide sequences that fork out about convergence or divergence. Alignment can be done by taking the entire length of the sequence or by taking substrings of the sequence; on this basis alignment is of two types: global alignment and local alignment, respectively. There are a few bioinformatics tool that provides the local and global alignment such as BLAST and FASTA. Genome comparison is a good source to find out the functions of other genome because similar structure nucleotides have most occurring chance of the same function (Hardison, 2003).

Comparative genomics facilitates the study of phylogenetic relationships. Phylogeny helps to know the evolutionary relationship among different species with the comparative results of a number of biomolecules or genes. Phylogeny brings forth the information about conserved genes between the species. It also tells us about the distance relationship among species along with description of matches between genomes. There are certain bioinformatics software such as clustal omega, COBALT, MAFFT, Kalign, and T-coffee that impart MSA to get phylogenetic results.

24.2.2 Microbial Genomics

The term "genome" itself comes to one's mind with big data itself. And if we think to get the whole genome of a particular species it seems unyielding! Is this true? It was a travail a few decades ago. Next-generation sequencing (NGS) is aiding researchers to get the sequenced data with no time. Microbial genomics pioneers the genome data along with its identification, characterization, sequencing, interactions. With the boom of bioinformatics tools, there is an ease to generate microbial genomic libraries so that microbial genetic diversity can be accessed (Quinn et al., 2001).

Being a vast diversity of microorganisms, it is an agony to live with harmful bacteria or microbes. Bioinformatics provides the tools for sequence alignment so that scientists can identify the harmful microbes by homology analysis. It also furnishes the way to identify pathogenic microbes that can help in diagnosis and treatment of a particular disease. Metagenomics dispenses a lot of information to the scientist to get a microbe in a detailed description manner that can be used for antimicrobial research (Fricke et al., 2014).

Microbial genomics aspect counterbalances boundless research done on humans as well as animals for the welfare of humanity. For instance insulin requirement of humans is still a hot topic for scientists as there are chances to derive insulin for humans from animals without killing them. Apart from these major incurable problems like malignant cancers and certain viral diseases, their treatment relies on genetic basis to make a cure which will be a big step toward animal and human health (Tomar et al., 2015).

24.2.3 PROTEOMICS VETERINARY SCIENCES

The term "proteomics" is used for the entire study of the galaxy of protein that covers structure, function, pathology, and various other aspects. Furthermore, veterinary science is a vast ocean that deals with the health of animals as well as the zoonotic aspect of diseases, therefore accounting for human health too. These two subjects are immensely related to veterinary science in a number of aspects such as anatomical, physiological, pathological, and microbiological.

As in anatomical aspects, if a person starts from the basics, then he must have knowledge about proteins because they play an important role in understanding the basic anatomy to complex anatomy, i.e., histology and embryology (Ghosh, 2018). Bioinformatics databases such as protein database, i.e. ProteomicsDB, PRIDE, PDB, help to get an idea about details of a particular protein of any of the species. In physical aspects the normal functioning and major interactions of body are done by the interactions of various molecules. If a researcher wants to know the interactions among different proteins or signaling molecules then he must go with the biological databases such as Kyoto Encyclopedia of Genes and Genomes (KEGG) to get the signaling pathways of a particular protein or many molecules involved in it.

Bioinformatics helps in understanding the pathogenesis of disease (Sastry, 2019). To access the information about the protein or related disease one can go with biology databases such as UniProt, Drugbank, NCBI, and PDB.

24.3 ROLE OF BIOINFORMATICS IN AGRICULTURAL RESEARCH

Agriculture is the primary source of food for the population of the whole world. As the population is growing with a rapid rate, there is necessity of sustainable agricultural practices to improve the yield, quality as well as quantity of crops. Bioinformatics and its branches, including omics technologies, namely, Genomics, Proteomics, Transcriptomics, System biology, Structural and Functional Genomics, NGS technologies of computer sciences, are making enormous and crucial changes in the field of agriculture. Bioinformatics provides information about the structural, functional, and even the genetics of an organism which support the modern advancements in the aspects related to the crop plants. Sections 24.3.1 to 24.3 cover the role of bioinformatics in different aspects of agriculture.

24.3.1 CROP IMPROVEMENT

The genetic-level information could be devised efficiently because of plant genomics which allows the accessing and storing of data of enumerable genes of different plant species with which one can embrace the biological properties and functions of various genes in different biological systems (Kushwaha et al., 2017). The first crop plant genome to be sequenced was of *Arabidopsis* published in 2000 (*Arabidopsis* Genome Initiative, 2000), after which various other crop genomes were sequenced and published such as of maize, soybean, and wheat. Genome sequencing is the major revelation and with the help of NGS technologies the task of sequencing is much feasible than the older methods of Sanger's or Maxam Gilbert's sequencing

TABLE 24.1

A List of a Few Plant Genome Databases

Database URL	Short Description of Database
https://www.ncbi.nlm.nih.gov/	Worldwide database having information related to genome of thousands of species
https://brassica.info/	Provides information for the various *Brassica* species
https://plants.ensembl.org/index.html	Genome centric portal for plants of scientific interests
https://www.asteraceaegenomesize.com/	Provides data related to *Asteraceae* family
http://pgdbj.jp/plantdb/plantdb.html	PGDJB, The Plant Genome Database of Japan's DNA Marker and Linkage database
https://www.plantrdnadatabase.com/	Comprises data of approximately 3,000 plant species

technologies. The genomic data along with other omics technologies is used for variable experiments. The genomic data is stored in databases from which one can access the sequences and other related information to any specific genes. A few of the plant genome databases are listed in Table 24.1.

24.3.2 Nutritional Quality of Improvement

Agriculture being the primary source of food for the population is very crucial for the world and it is difficult to meet the nutrition requirements of the growing population. To beat the hunger and malnutrition in the growing population, there is demand for improving crop nutrition. Nutrients are biomolecules required for the existential functioning of the body; further, nutrients are divided into macronutrients and micronutrients. There are six major classes of nutrients essential for human health: carbohydrates, lipids, proteins, vitamins, minerals, and water (Morris & Mohiuddin, 2021). Since the majority of these nutrients are consumed from the food crops, the deficiency of these nutrients in the food crops is one of the major issues. To overcome this problem, there is a need to grow nutrition-rich crops. Biofortification of food which means enhancing the nutritional value of the food crops to combat hunger came into existence and many of the new research started to make the food crops biofortified (Bouis et al., 2011).

Genetic engineering means the approach of modifying the crop by adding gene(s) of any desirable trait with help of suitable vectors and hosts. Bioinformatics have specific and crucial roles in the genetic engineering experiments which include finding gene sequences, gene function, the expression of genes in a biological system, and other information which is present over the biological databases, the omics tools of bioinformatics give new access for the making of "Transgenic Fortified Crops" in which nutritional quality of the crop is enriched by gene manipulation. One of the major stepping stones in improving the nutritional quality of crops was the "Golden Rice" which is a genetically modified crop or transgenic fortified crop which has the incorporation of beta-carotene gene which is a precursor of vitamin A and therefore the crop is rich in vitamin A.

TABLE 24.2

List of Databases Having Structural and Functional Information of Enzymes and Other Biomolecules

Sequence Databases	https://www.ncbi.nlm.nih.gov/nucleotide/ NCBI for nucleic acid sequences
	https://www.rcsb.org/ Protein Data Bank (PDB) for amino acid sequences
Bibliographic Databases	https://pubmed.ncbi.nlm.nih.gov/PubMed available at NCBI

The biosynthetic pathways of provitamin A (beta-carotene) were introduced in the rice endosperm (Beyer et al., 2002). The accession to the sequences and the other related information is possible because of bioinformatics databases, providing information regarding millions of sequences in various organisms and not only this the databases have information about various pathways too. The structural and functional information of enzymes and other biomolecules can be accessed from the databases mentioned in Table 24.2. One of the examples of transgenic fortified crops is to cope up with vitamin A deficiency in maize by finding sequences of different suitable vector organisms; designing primers with the help of primer designing tools was fulfilled via bioinformatics using bioinformatics tools (Shyamli et al., 2021).

24.3.3 PLANT BREEDING

Plant breeding is a technique of growing the crops with high number of favorable traits and selecting the ones which are best suited for cultivation. The major goal of plant breeding experiments is to get the better version from the existing varieties of that crop. The crop must have traits such as high yield, improved nutritional contents, stress tolerance, disease resistance, and resistance to pests and pathogens according to the requirements with respect to surrounding environmental conditions. The plant breeding methods are of two types: conventional breeding methods and modern breeding methods.

The conventional breeding methods became popular after Mendel's breeding experiments on Pea (*Pisum sativum*). The conventional breeding methods state crossing of two closely related species and selecting the filial generation having desired traits. However, this method had some limitations such as risk of unwanted traits transfer along with the desired ones. To overcome this disadvantage the modern methods of breeding came into existence. Modern plant breeding is achieved by the application of biotechnology, genetics, microbiology, agriculture, bioinformatics, and other allied fields of science. In the past two decades, technologies and tools related to biotechnology have been developed which have potential to give a better and wider range of options for plant breeders. The "Modern Biotech" (1980s) changed the picture of breeding experiments by introducing "Genetically Modified Crops" (Lusser et al., 2012).

The genomics branch of bioinformatics enables the new perspective of genomic prediction which means predicting and selecting the best genotype from the results of plant breeding experiments. Different methods of selection are used to select the accurate genotypes, including recurrent selection, combined selection, and best linear unbiased prediction (BLUP), but the most advanced method with the highest selection accuracy is with molecular markers (Heffner et al., 2009, Ordas et al., 2012, Bhering et al., 2013, Viana et al., 2011).

The advent of Next-Generation Sequencing (NGS) technologies has indeed revolutionized the field of vegetable crop breeding, as it has for many other areas of genetics and genomics. Genome sequencing, accelerated breeding, identification of beneficial traits are some ways in which NGS technologies have impacted and transformed vegetable crop breeding. The vegetable crops have much importance because of their high consumption among world's large-scale population; that's why it is essential to improve the quality, quantity, and other traits of these vegetable crops having wild relatives and modern cultivars (Hao et al., 2020).

24.3.4 PLANT DISEASE MANAGEMENT

Plant pathogens are a threat for agriculture causing several diseases in various crops. These diseases affect agriculture globally, leading to poor quality of crops, low productivity, and in extreme cases can cause senescence of the affected crop. The plant diseases have an indirect impact on human health and livelihood; that's why effective ways were required for plant disease management because of its impact on agriculture and humans, and also it affects the global food requirements. For strategizing the proper management, one needs to identify the causative agent, its genetics, interactions with host, symptoms of disease, and aftereffects of the disease. Bioinformatics has many practical applications in current plant disease management, including host–pathogen interactions, understanding of disease genetics, and pathogenicity factor, which contribute in designing the best management strategies (Kushwaha et al., 2017).

Bioinformatics and its tools play an important role in detection of plant pathogens. There are quantitative high-throughput image-based methods for phenotyping plant growth and development, which indicates changes in development pattern of plants which further helps in detection of symptoms of diseases (Balodi et al., 2017).

There are various genome databases specific to plant pathogens which have data related to host–pathogen relationship for studies of diseases related to them (Dong et al., 2021). Few databases are listed in Table 24.3. Some other databases which have data stored as images called the "Plant disease image Databases" are listed in Table 24.4 (Dong et al., 2021).

TABLE 24.3
List of Genome Databases Specific to Plant Pathogen

Database URL	Brief Description
http://www.phi-base.org/	PHI-Base is a database which identifies and presents the information about the host-pathogen interactions, pathogenicity, and the effector gene(s).
http://www.phytopathdb.org/	The integrative resource for plant pathogen genomics.

TABLE 24.4
List of Few Plant Disease Image Databases

Database URL	Brief Description
https://www.kaggle.com/datasets/emmarex/plantdisease	PhytoPath is the most popular database that has datasets of diseased images of plants.
https://data.mendeley.com/datasets/c5yvn32dzg/2	RoCole, a dataset that contains Robusta coffee leaf images.

24.4 ROLE OF BIOINFORMATICS IN INDUSTRIAL RESEARCH

Computing power of bioinformatics helps industries much by reducing their production time and calculation time using computational analysis and data science. Most of the industries use microbial production in their products, for example in dairy products, beverages, food production, cosmetics, enzymatic production, and many more. Bioinformatics provides microbial databases and its information more precisely in a cost-effective manner (Bogert et al., 2019). Below are the few sections which detail the industrial role of bioinformatics.

24.4.1 GENOME SEQUENCING AND ANNOTATION

We have seen the beneficial role of genome, genomics, proteomics, sequencing, etc. in the above sections. Nucleic acids and protein sequences play a great role in further studies of life science. Without sequencing, further results of protein structure, functions, gene products, comparative study, phylogeny, etc. are almost impossible. So to assist research in fields like genomics, proteomics, and phylogenetics, there is an utmost requirement of sequencing. There are various industries in the world that provide sequencing (Otero & Nielsen, 2010). Table 24.5 comprises a list of names

TABLE 24.5
Lists of Industries Provides Services in the Bioinformatics and Related Fields

Industry Name	Services
Illumins	Sequencing, microarray, proactive instrument monitoring
PacBio	HiFi sequencing, whole genome sequencing, targeted sequencing, RNA sequencing, metagenomics, data processing, data analysis
10xGenomics	RNA profiling, gene expression, spatial proteogenomics, CRISPER screening, immune receptor mapping
Bionanogenomics	Genome mapping, data processing and analysis, germ line DNA analysis,
Pierian	Sequencing, data visualization, QC analysis,
BioPharmaSpec	Primary de novo amino acid sequencing, N and C terminal sequencing, peptide mapping, extinction coefficient determination
mtoz-biolabs	Protein identification, protein sequencing, quantitative proteomics, Post-translational modifications (PTMs) identification
SGS	De novo protein sequencing, Primary peptide & protein structure

of the related industries. Tasks like whole genome sequencing (WGS) and molecular diagnostics are possible because of industrial research. The WGS of many of the bacterial and other species becomes possible by the support of bioinformatics and industrial research (Fricke & Rasko, 2014).

24.4.2 ENHANCEMENT OF PRODUCT QUALITY

Not only biological industries using bioinformatics approaches for their advancement, rather, many other industries like cosmetics, dairy, probiotics, and quality control also approach bioinformatics and related fields techniques for their product quality enhancement. Microbe databases facilitate the industries to select their perfect microbe for their research or production increment. For preparing beverages, food, jams, curds, and cheese, a variety of microbes are used. Bioinformatics provides the whole genome data so that an industry can select the perfect set of microbes for its advancement. In the same manner, cosmetics industries search for natural ways for their product production such as anti-ageing and beauty products and utilize bioinformatics databases such as plant databases and microbe databases for collecting their relevant information and analyzing the data according to their requirement.

The multiomics technology is in use for various breeding industries. One of the major crops consumed is soybean (*Glycine max*) and to fulfill the demands of growing population for soybean and related products, plant breeding experiments based on multiomics technologies have been performed to improve the quality and yield of the crop. The experiments were laid on the foundation of Quantitative Trait Locus (QTL) and mapping (Cao et al., 2022).

Forensic science is hugely used in determining the criminals and sorting many criminal records. It uses comparative genomics and genome sequencing techniques. Industries grossing much in providing sequence data such as DNA finger printing to the forensic labs and helping to solve the cases in the legal way (Massey, 2016).

24.5 ROLE OF BIOINFORMATICS IN BIOPHARMACEUTICAL RESEARCH

24.5.1 DRUG DISCOVERY

In order to find new therapeutic options, drug development employs a methodical process. Many different chemical and pharmacological approaches are used by the pharmaceutical industry to find novel compounds. Intense rivalry has arisen within the pharmaceutical industry as a result of persistent attempts to patent novel drug prospects (also known as new chemical entities, or NCEs) (Iskar et al., 2012). Thus, pharmaceutical companies spend heavily on all tactics that could expedite new drug moiety findings. The need to quickly and securely synthesize more substances drives bioinformatics' exceptional interest (Ortega et al., 2012). Computer-aided drug design (CADD), a new independent discipline, has been created to speed up this process (Song et al., 2009; Speck-Planche & Cordeiro, 2013).

24.5.1.1 Computer-Aided Drug Designing

Recently, computational techniques have become important for study effectiveness and drug component discovery (Murcko, 2018). CADD uses SBDD and LBDD (LBDD). SBDD techniques identify biologically relevant interactions and binding sites for each macromolecular target (Ferreira et al., 2015; Batool et al., 2019). Proteins and receptors are macromolecular targets. This knowledge could be used to build novel compounds that disrupt the target's key connections and inhibit biological processes required for activity (Figure 24.2). LBDD identifies target molecules and links their physiochemical properties to their biological effects (Mouchlis et al., 2021). This data could enhance existing drugs or help develop new more powerful ones.

24.5.1.1.1 Target Identification

Drug development begins with target selection and confirmation (Figure 24.2). Identifying druggable targets from tens of thousands of proteins is difficult. New tools solve this issue (Stanciu et al., 2022). Genetic and protein target-identifying methods dominate. The proteomic technique for finding a substance analyses gene expression regulation in a tissue or cell with or without a protein. This target picking method failed due to its complexity and duration (Imbrici et al., 2016). Thus, testing and statistical (in silico) target selection techniques have been developed such as sequence- and structure-based categorization. Sequence-based techniques give cellular networks functional and position data to pinpoint targets (Hughes et al., 2010). Structure-based techniques find drug-binding proteins from genomic or protein databases using statistical methods and then evaluate the analytical results.

24.5.1.1.2 Hit Identification using Virtual Screening and Molecular Docking

Virtual screening uses several hit detection methods (Cruz-Monteagudo et al., 2017). Three-dimensional ligand-based similarity searches use known chemical element types, connectivity, and structure to find novel findings. Ligand-based virtual filtering favors confirmed pharmacophores (Pereira et al., 2016). In silico screening employs a parametric three-dimensional configuration of molecular characteristics, such as an aromatic ring or a hydrogen bond donor/acceptor, that is important to the biochemical activities of one or more active molecules. Assessing big chemical collections requires QSAR modeling. QSAR programs describe molecule structures from huge data collections (Zhang et al., 2017; Lo et al., 2018).

Molecular docking also forecasts binding locations. Targets or homologs can be represented schematically to choose compound alignment and affinity. New virtual screening improvements may help drug compound discovery. Recent research shows the benefits of incremental focused screening (IFS) that integrates in silico and experimental screenings into design screen refinement cycles and serial and concurrent techniques (Kutchukian et al., 2017). Prediction models are used to study a new set of substances for trial in the next version.

24.5.1.1.3 Lead Optimization

Preclinical drug development requires lead refining. Hit-to-lead efforts pick potential hit series for drug research lead improvement (Kalyaanamoorthy et al., 2020). This step optimizes the lead series' biological activity and characteristics using an in vitro

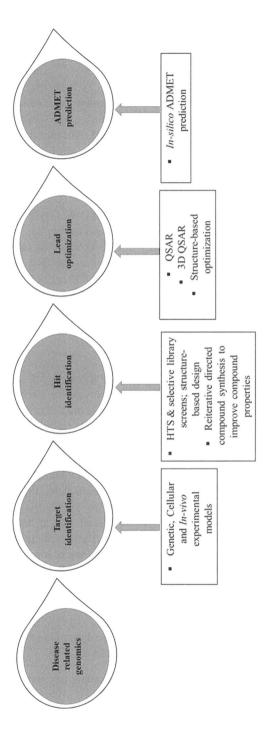

FIGURE 24.2   Applications of CADD in various steps of drug discovery.

and in vivo screening sieve. To select the finest substance for dosing and manufacturing, screening test physiochemical properties are assessed (Geromichalos et al., 2016). Data must be collected quickly and accurately to assess and create substances as perfect candidates. Quality experimental prospects improve clinical research.

24.5.1.1.4 Optimization of ADMET Properties

ADMET prediction tools' primary aim is to standardize drug solubility and safety assessments. ADMET research began with medication water solubility and in vitro tests (Wager et al., 2013; Maurer et al., 2020). Recently, automated forecast methods and in vitro and in vivo tests were shown to speed up drug finding and development (Smith et al., 2015). Drug creation and study have been used in silico methods for early ADME projection (Miller et al., 2002). Polar surface area (PSA, which affects fractional absorption) and atom-based LogP, two key chemistry variables, strongly correlate with PK characteristics in silico ADMET properties (AlogP98). P-glycoprotein substrate, inhibitor, cutaneous, gut, and membrane permeability also affect drug uptake. The logBB, CSF permeability, and VDss also affect medication diffusion. CYP models for substrate or blockage enable metabolic prediction (Landry & Crawford, 2019). The complete clearance model and kidney OCT2 substrate predict elimination. AMES toxicity, hERG suppression, hepatotoxicity, and cutaneous hypersensitivity indicate drug toxicity (Freitas & Schapira, 2017).

24.6   CONCLUSION

Bioinformatics is a Pandora's box full of tools and technologies essential for each and every field of biology. The impending future of biological experiments is bright because of the eminent light of bioinformatics. Bioinformatics resources like NCBI, EMBL, EBI, ExPASy, and EMBOSS update their data on a daily basis and provide an enthusiastic platform for the researchers to address various issues in a cost effective way. In July 2021 EMBL-EBI in collaboration with DeepMind developed an AlphaFold Protein structure database that makes the predicted 3D structure of almost all known protein sequences freely available. AlphaFold holds the whole proteome data of human beings in a short stretch of time. Apart from storing, retrieving, and analyzing the data, bioinformatics is playing a crucial role in fields like biotechnology, agriculture, industrial and biopharmaceutical research, drug discovery, and designing. However, further studies and advancement are needed in bioinformatics to understand science in a better way.

REFERENCES

Balodi R, Bisht S, Ghatak A, Rao KH (2017) Plant disease diagnosis: technological advancements and challenges Indian. *Indian Phytopathology* 70(3), 275–281. https://doi.org/10.24838/ip.2017.v70.i3.72487

Batool M, Ahmad B, Choi S (2019) A structure-based drug discovery paradigm. *International Journal of Molecular Sciences* 20, 2783.

Beyer P, Babili SA, Ye X, Lucca P, Schaub P, Welcsh R, Potrykus I (2002) Symposium: Plant breeding: A new tool for fighting micronutrient malnutrition. *The Journal of Nutrition* 132(3). https://doi.org/10.1093/jn/132.3.506S

Bhering LL, Barrera CF, Ortega D, Laviola BG (2013) Differential response of Jatropha genotypes to different selection methods indicates that combined selection is more suited than other methods for rapid improvement of the species. *Industrial Crops and Products* 41, 260–265.

Bogert BVD, Boekhorst J, May A (2019) On the role of bioinformatics and data science in industrial microbiome applications. *Frontiers in Genetics*. https://doi.org/10.3389/fgene.2019.00721

Bouis HE, Hotz C, McClafferty B, Meenakshi JV, Pfeiffer HW (2011) Biofortification: A new tool to reduce micronutrient malnutrition. *Food and Nutrition Bulletin* 32. https://doi.org/10.1177/15648265110321S105

Cao P, Zhao Y, Wu F, Xin D, Liu C, Wu X, Lv J, Chen Q, Qi Z (2022) Multi-omics techniques for soybean molecular breeding. *International Journal of Molecular Sciences* 23, 4994. https://doi.org/10.3390/ijms23094994

Cruz-Monteagudo M, Schürer S, Tejera E, Pérez-Castillo Y, Medina-Franco JL, Sánchez-Rodríguez A, Borges F (2017) Systemic QSAR and phenotypic virtual screening: chasing butterflies in drug discovery. *Drug Discovery Today* 22, 994–1007.

Dong A, Wang Z, Huang J, Song B, Hao G (2021) Bioinformatics tools support decision-making in plant disease management. *Trends in Plant Science* 26(9). https://doi.org/10.1016/j.tplants.2021.05.001

Ferreira LG, Dos Santos RN, Oliva G, Andricopulo AD (2015) Molecular docking and structure-based drug design strategies. *Molecules* 20, 13384–13421.

Freitas RF, Schapira M (2017) A systematic analysis of atomic protein-ligand interactions in the PDB. *Medicinal Chemistry Communication* 8, 1970–1981.

Fricke WF, Rasko DA (2014) Bacterial genome sequencing in the clinic: bioinformatic challenges and solutions. *Nature Reviews Genetics* 15, 49–55.

Ghosh RK (2018) *Primary Veterinary Anatomy*. Current Book International, 7th Edition. ISBN-13: 978-9385274275

Hao N, Han D, Huang K, Du Y, Yang J, Zhang J, Wen C, Wu T (2020) Genome-based breeding in major vegetable crops. *Theoretical and Applied Genetics*. https://doi.org/10.1007/s00122-019-03477-z

Hardison RC(2003). Comparative genomics. *PLoS Biology* 1(2), E58. https://doi.org/10.1371/journal.pbio.0000058

Heffner EL, Sorrells ME and Jannink JL (2009) Genomic selection for crop improvement. *Crop Science* 49, 1–12.

Hughes JP, Rees S, Kalindjian SB, Philpott KL (2010) Principles of early drug discovery. *British Journal of Pharmacology* 162, 1239–1249.

Imbrici P, Lianntonio A, Camerino GM, Bellis MD, Camerino C, Mele A, Giustino A, Pierno S, Luca AD, Tricarico D, Desaphy JF, Conte D (2016) Therapeutic approaches to genetic ion channelopathies and perspectives in drug discovery. *Frontiers in Pharmacology* 7, 1–28.

Iskar M, Zeller G, Zhao XM, Noort V, Bork P (2012) Drug discovery in the age of systems biology: the rise of computational approaches for data integration. *Current Opinion in Biotechnology* 23, 609–616.

Kalyaanamoorthy S, Lamothe SM, Hou X, Moon TC, Kurata HT, Houghton M, Barakat KH (2020) A structure-based computational workflow to predict liability and binding modes of small molecules to hERG. *Scientific Reports* 10, 1–18.

Kushwaha UKS, Deo I, Jaiswal JP, Prasad B (2017) Role of Bioinformatics in Crop Improvement. *Global Journals Inc. (U.S.A) Global Journal of Science Frontier Research: D Agriculture and Veterinary*. https://www.researchgate.net/publication/31403295

Kutchukian PS, Warren L, Magliaro BC, Amoss A, Cassaday JA, O'Donnell G, Squadroni B, Zuck P, Pascarella D, Culberson JC, Cooke AJ, Hurzy D, Schlegel KS, Thomson F, Johnson EN, Uebele VN, Hermes JD, Parmentier-Batteur S, Finley M (2017) Iterative focused screening with biological fingerprints identifies selective Asc-1 inhibitors distinct from traditional high throughput screening. *ACS Chemical Biology* 12, 519–527.

Landry ML, Crawford JJ (2019) LogD contributions of substituents commonly used in medicinal chemistry. *Journal of Medicinal Chemistry* 1, 72–76.

Lo YC, Rensi SE, Torng W, Altman RB (2018) Machine learning in chemoinformatics and drug discovery. *Drug Discovery Today* 23, 1538–1546.

Lusser M, Parisi C, Plan D, Creezo ER (2012) Deployment of new biotechnologies in plant breeding Nature America, Inc, *Nature Biotechnology* 30. https://doi.org/10.1038/nbt.2142

Massey SE (2016) Comparative microbial genomics and forensics. *Microbiology Spectrum* 4. https://doi.org/10.1128/microbiolspec

Maurer TS, Smith D, Beaumont K, Di L (2020) Dose predictions for drug design. *Journal of Medicinal Chemistry* 63, 6423–6435.

Miller RR, Madeira M, Wood HB, Geissler WM, Raab CE, Martin IJ (2002) Integrating the impact of lipophilicity on potency and pharmacokinetic parameters enables the use of diverse chemical space during small molecule drug optimization. *Journal of Medicinal Chemistry* 63, 12156–12170.

Morris L, Mohiuddin SS (2021) *Biochemistry*, Nutrients. StatPearls. *NCBI bookshelf* https://www.ncbi.nlm.nih.gov/books/NBK554545/

Mouchlis VD, Afantitis A, Serra A, Fratello M, Papadiamantis AG, Aidinis V, Lynch I, Greco D, Melagraki G (2021) Advances in De novo drug design: from conventional to machine learning methods. *International Journal of Molecular Sciences* 22, 1676.

Murcko MA (2018) What makes a great medicinal chemist? A personal perspective. *Journal of Medicinal Chemistry* 61, 7419–7424.

Ordas B, Butrón A, Alvarez A, Revilla P, et al. (2012) Comparison of two methods of reciprocal recurrent selection in maize (Zea mays L.). *Theoretical and Applied Genetics* 124, 1183–1191.

Ortega SS, Cara LC, Salvador MK (2012) In silico pharmacology for a multidisciplinary drug discovery process. *Drug Metabolism and Drug Interactions* 27, 199–207.

Otero JM, Nielsen J (2010) Industrial systems biology. *Biotechnology and Bioengineering* 105(3), 439–460. https://doi.org/10.1002/bit.22592

Pereira JC, Caffarena ER, Santos CN (2016) Boosting docking-based virtual screening with deep learning. *Journal of Chemical Information and Modeling* 56, 2495–2506.

Quinn PJ, Markey BK, Carter ME, Donnelly WJ, Leonard FC. (2001) *Veterinary Microbiology and Microbial Disease*, Wiley–Blackwell Publishing. ISBN-13: 978-0632055258

Sastry GA(2019) *Veterinary Pathology*, 7th edition, CBS Publisher and Distributor Pvt. Ltd. ISBN-13: 978-8123907383

Shyamli PS, Rana S, Suranjika S, Muthamilarasan M, Parida A, Prasad M (2021) Genetic determinants of micronutrient traits in graminaceous crops to combat hidden hunger. *Theoretical and Applied Genetics*. https://doi.org/10.1007/s00122-021-03878-z

Smith DA, Beaumont K, Maurer TS, Di L (2015) Volume if distribution in drug design. *Journal of Medicinal Chemistry* 58, 5691–5698.

Song CM, Lim SJ, Tong JC (2009) Recent advances in computer aided drug design. *Brief Bioinformatics* 10, 579–591.

Speck-Planche A, Cordeiro MN (2013) Computer-aided drug design, synthesis and evaluation of new anti-cancer drugs. *Current Topic in Medicinal Chemistry* 12, 2703–2704.

Stanciu GD, Ababei DC, Rusu RN, Bild V, Tamba BI (2022) Exploring the involvement of the amyloid precursor protein A673T mutation against amyloid pathology and Alzheimer's disease in relation to therapeutic editing tools. *Pharmaceutics* 14, 1270.

Tomar AK, Tomar SS, Singh R, (2015) *Animal Genetics & Breeding*. Daya Publishing House. ISBN-13: 978-9351303022

Zhang L, Tan J, Han D, Zhu H (2017) From machine learning to deep learning: progress machine intelligence for rational drug discovery. *Drug Discovery Today* 22, 1680–1685.

25 Industrial and Biopharmaceutical Research in Bioinformatics

Sai Padma

Bhavan's Vivekananda College of Science, India

25.1 BIOINFORMATICS IN INDUSTRIAL RESEARCH

Bioinformatics tools like algorithms, software, databases, and synthetic biology methods enhance quality and production of industrial products by engineered microorganisms (Kumar and Chordia, 2017).

25.2 INDUSTRIAL BIOCATALYSIS

Novel biocatalysts like keto reductases that break down larger substrates, ω transaminases, that convert β-keto esters to β-aminoacids have been designed using bioinformatics approaches (Liang *et al.*, 2010, Kim *et al.*, 2018). Synthetic biology methods have facilitated metabolic engineering of strains for increased production of metabolites like polyhdroxy alkanate (PHA) production and increased protein stability as in the case of halohydrin halogenase from *Agrobacterium radiobacter* (Zhang *et al.*, 2020, Suplatov *et al.*, 2015).

25.3 MICROBIAL BIODEGRADATION

Microbial strains with high catalytic efficiency and potency for biodegradation can be identified by using binning and functional algorithms (Tikariha and Purohit, 2018). Bacterial and fungal strains including *Burkholderia, Pseudomonas, Rhodococcus, Bradyrhizobiaceae Saccharomyces, Penicillium*, and *Trichoderma* degrade pesticides, hydrocarbons, and organophosphorus compounds (Rodríguez and Castrejón-Godíne, 2020, Tikariha and Purohit, 2020, Satpathy *et al.*, 2015). CREATE (CRISPR-enabled trackable genome engineering (Che & Men, 2019), a synthetic biology tool, generates newer microbial communities for biodegradation of less refined substrates. Few databases that store information related to the microbial degradation pathways are listed in Table 25.1.

DOI: 10.1201/9781003331247-28

TABLE 25.1

Representative List of Databases for Biodegradation

Database	Uses	Weblink
UMBBD	Useful for biocatalytic reactions as well as pathways for biodegradation	http://umbbd.ethz.ch/
Plastics Microbial Biodegradation Database (PMBD	Provides information on the biodegradation of plastics.	http://pmbd.genome-mining.cn/home.
MibPOP database	Resource for Persistent organic pollutants (POP)-degrading microbes	http://mibpop. genome-mining.cn/

This table provides few databases for microbial degradation of plastics and organic pollutants and their weblinks

25.4   WASTE MANAGEMENT

Metagenomics strategies find microorganisms that can be used for treatment of waste water, biological waste, fecal waste and feather waste (Hong *et al.*, 2020, Purohit *et al.*, 2016, Stachler *et al.*, 2017, Chang *et al.*, 2022). Synthetic biology approaches such as PURE (Protein synthesis using Recombinant Elements) system and metabolic engineering are useful in synthesis of thermostable enzymes used in environmental bioremediation (Lee and Kim, 2013), e-waste management, plastic biodegradation (Han *et al.*, 2022), and in paper industry (Mandeep *et al.*, 2020). Genomic scale metabolic model of B.megaterium, *i*JA1121, has also shown promising biorecovery of elements like copper and gold from e-waste (Aminian Dehkordi *et al.*, 2020).

25.5   MICROBIAL ENGINEERING

Metabolic engineering methods like design-based genome-scale models scale up expression of genes like those encoding plant isoquinoline alkaloid biosynthetic enzymes in *E.coli* and *S.cerevisiae* (Diamond and Desgagné-Penix, 2016). Optimization of microbial strains can be achieved through synthetic biology, systems biology and bioprocess engineering approaches (Vorapreeda *et al.*, 2016). Microbial engineering increases the yield of secondary metabolites with therapeutic potential (Asemoloye *et al.*, 2021, Jeandet *et al.*, 2018 Vibha Shukla *et al.*, 2022) and improves industrial strains in food biotechnology (Sardi and Gasch, 2017, Kuipers, 1999).

25.6   BIOREMEDIATION

Bioinformatics approaches including genomics, proteomics, transcriptomics, metabolomics, and fluxomics are part of the systems biology techniques for bioengineering of strains used in bioremediation of toxic compounds (Jaiswal *et al.*, 2019, Jaiswal and Shukla, 2020, Rodríguez and Castrejón-Godíne, 2020, Amrutha and Nampoothiri, 2022, Bouhajja *et al.*, 2016b, Pal and Sengupta, 2021).

25.7   COSMETICS AND PROBIOTICS

The designing of novel cosmetic formulations depends on a thorough knowledge of the ingredients, their metabolic pathways, and their safety assessment (Loei *et al.*, 2013, Cocuron *et al.*, 2014, Wada *et al.*, 2022 Jacques *et al.*, 2021). Databases like CosmetiC Europe database and NICEATM LLNA database and Green pharmadatabase, and tools like BIOVIA, ADME, Labmol VEGAHOB OChem, and Toxtree are useful for identifying ingredients for cosmetic formulations (Wilm *et al.*, 2018). Probiotics can be designed and screened using various computational, synthetic biology, and rDNA technology for producing a wide variety of therapeutics and neutraceuticals (Yadav and Shukla, 2019, Tao *et al.*, 2017, Sun *et al.*, 2022, Kiousi *et al.*, 2021, Garrigues *et al.*, 2013, Vyas and Ranganathan, 2012, Yadav and Shukla, 2020, Gurbatri *et al.*, 2020, Siezen *et al.*, 2004, Callanan, 2005, Naydich *et al.*, 2019, Mejía-Pitta *et al.*, 2021, Susanti *et al.*, 2021).

25.8   SYNTHETIC BIOLOGY FOR INDUSTRIAL STRAIN ENGINEERING

Synthetic biology methods help in strain improvement through evolutionary engineering that helps to engineer phenotype by developing novel genetic parts assembled into logic circuits that perform complex tasks (McCarty and Ledesma-Amaro, 2019, Yang *et al.*, 2019).

25.9   BIOINFORMATICS IN BIOPHARMACEUTICAL RESEARCH

The biopharmaceutical industries are involved in the synthesis and production of innovative drugs that are useful in the treatment and control of diseases (Figure 25.1).

The necessity for newer innovative drugs results in exploring the tools of bioinformatics that are helpful in designing as well as characterization of drugs. The outline of a typical drug discovery process is represented in Figure 25.2.

25.10   PHARMACOGENOMICS IN DRUG DISCOVERY

Pharmacogenomics is aided by the availability of public resources like (a) COXEN (Co-expression extrapolation) which identifies multigene pharmacogenomic biomarkers; and (b) COMPARE – a program that identifies compounds where drug sensitivities correlate with a molecular target of interest; (c) the Pharmacogenomics Knowledge database (PharmGKB); and (d) Pharma ADME that aids in pharmacogenomic drug discovery (Dancik and Theodorescu, 2014, Patrinos, 2018, Cowan *et al.*, 2019, Thorn *et al.*, 2010, Cacabelos *et al.*, 2014) (Table 25.2).

25.11   NEXT-GENERATION BIOPHARMACEUTICALS

Genomics, proteomics, and synthetic biology approaches are employed to synthesize next generation biopharmaceuticals by (a) modification of proteins by using an expanded genetic code called non-canonical aminoacid base protein engineering

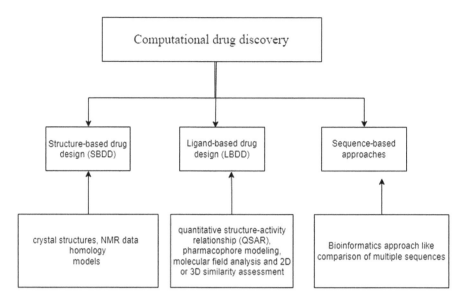

FIGURE 25.1   Computational drug discovery designs and the required input data for drug design.

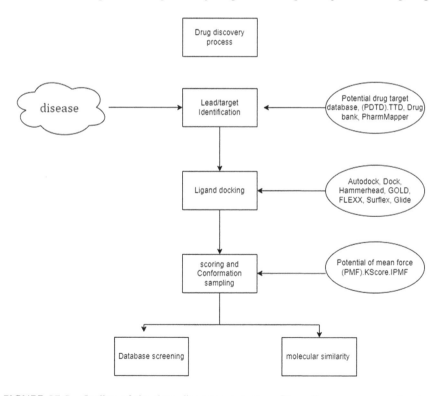

FIGURE 25.2   Outline of the drug discovery process – Drug discovery process involves three stages – Lead identification necessitated by disease followed by searching databases, ligand docking using Autodock or other tools and scoring of the docking.

TABLE 25.2
Therapeutic Compounds Identified for Select Diseases Using RNAi and Autodock

S.No	Disease	Compound	Bioinformatic Tools	Ref
1	Cardiovascular disease	Monoclonal antibodies – alorocumab, bococizumab, LGT209, RG7652 RNAi therapeutic ALNOCS502	RNAi	Dubé et al. (2016)
2	Ischemic stroke	Conivaptan), Avodart, Lumacaftor, Eltrombopag, Naldemedine Dihydroergotamine	Autodock-vina-molecular docking software	Chen et al. (2021)
3	Alzheimer's disease	Morusin (MRSN), Withanone (WTHN) and 27-Hydroxywithanolide B (HWTHN)	Docking	Borah et al., 2019

(Kang *et al.*, 2018), (b) synthesis of antibody cocktails (Logtenberg, 2007), (c) immunopeptidomics for untargeted discovery of bacterial epitopes (Mayer and Impens, 2021), and (d) use of endolichenic fungi (Singh *et al.*, 2017).

25.12 TRANSLATIONAL DRUG DISCOVERY

Systems biology contributes significantly to drug discovery, disease network, treatment response prediction, investigation of disease mechanism, and disease-associated gene prediction (Zou *et al.* 2013, Zhang and Wong, 2017). Translational bioinformatics make use of international databases and resources like M3C and eMERGE (Electronic Medical Records and Genomics) to predict the adverse clinical events of drugs (Wooller *et al.*, 2017 Mitsopoulos *et al.*, 2021, Rashed *et al.*, 2022, Li, 2015).

25.13 IMMUNOINFORMATICS

Immunoinformatics employs computational techniques including immune engineering (De Groot *et al.*, 2020), epitope production (Ramana and Mehla, 2020, Raoufi *et al.*, 2020), and vaccine development (Hegde *et al.*, 2018, Oli *et al.*, 2020, Ortega-Tirado *et al.*, 2020, Jain and Baranwal, 2021, Rezaei *et al.*, 2021, Lohia and Baranwal, 2020, Chaudhuri and Ramachandran, 2017). Web-based immunoinformatics tools like ImmunoNodes (Schubert *et al.*, 2017) and Drugena (Papageorgiou *et al.*, 2020) are useful in designing antibody drug conjugates to fight diseases like cancer and neurodegenerative diseases.

25.14 ARTIFICIAL INTELLIGENCE (AI) AND MACHINE LEARNING (ML) IN PRECISION MEDICINE

Artificial intelligence and machine learning strategies analyze data related to gene upregulation, target disease associations, protein structure predictions, and aid in devising drugs suited to an individual's genetic makeup (Kolluri *et al.*, 2022, Quazi, 2022).

The predictive analysis using AI/ML also facilitates advanced personalized medicine through whole exome sequencing and Big Data analytics (Suwinski *et al.*, 2019).

25.15 CONCLUSION

Bioinformatics approaches in industrial and pharmaceutical research aids industries in enhancing the quality and quantity of production. Microbial strain bioengineering impacts industrial biocatalysis, biodegradation, bioremediation, management of e-waste, cosmetic formulations, and design of probiotics for drug delivery. Predictive analysis using artificial intelligence and machine learning enhances the scope of personalized medicine.

BIBLIOGRAPHY

Amrutha, M., and Nampoothiri, K.M. 2022. In silico analysis of nitrilase-3 protein from *Corynebacterium glutamicum* for bioremediation of nitrile herbicides. *J Genet Eng Biotechnol*. 20(1):51.
Arbitio, M., Scionti, F., Di Martino, M.T., *et al*. 2021. Pharmacogenomics biomarker discovery and validation for translation in clinical practice. *Clin Transl Sci*. 14(1):113–19.
Asemoloye, M.D., Marchisio, M.A., Gupta, V.K., and Pecoraro, L. 2021. Genome-based engineering of ligninolytic enzymes in fungi. *Microb Cell Fact*. 20(1):20.
Azencott, C.A. 2018. Machine learning and genomics: Precision medicine versus patient privacy. *Philos Trans A Math Phys Eng Sci*. 376(2128):20170350.
Backert, L., and Kohlbacher, O. 2015. Immunoinformatics and epitope prediction in the age of genomic medicine. *Genome Med*. 7:119.
Bayat, A. 2002. Science, medicine, and the future: Bioinformatics. *BMJ*. 324(7344):1018–22.
Bober, J.R., Beisel, C.L., and Nair, N.U. 2018. Synthetic biology approaches to engineer probiotics and members of the human microbiota for biomedical applications. *Annu Rev Biomed Eng*. 20:277–300.
Borah, K., Sharma, S., and Silla, Y. 2019. Structural bioinformatics-based identification of putative plant based lead compounds for Alzheimer Disease Therapy. *Comput Biol Chem*. 78:359–66.
Bouhajja, E., Agathos, S.N., and George, I.F. 2016a. Metagenomics: Probing pollutant fate in natural and engineered ecosystems. *Biotechnol Adv*. Dec;34(8):1413–26.
Bouhajja, E., Agathos, S.N., and George, I.F. 2016b. Metagenomics: Probing pollutant fate in natural and engineered ecosystems. *Biotechnol Adv*. 34(8):1413–26.
Butte, A.J., and Ito, S. 2012. Translational Bioinformatics: Data-driven drug discovery and development. *Clin Pharmacol Ther*. 91(6):949–52.
Cacabelos, R., Cacabelos, P., Torrellas, C., *et al*. 2014. Pharmacogenomics of Alzheimer's Disease: Novel therapeutic strategies for drug development. *Pharmacogenomics Drug Discov Devel*. 175:323–556.
Callanan, M. 2005. Mining the probiotic genome: Advanced strategies, enhanced benefits, perceived obstacles. *Curr Pharm Des*. 11(1):25–36.
Chang, Su, Jin-Song, Gong, Anqi, Qin, *et al*. 2022. A combination of bioinformatics analysis and rational design strategies to enhance keratinase thermostability for efficient biodegradation of feathers, *Sci Total Environ*. 818:51824. doi: 10.1016/j.scitotenv.2021.151824
Chaudhuri, R., and Ramachandran, S. 2017. Immunoinformatics as a tool for new antifungal vaccines. *Methods Mol Biol*. 1625:31–43.
Che, S., and Men, Y. 2019. Synthetic microbial consortia for biosynthesis and biodegradation: Promises and challenges. *J Ind Microbiol Biotechnol*. Oct;46(9–10):1343–58.

Chen, G., Li, L., and Tao, H. 2021. Bioinformatics Identification of Ferroptosis-related biomarkers and therapeutic compounds in ischemic Stroke. *Front Neurol.* 12:745240.

Cherif, M.S., Shuaibu, M.N., Kodama, Y., *et al.* 2014. Nanoparticle formulation enhanced protective immunity provoked by PYGPI8p-transamidase related protein (PyTAM) DNA vaccine in Plasmodium yoelii malaria model. *Vaccine.* 32(17):1998–2006.

Cocuron, J.C., Anderson, B., Boyd, A., and Alonso, A.P. 2014. Targeted metabolomics of *Physaria fendleri*, an industrial crop producing hydroxy fatty acids. *Plant Cell Physiol.* 55(3):620–33.

Cowan, K., Macluskie, G., Finch, M., *et al.* 2019. Application of pharmacogenomics and bioinformatics to exemplify the utility of human *ex vivo* organoculture models in the field of precision medicine. *PLoS ONE* 14(12):e0226564.

Dana, D., Gadhiya, S.V., St Surin, L.G., Li, D., Naaz, F., Ali, Q., Paka, L., Yamin, M.A., Narayan, M., Goldberg, I.D., and Narayan, P. 2018. Deep learning in drug discovery and medicine; scratching the surface. *Molecules.* 23(9):2384. doi: 10.3390/molecules23092384

Dancik, G.M., and Theodorescu, D. 2014. Pharmacogenomics in bladder cancer. *Urol Oncol.* 32(1):16–22.

Dangi, A.K., Sharma, B., and Hill, R.T., *et al.* 2018. Bioremediation through microbes: Systems biology and metabolic engineering approach. *Crit Rev Biotechnol.* 39(2):1–20.

De Groot, A.S., Moise, L, Terry, F., *et al.* 2020. Better epitope discovery, precision immune engineering, and accelerated vaccine design using immunoinformatics tools. *Front Immunol.* 11:442.

Dehkordi, *et al.* 2020. A systems-based approach for cyanide overproduction by *Bacillus megaterium* for gold bioleaching enhancement. *Front Bioeng Biotechnol.* 8:528.

Denny, J.C. 2014. Surveying recent themes in translational bioinformatics: Big data in EHRs, omics for drugs, and personal genomics. *Yearb Med Inform.* 9(1):199–205.

Diamond, A., and Desgagné-Penix I. 2016. Metabolic engineering for the production of plant isoquinoline alkaloids. *Plant Biotechnol J Jun.* 14(6):1319–28.

Dubé, M.-P., de Denus, S., and Tardif, J.-C. (2016). Pharmacogenomics to revive drug development in cardiovascular disease. *Cardiovasc Drug Ther.* 30(1), 59–64.

Foley, C., Corvin, A., and Nakagome, S. 2017. Genetics of Schizophrenia: Ready to translate? *Curr Psychiatry Rep.* 19(9):61.

Fontana, J.M., Alexander, E., and Salvatore, M. 2012. Translational research in infectious disease: Current paradigms and challenges ahead. *Transl Res.* 159(6):430–53.

Gao, J., Ellis, L.B.M., and Wackett, L.P. 2010. The University of Minnesota Biocatalysis/ Biodegradation Database: Improving public access. *Nucleic Acids Res.* 38:D488–D491.

Garrigues, C., Johansen, E., and Crittenden, R. 2013. Pangenomics – An avenue to improved industrial starter cultures and probiotics. *Curr Opin Biotechnol.* 24(2):187–91.

Gurbatri, C.R., Lia, I., Vincent, R., *et al.* 2020. Engineered probiotics for local tumor delivery of checkpoint blockade nanobodies. *Sci Transl Med.* 12(530).

Han, P., Teo, W.Z., and Yew, W.S. 2022. Biologically engineered microbes for bioremediation of electronic waste: Way posts, challenges and future directions. *Eng Biol.* 6(1):23–34.

Hartung, T., Van Vliet, E., Jaworska, J., *et al.* 2012. Systems toxicology. *ALTEX* 29(2):119–28.

Hegde, N.R., Gauthami, S, and Sampath Kumar, H.M. 2018. The use of databases, data mining and immunoinformatics in vaccinology: Where are we? *Expert Opin Drug Discov.* 13(2):117–30.

Hong, P.Y., Mantilla-Calderon D, and Wang, C. 2020. Metagenomics as a tool to monitor reclaimed-water quality. *Appl Environ Microbiol.* 86(16):e00724–20.

Ishack, S., and Lipner, S.R. 2021. Bioinformatics and immunoinformatics to support COVID-19 vaccine development. *J Med Virol.* 93(9):5209–211.

Jacques, C., Jamin, E.L., Jouanin, I., *et al.* 2021. Safety assessment of cosmetics by read across applied to metabolomics data of in vitro skin and liver models. *Arch Toxicol.* 95(10): 3303–22.

Jain, S., and Baranwal, M. 2021. Immunoinformatics aided design of peptide-based vaccines against ebolaviruses. *Vitam Horm.* 117:157–87.

Jaiswal, S., and Shukla, P. 2020. Alternative strategies for microbial remediation of pollutants via synthetic biology. *Front Microbiol.* 11:808.

Jaiswal, S., Singh, D.K., and Shukla, P. 2019. Gene editing and systems biology tools for pesticide bioremediation: A review. *Front Microbiol.* 10:87.

Jeandet, P., Sobarzo-Sánchez, E., and Clément, C., *et al.* 2018. Engineering stilbene metabolic *pathways in microbial cells. Biotechnol Adv.* 36(8):2264–83.

Jensen, M.K., and Keasling, J.D. 2015. Recent applications of synthetic biology tools for yeast metabolic engineering, *FEMS Yeast Res.* 15(1):1–10.

Jérémy, A., and Bertin, P.N. 2016. The microbial genomics of arsenic. *FEMS Microbiol Rev.* 39:1–24.

Joel, T., and Dudley, A.J.B. 2010. Biomarker and drug discovery for gastroenterology through translational bioinformatics. *Gastroenterology* 2010 139(3):735–41.

Kang, M., Lu, Y., Chen, S., and Tian, F. 2018. Harnessing the power of an expanded genetic code toward next-generation biopharma.aceuticals. *Curr Opin Chem Biol.* 46:123–29.

Khetan, R., Robin, C., Deane, C.M., *et al.* 2022. Current advances in biopharmaceutical informatics: Guidelines, impact and challenges in the computational developability assessment of antibody therapeutics, *MAbs* 14(1):2020082.

Kim, G, Jeon, H., Khobragade, T.P., Patil, M.D., *et al.* 2018. Enzymatic synthesis of sitagliptin intermediate using a novel ω-transaminase. *Enzyme Microb Technol.* 120:52–60.

Kiousi, D.E., Rathosi, M., Tsifintaris, M., *et al.* 2021. Pro-biomics: Omics technologies to unravel the role of probiotics in health and disease. *Adv Nutr.* 12(5):1802–20.

Kolluri, S., Lin, J., Liu, R., Zhang, Y., and Zhang, W. 2022. Machine learning and artificial intelligence in pharmaceutical research and development: A review. *AAPS J.* 24(1):19.

Kuipers, O.P. 1999.Genomics for food biotechnology: Prospects of the use of high-throughput technologies for the improvement of food microorganisms. *Curr Opin Biotechnol.* 10(5): 511–6.

Kumar, A., and Chordia, N. 2017. Role of bioinformatics in biotechnology. *Res Rev Biosc.* 12(1):116.

Kumar, S., Dangi, A.K., Shukla, P., *et al.* 2019. Thermozymes: Adaptive strategies and tools for their biotechnological applications. *Bioresource Technology.* 278:372–82.

Lee, K.-H., and Kim, D.-M. 2013. Applications of cell-free protein synthesis in synthetic biology: Interfacing bio-machinery with synthetic environments. *Biotechnol J.* 8(11):1292–1300.

León-Buitimea, A., Balderas-Cisneros, F.J., Garza-Cárdenas, C.R., *et al.* 2022. Synthetic biology tools for engineering microbial cells to fight superbugs. *Front Bioeng Biotechnol.* 10:869206.

Li, L. 2015. The potential of translational bioinformatics approaches for pharmacology research. *Br J Clin Pharmacol.* 80(4):862–67.

Liang, J., Lalonde, J., Borup, B., Mitchell, V., Mundorff, E., Trinh, N., Kochrekar, D.A., Ramachandran, N.C., and Pai, G.G. 2010. Development of a biocatalytic process as an Alternative to the (–)-DIP-Cl-mediated asymmetric reduction of a key intermediate of Montelukast. *Org Process Res Dev.* 14:193.

Liu, Y., Shin, H.D., Li, J., and Liu, L. 2015. Toward metabolic engineering in the context of system biology and synthetic biology: Advances and prospects. *Appl Microbiol Biotechnol.* 99(3):1109–18.

Loei, H., Lim, J., Tan, M., *et al.* 2013. Proteomic analysis of the oil palm fruit mesocarp reveals elevated oxidative phosphorylation activity is critical for increased storage oil production. *J Proteome Res.* 12(11):5096–109.

Logtenberg, T. 2007. Antibody cocktails: Next-generation biopharmaceuticals with improved potency. *Trends Biotechnol.* 25(9):390–4.

Lohia, N., and Baranwal, M. 2020. An Immunoinformatics approach in design of synthetic peptide vaccine against influenza virus. *Methods Mol Biol.* 2131:229–43.

Mandeep, Liu, H., Luo, J., and Shukla, P. 2020. Effluents detoxification from pulp and paper industry using microbial engineering and advanced oxidation techniques. *J Hazard Mater*. 398:122998.

Mandeep, Liu, H., and Shukla, P. 2021. Synthetic biology and biocomputational approaches for improving microbial endoglucanases toward their innovative applications. *ACS Omega*. 6(9):6055–63.

Mathaes, R., and Mahler, H.-C. 2018. Next generation biopharmaceuticals: Product development. *Adv Biochem Eng/Biotechnol*. 165:253–76.

Mayer, R.L., and Impens, F. 2021. Immunopeptidomics for next-generation bacterial vaccine development. *Trends Microbiol*. 29(11):1034–45.

McCarty, N.S., and Ledesma-Amaro, R. 2019. Synthetic biology tools to engineer microbial communities for biotechnology. *Trends Biotechnol*. 37(2):181–97.

Mejía-Pitta, A., Broset, E., and de la Fuente-Nunez, C. 2021. Probiotic engineering strategies for the heterologous production of antimicrobial peptides. *Adv Drug Deliv Rev*. 176:113863.

Mitsopoulos, C., Di Micco, P., Fernandez, E.V., *et al*. 2021. CanSAR: Update to the cancer translational research and drug discovery knowledgebase. *Nucleic Acids Res*. 49(D1): D1074–D1082.

Moulahoum, H., Ghorbanizamani, F., Khiari, Z., Toumi, M., Benazzoug, Y., Timur, S., and Zihnioglu, F. 2022. Combination of LC-Q-TOF-MS/MS, network pharmacology, and nanoemulsion approaches identifies active compounds of two Artemisia species responsible for tackling early diabetes-related metabolic complications in the liver. *Phytochem Anal*.

Naydich, A.D., Nangle, S.N., Bues, J.J., *et al*. 2019. Synthetic gene circuits enable systems-level biosensor trigger discovery at the host-microbe interface. *mSystems*. 4(4):e00125–19.

Oli, A.N., Obialor, W.O., Ifeanyichukwu, M.O., *et al*. (2020). Immunoinformatics and vaccine development: An overview. *Immunotargets Ther*. Feb 26;9:13–30.

Ortega-Tirado, D., Arvizu-Flores, A.A., Velazquez, C., *et al*. 2020. The role of immunoinformatics in the development of T-cell peptide-based vaccines against *Mycobacterium tuberculosis*. *Expert Rev Vaccines*. Sep;19(9):831–41.

O'Shea, J.P., Faisal, W., Ruane-O'Hora, T., and Devine, K.J. 2015. Lipidic dispersion to reduce food dependent oral bioavailability of fenofibrate: In vitro, in vivo and in silico assessments. *Eur J Pharm Biopharm*. 96:207–16.

Pal, S., and Sengupta, K. 2021. In silico analysis of phylogeny, structure, and function of arsenite oxidase from unculturable microbiome of arsenic contaminated soil. *J Genet Eng Biotechnol*. 19(1):47.

Papageorgiou, L., Papakonstantinou, E., Salis, C., *et al*. 2020. Drugena: A fully automated immunoinformatics platform for the design of antibody-drug conjugates against neurodegenerative diseases. *Adv Exp Med Biol*. 1194:203–15.

Patrinos, G.P. 2018. Population pharmacogenomics: Impact on public health and drug development. *Pharmacogenomics*. 19(1):3–6.

Pazos, F., Guija, D., Valencia, A., *et al*. 2005. MetaRouter: Bioinformatics for bioremediation. *Nucleic Acids Res*. 33(Database issue):D588–92.

Planson, A.G., Carbonell, P., Grigoras, I., and Faulon, J.L. 2011. Engineering antibiotic production and overcoming bacterial resistance. *Biotechnol J*. 6(7):812–25.

Purohit, H.J., Kapley, A., Khardenavis, A., *et al*. 2016. Insights in waste management bioprocesses using genomic tools. *Adv Appl Microbiol*. 97:121–70.

Quazi, S. 2022. Artificial intelligence and machine learning in precision and genomic medicine. *Med Oncol*. 39(8):120.

Ramana, J., and Mehla, K. 2020. Immunoinformatics and epitope prediction. *Methods Mol Biol*. 2131:155–71.

Raoufi, E., Hemmati, M., Eftekhari, S., *et al*. 2020. Epitope prediction by novel immunoinformatics approach: A state-of-the-art review. *Int J Pept Res Ther*. 26(2):1155–63.

Rashed, W.M., Adel, F., Rezk, M.A., *et al.* 2022. MicroRNA childhood cancer catalog (M3Cs): A resource for translational bioinformatics toward health informatics in pediatric cancer. *Database (Oxford)*. 2022:baac013.

Rezaei, S., Sefidbakht, Y., and Uskoković, V. 2021. Tracking the pipeline: Immunoinformatics and the COVID-19 vaccine design. *Brief Bioinform*. 22(6):bbab241.

Rodríguez, A., Castrejón-Godíne, María Luisa, *et al.* 2020. Omics approaches to pesticide biodegradation. *Curr Microbiol*. 77(4):545–63.

Sandeep, K., Plotnikov, V.N., and Rouse, J.C. 2018. Biopharmaceutical Informatics: Supporting biologic drug development *via* molecular modelling and informatics, *J. Pharm. Pharmacol*. 70(5):595–608.

Sandlin, N., Russell, K.D., Kim, J., *et al.* 2022. Current and emerging tools of computational biology to improve the detoxification of mycotoxins. *Appl Environ Microbiol*. 88(3).

Santos-Merino, M., Singh, A.K., and Ducat, D.C. 2019. New applications of synthetic biology tools for cyanobacterial metabolic engineering. *Front Bioeng Biotechnol*. 7: 33.

Sardi, M., and Gasch, A.P. 2017. Incorporating comparative genomics into the design–test–learn cycle of microbial strain engineering. *FEMS Yeast Res*. 17(5).

Satpathy, R., Konkimalla, V.B., and Ratha, J. 2015. Application of bioinformatics tools and databases in microbial dehalogenation research (a review). *Prikl Biokhim Mikrobiol*. 51(1):15–23.

Schubert, B., de la Garza, L., Mohr, C., *et al.* 2017. ImmunoNodes - Graphical development of complex immunoinformatics workflows. *BMC Bioinformatics*. 18(1):242.

Scianna, M., and Munaron, L. 2016. Computational approaches for translational oncology: Concepts and Patents. *Recent Pat Anticancer Drug Discov*. 11(4):384–92.

Shukla, V., Runthala, A., Rajput, V.S., *et al.* 2022. Computational and synthetic biology approaches for the biosynthesis of antiviral and anticancer terpenoids from *Bacillus subtilis*. *Med Chem*. 18(3):307–22.

Siezen, R.J., van Enckevort, F.H., and Kleerebezem, M.B., *et al.* 2004. Genome data mining of lactic acid bacteria: The impact of bioinformatics. *Curr Opin Biotechnol*. 15(2):105–15.

Singh, B.N., Upreti, D.K., Gupta, V.K., *et al.* 2017. Endolichenic fungi: A hidden reservoir of next generation biopharmaceuticals. *Trends Biotechnol*. 35(9):808–13.

Singh, P., and Lembo, A. 2021. Emerging role of the gut microbiome in irritable bowel syndrome. *Gastroenterol Clin North Am*. 50(3):523–45.

Smiatek, J., Jung, A., and Bluhmki, E. 2020. Towards a digital bioprocess replica: Computational approaches in biopharmaceutical development and manufacturing. *Trends Biotechnol*. Oct;38(10):1141–53.

Stachler, E., Kelty, C., Sivaganesan, M., *et al.* 2017. Quantitative CrAssphage PCR assays for human fecal pollution measurement. *Environ Sci Technol*. 51(16):9146–54.

Sung, B.H., Choe, D., Kim, S.C., *et al.* 2016. Construction of a minimal genome as a chassis for synthetic biology. *Essays Biochem*. Nov 30;60(4):337–46.

Suplatov, D., Voevodin, V., and Švedas, V. 2015. Robust enzyme design: Bioinformatic tools for improved protein stability. *Biotechnol J*. Mar;10(3):344–55.

Susanti, D., Volland, A., Tawari, N., *et al.* 2021.Multi-omics characterization of host-derived *Bacillus* spp. probiotics for improved growth performance in poultry. *Front Microbiol*. Oct 20;12:747845.

Suwinski, P., Ong, C., Ling, M.H.T., Poh, Y.M., Khan, A.M., and Ong, H.S. 2019. Advancing personalized medicine through the application of whole exome sequencing and big data analytics. *Front Genet*. Feb 12;10:49.

Tao, L., Wang, B., Zhong, Y., *et al.* 2017. Database and bioinformatics studies of probiotics. *J Agric Food Chem*. Sep 6;65(35):7599–606.

Thorn, C.F., Klein, T.E., and Altman, R.B. 2010. Pharmacogenomics and bioinformatics: PharmGKB. *Pharmacogenomics*. 11(4), 501–5.

Tikariha, H., and Purohit, H.J. 2018. Assembling a genome for novel nitrogen-fixing bacteria with capabilities for utilization of aromatic hydrocarbons. *Genomics*. 111(6):1824–30.

Tikariha, H., and Purohit, H.J. 2020. Unfolding microbial community intelligence in aerobic and anaerobic biodegradation processes using metagenomics. *Archi Microbiol.* Aug;202(6):1269–74.

Umadevi, S., Aalfin, E.S., Ayyasamy, P.M., and Rajakumar, S. 2015. Computational Approaches in Waste Management: *Special Emphasis in Microbial Degradation Research & Reviews: Journal of Ecology and Environmental Sciences* RRJEAES| Integrated Waste management and Energy Recovery- S1, 2015 e-ISSN:2347-7830 p-ISSN:2347-7822

Voigt, C.A. 2020. Synthetic biology 2020–2030: Six commercially-available products that are changing our world. *Nat Commun.* 11:6379.

Vorapreeda, T., Thammarongtham, C., and Laoteng, K. 2016. Integrative computational approach for genome-based study of microbial lipid-degrading developing industrial microbial strains. *Nat Biotechnol.* 33(10):1061–72. enzymes. *World Journal of Microbiology and Biotechnology*, 32(7).

Vyas, U., and Ranganathan, N. 2012. Probiotics, prebiotics, and synbiotics: Gut and beyond. *Gastroenterol Res Pract.* 2012:872716.

Wada, K., Saika, A., Ushimaru, K., *et al.* 2022. Metabolomic evaluation of the central metabolic pathways of mannosylerythritol lipid biosynthesis in *Moesziomyces antarcticus* T-34. *J Oleo Sci.* 71(1):119–25.

Wang, W., Zhang, B.R., Liang, H., *et al.* 2014. Cancer v: A new assistant tool for malignant disease research. *Chin Med J (Engl).* 127(6):1149–54.

Weber, C.R., Akbar, R., Yermanos, A., Pavlović, M., Snapkov, I., Sandve, G.K., Reddy, S.T., and Greiff, V. 2020. immuneSIM: Tunable multi-feature simulation of B- and T-cell receptor repertoires for immunoinformatics benchmarking. *Bioinformatics.* Jun 1;36(11):3594–96.

Wilm, A., Kühnl, J., and Kirchmair, J. 2018. Computational approaches for skin sensitization prediction. *Crit Rev Toxicol.* Oct;48(9):738–60.

Wooller, S.K., Benstead-Hume, G., Chen, X., *et al.* 2017. Bioinformatics in translational drug discovery. *Biosci Rep.* Jul 7;37(4):BSR20160180.

Yadav, M., and Shukla, P. 2019. Recent systems biology approaches for probiotics use in health aspects: A review. *3 Biotech.* Dec;9(12):448.

Yadav, M., and Shukla, P. 2020. Efficient engineered probiotics using synthetic biology approaches: A review. *Biotechnol Appl Biochem.* Jan;67(1):22–29.

Yang, J., Kim, B., Kim, G.Y., *et al.* 2019. Synthetic biology for evolutionary engineering: From perturbation of genotype to acquisition of desired phenotype. *Biotechnol Biofuels* 12:113.

Yu, S., *et al.* 2022, iProbiotics: A machine learning platform for rapid identification of probiotic properties from whole-genome primary sequences, *Brief Bioinform.* Jan;23(1):bbab477.

Zhang, C., Chen, X., Lee, R.T.C., *et al.* 2021. Bioinformatics-aided identification, characterization and applications of mushroom linalool synthases. *Commun Biol.* Feb 17;4(1):223.

Zhang, R., and Wong, K. 2017. High performance enzyme kinetics of turnover, activation and inhibition for translational drug discovery. *Expert Opin Drug Discov.* Jan;12(1):17–37.

Zhang, X., Lin, Y., and Wu, Q., *et al.* 2020. Synthetic biology and genome-editing tools for improving PHA metabolic engineering. *Trends Biotechnol.* Jul;8(7):689–700.

Zhao, X., Bai, F., and Li, Y. 2010. Application of systems biology and synthetic biology in strain improvement for biofuel production. *Sheng Wu Gong Cheng Xue Bao.* Jul;26(7):880–7. Chinese.

Zhou, K, Pedersen, H.K., Dawed, A.Y., *et al.* 2016. Pharmacogenomics in diabetes mellitus: Insights into drug action and drug discovery. *Nat Rev Endocrinol.* Jun;12(6):337–46.

Zou, J., Zheng, M.W., Li, G., *et al.* 2013. Advanced systems biology methods in drug discovery and translational biomedicine. *Biomed Res Int.* 2013:742835.

26 Biotechnological, Agriculture, Industrial, and Biopharmaceutical Research in Bioinformatics

Shailja Singhal and Utsang Kumar
Barkatullah University, India

Megha Katare Pandey
All India Institute of Medical Sciences, India

Rekha Khandia
Barkatullah University, India

26.1 INTRODUCTION

Recent developments in molecular biology and genetic engineering techniques, which were crucial in the "*omics*" revolution, have been the prime factors in biotechnology sectors. The detection of novel organisms and metabolic pathways has recently been made possible by technological advancements in DNA sequencing and liquid/mass spectrometry, which were supported by studies in the field of bioinformatics and elevated computational science as shown in Figure 26.1. This has increased our understanding of biological systems. The possibility to undertake genetic alterations focused on obtaining the intriguing phenotypes of increased yields and resistivity or the formulation of novel substances which were synthesized earlier by exhaustible pathways is possible due to newly acquired knowledge.

After the COVID-19 pandemic, there was an upsurge in the development of a vaccine candidate for SARS-CoV-2 as well as for possible upcoming pandemics. Although all the studies are interdisciplinary and interrelated, findings from one study could be the primary source of another. An approach used in bioinformatics called codon usage analysis, which also involves codon optimization, can easily explain this. Codon optimization is an experimental method of improving the codon composition for a recombinant gene employing a variety of parameters without changing the sequence of amino acids. This is achieved only because of an amino

DOI: 10.1201/9781003331247-29

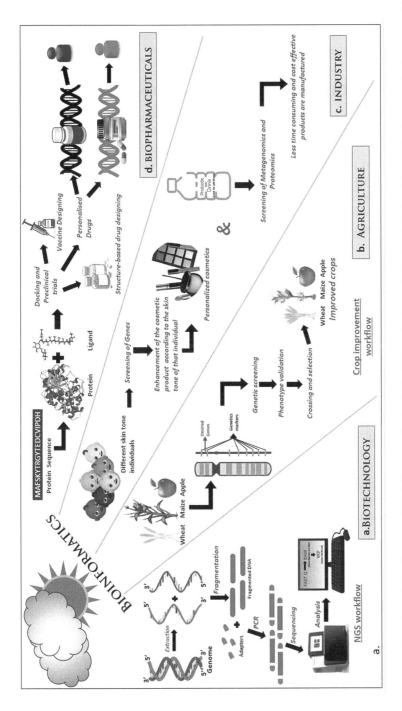

FIGURE 26.1 Overview of Significance of Bioinformatics in the field of Biotechnology, Agricultural, Industrial and Biopharmaceuticals sectors; (a) depicts the significance of Next Generation Sequencing, where the genomic data is processed for PCR following its sequencing and analysis; (b) depicts the crop improvement, via genetic mapping, phenotype validation, followed by crossing and selection; (c) shows the significance of bioinformatics and other *omics* datasets in industrial microbes processing, personalized cosmetics development, food and beverages production; (d) represents the steps involved in vaccine designing, customized drug development and structure based drug designing.

acid can be encoded by 2–6 codons. The applications of codon optimization frequently employed in biotechnology, agriculture, business, and biopharmaceutics research are discussed in this chapter. We will also talk about how codon optimization is an interdisciplinary method.

26.2 BIOTECHNOLOGICAL RESEARCH IN BIOINFORMATICS

Recently, numerous studies have been conducted based on the gene sequence, such as creating a complete genome sequence after joining contigs (small fragments) and predicting the regions of the gene sequence in plants and animals that code for proteins and act as promoters. Automated genome sequencing, gene identification and its functionality assessment, homology modeling, drug design and development, potential host identification, and understanding the complexity of genes and genomes are just a few applications of bioinformatics that can speed up study in the field of biotechnology.

26.2.1 Next-Generation Sequencing

Earlier, the Sanger sequencing method was employed, but it took over decades to complete the human genome's final draft. But now NGS (next-generation sequencing) is a well-known improved method of DNA sequencing that allows the entire genome to be sequenced in a single day (1). Various studies have been conducted using this technique till date. One among them is the study of genes associated with erythrocytosis in which one pathogenic variant (i.e., EPAS1 gene) was identified and the actual genetic cause of erythrocytosis was decided. NGS technique is extremely significant for the advancement of the screening of Slovenian patients with enigmatic erythrocytosis, including a further study on the pathophysiology of this unusual hematological problem (2).

Another study showed importance of NGS data to identify somatic mutations from specific tumor samples using a unique machine learning approach called svm-Somatic. This method is based on svm (support vector machines) algorithm dependent on NGS data (from individual tumor sample) to distinguish somatic single nucleotide variants (SNVs) from the normal state as multiple mutations and the presence of CVNs (copy number variations) that can hinder somatic SNV mutations (3).

Many studies are being conducted integrating NGS and CUB. These studies include the investigation of features of the whole genome of Galliformes (chicken, Guinea fowl, turkey, and Japanese quail) based on codon usage and evolution that indicated selection pressure dominance over mutational pressure and a bias toward synonymous substitution over non-synonymous mutation (4). Another study comprising the complete mtDNA and ribosomal operon sequence of *Parasaccocoelium mugili* (an intestinal parasite of mullet fish) was used following NGS for sequence cluster analysis that revealed a significant resemblance of *P. mugili* to *Plagiorchis maculosus*, whereas phylogenetic analysis showed a close resemblance to other *Paragonimus* species (5).

Current developments in NGS technologies have made it possible to create two sequencing assays that can either capture viral near-full genome sequences at single molecule resolution (FLIP-seq) or complete viral genome sequences including affiliated viral integration site (MIP-seq). Both of these assays are essential for the assessment of the actual viral genome and its survival in the host. Guinevere et al. (2021) reported in their study that HIV virus enters through viral DNA which includes both healthy and damaged viral genomes, each consisting of a unique entry site. So, these assays are helpful in differentiating the healthy and damaged HIV viral DNA genomes. Here, codon bias analysis can be utilized to modulate translation of protein and gene expression via synonymous codon usage which is crucial in determining the virulence and evolution of the viral genome (6).

26.3   BIOINFORMATICS IN AGRICULTURE

The significance of bioinformatics in agriculture may be seen in many different ways, including crop genome mapping, CRISPR-Cas9-based genetic editing, DNA profiling as well as inserting genes of interest in agricultural microorganisms are used for crop improvement. Codon usage analysis can also be used in crop improvement. Different studies based on CUB provide knowledge of phylogenetic relationships among species, the molecular evolution of genes, and the forces that shape evolution. The design of transgenes to boost gene expression levels by codon optimization is one of the most significant usage of codon bias analysis in creating the transgenic crops (7). Bioinformatics assists in studying the genetic architecture of microbes and pathogens by utilizing metagenomics and transcriptomics approaches to ascertain how several organisms impact the host plant. This allows us to design crops that are resistant to pathogens (8).

26.3.1   CROP GENOME MAPPING

Genetic markers make up the bulk of the genetic map. The rate of chromosome recombination and sharing determines its relative length. The construction of genetic maps is a very essential tool for the genetic improvement of commercially significant species (9).

An earlier study incorporating codon usage insight in five different Miscanthus plants (a perennial fiber bio-energy crop) and other two related species showed that A/T-bases and A/T-ending codons preference in the cp genomes of the species and natural selection force had an impact on the codon utilization profiles. Comparative examination of codon utilization frequencies between seven representative species and four model organisms (*Arabidopsis thaliana*, *Escherichia coli*, *Populus trichocarpa*, and *Saccharomyces cerevisiae*) inferred all model organisms except *Escherichia coli* could be considered preferentially best suited exogenous expression receptors. These findings may offer crucial background data for evolutionary assessment and also show how codon optimization might increase the efficacy of exogenous gene expression in transgenic studies (10).

26.3.2   GENETIC EDITING-BASED CRISPR-CAS9

The RNA serves as a guide, and the Cas9 enzyme makes up this system's two components. This method is quite simple, reliable, and effective because it combines site-directed mutagenesis, gene transcription, knockout, and knock-in/replacement. Single-stranded RNAs are used to modify genomes. Agricultural enhancement using CRISPR-Cas9 is common for economically significant features in crop plants (11).

A recombinant gene's codon composition can be improved experimentally using a variety of parameters without changing the amino acid sequence like codon-optimized version of Cas9. For the study of dicots and some monocot species, a codon-optimized version of Cas9 under the regulation of a potent constitutive promoter, such as CaMV (cauliflower mosaic virus) 35S promoter for dicots and ubiquitin promoter for mono-cots (maize), frequently results in mutations (homozygous, hemizygous, or bi-allelic) in the T0 generation and is heritable (12).

26.4   BIOINFORMATICS IN INDUSTRIAL RESEARCH

Industrial biocatalysts, which are often a type of microbial enzyme, are one of the primary areas in the spotlight as a way to replace or rebuild the conventional meth-ods of producing chemicals and pharmaceuticals. In the past few years, growth in bioinformatics and the genomic revolution have resulted in a significant rise in stud-ies of commercial biocatalysts. The retrieval of new biocatalysts using sophisticated DNA and protein sequence queries and their assessment utilizing various databases, algorithms, and programs is one of the important aspects of bioinformatics in bio-catalysis. Designing primers based on bioinformatics analysis paves the way to eas-ily extract the unidentified genes of microbial enzymes (13). Moreover, integrative research utilizing additional *omics* datasets like metatranscriptomics and metabolo-mics is required to enhance the efficacy of probiotics and enzyme discovery.

In this context, there has been an increase in economic interest in bioinformatics applications in the fields of food industries, beverages, probiotics, cosmetics, and biocatalysts, where microbial communities significantly contribute. In this aspect, an insight into a few industrial microbiome applications has been gained. For instance, in the dairy industry, lactic acid bacteria are employed in a range of food items and beverage preparation activities incorporating different processes. The availability or unavailability of strain-specific enzymes controls these processes. Culturing such strain is challenging due to uncertain growth factors. As an alternative, metagenome sequencing, assembly, and annotation might be used in yield optimization, to study these enzymes (14). Additionally, metagenome assembly is crucial for understanding the richness, diversity, and growth of bacteriophage population densities in different cultures. It is crucial to prevent phage infections that result in fermentation glitches and also to minimize the potency of phages to combat food-borne pathogens (15).

Another use of bioinformatics is in the identification of novel probiotics. Conclusions drawn from comparative studies of the gut microbiota illustrate the interaction between phenotypic characteristics like inflammation (16) and obesity (17) in particular bacterial populations when incorporated with other datasets (e.g., metabolomic, demographic, nutritional, and habits) may automate the characteriza-tion of newbie probiotic strains with reduced processing time, cost, and effort com-pared to the traditional culturomics approach (18).

Quality control of the finished products that consist of live micro-organisms is important (19). Since various microbial strains from a single species can exhibit varied behaviors, strain-level verification is essential to identify potential contaminants and to guarantee the presence of right strains (20).

Furthermore, in the context of cosmetic industries, an emerging market for customized skin products, bioinformatics plays an important role in determining the treatment's effectiveness. Apparently, the possible therapeutic investigations are frequently hindered due to the poor biomass of skin specimens, as a result, minor defilements (e.g., from adjacent skin or reagents) can readily produce false results. It also highlights the necessity for individual longitudinal investigations, where several statistical techniques can be used to evaluate connections between taxonomic or functional makeup and sample characteristics (21). In order to reduce the divergence from a covariate prior to authentication, the data can also be adjusted for one of the variables, such as "subject," which makes it easier to determine the treatment's effectiveness.

Finally, we anticipate that data science and bioinformatics together will play a key role in the cooperation between the academic and industrial groups. This interaction will be further boosted by the quick conversion of microbiome research into significant practical uses in health services, energy, and the food sector.

26.5 BIOINFORMATICS IN BIOPHARMACEUTICALS

In the biopharmaceutical industry, bioinformatics plays a significant role in designing different potential drugs by identifying the targets (receptors, ion channels, enzymes, and carrier molecules) and enhancing the effectiveness of drugs and finally reducing the wear and tear of drugs. Traditional expression systems have many restrictions in commercial biopharmaceutical production, which prompts efforts to identify, interpret, and explore substitute, reliable, and competent expression systems for synthesizing functional recombinant proteins. The interdisciplinary study has overcome these problems. Currently, *genomics* and *proteomics* are used in many studies on evolution, viral infection, and disease stimulation via different receptors and their mutations. Now these are also used in vaccine designing and novel drug designing.

26.5.1 Vaccine Designing

Codon usage bias, a bioinformatic approach, is widely used for prediction of suitable animal models for developing vaccines against emerging pathogens. The CUB develops strategies to modify the emerging pathogen's genomes to reduce their virulence and reveal the pathogen's reproductive effectiveness in human host (22, 23). Countless studies have been carried out to identify potential hosts that may allow COVID-19 and its strains to spread. According to some studies, the 3rd position of G or C nucleobases is poorly represented in SARS-CoV-2 favored codons. This imbalance of tRNA pools in infected cells may have a significant impact on the synthesis of host proteins and the translation rate of highly expressed genes that are linked to host proteins. It was discovered that these genes share the virus's codon usage pattern. Additional research on these genes leads to the conclusion that this epistasis mechanism may help explain how this virus escapes the immune system and the etiology of a few adverse effects brought on by viral replication (24, 25). These results, therefore, advance our perception of the SARS-CoV-2 pathogeneticity and may help in developing a live attenuated vaccine.

According to molecular evolutionary studies, CUB within and between species can be determined by a number of variables, including genome composition, expression level, G/C content, recombination rates, RNA stability, codon position, mRNA folding, gene length, and many others comprising adverse environmental conditions and population size. According to multiple studies, whole-genome sequencing of various pathogen and host species can illustrate how codon bias patterns differ within and among genomes and its adaptation to various pathogens (26).

An overview of genetic code variations, affecting variables of codon usage, nuclear and organellar gene CUB, computational techniques to detect codon usage, including the significance and applications of codon usage analysis in various fields (7), is shown in the Figure 26.2.

Codon usage parameters such as codon adaptation index (CAI), relative codon deoptimization index (RCDI), and similarity index were used to analyze CUB that defines NiV and host relatedness concerning codon usage (27). Understanding the pattern of codon usage helps to maximize protein expression in construction of a subunit vaccine candidate, in which a vaccine candidate is expressed in a prokaryotic or eukaryotic system. In addition to the subunit vaccine, codon optimization is helpful in developing several other viral vectored vaccine candidates, such as the Venezuelan equine encephalitis virus that carries the G and N protein of NiV and the viruses that cause rabies, canarypox, measles, and Newcastle disease. On the other side, comparable codon usage data can be considered to decrease the production of the NiV proteins throughout pathogen replication by selecting underrepresented codons and/or concurrently increasing uncommon dinucleotides like CpG and UpA. This rational, systematic strategy known as SAVE (synthetic attenuated vaccine engineering) allows for the adjustable attenuation of viruses (28).

Genetic stability and safety are important considerations for any proposed attenuated virus vaccine. Codon-pair bias de-optimization was added to the influenza hemagglutinin (HA) and neuraminidase (NA) genes. After being administered intravenously, the virus produced a virus phenotypic with negligible pathogenicity while simultaneously inducing a strong immune response. Thus, the health burden brought on by viral infection may be reduced by selecting underrepresented codons or uncommon dinucleotide like CpG and UpA, as a systematic strategy known as SAVE. Thanks to faster and more affordable nucleotide synthesis, it is now possible to create viruses with de-optimized codons. In a recent study, it has been speculated that the targeted gene segment and the number of codon alterations in influenza A viruses (with eight gene segments and variable genome recoding) can generate a range of attenuation that may target de-optimizing influenza A virus codons for the creation of potential vaccines (27).

Another approach for developing a potential vaccine is reverse vaccinology, which suggests the expression of genomic sequence (DNA) over the purified proteins obtained from the organism. Some pathogens like *Bacillus anthracis*, *Streptococcus pneumoniae*, *Mycobacterium tuberculosis*, and *Cryptosporidium hominis* are successfully applied for reverse vaccinology. Reverse vaccinology (RV) is the process of antigen discovery through the debriefing of an organism's complete antigenic repertoire coded in its genomic data (28). Immunoinformatics is the best tool for the mapping of epitopes that can stimulate cellular as well as humoral immune response (29).

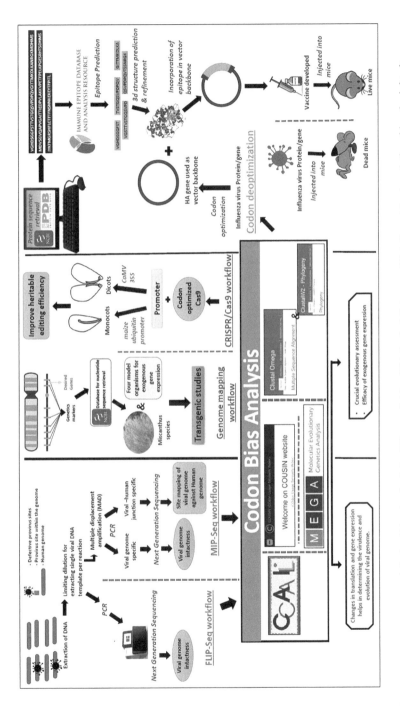

FIGURE 26.2   Importance of Codon Bias Analysis in different fields of Biological Sciences. Mutation at the translational level might alter gene expression, which helps in studying the viral genome evolution and estimating the efficacy of exogenous gene expression and could provide improved heritable editing efficiency through the CRISPR/Cas9 workflow. Altering the desired protein content of the viral genome or gene can be used to predict potential epitopes following vaccine development against evolving viruses.

26.5.2   Novel Drug Design

Drug development is a troublesome, risky, time-consuming, and costly process. Human and financial resources, rigid commitment to testing the quality, and manufacturing standards all are necessary for creating a novel drug. Bioinformatics and pharmacogenomics are two different fields that have had a favorable influence on medication development with reduced risk and expense. They also help to speed up the process at different stages and shorten the total time needed to complete the whole process (30).

Bioinformatics helps in the prediction, identification, and analysis of biological drug targets like proteins and nucleic acid. Different biological database repositories like Swiss-Prot, GenBank, and NCBI are widely used. Pharmacogenomics minimizes the side effects of medications by developing and prescribing drugs based on an individual's unique genetic makeup; this method is referred to as "personalized medicine." It may be possible to base treatment decisions on genetics when a gene mutation is linked to a patient's specific drug reaction, such as changing the dosage or selecting a different medication. Multigene analysis and whole-genome single nucleotide polymorphism (SNP) profiles are two contemporary techniques that are being employed clinically for the development of therapeutics (30). According to a study, the codon usage analysis of nucleotide sequences of Rossmann fold (GXGXXG motifs) revealed that a low guanine frequency at the third position of codons leads to the development of a new class of ribosome-directed antibiotics (31).

26.5.3   Structure-Based Drug Discovery

Similar to novel drug design, structure-based drug discovery (SBDD) requires high-purity protein that can be achieved by rearranging the native coding sequence to optimize expression in a specific host system, many protein targets are thus produced by heterologous expression of these recombinant proteins (32).

A drug discovery process broadly comprises the following four stages: discovery, development, clinical trial, and registry. The first stage involves the identification of a possible therapeutic target and active ligands, followed by cloning of the target gene, protein extraction, purification, and 3D protein structure determination. SBDD plays a crucial role in verifying the target protein's 3D structure in a complex with the effective ligand discovered. One of the main accomplishments of SBDD is the development of FDA-approved medications that block the human immunodeficiency virus (HIV)-1. Additionally, other medications discovered using the SBDD method include Norfloxacin [antibiotic] (33), Raltitrexed [thymidylate synthetase inhibitor] (34), and Amprenavir [a possible inhibitor of the HIV protease] (35).

26.6   CONCLUSION

Therefore, it can be concluded from this book chapter that codon optimization is an interdisciplinary approach applied in biotechnological research to increase gene expression levels and unveil the history and evolution of viral genomes. Bioinformatics with integration of different *omics* will aid in crop development research and can improve the effectiveness of foreign gene expression in transgenic investigations. It has great significance in the industrial sector for creating customized cosmetics, quick conversion of microbiome into beneficial commercial uses, and to automatize characterization of newbie probiotic strains. Lastly, however not the least, codon optimization plays a significant role in the pharmaceutical arena to design novel therapeutics, personalized pharmaceutical drugs, and viral vectored vaccine candidates.

REFERENCES

1. Behjati S, Tarpey PS. What is next generation sequencing? *Arch Dis Child Educ Pract Ed*. 2013 Dec;98(6):236. Available from: /pmc/articles/PMC3841808/
2. Kristan A, Pajič T, Maver A, Režen T, Kunej T, Količ R, et al. Identification of Variants Associated With Rare Hematological Disorder Erythrocytosis Using Targeted Next-Generation Sequencing Analysis. *Front Genet*. 2021;12:1222.
3. Mao YF, Yuan XG, Cun YP. A novel machine learning approach (svmSomatic) to distinguish somatic and germline mutations using next-generation sequencing data. *Zool Res*. 2021;42(2):246. Available from: /pmc/articles/PMC7995270/
4. Sarkar I, Rathore SS, Singh RP. An interplay between compositional constraint and natural selection dictates the codon usage pattern among select Galliformes. *Biosystems*. 2021;204:104390.
5. Atopkin DM, Semenchenko AA, Solodovnik DA, Ivashko YI, Vinnikov KA. First next-generation sequencing data for Haploporidae (Digenea: Haploporata): characterization of complete mitochondrial genome and ribosomal operon for Parasaccocoelium mugili Zhukov, 1971. *Parasitol Res.*. 2021;120(6):2037–46. Available from: https://link.springer.com/article/10.1007/s00436-021-07159-y
6. Lee GQ, Procopio A. Chemistry and Bioinformatics Considerations in Using Next-Generation Sequencing Technologies to Inferring HIV Proviral DNA Genome-Intactness. *Viruses* 2021;13:1874. Available from: https://www.mdpi.com/1999-4915/13/9/1874/htm
7. Parvathy ST, Udayasuriyan V, Bhadana V. Codon usage bias. *Mol Biol Rep* [Internet]. 2022;49(1):539–65. Available from: https://pubmed.ncbi.nlm.nih.gov/34822069/
8. Ballabh G, Ujjawal Kumar Singh Kushwaha B, Deo I, Prakash Jaiswal J, Prasad B. Role of Bioinformatics in Crop Improvement. Type Double Blind Peer Rev Int Res J Publ Glob Journals Inc. 2017;17.
9. Temesgen B, Husen Y. Genetic mapping in crop plants. *Open J Plant Sci*. 2021;019–26.
10. Sheng J, She X, Liu X, Wang J, Hu Z. Comparative analysis of codon usage patterns in chloroplast genomes of five Miscanthus species and related species. *PeerJ*. 2021;9. Available from: /pmc/articles/PMC8466072/
11. Hussain B, Lucas SJ, Budak H. CRISPR/Cas9 in plants: at play in the genome and at work for crop improvement. *Brief Funct Genomics*. 2018;17(5):319–28. Available from: https://academic.oup.com/bfg/article/17/5/319/4975473
12. Zhan X, Lu Y, Zhu JK, Botella JR. Genome editing for plant research and crop improvement. *J Integr Plant Biol*. 2021;63(1):3–33. Available from: https://onlinelibrary.wiley.com/doi/full/10.1111/jipb.13063
13. Yu H, Luo H, Shi Y, Sun X, Shen Z. [Application of bioinformatics in researches of industrial biocatalysis] - PubMed. [cited 2022 Sep 21]. Available from: https://pubmed.ncbi.nlm.nih.gov/15971599/
14. De Filippis F, Parente E, Ercolini D. Metagenomics insights into food fermentations. *Microb Biotechnol*. 2017;10(1):91–102. Available from: https://pubmed.ncbi.nlm.nih.gov/27709807/

15. Muhammed MK, Kot W, Neve H, Mahony J, Castro-Mejía JL, Krych L, et al. Metagenomic analysis of dairy bacteriophages: Extraction method and pilot study on whey samples derived from using undefined and defined mesophilic starter cultures. *Appl Environ Microbiol.* 2017;83(19):888–905. Available from: /pmc/articles/PMC5601343/

16. Andoh A, Kuzuoka H, Tsujikawa T, Nakamura S, Hirai F, Suzuki Y, et al. Multicenter analysis of fecal microbiota profiles in Japanese patients with Crohn's disease. *J Gastroenterol.* 2012;47(12):1298–307. Available from: https://pubmed.ncbi.nlm.nih.gov/2257 6027/

17. Kasai C, Sugimoto K, Moritani I, Tanaka J, Oya Y, Inoue H, et al. Comparison of the gut microbiota composition between obese and non-obese individuals in a Japanese population, as analyzed by terminal restriction fragment length polymorphism and next-generation sequencing. *BMC Gastroenterol.* 2015;15(1). Available from: https://pubmed.ncbi.nlm. nih.gov/26261039/

18. Lagier JC, Khelaifia S, Alou MT, Ndongo S, Dione N, Hugon P, et al. Culture of previously uncultured members of the human gut microbiota by culturomics. *Nat Microbiol.* 2016;1. Available from: https://pubmed.ncbi.nlm.nih.gov/27819657/

19. Fenster K, Freeburg B, Hollard C, Wong C, Laursen RR, Ouwehand AC. The production and delivery of probiotics: A review of a practical approach. *Microorg.* 2019;7:83. Available from: https://www.mdpi.com/2076-2607/7/3/83/htm

20. Huys G, Botteldoorn N, Delvigne F, De Vuyst L, Heyndrickx M, Pot B, et al. Microbial characterization of probiotics–Advisory report of the Working Group "8651 Probiotics" of the Belgian Superior Health Council (SHC). *Mol Nutr Food Res.* 2013;57(8):1479–504. Available from: https://onlinelibrary.wiley.com/doi/full/10.1002/mnfr.201300065

21. Van den Brink PJ, Ter Braak CJF. Principal response curves: Analysis of time-dependent multivariate responses of biological community to stress. *Environ Toxicol Chem.* 1999;18(2):138–48. Available from: https://onlinelibrary.wiley.com/doi/full/10.1002/etc. 5620180207

22. Kumar U, Khandia R, Singhal S, Puranik N, Tripathi M, Kumar Pateriya A, et al. Insight into codon utilization pattern of tumor suppressor gene EPB41L3 from different mammalian species indicates dominant role of selection force. *Cancers (Basel).* 2021;13:2739.

23. Khandia R, Singhal S, Kumar U, Ansari A, Tiwari R, Dhama K, et al. Analysis of Nipah virus codon usage and adaptation to hosts. *Front Microbiol.* 2019;10(MAY):886.

24. Alonso AM, Diambra L. SARS-CoV-2 codon usage bias downregulates host expressed genes with similar codon usage. *Front Cell Dev Biol.* 2020;8. Available from: https:// pubmed.ncbi.nlm.nih.gov/32974353/

25. Hou W. Characterization of codon usage pattern in SARS-CoV-2. *Virol J.* 2020;17(1). Available from: https://pubmed.ncbi.nlm.nih.gov/32928234/

26. Behura SK, Severson DW. Codon usage bias: causative factors, quantification methods and genome-wide patterns: with emphasis on insect genomes. *Biol Rev Camb Philos Soc.* 2013;88(1):49–61. Available from: https://pubmed.ncbi.nlm.nih.gov/22889422/

27. Baker SF, Nogales A, Martínez-Sobrido L. Downregulating viral gene expression: codon usage bias manipulation for the generation of novel influenza A virus vaccines. *Future Virol.* 2015;10(6):715. Available from: /pmc/articles/PMC4508661/

28. Del Tordello E, Rappuoli R, Delany I. Reverse vaccinology: exploiting genomes for vaccine design. *Hum Vaccines Emerg Technol Des Dev.* 2017;65–86.

29. Sette A, Rappuoli R. Reverse vaccinology: developing vaccines in the era of genomics. *Immunity.* 2010;33(4):530–41. Available from: https://pubmed.ncbi.nlm.nih.gov/21029963/

30. Katara P. Role of bioinformatics and pharmacogenomics in drug discovery and development process. *Netw Model Anal Heal Informatics Bioinforma.* 2013;2(4):225–30. Available from: https://link.springer.com/article/10.1007/s13721-013-0039-5

31. Mckie JH, Mckie SA. Synonymous codon bias as a basis for novel antibiotic design: from nucleotide wobble constraint to ribosomal garrotte. https://doi.org/104155/fmc-2017-0032. 2017;9(12):1377–400. Available from: https://www.future-science.com/doi/10.4155/fmc-2017-0032

32. Ranaghan MJ, Li JJ, Laprise DM, Garvie CW. Assessing optimal: inequalities in codon optimization algorithms. *BMC Biol.* 2021;19(1). Available from: /pmc/articles/PMC7893858/

33. Rutenber EE, Stroud RM. Binding of the anticancer drug ZD1694 to E. coli thymidylate synthase: assessing specificity and affinity. *Structure.* 1996;4(11):1317–24. Available from: https://pubmed.ncbi.nlm.nih.gov/8939755/

34. Anderson AC. The process of structure-based drug design. *Chem Biol.* 2003;10(9):787–97. Available from: https://pubmed.ncbi.nlm.nih.gov/14522049/

35. Wlodawer A, Vondrasek J. Inhibitors of HIV-1 protease: a major success of structure-assisted drug design. *Annu Rev Biophys Biomol Struct.* 1998;27:249–84. Available from: https://pubmed.ncbi.nlm.nih.gov/9646869/

Index

Pages in *italics* refer to figures and pages in **bold** refer to tables.